June 29, 1776 ✗ Action off Turtle
January 3, 1777 ✗ Battle of Princet
March 9, 1778 ✗ Action off Reedy Island, ~~~~~~~~~~
September 28, 1778 ✗ *Raleigh* against HMS *Experiment* and *Unicorn*
May 28, 1781 ✗ *Alliance* against HMS *Atlanta* and *Trepassey*
March 10, 1783 ✗ *Alliance* against HMS *Sybil*
August 23, 1798 ✗ *United States* captures the French schooner *Sans Pareil*
September 5, 1798 ✗ *United States* captures the French sloop *Jaloux*
February 3, 1799 ✗ *United States* captures the French schooner *L'Amour de la Patrie*
February 4, 1799 ✗ *United States* captures the French privateer *Tartuffe*
January 1, 1801 ✗ *United States* captures the French schooner *Diamaid*

TROPIC OF CANCER

Canton

Macao

Calcutta

Bombay

Madras

SOUTH

CHINA

SEA

SUMATRA

30°E   60°E   90°E   120°E

Str. of Sunda   Batavia

JAVA

I. de France

TROPIC OF CAPRICORN

1789

NEW
HOLLAND

Cape Town

1788

St. Paul I.
Amsterdam I.

JOHN BARRY

JOHN BARRY

AN AMERICAN HERO
in the
AGE *of* SAIL

TIM McGRATH

WESTHOLME
Yardley

Frontispiece: Portrait of John Barry by Gilbert Stuart, c. 1801. (*Bruce Gimelson Gallery/Private Collection*)

Westholme Publishing, LLC
904 Edgewood Road
Yardley, Pennsylvania 19067
Visit our Web site at www.westholmepublishing.com

First Printing May 2010
10 9 8 7 6 5 4 3 2 1

ISBN: 978-1-59416-104-9

Printed in United States of America.

For Cyd

CONTENTS

CONTENTS

List of Maps and Diagrams

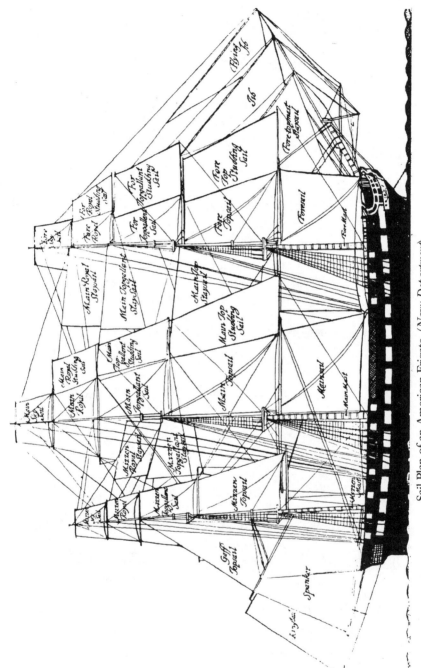

Sail Plan of an American Frigate. (*Navy Department*)

Sailing Vessels of John Barry's Time (not to scale). (*Navy Department*)

FOREWORD

THE STATUE STANDS TALL AND RESOLUTE, with a defiant expression on his face. His left hand holds a spyglass above a sheathed sword. His right arm points southward over Philadelphia: the same direction that the Delaware River takes toward the sea. To some who know the lay of old Philadelphia–and the location of St. Mary's cemetery–his gesture seems to say, "I'm buried over there." He has been guarding the south side of Independence Hall for a hundred years.

He paid no attention to the rain falling on September 13, 2003, as a hundred or so people made their way from his gravesite at St. Mary's churchyard at Fourth and Locust, working their way toward him under a colorful collection of umbrellas. They had just attended a ceremonial Mass and a simple, martial service at his resting place, commemorating the two hundredth anniversary of his death. They were led by an honor guard comprised of sailors from today's United States Navy and re-enactors dressed as Revolutionary War soldiers, marching in cadence as bagpipes played. They reached the statue and the pipes stopped playing (the rain kept falling); remarks were made by one priest, one admiral, and one mayor. The national anthem was sung, a benediction given, and the spectators left the statue to gather for lunch at the nearby Curtis Building.

After the meal, the vice consul of Ireland made a brief speech, and a plaque was presented by members of the crew from the latest U.S. destroyer that carries the same name as the statue. Descendants, veterans, and members of the various Irish and civic organizations that had sponsored the event toured an exhibit of artifacts, weapons, and paintings from the early days of the United States. Eventually everyone drifted out into the rain, and back to the twenty-first century.

Outside, it continued to rain on the statue's hat, his outstretched arm, his spyglass, his buckled shoes, and the pedestal that bears his name: "Barry."

A century earlier, when the statue was unveiled, thousands attended, and the event was front-page headlines in the newspapers of the day.

Philadelphia has two statues and a nearby bridge named after John Barry. There are other statues, in Washington, D.C., and in Ireland's County Wexford, where he was born. There are countless Commodore Barry Chapters of the Friendly Sons of St. Patrick and the Ancient Order of Hibernians. But as time passes, John Barry is being forgotten.

Barry is still called "Father of the American Navy" in some circles, although John Paul Jones and John Adams are two others that can lay claim to that title. But where Adams has eternal fame from being second President of the United States, and Jones still "has not yet begun to fight" in some high school history books, few can recall Barry's deeds. Two hundred years ago, it was a different story.

The fastest known twenty-four hours logged at sea in the eighteenth century? The *Black Prince*, captained by John Barry. The first and last successful battles fought at sea for the Continental Navy? Captain Barry. The fighting sailor who served with the Continental Army at Princeton? Barry. The veteran who seized the moment (and a couple of state assemblymen) to guarantee a quorum for Pennsylvania's ratification of the Constitution? None other. The merchant captain who helped establish trade with China and the man President Washington put at the top of the list to head up the United States Navy? The very same.

Why don't we know more about this man?

For one thing, he was not pompous. Take, for example, his desperate passage down the Delaware past occupied Philadelphia in 1778. It was a freezing winter night when he led forty threadbare and poorly armed sailors silently past British warships and helped conduct a legal rustling party with Anthony Wayne. The cattle they rounded up fed the starving soldiers at Valley Forge. John Paul Jones, always his own best press agent, would have written a poem describing his heroic exploits, full of bravado. Barry wrote, "I passed Philadelphia in two small boats." Other documents, personal and public, show his affection, anger, humor, and purpose. But they pale in comparison to the writings of his peers, many of whom wrote volumes more and accomplished much, much less. No wonder the historians at the Washington Navy Yard affectionately call him "Silent John."

His early time in Ireland left no paper trail. Irish and American historians once debated about where and when he was born. Was it in Ballysampson? Or Roostontown? Or Rosslare? Was it in 1739? Or 1745? The records are, as Celestine Rafferty (*the* Barry expert in Wexford) says, "A tad sketchy."

His youth is practically undocumented. For his first six years in Philadelphia, we don't know where he lived or whom he worked for. He married Mary Cleary, but her name is all we know about her. Tax records of 1767 list his household with their names and a "servant." Was this servant indentured or a slave? We don't know. During the British occupation of Philadelphia he was approached by a British sympathizer and offered a commission in the King's Navy along with 15,000 guineas. No documents from the Clinton or Howe papers mention who the go-between was, and Barry never told. Silent John. But most of those who knew him–George Washington, Robert Morris, even John Paul Jones–tendered him their respect and admiration.

Visit that statue on a bright sunny day, as the tourists leave Independence Hall and walk by. The cameras will come out, families will pose, and a stranger will offer to take a picture of all of them. Invariably one sightseer will look at the name and ask, "Who was Barry?"

Here are his times. This is his story.

CHAPTER ONE

OUT OF IRELAND

HE LAST THING AN ACTING COMMANDER needs is flagrant disobedience to orders. Lieutenant Stephen Gregory was well aware of that fact as he stood on the quarterdeck of the Continental frigate *Confederacy*; his crew intently watched him struggle to maintain both his poise and authority.

Although the 1779 calendar read October–usually a brisk month for Pennsylvania–this had been a pleasant, agreeably warm morning, with southerly breezes wafting up the Delaware River. For Gregory, it *had* been pleasant and agreeable enough, until this defiant brig sailed within hailing distance. Every other passing ship obeyed Gregory's commands to turn into the wind and be boarded, but this brig's captain showed no intention of doing so.

On the surface, the *Confederacy* lacked nothing. The New England vessel was considered the most beautiful ship built in America, even grander than her well-regarded "sister" frigate, the *Alliance*. Her lines were long and graceful, measuring an imposing 241 feet from bowsprit to taffrail, with a 37-foot beam.[1] Two ornate head frames, each adorned with a carved red fox, were joined at the bow by a handsome figurehead of a bearded warrior, his right hand on the hilt of his sheathed sword. Exquisite woodwork and filigree decorated the cabin windows. Sweeps were pierced between her gun ports; when becalmed, her crew could row her out of any doldrums or dangers. She carried thirty-six guns. Inside, the officers' berths were palatial by contemporary standards, with an adjoining great room that featured an eight-foot ceiling.[2] Built for diplomacy as well as battle, the *Confederacy* was the ideal combination of seventeenth-century luxury in a modern eighteenth-century warship. She lacked only one necessity: manpower.

Since arriving from Connecticut, the new frigate was moored in the Delaware River just twenty miles below Philadelphia, the capital of the young United States, where Captain Seth Harding had gone for last-minute instructions about his mission, a diplomatic errand to France.[3] Before departing, he gave Gregory strict orders to increase the ship's crew using the time-honored, Royal Navy method: the press gang.

Gregory carried out his assignment with gusto, manning a long-boat with the toughest thugs among his crew and arming them with boarding axes, cutlasses, and pistols—to intimidate, or worse.[4] Led by another junior officer, they boarded every merchantman or privateer that sailed by. Without fail, they rowed back with several protesting "recruits" whose names or marks now padded the ship's muster rolls. The frigate was christened *Confederacy* to symbolize the voluntary union of the colonies in a common cause. Now the impressment of fellow Americans was required to get her to sea: *Confederacy* by coercion.

All had gone well until this arrogant brig came upriver. Judging from her size, Gregory estimated her crew at about fifty—his men should be able to press at least a half dozen from this ship. Taking up his speaking trumpet, he ordered the brig's "main topsail hove to the mast" to slow her down for boarding. Her captain, in a strong voice with a hint of an Irish brogue, called back across the water that he could not obey "without getting his Vessel on Shore." Gregory could understand that. He did not want to see the brig run aground, he just wanted her men. He then commanded "that the Brig should come to anchor."[5]

The brig's captain neither replied nor complied. Instead, he maintained his course, "beating up with the Tide" in silent but unconcealed defiance. Seething at this show of disrespect, Gregory immediately ordered one of the *Confederacy*'s 12-pound guns run out. As the gunners rushed to their tasks, the longboat was lowered, manned with two officers and Gregory's hand-picked ruffians. Their oars sliced through the water as the cannon roared, the twelve-pound ball screaming overhead before it splashed into the river just in front of the brig.[6]

Soon the longboat bumped up against the brig's hull. Peering through his spyglass, Gregory watched his two officers clamber quickly up the side, jump aboard, and confront the captain—a tall, imposing figure looming over them from the brig's quarterdeck. Before Gregory could wonder why his men were not ascending to assist the officers he saw the reason: the gangway was blocked by some of the brig's sailors, brandishing "muskets, Pistols and Boarding pikes" and shouting threats to the *Confederacy*'s bullies below. In an instant, his two officers were climbing down to the longboat without a man-jack from the brig.[7] The press gang was still rowing back to the *Confederacy* when the incensed lieutenant ordered a second shot fired across the brig's bow, this one splashing a bit closer. There was no need to mask his anger now. Gregory meant business.

But so did the brig's captain. Gregory saw him shouting and gesturing orders to his crew. To the lieutenant's amazement, the brig's four starboard gun ports opened. His opponent was clearing his decks for action. Was he mad? The brig's guns were smaller in size as well as number—if it came to a fight, the *Confederacy* would blow her out of the water. A third warning shot boomed from the frigate, this one coming perilously close to the brig.[8]

Now the brig's captain took his speaking trumpet in hand, gruffly hailing the *Confederacy* and calling for the name of her commanding officer. Trying to sound equally threatening, Gregory gave his name. A second later, the brig's captain replied: "Lieutenant Gregory, I advise you to desist firing. This is the Brig *Delaware* belonging to Philadelphia & my name is John Barry."[9]

One sailor later wrote, "Nothing further was said or done by Lt. Gregory" for he "had been once under the command of Capt'n Barry and could not but know he was not to be trifled with."[10] Recovering his dignity as best as he could, the chastised lieutenant ordered the gun hauled in and his men back to their regular duties. The *Delaware* sailed on. For the rest of the day, Gregory vented his bruised ego on every ship that passed, pressing sailors from each of them.

My name is John Barry. One sentence against three warning shots.

By 1779, Barry had more than earned such extraordinary respect. His reputation was based not just on his consummate skills as a mariner, although these were well known by friend and foe. Neither was it his size, even if at over six feet, four inches, he towered over most of his contemporaries.[11] Nor was it his combative nature, a trait that gave his men heart in the direst of circumstances. He had learned to master fear, but it was not courage alone that made the mere mention of his name give others pause. Last, such esteem could not be attributed merely to his deeply rooted but unsatisfied ambition. It was all of the above.

———————

At the time of Barry's birth, no Irishman could conceive of reaching such heights. For a Catholic in eighteenth-century Ireland, mere survival was success enough.

By 1745, Catholic Ireland had been under Protestant Ireland's thumb for over fifty years. Catholics' hope for freedom, soaring when James II landed in Ireland in 1690 to reclaim his throne from William and Mary of Orange, was dashed after the bitter defeats at the Boyne and at Aughurim. James's exit strategy got him safely back to France, but left his bloodied forces behind in the besieged city of Limerick. After their heroic warrior-chief Patrick Sarsfield negotiated honorable terms, he departed for France, taking most of the Irish army with him into exile. Officially called the Irish Brigades, their skills as mercenaries in the employ of England's enemies soon won them a new name and legend: the Wild Geese.[12] Their departure meant the end of any organized resistance to English invaders and their Irish Protestant supporters who, in their "Ascendancy," used the new Penal Laws to reduce their Catholic neighbors to the status of slaves in everything but name.

The laws were officially called Acts for the Better Securing of the Government Against Papists.[13] Catholics were forbidden to own weapons. No Catholic worship or religious education was tolerated. To enforce these measures, Catholic clergy were ordered out of Ireland. Those caught returning faced being hanged, drawn, and quartered. Catholics could attain no profession or public office. Owning land was prohibited. The Gaelic language was banned. The right to vote was denied. Catholics could not inherit from any Protestant estate. Only one-third of a Catholic farmer's annual harvest could be kept. If it had been possible to pass a law barring the sun from shining on Irish Catholics, the Protestant Parliament would have gladly done so. This sentiment was carved into the Bandon city gates: "Enter here, Turk, Jew or Atheist, Any man except a Papist."[14]

The subjugation of Ireland was as successful as tyranny allows, which means that it failed somewhere, sometime. Despite the dangerous consequences, outlawed priests and teachers were sheltered, as they stole by night from cottage to village, celebrating the banned Mass in "farmhouse churches" and teaching Latin in "hedge schools." Over the decades, those outside the reach of the Penal Laws vigorously attacked them. Edmund Burke decried them in his "Tracts," and Montesquieu wrote, "They were conceived by demons, written in blood, and registered in Hell."[15]

By the mid-eighteenth century, no one under age sixty could remember an Ireland not under these conditions. Certainly James Barry could not, having been born years after Sarsfield's self-banishment. As a tenant farmer, Barry did not have enough hours in the day to pontificate over a long-lost cause. There was work to be done.[16]

For generations, the Barry family lived on the southeast corner of Ireland in County Wexford. For farming, Wexford was idyllic. One surveyor sarcastically remarked that while "Ireland has been said to be found of one immense rock on a bed of granite," Wexford, surrounded on three sides by the sea, had good soil, "being loamy as the depositions subsided towards the sea." Within ten miles of the coast, the ground could be replowed in wintertime, yielding an extra harvest.[17] However, a tenant farmer like Barry, moving from one estate to another, was master of nothing. His situation was as demeaning as that of sharecroppers in the post-Civil War American South. He put bread and potatoes on the table, but little else.

Years earlier, James met and married Ellen Kelly.[18] In those times, weddings were one of the few chances for a community celebration, as long as it was performed in as secluded a place as possible. A Protestant observer of the nuptials of this period marveled how the "ceremony was solemnized...much as in the same manner" as the English ritual. Afterwards, "Relatives and friends bring a profusion of viands of all kinds, and feasting and dancing continue all night, the bride sits veiled at the head of the table, unless called out to dance, when the chair is filled by one of the brides-maids. At every marriage an apple is cut into small pieces, and thrown among the crowd."[19]

The couple eked out their existence moving from one squire's estate to another, surviving the grim famine of 1740-41.[20] By the spring of 1745, they were living in a one room, thatched-roof cottage near Roostontown. Ellen and her sister Margaret were both in the latter days of pregnancy. On April 12–Good Friday–Ellen gave birth to a son. There was no doctor or midwife present; she was assisted by one or two women from the adjoining farms.[21] The proud parents named their son John. He was probably not their firstborn, but likely their first son. Margaret soon gave birth to a daughter.[22]

The storms over Wexford that spring were accompanied with word of political ones. In Scotland, Bonnie Prince Charlie led an uprising against the British, whose armies were in Europe fighting against the French.[23] In June, a ship docked in Wexford harbor, bringing grand news. French forces had met the combined armies of England, Holland, and Germany at Fontenoy in the Low Countries. The tide of the battle was turned by the Irish Brigades, who thoroughly routed the Coldstream Guards, winning the day (and the Low Countries) for France. It was the great hour of the Wild Geese.[24]

Repercussions from their victory were felt throughout Ireland. Protestant rulers feared that the Irish Brigades might return home with one purpose in mind–another war. This, coupled with the rebellion in Scotland, resulted in a suspension of some of the draconian Penal Laws, in hopes of stemming any Catholic support for the

Scottish Cause.[25] The outlawed hedge schools and farmhouse churches were no longer needed.

The town of Wexford blossomed. It had been nearly a century since Cromwell, not wanting "to restrain off the soldiers from their right of pillage," watched them massacre 2000 Wexford men, women, and children. [26] By 1745 Wexford was the most thriving port in all of Ireland; one British official cited its "very considerable importance in trade and shipping."[27] Wexford offered commerce and jobs. The harbor, sitting inside a "letter C" configuration of land, opened on its east to Loch Garman and from there to St. George's Channel.

Wexford merchants expanded their trade from England to France, Spain, and Portugal. Soon they were sending ships to the New World, bearing linen and sailcloth to the West Indies, Mexico, and the Spanish Main.[28] Irish Catholics began migrating to the Caribbean, where some eventually ran their own plantations on the islands of Jamaica and Montserrat.[29]

Despite the British yoke, Ireland in 1745 was exporting prodigious amounts of linen along with wool, ale, and beer. But its chief export was still young Irishmen (their unmarried sisters were sent off to convents or indentured servitude).[30] At the time of John's birth, there were three options for his future: remain home, and confront hardscrabble poverty; join one of the Irish Brigades far flung across Europe, and face death by battle or disease; or go to sea, and live a life fraught with hardships, risking mortality on the world's oceans in service to the British Empire. For many boys, the Wild Geese had their allure: it was estimated that between Limerick and Fontenoy as many as 250,000 Irishmen fought for France alone.[31] When the time came for a choice to be made, the Barrys had one blessing: geography. Wexford provided access to the sea. That had already been a way out for one relative, and a way up for another.

One family member was already in America. Jane Barry may have been the newborn's cousin or aunt; some think her an older sister from a previous marriage. She married John Wilcox, who had connections in the colony of North Carolina. John and Jane settled there too, determined to emulate another Wexford family, the Nixons, and established a shipping business, with an eye on moving north to the busiest American port, Philadelphia.[32] The Penal Laws had not crossed the Atlantic.

By far, the most successful of the Barry clan was James's brother, Nicholas. Sent to sea as a child, he was now a ship's captain, sailing the trade routes to European ports. Granted, there was a "canvas ceiling" that he could never cut through regarding ownership interest in any of his goods, but he certainly might have acquired enough money to build or purchase his own ship—one of the few things the Ascendancy forgot to ban. One Crown surveyor in Wexford told of a captain "building a ship by his own [hand], rigging the vessel by his own manufacture . . . freighted with the produce of the neighbouring lands and [sailing the] ocean for every port of Europe"—an apt description of industrious, ambitious Nicholas Barry.[33]

For James, the next few years saw little change except in new arrivals. Soon his brood numbered at least five children—John, Patrick, Eleanor, Margaret, and Thomas.[34] Booming business on the docks and relaxation of the Penal Laws did nothing to change James's lot. According to local lore, he faced eviction from one squire's estate and found another tenant farm to sweat over near the village of Rosslare, on the southern side of Wexford Harbor.[35] And it is probably here that young John's path was set. Now living even closer to the coast, the youngster could spend some time in Nicholas's company whenever he was ashore.[36] The captain must have looked absolutely heroic to his nephew, with his commanding presence and tales of life at sea.

John attended one of the charter schools while in Rosslare. Recently sanctioned by the government, they provided basic education to Catholic children aged six to ten. The price of instruction was conversion to the Church of Ireland, which many Catholic families subverted by pulling their children out of school as soon as those lessons began in earnest.[37]

For John, school was a welcome break from life on the farm. In later years, letters "from an old schoolfellow" would send him into idyllic reminiscence.[38] One friend, William Kearney, came from a family in the shipping business, who rented one of the village's handsomer homes.[39] The boys roamed the Rosslare waterfront, watching the ships sail to and from what were exotic destinations to the youngsters. The relative affluence of William's family was not lost on John, for whom new clothes or shoes was a rarity.

So many mouths to feed at home wore heavily on James, whose few acres and meager harvest could never supply enough. Young John's help on the farm could not equal what was needed to keep him clothed and fed. It was Nicholas who supplied the solution–a berth for his nine-year-old nephew as cabin boy on a Wexford merchant ship, probably his own.[40]

A later acquaintance of John's wrote how "at a very early age he manifested a strong inclination to follow the sea."[41] If the forthcoming voyage was an adventure in his eyes, it belied the worries of leaving home–poor as home was–and parting from family. At least a sailor's life included visits ashore, while offering escape from land plowed but never owned, air breathed but never as a free man.

The day came for the ship's departure. We do not know if any of John's family were at the dock to see him off, or if they bade farewell at the farm. With cargo stored and crew aboard, the boatswain ("bos'n") piped for all hands. The capstan and halyards were manned. On the timed response of a sea-chantey, spars were raised and the capstan driven until sails were set and anchor was weighed. Soon the ship headed out to St. George's Channel.

The world young John left behind must have seemed a life of leisure compared to his first weeks at sea. Nothing could have prepared him for life in the "wooden world." He was useless at first, as he earned his sea legs the way landsmen do–at the expense of his stomach. His first efforts at keeping his feet on the rocking ship resulted in a severe bout of seasickness, every movement sending his stomach into volcanic upheaval and increasing his dehydrated lightheadedness. One contemporary described his own first sailing days as a boy: "Soon after we [sailed], I became so seasick I could not go off the deck, and I should not have struggled if they hove me overboard!"[42]

Once he passed this ordeal, John began his unending tasks. A cabin boy on a merchant ship was also expected to serve as a seaman at the lowest level. Serving the captain's meals and being his on-

deck errand boy were just a fraction of John's duties. His survival–
and that of his shipmates–would depend on his skills. He needed,
very quickly, to learn the ropes.

Ropes were divided into standing and running rigging. Standing
rigging, tarred black and stiff, supported the masts and were secured
with deadeyes (cut and pierced wood, usually elm or ash). Stays
secured the masts and bowsprits fore and aft; shrouds secured them
to port (left) and to starboard (right). Tarred rope fastened across the
shrouds, called ratlines, allowed the shrouds to work as a rope ladder up the masts. John learned to worm (run small cords between the
strands to smooth the rope), parcel (bind tarred canvas around the
standing rigging), and serve (the final protection for the rigging–spun
yarn banged into the rope with a mallet). Soon he understood the
old adage: "Worm and parcel with the lay but always serve the other
way."[43]

Running rigging consisted of ropes that ran through block and
tackle, adjusting the sails and spars (called yards) to maximize use of
the wind. Halyards raised and lowered the yards; lifts steadied the
yardarms, raising or lowering each corner. Braces rotated and set the
yards in position. Young John quickly learned the ingenuity of block
and tackle: combinations of shell, shiv, and pin that allow the great
weight placed on running rigging to be pulled quickly and efficiently with muscle-saving ease. Once passed through the blocks, running
rigging was secured with a belaying pin, which resembled a small,
thin-handled baseball bat, inserted through the pinrail and secured
with a figure-eight knot for easy release.[44]

Sails were made of the coarsest Irish linen. The ship John sailed
aboard was probably a fore and aft rigged schooner or large sloop
that often carried a square sail at the top of the mast. In learning how
to reef and furl sail, John quickly overcame any fear of heights. On
the ratlines, he learned a mortal principle of physics: the higher one
ascended, the stronger the sway of the boat and wind, until he could
feel sheer force pressing him dangerously downward.[45]

Once aloft, he learned to move along the foot-ropes, those all too
slender lines that ran under the yards. Approached from the windward side so as to be blown in against the sails and not away from
them, John joined fellow crewmembers assigned to gather sail. Using

gaskets, they secured the folds of canvas to the spar from the middle out to the ends of the yards: daunting enough tasks on a smooth sea, but positively death-defying during strong winds and storms. And he learned the cardinal rule of self-preservation: never let go of one rope until another has been firmly grasped.[46]

On deck, chores for experienced hands consisted of mending sail and splicing cracked spars, while novices split those too severely cracked to be repaired. Swabbing the deck was a task for the entire crew. The deck was scrubbed with a holystone, humorously referred to as a "prayer-book" or "bible" depending on its size, and then mopped with "swabs"–mops made of unraveled rope.[47]

Life below deck held no creature comforts. It was dank and dark, lit by an occasional lantern, with a foul array of smells that intensified as the voyage lengthened. Bilge water, livestock, pitch, and unwashed bodies combined to create a unique, ghastly odor. Add the fact that the head–a hole in the deck at the bow, the designated place to relieve oneself–was not always used, and it became clear to any landsman that "going below" was barely any relief from the trials above. The crew's berths were toward the bow in the forecastle ("fo'c'sle"), alongside the cook's galley. The captain's cabin was aft, where the ship's movements were minimized–especially when compared to the heaving that was commonplace at the bow. The hold's cargo was securely lashed to prevent moving as the ship rolled. Ballast, consisting of heavy stone, sand, or gravel, was placed in the hold for balance when no cargo was aboard.

John was used to a meager board at home, but he must have found the ship's mess repulsive. Salt beef and biscuits were everyday fare: beef that would frequently spoil halfway through the voyage, and biscuits that were alive with weevils and worms. Occasionally pork, beans, cheese, potatoes, turnips, and rice found their way into the menu. Rancid butter and a half pint of vinegar were allotted on a weekly basis.[48] Grog–a mixture of water, lime juice and rum–was ladled out twice a day, a pint per man (boys like John received a half-pint).[49]

Being part of the crew had its interpersonal challenges as well. The fo'c'sle was as cramped as it was foul, and the same routine day after day with the same men did not bring out the best in them. It was a rare captain who could keep his men from fighting. Yet, at the same time, the constant labor served a purpose. The drudgery kept the men busy, while the dangerous aspects of work forced them to rely on each other. They further depended on their comrades while on watch. The crew was divided in half, alternating on the day's seven watches; five consisted of four-hour stints, and two "dog-watches" were of two hours each, guaranteeing that John would serve different watches on successive days.[50]

Time was marked with an hourglass or a ship's bell, eight bells per four-hour watch. Off watch, the men slept within inches of each other in hammocks. The roll of the ship kept them swinging and snoring in rhythm. Sailors' superstitions were explained to John whenever he inadvertently transgressed: never hand anything to someone through the ladder rungs; jabbing a pocketknife into a mast could bring a fresh wind; whistling at the wrong time, such as when the ship had head-way, would surely cause a storm.[51] Finally, he learned the inescapable fact for a sailor: he was almost always wet and, in wearing wool and canvas, had little hope of completely drying out.

As his maiden voyage progressed, the cabin boy also noticed the pecking order of life at sea. He had seen the esteem given Uncle Nicholas ashore. Now he watched the captain take full command of ship and crew, making the final decision on the ship's course, and liv-ing in what seemed like blissful elegance in his cabin. He was God on board. For John, at the bottom of the maritime ladder, having his own cabin was not a dream so much as a destination. It was a mat-ter of harnessing his desire to learn with his growing ambition.

John's voyages took him to the ports of Wexford's European trad-ing partners. Soon he could expertly hand, reef, splice, and steer.[52] As his trade kept him from finishing his education, the deck and the crow's nest became his schooldesk. In his mastery of navigation, the sun and the stars became his blackboard. Visits home were as wel-come for the portion of John's earnings put to use for the growing Barry family as for his presence. It was the beginning of a lifetime of charity to his land-bound relations.[53] His successful adaptation to a mariner's life convinced James to ship John's younger brother Patrick off to sea as well.

By the time John had spent a half-dozen years "before the mast," he was a teenager already on his way to clearing six feet in height, big-boned but lean, with a full head of dark hair pulled back and drawn into sealskin. His dark, thick eyebrows arched across piercing gray-brown eyes. A mole appeared between his right eyebrow and long nose.[54] He also possessed the classic Irish head: large, but with eyes, nose, and mouth cramped in the center of the face. The strong jaw line ended in a rounded chin. His skin, once fair as a toddler, had tanned and coarsened from his years at sea, exposed to sun and wind. His large hands were calloused from endlessly handling rope and canvas. His long sea legs had a sailor's grace; balancing the pitch and roll of the deck had become second nature to him.

He was also honing his powers of observation. The mark of a good sea captain lay in his ability to see everything at once. By now Barry performed his tasks, mundane or hazardous, with efficiency. He was well on his way to following in Nicholas's footsteps.

It was at Philadelphia in the colony of Pennsylvania where John Barry began his ascendancy. His coming to Philadelphia has been chronicled as that of the "poor boy made good," a Celtic Horatio Alger story passed down from one generation of Irish-Americans to the next. Actually, he was probably sent there. Irish immigrants had been coming to Philadelphia since 1719. James Logan, Philadelphia's "Secretary of Properties," called them "bold and indigent strangers." Earlier, Logan saw to it that a ship of "100 papists" bypassed his city and sailed upriver to Burlington, New Jersey. "It looks," he complained, "as if Ireland is to send all its inhabitants hither."[55]

By 1760, there was an established Irish presence in the city, including John's relative Jane Barry Wilcox, whose husband was one of a small but growing list of Irish-born merchants in Philadelphia.[56] This was where a Wexford boy with drive and ability could best succeed. So it was to Philadelphia that John Barry came, on a voyage that took two to three months' time. He was fifteen years old.[57]

The Atlantic crossing had its squalls and storms, but the sun was probably up as the ship (most likely another schooner) entered the

Delaware Bay–the gateway to Philadelphia. Off Cape May, the captain stopped and picked up a pilot, whose livelihood was a seemingly endless series of round trips to Philadelphia and back, applying his knowledge of the river's currents, rocks, and shallows to keep his charges from running aground. Depending on conditions, passage upriver could take as long as three days. The bay narrowed where the ship reached the river's mouth. While young Barry kept to his assigned tasks, he took notice of the distant flat and tree-covered shorelines. To starboard–the colony of New Jersey–tiny fishing villages were soon seen, their inhabitants only recently free from the depredations of pirates who once plagued this waterway.[58]

As the ship tacked upriver, traffic increased. Shallops-skiffs propelled by oars or sails–headed north, bearing grain from Maryland and hugging the Delaware colony's shoreline as they passed. Schooners sailed toward the Capes, their holds full of timber, iron, grain, cattle, and salted fish, bound for the West Indies. Others returning from those destinations accompanied John's ship northward, bearing molasses, sugar, and rum. Finally, there were the merchantmen: large, three-masted vessels carrying massive shipments of iron, timber, and furniture to England.[59]

The river became serpentine as it narrowed. Flatboats and small craft were coming out of the creeks, loaded with fish and game for the markets in Philadelphia.[60] The pilot may have pointed out Reedy and Pea Patch Islands as he passed them to port: small, peaceful spits of land. If the passage upriver was uneventful weather-wise, the ship was well into its second day when, to port, the mills of Delaware came into view followed by the first significant towns of Pennsylvania: Marcus Hook and Chester, nautical way stations for passing ships.

As John's vessel approached the mouth of the Schuylkill River, he could make out Philadelphia as a tangle of masts and spars along the wharves, and beyond, an evenly distributed density of redbrick buildings under the afternoon sun. The spire of Christ Church rose over them, a testament to the presence of the Church of England. This was easily the largest city John had seen, never having been to London. Soon all of its sights, sounds, and smells greeted him as the ship docked.

The city John would call home for the rest of his life held the largest population in the American colonies, and was the second largest English-speaking city in the world. By 1760, Pennsylvania's population had reached about 200,000; in Philadelphia the population neared 30,000. It was already written that "Philadelphia is not only the busiest port on the American continent, it is probably busier than any port in England except for London and Liverpool."[61]

All of this awaited John's discovery, but for now there was the matter of finding the Wilcox home. We do not know if their hospitality extended past one night. Perhaps, like other bachelor sailors, he found lodging at one of the meager boardinghouses along the waterfront.[62] In the morning, while venturing back to the waterfront to find a berth on an outgoing ship, young Barry got his bearings of Philadelphia. The evenly spaced streets ran from Front west to Eighth and from Cedar north to Vine, where the township of Northern Liberties began, stretching several miles along the Delaware up to the village of Frankford. The houses on each block stood like redbrick battle squares. Here lived citizens of wealth and property: professionals, businessmen, and gentlemen of leisure. Their servants and slaves were quartered in the small backyards, along with any horses or other livestock (chickens and pigs were common). Along the alleys that split the streets directly behind these homes were shacks and shanties that housed the working class. Only a few feet separated their living quarters from those of Philadelphia's well-off. Artisans–silversmiths, furniture makers, and coopers among them–actually lived in both parts of the block, their place of residence based more on financial success than class status. Their work ethic was legendary, having long abandoned the old city workweek that included a second successive day off, known as "St. Monday."[63]

Young Barry found the appearances of Philadelphians as diverse as the people themselves. Quaker men still favored their simply cut suits of black or gray cloth, topped with the unadorned, broad-brimmed hats that had defied fashion trends for eighty years. Other Philadelphians wore knee britches and broad coats, their oversized cuffs kept in place with starch and large brass buttons. Buckled shoes and a tricornered hat completed the outfit. Leather vests and aprons identified the artisan, buckskin and coonskin the woodsman selling his furs. The most colorful apparel was worn by the "Macaronis," young rich men in tight, colorful clothes with a knot of hair fastened at the nape, strutting through town carrying decorative five-foot walking sticks. Women wore the colorful clothing of the day. Among their accessories they carried a "pocket"–a purse drawn shut by leather or ribbon, tied around the waist or neck–as women's clothing had no actual pockets.[64]

The city's many taverns, coffeehouses, and inns catered to one certain class or another. The largest was the London Coffeehouse on Front and High streets, the gathering place of choice for Philadelphia's merchants. Coffeehouses served a special purpose; their common rooms and upstairs parlors were eighteenth-century conference centers for deal making and political discussions.[65] Standing in the street, John heard the men inside discussing the war with France, the latest ship arrivals, and gossip on every subject. Their voices created a steady hum that competed with the auctioneer on the front porch, busily selling everything from unloaded cargo to slaves. By the time of John's arrival, efforts to abolish slavery in Pennsylvania were well under way. Still, the "Droves"–long lines of slaves, chained two by two, were paraded through the streets, and Philadelphia's most successful merchants, Willing and Morris, advertised the sale of "170 Negroes from Barbados."[66]

Shops were plentiful along High Street, called "Market" for its array of stores and stands. Smithies were busy, making everything from nails to anchors. Others tradesmen offered tea kettles, coffee pots, and ovens. Bookbinders thrived. Pottery, glassware, and leather goods were sold. The two top newspapers, the *Pennsylvania Packet* and Benjamin Franklin's *Pennsylvania Gazette,* were in demand throughout the colonies and in Europe. By 1760, Philadelphia had more newspapers than London.[67]

Walking one block north of Market, Barry saw the Arch Street Ferry, the most direct route for crossing the river to New Jersey at Camden. Ownership of the enterprise had given Samuel Austin wealth, property, and his own pew at Christ Church, where his family joined the Merediths, Hopkinsons, and Franklins at Sunday services.[68]

Further uptown was the seat of government. The state house dominated Chestnut Street between Fifth and Sixth Streets, where some farms still existed.[69] The last building of size and importance was Pennsylvania Hospital, co-founded by Franklin and ensconced at the unofficial end of town on Eighth Street between Walnut and Pine, a bucolic area of farmland and (sometimes) clean country air. Prior to its construction, the care for the sick and insane was left to the poorhouses, where they coexisted with debtors. Here, too, lived the wives and families of Philadelphia's sailors, whenever their money ran out.[70]

The docks bustled with activity unlike anything John had seen. The riverfront was packed with sailors, laborers, peddlers, and the occasional inspection officials. Their voices rose in cacophony over the endless clanking of the windlasses that raised the cargo out of ships' holds, to be carted off to the merchant warehouses. Permeating everything was the foul smell of a tannery behind Carpenters' Hall, its waste seeping into Dock Creek and thence into the Delaware, while its odor drifted across the city, even reaching ships downriver if a northern breeze prevailed.[71] North and south of the docks lay the shipyards, each one just long enough and wide enough to hold the skeleton of any craft from shallop and sloop to brigantine and schooner.[72] The larger merchantmen were built downriver in Southwark, where John Wharton owned the largest shipyard in Philadelphia. Rope-makers, sail-makers, and chandlers never lacked for work in this city.

This was Barry's new home. Years after his death, two longtime acquaintances wrote a magazine article about his life. In their narration of his first days in Philadelphia, they did not describe his impressive physique. Instead, they told of his brains and spirit; how he was "possessed of a strong and active mind" with "indefatigable industry." For such a willing lad, a berth on an outgoing vessel was never in doubt, and "he was not long without employment."[73]

The West Indies were the cornerstone of Philadelphia's merchant trade. The city was "one-stop shopping" for practically everything the islands needed, and West Indies' coffee, rum, molasses, sugar, ginger, pimento, and pepper were sold in Philadelphia and reshipped to England and the other twelve colonies. Profit margins were wondrous; during the French and Indian War, Philadelphia merchants saw a 10 percent higher volume on outbound cargo to the Caribbean.[74] Over the next six years, this lucrative trade gave John the chance to demonstrate "his nautical skill, the steadiness of his habits, and the integrity of his character."[75] By the end of his teens, he had risen to a mate's status. Merchants and captains came to the same conclusion: young Barry could be trusted.

Earlier biographers told as fact the legend that he served as a mate on Charles Carroll's voyage from London to Maryland in 1764, but no document substantiates this. A letter written that same year from a Basseterre businessman sent "by this opportunity of Mr. Barry going to Dominique" regarding payment arrangements and the request "Please send my Sword by Mr. Barry" verified his activities in a more realistic light.[76] James Fenimore Cooper, in his "Sketches of Naval Men," written in 1839, told the following anecdote:

> A riot occurred among some stevedores, and a ship owner of respectability was threatened with injury. Barry interfered, and manifested so much in intrepidity and personal prowess, as at once to procure for him a reputation in the then peaceable town of Philadelphia . . . Barry had grappled one of the stoutest of the stevedores in the presence of the owner, who was a "Friend," [crying] "Give it to him, Johnny, now thou hast him."[77]

By 1766, he possessed leadership skills and a detailed knowledge of the West Indies trade. Merchants, always judging talent, were rarely willing to risk ship, crew, and cargo to an untried mate. Established firms retained the more experienced captains, frequently offering them some equity in the vessel they commanded—an eighteenth-century version of "golden handcuffs." Although there were five hundred merchants in Philadelphia between 1756 and 1765, just fifty-two of them, in thirty-seven firms, were the foundation of Philadelphia trade.[78] It was usually a merchant outside this circle, successful enough to own at least one ship, who gave someone like John a chance at command.

For Barry, that man was an elderly merchant named Edward Denny. His had been no meteoric rise; his name was not spoken with the hushed, revered tones that accompanied mention of Meredith, Willing, Drinker, or Morris. True, he worked on a smaller scale than these illustrious men, but he shared one thing in common with them. He traded in slaves.[79]

Quakers had long abandoned this traffic, leaving it to Anglican merchants, who happily picked up both the slack and the profit. Where a vacuum exists, an entrepreneur will seize the moment, and Denny did just that. For twelve years he published notices like the following: "A LIKELY Barbadian fellow, about 23 years of age, he has had the Smallpox, and is fit for any business. Likewise three Negroe girls[.] Enquire of Edward Denny, at Captain Arthur'[s] in Walnut St."[80]

By 1766, Denny's services as middleman in the slave trade provided him enough money to purchase his own schooner, the *Pitt*.[81] With his own ship, he became a true merchant of respectable goods. Schooners cost roughly £500 cash, a high figure for a merchant to have available. Denny's success in the slave trade allowed him to escape it.[82]

However, it did not leave him enough funds to employ a seasoned captain. He had to take a chance on a first mate whose references would attest to skills as a sailor, navigator, businessman, and leader. Denny's peers and maritime contacts brought him and Barry together. After meeting the twenty-one-year-old Irishman, Denny felt comfortable placing his ship in the youth's hands. There was no question in Barry's mind if he wanted to assume such responsibility. Denny's offer was quickly accepted. On September 29, 1766, the new shipowner and shipmaster walked the cobbled streets together to the Custom House, where they registered the *Pitt,* a "Square Stern'd Vessel of the Burthen of sixty Tons or thereabouts." They also gave her a new name: the *Barbadoes*.[83] She was one of the larger schooners registered that year.[84]

The size of Barry's first command can be guessed from plans of a ship of similar tonnage: about fifty-five feet in length, seventeen feet in breadth, with an eight-foot depth of hold. The captain's cabin was about five and a half feet in height, and with the deck beams lowering the ceiling by another foot at some points, the young shipmaster could stand erect only above deck. A small cubbyhole served as the mate's quarters. The galley and fo'c'sle were about ten feet combined, with a brick oven toward the front that further cramped living quarters of a crew of five or six. Above deck, she carried a fifty-foot mainmast and a smaller foremast.[85] A trim craft, all in all, well-suited for its purpose.

The crew's scant number was not unusual for Philadelphia merchants, notorious for employing "skeleton crews" for every voyage. To them, the peril of becoming further shorthanded from storm, accident, or disease was not sufficient risk to hire more hands. Safety in the number of sailors shrunk profits.

Barry's personal life was also changing, thanks to an Irish girl named Mary Cleary. Like John, she was twenty-one years old. No record exists of where, when, or how they met. Any courtship was constricted by Barry's career choice—away for months, home for a few weeks at best; but at least it gave Mary an inkling of marriage to a seafarer. Still, a captain's income, coupled with Barry's good looks and charm, certainly made him a great "catch" to Mary, who may have been a house servant fresh from indenture or the daughter of a poor family. There are no Clearys in the Philadelphia annals of the time, and Mary left no letters or other information for historians.[86]

Barry assumed his first command just as mercantile America won a temporary victory over the mother country. Merchants were already coping with the Navigation Laws and the Sugar Act by mastering smuggling as a business practice (in Boston, John Hancock was so successful at it that he earned the dubious nickname "King of Smugglers").[87] While smuggling was the option most used to circumvent previous British laws designed to restrain private profit while increasing government revenue, the Stamp Act—Parliament's latest measure to cover postwar colonial expenses—was opposed outright by the merchants and their associates. Their unified opposition forced its repeal in Parliament.[88]

There was still ample British influence over Barry's new venture. Under the law, the *Barbadoes'* cargo was limited to goods produced in Pennsylvania and New Jersey. For days, stevedores labored up and down the schooner's gangplank under the novice captain's watchful eye, until every item on his cocket was stowed in the hold: thousands of barrel staves, headings, and shingles; bundles of hoops; dozens of chains, and bars of iron. Barry and Denny attested to their being "firmly bound unto our Sovereign Lord George III, by the Grace of God etc." and that, in compliance with the Navigation Laws, all goods were guaranteed delivery to Barbados and nowhere else.[89]

On October 20, 1766, with his small crew and a pilot aboard, Barry ordered the yards hoisted, the anchor weighed, and the sails unfurled. Denny was among the onlookers seeing Barry off, watching his investment stand down the Delaware. For Mary it would be months before her young lover returned—unless some tragedy took him away forever. John Barry had begun his career as a ship's captain.[90]

The new master discharged his pilot at Cape Henlopen and set a course east southeast toward Bermuda. From there Barry sailed south by east, a route he knew well. If meteorological conditions were good, the trip could be made in three weeks. Barbados is the easternmost of the Windward Islands, which comprise the lower half of the Lesser Antilles. Like a bent longbow, the islands curve gracefully, starting north at Puerto Rico and finishing at Grenada. Only Barbados juts out of place.

Its capital, Bridgetown, lies southwest on the island, facing Carlisle Bay. The established route that ships took was to round Barbados to windward and sail into the harbor.[91] Barry arrived in Bridgetown in November, docking at the Stepping Stones Wharf.[92] After meeting with customs officials, Denny's agent, and unloading the cargo, there was no rush to return home. Denny had arranged to keep the *Barbadoes* south and out of the winter storms, with instructions that Barry make two short hauls to the Carolinas and back to Bridgetown.[93]

The long layover allowed Barry and his crew to help save Bridgetown from infernal disaster. On the night of December 27, fire broke out in one of the waterfront stores. Winds spread the flames to the warehouses and soon threatened to engulf the entire town, already a victim of a devastating conflagration months earlier. Soon the winds sent the fire back toward Stepping Stones Wharf, licking at the *Barbadoes* and the other docked ships. Along with the towns-folk and other mariners, Barry and his sailors tirelessly worked the bucket brigades. By morning they had contained the damage to approximately forty buildings.[94]

Staying south to avoid the winter weather as planned, Barry made his round trips to the Carolinas. After his second ended, he had the hold filled with rum, sugar, and molasses, returning to Philadelphia in June 1767.[95] During this passage homeward the *Pennsylvania Gazette* published its first news report from Barry. It was customary for captains to inform newspapers of the ships they sighted or "spoke," giving their readers (especially owners and family members) any updates regarding those at sea:

> Captain Barry, from Barbadoes, informs, that a brig, Captain Duncan of this Port arrived there from Maryland, on the 10th of last month, and sailed again on the 12th for Antigua. On the sixth instant, in Lat 29, Long. 68, he spoke a Brig from Antigua for Virginia, 7 Days out, all well, but could not learn the Master's Name; and on the seventh in Lat 32:30 Long. 71, he spoke a Sloop, Captain Williams 15 days from Barbados, but last from St. Eustatia bound to New London.[96]

Barry's safe return with a hold full of profitable goods met with Denny's satisfaction, and he was back to sea in August. The young skipper sailed again to Barbados with a cargo similar to that of his first voyage. This junket, a true round trip, was one that fully tested his skills and nerve. On October 15, he began a forty-eight-hour sail through one of the more horrific storms that attacked the Atlantic coast. The *Pennsylvania Gazette* reported how "Captain Barry's Vessel was thrown on her Beam Ends for 24 hours, shifted her Cargoe, and he lost his Mainsail and Topsail."[97]

"Thrown on her Beam Ends" meant that the *Barbadoes* was sail-ing almost sideways, her sails reefed or in tatters, and perilously close to capsizing. The storm tossed the schooner about like a fragile toy, threatening the ship not only with gale force winds and high seas but with motion itself. Working under terrifying conditions day and night, the hardy men of the *Barbadoes* proved their seamanship.

This issue of the *Gazette* was filled with reports of a host of ships, bound from Europe as well as the Caribbean, assailed by what must have been a hurricane of monstrous proportions. To have sailed his schooner successfully through such a force of nature was a real accomplishment for Barry. Keeping a ship safe in a storm tested a captain's ability to handle life-and-death issues in rapid succession. By this time, Barry was familiar with how his schooner handled strong wind and dangerous seas. He also knew the measure of each man aboard. Doubtless his sailors had gotten to know him as well. With a crew this small, each person's capabilities were constantly tested.

Barry brought the *Barbadoes* back to Philadelphia on October 26, and wasted no time with his nuptials: on October 31, John and Mary were married in a simple ceremony. The newlyweds settled in the South Ward, which was affordable and close to the riverfront–although within reach of the tannery's stink.[98]

Their adjustment to married life lasted just a month, for Barry sailed again on November 28. Mary's first Christmas as a captain's wife was spent without her bridegroom. Word did not reach Philadelphia of John's safe arrival until January 23, 1768.[99] One month later, the *Gazette* ran another report from Barry about the aftermath of another severe storm. Mary–if she were literate–could read about the hazards of her husband's profession:

Captain Barry, also from this Place for Barbados, in his Passage, Lat. 29, spoke a Sloop, Captain Winters, from Maryland for Halifax, who had been blown off the Coast, and was then standing for the Grenades, 7 Weeks out; that a Sloop from Maryland for Boston, and a Schooner from St. Eustatia for Connecticut, being blown off, were arrived at Barbados, the Captain of the latter died 9 Days before she got in; that Captain Forbes, in a Brig from New London arrived there in a shattered Condition, having . . . in a Gale of Wind, shipped a Sea, which carried away his Awning, and 40 Horses, also his Mainsail, Boom, Outer, Rails, Stanchions, Binnacle,

Companion, Tiller, and every Thing off his Deck with one of his Men, who was drowned; that another Brig from the same Place, also arrived there, having lost 17 Horses, her Main, Topmast, and two Men, in the same Gale.[100]

Welcome, Mrs. Barry, to news from the sea.

Under the same schedule as the previous fall, Barry returned in May.[101] He made no fewer than four voyages to Barbados in 1768 alone.[102] While Mary adapted to her lot as a captain's wife, Barry's successes earned him recognition by his peers. In 1769 he was elected to the Society for the Relief of Poor, Aged and Infirmed Masters of Ships, and Their Widows and Children, better known as the Sea Captains Club. Membership in this organization was a sign that young Barry had arrived. Its roster of captains and owners was a veritable Who's Who of the Philadelphia maritime, and many of them would play a part in Barry's future adventures.[103]

The club's dinners at the City Tavern gave Barry an opportunity to put his talent for observation to use in a different world: the gentleman's dining room. While some members came from the same rough-and-tumble world as he, there were others like Charles Biddle, raised in a more genteel environment yet equally at home on a merchantman's deck and in a salon. Barry watched Biddle and the other gentlemen with a quiet intensity, scrutinizing their posture and language right down to which fork they used for what course. He saw admittance in the Sea Captains Club not so much an honor as a steppingstone—a chance to some day enter Philadelphia's upper class.

Barry's voyages on the *Barbadoes* were undertaken while another political shoving match took place between the colonies and England. William Pitt, America's champion in Parliament, was mentally and physically ill. In a naked power play, his mantle was seized by Charles Townshend, whose agenda, passed by Parliament and bearing his name, included blank search warrants ("Writs of Assistance"), new duties on goods, and laws imposed on the colonies intended to increase British influence and profits. Among other odious practices under the Townshend Acts, the new position of "port collector" was handed to cronies of the royal governors, who weathered the animosity and disdain of merchant and captain alike.[104]

Merchants began attacking the issue of Crown taxes with a different weapon: their rights as British citizens. It was the start of their own personal tug of war, pitting their civic hearts against their financial souls. These same political and economic issues were discussed by the Sea Captains Club over pipes and bowls of punch at the London Coffeehouse. The new laws and duties dictated from on high across the Atlantic had a direct bearing on their livelihood, and they sided with their employers. The merchants won another economic victory when Parliament abolished all duties—except those on tea.[105]

Barry finished an eighth voyage commanding the *Barbadoes* in May 1769, and was back to sea before the month was over. Mary must have taken comfort that the summer voyages were always demonstrably shorter: no sooner did she read on August 17 that Barry was in Barbados than she saw his ship come in a few days later. As usual, the reunion was all too short, after a flurry of refitting and resupplying the schooner, Barry departed in early September on his longer winter mission. The *Gazette* reported that on his southern passage, the schooner ran aground near Barbados and "it is hoped will also be got off with little Damage." By the end of the month, Mary, Denny, and other readers learned that "all [was] well."[106] The Barrys, married two years, spent their third Christmas apart.

After several more trips in 1770, Barry made his last voyage in the *Barbadoes* that September. Whether Denny was ill or just looking to retire is not known. Over the previous year, Custom House tonnage reports listed the well-known merchant Reese Meredith as cosigner in Denny's stead.[107] The log for this voyage is the oldest surviving document in Barry's hand. The *Barbadoes* departed Philadelphia for Antigua on October 7—at the height of the hurricane season—with a "Pleasant Breeze and Clear Weather attended with some squalls. / People employed on Sundry."[108] There was "Fresh Breezes and Clear Weather with all sails sett" for the next two weeks.

Then the weather took a violent turn: "Strong Gales and Cloudy W[eather]. At 9 AM Close Reeft four top Sail at 10 AM Duble Reeft foresail M.S. [mainsail] and Took the Bonnet of[f] the Jib." The gale threatened to overwhelm the schooner. Barry, anxious to keep his course and use the wind as far as risk allowed, shortened and trimmed all but his mainsail. The next day, the *Barbadoes* "Pitched her Bowsprit in and Carreyed away the flying Jib Boom and washed away Some of the Jib." Without the lead sails working, Barry was forced to steer the schooner like a crab over the water. Repairs could not be made until the gale subsided two days later, when he entered in the log, "I find my self in the Gulfstream."[109]

The tempests returned: "Dark Rainey" storms dogged the *Barbadoes*, forcing Barry to sail through "a large Sea [and] hard Gales." Barry tenaciously held his course as close to south-southeast as possible, while green seawater washed over the bulwarks and poured down the hatchway, keeping his sailors hard at the pumps when not fighting the storm on deck or aloft. On October 30, Barry finally entered the words "MOD[erate] B[reezes] and Clear . . . with all sails sett." Cloudy days with no observations followed, but by now the master of the *Barbadoes* was an expert at dead reckoning: accounting for the ship's position when conditions prevented astronomical observations.[110] By November 11, the *Barbadoes* was safely in Carlisle Bay.

When he returned to Philadelphia Barry learned of Denny's retirement, putting the young captain out of work; the deck of the ship he considered his own had been sold right out from under his feet. Success did not satisfy him—it merely stoked his ambition further. Only twenty-five and already an accomplished sailor and captain, Barry had a new goal: ship owner.

CHAPTER TWO

STORMS

BARRY'S ACHIEVEMENTS WERE QUITE A TOPIC among the mariners and merchants at the London Coffeehouse and City Tavern. As he was without employ upon his return to Philadelphia, Barry's services as captain were "recommended . . . to some of the most respectable merchants."[1] Each voyage of the *Barbadoes* netted owner Edward Denny a 10 to 15 percent profit.[2] Barry's was the latest success story along the waterfront.

Philadelphia's merchants and captains faced new risks. The economic downturn after the end of the French and Indian War, followed by the Stamp Act and the Townshend Acts, compounded the ever-present risks of fickle markets and the loss of ships at sea. Established firms, some in their second or third generation, weathered these challenges better than fledgling newcomers could. Quaker mercantile dynasties competed against firms with Anglican names like Willing, Coxe, and Morgan. Some of their suppliers and employees looked at the merchants' wealth and position with envy. Others, like Barry, saw their riches as an objective worth striving for. He was among the mariners, vendors, and artisans who, seeing that their talents and efforts did not produce similar financial rewards, concluded that becoming a merchant was their best chance at getting rich.[3]

In the early winter of 1770, Barry returned to Philadelphia with a plan, if not a ship. Already managing his earnings in a manner reflective of his penurious upbringing—dividing it between his expenses at home and his family in Wexford—he and Mary saved whatever remained. (Barry's prolonged absences gave her a freer hand on the purse-strings.)[4] While lacking sufficient funds to purchase his own ship, there was enough to contribute to a joint venture, and he had partners in mind: John Dugan, a shopkeeper, and Stephen Barden, a grocer, two acquaintances from Dock Ward.[5] Both Irishmen were doing well in their chosen fields, but like Barry they wanted more. A partnership was formed.[6]

By the end of the 1760s the concentration of wealth in Philadelphia's upper class was accelerating. Poverty—one of the ills William Penn hoped to leave in England—had come to stay, making its presence felt in the social fabric of the New World's largest city.[7] "It is remarkable what an increase of the number of Beggars there is about this town in the winter," one Quaker sadly commented.[8] This development carried economic consequences, increasing the risk factor for new ventures, especially ones funded by those from modest beginnings, gambling everything they owned. For every success story like Barry's, there was a fistful of failures.[9]

For the first time in Barry's marriage Christmas was spent with Mary, attending Mass at St. Joseph's, the small church sequestered off Walnut Street. Rumors of war between England and Spain over the Falkland Islands were fresh in the wintry air when another merchant, John Gibbon, approached Barry with a wrinkle in his plans with Dugan and Barden.[10] Gibbon owned the brig *Patty and Polly*, whose captain had died on the most recent voyage. With the brig's hold full of supplies for the Virgin Islands, Gibbon asked Barry to assume command. Although the dead of winter posed a challenging time for such an enterprise, Barry accepted.[11]

The Delaware was "so full of Ice that all Navigation is Stopped," and Barry could not depart until the end of February, 1771.[12] "Hard Squalls" dogged the brig; one vicious storm forced her to ride under "bare poles"—without sails. For forty hours the masts didn't carry so much as a rag of canvas, as tremendous waves washed over ship and crew. Barry did not find himself in peaceful waters until the end of

March. After a month of refitting and loading new stores in St. Croix, Barry returned to Philadelphia in May.[13] By then the threat of war with Spain had passed, and Barry renewed his search for a vessel that would suit his new venture.[14]

In August he found it: the schooner *Nancy*, for sale by her owner, an acquaintance of Barry's. After his thorough inspection found her seaworthy, Barry convinced Dugan and Barden of her merits. The three partners purchased her, registering the vessel under her new name, *Industry*.[15] With a growing reputation as a good captain, Barry had no trouble hiring a crew, and in one week had enough hands and a cargo loaded for delivery to a Virginia merchant.[16] The *Industry* departed Philadelphia on August 28.[17]

Barry titled his log "A Journal of a Voyage from Philadelphia Toward James River Virginia in the Good Schooner *Industry*."[18] At twenty-six, he was a ship owner, the equal of his Uncle Nicholas. Barry's Catholicism, lack of extensive education, and family status—insurmountable obstacles in Ireland—were, in Philadelphia, merely incidental facts about the man. The pride in the log's title was merited.

Industry hugged the coast of Maryland until Barry sighted Chincoteague on August 30 and headed the schooner up the James River. On the morning of September 1, wearing his finest clothes, Barry came ashore to register at the Williamsburg Custom House. It was a beautiful day; the streets full of well-dressed Virginians on their way to church. Barry returned to his ship. "Went up to Williamsburg Could Do No Businis," he sheepishly wrote, having forgotten it was Sunday.[19]

For several days, a lingering storm prevented the unloading of Barry's cargo. The downpour slowed refilling the *Industry*'s hold as well. Weeks dragged by before she left Virginia, arriving in Philadelphia on September 21. So far, the *Industry* was performing to her captain's liking, and she took on another merchant's cargo for New York, departing on November 4.[20] For the first time in Barry's marriage he was home for his wedding anniversary. Things looked rosy for John and Mary as they began their fifth year together, thanks to the initial success of Barry and his partners.

Their ardor soon cooled after a marked change of luck for the *Industry*. Just five hours after leaving Philadelphia, an errant shallop carried away her jib boom. Repairs were no sooner completed the following afternoon when Barry's "Raskill of a Pilot" ran the schooner aground at Cape May. For an entire day, an irate Barry scribbled soundings and fathoms, making every effort to get the *Industry* offshore, all the while calling the "Raskill" other names not entered in the log for posterity. The usually short trip to New York was also plagued with a vicious nor'easter, "Keeping all Hands at the Pumps." As the ship took in wave after wave of water, Barry headed further and further south to escape the storm. Soon he was far off course, estimating that the *Industry* was fifty miles off the Delaware coast. When "Pleasant Breezes" returned, Barry "spoke a pilot boat" off Cape May, the exact spot the *Industry* had been one week earlier. Four days later, the schooner "Run up to [New] York in Company with several other Vessels."[21]

The return trip was no less vexing. "Strong Gales and Dark Snowy weather" damaged the *Industry*'s rigging and sails. The next day "An abundance of Snow" prevented Barry from making any observations. Once again his efforts to keep the ship safe resulted in a further loss of time. After being driven below Maryland, Barry and his crew brought the *Industry* northward with great difficulty, finally spotting the Cape Henlopen lighthouse after three sleepless days and nights. The *Industry* returned to Philadelphia on December 12.[22] The shortest roundtrip of Barry's career was one of his most hazardous.

That storm was a harbinger of bitter weather to come. With their financial situation threatened by weather and the calendar, the *Industry*'s owners rushed into another voyage, this time to Nevis.[23] The Delaware was so icebound that few ships arrived in port and even fewer departed.[24]

Shortly after New Year's Day 1772, enough ice melted for the *Industry* to stand down the Delaware, but pleasant weather only accompanied her to Cape Henlopen. "Fresh gales" pushed the schooner eastward and further off course, as "Large Seas" broke over her rails and "Caried away sundry small things." After two weeks, the weather changed to "Mod[erate] Breezes and Cloudy," allowing the crew to repair "The Flying Jibb Gear and Boom." On January 19, under a beautiful, starry, midnight sky, the *Industry* "Came to Anchor in Nevis Road."[25]

This voyage marked a return to the winter schedule of Barry's *Barbadoes* days; he remained in the Caribbean until March, returning with the usual cargo of rum, molasses, and sugar. Navigating the treacherous and oddly named shoals around Nevis was a challenge, but Barry safely sailed the *Industry* through "the Dog and Prickelly Paire." "Pleasant and fair all sails Sett" marked Barry's departure but, as befitting the *Industry*'s luck, "Fresh Gales" accompanied her homeward, with more sails, blocks, and yards lost, and more water "shipt" until reaching Philadelphia at month's end.[26]

The *Industry*'s last voyages put an end to her owners' enthusiasm for their venture. Repairs ate substantially into profits. The challenge of ownership differed for each man. Anxiety over the whims of nature playing with his investment sent Dugan back to full-time shopkeeping. Barden found that cockets and customs laws did not suit him as well as selling Jersey produce.[27] Lacking the stomach for the uncertainties of mercantilism, Dugan and Barden wanted out. As for Barry, he had been tested at sea like never before, and was the better captain for it. Whether he wanted to keep the schooner was a moot point—he could not afford to buy out his partners. The best-laid plans of grocer, shopkeeper, and sailor had gone awry.

They agreed to sell the *Industry* after her return from a voyage to Halifax, Nova Scotia, where Barry not only found a prospective buyer but also discovered a sloop for sale, named *Frugality*.[28] She was the classic model of what was popularly called a Bermuda schooner: three lateen sails started from her bowsprit to a single mast, which held a fore- and aft-rigged mainsail and one square-sail atop.[29] After inspecting the craft he took an option on her.

The homeward trip gave Barry time to mull over his future by examining his past. Denny's retirement had left him high and dry, and now his partners' decision to return to the relative safety of their old occupations did the same. Without the wherewithal to buy the *Frugality* himself, he needed an employer of substance, a merchant who would see his availability and that of the *Frugality* as a profitable combination. He knew such a man. The *Industry* no sooner docked in Philadelphia than he was off to see Denny's friend Reese Meredith.[30]

Meredith, reputedly worth £80,000 (a multimillionaire's fortune today), was one of Philadelphia's most respected and experienced merchants, at ease with the ebb and flow of profit and loss, with profit being his usual outcome. His partner, George Clymer, was a man of unquestioned integrity and civic-mindedness, if not possessing his partner's zeal for trade. Well-born and well-off, Clymer, who would later sign the Declaration of Independence, was not in love with his profession, actually instructing his children *not* to follow in his footsteps.[31] Meredith and Clymer expanded their business and their fleet with methodical surefootedness.

Barry's hunch was correct. Meredith not only saw the merit in his proposal, but offered to add Barry to his roster of captains and purchase the *Frugality* for his command.[32] Another captain in Barry's predicament might have cursed his bad luck and the "bare poles" that put him in such a financial crisis. Barry turned his dilemma into career advancement.

Meredith's newest captain sailed the *Industry* back to Nova Scotia that summer, returning aboard Meredith's newest acquisition in September. The sloop's sailing capabilities were a delight to her new master. His reunion with Mary in Philadelphia was a special one, for she had exceptional news: John's brother Patrick was in town, as shipmaster of the schooner *Amelia*, out of St. Kitts. Mary met not only Patrick but his fiancée, Mary Farrell, as well. Plans were made for an October wedding upon Patrick's return from sea.[33]

With his own star rising again, John moved Mary to a larger home in the Walnut Ward, between the docks and the business district. Tax records listed three residents: "John Barrey, wife and servant"—but did not indicate if this servant was indentured or a slave (due to Barry's prolonged absences it was most likely a young woman).[34] She could also have been another Irish immigrant, many of whom were already bond servants before leaving Ireland or, arriving penniless, were forced into indenture at the Philadelphia docks.[35] This "acqui-

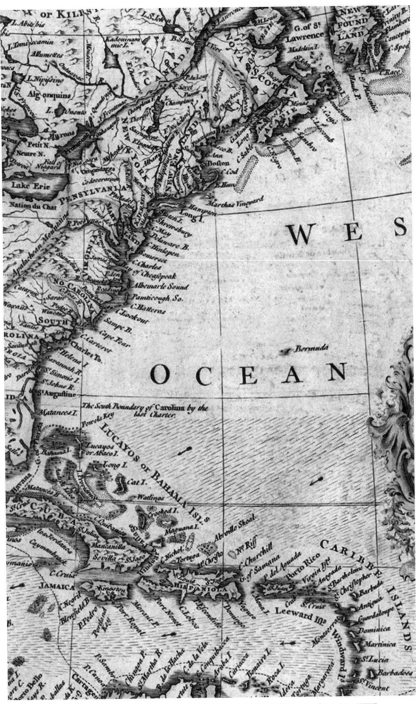

The Eastern North American Seaboard and the West Indies in 1775.
(*Library of Congress*)

sition" to assist Mary with her housekeeping was as much a sign of success to Mary as was Barry's new position. The injustice of slavery and indentured servitude received very little thought among most white colonists. But the irony that an exile from the demeaning Penal Laws would see nothing amiss in the ownership of another human being was evidently as lost on Barry as it had been on the Irish plantation owners in the West Indies or other successful Irish émigrés.

Barry spent the next several weeks refitting his new ship, now called the *Peggy*. Shipping records of the day abound with vessels given a lady's name beginning with the letter "P," in sound and speech easy to understand whenever captains "spoke each other" at sea. Refitting took longer than anticipated, allowing John to be present for his brother's wedding—barely. Patrick was docking the *Amelia* while Barry and Meredith registered the *Peggy* at the Custom House on October 9. The next day's tide table gave Barry the chance to stand at Patrick's side just long enough to witness the vows. Then he scrambled to the waterfront to sail off in the *Peggy* for St. Eustatia. After finding living quarters near John's in Walnut Ward, Patrick too was off, dividing his voyages on the *Amelia* between New Orleans and Barbados.[36]

Barry reached Oranjestad, St. Eustatia's capital, at month's end. The island's vast roadstead could hold two hundred ships, and as Barry brought the *Peggy* into the harbor he saw seemingly countless warehouses built right up to the waterfront. Beyond them was a natural plateau, rising over the town and below the peak of an ancient volcano. An array of luxurious tropical mansions, built by the rogue merchants of this freewheeling isle, made the vista even more imposing. The *Peggy* dropped anchor at the busiest and richest settlement in the western hemisphere.[37]

In one major respect, St. Eustatia was different from Barry's other Caribbean destinations. "Statia" was a free port. Trade was open to every country, and the legitimacy of one's trade was no concern at all. Dutch-owned and perpetually neutral, St. Eustatia was nestled among British, French, Spanish, and Danish islands, thereby becoming the principal port for goods coming from and going to America and Europe.[38] No wonder Statia was called "the Golden Rock."

Meredith and Clymer's agent met Barry as he docked, introducing him to the tiny island's carefree business transactions while the *Peggy* was relieved of her cargo. Nothing in Barry's return cocket was home produced. St. Eustatia did not make or refine anything; it served as a way station for everyone else's goods. The mile-long main street in Oranjestad consisted of shops, taverns, and storage depots one after another. Goods from the world over were traded: rum from Jamaica, furniture from the North American colonies, clothing from England, all interspersed with French silks, Danish coffee, and artisans' crafts from everywhere; all sold at the lowest prices in the world. The "Golden Rock" was an international eighteenth-century traders' paradise.[39]

A popular Holland product, gunpowder, was not yet banned from sale to the colonies by England, as Parliament saw no need to deny Americans the right to protect themselves against hostile Indians. Not that banning anything in Statia would matter. Smuggling was tacitly accepted by even the most upstanding of merchants. Meredith, Clymer, and now Barry engaged in "business as usual" at this intriguing port. An honest business transaction in St. Eustatia was rarely a good one. By 1772, smuggling was one of the underpinnings of colonial business.[40]

After another round trip to Statia, Meredith sent Barry to a new destination that spring: Montserrat, twenty miles southeast of St. Eustatia. Barry made another voyage to Statia in June, returning to Philadelphia in August. The *Peggy* was a fast ship with a contented captain at the helm.[41] One of the items not listed on Barry's cockets during his travels, but one he brought back nonetheless, was tea.

By 1773, no other product was so identified with the British Empire—or its increasingly strained relationship with its American colonies. Now tea became a Parliamentary weapon. For over a century, the East India Company had been the major player in the world's largest economy. Now facing bankruptcy, it needed government assistance to keep it (and therefore the British economy) from sinking. East Indiamen, ships that resembled floating cities in size, were the symbol of British mercantile power. Now, "John Company's" warehouses held seventeen million pounds of tea, with nowhere to ship it.[42] Accordingly, Parliament passed the Tea Act of 1773, giving the East India Company a free hand in dealing directly with American merchants.[43] The decade-long conflict pitting profits against patriotism came to a head over tea.

News of the Tea Act reached Philadelphia that spring, with loyal merchants petitioning to handle the new trade while their unhappy colleagues railed against it.[44] That autumn, a broadside warned "the Delaware Pilots" that "Tar and Feathers" awaited anyone who would bring up the "Ship *Polly,* Captain Ayres, a Three Decker which is hourly expected . . . on a Voyage from London to Philadelphia." It was signed by "the Committee of Tarring and Feathering," who made their intentions clear: "Pennsylvanians are to a Man, passionately fond of Freedom . . . and at all Events are determined to enjoy it . . . what think you, Captain, of a Halter around your Neck–ten Gallons of liquid Tar decanted on your Pate–with the Feathers of a dozen Geese laid over that to enliven your Appearance?"[45]

The broadside found its way to New England; John Adams later admitted it gave the Sons of Liberty the idea to stage the Boston Tea Party in December.[46] It also inspired Philadelphia's own, when another ship was boarded by Pennsylvania and New Jersey patriots who unloaded the tea, took it ashore, and destroyed it. (Afterward one of the participants, Henry Stacks, was discovered with his pockets bulging with the vile black leaves: he was derisively branded "Tea Stacks" for the rest of his life.)[47]

All of this activity brewed while Barry was sailing homeward, returning to Philadelphia in December.[48] Reports of Boston's Tea Party were fresh in the papers when, on December 27, Captain Ayres was taken off the *Polly* at Gloucester Point and escorted to Philadelphia by the "Committee of Tarring and Feathering." Barry was part of the boisterous crowd that filled the State House yard, loudly proposing and passing several "resolutions" as Ayres fearfully eyed the swinging halter and inhaled the bubbling tar's noxious bouquet. To be tarred and feathered was not only degrading, it was excruciatingly painful. Assuring all that he would sail home on the next tide, Ayres was returned unharmed to the *Polly.* The next day, Barry sailed for St. Eustatia in the *Peggy,* clearing the Capes with the

Polly just ahead of him.[49] Barry's voyage went smoothly; 1774 began with promise.

While he was in St. Eustatia, Mary died. Patrick, having returned to Philadelphia in January, was present with John's wife at the end, and handled the funeral arrangements. There is no documented record of what illness or accident befell Mary, only that she passed away on February 9. A plain headstone was erected, and her name and age—"29 years, 10 months"—were all that appeared on it.[50] Two weeks later, the *Gazette* relayed the news that "Barry, from St. Eustatia" had "arrived at our Capes, and may be hourly expected up."[51] As the *Peggy* approached Philadelphia, a rowboat took Patrick out to the sloop, where he broke the news to his brother.[52]

In later years, Barry wrote in passionately plain language about his deeds as a sailor and patriot. Letters to family members were simply worded and affectionate. But no writings exist regarding Mary. When Barry's days ashore are calculated, they were together for less than six months in a marriage of just over six years. If one of them was destined to die young, odds would have made it the sailor on the high seas, not the spouse living in the most civilized city in the colonies. At twenty-eight, John Barry found himself a widower.

In the midst of his mourning came a new career opportunity, one that would move the young captain to the pinnacle of Philadelphia's merchant trade. In March 1774, Barry received a message from Robert Morris, requesting a meeting.[53]

––––––––––

Benjamin Franklin may have been the most renowned Philadelphian of the time, but Robert Morris was by far the richest. Like Franklin, Morris came to Philadelphia as a young man. Born in Liverpool in 1734, he was raised by his grandmother after his mother died and his father, Robert Senior, migrated to Maryland, where he became a Chesapeake merchant. In 1747, he summoned his son to come live with him.[54]

Physically immense, Robert Senior was an accomplished businessman, raconteur, and politician—attributes that would become even more pronounced in his son. Young Morris was unimpressed with his father's burgeoning library; the only books that caught his fancy were accounting ledgers. This, combined with his open animosity for Robert Senior's lover, forced father to exile son to Philadelphia, where his continued disinterest in scholarly pursuits brought about an apprenticeship under Charles Willing, one of Philadelphia's foremost merchants. Willing's firm traded directly with both the West Indies and England, advertising "European and West India goods . . . West India rum, muscavedo sugar, Bohea, and Hypon teas, Bristol beer, Herefordshire cyder, Gloucester cheese, anvils, hammers, sledges and vises, Vidonia and Sherry wines, long and short pipes, cortage and anchors, window glass . . . and Welsh and West country servants."[55]

Willing soon realized that he had two bright boys under his tutelage: his son Thomas and young Morris. Only sixteen, Morris showed an acumen for business far beyond his years. Once, while Willing was away, he learned from a captain just back from London that the price of flour had gone sky high in England. Morris bought every sack he could get his hands on, to the bemusement of the uninformed merchants. The next morning, they learned why Willing's apprentice had cornered the Philadelphia flour market, and Morris was never underestimated again. With Charles Willing's death in 1754, Robert assisted his grieving friend Thomas, managing company affairs and substantially increasing the firm's profits during the French and Indian War. He was rewarded with a partnership. When Barry arrived in Philadelphia in 1760, the firm of Willing and Morris was as successful as any in the colonies, with a fleet of over twenty ships.[56]

At thirty-five, Morris married the beautiful teenager Mary White in 1769; five years later, his family included two sons and a daughter. His vast wealth allowed him to satisfy his appetites for politics and ostentation. After leading the opposition to the Stamp Act, he immersed himself in the growing schism between the colonies and Parliament. To complement his huge mansion in Philadelphia, he built a summer estate on the Schuylkill, where he grew hothouse oranges and pineapples.[57] If Franklin was the example of how high an artisan could rise in the colonies, then Robert Morris was the perfect role model for every apprenticed clerk.

Morris's request to see Barry did not result in a meeting until springtime. Compared to the average height of the day (about five feet six inches) both men were tall, physically intimidating figures, with resumés to match. Morris had followed Barry's career with more than passing interest. He offered the young widower a choice of two possibilities: one, take command of the recently purchased brigantine, the *Venus*, or two, remain with Meredith and Clymer until construction was completed on the *Prince Edward*, a two-hundred-ton merchantman.[58] Barry quickly accepted the latter offer while proposing his brother Patrick for the former. Patrick's success aboard the *Amelia* was known to Morris from the newspapers and Coffeehouse chatter. He readily agreed to hire both brothers.[59]

Before Barry sailed the *Peggy* to Montserrat on March 20, he notified Meredith that his services would end that fall. Eight days later, the "Brigantine *Venus*, forty-tons, Patrick Barry, Captain," was registered at the Philadelphia Custom House, and then sailed with a cargo of wheat and lumber to Jamaica and the Mississippi.[60] John returned to Philadelphia in June, docking the *Peggy* in the midst of political and economic upheaval.[61]

Parliament and the Crown had spent the past decade dealing with the colonies like a stern but befuddled parent trying to figure out how to discipline rebellious teenagers. Punishing steps were implemented, then reversed; the Stamp Act Congress, the Townshend Acts, the Boston Massacre, and the *Gaspee* affair were usually dealt with by putting a foot down, then relenting. But the Boston Tea Party called for severe measures. Parliament passed the Boston Port Act, closing the port of Boston. Soon British reinforcements to those stationed at Castle William began arriving in dozens of transports, clogging the King's Roadstead in place of merchantmen. The harbor's closing was a virtual death sentence, threatening Boston's economic survival. Only restitution for John Company's destroyed tea, plus all prospective duties on its sale, would restore Boston's privileges.[62]

News of the port's closing was carried on horseback by silversmith-turned-courier Paul Revere, who stopped in Philadelphia en route to Virginia, his saddlebags bursting with letters requesting support for Boston from fellow colonists.[63] Staunch loyalists saw the

Boston crisis as proof that a harsh price awaited rebellious colonists for their protests and sometimes violent acts against the Crown. If this could happen in Boston, could it not happen in Philadelphia? Nearly every Quaker merchant—and many Anglican ones as well—were vociferous in their objections to any support for Boston. One admonished his colleagues to "keep the transactions of our City within the limits of Moderation, and not Indecent or offense to our parent State."[64]

On the evening of May 20, a meeting was held among Philadelphia's politicians and merchants at the City Tavern (nearly all of the Quakers were conspicuously absent, as a sign of support for the Crown). Over dinner they scripted a set of resolves, calling for "a day of mourning," a special meeting of the Pennsylvania Assembly, and the establishment of a Committee of Correspondence between Philadelphia and Boston. Thomas Willing was appointed chairman.[65] On June 1, the designated "day of mourning," shops were closed and the bells of Christ Church tolled throughout the day. Barry flew the *Peggy*'s flag at half-staff, an action taken by sympathetic captains as a sign of support for besieged Boston.[66]

Barry refitted the *Peggy* for his last cruise for Meredith and Clymer (Clymer, one of the resistance's ringleaders, became so involved that he left Meredith with the task of running their firm).[67] As witnessed by his attendance during the *Polly* affair, Barry's own political sympathies were with the Cause. There was not one tug of conscience regarding the rights of the British Empire in the heart and mind of this Irishman, exiled because repression and religious intolerance reigned over his native land. If the time came to fight, John Barry would fight.[68]

As Barry oversaw stowing of the *Peggy*'s cargo, Meredith and Clymer attended a meeting at the State House co-chaired by Morris, where it was proposed that a Continental Congress convene in September, with each colony to send representatives. On June 25, Barry headed down the Delaware, taking the *Peggy* to Montserrat on an uneventful voyage. He left the magnificent view of smoldering Mont Soufrière in his wake in late August. At the Capes south of Delaware Bay he was pleasantly surprised to encounter the *Venus*.

Over the past two years John and Patrick had rarely seen each other. They sailed upriver together, docking in Philadelphia on September 21.[69]

Down the street from the waterfront at Carpenters' Hall, the first Continental Congress was in its third week of deliberations. Eleven colonies had sent representatives—men with disparate tastes, backgrounds, and education. For many it was their first time away from home. Virginia's delegation included the firebrand Patrick Henry and soldier-turned-tobacco planter George Washington. Among the Massachusetts representatives was the brilliant lawyer who had defended the British troops involved in the Boston Massacre, John Adams; and, wearing a claret-colored suit, his more rambunctious and rebellious cousin, Samuel. The men from Massachusetts and Virginia drove the agenda during these meetings.[70]

Shielded from the warm September sun, Congress questioned, probed, and argued over each issue. As autumn began, conservative members seemed on the verge of reining in their rebellious colleagues. The session was about to conclude with a tepid letter of protest to the Crown when Paul Revere arrived with the latest news from New England.[71] Resolutions had been passed by the citizens of Suffolk County, Massachusetts, vehemently denouncing the latest British laws, declaring that "no obedience is due from this province to either or any of the Acts."[72]

The reading of the Suffolk Resolves resulted in bedlam. As radical battled conservative, the Resolves became the basis for a declaration of colonial rights of life, liberty, and property. Economic sanctions against England were enacted, to remain in place until the Coercive Acts, Intolerable Acts, Tea Tax, and the like, were repealed. Effective December 1, 1774, no goods would be imported from England and Ireland, with exports to Great Britain and the West Indies ceasing the following September. Congress adjourned, to reconvene in May 1775.[73]

At the Southwark shipyard, the final touches were being made to the *Prince Edward*. Barry's new ship would take him back across the Atlantic for the first time in fifteen years—to England, of all places. While he was attending the annual meeting of the Sea Captains Club at the London Coffeehouse, his appointment as captain of Philadelphia's grandest merchantman was announced, and cheers and glasses were raised in his honor.[74] Life was certainly looking up as far as his career was concerned, but even the arrival in port of another brother, Thomas, was not enough to keep Mary from his thoughts, especially as he marked his wedding anniversary–ironically ashore.[75]

The bookish Thomas came to Philadelphia in hopes of furthering his career as a clerk; he also brought news for John and Patrick of the family remaining in Ireland. Their aging parents were living off what money John and Patrick sent home. Their sisters, Eleanor and Margaret, were married with children. Eleanor Hayes had three: Michael, Patrick, and Eleanor; Margaret Howlin had several children, the oldest a daughter.[76] This reunion was short for Patrick, soon bound for Tobago. Some days later, standing on the Willing and Morris dock, John and Thomas waved farewell as the *Venus* stood down the Delaware, slowly vanishing from sight. John never saw Patrick again.

The *Prince Edward* had five owners: Thomas Willing, Robert Morris and his brother Thomas, John Nixon from County Wexford; and her builder, John Wharton.[77] Launching took place while Congress was in session, and Wharton and Barry worked tirelessly to have the ship ready to sail by year's end. Willing and Morris were well aware that the Congressional resolves would bring severe repercussions from the Crown, although how severe was yet to be fathomed. Both partners, while stridently advocating the rights of colonials (especially colonial businessmen), still hoped that all would end amicably, although Willing was beginning to view the radical prospect of independence "as an economic consideration, not a political one."[78]

The new ship was beautiful to behold: 91 feet 5 inches long, 26 feet 1 inch at the beam, with the blunt bow and raised quarterdeck easily recognized on both sides of the Atlantic as that of a Philadelphia merchantman.[79] When Barry and Nixon registered her they also changed her name, if not her namesake. Prince Edward was called "the Black Prince" for his wartime heroics as much for his appearance, and that sobriquet was now the ship's name. Her figurehead was a handsomely carved knight, sword and shield at the ready.[80]

In a last flurry of activity, Barry signed on a crew and oversaw the loading of cargo. The hold was packed with 1,246 barrels of flour, 16,203 bushels of wheat, 800 boards, and 3,840 pipe and barrel staves, all for delivery to Bristol, England. On December 28, the *Black Prince* stood down the Delaware, the prize float in a two-day parade of outgoing vessels, all sailing for British ports of call. She was the last ship to depart Philadelphia in 1774.[81]

The year 1775 began under "Squall[s] with rain" which did little to slow the *Black Prince*'s speed. Over the next two weeks, despite the weather changing from bad to worse, the new merchantman made terrific headway, logging nearly five hundred miles over three days. On January 10, "A Varrey Dangerous Sea" began washing over the deck, and Barry ordered lifelines run to keep his men from being swept overboard. "Hail, rain, [and] much lightning to the E'ward" beset both ship and sailor. For days there were "No Observations"; by now Barry was an old hand at maintaining course by dead reckoning.[82]

Reading Barry's entries of this voyage one can hear the awful howl of the wind, the roar of pounding seas as they crashed over the *Black Prince*'s bulwarks, and the gruff shouts of orders to his crew over the din of the tempests. The phrases "Peopel Employed on weaving mattes, and knitting of yarns," interspersed with "set Doubel Reef main to fore topsails and jibb" encapsulate long, dangerous days when the crew was constantly occupied with the repair of rigging and sail after a perilous watch aloft on the footropes, desperately leaning into yard and canvas, reefing sail in an effort to keep their ship afloat and themselves alive. Respite finally came on January 16, with "Light airs inclinable to Calm" and "Peopel Employed in making [repairs to] the sail and rigging." For the next few days, Barry's log reads like an elongated sigh. The *Black Prince* continued eastward.[83]

The dreadful nor'easters proved the excellence of the ship's construction to captain and crew alike. No masts gave way, no yards were lost. Another storm struck the ship on January 19, and for a solid week, the gales were too fierce to be heard over; on January 22, Barry "spoke a brig from Philadelphia Captain McGurney But Could not understand what he sayed it blowing hard."[84] Three days later, the *Gazette* informed Willing and Morris that the *Black Prince* had been sighted: "the ship *George* Captain Pinkerton, from this port for our Capes he spoke the ship *Black Prince*, Captain Barry, from this port for Bristol."[85]

That very day, January 25, Barry literally turned the *Black Prince* around to survive Mother Nature. Besieged by the elements, the merchantman could only make one or two knots, as winds shifted quickly and unexpectedly throughout the day. The constant change of direction meant painstaking tacking of the *Black Prince* until, after no less than fifteen hours with all hands aloft or on the braces, Barry finally ordered "wear ship!"[86] With a collective groan that seemed to come from her keelson, the *Black Prince* slowly came around on the opposite tack, her bow wearily turning away from the howling wind. Barry ordered the mainsails brailed up and the foresails braced around to catch the gale and bring the bow around with the stern coming through the wind.[87] Barry's drenched, exhausted sailors more than earned their salt that day.

By this time, the crew had a healthy respect for their captain; one sailor recollected Barry "possessed courage without rashness."[88] Barry's leadership skills were now second nature to him: a winning combination of seamanship, fearlessness, and honesty. Keeping his emotions just beneath the surface, he applied his wit or his temper to emphasize a point or an order. His reputation for fairness and hard work was already well known on the Philadelphia waterfront.[89] Now these sailors saw it firsthand.

Soon the *Black Prince* was on top of the British Isles–the closest Barry had been to Ireland in fifteen years, but on a course that would not take him any closer. He was near enough to the English coastline on January 26 to record a sounding of fifty fathoms, with "Pebel stone and schalaps shells and mud." Land was sighted the next day, and Barry arrived in Bristol Channel under "light Breezes and fluttery" conditions. "Hard gales with a Constant Rain" accompanied the *Black Prince* past the Avon River's shoals. Just thirty-one days after leaving Cape May, Barry dropped anchor in Bristol harbor.[90]

Congress' trade policy was already the talk of Bristol taverns and coffeehouses, and Barry's order for ballast in lieu of trade goods was not welcome news to merchants or officials. In tacit retaliation they purposely took their time getting the *Black Prince*'s hold unloaded.[91] Barry found the talk regarding Anglo-American relations pessimistic. Although many Bristol merchants were sympathetic to the colonists' plight, others spoke "with contempt of the firmness of America."[92]

For the next two weeks, Barry seethed as stevedores "Employed on Dischargging part of the Cargo" worked at a snail's pace, with "Nothing Rec'd on Board."[93] On one of these lethargic days, another ship broke her lines and smashed into the *Black Prince*'s stern, damaging her quarter rail and breaking the cabin windows. Dockhands continued to slowly, ever so slowly, bring Barry's cargo out of his ship's deep hold; sometimes only three hundred barrels a day were removed.[94] Willing and Morris agents informed Barry that the market would not pay the firm's requested price for the wheat and flour.[95] Frustrated by accidents, glum businessmen, and boredom, Barry turned command over to his first mate and accompanied other American captains to Bath, the old Roman city southeast of Bristol, whose warm mineral springs had just been rediscovered by the local gentry. The two-day soak did him good, and no doubt his crew enjoyed the break from their captain's darkening mood.[96]

Not until March 1 did the *Black Prince* have sufficient ballast to sail. Once again, storms forced the ship to anchor downriver. Eleven days later, still in the roadstead, an irritated Barry wrote "at 5 AM one Snow pembrook drove fowl of us Caryed away his jib boom." Two days afterward, the relieved captain departed "with several sails in Company" and "all sail set."[97]

––––––––

The first leg of this voyage passed smoothly, as Barry took the *Black Prince* southward toward the Azores. From there, "heavy tumling seas for the W'ward" propelled her homeward; even a ship of this size could be sent bobbing up and down on a high, rolling ocean. On April 11, 1775, Barry let the merchantman race a bit, running up to ten knots, but in doing so "splitt the main topsail" and then "splitt the fore topsail." She was also being driven south of her intended course, and in five days was at the latitude of the Carolinas. The following days were blessed with favorable conditions, and the *Black Prince* plowed northward, covering 350 miles. By April 21, Barry was outside the Delaware Capes under "Light Breezes" and picked up a pilot at Cape May. Fog kept him below the bay's entrance until the twenty-fourth, when the pilot took the ship upriver, reaching Chester by nightfall. That night the *Black Prince* rode at anchor. Her captain and crew turned in, knowing they would be home in the morning.[98]

In Philadelphia that same day, the St. George's Society for the Assistance of Englishmen in Distress held its annual banquet at the City Tavern.[99] Over a sumptuous meal, the hundred members discussed the growing divide between king and subject. After dessert, the society's vice president, Robert Morris, stood to propose a toast to the health of George III. Members rose to drink to their king and patron saint's namesake. Suddenly, a panting dispatch rider burst through the front door with news: musket fire had been exchanged between Massachusetts Minute Men and British "Lobster-backs" at Lexington and Concord.[100] The members of St. George's Society, spilling glasses and upending chairs, bottled up the doorway in their mad rush to spread the news. According to legend, Morris, now alone in the room, changed his toast to a vow of support for the Colonial cause, and downed the contents of his glass. Then he stepped out of the tavern and into the uncertain, dangerous future.[101]

The following day, under "fine clear sunshine weather," the *Black Prince* nestled against the Willing and Morris dock, and Barry saw firsthand the pandemonium created by the previous day's news: a "River covered with ships and the wharves covered with inhabitants." The waterfront and adjoining streets were hopelessly clogged with carts, drays, and wagons: full ones heading to the docks to be unloaded; empty ones heading toward the warehouses to be refilled and unloaded again. Cargo was not laded into the holds so much as tossed. There were no idle longshoremen that day; "there were as many hands as could work" without inadvertently jostling a fellow dockhand into the river. Those merchants with ships in port were beseeched by their unluckier colleagues with exorbitant offers to allow them space for their wares, to no avail.[102]

On nearby streets, approaching the chaos, millers came with more wagons full of grain. Shallops and row-galleys crossed the river from Camden, weighted down with goods. Outside the State House, speakers exhorted their fellow countrymen to enlist in the coming fight while men drilled on the square. Once outspoken loyalists cowered in their homes, fearing a mob of "rebels" might attack them and destroy their property.[103]

Along the waterfront, a truth of human nature lay just beneath the surface disorder. Merchants had been in the forefront of resistance against England, not necessarily as much over patriotism as over profits. Now, after a decade of Crown affronts to their citizenship and commerce, after a decade of warning king and Parliament that they would fight for their rights, they learned their fellow Americans in Massachusetts had done just that. Further, the imminent session of the Second Continental Congress would surely approve a plan of resistance that would terminate all business with England indefinitely. Colonial merchants had been walking a narrow path as ardent advocates of American rights and shrewd icons of commerce. The merchants were patriots, but they were still businessmen. Now, seeing a future pitting them in a war against a great international power, they hoped for just one more killing in the marketplace before any actual killing came to Philadelphia.

Willing and Morris found Barry's arrival more than opportune, and gave him no chance to relax. Outside of a brief visit to the *Gazette* offices to report the news from Bristol and the ships he "spoke," his waking hours were spent supervising the *Black Prince*'s refitting and the stowing of cargo; 2,623 bushels of wheat were stored in one day (compared to 320 bushels being unloaded in one day back in Bristol).[104] On May 6, as Barry continued his manic pace to get his ship ready for sea, thousands crowded the docks to welcome the *Pennsylvania Packet*, carrying home Philadelphia's favorite son, Benjamin Franklin, after his long absence in England. From the

Black Prince's quarterdeck, Barry could see Franklin disembark "to the satisfaction of his friends and the lovers of Liberty."[105]

The following day, less than two weeks after docking and without an inch of empty space in her hold, the *Black Prince* stood down the Delaware, accompanying the brig *Nancy* and the merchantman *Aurora*, captained by Barry's friend Thomas Read. All three were bound for the British Lion's den itself: London.[106] Practically every remaining Philadelphia ship accompanied them downriver, headed for England or the West Indies. The Delaware was a wild traffic jam as ships of all size came dangerously close to each other, tacking their way to the Capes. It looked as if all of Philadelphia was leaving home.[107]

The *Black Prince* was sailing under the first mate's command. Barry remained in town for last-minute discussions with Morris regarding a scheme to sail from London to St. Eustatia, to smuggle home a shipment of gunpowder. The idea was dismissed, and Barry came aboard at New Castle in Delaware on May 9.[108] The *Black Prince* discharged her pilot and cleared Cape Henlopen two days later. That same day the Second Continental Congress went into session.[109]

Once at sea, Barry found the *Black Prince* "Vastly out of trim" due to the rushed preparations for this voyage. The Atlantic weather, usually peaceful in May, was again unkind. Storms returned in full force, and while the *Black Prince* still kept company with the *Aurora* and *Nancy* over the next two days, conditions became even more dangerous: "a hollow grown sea" with gale-force winds "splitt the forestaysail and the mainsail." All three ships turned into the wind until the tempest passed. Only fifty miles were made the following day. As his crew repaired the torn canvas, Barry watched the less damaged *Aurora* and *Nancy* disappear over the horizon.[110]

It seemed foreordained that storms would stalk the *Black Prince* on this voyage. Barry did not sail in favorable conditions until the middle of June, when he sent his ship speeding eastward. On June 17, a "Steady Breeze and Pleasant Weather" allowed "all sails sett" and he soon "spoke Captain Read"; the *Black Prince* had overtaken the *Aurora*. The ships proceeded together up the English Channel. One week later, Barry "got the Pilot John Abraham on Board at Dover," and on June 27, the *Black Prince* docked in London after forty-eight strenuous days of sailing.[111]

The fighting at Lexington and Concord seemed the only topic of discussion in London when Barry and Read came ashore. Neither captain carried news that London had not already heard. In fact, London had news for them. Rebel forces had captured Fort Ticonderoga, its much-needed artillery now in colonial hands.[112] The two captains read an ominous comment in the London *Public Advertiser* that Parliament "Will either keep Possession with Troops of all the great Towns on the Coast of America and shut all her Ports with Frigates, or . . . finish the War at once, by reducing with a military Force, the Provinces of New England to Obedience."[113]

Stuck in London, Barry did not venture far from his ship, sleeping in his cabin rather than taking a room in the city—a decision made as much for his safety as for convenience. The slow discharge of cargo, similar to his experience in Bristol four months earlier, was concern for worry, especially when he contemplated the very real possibility that the *Black Prince* could be seized and he and his crew imprisoned. Mundane entries in the ship's log of "Tarrd the For Topmast Shrouds and Back Stays" and "Disch[arged] 7 Casks of Bees waxe" belied the churning anxiety Barry shared with other Americans, waiting to refit and leave what was now the enemy capital.[114] Fresh reports of the battle at Bunker Hill, and the heavy British casualties, did little to ease the fraying nerves of American sailors.

Most of the other American ships had already left London when, on August 5, the *Black Prince*'s hold was empty and ballast could be loaded. Barry decided that any unfinished repairs would be completed at sea. On the eighth, he met with Morris' agent while the first mate took the ship downriver. Barry rejoined his crew the following day.[115] "Sailed, the *Black Prince*, Barry for Philadelphia," read the clearance of the British officials.[116]

Any hope of smooth sailing was short-lived. Shifting winds kept Barry tacking back and forth until the nineteenth, when the *Black Prince* finally reached the Atlantic—and more bad weather. Distances traveled on these days ranged from average to dismal; only thirty miles were tallied on the twenty-third. Conditions varied from calm to stormy, and Barry recorded them in clipped, frustrated sentences. His entry for September 3 was only forty-nine miles; the following week was more of the same: fits and starts, but mostly fits. On September 10, thirty days after leaving London, the mast-header finally sighted the Azores.[117]

In eight months of sailing the *Black Prince*, Barry had pitted her against whatever the elements brought to bear. For the next twenty-four hours, the weather gods smiled.

On a course of "NNW, the winds bearing ESE," Barry started the September 11 entry at noon, the official beginning of a day at sea: "This 24 hours a fresh gale and Cloudy attended with light Showers of Rain." The *Black Prince* was cruising at eight knots. Soon, nine: as the winds shifted "to the So'ward," Barry ordered steering sails set to maximize the wind. The *Black Prince* was doing ten knots when, at 6:00 P.M., the gale "Carried away the M[ain] Top G[al]l[an]t Royal yard," the highest sail and spar aboard ship. Not wanting to lose a second, Barry sent his top-men aloft and "got the mizen top gallant yard up in his Place." This quick fix only held for two hours when a fresh gale "Caried [it] away" under darkening clouds, but its loss was not enough to stop this one-ship race.[118]

Barry ordered a smaller yard hauled up to the awaiting top-men, who finished their high-wire act above the deck, only to see their repair come crashing down below. No matter. The rest of the sails were more than doing the job, the masts, yards, and stays groaning from time to time under the full press of canvas.[119] Strong as the winds were, Barry was determined to make up for lost time—in actuality, lost days—as long as the winds were favorable. To him, this gale was a blessing. The very act of sending the *Black Prince* hurtling over the waves gave him joy, and his mood was contagious: one did not get many days like this one; best to enjoy it.[120]

The prize ship of Philadelphia now raced into darkness at eleven knots. At 2:00 A.M. the wind shifted yet again, blowing east. Barry had the night watch "Set the foretopmast Steering [sail] for a

Driver."[121] Under another soaking squall, sailors took the steering sail and set her at the end of the spanker boom, giving them one extra square sail aft to maintain–if not increase–the *Black Prince*'s speed.[122] In the gloom of this rainy, windy night, with "the Carpenter Employd making a new Royal yard," Barry worked his men without rest, sending them up and down the ratlines replacing canvas while he thought up spur of the moment solutions that kept the *Black Prince* flying at top speed.[123] Her bow literally hummed as it cut through the water.

Back to ten knots, a speed the *Black Prince* would keep into the next day's entries. "No Observ. to Day" is the last entry on the right hand side of the log. On the left, "Dist. logged–237."[124]

Two hundred and thirty-seven miles. There is no faster known twenty-four hours of sailing in the eighteenth century.[125] For one glorious day, Barry had the right combination of seas and wind.

On September 13, foul weather returned, as strong winds carried away the main topmast. Ten days later, "High Seas Attended with Thunder and Lightning" attacked the ship, driving her off course toward Sandy Hook, New Jersey. On the twenty-eighth, Barry "herde the Main yard crack" and made his last repair on the *Black Prince*. He finally sighted Cape Henlopen through his spyglass on October 4.[126]

Barry awaited a pilot boat. None came. The *Black Prince* rocked at anchor, her decks cleaned and sails furled. Aboard any of his previous ships Barry would have headed into the bay, but the draft of the *Black Prince* was over fifteen feet; he dared not risk her passage up the Delaware without a pilot.[127] Nor did he know, five months away from home, what had become of home. Barry sent his mate ashore to find a pilot. He found one hiding from the British in obedience to orders from the newly formed Committee of Safety.[128]

As the *Black Prince* made this last leg homeward, the pilot told Barry he was wise to have waited for him. There was a new, man-made hazard in the Delaware, the *chevaux-de-frise*. These crisscrossing, pointed stakes were anchored by up to forty tons of stone at the river bottom. Their frames were thirty feet wide, pierced with protruding spikes two feet wide that reached up to sixty-five feet in length. Sunk at different depths, but not more than six feet below the surface at low tide, they were designed to rip apart the hull of an unsuspecting (and unpiloted) enemy ship.[129] Only trusted pilots knew of their whereabouts. On Mud (now renamed Liberty) Island, construction was under way to complete what was commonly called "the mud fort." The waterway to William Penn's peaceful kingdom was being prepared for the British warships that were sure to come.

Barry docked the *Black Prince* at the Willing and Morris wharf. When he departed in May, the world he knew seemed to be on the verge of monumental change. By the time he returned, that change had become a reality.

CHAPTER THREE

THE LEXINGTON

HE DAY AFTER BARRY'S RETURN, he and Thomas Read (his
Aurora beat the *Black Prince* into port by a day) walked the
streets together to make their reports, visiting Morris, the Committee
of Safety, and finally the newspaper offices. The information Barry
provided, while dated, included intelligence that the British planned
to garrison three thousand troops in Philadelphia and increase the
amount of armed ships along the coast.[1]

He saw firsthand how the war was turning Philadelphia upside
down. From that spring day when he sailed the *Black Prince* back to
England, Philadelphians began converting their beloved city from
British port of call to American capital, with all of the bravado, inse-
curity, and paranoia that came with the rebellion. But not everyone
succumbed to the patriotic fervor. Just as many townsfolk opposed
it, believing proponents to be nothing more than a "Licentious and
Rebellious Mob." Any family could find more than one opinion
under their roof: Franklin's own son William, Governor of New
Jersey, remained loyal to the king.

Philadelphians looked to Franklin for leadership and counsel in
every conceivable area pertaining to the war. One responsibility after
another was piled on his sixty-nine-year-old shoulders: delegate to

the Second Continental Congress, Postmaster General of the thirteen colonies, and president of Philadelphia's Committee of Public Safety.[2] Without delay, he began plans for the city's defenses, including those to repel an "Insult by water."[3] Armed forces were recruited, redoubts were built, and the committee hurried construction of the "Mud Fort," just south of Philadelphia on the Delaware, following the plans of its designer, British army engineer John Montresor.[4] More chevaux-de-frise were constructed and, though not yet tested against enemy ships, were nonetheless effective. One merchant's brig, "loaded with Sugars, Molasses and Coffee" and sailing upriver without a savvy pilot, ran "upon the Chevaux De Frise and immediately sunk in five-fathom water."[5]

A "Pennsylvania Navy" was proposed, primarily consisting of row-galleys.[6] Twenty oars and two short masts, rigged for lateen sail, would propel them through the water, with a porthole at the bow "for one 18 or 24 pounder . . . and 2 Swivels on the Bow."[7] With the row-galley, the committee updated the Viking ship for eighteenth-century warfare, replacing the dragon's head at the bow with a single cannon—not as fierce looking, but deadlier.

Among those who made their living on the Delaware, the onset of war was cruelest to the river pilots. Led by Delaware's Henry Fisher, they petitioned the Committee of Safety in September. The pilots, "many of whom have large families, find themselves destitute of their usual means of obtaining support for themselves."[8] The committee made a list of pilots considered patriotic enough to be informed of the whereabouts of the river's booby traps.[9] Fisher's pilots would prove invaluable to the war effort.

Franklin's committee also established an alarm system devised to warn Philadelphia of approaching British warships. Should enemy ships be sighted at the Capes, dispatch riders would gallop posthaste from Lewes to Philadelphia, acting as an early Pony Express. Way stations were set up along the route for fresh riders and mounts. Should the couriers be caught, cannons mounted at each station would be fired, relaying the news to the next station until, by rider or cannon fire, the alarm reached Philadelphia.[10]

Barry's return coincided with the debate in the State House over creation of a navy. By October Congress had assumed broad powers, flexing financial, military, and political muscles unthought-of before Lexington and Concord. In addition to raising an army and making Washington Commander-in-Chief, Congress issued two million dollars in credit to run the new national government. Direct negotiations commenced with Indian tribes, usurping a British prerogative. A working relationship with each colony's government was established that included a national postal system. Although the thirteen colonies did not yet officially see themselves as a nation, their representatives were taking national measures, building on the sense of unity first witnessed in the days of the Stamp Act Congress. The only thing Congress had yet to do on a major scale–apart from declaring independence from England, of course–was address the issue of a navy.[11]

In the early days of this session, John Adams suggested a Continental Navy, only to see his proposal dismissed out of hand.[12] While all of the colonies were dependent on maritime trade to some extent, only a few were in immediate need of defense at sea: Massachusetts, where Boston's harbor had been closed to business for over a year; Rhode Island, whose coast had been ravaged for months by the British Navy (particularly by Sir James Wallace, captain of the frigate HMS *Rose*); and Virginia, where a combination of armed loyalists and British warships under Royal Governor Lord Dunmore was terrorizing the Chesapeake.

In August 1775, Rhode Island's General Assembly, tired of congressional inaction, passed a resolution calling for "the building and equipping of an American Fleet."[13] Presented to Congress on October 3, this resolution set off a firestorm of debate, luckily assisted by reports of Washington's tactics in besieging British-held Boston. With his troops in need of munitions and supplies, Washington chartered and armed small schooners and shallops, with orders to seize unsuspecting (and unarmed) British merchant ships. He also requested naval assistance from Rhode Island, asking that a ship be outfitted and sailed to Bermuda to procure gunpowder.[14]

With visible threats on the coastline, and Washington's example for support, John Adams again applied his political skills to the need for a navy. On October 13, Congress passed its first naval legislation, creating a Naval Committee and authorizing acquisition of two armed vessels. The Continental Navy was born. What Samuel Chase of Maryland called "the maddest idea in the world"–taking on the greatest naval power on earth–was becoming a reality.[15] Over the next two months, Congress increased its size from two ships to four and then to thirteen. The first ship purchased by Congress was the *Black Prince*.[16]

The Naval Committee was comprised of seven Congressmen from different colonies: John Adams, Massachusetts; John Langdon, New Hampshire; Silas Deane, Connecticut; Stephen Hopkins, Rhode Island; Richard Henry Lee, Virginia; Joseph Hewes, North Carolina; and Christopher Gadsden, South Carolina.[17] They met practically every night at the City Tavern for dinner and brainstorming.

Rhode Island's ancient mariner, Stephen Hopkins, dominated discussions from the time the committee stepped outside the State House, through their dinners, pipes, and evening farewells. With his plain-cut dark clothes and broad hat atop his untied, long gray hair, he looked more like a Philadelphia Quaker than an old merchant-sailor whose relationship with the sea was out of the Old Testament: it had made him rich, but claimed three sons. His rollicking story-telling and deft political skills easily won over his fellow committeemen, none more so than Adams, who found the man's company both convivial and informative.[18] Adams drew up the "Rules for the Regulation of the Navy of the United Colonies," whereby its commanders were to "shew in themselves a good example of honor and virtue to their officers and men."[19] In his own zeal for this venture, Adams wanted "to know what is become of the Whalemen, Codfishers, and Other Seamen [who] might be inlisted into the service of the Continent [and] be qualified to serve as Commanders And Officers."[20]

One candidate for a commander's position was right under the portly New Englander's nose–but Barry's capabilities were not considered during the selection of officers. The names of the new navy's captains were announced on November 5. Stephen Hopkins's fingerprints were all over the commission papers.

Only one Philadelphian was named: Charles Biddle's younger brother and Barry's friend, Nicholas, who had served as a midshipman in the Royal Navy (Horatio Nelson was a messmate).[21] He was joined by Dudley Saltonstall of Connecticut, brother-in-law of Silas Deane; Hopkins's nephew, John; and a friend of Hopkins's, old salt Abraham Whipple. To lead the fleet, with the honorary title of "Commodore," the committee picked Stephen's brother, John's father, and Abraham's brother-in-law: mariner, politician, business-man, and Rhode Island General Esek Hopkins.[22] In the com-modore's councils of war, Biddle would be surrounded by New England accents. Even if Barry's name was raised during the selec-tion process, he did not command enough influence with a commit-tee that had not one Pennsylvania member.

The navy soon had five ships and renamed all of them, as John Adams related: "The first We named *Alfred* in honor of the founder of the greatest Navy that ever existed. The second *Columbus* after the Discover[er] Of this quarter of the Globe. The third *Cabot* for the Discoverer of this northern Part of the Continent. The fourth *Andrew Doria* in memory of the Great Genovese Admiral and the fifth *Providence*, for the town where she was purchased."[23] The *Providence* came with its own commander, John Hazard, yet another Rhode Islander. The *Alfred* was the fleet flagship, and the new name of Barry's *Black Prince*. The figurehead of Prince Edward now did dou-ble duty as King Alfred.

With the captains chosen, a long list of tasks loomed regarding the newly purchased ships of war, given the fact that they were not ships of war. Substantial renovations were in order—beams, timbers, and bulwarks required bolstering; gun ports needed to be pierced; outfitting and rerigging was necessary; and supplies, arms, and ammunition required procurement—and everything needed to be done immediately. The Naval Committee gave these assignments to three local experts. To John Wharton's able protégé, Joshua Humphreys, went the assignment of structural strengthening. Nathaniel Falconer, another familiar face from Philadelphia's mer-chant circles, was put in charge of purchasing and procurement. The task of rerigging and outfitting the ships, beginning with the *Alfred*, fell to John Barry.[24]

Barry did not rise from sailor to captain without an ego that matched both his ambition and his skills. Changing his ship's name—and her captain's—was hard to bear. He had earned his station by talent and courage, not by political influence. Nevertheless, Dudley Saltonstall now commanded the *Alfred*. It was not easy to give up command of the finest ship in the colonies (Esek Hopkins's use of it as his flagship being the proof), but Barry immediately saw to his duties, "employed by the Congress to fitt for Sea the first fleet that sailed from Phila."[25]

Congress appropriated £100,000 to refit the four ships, and Wharton's charge book was soon filled with orders for "Scrapers, WhiteWash Brushes, and Empty Tarr Barrells" as Barry directed the clean-up of his old command. He purchased miles of rope to rig the *Alfred* as a proper ship of war.[26] Every morning she swarmed with laborers. As Humphreys's carpenters increased the ship's gunwales from two inches to six, reinforced the ship's hull, and pierced her bulwarks for the twenty-four guns she would mount, Barry's men toiled on deck and aloft, working with tallow and lampblack to turn stout rope into standing rigging. By twilight their faces and hands were as blackened as the new ratlines.[27] As the work progressed, Barry and Humphreys developed a deep respect for each other's talents. The Irish sailor and the Quaker shipwright–although Humphreys would be disowned by the Quakers for building ships of war–became lifelong friends.

The speed at which the *Black Prince* became the *Alfred* was the talk of the waterfront. News of her progress soon reached ally and enemy alike: "The ship *Black Prince* is to be finished this day, and mount 30 guns," one Marylander reported on November 11, while a Tory sent word to England how the *Black Prince* was "a fine vessel" that "mounts from twenty to thirty 12 and 16 pounders."[28] Under the renovation team of Barry, Humphreys, and Falconer, the four ships were finished by December (the *Providence* arrived in port battle-ready). Junior officers were assigned to each vessel. Adams, pleased with the progress being made, drew up a "list of Persons Suitable for Naval Commands" with twenty-two names on it. Barry's name was again among the missing.[29]

Soon there were three more vessels added to the fleet: the schooners *Wasp* and *Fly* and the sloop *Hornet*. A Marine Corps was established. Congress' plans to expand the infant navy with thirteen new frigates also meant an increase in appointees to the Marine (erstwhile Naval) Committee, Robert Morris among them.[30] If Barry thought the addition of Morris to the committee would give him the required influence to be rewarded for his good work thus far, he was disappointed. The committee passed over him again.

While the fleet shared dock space with the fourteen new row-galleys of the Pennsylvania Navy, crews were enlisted and supplies began to be loaded aboard each Continental ship.[31]

On December 3, the "Grand Union" flag—thirteen red and white stripes with the British colors in the upper left corner, or canton—was raised on the *Alfred* by her new lieutenant, a former Scottish merchant captain who earlier had declined a captaincy upon his arrival in Philadelphia. John Paul Jones came with a mysterious past, a reputation for feistiness, and an ego larger than his diminutive size.[32] Two days later, Congress passed a resolution that detailed policy regarding captures and the distribution of prize shares, and that "the seamen and marines be enjoined for the first of January, 1777, unless sooner discharged by Congress."[33] All that was needed to get the new navy to sea was a full crew for each ship, and the presence of the new commodore.

Esek Hopkins was still in Rhode Island. The stout, moon-faced, fifty-seven-year-old was finishing up business and political chores, and did not reach Philadelphia until the New Year. His appointment as "Commander in Chief of the Fleet of the United Colonies" put him in charge of the Navy, but Congress by no means considered him the maritime equal of Washington.[34] They ordered him to sail into harm's way, proceeding "directly to Chesapeak Bay in Virginia . . . Search and attack, take and destroy all the Naval force of our Enemies That you find there."[35] To most congressmen, and each Virginian, that meant going after Lord Dunmore.

John Murray, Lord Dunmore, was Royal Governor of Virginia. Sir Joshua Reynolds painted him in his tartan, his legs bowed from a lifetime spent in the saddle. His long nose rested above pursed lips, with reddish-brown hair beneath his tam. After hearing of Lexington and Concord, he ordered the gunpowder stores removed from the magazine at Williamsburg to keep them out of patriot hands. Patrick

Henry wasted no time in leading the local militia to Williamsburg, seizing the magazine with such a show of force that Dunmore took his family and fled town, via the British man-of-war *Fowey* under young Captain George Montagu. Montagu (who years later would be sent to Tahiti in search of the mutineers from the HMS *Bounty*) put the *Fowey* and her tender, the sixteen-gun *Otter*, under Dunmore's orders. They would be the start of a loyalist and British force that Dunmore would use in his attempts to subjugate the rebels along the Virginia shore.[36]

Dunmore declared martial law and proceeded to secure his colony as best he could from the *Fowey*'s cabin, raiding the coastline while using the city of Norfolk as his base of operations. Over five hundred runaway slaves joined his forces and became known as his "Ethiopian Regiment."[37] News of their participation in the fight against their former owners quickly spread throughout the colonies. The *Pennsylvania Evening Packet* pointedly inquired, "Are not the Negro slaves, now on board the *Fowey* [and]under the G[overnor]'s protection, in actual rebellion? And punishable as such?"[38] Then, on November 7, Dunmore delivered a bombshell, declaring "all indentured Servants, Negroes Or Others (appertaining to Rebels), free that are able and Willing to bear Arms," if they fled their rebel masters and joined his forces.[39]

Dunmore's emancipation proclamation, preceding Lincoln's by four score and seven years plus one, only freed the slaves of rebellious masters; slaves belonging to loyalists were returned.[40] White Virginians were rebelling against the Crown; what better justice—in Dunmore's eyes—than to fight them with their own slaves? Dunmore envisioned a virtual rebellion against the rebellion. In quick response, slaveholders quickly told their "property" that Dunmore's offer was a lie; merely a ruse to resell them to the West Indies sugar plantations. Thomas Jefferson wrote that Dunmore's actions "raised our country into a perfect phrensy."[41]

If Dunmore's proclamation put fear of a slave insurrection in the minds of the white population in the southern colonies, it also focused their efforts as nothing else could to eliminate him once and for all: hence the wish of Congress for Hopkins to sail to the Chesapeake and destroy Dunmore's operation. Barry could only watch as the Continental Navy made sail on January 4, heading down a river so full of ice that it would take weeks for the ships to clear Cape Henlopen.[42] As Hopkins's fleet lay trapped in the icy Delaware, Dunmore abandoned Norfolk, burned to the ground by Tory and patriot torches alike.[43]

Thanks to the speedy success of their work with the fleet, both Congress and the Committee of Safety gave Barry, Humphreys, and Falconer more ships to overhaul. The latter contracted a Southwark shipwright named Simon Shurlock to build a warship for Pennsylvania.[44] A subcommittee consisting of Morris, Clymer, and Nixon was formed to oversee construction and prod it along, as Shurlock worked much too slowly. Needing a man they could trust to get the job finished, they sent for Barry.[45] Once more he went to the shipyards, taking charge and keeping John Wharton's chandlery busy filling orders. Under his supervision, the ship became a trim fighting craft: fourteen guns, eight swivels, and sixteen cohorns (mortarlike cannon that could lob shells from the main top as well as the deck).[46] Christened the *Montgomery*, she was given a captain deemed worthy of her potential. Once more Barry was disregarded; command went to his friend from the *Aurora*, Thomas Read.[47]

No sooner was the *Montgomery* off the ways than Barry was sent to review the construction of the four frigates recently assigned to the Philadelphia shipyards.[48] This was followed with another clerical assignment, overseeing the disbursement of funds for the refitting of other ships, such as £21 payment for "Iron work, Tubs as needed" requested by Captain James Nicholson, a former Royal Navy officer from one of Maryland's best known maritime families along the Eastern Shore.[49] It was Barry's first encounter with one of the Nicholson brothers, whose careers would intersect with his over the next twenty-five years—not always pleasantly. As before, Barry carried out his duties with speed and thoroughness.

In fact, Barry may have been *too* good at these jobs. After a decade spent commanding his own ships, he now found himself literally dry-docked, preparing other captains' vessels for war and watching them sail away. Whether Barry complained of his lack of a ship is not documented, but it must have tested him sorely. When would his turn come?

Luckily, it had not come with Esek Hopkins. As the commodore's fleet sailed into the Atlantic, his mind was preoccupied with his orders to confront, fight, and defeat Lord Dunmore and his British ships. Reading and rereading his orders, Hopkins found one section of particular interest, included out of deference to his experience: "if bad Winds or Stormy weather ... disable you so To do, You are then to follow such Courses as your best Judgement shall Suggest."[50]

Weighing Dunmore's dangerous ships on one hand and meteorological conditions on the other, Hopkins concluded that this was literally an escape clause. "Bad Winds or Stormy Weather" gave him an out, and he elected to take it. Bypassing both the enemy and his orders, Hopkins headed to New Providence (now Nassau) in the Bahamas to capture its supplies of cannons and gunpowder.[51] His decision left the Chesapeake Bay and Virginia coast in the hands of the one enemy the American fleet was principally created to destroy.[52]

As winter ended, the British began acting on their plans to occupy Philadelphia, seeking to be as fully informed as possible before they came to call. On February 23, 1776–just five days after Hopkins cleared Delaware Bay–Captain Andrew Snape Hamond of the frigate *Roebuck* ordered his subordinate, Captain Alexander Graeme of the *Kingfisher*, to "Proceed to the mouth of the River Delaware, and use every Act and Stratagem in your power to obtain as many Pilots for that River as you possibly can, also as much information concerning the Fortifications and Machines which are placed to Obstruct the Navigations to Philadelphia, as you may be Able to Learn."[53]

On March 3, Commodore Hopkins sailed his fleet into the waters around New Providence and captured Nassau's fort without firing a shot.[54] It was the first wartime success for the old *Black Prince*, hollow as it proved to be: the island's governor had removed the bulk of the powder from the fort, and only twenty-four barrels remained to be "seized."[55] After giving some thought to pitting his fleet against a British squadron off Georgia, Hopkins once more decided not to test his unproven sailors in a fight against experienced British gunners. Instead, he set a course for Rhode Island, taking eighty-eight cannons and a "Part of a Cask of Spirits" along with the two dozen barrels of powder.[56] On his way home, Hopkins again sailed past Lord Dunmore and his own orders from Congress.

Also on March 3, Richard Boger, a young British lieutenant, took advantage of Hopkins's absence along the Virginia coast. Commanding the *Edward*, a sloop acting as tender to HMS *Liverpool*, Boger was cruising in search of American prizes. He proved his capabilities soon enough, capturing an American sloop "loaded with salt taken from the Rebels."[57] Some days later, the *Edward* pursued a northward bound American brigantine, the *Wild Duck*, under Captain James Tribbett, heading to Philadelphia from St. Eustatia with her hold full of powder and arms.[58] To Boger's dismay, the *Wild Duck* narrowly escaped.[59] On March 12, Charles Carroll of Carrollton joyfully wrote from Philadelphia that "An armed vessel purchased for our province in Statia is arrived here with 2000 lb of powder."[60]

Congress wasted no time in purchasing the *Wild Duck* for the Continental Navy.[61] John Hancock and Robert Morris had the pleasant task of summoning Barry and informing him that his days ashore and out of action were about to end.[62] The offer to command the brigantine was made, and Barry "accepted the command with a determined resolution of distressing the enemy as much as in my power." As president of Congress, Hancock signed Barry's commission papers.[63]

Once the *Wild Duck* went to Wharton's shipyard, now the de facto navy yard, Barry and Humphreys began her refitting. She already carried her guns—sixteen 4-pounders and twelve swivels. She was 86 feet long, with a 70-foot deck, a 25-foot beam, and weighed about 140 tons. To give some idea of her size, if she was placed at home plate on a baseball field, her hull would stop four feet short of first base. Originally built in Bermuda as a sloop, she had been converted to a square-sail brigantine in New York.[64]

While Humphreys directed the recaulking of the *Wild Duck*'s seams and the scraping of her hull, Barry inspected the sails and rigging and found them suitable.[65] Quick and thorough as he was at converting all of the previous ships assigned to him, Barry was breathtaking in the speed in which he got the *Wild Duck* ready for sea. The entire job was finished in just two weeks. She had a "square-tuck Stern painted yellow, and a low, rounded stem painted lead colors, black sides and yellow moldings."[66] The *Wild Duck's* supplies were put to use for other ships as well: another of Barry's refitting assignments, the Maryland ship *Defence*, took aboard "One Barrell with Grape Shott" and "Ninety-Six Cutlashes" from the brigantine's stores.[67]

Nor were Barry and Congress the only ones interested in the renovation of his new command. One Tory informant wrote the Admiralty: "She . . . is to carry 110 men and to Mount Sixteen 4 pounders and 16 Oars . . . is now called the *Lexington* Captain Barbut."[68] Future spies would come to know Barry's name well enough.

Among the officers the Marine Committee assigned to serve under Barry was First Lieutenant Luke Matthewman, who would share more than one adventure with his new captain during the war.[69] Matthewman took charge of the rendezvous—the enlistment of a crew—beginning, fittingly, on St. Patrick's Day. Accompanied by fife and drum, Matthewman and a midshipman, their uniforms clean, sword hilts and shoe buckles spit-polished, paraded the streets along the Philadelphia waterfront, stopping at Allen Moore's tavern after the music had drawn a crowd.[70] Next, Matthewman or the midshipman—the one with the better singing voice—lustily sang the following, to the tune of "the British Grenadier":

> *All you that have bad masters*
> *And cannot get your due,*
> *Come, come my brave boys,*
> *And join with our ship's crew.*[71]

Matthewman called for silence and, with patriotic fervor, made a stem-winding speech about the war, the *Lexington's* approaching cruise, her well-known captain's prowess, and the prize money sure to be jingling in the pockets of each and every sailor upon return to port. Here was a chance at adventure, patriotism, and wealth—all at the expense of Congress and King George, God willing. Then he invited the crowd inside for a free round of drinks, his enlistment sheets at the ready.[72] Within a week, seventy men signed their names or made their marks on Matthewman's papers, with quite a few coming from the *Wild Duck*'s crew.[73] It was a significantly smaller number than Barry had hoped for, far less than the 110 men the *Lexington* could comfortably hold. One man's name was not on the muster rolls: a slave, name unknown, purchased by Barry as his personal servant for the cruise.[74]

One deterrent to the success of the *Lexington*'s rendezvous was the initial disparity concerning the enemy's regard for American sailors as opposed to American soldiers. Yankee tars were well aware that, in the eyes of the British, a captured Continental Army regular or militiaman was a prisoner of war. A captured Continental sailor or privateer was considered a pirate, and treated as such. In accepting his commission, Barry not only chose to fight the British but risked the gallows. More than one merchant captain declined a naval commission because he "did not choose to be hanged."[75] That went for sailors as well.

Barry and his crew were now serving under the Articles of War drawn up by Congress. The Articles clearly defined what punishments were to be meted out for each specific offense. They were also less severe than those of the Royal Navy. While blasphemy was punishable by the wearing of "a wooden collar, or some other shameful badge of distinction," and confinement in irons was what the Marine Committee wanted to do with a drunken sailor, twelve lashes were the limit aboard a Continental ship for more serious offenses. An officer was required "to apply to the Commander in chief of the Navy" if he felt an offense required a higher number of stripes.[76]

While monthly pay for the American sailor was better than his British counterpart, monthly compensation for American officers was substantially less:

Captains–$32.00
Petty Officers $9.00–15.00
Lieutenants/ Marine Captains–$20.00
Able Seamen–$8.00
Surgeons–$21.33
Landsmen (Ordinary Seamen)–$6.66[77]

Congress also passed a "Mess Bill" allotting each sailor a daily ration of a pound of bread, a pound of beef or pork, a pound of potatoes or turnips (or 1/2 pint of peas), and a half-pint of rum. Butter and cheese were issued twice a week, usually on Tuesdays and Fridays. On Wednesdays, the Royal Navy custom of "banyon" was adopted: only bread, butter, cheese, and rice were issued. A pint and a half of vinegar was split among six men per week.[78]

Next, Congress ordered "the Secret Committee" to "supply the Brig *Lexington*, Captain Barry, with one ton of powder."[79] On a visit to Wharton's shop, Barry purchased a pistol with a stock large enough to fit comfortably in his huge hand. Wharton delivered it to "Capt. Barry for ye Brig *Lexington*" for "£1, 0, 0."[80] For a few days, it looked like Barry's pistol would have to be shared with his officers and crew, as it was the only hand-held weapon aboard ship. Barry had the *Lexington* ready, but now needed to prod Congress to arm his sailors. The Marine Committee ordered "thirty stand of arms . . . & 26 Muskets" from the Pennsylvania Committee of Safety on March 25.[81]

That evening, Henry Fisher, in keeping with his responsibilities of informing the Committee of Safety of any developments in the bay or river, scribbled a dispatch that a British "Sloop of War . . . with a Small Tender" was heading up the Delaware. Knowing such news was urgent, and anxious to get his courier to horse, Fisher kept the note brief, omitting the flowery formalities ("I am, Sir, Your Obedient and Humble Servant") found in other reports. "Yours in Haste" is probably the most appropriate signoff found in any document from the Revolutionary War.[82]

The committee immediately ordered four row-galleys to Reedy Island, about fifteen miles south of Wilmington, adding that "The said Boats [are] to Act in concert with, and by the order of Cap't Barry, of the Brig *Lexington* . . . and exert their utmost endeavors to take and destroy all such Vessels of the Enemy as they still find in the River Delaware." However, the *Lexington* and the row-galleys were not going anywhere, as Barry still awaited his powder and arms. All day on the twenty-seventh he traversed Chestnut Street, keeping his temper under his hat and his hat in his hand while going back and forth to the Marine Committee's office and the Committee of Safety's headquarters, beseeching both groups for his weapons.[83] They finally arrived at dockside at midnight, March 28.

With the ship lit only by lanterns and the dim spring stars peeking through the clouds, Barry's crew carried the half-barrels of powder and small arms including "13 Dutch Firelocks" up the gangplank, storing them in the magazine and weapons chests, respectively. Barry's commands and the heavy footsteps of the crew were the only discernible sounds of activity on the docks in those wee hours.[84]

His quickly drawn itemization "For First Cruize" was rushed to Congress. The messenger was no sooner off the gangplank when Barry ordered it cleared away. The *Lexington* stood down the Delaware while the city still slept.[85] The early morning light showed the brigantine's Grand Union flag (made by one Mrs. Bridges, who was paid £7.10 for her needlework) fluttering in the light breeze.[86]

Spring is a season of fits and starts along the Delaware: a balmy seventy-degree day with pleasant skies can be followed with snow squalls on the next, but by the end of March the threat of ice on the river had passed. The *Lexington* headed downriver as Barry's pilot steered the brig away from the treacherous chevaux-de-frise to the safety of Port Penn and Reedy Island. Due to Fisher's message, Barry was under the assumption that he would soon be confronting a British sloop. But while the *Lexington* made for the bay, Fisher sent a courier galloping to Philadelphia, an updated report in his saddlebags. The enemy ship was in fact the *Roebuck*, the aforementioned forty-four-gun frigate under the experienced command of Captain Andrew Snape Hamond.[87]

Hamond was already an accomplished captain with over twenty years in the British Navy. A painting of him shows a handsome, proud man with dark, piercing eyes set apart by a strong nose; his lips in a half smile above a strong chin: the perfect portrait of the quintessential frigate commander. His orders from the Admiralty were to proceed up the Delaware, "destroy the floating Batteries," and "render useless the Machines sunk in the Channel of the River Delaware."[88] To carry out his mission he requested reinforcements, including a landing force. While waiting at the Capes for an answer,

Hamond and his tenders preyed upon defenseless American shipping.[89]

On March 28, off Cape May, one of Hamond's tenders, the *Maria*, sighted the Continental schooner *Hornet*, under Captain William Stone, recently broken off from Hopkins's fleet. At first, the *Hornet* pursued the *Maria*, but once Stone caught sight of the *Roebuck* he changed course for Cape May. Now Hamond returned the favor and pursued the *Hornet* until 10:00 P.M., when the frigate's mast-header "lost sight of the chace."[90] Stone got the *Hornet* by Cape May and continued fleeing until he ran aground at Egg Harbor Flats. He was lucky. Hamond was an excellent commander who would have probably taken the *Hornet*, but on the twenty-eighth he was "so excessively ill, with an inflammation in my Bowels, that it was not possible for me to attend to the duty of the Ship." Stone escaped the *Roebuck* while she was under the command of Hamond's temporary replacement, the ironically-named Lieutenant Leak.[91]

Barry ordered the row-galleys that accompanied the *Lexington* downriver to remain at Reedy Island. From there the *Lexington* went on alone to face the enemy's ships. Barry, while outnumbered and completely outgunned, did have some advantages. The river and bay were his bailiwick, and the *Lexington*, with her shallow draft, could enter the familiar shoals alongshore where the much larger *Roebuck* dared not go. If the frigate's tender was to pursue the American ship into the shallows, that would constitute a fair fight in Barry's eyes.

Merchant ships carried one or two cannon and arms for defense against pirates, and Barry was doubtless familiar with the workings of a gun crew. But most of his sailors lacked that experience, and Barry was determined to give them what practice he could. Of all the drills he put his men through, from beating to quarters to clearing the decks for action, developing his men's proficiency with the guns would be the singular difference between victory and striking one's colors.

Ships' cannon were classified by the weight of the cannonballs they fired. The *Lexington*'s 4-pounders (two 6-pounders were added later) were among the smallest in size; some British frigates and all of their ships-of-the-line had 18-pounders onboard. A "4-pounder" gun actually weighed between 1,000 and 1,200 pounds.[92] Mounted on carriages, the guns used two sets of rope and tackle connected to ring bolts driven into the bulwarks. One set allowed the cannon to be run out the gun-port when ready to fire; the other absorbed the shock of the gun's recoil and kept it from flying across the deck.[93] Spare ringbolts were usually set in case the strain of the recoil pulled the original bolts out of the bulwark. A handspike set the gun carriage in place.[94]

All the way down the Delaware, Barry had the commands for gunnery practice endlessly drummed into his men's ears. When he bellowed, "Clear decks for Action," all fires were immediately doused aboard ship, from cooking fires to lanterns, while the gun crews hastened to their battle-stations.[95] The chief gunner (sometimes a midshipman) made sure that each gun's equipment was in place. This included a rammer/sponger, a tub of water, powderhorn, crowbar, and quoin (a notched wooden wedge used for elevating the gun).[96] Under battle conditions and typical drills he checked to see that there was a full supply of balls and powder charges in the designated boxes. These would be replenished by the ship's boys, later known as "powder monkeys" as much for their duty as their agility.[97]

The sequence of orders to prepare and fire the cannons followed. "Cut loose your guns," Barry would bark, and the lashing that fastened the barrel of the gun to the gunport was removed. "Load your guns," and the cannon's barrel was set parallel to the deck. "Take out your tompions," and the stopper was removed from the gun's muzzle. "Load with cartridge," and the bag of powder, along with a wad placed right behind it was rammed down the muzzle. "Shot your guns," and the cannonball was rammed down. "Run out your guns," and the muzzle was pushed out the gunport, with the tackle in place, ready for recoil (and hopefully away from anyone's feet). "Prime," and gunpowder from the powderhorn was put in the cannon's touchhole. "Point your guns," and the cannon was adjusted while the cannoneer of the crew kept the slow match lit by gently blowing on it. "Elevate," and aim was taken on the target, a handspike raising the gun. Then the quoin was slipped into the proper notch, keeping the gun in position to hit its target.[98]

"Fire!" and the lit match was applied to the touchhole, usually on the ship's uproll. After the gun's recoil, Barry yelled, "Sponge your guns," and a wet sponge attached to a long handle was rammed down the muzzle and rotated, extinguishing any sparks or smoking remnants of the cartridge bag. An experienced gun crew could accomplish all this in less than two minutes. If the drill was to continue, the orders were repeated. If not, the order was given to worm the gun, using the long-handled corkscrew that removed remnants of shot, paper, and powder.[99]

Cannonballs–cast iron solid shot–were not the only projectiles rammed down the muzzle in a fight. There was bar-shot (two halves of a ball joined by an iron rod), and chain shot (two balls connected by a chain), used to cut enemy rigging. Grapeshot (walnut-sized iron balls set in a wooden frame, looking like a bunch of deadly grapes) and canister (metal shards or musket balls wrapped in paper) were extremely deadly at close range. Bags of nails, heated red-hot, were fired at sails to set them ablaze. The smaller swivel guns, mounted on the quarterdeck, were anywhere from twenty-eight to thirty-six inches long, and served as high-powered shotguns at close range.[100]

Like muskets, cannons were smooth-bored, and while they could fire a cannonball up to a mile in distance, accuracy was not guaranteed. Gunners learned their weapon's foibles and adjusted to them. A 4-pounder was considered to be accurate at one hundred fifty yards, allowing for the wind and the roughness of the sea.[101] All that flying iron could turn an enemy ship into a death trap. Cannonballs tore into bulwarks, gunwales, and masts, smashing loose long, jagged splinters that flew about a ship's decks and innards with lethal speed. Falling masts and spars, weighed down with canvas and rigging, became instant weapons against a ship's own crew.

Once battle began, other weapons would be brought to bear. The marines were expected to be well-practiced marksmen: after climbing to the tops, they fired their muskets in volleys, to sweep the enemy decks of their sailors. As the ships closed in on each other, grappling hooks–iron claws attached to long lengths of rope–were thrown across the water to the enemy ship. Digging into the gunwales, they were then pulled by the crew to bring the enemy ship close enough for boarding. Pistols, some with a folding blade, joined cutlasses, short swords, axes, and even boathooks as the hand-to-hand weapons of choice.[102]

Barry and his officers needed to quickly assess each sailor's fighting ability, determining who among them was suited for combat while the rest would serve the ship best during a fight by manning rope and sail. The men aboard the *Lexington* faced an enemy with a long tradition of warfare; the "wooden world" of the Royal Navy was full of bloody contests that habitually ended in a British victory. As the *Lexington* headed ever closer to the *Roebuck* and her tender, Barry got in as much gunnery practice as possible. But the drills were most likely done without firing any ammunition, save perhaps for the last round. Barry could not afford to waste any cannonballs or powder. He and his crew were shadowboxing.[103]

Congress, however, was full of fight. One member wrote home that "the Coast is much infested with pirates," alluding to the presence of the British. With news that "A 40 gun ship is at the Capes"– meaning the *Roebuck*–he went on to announce, "the *Lexington* is gone down," as if Barry's little brigantine would be more than a match for Hamond's frigate.[104] Barry knew better, and kept the *Lexington* along the eastern side of the channel, passing Egg Harbor Flats where the *Hornet* had recently run aground. At dawn on March 31, keeping his ship along Cape May, he soon sighted the *Roebuck* through his spyglass. The frigate's lookout also spotted the *Lexington* on the horizon, and Hamond gave chase: "At 6 in the morning weighed and made Sail after a Brig under Cape May, but being obliged to go round the overfalls, at 8 lost sight of her."[105]

Taking advantage of the *Lexington*'s shallower draft, Barry sailed for the "Overfalls"–the shoals that encircle Cape May–to keep his brigantine safely out of range of the *Roebuck*'s long guns, then disappeared from Hamond's sight altogether as she rounded the cape. Hamond's entry was the first mention of Barry by the Royal Navy. It would not be the last.

CHAPTER FOUR

BATTLE

*I*N HIS REPORT TO THE COMMITTEE OF SAFETY on April 1, 1776, Henry Fisher noted Hamond's chase of the *Lexington*: "The Brig [with] Capt. Barry came down under Cape May Around on Sunday Morning went out–the Ship and Tenders put out to Sea after the Brig but returned on Sunday evening into the road."[1] Although anxious to see action, Barry knew the *Lexington* was no match for one of His Majesty's frigates. He proceeded up the New Jersey coastline.

After two days without so much as sighting a sail, he reversed course above Barnegat Bay, and came down to Little Egg Harbor. Once ashore he learned that the tender for the HMS *Phoenix* had captured three prizes and sent a landing party ashore. The British tars terrorized a family in their home on the Absecon beach, taking "even the clothes on the children's back[s]."[2] Deducing that the tender and her prizes had already reached New York, Barry returned to the *Lexington* and headed south for Virginia.[3]

On April 4, the *Lexington's* mast-header sighted a sail on the horizon. The brigantine gave chase and quickly overtook a sloop from St. Croix.[4] Despite the protests of the captain that he was on an innocent mission to New York, Barry turned the sloop over to a lieutenant and a small detachment of the *Lexington*'s crew, with orders to sail to Philadelphia.[5] The *Lexington* accompanied the sloop to Cape May, where Barry received a signal from Fisher.

That evening, the resourceful pilot was rowed out to the brigantine and delivered a letter to Barry from Nathaniel Falconer: a small fleet of merchant ships under the Cape was in need of escort. The next day, with overcast weather acting as a perfect shield, Barry convoyed them past the usually watchful *Roebuck* on April 5. Once the merchantmen cleared Cape May, they headed northward. Barry continued his southerly course.[6]

Hamond, meanwhile, received word regarding Esek Hopkins: the "Philadelphia Squadron having been at [New] Providence & St. Augustine . . . were certainly on their return to Philadelphia. . . . Upon receipt of this Intelligence I took care to place my Ship in the best Manner I could to intercept them."[7] Hopkins's fleet, which Hamond's report listed as seven ships, was much more appealing prey than Barry's small ship, as far as the intrepid captain of the *Roebuck* was concerned. His change in plans and direction allowed Barry to slip past the Capes undetected. By Sunday morning, April 7, the *Lexington* reached Cape Charles, Virginia, the home waters of Lord Dunmore's fleet of "Royal Pirates," just a short distance from the charred remains of Norfolk. There would certainly be a chance for action there.

That afternoon, the *Lexington*'s lookout spotted a sail coming from the southwest. Believing her to be a sloop of war, Barry ordered, "Beat to quarters!" Still keeping the *Lexington*'s gun ports closed, and not flying the "Grand Union," he gave orders to head eastward, giving the impression that the Americans were trying to escape.[8] With his bait set, the sloop took up the chase, and soon began to overtake the *Lexington*. Barry's suspicions that she was a tender to one of the British frigates proved correct; as the sloop sailed closer, the old tars from the *Wild Duck* recognized their pursuer from weeks earlier. It was the *Edward*.[9] Barry issued orders to load the *Lexington*'s cannons, but still kept the gun ports closed.

The Americans waited quietly at their stations. Soon captain and crew would know if the drills and gunnery exercises had prepared them well enough for combat. All felt a mixture of anxiety, fear, and readiness as they waited for the fight to come to them. Barry's commanding presence on deck and his jocular comments kept many a sailor's knees from knocking. All the men could hear was the lapping of the waves against the *Lexington*'s hull, the wind snapping at the canvas, and their captain's occasional low exhortations to keep calm . . . when suddenly the *Edward* fired a warning shot over the *Lexington*'s bow.[10]

Lieutenant Richard Boger had an experienced crew of twenty-nine men aboard the *Edward*. The sloop carried six 3-pounders and several swivels; it was not as well armed as the *Lexington*, to be sure, but her crew was battle-tested and eminently more familiar with their guns than the *Lexington*'s sailors were with theirs. The *Edward* had just finished escorting a packet through the Virginia Capes when she sighted Barry's ship.[11] With orders to "intercept and carry into Virginia" any rebel vessels, Boger saw the brigantine as easy pickings. The *Lexington* again changed course as if to elude the little warship.[12] As the *Edward* closed in on her prey, Boger took his speaking trumpet and bellowed orders for the *Lexington* to identify herself and "heave to": bring the ship into the wind, in order to come to a complete standstill.[13]

Barry's response to Boger's demand was threefold. First, he took up his own speaking trumpet: "Continental brig *Lexington*," he shouted over the water. Second, he ordered the Grand Union raised and the gunports opened. Finally, he roared, "Fire!" The port rail of the brigantine disappeared in the smoke of a broadside aimed at the *Edward*'s starboard hull and bulwark. The battle was joined. Barry ordered the mainsail and main foresail reefed to keep better control of the ship during the fight and minimize damage to them.[14]

The *Edward* only took a hit or two from the broadside, fired by Barry's gun crews with more nervous enthusiasm than accuracy. But the broadside proved enough of a shock to Boger that he decided to change course, losing headway in the process. As he brought his sloop back into the wind, she ran into another broadside. Again, the results were negligible.

While Barry's greeting surprised Boger and his crew, they wasted no time responding. Boger kept his course west-southwest, heading for the Chesapeake. If he could put distance between himself and this rebel's superior firepower, he might reach other ships from Dunmore's fleet for assistance. The *Edward*'s smaller guns, more accurately handled, soon proved deadly. Her cannonballs found their mark, splitting the rails and bulwarks of the *Lexington*. One shot felled three of Barry's men, killing two and wounding the other.[15]

It was a running battle. Despite the surer aim from his more seasoned hands, Boger could not scare off the *Lexington* and free his ship from the tenacious brigantine. Gunwales splintered, deck bloodied, the rebel ship still would not back off. Barry kept his men to their assigned tasks. Slowly but surely, his gun crews found their range and improved their accuracy.[16] The *Lexington*, larger in size, sail area, and manpower, kept up its pursuit. Soon Barry took control of the fight. Now the *Edward*'s bulwarks were being shot into splinters, menacing the crewmen and tearing her rigging and sails.[17] For an hour, the two ships kept at their small guns; two young lightweights crudely pawing at each other while dancing around the ring.

Finally, Barry saw the opportunity he hoped for: the *Lexington* "crossed the T," coming across the *Edward*'s stern.[18] For a few brief moments, the sloop was defenseless. The next round of cannon fire from the Americans resulted in a shot as lucky as it was deadly, smashing the *Edward*'s stern just at or below the cabin, killing a British sailor. Water poured in fast; Boger sent a man to find a "plug"–a stanchion large enough to stop the incoming seawater–but none could be found of sufficient size. With his crew too small in numbers to maintain the fight, sail the ship, and keep the *Edward*'s stern from flooding and eventually sinking, Boger was forced to reach for his speaking trumpet, ask Barry for quarter, and strike his colors.[19]

The crew of the *Lexington*, bloodied and exhausted, had just won their first victory at sea. It was also the first time British colors were lowered by a British ship of war in combat with the Continental Navy.[20]

The Americans quickly boarded their prize and assisted in plugging the *Edward*'s stern, rendering her seaworthy for the voyage back to Philadelphia. Barry placed a prize crew on board and turned command over to his sailing master, Lieutenant Scott. The *Lexington* escorted the *Edward* back to the Delaware Bay.[21] Before they departed, Barry handed Scott a euphoric report of his victory, to be delivered to John Hancock in Philadelphia:

In sight of the Capes of Virginia, April 7, 1776.
To the Continental Marine Committee:

Gentlemen, I have the pleasure to acquaint you that at one PM this Day I fell in with the sloop *Edward,* belonging to the Liverpool frigate. She enjoined us near two glasses. They killed two of our men, and Wounded two more. We shattered her in a terrible manner, as you will see. We killed and wounded several of her crew. I shall give you a particular account of the powder and arms taken out of her, as well as my proceedings in general. I have the pleasure to acquaint you that all our people behaved with much courage. I am gentlemen {& c}

John Barry[22]

It was a succinct account with not one wasted word. Barry awarded no accolades to himself for his ruse, leadership, or courage. The praise was for "all our people." His skills as a sailor and qualities as a commander were between the lines of his report. It would later be said that he was as popular with his men as any captain in the navy: with a minimum of casualties, a victorious battle under their belts, and a prize ship heading home (and shares in its condemnation awaiting them), the Lexingtons were ready to follow Barry anywhere.[23]

The ships parted company at Cape Henlopen. Sending the *Edward* limping up the Delaware to Philadelphia, Barry sailed the *Lexington* back to Little Egg Harbor, to repair his own ship and dispose of his prisoners.[24]

———

As the battered *Edward* struggled upriver, Philadelphia finally received news of Esek Hopkins's squadron, as the schooner *Wasp* and Captain Hallock sailed into town. The fleet departed the

Bahamas on March 17, heading north with their holds full of captured ordnance and three prisoners, including the lieutenant governor of Nassau. Some of the Americans came down with "tropical sickness"–perhaps a euphemistic way of saying that the "Cask of Spirits" mentioned earlier resulted in everything from hangovers to alcohol poisoning.[25] And while some sailors suffered the excesses of demon rum, others also complained of ill health, with pustules breaking out on their skin–symptoms of smallpox.[26] Hopkins ordered the fleet to rendezvous at Block Island Channel below Rhode Island.[27] On the way home, the *Wasp* was separated from the squadron by a storm; with his ship damaged and "14 Sick people" aboard, Hallock returned to Philadelphia.[28] The *Wasp* barely made it upriver, in what Robert Morris called a "leaky and sickly" condition– also an apt description of her crew.[29]

Along the way, the *Wasp* passed the *Betsy* at Gloucester Point. The *Betsy*'s destination was France, and among her passengers was Silas Deane, the first American envoy to the court of Louis XVI.[30] Morris and Deane wrote back and forth to each other as the *Betsy* sailed toward the Capes. Deane nervously hoped "that as Capt. Barry has got out and will Cruize from Sandy Hook to the Capes of Virginia, No small [British] Vessels of war, will keep the Coast," and attack Deane's ship.[31] Morris planned to send the *Wasp* back downriver to escort the *Betsy*, if the latter would wait for her, but "I cannot find the Captain." Morris wrote, "however I will have her fitted quick." Four days later, the *Wasp* was ready.[32]

The *Wasp* reached Chester on April 9, and saw the battered *Edward* in the river, having picked up a pilot to get her to Philadelphia safely. Also at Chester was Lieutenant Colonel Francis Johnson of Anthony Wayne's regiment, who immediately penned a letter to his superior stating "that Captain Barre has been amazingly successful" and that "All The Prisoners are to go to Philada Thro' Jersey (saving one or two Seamen and three or four Negroes)."[33] The letter, delivered by a dispatch rider, got to Philadelphia before the *Edward* crawled into the harbor. Quite a crowd turned out to see her; from Congressmen to servants, they beheld the first captured warship to arrive at an American port.[34]

News of Barry's victory sped throughout the colonies. In a letter praising his actions, the Marine Committee promised that the *Edward* "shall be immediately libeled in the Court of the Admiralty . . . the share thereof belonging to you, the Officers and Crew shall be deposited in the hands of your Agents and in every respect the utmost Justice Shall be done to all concerned. . . . We report our approbation of your Conduct, And beg you may signify to your Officers and Men that the Marine Committee Of Congress highly applaud their Zeal and bravery."[35] Eventually, the news reached London, in an "Extract of a Letter from Philadelphia" published in the *Public Advertiser* with a dateline of April 15: "This Morning was brought in here a Sloop mounting six three pounders and ten swivels belonging to the *Leverpool* Man of War. . . . She was taken off the Capes of Virginia by . . . Capt. Barry."[36]

True to their word, the Marine Committee sped through the condemnation process of the *Edward*. Back at Little Egg Harbor, Barry procured what few stores the little village possessed to mend damages incurred during the battle. On April 8, with Lieutenant Scott and the first "prize" having arrived in port, the Marine Committee wrote to Barry that the St. Croix sloop "does not prove to be a prize, yet as the circumstances attending her Suspicions you did right."[37] Further, the committee sent "your Lieut. of Marines and some men" with Captain Hallock and the W*asp*, to be landed at Cape May; Lieutenant Scott took a similar message with him to Little Egg Harbor should Barry still be there. The letter concluded with orders that the *Lexington* join the *Wasp* in giving safe escort to the *Betsy* "until you and Mr. Deane Shall think her out of danger of the Enemies Tenders and Cutters."[38] Scott arrived on or around April 12, but it wasn't until the fifteenth that Barry could comply with the committee's orders to catch up to the *Betsy* and escort Deane and Co. past the Capes. That day, Barry commanded the local militia's captain to "deliver the prisoners which I have taken out of the Sloop *Edward*, and to supply them with sufficient meat Drink and Lodging during their journey. . . . Mr. Robert Morris will satisfy you."[39] By noon Barry rounded Cape May, where Hallock "Sat [set] Capt. Barrey['s] pepel on Shore." While retrieving them at Cape May,

Barry learned that the *Roebuck* had pursued the *Wasp* until Hamond called off the "game" on account of darkness.[40]

Barry endeavored to catch up to the *Betsy*, following a course toward Bermuda he believed the *Betsy* would take before turning eastward so as to avoid British ships. By this time, Barry and the *Lexington* were becoming an obsession with Hamond. In a letter to Lord Dunmore he poured out his frustrations regarding Barry:

> It is with great concern I acquaint yr Lordship, that Mr. Boger . . . was taken by this Brig I mentioned to you in my letter . . . she is now fitting out with great expectation as a Privateer and will undoubtedly be sent to the Capes of Virginia: and by not being known for an Enemy . . . will do a great deal of Mischief. . . . I would give more than I can express to have the *Otter*, or even the *Otter*s Tender here for a few days, as without a small Vessel that can go in shallow water it is totally impossible (or at least very unlikely) that I shall be able to do any thing with this Brig *Lexington*. All the North side of Delaware Bay is encompassed with shoals & shallow water, having a channel of about 13 or 14 foot water within them; and this passage Mr. Barry is at present master of. I have chaced him several times but can never draw him into the Sea. . . . However, I trust if my good stars will be but propitious enough to me to send me any Vessel that can carry 50 Men, his reign will be of short duration, especially as his success of late has made him bold.[41]

As Hamond penned this letter, the *Lexington* was six hundred miles away, near Cape Roman on the South Carolina coast.[42] On April 27, the *Lexington*'s lookout sighted no less than seventeen sail to the southeast. Barry kept a watchful eye on them; when one of the larger ships began to stand toward him, the *Lexington*'s captain took enough time to discern it to be a frigate, and gave orders to head northwest in a hurry. The chase was on. Barry ran out every inch of the *Lexington*'s canvas.[43]

The hound in the hunt was the HMS *Solebay*, twenty-eight guns, led by Captain Thomas Symonds. The seventeen ships sighted comprised the British fleet under Sir Peter Parker, escorting British merchantmen. Symonds, "seeing sail in the NW Qr our Sigl to Chace could not come up with her ha[u]l'd our wind" and rejoined the convoy.[44] The *Solebay* chased the *Lexington* for "eight hours . . . when the man of war quitted the chace and joined his convoy. Barry then reversed course and followed, with design to pick up some of the fleet, but discovering his foremast was sprung, he was obliged to alter his course."[45]

With so much pressure from the wind on the *Lexington*'s sails, her foremast was carried away. But despite this accident, the *Solebay* couldn't catch up with the American ship. Barry kept the wind at his favor, and nothing Symonds tried brought the *Lexington* within range of his bow-chasers. Given that the fleet seemed to be heading for Virginia (actually North Carolina), Barry set his course for home. Cloaked in the dusk, the *Lexington* slipped past Cape May on May 4.[46]

Daylight found not one but three British warships in Whorekiln Road, heading up the Delaware to Philadelphia, the *Roebuck* having been joined by the *Liverpool* and the *Fowey*. Once the *Roebuck*'s mastheader spied the *Lexington,* Hamond instantly recognized her and began pursuit, running "with all my Studding sails."[47] Barry kept his ship hugging the Jersey shoreline and its shallows, eluding Hamond once more.[48] The vexed Briton fired a long gun in frustration at his nemesis, and Barry sardonically returned the backhanded compliment with one of his diminutive 4-pounders.[49] Low on supplies and ammunition, the Irishman gave orders to head upriver and home.

Philadelphia gave him a hero's welcome. "Capt. Barry in the brig *Lexington* returned from a cruise against the English Pirates" was the lead in the *Pennsylvania Journal*'s article on his return.[50] His deeds were the talk of the town, especially in light of the latest news regarding Esek Hopkins.

The Continental fleet was sailing back to Hopkins's home port, Providence, Rhode Island. They had just captured two British ships: the schooner *Hawk* and bomb-brig *Bolton*.[51] On April 6, another sail was seen on the horizon, and the four largest American vessels took up the chase, catching up with her off Block Island.[52] She proved to be the frigate *Glasgow*, under Captain Tyringham Howe, Charleston bound. Her twenty guns made her a formidable opponent, but as she was outnumbered four to one, Hopkins gave the orders to engage.

Where British tactics would have dictated forming a line of battle in order to pound the *Glasgow* into submission, the inexperienced Hopkins sent his ships at the frigate one at a time. Like a gang of young toughs that had cornered an experienced street fighter in an alley, each vessel took its turn at the *Glasgow* and came away the worse off. For over two hours, the outnumbered British ship bravely outran and outfought her enemy. The *Alfred* alone "receiv'd considerable damage . . . our, wheel, rope and blocks shot away."[53] Finally, the four American ships, their holds heavy with captured cannon and ammunition, and their bottoms foul from their round trip to the Bahamas, broke off the engagement.[54]

At first, Congress and the public believed Hopkins's version of the battle, as originally reported by the press. But soon writs from the crews about lack of payment (soon followed by similar complaints from officers) were quickly augmented by allegations of cowardice aimed at Captains Hazard and Whipple, and rumors of incompetence regarding Commodore Hopkins himself. Courts of inquiry were called. Whipple's court-martial, which questioned his judgment during the fight, cleared him; Hazard's found him guilty. Hopkins's politically connected appointment was beginning to look like a poor choice.[55] He was later censured by Congress for his conduct, yet retained his command. The American Navy might not have yet learned how to fight like the British Navy, but Congress had learned the importance of family connections, in meting out levels of blame as well as in appointments.[56]

Barry also learned that the *Edward* was condemned at an Admiralty hearing. George Campbell, "Presenter for the Libellists," presented "the Bill of John Barry Esquire [and] the Officers Marines and Seamen" of the *Lexington* and the "Thirteen united Colonies of North America" against "The *Edward* with her Guns Tackle Furniture and Apparel." The *Lexington* fitted out for the "Defence of American Liberty . . . sailing on the high Seas . . . did discover pursue approach the *Edward* . . . burthen about fifty Tons . . . employed in the present cruel and unjust War." The inventory included everything from "Guns Tac[k]le Furniture" to "10 E[m]pty Hammocks" and was promptly itemized for condemnation.[57]

Interrogations were administered; Lieutenant Boger did "declareth and confesseth" to the truth of the statements, including in his testimony "that there were four Negroes on board the said Sloop at the Time of her Capture that one of them called Pompey White he hath heard and believes is free. That the other three he believes are Slaves and one of them named James he has been told belongeth to one Mr. Anderson of Hampton that as to the other two knoweth not to whom they belong." Along with the items Boger had seized from the ship *Philadelphia Packet,* the slaves were removed from the Court's list, to be returned to their owners.[58]

On May 1, the *Pennsylvania Gazette* ran an "Advertisement of the Sale of the Prize Sloop *Edward.*" The auction was held at the London Coffeehouse on the following day.[59] The Marine Committee purchased the *Edward,* giving her to Joshua Humphreys for repairs; his talents soon transformed her into the ten-gun Continental sloop of war *Sachem.* She was the second acquisition of the Continental Navy since the *Lexington*'s first cruise. Another brig, the *Molly,* had been refurbished by the tireless Humphreys and given to another Willing and Morris merchant captain: Lambert Wickes. He joined the roster of naval commanders with his renamed ship, the *Reprisal.*[60]

Barry's officers and crew got their first taste of prize money. Congress had broken down the disbursement of shares in the following manner: 10 percent to the captain: 15 percent divided between the marine captain, lieutenants, and masters; 12 1/2 percent divided between the marine lieutenants, surgeons, chief gunners, and carpenters; 15 percent between the midshipmen, warrant and petty officers; and the remaining 48 1/2 percent distributed among the rest of the crew. Handsome as it sounded, there was a catch—a very large catch. Since 50 percent of the full amount went to Congress, the above percentages for shares were actually only worth half as much—a far cry from the "captain and crew take all" approach of His Majesty's Navy.[61]

Precedent was also set for Barry's prisoners of war. Under the watchful eyes of the Pennsylvania Committee of Safety, Richard

Boger and his junior officer signed a parole, swearing "We would not go farther than two Miles from Germantown, where we are ordered to reside, with leave of the Committee . . . that we will not bear arms against the said Colonies, nor carry on any Political Correspondence . . . nor give any Intelligence to any Person whatever . . . so long as we remain a Prisoner."[62] The committee passed a resolution that the "Mariners taken Prisoner by Captain Barry" were to be offered similar terms for parole, with instructions "to provide the Lodging on the most reasonable Terms."[63] Such gentlemanly arrangements for British prisoners were in stark contrast to the treatment of American sailors captured by the British (the prison hulks in New York harbor rival the Civil War's Andersonville for inhumanity). As an officer, Boger would be a valuable chip in negotiations over prisoner exchange.[64]

Once set ashore, Barry's prisoners were better treated than one of his own crew, who presented his "Petition of a Slave to the Pennsylvania Committee of Safety":

> Sheweth that your poor Petitioner was Bought by Captain John Barry and taken to Sea in the Brig Lexington belonging to the Honorable the Congress and has since Sold him for the Same Money That he Paid for Him Besides Having Receved Your poor Petitioners wages and Prize Money–Therefore your Humble Poor Petitioner Requests that you Would take his Case unto Your Serio[u]s Consideration and order Him Such part of the Prize Money as you shall Deem fit and In so doing Your Humble Petitioner Will be for ever bound To pray and C
>
> Servant to Capt. Barry[65]

No record exists about the outcome of the slave's petition. Throughout the war, wages and prize shares earned by a slave at sea were paid out–to his owner.[66]

Barry's arrival in Philadelphia coincided with Hamond's return to the Delaware. With the *Liverpool* and her twenty-eight guns for company, Hamond sailed the *Roebuck* upriver to replenish her water supply and "reconoitre the enemy[']s force of the River."[67] Henry Fisher's alarm system went into action immediately. Signal guns were fired sequentially along the river while couriers galloped to each way station, handing Fisher's warning to the awaiting rider. Within minutes, Philadelphians knew enemy ships were approaching; within hours, they knew what ships were approaching. Barry and Humphreys busied themselves with refitting the *Lexington* and completing repairs.

The *Roebuck* and *Liverpool* were alongside Wilmington the next day. Their long guns put Philadelphians "into some Consternation for a short time," Richard Bache noted in a letter to Franklin.[68] Morris, as the vice president of the Marine Committee and as a member of the Pennsylvania Committee of Safety, ordered Barry to "Collect your officers and Men" and assist in the defense of Philadelphia. Barry and at least seventy of his men from the *Lexington* joined Captain Read aboard the *Montgomery* and Captain Wickes on the *Reprisal*. Every warship, row-galley, and floating battery from both the Pennsylvania and Continental navies headed below the crest of Fort Island (later Fort Mifflin), to give as warm a welcome as possible to Andrew Snape Hamond, R.N.[69]

Barry and Read got to the battle line on May 9 and were briefed on the previous day's actions. Thirteen row-galleys positioned themselves in the shoals—putting them about a mile from the frigates—and began firing at the *Roebuck* and *Liverpool*. The frigates, trying to maneuver to a point in the river where their guns could destroy the small American boats, returned fire. Most of the cannonballs from both sides splashed in the water, yards away from their targets. At dusk, the *Roebuck* attacked from the Jersey side of the river near Helen's Cove. Hamond intended to take out the row-galleys before nightfall. In his haste he forgot about the *Roebuck*'s eighteen-and-a-half-foot draft; perhaps he had no pilot. Without warning, the *Roebuck* ran aground.[70] The guncrews on the row-galleys kept firing their cannon until they were too hot to handle. That night, Hamond put some of his crew in the *Roebuck*'s boats, serving as a night patrol against possible assault by the Americans. Captain Bellew sailed the *Liverpool* as close as he could to the *Roebuck* to protect the entrapped ship and serve as a getaway for Hamond's crew if required. When the tide began to rise, Hamond used every man and boat available to free his ship. After putting every British sailor to their utmost exertion, Hamond got the *Roebuck* off by 4:00 A.M.[71]

That morning, with ammunition and supplies running low, Barry fired off a note to Morris that "if the *Lexington* was Fit[t]ed she might be of service, for the More Thare is the Better . . . we shall keep them in play."[72] The second day's fighting was more of the same, with both sides jockeying for position, taking care to avoid the *Roebuck*'s mishap. Finally, the British ships broke off the engagement. Hamond knew he was lucky; Charles Biddle "heard that Captain Hamond then said if the commanders of the galleys had acted with as much judgment as they did courage, they would have taken or destroyed his ship."[73]

Philadelphia's citizens, having heard the constant echo of cannon fire for two anxious days, considered the *Roebuck* affair more a victory than a draw. The brave little row-galleys had served their purpose. John Adams wrote his wife, Abigail, "There has been a gallant Battle . . . in which the Men of War came off second best–which has diminished, from the Minds of the People . . . the Terror of a Man of War."[74] With the wood and canvas chess pieces back to their accustomed places on the board, it fell to the Marine Committee to come up with a plan to get the arriving merchantmen escorted past the Capes and safely upriver with their badly needed goods.

There were now four Continental ships at Philadelphia: Barry's *Lexington*, Wickes's *Reprisal*, the *Hornet* under Captain Hallock, and the *Wasp*, now under Captain Charles Alexander. The Marine Committee ordered them to work in concert along Cape May (where there was more shallow water in the bay than on the Cape Henlopen side), providing escorts at the Capes to arriving merchantmen when not harassing the enemy. Keeping to the Jersey shore and sailing into the bay at night gave the Americans a fighting chance in keeping the merchantmen–many carrying gunpowder and munitions–out of British hands.[75]

Thanks to Barry's recent achievements, his rendezvous for the *Lexington*'s second cruise was quick and successful. Barry soon had a full complement of 110 men.[76] After presenting his expenses for refitting and supplies on May 21, he sent the *Lexington* down the Delaware, picking up his fellow ships along the way.[77]

Barry discovered that Hamond and the *Roebuck* had departed Delaware Bay. Responsibility for the attack and capture of American shipping now fell to Captain Bellew and the *Liverpool*. With only one minor incident—Barry ordered a snow that had been bound for New England to return to Philadelphia due to its deep draft—the squadron came together under Cape May. Learning that the *Liverpool* had sailed beyond the Capes, Barry and Alexander sailed over to Cape Henlopen and met with Henry Fisher, who informed them that the *Liverpool* had taken a prize: "A Snow . . . she appears to be in ballast. . . . On Sunday [May 26] the *Liverpool* and her prize . . . went to sea. I am persuaded that the *Liverpool* was scar'd. . . . I went on board to give them [Barry and Alexander] the best information that I could in regard to the *Liverpool*. . . . They went on to Cape May for the rest of their fleet, and now they are all under our Capes in quest of the Pirate."[78]

Barry and Alexander returned to Cape May, where they found the *Reprisal* and *Hornet* with a privateers' prize, the *Juno*, which had been chased by the *Liverpool* and gotten to the shallows of the Overfalls, the same tactic Barry had used with Hamond and the *Roebuck*. That gave Barry an idea. Leaving the *Wasp* to escort the *Juno* up the Bay, the other three American ships headed back to Cape Henlopen and out to sea. At 7:30 A.M., despite "Fresh Gales and hazey" conditions, the *Liverpool* "Made a chace to be [a] Ship a Brig and a sloop arm'd Vessels belonging to the Rebels."[79] It was an encore performance of Barry's cat-and-mouse game with Hamond.

For three hours the *Liverpool* chased the smaller vessels. At 10:30, Barry ordered "heave to," and the three American vessels turned into the wind, coming to a dead stop almost immediately. Aboard the *Liverpool*, Bellew ordered "Beat to quarters!" It was obvious that the *Liverpool* would easily overtake the Americans ships. Bellew must have relished this chance to finish off the rebel captain who had sorely frustrated Hamond. Another half-hour put the *Liverpool* ever closer to the three Yankee ships.[80]

Though caught up in the moment of the chase, Bellew still had the foresight to order soundings, sending a midshipman toward the bow with the "lead line"—a twenty-fathom (about 120 feet) line of rope with a six- to nine-pound lead weight attached, hollowed out at one end and filled with tallow. The young officer swung the line over his head several times in an arced, pendulum-type motion, then flung it into the water in front of him; by the time it came back alongside where he was standing it was perpendicular to the bottom, where it could measure depth as well as give the nature of the seabed itself, with samples sticking to the tallow.[81] Every couple of minutes, the midshipman called back his findings to the quarterdeck.

Suddenly, at 11 o'clock, Barry ordered his ships under way. With the wind filling their sails, they headed for the Overfalls, where soundings vary from as much as seventeen and a half to three and a half feet within as little distance as two hundred yards.[82] Bellew continued his headlong pursuit; soon his quarry would be within range of his guns. Then the midshipman's alarmed cry rang out from the bow: the *Liverpool* was in only four fathoms of water. Quickly, Bellew gave orders to wear ship. In an instant, his crew's emotions swung from excitement to dread. They fairly jumped to their orders; now it was the *Liverpool*'s turn to swing into the wind to keep from running aground and becoming a sitting duck for the rebel ships. Shortening sail, the frustrated Englishman headed back to Cape Henlopen.[83] Barry came within seconds and inches of another capture.

Barry's attempt to run the *Liverpool* aground gave him the chance to see the *Hornet* in action. Leaking and slow, she would not be of much use in future encounters with His Majesty's warships. Barry kept her anchored at Cape May as more of a presence than a true threat.[84] He sent Wickes and the *Reprisal* to convoy the merchantmen out of the bay.[85]

The *Liverpool* soon disappeared from the Capes; Bellew sailed in pursuit of "several sail" and headed hundreds of miles below Cape Henlopen in chase.[86] At the same time, Congress declared that the "Committee of Safety of Pennsylvania be empowered to negotiate with Captain Bellew . . . for an exchange of the prisoners on board of the *Liverpool* . . . to deliver up Lieutenant Boger and Lieutenant Ball in the exchange."[87] Congress was determined to be honorable and aboveboard in its treatment and actions toward naval prisoners of war. British officials, as we shall see later, were not so disposed.

Bellew wrote a report to Admiral Shuldham at Halifax of his encounter with Barry's squadron in "Cape Mary Road," describing it as "a large Privateer Ship at Eighteen Three Pounders, a Brig of

Sixteen Sixes and Fours, and a Sloop of Ten Six Pounders." While reporting the loss of his tender, and the other Continental successes along the coast, he did find solace in the fact that he captured "a small vessel laden with linen and Twelve thousand Dollars . . . the property of Willen and Morris . . . two most Notorious rebels."[88]

Now back to sea and on the prowl, the *Lexington*'s lookout sighted two sail: one due east, too far to be recognized; the other a sloop of war, coming out of Whorekiln Road to the southeast. This was the *Kingfisher*, captained by Alexander Graeme, recently from Nova Scotia and a cruise in the Bay of Fundy, with orders to join the *Liverpool* at the Capes.[89] Seeing the *Kingfisher* stand for the other ship, now identifiable as a merchant brig, Barry lost no time in making for the same target. With the advantage of the shorter leg in this triangular pursuit, Barry brought the *Lexington* alongside and boarded her around 5:00 P.M. She was a Wilmington brigantine under one Captain Walker, returning home with a hold containing powder and arms. Sizing up the situation, Barry ordered the munitions transferred aboard the *Lexington*. He offered to bring Walker and his crew aboard as well, but Walker declined abandoning his ship to the enemy–a decision that Barry understood. With the precious cargo in his hold, Barry departed at sunset. Within an hour Graeme captured yet another prize for the British.[90]

Vigilant Henry Fisher, in his report to the Committee of Safety on June 11, noted that "lucky for us before the Pirate [Bellew] Boarded our Brave Capt. Barry had been on board . . . in sight of the *Kingfisher.*" Fisher's report was "delivered by the Whale Boats as far as New Castle, and from there, by Land, the Torys having Cut that Communication."[91] It was becoming increasingly risky for Fisher to carry out his very dangerous and often unappreciated job.

In recognition of his actions against the enemy, Congress awarded Barry command of the *Effingham*, one of the four frigates being built in Philadelphia.[92] At Cape May, Barry got word of his imminent appointment from John Baldwin, newly appointed commander of the *Wasp*. When this news reached the ambitious Samuel Davidson at Fort Island, he immediately wrote Robert Morris: "Permit me Sr; to Beg your Interest to command the *Lexington*, when Captain Barrey Resigns."[93]

The details and paperwork for Barry's new command went through the office of the Marine Committee's Secretary, John Brown. Like Barry, Brown had emigrated from Ireland to Philadelphia as a young boy, and was soon working for Willing and Morris. Darkly handsome, with piercing brown eyes and an Irishman's "gift of the gab," Morris trusted Brown implicitly. Three years Barry's junior, Brown was already a good friend; the war years only deepened their admiration for each other. In Brown, Barry had both a confidant and trusted adviser.[94]

Baldwin also had new orders in hand: the *Reprisal* was to sail on a diplomatic mission to Martinique, the *Hornet* to return to Philadelphia for repairs, and the *Wasp* to rejoin the *Lexington* at the Capes.[95] Baldwin also carried a dispatch from Morris. Under his responsibilities with the Committee of Safety, Morris alerted Barry of the arrival at the Capes of the brigantine *Nancy*, commanded by one of Barry's old friends, Hugh Montgomery. The *Nancy* was returning to Philadelphia with that most valuable and volatile of cargo–gunpowder–from St. Croix and St. Thomas: 386 half-barrels, to be exact.[96]

The *Reprisal*'s mission to Martinique was thwarted by the arrival of a third British warship, the frigate *Orpheus*, Charles Hudson in command, having finished a "Cruze between the West end of Long Island and Cape Henlopen."[97] With a growing fleet of merchantmen assembled at the shoals under Cape May, Barry told Wickes to wait for the best opportunity to slip past the British. The large number of ships was duly noticed by the British on June 24, as the *Kingfisher*'s Graeme recorded: "Saw fifteen sail at anchor under Cape May Lighthouse WbS 5 or 6 miles." The next day's report shows a further increase in ships: "8 am saw 18 Sail of Pirates and Merchants . . . at anchor off Cape May." Tensions were mounting on both sides.[98]

By mid-morning on June 28, 1776, the weather worsened: "Mod't with rain," was how Hudson described it in his journal.[99] Soon his lookout called out, "Sail Ho!" It was the *Nancy*, already pursued by the *Kingfisher*–Graeme had been "in chace" since 3:00 A.M. The *Orpheus*, off Cape Henlopen lighthouse, spotted the incoming *Nancy* "at 11 AM [and] gave Chace to sail to the No[rth]ward." By late afternoon the *Nancy* was "standing in for Cape May," and the *Kingfisher* "weig'd and stood for the Cape as did the *Orpheus* and Tenders."[100]

Eminently aware of his surroundings, Montgomery sailed the *Nancy* toward the shallower waters outside the oddly named Turtle Gut Inlet, about seven miles northeast of Cape May. The darkness and shallows were a good defense against the British ships and their following tenders, and the enemy's unfamiliarity with the waters guaranteed there would be no pursuit or attack on the brig until dawn. Miles away, the *Lexington's* lookout saw the approaching ships come over the horizon and hailed Barry of the *Nancy's* arrival, along with her pursuers.

Now with darkness came the waiting game. Barry signaled Wickes and Baldwin to come aboard the *Lexington*. The captains and their officers were no sooner up the gangway when they were brought to Barry's cabin for a council of war to create a plan of action.[101]

The three captains determined that the "light winds" would keep the *Reprisal* from taking part in any action, so Barry and Wickes decided that *Reprisal's* barge would assist the other two Continental ships. Lambert's younger brother, Richard, insisted on commanding the barge. After he "refused several Times," the older brother "at Las[t] was prevailed on to let him go." Elated with this chance to prove his courage and leadership, Richard set out in the barge, joining the *Lexington* and *Wasp*, who were at anchor off Cape May. Barry ordered the ships to drop anchor in Whorekiln Road, where he could observe the unfolding action and take steps accordingly.[102] His crew attended their watch or lay in their hammocks, sure in the knowledge that morning would bring battle.

Aboard the *Nancy*, Montgomery had assembled his meager crew and laid out the situation they were facing. He also gave them a choice: those who wished to go ashore in the ship's boat were free to do so, but he was determined "to defend the munitions of war at all hazards." Not a man departed the ship, now riding at anchor several miles off of Turtle Gut Inlet.[103] The inlet would give Montgomery the chance to unload his cargo and get it ashore. The shallow water surrounding its entrance would prevent the larger British ships from entering. Although the *Nancy* would still be in range of their guns, the British would have to send boarding parties in longboats to make a fight of it.

The *Orpheus*'s Hudson began the day with breakfast and a flogging: he "punished Thos. Sandower for Breach of 2 Articles of war w[ith] one Dozen Lashes." Hudson either liked the cat-o'-nine-tails or had a difficult crew; he had a dozen lashes meted out to another sailor just two days previously. The morning weather was more of the same: "Light breezes and hazy and small rain." One of Barry's favorite allies showed up that morning–fog.[104]

Gray daylight gave witness to the resumed chase: "3 Leagues Dist to the Et Ward"–about ten miles–the *Nancy* was sighted and pursued once again by the *Orpheus*, the *Kingfisher*, and "2 Tenders in Chace." Barry, seeing that the *Lexington* and *Wasp* could not be of any assistance on the *Nancy*'s behalf in open water, told young Wickes to send his barge immediately out to the *Nancy*, board her, and sail her into shore, once again using the shallows as a defense against the British warships and their larger drafts.[105]

No sooner had Wickes departed for the *Nancy* than Barry ordered that the barges from the *Lexington* and *Wasp* also be lowered. Deciding that the "light winds" would keep the other two American ships from playing a role in the fight, Barry got into the *Lexington*'s barge: he would personally lead the action.[106] He also made sure that his best gunners came along. Under his command, the sailors in the barges manned their oars and began rowing furiously up the coastline toward Turtle Gut Inlet. They could hear the gunfire of the enemy ships' bow-chasers at the *Nancy*. The brigantine, her hold full of gunpowder, was one chance shot from being blown to bits.

Young Wickes's barge reached the *Nancy* at the entrance to the inlet. After a quick introduction, he and Montgomery determined that the quickest and safest course of action was to "cut her Cable and runn her a shore in order to save her Cargo if possible."[107] The enemy cannon began to boom at them, though not yet finding their range. The *Nancy* headed for the shoreline, entered the inlet, and soon struck ground hard and fast. It was now just past sunrise.

Within minutes, Barry's barge reached the *Nancy*. Once aboard, he hardly had time to greet his old colleague Montgomery and young Wickes. He immediately issued orders to unload the gunpowder, while he and his men manned the *Nancy*'s six 3-pounders. As his men "cut loose the guns," Montgomery's crew and the sailors from Wickes's barge began unloading the nearly four hundred half-barrels of powder in the hold.[108]

The *Kingfisher*, her draft much lighter than that of the larger *Orpheus*, got as close to the inlet as Graeme could manage without running aground. Her first broadside sailed over the *Nancy* and the feverishly working Americans. Operating like a bucket brigade, they passed each half-barrel one man to the next, up from the hold to the deck, and down to the *Nancy*'s boats. By now, the two enemy tenders reached the *Kingfisher* and added their guns to the bombardment. Once Graeme's gunners found their range, he ordered four rowboats lowered to attack the Americans.[109]

The gunners from the *Lexington*, their courage already proven during the taking of the *Edward* and the battle with the *Roebuck*, had the *Nancy*'s 3-pounders primed and ready. Along with other sailors armed with muskets, they awaited their captain's orders. Barry, too, was patient. Once the enemy boats were within musket range, Barry's gunners took dead aim at them, and he bellowed, "Open fire!"

A furious broadside and a volley of musketry swept the attackers with deadly results, and "these Boats were soon beat of[f] & sent back from whence they came." Barry's men did their job well, damaging one longboat so badly that she was of no further use in the battle. As the British rowed hurriedly back to their ship, Barry directed his gunners to take aim at the *Kingfisher* and her tenders. All the while, their comrades kept unloading the gunpowder onto the boats on the leeward side of the *Nancy*. Once so full that they were about to swamp, the boats were rowed to shore, quickly unloaded, and sent back again for more half-barrels.[110]

Around 8:30 A.M., the *Orpheus* closed in.[111] Her 9-pounders opened up in concert with the *Kingfisher*'s guns. The *Nancy* was being pulverized. Her hull was shot full of holes, the main mast shot in two, and her deck was littered with spars, canvas, rope, and tackle.[112] Graeme ordered the *Kingfisher* run within "3 or 4 Hundred yards" of the *Nancy*, putting his ship right at the entrance to the inlet.

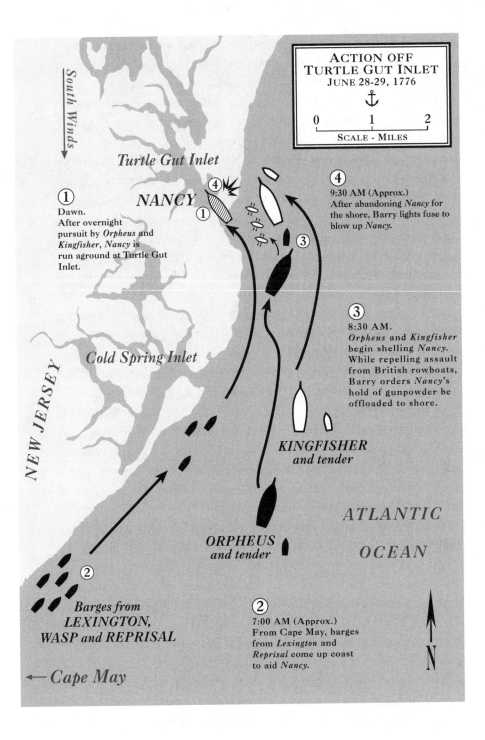

ACTION OFF TURTLE GUT INLET
JUNE 28-29, 1776

⚓

0   1   2
SCALE - MILES

South Winds

Turtle Gut Inlet

NANCY

④

①

① Dawn. After overnight pursuit by *Orpheus* and *Kingfisher*, *Nancy* is run aground at Turtle Gut Inlet.

④ 9:30 AM (Approx.) After abandoning *Nancy* for the shore, Barry lights fuse to blow up *Nancy*.

③

③ 8:30 AM. *Orpheus* and *Kingfisher* begin shelling *Nancy*. While repelling assault from British rowboats, Barry orders *Nancy*'s hold of gunpowder be offloaded to shore.

Cold Spring Inlet

NEW JERSEY

KINGFISHER *and tender*

ATLANTIC

ORPHEUS *and tender*

OCEAN

②

Barges from LEXINGTON, WASP and REPRISAL

② 7:00 AM (Approx.) From Cape May, barges from *Lexington* and *Reprisal* come up coast to aid *Nancy*.

N

← *Cape May*

The British bombardment went on for another half an hour. Amazingly, for all of the flying iron, lead, and splintered wood, only one American sailor had been wounded thus far.[113]

At 9:00 A.M., Hudson ordered two boats from the *Orpheus* to join the *Kingfisher*'s three remaining boats in a new assault on the battered *Nancy*.[114] As Barry watched them come on, another British broadside whistled across the inlet. One of the cannonballs slammed into the *Nancy*'s galley, smashing it to pieces.[115] The combination of more advancing enemy boats and the improving aim of the British gunners now made the situation aboard the *Nancy* untenable. Barry's next order was immediate and direct. While his gunners continued to return fire from the *Nancy*, the barges took the other Americans to the shore, with orders to return for Barry, Montgomery, and the gun crews.

Only 121 of the 386 half-barrels remained aboard. Barry was determined that the *Nancy* and her remaining gunpowder would never be taken by the British. He ordered the gun crews to move 30 or 40 half-barrels from the hold to the captain's cabin. With Montgomery in tow, he laid a fuse-like line of gunpowder running from the cabin along the deck and down into the hold. Next, taking the ship's mainsail, the two captains poured 50 pounds of powder onto it and folded the canvas several times over. Dropping two red-hot coals on the sail's edges, he ordered the remaining men to scramble over the side, into the last barge.[116]

While the Americans had removed "265 heavy Barrels of Powder[,] 50 Muskets[,] 2 three Pounders[,] the Swords[,] and about 1,000 pounds wort[h] of dry Goods" from the *Nancy* during the fighting, Barry had forgotten to haul down the ship's colors.[117] One "daring but fool hardy seaman," coincidentally named John Hancock, leapt back onboard, took down the Grand Union, jumped into the water, and was hauled into Barry's barge.[118] As they rowed to the beach, the advancing British boarding party was being peppered by musket fire from the Americans already ashore. It took the British nearly half an hour to reach the abandoned *Nancy*, "during which Time they [the Americans] killed several of their Men which they saw fall over board and others wounded."[119] Barry's makeshift fuse continued to slowly burn its way toward its two destinations of cabin and hold.

The *Kingfisher's* longboat took the lead in the race toward the abandoned *Nancy*. Despite the brigantine's decimated condition, a prize is still a prize–especially one so fiercely contested. Once he waded onto the strip of beach, Barry again took command. With "one or two small cannon mounted onshore"–probably swivels–he directed the firing on the enemy rowboats from the beach.[120]

At last the crew of the *Kingfisher's* longboat, commanded by her master's mate, came under the *Nancy's* stern. Armed to the teeth, they scrambled aboard with the cheers from their fellow sailors ringing in their ears–just as the sparks from Barry's fuse reached the barrels of gunpowder in both cabin and hold. In that split second, with a deafening blast, the *Nancy* and the British boarding party disappeared.

It was said that the explosion was heard "40 miles above Philadelphia." It sent the men aboard the *Nancy* and those in the closest rowboats flying "30 or 40 yards high," along with pieces of the exploded ship. As the smoke cleared, sailors on both sides could see the gory debris fall back into the inlet, as if the heavens refused it. "Eleven bodies, two laced hats, and a leg with a white spatter dash" dropped back into the water along with the shattered remains of the brigantine.[121] The surviving, dumbstruck British tars, their remaining boats "in a shattered Condition [and] weakly man[n]ed," rowed back to their ships.[122]

The guns on both sides were silent until they returned. Suddenly, a fierce cannonade from the British ships exploded onto the beach at Turtle Gut Inlet, but only one American was hit, "Shott through the arm and body." It was Richard Wickes. A cannonball took his arm and half his chest away. Fresh from the *Reprisal,* Lambert Wickes arrived on the beach at the head of his reinforcements just as his younger brother died: "I arrived just at the Close of the Action Time enough to see him expire . . . Captn Barry . . . says a braver Man never existed."[123]

Taking Richard Wickes's body, the American sailors left the spit of sand they fought over that morning. The powder was stowed in the *Wasp's* hold and sent up the Delaware. "At 2 weighed and made

Sail," Hudson briefly noted in his journal.[124] The British returned to Cape Henlopen.

As before, Barry had taken long odds, assessed the best plan that could succeed, and beaten the British. The *Nancy* was destroyed, but the *Wasp* would reach Philadelphia safely with the desperately needed gunpowder. Despite superior firepower, the "butcher's bill" was far heavier for the British. But the victory brought no cheers or satisfaction among the Americans, and Barry was particularly saddened by the death of the gallant young Wickes.[125]

The next morning–Sunday, June 30–the men of the *Lexington* and *Reprisal* gathered to mourn their shipmate at the log meetinghouse in the small village of Cold Spring, just north of Cape May. Under the same light breezes of the day before, the American sailors, with "bowed and uncovered heads," filed inside and sat on the long, rough-cut wooden pews. After "The Clergyman preached a very deacent Sermon," Lambert Wickes and the *Reprisal's* officers silently hoisted the coffin. Shuffling under its weight, they carried it outside to the little cemetery, and laid their comrade to rest.[126]

Lambert Wickes now faced the task of informing his family in Maryland of Richard's death. On July 2, in a sad but disjointed letter to his brother Samuel, he mentioned Richard's death among a list of the items–including the sugar and "one Bagg Coffee" that accompanied the letter. "You'll disclose this Secret with as much Caution as possible to our Sisters," he pleaded. He quoted Barry's report that Richard "fought like a brave Man & was fore most in every transaction of that day," dying for the cause of the "united Colonies."[127]

By the time Lambert's package reached his family in Maryland, the "united Colonies" ceased to exist as well. The same day Wickes posted his letter, Congress approved the Declaration of Independence. Barry, Wickes, and the rest of the Continental Navy were now fighting for the survival of a new country: the United States of America.

CHAPTER FIVE

INDEPENDENCE

On July 8, 1776, THE *Sachem*, UNDER COMMAND of Captain Isaiah Robinson, sighted the *Lexington* near Cape May. As she approached, Barry recognized her immediately as the old *Edward*. It must have given him pleasure to see her so well repaired, now heading back into action under American colors. While copies of the Declaration of Independence were available by the time Robinson departed Philadelphia, it is not known if he had one aboard or the latest issue of the *Pennsylvania Gazette*, boldly announcing that "the CONTINENTAL CONGRESS declared the UNITED COLONIES FREE and INDEPENDENT STATES."[1] This news certainly resulted in cheers from the Lexingtons, and Barry in particular must have welcomed it. As a Continental officer he already risked the gallows or imprisonment if captured by the British. Now he and his sailors were no longer fighting for redress of grievances, peace, or reconciliation. Robinson delivered new orders from John Hancock and the Marine Committee to Barry:

> As we find our coast is now lined with Men of War of too great a force for you to cope With, We think it can be of little use for you to remain cooped up at Cape May, and as the frigate You are to command is not yet launched, her guns and anchors not

yet ready, We think it a piece of justice due to your Merit to take a Cruize in the Lexington for one or two months, in hopes that fortune may favor your industry and reward it with some Prizes.[2]

The letter accompanied a "copy of the resolves of Congress respecting Prizes . . . what to take and what to let pass" and suggested that Cape May and Egg Harbor were the safest destinations for Barry's future prizes.[3]

The Marine Committee's letter noted that the *Sachem* had "liberty to make a cruise and it may be advantageous that you go in concert." Barry and Robinson conferred and decided to depart Cape May together before splitting up. With the *Kingfisher* already sailing north and the *Orpheus* at Cape Henlopen, the two American captains sailed away undetected. The *Lexington* headed east by south, with Barry's intention to cruise for prizes in the same waters where he had taken the *Edward*.[4]

Two weeks passed; the *Lexington* was within a day's sail of Bermuda on what had been thus far an uneventful cruise. By now, Barry's officers and crew knew his moods pretty well; this unproductive sailing was never enjoyable for him. Finally, at dawn on Saturday, July 27, the *Lexington*'s lookout sighted a sail: a sloop whose captain soon realized that his ship was too small to fight Barry's brig. The sloop changed course before the wind with the *Lexington* "right through the windward."[5] Barry ordered the *Lexington* after her, the beginning of a six-hour stern chase.

The sloop's captain, using a "three pounder out of My Cabin windows," fired futilely at the *Lexington* in hopes of scaring her off.[6] But Barry continued his dogged pursuit, his bow-chasers returning fire. While not hitting his quarry, each cannonball splashed closer to his target as the chase went on. As the *Lexington* closed, the pursued commander became desperate, "Giving [the] sloop a yaw and fetching some of my after guns to bear upon her"—that is, turning his ship and firing a small broadside in an effort to slow the *Lexington* and increase the distance between them. The maneuver only gave Barry more of a chance to catch his prey. With "her Bough guns aplaying upon me," the *Lexington* came up alongside the sloop. "Having but 10 men on board 6 of which was down with the Small pox and 2 more not worth their salt," the captain asked Barry for quarter. Barry gave it.[7]

The sloop was the *Lady Susan* of Virginia. She carried one less gun than the number of her crew: eight 4-pounders in addition to the 3-pounder in the cabin. Her captain, William Goodrich, was a son of Virginia shipbuilder John Goodrich. William was described as "A well made lusty man, about 34 years of age, about 5´8˝ inches, stoop shoulder'd, with forced full features, and sometimes looks reddish about the eyes [with] short light or yellow coloured curly hair."[8] Cronies of Lord Dunmore, the Goodrichs were anathema to American sailor and congressman alike.[9] Dunmore dispatched the *Lady Susan* to purchase an eighteen-gun brig believed to be in Bermuda, but the errand proved to be a wild-goose chase. Goodrich found "there was no such Vessil to be had" and was sailing home when the *Lady Susan* encountered the prize-hungry *Lexington*.[10]

Goodrich, "When carryed onboard of the Brig," was greeted "with A Grate Deal of Joy" by Barry, who gave Goodrich "a harty welcom onboard of the *Lexenton*." The clueless Goodrich could not comprehend why his captor "never was . . . gladder to see any man in all his life altho we never Saw each other before."[11] Perhaps allowance should be given the well-born Virginian: being captured by an Irishman was a new experience for him. On the other hand, after two luckless weeks at sea, Barry's joy in taking a ship –and one of Lord Dunmore's, at that– was a perfect occasion to let his wry humor surface.

Happily, Goodrich's crew did not seem physically ill as much as sick of being in Dunmore's service. No less than seven of them signed the *Lexington*'s muster roll. One, Richard Dale, was a young adventurer with eight years at sea under his belt. Dale was a lieutenant in the Virginia State Navy when his ship was captured and he agreed to join Dunmore's Navy. Now here he was, captured again. Barry persuaded Dale to accept a midshipman's berth aboard the *Lexington*. That day, Dale began a lifetime friendship with his new captain, and a lifetime of service to the United States.[12]

Below deck, the Lexingtons also discovered eight slaves. According to Congress, they were property, and therefore part of the libel and condemnation process by the Admiralty Court in Philadelphia.[13] Barry placed a prize crew aboard the sloop and sent her to Philadelphia. Her arrival on August 2 was cause for more celebration; John Adams noted that "Barry has taken another Tender," and fellow Congressman Josiah Bartlett happily wrote home that "Captain Barry in the *Lexington*" had "taken and sent here a privateer of six carriage guns commanded by another of them infamous Goodrich's of Virginia."[14]

The *Lexington* cruised through another fruitless period lasting nearly a month, when another enemy ship was sighted northeast of Cape Charles on August 24. With no flag flying atop his mast, Barry hoisted a British flag and came alongside the unsuspecting sloop, the *Betsy*, Samuel Kerr, Master. The ruse worked: Kerr believed the *Lexington* to be a British tender. Relieved, he ordered the *Betsy*'s crew to give three cheers for their presumed comrades. The sardonic Barry ordered the three cheers returned by his men. Taking speaking trumpet in hand, he informed Kerr of his true identity, and of Kerr's new standing in the war: as a prisoner of the Continental Navy. "I was hartily sorry for Mr. Kerr's loss," the hapless Goodrich recalled, "but could not keep myself from laughing at him."[15]

Kerr was sailing under orders from both Dunmore and Hamond, his sloop carrying a cargo of "several Kinds of Merchandize and other Effects" for Dunmore's fleet. Another prize crew sailed her to Philadelphia, with Goodrich along as well. The captures of the *Lady Susan* and the *Betsy* did as much for the morale of Barry and his crew as the knowledge that a considerable sum of prize money would soon be jingling in their pockets.

But the mood soon changed from merriment to fear. The *Lexington* encountered a terrible thunderstorm. An old hand like Barry had seen enough storms before; once he determined the crew had things well in hand against the rain, wind, and thunder, he turned in for the night. Suddenly a bolt of lightning struck the ship. At that very instant, everyone on deck, young Dale among them, "was prostrated [and] senseless." The crackling blast brought Barry immediately out of his cabin and onto the deck. Calling for all hands, Barry soon brought the ship under control. Luckily, each stricken sailor was "providentially restored in a few minutes." The *Lexington*'s shredded and charred rigging could only be repaired in a hurried, makeshift fashion.[16]

Barry got the *Lexington* through the Capes, picked up a pilot from Fisher's steadfast group, and sailed up the Delaware to Philadelphia without further incident, arriving on September 26. He relinquished command of the brigantine two days later.[17] For the rest of his life, Barry remained proud of his accomplishments aboard the *Lexington*, with which he "Cleard the Coast of all Small Cruisers that was out on it by taking some of them and Keeping the others in port[,] All tho at that time there was a forty-fore gun ship and two Frigates of the Enemy in the Capes."[18] Thanks to the published reports of his deeds, he was quite the celebrity in his hometown. Already renowned for his skills as a mariner, his deeds aboard the *Lexington* only added to his reputation. Philadelphians, congressmen, and even the British saw him as the embodiment of the American fighting sailor.

Command of the *Lexington* passed on to William Hallock. Barry attended to the reports on his cruise, and kept track of the Admiralty's trials on the libel and condemnation of his two recent prizes. The *Pennsylvania Packet* published a "Libel of Captain John Barry Against Eight Negro Slaves" whose owners "may appear and shew cause . . . why the same should not be condemned" and then resold into slavery. The premium paid for them went toward the *Lexington*'s prize money.[19]

Interestingly, the three men from the *Lady Susan* who declined Barry's offer to join *Lexington*'s crew were not imprisoned but "dischargd and permitted to go to their Families in Maryland."[20] The condemnation of the *Lady Susan* was appealed by its original owner, Joseph Hickson from Bermuda, who stated that his ship had been seized and confiscated by Lord Dunmore. He was rewarded with one half the purchase price of the *Lady Susan*'s sale, which cut deeply into the total prize money. Barry and his men received one third of the remainder—or, using Continental Congress math, a little over 8 percent.

While Barry was on his last cruise with the *Lexington*, Congress turned to the business of ordering uniforms for the navy. Captains were issued a "blue coat with red lapels, a slash cuff, a standup collar, flat yellow buttons with anchors on them, red waistcoat with narrow gold lace, and blue Breeches." A simple cocked hat topped the captain's uniform. Those for lieutenants and masters were similar, minus the gold lace and slashed cuffs. Midshipmen's attire was distinguished by "red facings on the cuffs and red stitching" on the coat's buttonholes; Marines wore a "dashing green coat with white [piping], white breeches edged with green and black garters." There was no uniform designed for sailors, although green shirts were suggested "if they could be provided."[21]

What Barry thought of the uniform, we do not know. John Paul Jones did not like it one bit, and would later design a smarter-looking uniform that mirrored that of a British captain—a blue coat with white breeches and waistcoat. It was so close in resemblance that it would assist in deceiving the enemy into believing a sighted American ship was British, as American commanders needed to display cunning as frequently as courage. Jones also added epaulettes, a French twist that would help a shorter man's shoulders artificially "grow" an inch or two.[22] Barry, arriving in late September, was one of the last captains fitted with the new uniform.

On the heels of the issuance of uniforms came another decree from the Marine Committee, one few officers found to their liking. It listed "the rank of the captains of the navy" along with their ship assignments:

Captain, Ship, Guns.
1. Jas. Nicholson, of the *Virginia*, 28
2. John Manly, *Hancock*, 32
3. Hector M'Neil, *Boston*, 24
4. Dudley Saltonstall, *Trumbull*, 28
5. Nicholas Biddle, *Randolph*, 32
6. Thomas Thompson, *Raleigh*, 32
7. John Barry, *Effingham*, 28
8. Thomas Reed [*sic*], *Washington*, 32

9. Thomas Grenell, *Congress*, 28

10. Charles Alexander, *Delaware*, 24

11. Lambert Wickes, *Reprisal*, 16

12. Abraham Whipple, *Providence*, 28

13. John Hopkins, *Warren*, 32

14. John Hodge, *Montgomery*, 24

15. William Hallock, *Lexington*, 16

16. Hoyste[a]d Hacker, *Hampden*,

17. Isaiah Robinson, *Andrew Doria*, 14

18. John Paul Jones, *Providence*, 12

19. James Josiah [no ship assigned]

20. Elisha Hinman, *Alfred*, 28

21. Joseph Olney, *Cabot*, 16

22. James Robinson, *Sachem*, 10

23. John Young, *Independence*, 10

24. Elisha Warner, *Fly*,

Lieut. [John] Baldwin, *Wasp*, 8

Lieut. [Thomas] Albertson, *Musquito*, 4[23]

The list created a tempest of ill feelings. Given a chance to review the performances of over a dozen captains appointed since November 1775, the enlarged Marine Committee picked up where former member Stephen Hopkins left off, emphasizing political connections over talent.[24] Naval historian Samuel Eliot Morison described the list as "a vanity of localities," believing that wiser, less politically concerned leaders would have placed Jones, Barry, Biddle, and Wickes in the top four. James Nicholson could thank Richard Henry Lee for his being placed at number one; while he had spent time in Maryland's Navy, he was still waiting to serve his first day on board a Continental vessel.[25] Manley and McNeill, veterans of Washington's navy, as well as Thomas Thompson, could thank John and Sam Adams for their high placement. Numbers four and five, Saltonstall and Biddle, had at least served in the navy. Biddle well deserved his position, while Saltonstall had yet to impress.[26]

Barry's seventh-place finish was as high as his success (or Morris's support) could get him. Wickes, Read, and Robinson were farther down the list, while John Paul Jones, who had turned down offers of command in Hopkins's fleet before demonstrating his capabilities captaining the *Providence* and *Alfred*, ranked eighteenth. With Joseph Hewes his only backer in Congress–and Hewes was away when the list was compiled–Jones lacked the pull to place higher. He remained bitter until the end of his life over this list.

And Barry? "If Barry complained," an earlier biographer wrote, "no record of such survived."[27] Barry had been through all of this the year before. And, unlike Jones, there was a frigate being built for him, literally in his own backyard.

The four Philadelphia frigates were in various stages of completion. Getting them built, launched, outfitted, and armed was too much of a strain on the Marine Committee's budget. The *Randolph* and *Delaware* were launched in July; the *Washington* finished in August. The *Effingham*, named after one of Queen Elizabeth's "Sea Hawks," was still in Grice and Company's shipyard above Philadelphia and Kensington. She was finally launched on October 31–Barry's wedding anniversary. Besides her captain, the frigate had other admirers, among them Joseph Hewes, who called her "the finest vessell of the whole."[28]

By November the *Randolph* and *Delaware* received their supply of guns, leaving few for the *Washington and Effingham*–although the guns cast in the Philadelphia area were best known for their unreliability, frequently splitting when "proved." In getting the *Delaware* ready, the coal supply ran out, ending labor on her anchors and other ironwork.[29] If the *Effingham* was ever finished, she promised to be a formidable fighting ship. Over 126 feet long, with a 34-foot 4-inch beam and at 682 tons, she would dwarf the *Lexington*. Her plans called for twenty-eight guns, 12- and 9-pounders–how maddening these delays must have been for Barry.[30]

The patriotic euphoria ushered in by the Declaration of Independence in July was cooling with the autumn weather and the latest news from the battlefront. The war was not going well.

Washington's Continentals, routed out of New York, were in retreat to Philadelphia, hoping to keep the Delaware River between them and the victorious British army, comprised of redcoats and Hessian mercenaries under Generals Howe and Cornwallis. One Philadelphia Tory described the bedraggled American soldiers as "diseased and covered with Vermin to a loathsome degree."³¹

On November 19, 1776, just as Fisher sent word that seven British warships were off the Capes, and another series of chevaux-de-frise were ordered for the river's defenses, two Philadelphians, David Rittenhouse of the Council of Safety and Thomas Mifflin, the Continental Army's Quartermaster General, spoke at a rally at the State House yard.³² Their appeals for service inspired 2,000 citizens to shoulder their muskets (if they had them) and join the newly formed Philadelphia Brigade.³³ "The enemy intends to make a push for Philadelphia," one diarist wrote, and to many Philadelphians, it seemed certain that nothing could stop them.³⁴ From his cabin on the *Roebuck*, Hamond celebrated the American's bad fortunes, with "The Rebel army being in a manner broke up & dispersed" and "Lord Cornwallis in the Jersey driving the Enemy everywhere before him."³⁵ By December the Continental Army had been reduced by thousands, not from casualties so much as mass desertion–now a daily occurrence.

As the crisis escalated, Barry and the other four Continental captains in port–Biddle, Read, Alexander, and John Nicholson–met to discuss raising a company of sailors and bringing their cannon ashore. They presented their offer to Congress, who "Ordered, that it be referred to the Marine Committee, who are determined to pursue such means as they think proper in consequence there of." With the *Randolph* and *Hornet* ready for action, Biddle and Nicholson were ordered to stand by their ships and get to sea as soon as possible. The other three were taken up on their offer.³⁶ After he reviewed the most recent bill of naval stores for the *Effingham*, from "two thirds gallons of wine" and "two hundred Lines" to "Beef for Lunch" and "one and one half load of Boards," John Barry joined the army.³⁷

Barry and Read hoped to raise volunteers among the sailors, dockhands, and carpenters now idle on the Philadelphia docks and shipyards, only to find that practically every able-bodied patriot was already bearing arms or performing some indispensable duty. They did recruit about five dozen seamen from idle privateers. With some cannon now remounted to wheeled carriages and in their new uniforms, Barry, Read, and their volunteers were placed under command of another Philadelphian, Colonel John Cadwalader.[38]

The blue-blooded Cadwalader, thirty-four years old, was an expert foxhunter and considered one of the finest skaters in Philadelphia.[39] Set up by his father in the merchant trade while still in his teens (around the same time that Barry arrived in Philadelphia), he tired of the business after a few years. He was an early and ardent supporter of the Revolution, organizing and leading the "Philadelphia Greens," now with the Pennsylvania Militia. Washington sent Cadwalader orders directing that "the Marines, sailors & ca. from Philadelphia" be placed under Cadwalader's command while asking if the tars "came out resolved to act upon Land or meant to confine their Services to the Water only."[40]

Barry and Read, along with their men and artillery, reached Bristol, Pennsylvania, on December 11. Read was put in command of the men and a battery, while Cadwalader assigned Barry to his personal staff as his aide.[41] Also on the eleventh, Philadelphians watched "Congress leave this City for Baltimore, the Militia going out fast for Trentown, Streets full of wagons going out with goods."[42] Smallpox and camp fever raged among the soldiers, with countless dead Continentals and militiamen lying in shallow graves near Walnut Street Prison (what is now Washington Square).[43] The city began to resemble a ghost town.

One congressman remained. "I am now the only member of Congress left in this City," Robert Morris wrote to Silas Deane, informing the envoy to France of the recent disasters.[44] Morris not only told Deane of the loss of New York and New Jersey, but also that "We are told the British Troops are kept from Plunder but the Hessians & other Foreigners looking upon that as a right of War, Plunder where they go." Like an American Job, Morris ended his lamentations with hope: "France should therefore strike with us & she will reap an immediate Harvest," including everything from "tobacco and iron" to "Bees Wax and Whalebone."[45]

About 1,400 Hessians under Colonel Johann Rall were quartered in Trenton, part of the 12,000-man army Howe had brought down from New York.[46] Washington, needing a miracle, was planning to cross the Delaware and surprise the Hessians. The freezing cold weather and the ice along the Delaware were not welcome factors at all. "The Ice has driven off the Gallies," Cadwalader complained to the Council of Safety.[47] But if the weather was an obstacle for Washington's plans, it also served as an ally.[48]

Washington began Christmas Day with a letter to Morris back in Philadelphia: "I agree with you, that it is in vane to ruminate upon . . . our past Misfortunes, we should rather exert ourselves and look forward with Hopes, that some lucky Charm may yet turn up in our Favor. Bad as our prospects are, I should not have the least doubt of Success in the End." Next, Washington addressed the lack of manpower for the "Continental Ship of War in the Delaware," suggesting "two New England Regiments," mostly "Watermen" who "would willingly . . . navigate them round to any of the ports in New England." He updated Morris on the enemy's "Intentions . . . to cross the Delaware as soon as the Ice is sufficiently sturdy." Before wishing that "the next Christmas will prove happier than the present to you," he reviewed the possible exchange of Richard Boger–the British officer Barry had captured from the *Edward*–for an American naval officer. The biggest event thus far in Washington's life was only hours away, and he still found time to encourage a fellow patriot, come up with a possible solution for manning the frigates, relay the plans of the enemy, and inquire about the exchange of Barry's highest ranking prisoner. He then sent a message to Cadwalader that "I am determined, as the night is favourable to cross the River and make the attack."[49] With 2,400 men to strike Rall at Trenton, Washington crossed the Delaware.

Barry and Cadwalader did not. The legend that Barry fought at Trenton is a false one. Cadwalader's forces were to cross at Bristol and attack the Hessians from the rear, but Cadwalader found "It is impossible to pass above Bristol with the ice" and saw no way to get the cannon Barry had delivered across the river.[50] By the time Cadwalader's force got to New Jersey on December 26, not only was the battle of Trenton over, but the victorious Washington had crossed back to the west side of the Delaware.[51]

Washington's victory at Trenton is the most written about battle of the Revolution, but rarely from a British perspective. In his captain's cabin, Andrew Snape Hamond wrote, "From my other intelligence I learnt that [Cornwallis] was gone to his winter quarters at Brunswick: and that a Brigade of Hessians which he had left as an out guard near Trentown on the Delaware, under the Command of Colonel Rhole [Johann Rall], had been surprized by the Enemy; and that 700 Men, with all their Baggage Camp Equipage & several Field Pieces had fallen into the Rebels hands. A most sad blat!"[52]

Cadwalader took his men up to Bordentown and headed east toward Crosswicks, New Jersey, in pursuit of the enemy's baggage train. "I hope to fall on their rear," he wrote Washington. He received an immediate reply from the commander-in-chief, ordering him to return to Crosswicks until further notice.[53] Washington had other plans for Cadwalader and his men.

Some of Cadwalader's forces were assigned to a defensive line along Assunpink Creek, running east of Trenton. On January 2, 1777, Barry gave Thomas Read orders to station his battery at the stone bridge over the Assunpink; he then rode off to meet Cadwalader. British and Hessian forces–part of General Cornwallis's army he had personally led to Perth Amboy–advanced on the bridge, in an attempt to strike at Washington's main camp. The American sailors were part of the line that repulsed the British attack.[54]

As aide-de-camp, Barry joined Cadwalader and the rest of his force in an open field a mile north. Washington left four hundred men in Trenton to build scores of bonfires, creating the illusion that the entire army was camped down for the night. At his own headquarters, Cornwallis bragged to his subordinates that they would "bag the fox" the next day.[55] But the fox was behaving . . . like a fox. On that cold, windy night, Washington led a combined force of regulars and militia around Cornwallis's encampment and north to Princeton, to attack the British forces remaining there.

Barry may have missed action the day before, but he saw plenty of it the next morning. Cadwalader's troops were behind General Hugh Mercer's Delaware "Blue Hens." Mercer's men surprised British forces under Colonel Charles Mawhood, marching south to reinforce Cornwallis. In the fighting, Mercer was bayoneted to death, and his retreating men ran pell-mell into Cadwalader's soldiers. While some Pennsylvanians also fled, others stood their ground, including Cadwalader's artillerymen, firing grapeshot from their 4-pounders point-blank at the enemy. Their example helped Cadwalader, Barry, and the other officers convince their fellow Philadelphians to turn and fight.[56]

Just then Washington arrived, astride his white horse, and took over field command, giving reassurance to Mercer's men while he advanced with Cadwalader's. At one point, with the British only thirty yards away, Washington ordered "halt and fire!" Both sides blasted away. One of Washington's aides covered his eyes, not wanting to see his general shot down. When he reopened them, the charmed Virginian was still in his saddle. In a full, violent day, Washington led his troops to a complete victory over the British, whose muskets, canteens, and knapsacks lined the path of their retreat. "It's a fine fox chase, my boys," the fox lustily declared as he led the pursuit.[57]

At battle's end, Washington's army left Princeton heading north, just as the outwitted Cornwallis and the main portion of his army came in from the south, too late to have any impact on the battle. The Americans marched to the high ground at Morristown. Cornwallis returned to New Brunswick. Of this novel experience of war on horseback, the tight-lipped Barry merely recalled in the third person, that "the services he rendered here, being in an Element new to him, must be judged by his Superior officers and his Country."[58]

On January 7, Cornwallis dispatched an envoy under a white flag with a letter asking Washington's permission to send a British surgeon, medicines for the care of the British wounded, and the baggage and other personal belongings of the captured Hessians from Trenton. The latter had been sent to Philadelphia (a safer place for them due to their plundering of New Jersey along the route to Trenton). Washington gave his permission, sending "Captain Barry the Bearer of this [letter], to give a safe conduct to the Hessian Baggage as far as Philadelphia, and the Surgeon and Medicines to Princeton."[59]

Previous biographers have cited this letter and told the tale of John Barry's meeting Cornwallis and leading this wagon train back to Philadelphia. The facts prove otherwise. Miltary historians and experts on Washington's papers are convinced that this "Captain Barry" is actually Captain Thomas Berry of the Eighth Virginia Regiment, which was principally made up of German-speaking patriots from western Virginia.[60] It was only appropriate for Washington to use a German-speaking officer for this errand. As we will see, Washington and John Barry would cross paths often, but that lay in the future.

Washington's victories at Trenton and Princeton lifted patriot hearts and renewed the will to keep fighting. In one week, his leadership and courage brought his army and country back from complete collapse. Dubbed the "Year of the Hangman" due to its three 7's resembling three gallows, 1777 was off to a good start for the American cause.

The land service of the navy captains came to an end later in January. They and their volunteers were mustered out of Cadwalader's brigade, and their valuable cannon returned.[61] Barry and his men arrived back in Philadelphia just as many other citizens were returning home, now that the British invasion plans were as cold as the Philadelphia winter. It would be another two months before Congress returned from Baltimore.

Barry paid a courtesy call on Robert Morris, who briefed him on what had happened to his naval colleagues while he was away.[62] Despite the recent prize takings of the *Roebuck* and her consorts along the Capes, not all of the news was bad. Barry learned that his old command, the *Lexington*, had been captured by the British only to be recaptured the next day by her crew, including Richard Dale.[63] The *Andrew Doria* had sent more good news into port via the captured British sloop *Racehorse*. The American ship also received the first salute of the American flag in a foreign port at St. Eustatia.[64] Then, there were the further adventures and accomplishments of John Paul Jones, easily the most successful officer from Hopkins's original squadron. Biddle was preparing the *Randolph* for a cruise with the *Hornet* as consort, but Morris complained that "our River is so full of Ice and our Bay pestered with British Men Of War" that it was impossible to tell when Biddle could depart.[65]

As for the *Effingham*, Morris could only tell Barry that nothing had been done in his absence. As senior naval officer in Philadelphia, Barry divided his time between his futile efforts to get the *Effingham* further along and presiding over courts of inquiry.[66] For the next two months, he watched as the *Randolph, Hornet, Independence,* and *Sachem* all left Philadelphia and slipped past the Capes while next to nothing was done regarding the *Effingham* and *Washington.* Barry and Read were dry-docked.

Congress returned to Philadelphia in March, adding the task of completing the *Effingham* and *Washington* to its "to do" list.[67] All of the carpenters, rope-men, iron workers, and sailmakers were back from their stint under Washington's command and at the shipyards. The Marine Committee and Navy Board reconvened to discuss procuring the canvas, wood, and iron required to finish the ships and enlist crews. However, with no materiel to continue construction, there were no ships ready to recruit a crew for. The double-edged sword—no progress on the *Effingham* or *Washington,* and therefore no need to enlist a crew—still hung over Grice and Company's shipyard.

There was one upside to the lethargic progress on Barry's frigate. He had time to fall in love.

Sarah Austin was twenty-three years old when she met John Barry. She was a descendant of the Kyn family, one of the first Swedish families that settled around Philadelphia in the 1620s. The name had been anglicized by the influx of Quakers and other English-speaking settlers to Keen well before Sarah's birth. Her mother, also named

Sarah, was twice married; Samuel Austin, her second husband (and Sarah's father), owned and operated the Arch Street Ferry, which traversed the Delaware to Camden and back. Sarah and Samuel married in 1746. The bride brought with her a daughter from her first marriage, Christiana Stille. The Austins eventually had three children: William (1751), Isaac (1752), and finally Sarah (1754), known as Sally to friends and family her entire life.[68]

Running what became known as the "New Ferry" made Samuel a fairly rich man. He soon owned a fine house at Arch and Water streets, as well as the ferry, ferry house and wharf, along with several "tenements" by the river (one which son Isaac would use as his watch repair shop).[69] As a further sign of status, he had his own pew at Christ Church.[70] Samuel also owned slaves. One of them, a man named London, "about 5 Feet 3 Inches high, born in Barbados," had run off near the end of Samuel's life. Between October 1765 and February 1767, he ran several advertisements for London's capture and reward. With London "Apt to hire himself on board of Vessels," Samuel Austin offered anywhere from forty shillings to eight dollars for his return.[71]

Shortly before his death in 1767, while "indisposed in body, but blessed be God of sound mind," Samuel drew up his will, leaving his estate to his wife, except for the watch repair shop which went to Isaac.[72] After the funeral services, Mrs. Austin and her eldest son, William, published a notice in the *Gazette* that all debts were to be paid, all bills to be given to her as executrix, and that "the ferry will be continued by Sarah [widow] and William Austin," who "take this opportunity of returning thanks to their former customers, to whom they shall be obliged for a further continuance of their favours, etc."[73] In one stroke of business savvy William began catering to "commuters," offering the reasonable sum of two shillings "including baggage" for "a round trip to New Jersey and back."[74] Under William's management, the family business thrived. His personal life was not so charmed; he and his wife had several children, but only one would live to adulthood.[75]

As a girl, Sarah's "prudence, fortitude and active benevolence were extremely exercised" and she "commanded the respect, esteem, and tender affection of all those who had the happiness of an intimate acquaintance with her."[76] With that kind of regard, added to her family's prestige in the community and her good looks, she was certainly a young lady of note in social circles. By 1775 she was involved with a group of women at Gloria Dei Church, whose sewing circle was kept busy making flags. The best known of these "stitch-sisters" was a seamstress and upholstery maker, Betsy Ross.[77] On June 14, 1777, Congress adopted the Stars and Stripes as the official flag of the United States and appointed John Paul Jones captain of the sloop-of-war *Ranger*. He was presented with one of Sarah's flags. It was the first one to be saluted in Europe.[78]

Sarah's brother Isaac had shouldered a musket and marched with Washington to Trenton and Princeton in December 1776, a fact he was proud of all his life. William Austin was not so inclined. He was just as staunch in his support of King George, and remained in Philadelphia to run the ferry.[79] Their half-sister Christiana's husband, Reynold Keen, also fought at Trenton—but with seven children and an eighth on the way, was wavering in his support of the Cause.[80]

No documents or family stories were handed down to tell us where and how John and Sarah met, although her service in making flags for the navy provides grounds for an encounter. Sarah certainly had plenty of suitors. But it was the older, tall Irishman, resplendent in his Continental uniform, who won out over the other gentlemen callers. No doubt romance was behind Barry's pursuit of Sarah, but her family's wealth and social status would not go unnoticed by such an ambitious man.[81]

The first celebration of the "Glorious Fourth" set the tone for future observances. At noon, "armed ships and galleys" fired thirteen-gun salutes "with their gay streamers flying." After Barry attended "an elegant dinner" for congress and military officers, he joined Sarah and thousands of Philadelphians for a "ringing of church bells, a grand exhibition of fireworks on the commons, and an illumination of the houses."[82]

Three days later John and Sarah were married at Christ Church. The steeple had been struck by lightning just four weeks earlier, but the carpenters and roofers stopped their hammering long enough for the ceremony to be conducted peacefully. The extended Austin family was present in force, along with the mutual friends of the bride and groom, including Robert Morris, Mr. and Mrs. Thomas Barry, and Patrick Barry's wife, Mary. Reverend William White presided over the marriage ceremony. The Anglican minister, his sympathy for the American cause well known throughout the city, took his place at the "wine-glass pulpit." Sarah and John stood at the altar; the bride in a colorful dress (as was the fashion of the day), the groom in his spotless blue and red uniform.[83]

So, on July 7, 1777, the most hangman-like day in the "year of the hangman," John Barry once more became a husband. The new bride was certainly aware that there were challenges and difficult days ahead, due in no small part to her groom's profession and the seeming inevitability of a British invasion. Sarah had no idea how immediate—and formidable—those challenges would be.

CHAPTER SIX

LOW TIDE

IRST AND FOREMOST, FRANCIS HOPKINSON was a patriot. Only thirty-nine, he had already eclipsed his father in accomplishments–and that was saying something. Thomas Hopkinson had been an influential Philadelphian in his day, a successful lawyer and a member of City Council. A confidant of Franklin, Thomas was a director of the Library Company when Franklin enlisted him to serve as president of the newly formed American Philosophical Society in 1744.[1] Thomas was also one of the first trustees of the College of Philadelphia, soon called the University of Pennsylvania, and young Francis would be its first student, graduating in 1757 at the age of twenty.[2]

Small in stature but bursting with ambition, Francis began clerking in Benjamin Chew's law office upon his graduation and was admitted to the bar in a year's time.[3] He was proficient on the harpsichord and displayed a knack for composing clever little airs, which he eagerly performed in public.[4] He is credited with writing and publishing the first "American" song in 1759, entitled "My Days Have Been So Wondrous Free."[5] After several years of practicing law he went to London in 1766, in hopes of making a name for himself. He took painting lessons from a family cousin, the artist Benjamin West.[6]

When other relations, including the bishop of Worcester and Lord North, offered little assistance to his aspirations, Hopkinson came home.[7]

Soon after his return to Philadelphia he married Ann Borden, whose father had founded Bordentown, New Jersey. For a short while he ran a dry goods store, but he found that boring, and returned to work as an attorney in earnest, specializing in maritime law, which led to his appointment to the Governor's Council and to the position of Customs Collector for the port of New Castle, Delaware.[8] His skills as a politician were complemented by his other talents in science, music, inventions, and satire. When matters came to a flashpoint between the colonies and England, Hopkinson threw in his lot with the Cause and was elected to the Continental Congress. He proudly signed the Declaration of Independence, and insisted to the day he died that the design of the American flag was his and his alone.[9] Hopkinson was recognized by his fellow Congressmen as a man of biting wit and eloquence. John Adams took notice: "His head was no bigger than an apple. . . . He was a pretty, little, curious, ingenious man; I have not met with anything in natural history more amusing and more entertaining than his personal appearance."[10]

His knowledge of maritime law made him an obvious choice for the new Navy Board, and he dove passionately into his duties. On February 22, 1777, Congress ordered the board, consisting of Hopkinson, Thomas Wharton, and John Nixon, to "Push forward with the utmost vigilance [diligence] the fitting out of the Continental Fleet under your directive."[11] Hopkinson took the orders to heart, doing whatever was possible to procure supplies and equipment. This work exhibited his flair for a most diplomatic writing style ("We write to you . . . requesting you to return Three Guns you borrowed from the Sloop *Race Horse*. . . . We are sorry to be this troublesome, but Affairs are not so [critical] that we must ware Ceremony"), but he could also be brusque: "All Sargents and Warrant Officers . . . belonging to the Navy of the United States . . . are hereby directed to give personal attention at the . . . Navy Board, every Monday and Thursday . . . to receive orders of the said Board."[12]

Hopkinson's leadership also impressed Adams, who observed that "The Business of the naval and marine Department will be some point in a better Train than it has been."[13] Yet, for all of the board's successes, it could not procure the supplies, ordnance, or manpower necessary to complete work on the *Effingham* and *Washington* and send these frigates into action.

Nor did the Navy Board or Marine Committee solve the issue of who would lead Philadelphia's defense on the Delaware. The Marine Committee issued a request to Congress as to whether the senior Continental Navy officer in port (Barry) or the head of the Pennsylvania Navy (John Hazelwood) should command. Congress referred the decision back to the Marine Committee.[14] It was a responsibility Barry was clearly qualified for, but the Marine Committee and the rest of Congress were timid regarding this question, as it was an issue of state's rights: Philadelphia might be the nation's capital, but it was also Pennsylvania's. Another officer with a greater talent for self-promotion, such as John Paul Jones, would have written paeans about his qualifications for the position. Barry simply left it up to Congress.

As the summer lengthened, the possibility of another British move on Philadelphia became more a matter of "when" than "if." Earlier General William Howe (his brother was the British admiral Richard Howe) had marched into New Jersey, hoping to tempt Washington into a fight. When Washington did not take the bait, Howe returned to New York. Washington was also notified that a second British army under Lieutenant General "Gentleman Johnny" Burgoyne had marched south from Canada, retaken Fort Ticonderoga, and now threatened to sever New England from the rest of the United States.[15] On July 22, 1777, Howe's army, stowed aboard 267 ships, departed New York harbor. Oddly, no sooner had Henry Fisher seen Howe's invasion fleet arrive at the Capes, and informed the Council of Safety of its presence, than he watched it sail out of sight as quickly as it had arrived.[16] What was Howe up to?

This news was greeted with more dread than the first approach of British forces at the end of 1776. "I can well remember the . . . gloom spread over the minds of the inhabitants, from the time it was thought the enemy would advance through the Jerseys," one Philadelphia woman later recalled.[17] Fear of invasion heightened the political tensions in Philadelphia. The Pennsylvania Executive Council, under recommendation of Congress, began arresting prominent Quakers "disaffected to the American cause," sending them to the city jail or to exile in Virginia.[18] Other loyalists, like William Austin, maintained their silence.

A possible British move on the city failed to affect the profiteering of Philadelphia's merchants. Washington's Quartermaster General, Thomas Mifflin, now had the wherewithal to invest in several ships that eluded capture while sailing to the Caribbean and back for much needed goods, yielding him better than a 50 percent profit on his investment.[19] Robert Morris, for all the countless hours he devoted to his country's finances, still found time to ask an old colleague to "buy a good prize vessel, double-decked[,] and pick up a cargo . . . from France . . . masts, spars, beeswax . . . perl and polish, fish . . . are wanted in our country and will answer well if laid in at modest prices."[20] Once a businessman, always a businessman, at least until those 267 British ships showed up.

While Congress pondered action and Philadelphians tried to keep a lid on panic, Barry dealt with a crisis of authority. On July 23, he issued a summons to other Continental officers in port to serve on a court martial.[21] No officers showed. Instead, he received a group reply from the twelve lieutenants he had summoned to duty: "As we, the Subscribers are determined not to act upon any Court Martial, or others on Board any Vessel of War until our Grievances are redressed . . . we beg you will not take it amiss at our not attending your summons."[22] If this was not mutiny, it was close.

Their "Grievances" could be summed up in one word: money. They had petitioned the Marine Committee for an increase in pay, as the navy's surgeons had recently done. But while Congress approved the surgeons' request, they denied that of the lieutenants. A meeting with Robert Morris brought no further assistance on their behalf. They saw Barry's orders as an opportunity to show their solidarity on the issue. Barry immediately notified Congress, which replied that very same day: it was "necessary for the public service to make examples of such offenders," and resolved that the lieutenants be "dismissed the Continental service . . . and their commissions rendered void and of no effect." To Barry's chagrin, his first lieutenant from the *Lexington*, Luke Matthewman, was among them.[23]

But Congress's speedy dismissal of all twelve officers resulted in their own swift response: an apology. One of the twelve, Thomas Vaughn by name, petitioned Congress the very next day, stating that he had not "signed the paper addressed to John Barry, Esqr."[24] Henry Laurens, writing on July 25, noted the success of Congress's actions: "This Resolution proclaimed humble Petitioners from the whole. They are now reinstated and I suppose Business will go forward again."[25] In the rebellion for independence, rebellion in the service would surface and resurface throughout the war, on land and sea.

That challenge to authority resolved, Hopkinson informed Barry and Read on July 31 that they were "hereby authorized to look at and take such Rigging" and "bend as much Sail as you may enable to run [their ships] up the River to some Place of Safety." With further orders to give "a Recpt to the Owners for whatever you take" and a condescending, parting directive to "conduct this Business with all Decency and Direction," the two captains found what sails and rigging they could. Soon their unfinished warships were ready to sail up the Delaware.[26] Barry found the order to flee the coming fight an odious one. For the meantime, the frigates remained docked in Philadelphia.

The order served as a twofold message to Barry, who had no trouble reading between the lines. Hopkinson was tacitly acknowledging that the *Effingham* and *Washington* would not be finished in time for the impending British advance, and sailing them north made it unlikely that he would command the combined naval forces in defense of the Delaware. The city's most experienced captain, with the most successful record against the British, faced being shunted aside yet again.

On August 22, Congress received word that the Brothers Howe had sailed up the Chesapeake and reached the Head of Elk, where William's army marched north in a "back door" advance through southeastern Pennsylvania.[27] Howe issued a "Declaration" on August

27, addressed to Washington's army and offering "a free and general pardon to all such Officers and private Men as shall voluntarily come and surrender themselves to any Detachment of his Majesty's Forces."[28]

Washington, in an attempt to raise the city's morale (and give some degree of pause to the city's expectant Tories) marched his Continentals through Philadelphia, his soldiers wearing optimistic sprigs of green leaves in their hats. They headed south, where they met Howe's redcoats three weeks later on September 11 at Brandywine Creek. Over a long, bloody day, Howe once again outmaneuvered and outfought Washington, claiming the field. By the nineteenth, British skirmishers reached the outskirts of Philadelphia.[29] That day, Washington's young aide Colonel Alexander Hamilton carried a message to Hancock, informing him that Congress should leave Philadelphia immediately. "Congress was chased like a covey of partridges from Philadelphia to Trenton, from Trenton to Lancaster," John Adams wrote before he rode to safety on his own swift mount.[30] As the enemy advanced, seizing food and supplies along the way, British soldiers under Major General Charles "No Flint" Grey assaulted Anthony Wayne's brigade just before dawn at their Paoli encampment. Bayonets, sabers, and claymores cut down many an American soldier.[31]

While they did not flee with the speed of Congress, Philadelphia's patriots began their exodus as well. Most of the Austin family made their preparations to go to the family summer home in Reading, thirty-five miles northwest of Philadelphia. Barry barely had time for a proper farewell to Sarah. She and her brother Isaac helped Reynold Keen assist his pregnant wife Christiana and their children pack their belongings. After kissing Sarah goodbye, Barry returned to the *Effingham* and his preparations for sailing up the Delaware.[32] Keen, along with William Austin and his family, remained in Philadelphia.

The panic along the waterfront was reminiscent of Barry's departure on the *Black Prince* two years earlier. But this time, carts and wagons were not hauling market goods to the ships in port. As soon as they were overloaded with goods, they were driven out of town, up King's Road to York, Reading, and Lancaster.[33] They would not be escaping on the Arch Street Ferry. Philadelphia's leading Tory, Joseph Galloway, asked William Austin "to take care that no Goods" be "carried away from this City."[34] Austin's devotion to his duty would prove costly, beginning that very day. While keeping the ferry free from patriot misuse, one thousand gallons of spermaceti–just purchased by Austin for immediate and profitable resale–was stolen. He estimated its worth at over £225.[35]

The *Effingham* and *Washington* departed on September 25. Barry and Read, with skeleton crews consisting of a few seasoned hands and invalid soldiers, got all of the Navy Board's supplies and documents aboard their ships. Hopkinson and Wharton took passage on the *Mercury* packet, accompanying the frigates upriver. John Nixon, Barry's old employer and member of the Navy Board triumvirate, remained in Philadelphia with his militia battalion.[36] For all intents and purposes, the Navy Board was now a twosome, dominated by Hopkinson.

Congress might have delayed in making their choice between Barry and Hazelwood to command the coming fight against Admiral Howe's ships, but Washington now made his preference known: he wanted Hazelwood.[37] His decision was sound; being relegated to Delaware the past two years, Hazelwood had a better knowledge of the river and its defenses than Barry and was therefore best suited for the job.

"Black Dick" Howe was coming, his mighty fleet having reentered the Delaware Bay.[38] This was not going to be a nautical dustup like the *Roebuck* affair the year before. This was the full might of King George's Navy paying a call; the British would not stop the forthcoming attack until every American ship in sight was sunk or captured, and every American sailor was in retreat, in irons, or dead. Lewis Nicola, one of the erstwhile designers of the Delaware gun boats and now a "Colonel of Invalids," ordered "every decked Vessel" be "taken up to Burlington & put under care of the naval officer commanding there."[39] The river was being cleared for fighting.

Barry's passage up the Delaware bore one intriguing incident. "A few miles from Philadelphia," Barry later recalled, a rowboat approached the *Effingham*, bringing a messenger to see the captain.

Barry ushered him into his cabin. Now that they had their privacy, the messenger presented Barry with "a large offer of 15,000 Guineas" if Barry would "come in with the ship." Barry's visitor offered another enticement: if he wished, Barry could retain command of the *Effingham* under British colors, with "the Com[mission] of her in the King's Service."[40] Acceptance of the proposal would make Barry very rich, indeed.

At first, the offer to turn traitor stunned Barry, but it soon triggered his temper, especially coming after the piled-up events of invasion, parting from his new bride, and his bitter retreat upriver and away from the coming fight. With an angry, clear voice, Barry "spurned the eydee of being a Traitor to [my] Country," and sent the emissary back where he came from.[41]

The notion that the agent acting on Howe's behalf was someone Barry knew well has been a subject of conjecture by historians. William Bell Clark, for one, wrote that "from Barry's extreme reticence on the subject, we would surmise the visitor was actually a close friend." Clark opined that "only a life-long friend could have come away unscathed at liberty from the *Effingham* after proposing such treason to John Barry."[42] As a captain's commission was inferred, the offer probably originated from Lord Howe. There were certainly enough British naval officers, starting with Hamond, who could attest to Barry's fighting capabilities.[43]

It is extremely rare for any cloak-and-dagger escapades to leave a paper trail. That is the best way to get caught–John André comes to mind. Historians have suggested that the offer could have been made by one of Barry's merchant contacts with Tory connections. For example, Thomas Willing remained in Philadelphia after the British took over. He sent Barry's friend John Brown to Robert Morris, with an offer from General Howe to end the war if Congress renounced the Declaration of Independence. Brown was immediately suspected of being a traitor and jailed by the Council of Safety. He was released only after Morris risked his own reputation in defending Brown's innocence.[44]

Two figures that beg suspicion are Barry's in-laws, William Austin and Reynold Keen–especially Austin. Where Keen enlisted in a loyalist regiment, Austin, in addition to his duties with the ferry, "was active as a Guard," serving watch at night "to prevent the Town being set on fire by the Rebels." Once General Howe was ensconced in Philadelphia, Austin "exerted his best Services in procuring Provisions for the Troops."[45] But he did not stop there: throughout the British occupation, he tirelessly worked "obtaining Intelligence for the Commander in Chief" and accepted a commission in a loyalist regiment. Austin later wrote to Sarah that his "treasonous offense" saved their home and business from confiscation by the Crown.[46] Some historians call the Revolution America's first civil war, and Barry and Austin certainly prove their point: brother against brother-in-law.

Whether Austin or Keen was Howe's envoy to Barry is not known. Later, Barry would spend considerable time and effort trying to keep these two wayward relations (especially William) out of both prison and the hangman's noose. But the only known facts of the incident are that (a) Barry turned the offer down and (b) he never revealed who made it.[47]

From Lancaster, the Marine Committee sent out a flurry of orders that same day, responding to the imminent approach of Lord Howe's armada. Plans were hastily made for the defense of Philadelphia's waterway. Following Washington's lead, they placed the Continental ships in port under Hazelwood's command.[48] With orders to "defend the passage of the River to the last extremity" they gave him complete authority over every ship, row-galley, floating battery, and fireship.[49]

Howe kept the main force of his army with him outside the city in nearby Germantown and sent Cornwallis into Philadelphia on September 26, leading a force composed mainly of British and Hessian Grenadiers. They were welcomed by crowds made up of Tory and Quaker families.[50] Accompanying Cornwallis at the head of the procession was a contingent of loyalists led by Joseph Galloway.[51] One Philadelphia boy recalled in later years that

> I went up to the front ranks of the Grenadiers where they had entered Second street when several of them addressed me thus: "How do you do, young one. —How are you, my boy."– In a benefactory tone. . . . They reached out their hands . . . and

caught mine and shook it . . . with a sympathizing tone for the vanquished. The Hessians . . . their looks to me were terrific–their brass caps–their mustaches–their countenances, by nature morose; and their music, it sounded better English then they themselves speak–plunder–plunder–plunder–gave a despairing, heartbreaking effect . . . to me it was dreadful.[52]

That same afternoon the *Effingham* and *Washington* reached Burlington, New Jersey. The following morning, Barry and Read took on some militiamen no longer in condition to join the fighting. Lack of wind kept the retreating ships from making any significant progress the next day. From the south, Barry could hear the echoes of cannon fire. The battle for the Delaware had begun.[53] With the British occupying and fortifying Philadelphia above the American forts and ships, and Howe's mighty fleet sailing upriver behind them, the outcome was foreordained.

On September 27, a small squadron led by the *Delaware, Fly,* and state ship *Montgomery* approached Philadelphia to bombard Cornwallis's batteries. Charles Alexander, in charge of the attack, carried a letter admonishing "the Commanding Officer of the British Army at Philadelphia" that "the Blo[o]d of the Women & Children [would] lay at your Door."[54] Alexander brought the *Delaware* closer to the wharves, but not to deliver his letter. "At 1/2 past 8 . . . Two of the Rebel Frigates and 5 row Gallies came up with the Tide," recalled Captain John Montresor, Cornwallis's chief engineer and the man responsible for the speedily placed British batteries (as well as the design of the river fort now occupied by the Americans). "We opened upon them and the artillery being extremely well directed [at] their best Frigate the *Delaware* which got somewhat aground, struck to us."[55]

Alexander's surrender gave the British a captured frigate for their use above the American line of defense. The *Delaware* had six of her sailors wounded and one killed–her cook, decapitated by a cannon-ball.[56] If anything, the battle was a testimony to the deadly accuracy of the British artillerymen. The *Montgomery* was dismasted in the battle, and two other schooners ran aground. Those American ships that could withdraw did, sailing back to Fort Mifflin.[57]

Much to their frustration, Barry and Read literally remained above the fray while their boss, Hopkinson, wrote to Washington, informing him that "We have Cannon [and] Ammunition . . . but have not men."[58] Washington was too busy with his own plans to reply. On October 4 he attacked the British forces at Germantown, the violent cacophony within earshot of Philadelphians. By dusk a victory nearly won became just another bitter defeat.[59] It was one more wave in a seemingly endless cascade of bad news for the Americans. Downriver, Barry's fellow patriots were locked in a desperate fight while he remained in safety at White Hill, captain of a beautifully built but unfinished and barely armed frigate. He could hear the hated British guns as they conquered his adopted home.

After Germantown the focus of battle shifted back to the Delaware. Faced with a shortage of seamen for Hazelwood and soldiers for Forts Mifflin and Mercer, Washington ordered all sailors in the Continental Army to report to Hazelwood, and then sent an emissary to White Hill to summon sailors from the *Effingham* and *Washington*. In a rare instance of defiance to Washington, Hopkinson refused, citing the need to defend the frigates.[60]

Vexed by their inability to contribute to the American effort, Barry and Read were nonetheless busily preparing to defend their ships. Although short of men, cannons, and ammunition, Barry believed that he and Read "had taken every measure to defend their vessels from all [future] attempts of the enemy." Requisitioning every piece of ordnance they could get their hands on from nearby merchant ships, they came up with twenty-three guns between them: "twelves, sixes, and four pounders." Realizing that arming the frigates was the best defense for their own ships, the merchant captains readily turned them over, along with enough sailors to give each frigate approximately eighty hands, "ready for action at the shortest notice." Furthermore, Barry and Read had a barge and longboat each armed with small cannons, and were asking "men from the shallops that were coming down from Trenton" to join them.[61] If he could not go to war, at least Barry would be ready when the war came to him.

He returned to the phantom gunnery practice from his *Lexington* days. During the drills and preparations being made on October 23, he and his men heard a deafening blast from downriver, the likes of which had not occurred in that part of the country since Barry blew up the *Nancy*. Under fire from Fort Mifflin's guns and those from Hazelwood's row-galleys, the British ship-of-the-line *Augusta*, sixty-four guns, ran aground. She caught fire and soon exploded, the largest British ship ever lost to Americans in wartime.[62]

But this victory only delayed the inevitable. On November 10, the British began the heaviest bombardment of the entire war, directed at Fort Mifflin. Each British gun was ordered to fire eighty rounds of shot that day. The Americans in the fort, outnumbered and out-gunned, were so lacking in ammunition that they bravely retrieved British cannonballs and fired them back at the enemy. At nighttime they worked frantically to repair as best they could the damage done to their ever-weakening walls. American gunners also inflicted casu-alties among the enemy, and Montresor's men were kept busy at night replacing smashed guns and repairing their defenses.[63]

On November 11, Lieutenant Colonel Samuel Smith, the fort's commander, was severely wounded.[64] By the fourteenth, the fort was reduced to unrecognizable rubble. On the fifteenth, the garrison real-ized that they could no longer withstand the siege. The heroic sur-vivors set fire to what was left of the fort and abandoned it that night, crossing over to Fort Mercer.[65] Within a few days, that fort's position became untenable. With help from Hazelwood, the Americans evac-uated Fort Mercer on November 20. The British were in possession of the Delaware from Philadelphia to the sea.

The defeat resulted in finger-pointing from both sides. Sailors blamed soldiers for not attacking the shore batteries and soldiers blamed sailors for not doing more from their vessels. The only bright bit of news during this bleak autumn came from New York, where an army under Major General Horatio Gates (brilliantly led, in truth, by Benedict Arnold) thoroughly defeated the British forces under Burgoyne at Saratoga. It was heartening news, especially to Benjamin Franklin in Paris, who now finally had the legitimate victory he needed to support his plea for an open French alliance.[66] And it was certainly more accurate than the news Franklin had received from a misinformed congressman who had written him that "Captain Bar[r]y has recaptured the frigate *Delaware* recently took by the English."[67]

Throughout October, Washington deliberated over what to do with the *Effingham* and *Washington*. At month's end he decided on their fate, and relayed his wishes to Hopkinson on October 27:

> The more I reflect upon the evil that may arise from the Enemies Possessing themselves of our Frigates up the Delaware, the more convinced I am of the indispensable obligation we are under to prevent it, effectively. If no other method could be devised, I should be for absolutely burning them; but scuttling them and sinking [them] . . . will, in my judgment answer the end... At present, these Ships are of no use to us, whilst the hands are greatly wanted. . . . If I have stepped out of line of my duty to make this request, I am persuaded you will excuse it.[68]

Upon receipt of Washington's dispatch, Hopkinson and Wharton ordered Barry and Read to make a list of "returns" of their crews without telling them the reason behind this order. Unaware that the end result was to be the sinking of his command, Barry immediately presented his list, including officers, crew, and those recently assigned militiamen. Then Hopkinson, using his best diplomatic language, wrote Washington that his orders were being followed—to a point. Hopkinson intended to lighten the frigates and bring them up the shallow waterways along the Delaware above Bordentown. But, while the general's request was "a Law to us," he did not want to scuttle the ships "till the Enemy has got up to the City with their Shipping."[69]

Washington immediately responded with his second letter of the day. Citing the "letter which I wrote you a few hours ago . . . urging the necessity of Scuttling the Frigates immediately," he then pressed his demands, based on a report from "An intelligent Lad from Philadelphia" who "says they [the British] may have their Eye upon the Frigates above." Therefore, Washington "advise[d]" Hopkinson "to sink, not only them, immediately upon receipt of this, but every other Vessel."[70] These new orders immediately became a law to Hopkinson and Wharton. They dispatched a messenger to Barry and Read: they were to sail their ships back down to White Hill, two miles below Bordentown, and await further orders.[71] Three days of punishing rain had raised the river, giving Barry and Read a muddy two-mile journey to make. The next day, they were summoned to Bordentown.

Upon their arrival at the Navy Board's "office"–one of the homes on Bordentown's riverbank–only Barry was brought in to meet Hopkinson and Wharton.[72] Dispensing with any pleasantries, Hopkinson handed Barry his orders: "As we understand your Ship is now scuttled & ready for sinking, you are hereby directed to remove her a little below White Hill, and having found a suitable Birth where she may lye on a soft Bottom and be easily got off at a common Tide, you are to sink her there without further Delay. We expect this Business will be completed by Sun-Set this Evening, and report thereof made to this Board."[73]

The more Barry read, the angrier he became. With no explanation to support the frigates' sinking, and no acknowledgment of the trip the two captains had made in the pelting rain to receive an order that could have easily been dispatched to them as before by messenger, Hopkinson summarily dismissed the drenched and speechless Irishman.[74] Barry stomped out the door to find his voice and fellow captain.

Returning to their ships, Barry and Read vented their anger over both Hopkinson's orders and his conduct. Here were two captains pent up for weeks above the desperate battle for their home. Washington had called for their men, but not for them. And now, to be treated like a couple of shavetails by Wharton and Hopkinson–especially Hopkinson–was truly demeaning. They were men of action, not words, and now the call to action they had been waiting for turned out to be instructions to sink their untried ships of war.

But orders were orders. Being shorthanded, it took longer than Hopkinson expected or wanted for the captains to remove the ordnance, ammunition, and other supplies from their ships. There was no way they could keep to Hopkinson's timetable. At noon on the following day, Read went back to Bordentown to hire more men. He returned empty-handed, except for new orders from Wharton: the frigates were to be sunk, either that evening or the following morning.[75]

If Read was angry upon receipt of these commands, Barry was apoplectic. They stormed back to the Navy Board offices, barging in on Hopkinson and Wharton. Barry's temper already was on a short fuse, and now the disdain in which the previous day's orders were given ignited a two-man war. In one corner, Francis Hopkinson: "well over four feet" as the Irish say of short stature, whose brilliance outshone almost all of his contemporaries. In the other corner, John Barry: six feet four, and as able a fighter and sailor as in the navy. One of the best educated patriots versus one of the least educated. Unctuous flattery to superiors and imperiousness to subordinates opposed honesty and directness. The brightest man in the room was pitted against the bravest man in the room.

Barry confronted Hopkinson with the news of Wharton's order to Read, a repeat of the one Hopkinson handed Barry the day before. Hopkinson, whose dealings with Barry were patronizing at best, verified Wharton's order and repeated to Barry that the ships were to be sunk immediately. Barry, not for the first time, brought up the measures he and Read had taken, adding that the "heavy fresh in the river, occurred by the great rain which fell at that time, made it impossible for the Enemies' boats to come up." Barry felt the two frigates could be "easily destroyed" anytime and told Hopkinson that "were General Washington fully acquainted with the setting of the ships, he would not order them sunk." Agreeing that they *could* be sunk "should the event happen," Barry offered "to go to his excel[lenc]y the General and give him full information of all that had been done."[76]

Hopkinson's reply was cuttingly cool: sinking the ships would not be a mistake, although he himself thought so only a few days before. In fact, Hopkinson pointed out, the board already wrote Washington that the ships would be sunk and that "should [Hopkinson] disobey one jot of [Washington's] orders they would rather the whole thirteen frigates should be sunk." Hopkinson then informed Barry and Read that "His Excellency the General had been informed by a lad from Philadelphia that the enemy were preparing boats, and the frigates might possibly be their object." In his explanation Hopkinson stressed Washington's authority, but what Barry heard was that the decision to sink the frigates was based on the word of a mere boy. He reiterated that "Boats could not board us." Hopkinson's reply was that "he would take General Washington's opinion" over Barry's.[77]

The lawyer had been using his words and tone to make Barry cower, but Hopkinson's last barb only provoked him further: "I told [Hopkinson] I did not doubt that," he replied, "but . . . *nevertheless I knew more about a ship then General Washington and the Navy Board together.*"[78]

Barry let the remark lay there. Then he struck at Hopkinson's weak spot–his vanity. He told Hopkinson that in Barry's opinion, only the Marine Committee could direct him to sink his ship: "I was commanded by Congress to command her, and therefore expected to be consulted before she was destroyed."[79] The lawyer had played his trump card, invoking Washington's seniority over Barry's. Now the sea captain's trump was played, invoking the authority of Congress over Hopkinson.

Barry's defiance sent the little lawyer into a tantrum. Abandoning his usual sing-song tone, Hopkinson screamed, "You shall obey our orders!" Read, seeing his friend "In a high dudgeon," realized that no good was coming of this escalated bickering, and led (perhaps shoved) Barry out the door.[80]

A thick fog accompanied by a heavy frost greeted Barry, Read, and their crews at daybreak on November 2, as they assembled at the riverbank for the distasteful task.[81] Overnight all remaining stores and ordnance were removed from the *Effingham* and *Washington*. Their masts were brought down, taking away the frigates' majestic appearance. Stout lines, purchases, and every set of block and tackle in White Hill were in readiness to secure the ships, while their anchors would be dropped at the appropriate second to offset the pressure from the water that would be rushing into the ship after her plugs were removed. Barry sent word to Hopkinson that all was ready.[82]

Sinking the frigates in a manner that would allow them to be recovered afterward required precision and near-perfect timing. The object was to sink them into the Delaware's banks, thereby ensuring that they would not pose a hazard to traffic in the river. It required them to be sunk at the peak of high tide. Move too early and the tide would push the frigates forward and possibly break the ships apart. Wait too long and the commencement of low tide would pull the ships inexorably into the middle of the river. It was also a dangerous process, especially for the carpenters below deck, whose job it was to hammer out the plugs. The water would immediately rush into the ship so fast that it could suck them under before they escaped. One mariner who wrote of his success in sinking two ships recounted how:

> The tide bore upon us very heavy, we found that [the ships] would sink in two minutes . . . in an instant the cable parted from the ship we were on board of, which carried her bow round about thirty degrees before she struck the bottom . . . we sprang to the boat, and the vortex was so great it was with difficulty they could prevent the boat from following the ship, although they sprang at the oars with all their might. . . . The torrent of water in upon her was indescribable, and the water that came from her gangway ascended nearly twenty feet into the air.[83]

Later that afternoon, Hopkinson arrived at White Hill, and quickly gave orders to "head the ships ashore." There was enough remaining daylight to sink them by sunset, just as he ordered. Then he did the unthinkable.

Hopkinson had himself rowed aboard the *Effingham* to personally supervise her sinking. Whether he did this to establish his total authority over the act, to publicly humiliate Barry, or for both reasons, he never bothered to explain. "Not satisfied with giving orders, Mr. Hopkinson came on board my ship himself," Barry recalled. The captain obediently stepped aside, and Hopkinson gave orders to haul both ships on shore and sink them.[84] Barry might object to sinking his own ship, but Francis Hopkinson–lawyer, congressman, designer of the American flag, and Navy Board official–was more than willing to do so. In stepping aside, Barry cooperated.

The tide, however, did not. Hopkinson may very well have known maritime laws as well as any man alive, but he was evidently ignorant of the laws of nature. Nor was he aware of the watchlike precision this procedure required. With his pen dipped in sarcasm, Barry later wrote, "This was the wrong time of the tide." Still, Barry stepped aside, and watched in silence as his ship struck "soft bottom."[85] Barry recalled, "As soon as she struck ground, he [Hopkinson] ordered the plugs out."[86] Upon hearing the order from above deck, Barry's carpenters swung their heavy mallets at the plugs. Blessed with Hopkinson's absence on his own deck, Read could only watch in horror at what happened next.

Standing next to Hopkinson, Barry had a perfect view of the consequences of Hopkinson's orders. Rather than heel toward shore and sink against it, the water rushed into the frigate "so fast we could not heel the ship to the bank, in consequence which she lay upon her beam ends, and was very near oversetting," her captain reported.[87] Francis Hopkinson and the *Effingham* were victims of the tide table. A waterspout gushed through the frigate's hatchway as the carpenters, thoroughly soaked, struggled to reach the deck. The ship came perilously close to "turtling"–capsizing. With a salon dancer's agility, the head of the Navy Board managed to get off the frigate without hurting himself and ordered his boat rowed to shore.

It is not known whether Hopkinson officially returned command back to Barry, but once the omniscient lawyer abandoned the sinking ship, Barry reassumed responsibility for his men's safety. He ordered them back to their boat, and then got in himself. By the time they reached the riverbank, Hopkinson had already slunk off to Bordentown. To Barry the sight of his frigate lying on her beam-ends in the Delaware seemed like a monstrous practical joke, played on himself.[88]

Hours later Read, acting without Hopkinson's assistance, brought the *Washington* alongshore and removed her plugs at the proper time, sinking her correctly and safely. The next morning Barry visited his frigate, her massive hull half-drowned in the river. The *Effingham* was literally a trapped derelict. With a sigh, he rode to Bordentown to acquaint Hopkinson of the ship's wretched condition.

Where Barry–having seen that his silent obedience had resulted in his beautiful ship's wretched state–was in a more docile mood, Hopkinson had recovered from his embarrassment and rediscovered his considerable ego. After Barry "acquainted the Board with the situation of the ship," Hopkinson replied that "it was a misfortune, and that we must do the best to remedy it." The captain replied that "nothing on my part should be wanting." With Hopkinson's permission to "hire all the hands I wanted," Barry returned to White Hill and the task of correcting the all but uncorrectable.[89]

And it was uncorrectable. Barry could not obtain close to "all the hands I wanted" without having to "coax them [with] extravagant wages." Two efforts over the next three days to raise the *Effingham* failed. Unable to succeed with this combined force of his own crew, the sailors from the *Washington,* and his few, high-priced "volunteers," Barry knew that a third attempt would require considerably more men. Hopkinson, however, viewed Barry's failures as a further slap at his authority.[90]

To make matters worse for Hopkinson, he had just received a letter from Washington who, unaware that his orders were not exactly obeyed, ordered that "all other vessels being capable of being converted into armed ships" be immediately sunk.[91] Hopkinson, in humble tones that would have made Uriah Heep blush, replied immediately: "The Frigates have been long since sunk, & now lie fit aground in a Place where they can receive no Danger from the Ice & cannot possibly be got off by the Enemy . . . we have a secret Gage that will enable us to raise them with Ease when a suitable Time shall offer." With the innocuous disclosure that "in sinking of the [*Effingham*], she unfortunately lay against a steep Bank whereon the Tides falling, caused her to heel outwards from the Shoar"–a comment that spared him any responsibility–Hopkinson dispatched his letter to Washington's headquarters in Whitemarsh.[92]

An early snow fell on the Delaware Valley over the next two days.[93] Afterward, Barry sent notice to the board that he would make a third attempt to raise the *Effingham,* and received word that "Mr.

Hopkinson would come down and raise her himself. This insult I overlooked," Barry recollected, "having the getting of the ship much at heart." The sky cleared around ten that morning, and Barry requested as many of Colonel Lewis Nicola's invalids "as they could send," believing that in getting as many hands as possible the third try would be the charm. Barry and his men waited in the cold for Nicola's men to show up.[94]

Finally, at "About one o'clock a sergeant & six or seven invalids came to my assistance." If Hopkinson saw Barry's failure to raise the *Effingham* as insolence, Barry judged Hopkinson's failure to cooperate as downright incompetence. When he asked the sergeant why so few men had arrived for the prodigious task, he was told that Hopkinson and Wharton called only for "men as were well-attired" to come and assist.[95] With his own crew listening to this conversation in tattered sailcloth and rags, while the cold wind swept upriver, stinging the men's faces and setting their teeth to chattering, Barry sent everyone back to the task at hand.

Having "collected all the seamen I could," Barry gave orders "and [the men] began to heave upon the purchases."[96] The "purchases"– consisting of every means of increasing power and leverage Barry could find, from block and tackle to a jury-rigged windlass–needed more manpower than Barry had mustered.[97] Twice he had failed at raising his beloved frigate with only "twenty or thirty five men," and now to have but a handful more kept the task both impossible and demeaning. Taut lines creaked, men swore under the strain, but their labors brought no success. The *Effingham* was immovable in the Delaware's mud.

True to his word, Hopkinson soon showed up to assume command once again, although he failed to bring with him "the secret Gage" that would effortlessly raise the *Effingham*. "Captain Barry," he called in his superficially cheery fashion, barely hiding both condescension and contempt, "doth she rise?"

In a voice that did not bother to conceal his own contempt for the questioner, Barry responded, "No, sir. How can she rise when you keep the people back?"

"Pooh," Hopkinson snorted, "You are always grumbling."

"What did you say?" a furious Barry asked.

"Go along, and mind your own business, you scoundrel!" was Hopkinson's scathing rejoinder.

Once more Hopkinson's spurs got under Barry's skin. His baleful stare gave way to outright rage. "It is a lie!" he shouted.

"What! Do you tell me I lie?" Hopkinson retorted.

Barry ordered the sergeant of invalids to approach and report to Hopkinson what he had told Barry, and he repeated Hopkinson's orders verbatim. Trapped by his own words and angered by his subordinate's wrath, Hopkinson told Barry that he "would bring [him] to account for this." The two men had reached the point where civility, authority, and mutual respect were as sunk as the *Effingham*. "Damn you," Barry said scornfully. "I don't value you any more than my duty requires."

"Sir," Hopkinson sneered, "you never minded your duty."

Barry's reply was immediate and withering. "You're a liar. The Continental Congress [knows] that I have minded my duty, and had [you] made yours as well, this ship would not be in its present condition."[98]

Throughout this exchange, Hopkinson had stood his ground like a bantam cock, but now Barry's words, how he said them, and his menacing physical presence were enough of a combination that Hopkinson chose to withdraw from the scene.

The Irishman's vitriol seemed strong enough to raise the *Effingham* from its sheer energy alone; nevertheless Barry returned to the more conventional method of trying to free his pitiful ship. As Hopkinson was leaving, "I pursued my business," Barry reported, "until one of the purchases gave way." The sudden snap of the lines threw the men backward, and the frigate settled deeper into the muck. The third and last attempt to raise the *Effingham* had come to nothing. With no further need to keep the exhausted men out in the cold, Barry ordered them to break down the equipment and sent them back to town. Later that day, Washington wrote a conciliatory note to the Navy Board explaining that he was glad to hear that the frigate had been sunk.[99]

In the pre-dawn hours of November 21, cloaked in darkness, Hazelwood's surviving row-galleys slipped past the British batteries at Philadelphia. Sometime later Barry, Read, and the sailors exiled in

Bordentown saw smoke south on the river. Isaiah Robinson, former captain of the *Sachem*, had attempted to bring up the remaining Continental Navy vessels: the *Andrew Doria, Hornet, Wasp, Racehorse,* and *Fly*, along with the Pennsylvania Navy xebecs *Repulse* and *Clymer* (xebecs were sleek, two- or three-masted vessels with square-rig foremasts but lateen sails on the other masts). He was not as lucky as Hazelwood. Seeing the futility in running the gauntlet of British batteries in daylight, Robinson ordered the ships stripped of anything useful that could be removed, from tools to sailcloth. Then they were burned, less than two years after some of these same ships had sailed so proudly from Philadelphia in that first Continental fleet. Like Viking funerals they drifted afire until they slowly sank into the river's depths.[100] Over three hundred cold, wet, and hungry officers and sailors slogged the twenty miles to Bordentown.[101]

There was no respite for Hopkinson after the *Effingham* affair. His brother-in-law, Jacob Duché, the rector of Christ Church and a former patriot, had been imprisoned by General Howe. There he recanted the error of his ways in a notorious letter to Washington that urged him to turn his back on the fight for independence. The letter quickly gained widespread notoriety and was an obvious embarrassment to Hopkinson, who immediately reaffirmed his support for the patriot cause–a cause which had, in fairness, put Hopkinson's future at risk. Writing "for true and brother Love," Hopkinson belittled Duché's "vain and weak Effort attempted [at] the Integrity of one whose Virtue is impregnable to the Assaults of Fear and Flattery."[102]

Hopkinson did not post the letter to the rector. Instead he sent it to Washington, beseeching him to forward it to Duché (as if Washington would); but we do not know whether he sent it to the general from fear of his connection to Duché, or in the hopes of mollifying Washington with his sycophantic flattery.[103]

The arrival of the sailors in Bordentown allowed the sunken frigates to serve as yet another punch line. Lacking enough rooms to quarter so many sailors, Hopkinson and Wharton wrote the Marine Committee requesting instructions as to what to do with them all. Unaware of what had transpired, the committee immediately replied, "By all means keep them together in good humor and in Action until you hear further from us on the subject." To Hopkinson, that meant one thing; composing yet another fawning epistle to Washington, he suggested the two frigates be raised to be used as a floating barracks for the homeless sailors. An exasperated Washington responded with a terse note. While he would "leave the matter to [the Navy Board's] judgment," he saw "no reason for changing my former opinion, in request to Sinking the Frigates."[104] Once again, Washington's word was law to Hopkinson; the ships remained in watery hibernation, and Hopkinson's "secret Gage" forever remained a secret.

A court-martial gave Barry the chance to take his mind off the *Effingham* and Hopkinson. On November 25, he presided over the trial of five members of the crew of one of the xebecs accused of desertion in the recent fighting. Using the merchantman *Lyon*'s cabin, Barry and eleven other officers (among them Read) reviewed the evidence, including testimony from eyewitness Luke Matthewman, serving aboard the sloop *Surprize* at the time of the incident. The five accused—the master's mate, master of arms, armorer, quartermaster, and "a Boy"—were found guilty "upon a due and impartial consideration." The men were sentenced to "be hung off the Yard Arm of any Continental Vessell," while "the Boy" was sentenced to "Thirty Six lashes on his bare back with a Cat-Of-Nine-Tails as being a Boy and called out of his Bed." The prisoners were put in close confinement "in Burlington Gaol"—presumably until any "Continental Vessell" could be found (or raised) to provide the necessary yardarm. Congress later pardoned the five on condition that they join the army and serve throughout the war.[105]

The next day, Washington received word that "thirty Sail of Transports came up the River, above one hundred now lie opposite the City" and troops were now being landed in Philadelphia.[106] December 1777 was the same as, yet different from December 1776: Washington's army was near Philadelphia, not poised for a desperate attack to save the city, but defeated, in rags, with little food. Congress had fled, as they had the year before, not due to a threat of a British takeover but because of an actual one. The Delaware, used by Barry and his cohorts Wickes and Biddle to harass and stymie the Royal Navy, was now completely in enemy hands. And, while John Cadwalader and other officers proposed attack, Washington sent his forces to winter encampment at nearby Valley Forge.[107] Howe and his loyalist supporters had Philadelphia all to themselves. The British Empire had certainly struck back.

In Bordentown, Barry was close to stir-crazy. Ordered to retreat from the fight on the Delaware, separated from his bride, approached by an acquaintance to turn traitor, having witnessed and failed to rectify the disastrous sinking of his ship, he found that the bitter acrimony between himself and Hopkinson had sapped his patience, if not his self-respect. Yet while he was forced into idleness, his heart and brain were restive. He had an idea of how to harass the enemy, but it was not one he dared share with the imperious Hopkinson.

Accordingly, Barry bypassed the channels of command. Instead of approaching the Navy Board, he applied directly to the Marine Committee requesting leave, presumably to spend Christmas with Sarah and her family in Reading. Upon receiving permission on December 13, he notified Hopkinson and Wharton that he was leaving town.[108]

Hopkinson not only saw Barry's absence as "French Leave," but also as the perfect opportunity to settle accounts with him once and for all. He and Wharton drafted a letter to the Marine Committee. Hopkinson–who, judging from his choice of words, was clearly relishing his own narrative–told how "in the presence of several Strangers he [Barry] in the most indecent terms refused to execute our orders" and that his "insolence, disrespect and ill treatment warranted suspension from the service at the very least."[109]

Once more Hopkinson could not resist being clever with how he mailed a letter. It was sent directly to committee member Robert Morris, but not to his Congressional address in York. Rather, Hopkinson sent it where he believed Morris would be, at his estate in Manheim. Once again, Hopkinson asked a superior to act as personal postman after his letter was read. Thus would the influential Morris be informed of Hopkinson's side of the affair before Barry got the chance to tell his old employer his somewhat different account.

Unbeknownst to Hopkinson, Barry took a circuitous route to Reading via Valley Forge, arriving on December 19. He rode there specifically to see Washington, who that very day arrived from nearby Whitemarsh. Directed to the fieldstone house Washington had just moved into as his winter quarters, Barry waited inside the front door until Washington's secretary, Lieutenant Colonel John Fitzgerald, escorted him past a tall sentry and into the parlor, converted into the general's office only hours earlier.

After a brief introduction, Washington and Barry sat by the fireplace at one of the four mahogany tables, each covered with a green tablecloth. Whether Barry recounted his feud with Hopkinson is unknown, but doubtless he shared the plan he wished to undertake that would allow him to resume his role as a fighting sailor. It met with the general's approval.[110] And, as a further bonus for the extra miles the sea captain rode, Barry also encountered none other than Robert Morris. Barry launched into a harangue against Hopkinson, but Morris cut him short, later recalling that Barry "wanted to Relate to me the Substance of his dispute with the Navy Board, but I had neither the time or inclination, neither did I think it proper to hear one Story without the other as it was possible I might some day become a judge in the affair."[111] Mollified that his old employer would give him a fair shake, Barry mounted his horse and headed to Reading.

Morris returned to Manheim to find Hopkinson's letter waiting for him, which he forwarded to the Marine Committee as Hopkinson anticipated. But Morris also enclosed his own letter, writing, "Capt. Barry thinks himself capable of making a defence against the accounts of the Board and Submitting the matter entirely to the deliberation of the Committee."[112] The first part of Hopkinson's plan to destroy Barry had failed, thanks to blind luck.

Barry reached Reading in the hopes of finding solace, peace, and a chance to catch his breath from the trials of war and bureaucratic discord. Sarah should have been glad to see her husband; instead, she matched her husband in tales of woe. At the same time Barry was trying to unsink the *Effingham*, Sarah's half-sister, Christiana Keen, died during childbirth. Now her eight children looked to Sarah and Isaac for all that parents provide. Sarah told her husband how William Austin and Reynold Keen had joined loyalist regiments, and that local officials were attempting to seize Reynold's possessions after hearing of his treasonous act. Keen's numerous creditors now demanded payment of his debts from Isaac and Sarah.[113]

The snow that fell that week on Mount Penn and the hills around Reading gave the town a holiday luster in contrast to the gloom pervading the Austin household.[114] Further south and east, the wind and snow signalled the first in a series of storms that ripped through the hurriedly constructed cabins at Valley Forge, held together by sod and mud. The wind seemed to echo the moans of Washington's freezing, hungry soldiers. In Philadelphia, the Howe brothers and Cornwallis enjoyed the finest food William Austin and other loyalists could provide, the finest houses abandoned by the aristocrats of the American cause, and the finest mistresses that a handsome red uniform could attract.[115]

On December 30, Barry received a letter from John Brown, now Secretary of the Marine Committee. With his letter came copies of the committee's latest two resolutions, passed after reviewing Hopkinson's tirade: "Resolved, That Captain John Barry be required immediately to attend Congress, to answer to the complaint exhibited against him, and that he be furnished with an extract from the letter of the navy board." This was hard enough for Barry to swallow, but the second resolution was even more wounding:

> Whereas, it is essentially necessary to the marine service, that the affairs of the Officers of the Navy of the United States of America should pay obedience to such orders as the navy board's and the respective districts may at any time find necessary to give them [and] that all the officers in the said navy should treat the said navy boards with decency and respect: resolved, that the navy boards be, and they are hereby impowered to suspend any officer of the navy . . . who shall refuse to

pay obedience to such orders as they may think necessary to issue, for who shall treat them with indecency and disrespect: and the said navy boards are hereby required to give immediate notice to the Marine Committee of any such suspension, with the venue thereof.[116]

Brown also enclosed a copy of Hopkinson's complaint. Having proven that he could stand up against prejudice, the elements, tyranny, and war, Barry now faced a new obstacle: intrigue. And his opponent was a master.

The year of the hangman ended with every aspect of Barry's life beset by troubles. As his mount carried him over the snow-covered road to York to confront Hopkinson's cronies in Congress, Barry knew that his future in the navy could only be saved by political, not nautical, skills.

CHAPTER SEVEN

VINDICATION

As JOHN BARRY JOURNEYED TO YORK, Washington's army was freezing at Valley Forge. Private Joseph Plumb Martin, at sixteen already a survivor of the mud and lethal bombardment at Fort Mifflin, described the rations meted out as "a leg of nothing and no turnips."[1] The soldiers were perpetually starving. They went about in rags, taking shelter in the drafty log huts they built for winter quarters (one guard kept his post while standing on his head to keep his bare feet out of the snow).[2] The horrifying condition of the troops was not due to lack of congressional funds as much as lack of congressional foresight. From Maine to Georgia, farmers reaped a truly grand harvest the previous fall. But neither Congress nor Quartermaster General Thomas Mifflin—who was working around the clock with other officers and congressmen to have Washington replaced with General Horatio Gates—tried hard enough to get food and supplies to America's soldiers.[3]

In nearby Philadelphia, empty but for the small population of loyalists—including William Austin and Reynold Keen—and the warm and well-fed British Army, British commanders settled into the best Philadelphia homes. General Howe and his mistress moved into a handsome home on Sixth and High (Market) Streets, inspiring this bit of patriotic satire:

Sir William he, snug as a flea
Lay all this time a snoring
Nor dream'd of harm as he lay warm
In bed with Mrs. Loring.[4]

"Black Dick" Howe took up residence on Chestnut Street in a home so impressive that it later became the headquarters of a bank. Cornwallis ensconced himself in David Lewis's magnificent abode on Second and Spruce. Major John André, a favorite of Howe's due to his flair for theatrics, "dwelt in Dr. Franklin's mansion." The Hessian Commander, Baron General Wilhelm von Knyphausen, "very honorable in his dealings," took over John Cadwalader's home on South Second, where "exalted as he was in rank," Knyphausen "used to spread his butter on his bread with his thumb."[5]

British officers "held frequent plays at the old theatre, the performances by their officers."[6] The dates and addresses of their balls were published in the *True Royal Gazette*, one of the Tory papers now flourishing in the captured capital. Upon hearing of the British occupation of his hometown, Franklin acerbically commented that Howe had not taken Philadelphia. Philadelphia had taken Howe.[7]

Barry arrived in York, hoping to rely on his friends in Congress, especially those on the Marine Committee. It never occurred to him to refrain from confronting his accusers directly and immediately. His first supporter was his old employer. Morris, while asserting his neutrality regarding the *Effingham* affair, nevertheless put the committee's secretary, John Brown, at Barry's disposal, giving Brown two tasks: one, to keep Barry calm; and two, sequester him in a tavern room, where the accused captain could pour out his version of the events that brought him there in the first place.[8] Brown, still smarting that Hopkinson's friends in Congress had thrown him in jail weeks earlier just for bringing them Howe's peace feeler, was more than happy to counsel Barry.[9]

The final draft, five long pages in Barry's own hand, was a thorough, well-delineated effort, in which he narrated what happened and his reactions. It did not sugarcoat his words or conduct. Brown may have smoothed over the rough edges and suggested a phrase or two, but it is pure Barry from beginning—"I think it necessary that this period to exculpate myself...nor do I aver that the following conversation passed only in the presence of Captain Read and the Board"–to end–"This Gentlemen is a true relation, as nearly as I can recollect, and I submit to your Honors judgment how far my conduct has been Blameable . . . . For my part, I shall think myself unworthy of the Commission the Honourable Congress has been pleased to give me could I tamely put up with differently Treatment."[10]

While he confined his account to the *Effingham*, he did take one swing at Hopkinson for his pompous attitude toward Barry and Read, in the hopes that Congress would discuss the issue of respect for the military by their civilian superiors: "I shall only add that it has been a principal Study with me to behave with the greatest respect to the Navy Board ever since their appointment and I would just suggest to your honors whether the good of the Service does not require the Captains of the Navy to be treated as Gentlemen with respect and as Gentlemen so long as they observe their Duty."[11]

Barry's case was taken up as "new business" by Congress on January 10, 1778.[12] Whatever cunning ploys and gamesmanship Hopkinson's friends might play behind the scenes, Barry's defense, bereft of apology for his words or actions, did garner support among those congressmen unfamiliar with the incident. It also won over some of Hopkinson's colleagues who had been similarly treated by Barry's antagonist.

Barry's defense was read into the minutes of Congress on January 13, and immediately referred back to the Marine Committee for resolution. (That same day, they wrote Thomas Read, rewarding his desire "to be active in the service of your Country" with "Command of the Continent Brig *Baltimore*." Read left hearth, home, and wife– his new bride having joined him in White Hill–and departed for Baltimore.[13])

By this time Barry's plan of action against the British was being discussed openly. Since his forced exile at Bordentown, he had been developing a scheme to strike back at the British along the Delaware, hoping to take the barges of the *Effingham* and *Washington* below Philadelphia, manned with the seamen becalmed at Bordentown.

Once south of the city, they could harass and perhaps even capture British supply ships. The Royal Navy was the main source of supplies to Howe's army, and the Delaware their only route. Barry's plan met with approval from Washington when he visited Valley Forge, and now the Marine Committee expressed enthusiasm. Further, Barry's friends on the committee saw his plan as their opportunity to support the captain openly against Hopkinson without getting personal.[14]

In Bordentown, Hopkinson and Wharton were still beset with problems. There were now close to five hundred sailors in town, and their need for food and clothing was as great as that of Washington's army. Morale, already low, had plummeted like the thermometer. Food was intermittently distributed, but at least it came more often than pay.[15]

Like Barry, Hopkinson was involved with plans to strike back at the British, but these only proved to be acts of overly clever desperation and insufficient planning. The first two involved the French engineer Major Fleury. He proposed setting twelve boats afire, with sharp iron pikes at their bows to attach themselves to enemy ships and sending them south in favorable winds. This did not pass a test run. Next, he wanted several volunteers to carry shirts packed with sulfur across the river below Bordentown at Cooper's Ferry by walking across the ice, then set fire to the shirts once they got close to British ships. This far-fetched scheme was never attempted: cold as it was, it was not cold long enough to allow the Delaware to thoroughly freeze. Curiously, Washington liked the idea, if "some desperate fellows" could be found to (a) travel the river when it did freeze and (b) carry such a flammable garment with the degree of stealth and fool's courage the gambit warranted.[16] No takers came forward.

Hopkinson's father-in-law, Colonel Borden, was enamored of a plan by David Bushnell, one of the first pioneers in developing the submarine. Bushnell came up with a weapon comprised of underwater mines floated by buoys and kegs. On January 5, Bushnell let loose his kegs on the Delaware. For all his calculations, and the ardent support of Borden and Hopkinson, Bushnell did not seek out assistance or advice from Hazelwood, who certainly knew the Delaware as well as anyone in Bordentown. Perhaps Bushnell knew Hazelwood would not approve such a far-fetched idea.[17] Years later, one Philadelphian recalled that "when the scheme was set in operation, the British fearing the making of ice, had warped in their shipping to the wharfs, and so escaped much of the intended mischief."[18] Apparently, the kegs floated harmlessly down the river without a chance to strike the safely moored British vessels.

Barry's plan, lacking burning shirts and kegs, involved boats, men, and risk, but he would not be in command if Hopkinson had anything to do with it. As soon as he received word of Barry's proposal from his informants in Congress, Hopkinson sent Charles Alexander, late of the captured *Delaware*, to visit Washington with a similar proposal nominating Alexander as commander.[19] Hopkinson also began holding Congress' feet to the fire as far as his accusations against Barry were concerned. More than two weeks had passed since their summons to Barry, yet he not only remained unpunished, but obviously still in favor with the Marine Committee. Tipped off that the committee's cooperation with Barry would make his plan a reality, Hopkinson again wrote his congressional allies on January 19.[20] Upon receipt, they worked behind the scenes, currying votes against Barry—just as Barry's supporters were doing on his behalf.

Ten days later, Hopkinson's allies passed a motion "that Captain Barry be not employed on the expedition assigned to his conduct by the Marine Committee, till further orders from Congress."[21] The motion was put to a vote. The time for gamesmanship was over; Congress must now decide between the lawyer and the sailor. Every representative's name was called, and each vote was cast and recorded.

The vote was a tie.

As such, the motion "passed in the negative." One less vote and Barry's next adventure would have taken place without him. While Congress "adjourned to 10 o'clock to Morrow," the Marine Committee wasted no more daylight.[22] They immediately issued orders that Barry "employ the Pinnace and Barges belonging to the Frigates" and "employ such Continental Navy Officers not in Active Service" for his mission. Further, adding insult to injury, the committee directed Hopkinson to provide Barry "with everything necessary for equipping your little fleet. . . . You will give immediate notice to General Washington of such stores as you may Capture which are necessary for the use of the Army."[23] Wishing Barry success, and asking that he "Write us frequently," the committee sent their own instructions to Hopkinson—not exactly a veiled rebuke of him as much as emphasizing their support of Barry: "We have directed Captain Barry to employ the Pinnace and Barges . . . in annoying the enemies Vessels in their Passage up and down the Delaware. . . . We desire that you would deliver him such War-like Provisions and other necessaries as he may think necessary for equipping and victualling the Said Boats."[24]

With a world of scheming and contrivance lifted off his broad shoulders, Barry lost no time in leaving York. For the first time in months, he could focus on his duties and leave the politicians behind.

There was much to do. For Barry's plan to work, the barges would have to elude the British in Philadelphia. South of the city, the Delaware widens; numerous creeks and streams would provide refuge from any pursuing British craft. Most of the traffic on the river would consist of supply transports. The ice, and British lack of knowledge regarding the Delaware's tributaries, would also serve to his advantage. Barry saw the coming action as a chance to attack the enemy with speed and surprise; any resultant captured supplies that could be sent to Valley Forge would be a welcome residual.[25] That said, he still faced overwhelming odds: the enemy was sure to respond with superior numbers of barges and men. Add the fact that there were enough loyalists living on the riverbanks who would offer neither succor nor silence, and Barry's mission carried no guarantee of success.

Barry departed York on January 30, visiting Morris in Manheim at John Brown's request, dropping off a letter regarding Barry's brother. Patrick was in Edenton, North Carolina, preparing a privateer for a voyage to France.[26] It was the first bit of news Barry had of Patrick in over a year.

From Manheim, Barry went back to Valley Forge for a brief meeting with Washington and to request Washington's intercession with General James Varnum in Burlington, New Jersey. Realizing that the Marine Committee's letter called for "volunteers," Barry wanted an order giving him use of the same soldiers Washington assigned in the fall to the Pennsylvania Navy, and Washington happily obliged.[27]

The Marine Committee's orders to Barry were strict instructions as to how to handle every conceivable issue his venture might encounter:

> As you will have frequent occasion to land on each Side of the Delaware during your Cruze you will take effectual care to restrain your officers & men from plundering, insulting or in any way treating ill the Inhabitants of the Country. Humanity, good Policy and your reputation demand that they should be treated with kindness–you may want supplies from them and their assistance in moving to a place of safety such effects as you may capture . . . you shall take with you or appoint on Shore some honest, faithful persons who are well acquainted with the Country and will undertake to procure wagons for the speedy removal to a place of safety and take care of such goods as you may Capture. . . . We would have you Sink or otherwise destroy the Hulls of all such Vessels as you may take which cannot be removed to some place of Safety. The Vessels which you take and preserve and the goods which you Capture must be libeled in the Court of Admiralty in the State which they are carried–you will therefore employ some suitable Attorney to libel for the same. . . . The Success of your Cruze depending upon your dispatch, activity, prudence and valour we hope you will exert the utmost of your abilities on this occasion.[28]

The committee's orders that Barry receive supplies and support from the Navy Board must have been gall and wormwood to Hopkinson. Nonetheless, Barry encountered no resistance from him. Hopkinson's days in his hometown were numbered anyway. Congress already decided "As that part of the Continental Navy late in the Delaware are either lost or rendered useless, there appears no necessity of your continuing in Jersey." Hopkinson and Wharton were ordered to Baltimore, with further instructions to pick up John Nixon from his militia post along the way.[29] Hopkinson's recent mail was not personally very cheerful for him; he also got a note from Washington approving Alexander's mission, but only if it was "in conjunction with the other Gentlemen of the Navy"–that is, under Barry's supervision. The general closed with regrets that he would not be Hopkinson's personal mailman: "Having never found an opportunity of conveying the Letter, which you sometime ago sent to me for Mr. Duché . . . I return it to you again."[30]

Once in Bordentown, Barry discovered that his biggest obstacle was not the little attorney but his choice of vessels: only two of the barges were in suitable condition for the venture. The pinnace and the other barge were in need of time-consuming repairs. He ordered the two serviceable barges overhauled for the expedition, with a four-pound cannon mounted on each bow, and swivel guns placed along the gunwales.[31]

The recruitment of a crew began with finding a second-in-command. Barry's first choice, Luke Matthewman, accepted immediately. Upon his arrival in Bordentown following the fighting at Fort Mifflin, Matthewman was made "Commisary for the Seamen of the Late Fleet," a position with much responsibility but little authority or success in providing food and clothing for his fellow sailors. Midshipman Matthew Clarkson, another *Lexington* veteran, also decided to face the icy Delaware rather than wait in boredom for infrequent rations at Bordentown. Marine Lieutenant James Coakley was the only other officer who enlisted.[32]

Few Continental sailors volunteered, due to the bitterly cold conditions and recent memories of the defeat that put them in Bordentown in the first place. Out of the hundreds in town, only two dozen volunteered. Barry's trip to Burlington to recruit volunteers from Varnum's and Hazelwood's forces was minimally successful; only fifteen of Varnum's "landsmen" signed on.[33] Hazelwood told Barry that six of the Pennsylvania Navy's row-galleys had just embarked on a similar mission. Two reached Cooper's Ferry, across from Petty's Island, but their crews deserted in the dead of night. The other four boats, under command of Captain Joseph Wade, were painstakingly lugged overland. Hazelwood had not heard from them since.[34]

After a week of preparation the barges were ready. Taking command of one, Barry placed the other under Matthewman and assigned twenty men to each boat. Although the Delaware was

150 • JOHN BARRY

frozen at Bordentown in late January (there were still no takers for Major Fleury's booby-trapped shirts), a recent thaw broke the ice into floes. Barry was not about to follow Wade's overland route. Instead, he would head downriver under cover of darkness, risking detection and capture by the British. News of his plan was already inspiring other officers to follow suit. Two Pennsylvania Navy captains applied to the Pennsylvania Council of Safety for permission to do so but, while the council commended Barry's "spirit of enterprise," they withheld permission until "Capt. Barry's example" proved successful.[35]

Around the time this letter was sent (the specific date is not known), Barry left Bordentown. Boarding one of the barges at dusk, he gave orders to push off. With oars muffled and oarlocks greased to eliminate squeaking, the sailors propelled the crowded barges as silently as possible. Barry kept them to the Jersey side of the river.

By midnight they reached Philadelphia. From their boats they could make out the illuminated homes just past Dock Street. The music from any boisterous frolic at a loyalist household carried over the water through the thin winter air. They could make out the wards where Barry and some of his men had lived, and the wharves from which they had sailed. They saw the silhouettes of the redcoat guards, their bayonets occasionally reflecting the lamplight along the docks or on the ships where they stood watch. Among the ships they slipped past was the *Roebuck*, finally docked in Philadelphia after nearly two years of Andrew Snape Hamond's attempts to do so.

One of the sentries on an anchored warship heard something suspicious across the water, and called out. In a strong whisper Barry ordered his men to stop rowing. A musket was fired over the water but found no target. With a nod from their captain, the Americans continued their muffled rowing. Soon Barry and his men were past the captured city.[36]

As dawn rose, Barry's men, exhausted and numbed by the cold, pulled into one of the Delaware's streams for cover from the spyglasses of British deck-officers. Then, after dusk, they were at it again, passing Chester and Marcus Hook, then rowing across to the Christina River in Delaware. The following morning, Barry made his arrival known to General William Smallwood, the commander of the

Continental forces in Wilmington.[37] Of his trip downriver, Barry wrote, "I passed Philadelphia in two small boats," his total recounting of this desperately silent journey.[38] Matthewman's report was equally lacking in detail: "Capt. Barry and myself and two barges passed Philadelphia through the ice."[39]

Nor were just American barges heading into the icy river. On February 11, Hamond wrote out orders "for the Defense of this City, and the better exerting the King's Service in the River Delaware," that an armed "Row-Galy" named the *Philadelphia* be put to use against any rebel opposition they may encounter.[40] Whether he was tipped off by Tory informants, or simply sniffing at something in the wind, Hamond, as usual, was leaving nothing to chance.

One week later, three hundred Continental soldiers led by General Anthony Wayne arrived in Wilmington. Wayne's orders were to cross the Delaware to the New Jersey side and purchase or requisition cattle from the farms dotting the river's shoreline. Most livestock owners would call Wayne's band a large rustling party. Their mission was that pure, simple, and necessary. The Continentals were also directed to destroy any forage they found before it could be seized by British dragoons for their horses.[41] It was Wayne's first solo action since the Paoli Massacre. Although cleared of any wrongdoing in that disastrous incident, he was anxious to redeem himself. If the theft of beef on the hoof was his first opportunity, then so be it.

Wayne also reported to Smallwood, inquiring about any boats and men available to take his soldiers across the icy river. Smallwood had no boats to speak of, but told Wayne of Barry's arrival in the Christina River. By this time Barry had been joined by Wade and his barges. Smallwood put Barry and Wayne together, the beginning of a lifelong friendship.

On February 19, Barry's "fleet" transported Wayne's soldiers to New Jersey in broad daylight—there being no British craft in view on the river; nor could any Tory spies warn General Howe back in Philadelphia in enough time to prevent the crossing. Wayne's men marched into Salem while Barry's barges and boats passed Finn's Point, making for Salem Creek. The next four days were spent with the "rustlers" trying to carry out their mission. Wayne's soldiers were unfamiliar with both their assignment and the countryside. The Jersey farmers, whether patriot, loyalist, or neutral, were in no way desirous of having their cattle taken outright or paid for in worthless Continental scrip–especially when the British, under Howe's gentlemanly orders, would pay better (and in British pounds) for the same beef. Instead, they hid their cows and steers in nearby swamps or in the dense pine backwoods, out of sight of Wayne's soldiers.[42]

By the twenty-third, Wayne "had got together upwards of One hundred and fifty Head." Soon he had nearly five hundred, with enough commandeered wagons loaded with hay to feed them.[43] The problem was getting his herd to Valley Forge. By now the British were aware of Wayne's activities, and he received word that a large British force was marching north of Philadelphia to cross the Delaware at Burlington and capture or kill any American soldier, sailor, or steer.[44] Rather than march north with the herd, Wayne and Barry attempted to transfer the cattle using the barges, but they proved unsuitable for the reluctant, four-legged recruits, who showed no enthusiasm for a boat ride.[45]

During a council of war with their officers to determine a course of action, Wayne and Barry decided to send the cattle and hay wagons north along the road that led from Salem to Mount Holly–a distance of approximately fifty miles–with Wayne's men keeping between the road and the river to repel any British or loyalist forces. Barry and his men would act as decoy. Taking his forty sailors and soldiers, he would send his boats upriver to Mantua Creek just above Billingsport.[46] From there they would proceed southward "and Burn all the Hay along the Shore from Billingsport to this place [Salem] taking any acct. of the Persons Names to whom it belongs." While such a measure deprived the British of the forage, Wayne, citing Washington's desire "that Private Property not be Sacrificed to Public Good," directed Barry to "transmit to headquarters the Names . . . with the Quantity of forage belonging to each" for "Recompence at a future day."[47]

Barry's ruse would be tedious, unpopular, and dangerous. It was one thing to "request" hay for the Continentals and pay for it with near-worthless paper money. It was another to burn the hay and, in doing so, not only raise hackles with fellow countrymen but also incite the enemy to chase after him, while Wayne endeavored to get his cattle above Mount Holly, cross the Delaware, and swing west of Philadelphia back down to Valley Forge. Reinforced by twenty more men from Wayne's force, Barry promised to land them "on the Pennsy[lvania] Shore" as soon as he "Effected the Business on which he is ordered."[48]

At dusk on the twenty-third, Barry's flotilla left Salem Creek and headed up the Delaware. Rowing without rest throughout the long, cold night, they reached Mantua Creek in the early morning hours– a distance of thirty-five miles.[49] There was no time for as much as a catnap. All that morning, under clear skies and carrying their hastily made torches, Barry and his men entered every creek and stream as they moved southward along the Jersey shore.[50] Complying with his orders, Barry took down the names of each farmer–all bitterly protesting their loss regardless of their politics. Barry estimated each and every haystack in quantity and worth, from "John Kelley's 100 tons at Rackoon Creek" to lesser totals from the smaller farms stretching from the riverbank to the woods. Then they were put to the torch.[51]

One plume of smoke followed another, until it looked to the British in Philadelphia as if all South Jersey was ablaze. That afternoon, as he made his way to Haddonfield, Wayne saw the smoke signals southward as evidence that Barry and his men were keeping to the plan. Then, swinging his spyglass westward toward Philadelphia, Wayne recognized that Barry's pillars of fire were having the desired effect on the British. The smoke misled the enemy into thinking Wayne was unaware of their maneuver; now they called a halt to their crossing at Burlington. With "Thick hazey w[eathe]r" coming across the river, a fuming Hamond, watching from the *Roebuck*'s quarterdeck, ordered "out the *Pembroke* (Tender) & half Galley's."[52] When Barry finally called it a day below Carney's Point across from Wilmington, his detachment had come within ten miles of Salem, their entire route south lit by fire.[53] It took hours for the British to finish their preparations for pursuit. When "the *Pembroke* with the two Galleys" and "a Great No. of Flatt Boats" departed the *Roebuck*, it was already 11 P.M.[54] Back in New Jersey, Barry set up watches, allowing his dog-tired men to get some sleep at their oars in the frosty air.

"Dark, cloudy weather" greeted Hamond the next morning as he scanned the river to see how much progress his enemy had made overnight. Barry's firebrands were already at work, heading southward past Finn's Point and back up Salem Creek. From the opposite shore, Barry peered through his spyglass and saw at least a score of flatboats heading his way, each filled with redcoats.[55] With his expert knowledge of the Delaware's idiosyncrasies and current, Barry judged that he had enough time to continue with his fiery harvest.[56]

By dusk, his sooty and sweat-stained men were exhausted. After some furious rowing they reached Alloway Creek, five miles below Salem, just as the British boats reached Finn's Point.[57] Realizing that remaining in New Jersey now meant capture, Barry looked across the river to his planned place of refuge, Reedy Island, roughly two-thirds the distance to the Delaware shore. Prompt orders were issued and obeyed. In complete darkness, Barry took his barges back into the river.

At 11 P.M., the commander of one of the British galleys, the *Cornwallis*, "Saw 6 boats" and "weighed and Gave Chace."[58] Seeing one within range he ordered the galley's huge 24-pounder to fire. Twice the gun roared and the immense cannonballs flew past the barges, soaking the Americans with freezing water. Once again, luck was with Barry, this time in the form of the sudden appearance of two mysterious ships. The *Cornwallis* tailed them until they were identified as British, giving the Americans time to row out of danger. Before dawn the barges passed Reedy Island, reaching the Delaware fishing village called Port Penn. The villagers put Barry and his men up in their cottages. For the first time in over two weeks each sailor slept under a roof.[59]

The following morning, February 26, Barry wrote to Washington:

Sir,

According to the Orders of General Wayne, I have Destroyed the forage From Mantua Creek to this Place the

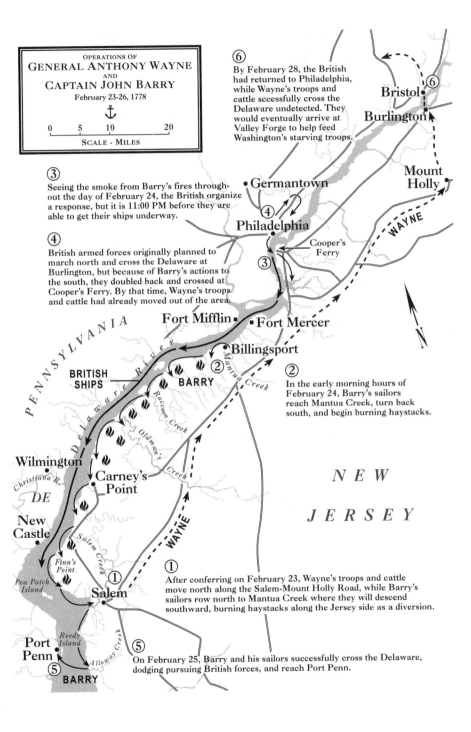

OPERATIONS OF
GENERAL ANTHONY WAYNE
AND
CAPTAIN JOHN BARRY
February 23-26, 1778
⚓
0   5   10   20
SCALE - MILES

③
Seeing the smoke from Barry's fires throughout the day of February 24, the British organize
a response, but it is 11:00 PM before they are
able to get their ships underway.

④
British armed forces originally planned to
march north and cross the Delaware at
Burlington, but because of Barry's actions to
the south, they doubled back and crossed at
Cooper's Ferry. By that time, Wayne's troops
and cattle had already moved out of the area.

⑥
By February 28, the British
had returned to Philadelphia,
while Wayne's troops and
cattle sccessfully cross the
Delaware undetected. They
would eventually arrive at
Valley Forge to help feed
Washington's starving troops.

Bristol
Burlington
Mount
Holly
• Germantown
Philadelphia
Cooper's
Ferry
WAYNE

Fort Mifflin ▪   ▪ Fort Mercer

• Billingsport
Mantua Creek

BRITISH
SHIPS
BARRY
Raccoon Creek
Oldman's Creek
Delaware River
PENNSYLVANIA

②
In the early morning hours of
February 24, Barry's sailors
reach Mantua Creek, turn back
south, and begin burning haystacks.

N E W

J E R S E Y

N

Wilmington
Christiana R.
DE
Carney's
Point
New
Castle
Salem Creek
Finn's
Point
Pea Patch
Island
WAYNE
Salem
①

①
After conferring on February 23, Wayne's troops and cattle
move north along the Salem-Mount Holly Road, while Barry's
sailors row north to Mantua Creek where they will descend
southward, burning haystacks along the Jersey side as a diversion.

Port
Penn
Reedy
Island
Alloway Creek
⑤
BARRY

⑤
On February 25, Barry and his sailors successfully cross the Delaware,
dodging pursuing British forces, and reach Port Penn.

Quantity Destroyd is about four Hundred Tons and Should have Proceeded farther had not a Number of the Enemies' Boats appeared in sight and Lining the Jerzee Shore Deprived us the Opportunity of Proceeding Further . . . have thought Proper to Detain four of Your Men to assist in getting the Boats away as some of my Men are Rendered Incapable of Proceeding Thro Fatigue. But shall again Remit by the First Order of Your Excellency having no further Occasion for the Remaining Part of the Detachment under my Command here thought proper to Discharge them.[60]

Giving the letter to their senior officer, Barry sent the men detached from Wayne's forces back to Valley Forge.[61] It would be weeks before Barry learned how successful his feint was. On the same morning that Barry began his fiery march, 2,000 redcoats crossed the Delaware, but at Cooper's Ferry, not Burlington. The southward shift in plans allowed Wayne's cattle drive to get past Haddonfield, up to Mount Holly, and cross the Delaware undetected. Wayne's success inspired other "roundups" that would feed Washington's men until springtime.[62] The redcoats, finding no sign of the rebel arsonists, returned to Philadelphia on February 28; it took some degree of courage to inform Hamond that their mission had failed.[63] Subsequent British foraging parties would reap nothing but ashes.

His haystack burning days over, Barry returned to the original purpose of his mission, posting guards daily on Reedy Island to keep a weather eye out for enemy sail. None appeared. The Delaware returned to its wintry icebound state. No ship was seen for a week. Finally, the temperatures warmed enough to break up the ice. It was "thick, foggy Weather" on Saturday, March 7, 1778, when a lookout spotted three sails to the southward, off Bombay Hook.[64] Two transports were heading upriver, navigating their way through the ice floes.[65] An armed schooner was moving along to catch up to them. On Barry's orders, the bos'n's whistle pierced the wintry stillness–the signal for his men bivouacked in the fishing village's cottages to meet him at the boats.[66]

As soon as the sailors gathered, Barry addressed them. After a week of inactivity, here was a chance to strike at the enemy. Knowing that the transports would be lightly armed, he gave quick, direct orders. Matthewman would command three of the barges, while Barry led the other four. The crews hastened pell-mell to their oars. It was obvious that the British did not suspect an attack, having enjoyed sole possession of the river for nearly four months.

The element of surprise was on Barry's side as his barges burst past their island cover, rowing furiously out to midriver to intercept the transports. His hunch was correct; they were lightly armed, each with a fourteen-man crew. Matthewman's barges closed in on the nearest vessel, the *Mermaid*, armed with two swivels. Barry's four barges headed straight toward the second ship, the *Kitty*, his men rowing furiously in unison. As they neared their quarry, they saw that she was the better armed of the two, mounting six 4-pounders.[67]

Matthewman gave orders to board the *Mermaid*. The ten-man crews of his barges scrambled over the gunwales, weapons brandished, overcoming the enemy so fast that not a shot was fired. The *Mermaid*'s commander immediately surrendered. Matthewman found his prize loaded with much-needed forage for the horses of the British dragoons.[68]

Barry's sailors, on the other hand, watched as the *Kitty*, having more time to react to the swift attack, ran two 4-pounders out of her forward gunports. Her commander, J. Mallet, gave the order to fire and the *Kitty*'s guns went off, but the inexperienced gunners hit nothing but water. Barry ordered his rowers to "trail oars," slowing their boats while keeping them straight. Thus steadied, the Americans fired their 4-pounders and hit their mark, smashing into the *Kitty*. Barry ordered his crews to resume rowing, and as the Americans continued their speedy advance, Mallet struck his colors. Barry, cutlass in hand, led his men as they clambered over the bulwark to find they, too, had captured a British ship loaded with forage.[69] The entire attack took about half an hour.[70]

But there was not one second to rest. The British schooner was coming ever closer to the transports and barges that were now stopped dead in the water. Barry had to make a snap decision—cut and run with the first two British captures in the river in months, or risk making an assault with his barges and captured transports on the surely better-armed schooner. "Curage alone," as Barry would later write (with his distinctive spelling) would not suffice; a "Grate dale of Art" would also be required to take the schooner.[71] The decision was easy: attack.

Barry's "Grate dale of Art" consisted of a hurried improvisation. Sending the British crew below and battening down the hatch over them, he ordered "Wear ship!" The *Kitty* turned through the wind. Seizing Mallet's trumpethorn, Barry bellowed orders to Matthewman for his barges to stay to the *Kitty*'s starboard, while he sent his barges to *Kitty*'s port. Once the *Kitty* turned, the makeshift squadron headed right at the schooner, with all guns trained on her.[72]

Standing by his ship's wheel, the schooner's commander assessed his situation. Several barges and one captured transport gave him plenty of targets to choose from—perhaps too many. The barges, under Barry's orders, kept enough space between themselves to be difficult to hit, while coming closer to the schooner.[73] Barry's lust for the next capture, evident in his rousing commands and the fire in his eyes, was contagious; his men were as eager for battle as he was.

To their surprise, no gunfire came from the schooner. Instead, she struck her colors. Barry immediately ordered Matthewman, whose barges were closest to the ship, to hoist a flag of truce and propose honorable terms. The British commander, a lieutenant of engineers named Daniel Moore, accepted Matthewman's offer and surrendered.[74]

The ship was the schooner *Alert*, assigned to the Engineering Department of the British Army.[75] Carrying "eight Double fortified four-pounders & twelve four Pound howitzers," and with a crew of thirty-three plus a company of artifice-mechanics aboard, Moore had enough gunfire and hands to have made a fight of it.[76] As soon as he boarded the *Alert*, Matthewman found the reason for Moore's quick surrender—three officers' wives were passengers. Moore had opted for their safety rather than risk their lives. Matthewman also recognized the ship's pilot. He was from Fisher's company, either pressed into service or turned loyalist. Hastily drawn up "Articles of

Surrender of the British Army Schooner *Alert*" guaranteed that "Every Lady in the Ship is to have their Baggage & belongings to their own Private-Property[.] The Lady's are to be Sent to Philadelphia By the first Conveyance[,] The Men to Remain Prisoners of War 'till Exchange Dilworth the Pilot to Be held as a Prisoner of War." When Barry came aboard he added his signature, thereby agreeing "to keep the above Articles sacred."[77]

Far to the south, the Americans could see more British sail, with at least two men-of-war among them. Once again, there was no time to waste. Barry ordered all craft back to Port Penn. They docked there at nightfall.[78]

Barry's stirring victory in broad daylight did not give him any excess of confidence. He knew full well that the British would come to reclaim their ships, and that their landing parties and long guns could easily turn his victory into defeat. The next day, March 8, Barry sent a courier to Smallwood requesting reinforcements, but only a few local militiamen came, accompanied by Delaware Congressman Nicholas Van Dyke. He and Barry conferred regarding the three ladies (who must have been terrified at being held captive by the American brigands) and the fate of the British prisoners. It was decided that the ships would be unloaded at Port Penn, and that Moore and another officer would be paroled to conduct the ladies to Philadelphia.[79]

Barry also wrote a letter to the Marine Committee, relaying his good news and urging them to purchase the *Alert*. In his eyes she was another *Lexington*: small, fast, and capable of inflicting substantial consternation and damage to the enemy. The missive was given to a courier, who would reach York on March 11.[80]

The unloading of cargo from the three captured ships continued into Sunday afternoon, when a sailor came up the *Alert*'s hatchway with news that her hold was full of engineering tools and a huge compilation of correspondence, mostly belonging to British Chief Engineer Montresor and Hessian General Knyphausen. While ransacking the galley, other sailors came across a well-stocked pantry, including a huge cheese "together with a Jar of Pickled Oysters."[81] Barry commandeered the cheese and oysters, but not for himself. He earmarked them for delivery to Washington.

Barry ordered the *Kitty's* 4-pounders transferred to the docks, leaving the *Alert's* guns on board; for Barry's plan to work, his best prize would need her guns. When all that could be done to defend Port Penn and his three prizes was done, Barry sent a lookout aloft to inform him of the northward progress of the British squadron heading toward the island.[82] Van Dyke and a few of the militiamen prepared to escort the British prisoners to Wilmington. After agreeing to act as Barry's agent regarding the captured ships, Van Dyke set off with his caravan of militia, prisoners, engineering tools, and military correspondence.[83] Every possible variable for the coming engagement, including the defense of the ships using the small 4-pounders, the shallow water between Port Penn and Reedy Island, and the tide tables, were factored into Barry's plan of defense—and escape.

His opponent in the coming fight was none other than Captain Sir James Wallace, the very same commander who had terrorized the Rhode Island coast at the onset of the war. Wallace now commanded the ship-of-the-line *Experiment*, fifty guns, a worthy promotion for so successful a warrior. In January the *Experiment* had entered the Delaware Bay, which Wallace found as ripe for prize taking as the waters off Rhode Island. His journal was replete with entries of captured American prizes, sent to New York for libel and condemnation.[84]

Barry's three captures were actually part of a convoy Wallace was escorting from Rhode Island that included a merchantman loaded with troops from Ireland, three smaller warships, and eight transports carrying forage. The commanders of Barry's prizes had ignored Wallace's orders "to remain with the squadron—they had passed the *Experiment* at Cape Henlopen without taking notice of him."[85] They then sailed ahead of the convoy and right into Barry's waiting arms.

Now Wallace was coming for them. At 7 A.M. on March 9, with "Light Breezes and Hazy" conditions, he ordered *Experiment's* anchor weighed, and made for Reedy Island and Port Penn. Wallace did not come alone. He brought a small squadron: the frigate *Brune*, twenty guns, and the sloops-of-war *Dispatch* and *York*. The coming fight did not stop him from his other duties; he found time to

"Punish John Julim for Mutiny" while his ship began "working up the River Delaware." As they tacked their way northward, avoiding the few remaining ice floes, the skies darkened ominously.[86]

The *Experiment*'s draft was much too large to get through the shallows at Port Penn. Wallace ordered the rest of squadron to wait for the tide to change through the morning hours. Another British sloop, the *George*, came sailing by. Sizing up the lay of Reedy Island while visualizing what his opponent's coming moves would be, Wallace had a boat lowered, and "Sent [his] Lieut. On bd. the *George*" with orders that her captain cross the northern passage above the island. By 2:00 P.M., with their guns loaded and run out, Wallace's three smaller ships "Stood into the East End of the Island." By now the winds were howling and a whipping snowstorm began.[87]

Barry was already alerted to the arrival of enemy ships. While his forces awaited his orders, he remained inside the *Alert*'s cabin, penning another letter to Washington:

> 'Tis with the Greatest Satisfaction Imaginable I inform you of Capturing two Ships & a Schooner of the Enemy. . . . [There] are a number of Engineering tools . . . by the Bearer Mr. John Chelten have Sent You a Cheese together with a Jar of Pickled Oysters which Crave Your Acceptance.[88]

Suddenly his composition was interrupted by cannon fire. Wallace "Saw a Schooner and Ship within Reedy Island," and, with the tide coming in, gave orders to begin the attack. The *Dispatch* was the first British vessel to enter the shallow passage. Once she was in range, the American gun crews on the docks let loose with their 4-pounders.[89] One of Barry's officers burst into his cabin to tell him the news. The battle was joined.

Barry's main concern was the *Alert*, "a most Excellent Vessel for our purpose" that he was "Determined to hold . . . at all events." And while his plan did not include letting Port Penn be destroyed by British guns, he had no qualms in sacrificing the transports. With enough hay remaining aboard both vessels to start a quick and devastating fire, Barry ordered the officer to torch the *Kitty*, and resumed writing Washington that "a fleet . . . appearing in Sight Obliged me to Burn One of the Ships & [I] am afraid the Other will share the same fate after Discharging her."[90] As the British gunfire increased, Barry calmly sealed his letter. Then he gave it, the cheese, and the pickled oysters to John Chelten, with orders to head for Valley Forge.

Now Barry turned his full attention to escape. As he came outside he saw that the nor'easter was peaking, its winds blowing snow and sleet on the meagerly clad Americans. The gun crews on the docks blew on their cramping fingers to warm them for a second or two. In this kind of storm cold became bitter; wind became raw.

Once on deck, Barry gave orders to get the *Alert* and the barges underway. In minutes the schooner headed north, under cover of the smoke from the burning transports. He had always foiled British captains before, but now he was up against a wily commander with years of experience in dealing with other clever American adversaries. With the *George* crossing above Reedy Island to head off the *Alert*, Wallace now employed his other nautical chess pieces. The *Brune, Dispatch*, and *York* continued to pour fire at the battery on the Port Penn docks, while abandoning plans of landing troops to attack. Instead they pursued the departing *Alert*.[91] Seeing that "The Schooner made Sail out," Wallace "fired several Guns at her over the Island."[92] The *Experiment*, a two-decker and officially a "fifth rate" ship-of-the-line, carried 18-pounders among her arsenal. These long guns easily had enough range to fire over Reedy Island.[93]

Barry's only chance at success lay in keeping ahead of his pursuers and getting past Reedy Island. Then he could head back into the Christina River near Hamburg.[94] The captains of the *Brune* and *Dispatch*, with orders to "stand in between Port Penn and Reedy Island," watched as Barry's "Schooner and several Gun Boats went out [the] Opposite End of [the] Passage." The Americans left behind on the docks "fir'd several Shots at us from a Battery, which we return'd with several Broadsides as we Past," one commander noted. Meanwhile, the rest of Barry's fleet made a hasty getaway, manning the barges and rowing east: "Some Gun boats & a galley got on the Jersey shore," Wallace later recalled. While the American "Gun Boats [barges] row'd within the Shoals" and got away, the *Brune* and *Dispatch* joined the chase of the *Alert*.[95]

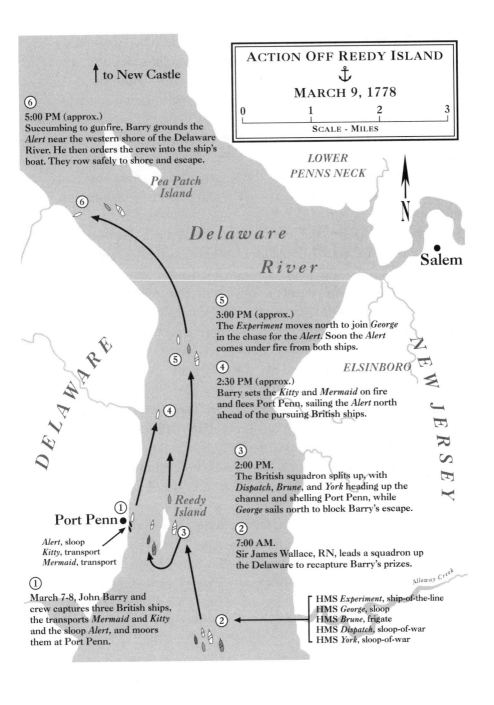

ACTION OFF REEDY ISLAND
⚓
MARCH 9, 1778

0   1   2   3

SCALE - MILES

to New Castle

⑥
5:00 PM (approx.)
Succumbing to gunfire, Barry grounds the
Alert near the western shore of the Delaware
River. He then orders the crew into the ship's
boat. They row safely to shore and escape.

*Pea Patch
Island*

LOWER
PENNS NECK

Delaware

River

•
Salem

N

⑤
3:00 PM (approx.)
The *Experiment* moves north to join *George*
in the chase for the *Alert*. Soon the *Alert*
comes under fire from both ships.

④
2:30 PM (approx.)
Barry sets the *Kitty* and *Mermaid* on fire
and flees Port Penn, sailing the *Alert* north
ahead of the pursuing British ships.

ELSINBORO

DELAWARE

③
2:00 PM.
The British squadron splits up, with
Dispatch, *Brune*, and *York* heading up the
channel and shelling Port Penn, while
George sails north to block Barry's escape.

*Reedy
Island*

Port Penn •

Alert, sloop
Kitty, transport
Mermaid, transport

②
7:00 AM.
Sir James Wallace, RN, leads a squadron up
the Delaware to recapture Barry's prizes.

①
March 7-8, John Barry and
crew captures three British ships,
the transports *Mermaid* and *Kitty*
and the sloop *Alert*, and moors
them at Port Penn.

NEW JERSEY

Alloway Creek

HMS *Experiment*, ship-of-the-line
HMS *George*, sloop
HMS *Brune*, frigate
HMS *Dispatch*, sloop-of-war
HMS *York*, sloop-of-war

Actually, Wallace *allowed* the barges to escape. The *Experiment*'s captain was not used to losing so much as a marlin-spike, and now two of his transports were burning out of control before his eyes, with the perpetrator escaping on another vessel assigned to his guardianship. If his correspondence is any reflection of his personality, Wallace was cold and cunning, and his anger equally icy. The *Experiment* now joined the pursuit of the schooner, coming around the east end of Reedy Island. Let the barges go: more than anything else, Wallace wanted to retake the *Alert*, and personally capture this rebel upstart.

Barry did what he could to increase the distance between the *Alert* and her pursuers. The small schooner was a hard target to hit, but not for lack of British effort. Cannon fire dogged her escape. The *Alert*'s crew heard the enemy's long guns fire, followed by the screaming whistle of the approaching cannonballs and the heavy splash as they hit the water around them, or the split-second rip of canvas overhead as the flying iron made perfectly round holes through the sails.[96] The *Alert*, like a fox brought to bay by British hounds, began to lose the race.

A handful of Americans lost their nerve. They "le[a]ped into the long boat and were preparing to desert." Barry left his post by the schooner's wheel. In several long strides he reached the bulwark and stopped them in mid-act, with his "presence of mind and singular address."[97] Whether they were reassured or cowed by his physical presence, the men returned to their duties.

It had been two hours since the opening cannonade. The *Alert* passed Reedy Island, but British guns–especially the *Experiment*'s bow-chasers– began smashing into the *Alert*'s stern.[98] The *Experiment* and *George*, "with all the sail they could [carry]" were drawing ever closer, and would soon be in range to fire broadsides–something that the *Alert* and her "double fortified 4-pounders" could not possibly withstand.[99]

Having "maintained an obstinate fight," Barry saw that if escape with the *Alert* was no longer an option, escape without the schooner was. After ordering the schooner's guns overboard, Barry roared, "Hard a port!" From the *Experiment*'s quarterdeck, Wallace watched "the schooner Run aGround." As water rushed into the *Alert*, Barry ordered all of his crew to man the schooner's boat. Then they rowed to shore, making their escape.[100]

"The Schooner was onshore and taken," reported Captain James Ferguson of the *Brune*, but Barry and his crew got clean away.[101] Not one American sailor perished; in fact, not a man from Barry's original barges was killed throughout these missions.[102] That night, longboats from the *Experiment* and *George* reclaimed the *Alert* "in 3-1/2 fathoms Found the Schooner full of Water." At Port Penn, one British officer reported that the *Kitty* "was Burnt," and "the *Mermaid* so effectively on Fire that it was out of the powers . . . to extinguish it." With no damage other than "some Shrouds and running Rigging cut by the Shot from their Battery," Wallace's squadron "joined the convoy that Night and Anchored below New Castle."[103]

If Wallace won an empty victory, Barry won a moral one, and news of it soon spread from Philadelphia to Valley Forge, York, and beyond. Washington's young aide, Colonel John Laurens, wrote "of Capt Barry's success with two or three armed boats on the Delaware . . . it will give me great pleasure to dwell upon the praises due to Capt Barry. Among other things taken on board...are a number of German letters and papers . . . from whence we hope to gain some useful intelligence. Gen'l Knyphausen's order of the Lion d'or is likewise taken, but will be sent unto him."[104] The citation was soon delivered to Knyphausen's unbuttered hand.

The *Pennsylvania Gazette* published a lengthy "Extract from a Gentleman Near Head Quarters" how "Captain Barry has distinguished himself exceedingly on the river." Describing the long odds taken and the bravery of Barry and his men, the "Extract" called it as "gallant an action as any during the war, and does great honor to the brave officer and his associates who planned and executed it."[105]

The Marine Committee wrote Barry on March 11, congratulating him "on the successful commencement of your expedition and hope it will be attended with Similar advantages to the Public and Glory to the gallant Commander, brave officers & men concerned in it." Having not yet heard of the *Alert*'s recapture, they also gave Barry orders to purchase her and rechristen her the *Wasp*.[106] But the finest praise came from Washington himself:

> Sir–I have received your favor of the 9th inst. I congratulate you on the Success which has crowned your Gallantry and Address in the late Attack upon the Enemie's Ships–although circumstances have prevented you from reaping the full benefit of your Conquest, yet there is ample consolation in the degree of Glory, which you have acquired–You will be pleased to accept my thanks for the good things which you were so polite as to send me, with my wishes that your suitable recompense may always attend your Bravery.[107]

Barry's success with the barges gave some in Congress hope for more of the same. "I expect every day to hear of their further Success," wrote Congressman William Ellery, a staunch naval advocate, adding that "These boats will annoy and injure the enemy more, in my opinion, than both the Seventy-Fours would if they were built, equipped and manned, at least upon the Delaware."[108]

Even though Barry had escaped back to Wilmington, his insurgency on the Delaware was short-lived. From the *Roebuck*'s cabin, Hamond ordered other British captains to keep "between Bombay Hook and Reedy Island and use your best endeavors to take or destroy any of the Rebel Armed Boats you may meet with."[109] The river was soon clogged with enemy vessels, from the frigate *Pearl* to the row-galley *Cornwallis*, patrolling the length and breadth of the Delaware (the British soon captured Wade and his men in Red Lion Creek, within eyesight of Reedy Island). Hamond was determined not to let as much as one Yankee sailor stir a finger on the river. "For the past two Days the Enemies Fleet have been passing by here, to Amount of 150 Sail," Smallwood wrote to Washington on St. Patrick's Day.[110] Barry was safe, but once again high and dry.

Back on the mainland, Barry replied to Washington's letter, enclosing "an Invoice of the Goods taken" from his prizes, regretfully notifying Washington that Montresor's valuable "Intrenching Tools . . . are Stolen by the Inhabitants together with about one-fourth Part of the Cargo taken out of the Vessels." All of Montresor's tools, along with some of his cargo, had "disappeared"–taken by the very militia charged with their delivery and safekeeping. Barry further informed Washington of the increased British traffic on the river, some "forty Sail of Vessels up Salem Creek & about thirty more on the Delaware." Now it was the redcoats' turn to raid for forage and cattle, and with "about fifteen hundred Men Landed" on both sides of the Delaware, both Barry and Smallwood saw the futility in any further actions against such overwhelming numbers.[111]

Having heard of the *Alert*'s recapture, the Marine Committee commiserated with Barry over his loss, regretting that "the Militia instead of offering you Assistance had pilfered so much of the goods." After wishing him success in future attacks, they came to the unpleasant subject of money: one-half of what remained, of course, went to Congress, as per their Resolution of October 30, 1776. They noted that, had Barry managed to keep the *Alert*, "She would have been solely the property of the Captors." As for any reward from Congress for burning the *Kitty* and *Mermaid*, alas: such bounty "was confined exactly to the fire Ships fitted at Philadelphia last fall." After telling Barry what he was not entitled to, they did send him an $800 advance, with the understanding that he would be accountable for it later.[112]

He attended the sale of his remaining captured goods on April 6, writing Washington that one "Major [Ichabod] Burnet purchased all the Knives and forks to be equally divided between Your Excellency and General Green[e]." Burnett purchased everything from "6 loafs of Sugar" (about 42 pounds) to "1 doz[e]n White Kid Gloves" and "12 lbs. best hair Powder." The sale raised $356; after Congress took its 50 percent, Barry and his men split a grand total of $178.[113]

Springlike weather arrived on the Delaware in April. Barry wrote again to his commander-in-chief, expressing his wish to "have one more sweep at" the British "before we give up." He also reported that the soldiers loaned to him by General Varnum wanted new clothes "and the[y] Grumble Very much About it . . . I fear thare Is some of them that will not stay unless the[y] can be suplyed with them." Assuring the general that Varnum's men will be "sent to join Thare Respectave Regiments," and that "we can be of use for some little time yet," Barry sent the letter along with the goods purchased for Washington and Green. Washington's reply requested that Varnum's men be returned by May 1, quickly enough in the general's view that "I cannot think it necessary or right that they should receive their Clothes until they join their Corps."[114] Having neither the inclination nor funds to purchase slops for the army, Barry instantly relieved them of their duties. Smallwood also departed for Valley Forge.

Barry, too, closed up his Delaware operation.[115] Luke Matthewman headed to Maryland to serve with Count D'Estaing and the newly arrived French Navy.[116] Barry returned to White Hill, arriving in a driving rainstorm on May 7.[117] Bordentown and White Hill were all but abandoned by American personnel. All that remained from Barry's regrettable exile there were the hulls of the *Effingham* and *Washington*, half exposed during low tide.[118] By now he had learned of the French treaty with the United States, brilliantly engineered by Franklin. In Philadelphia General Clinton, who had replaced Howe as commander of British forces, was concerned over what was surely heading his way—a French fleet and army at the very least, to fight beside Washington's Continentals.

Upon his arrival in White Hill, Barry called on Mary Peale Read, who had not yet departed to join her husband, Thomas, in Baltimore. Barry graciously accepted her offer that he stay the night. Unknown to Barry, before evacuating Philadelphia, Clinton left one last calling card for the Americans to remember him by. In concert with Admiral Howe, Clinton sent a detachment of British light infantry under Major Maitland of the Marines on an overnight trip upriver to Bordentown and White Hill to destroy any remaining boats, barges, and supplies that might be used to harrass British forces during their move north to New York. They left on "flat boats," accompanied by British row-galleys, one brig, and a schooner. The combined force was close to 800 in number.[119]

On the morning of May 8, about fifty American "light horse and their like number of militia men" made a stand of resistance against the approaching redcoats but "were instantly dispersed." As they entered White Hill, the British learned that one rebel sea captain remained in town. Informants gave them Mrs. Read's address.[120]

A manuscript handed down through the Read family for generations related what occurred next. After a servant spotted British troops marching toward the house, Mrs. Read immediately knocked on the door of the guest room. Barry greeted his hostess, "holding a razor in his hand, his face lathered over preparing for his morning shave." She quickly told him of the approaching soldiers and begged him to leave as quickly as possible. Then,

> With great tranquility he cleared his face and put his razor away. She urged instant flight, "If you don't go they will take you Prisoner!" He laughingly replied: "They won't catch me today," calmly went downstairs, mounted his horse, which was in readiness, and rode off rapidly, concealed by the outbuildings and dwelling from the British soldiers, who presently arrived, surrounded the house and demanded him.

Coming to the door, Mrs. Read now played the coquette:

> Mrs. Read said, "He is not here," but went to deliver up all keys that the search might begin, and thus delay them. After their fruitless efforts to find Capt Barry, she invited the officer to a good breakfast and sent out rum to his men. She was very graciously entertaining, so the meal was prolonged . . . the soldiers being fatigued from their night march made no further effort to pursue one already beyond their reach.[121]

Barry escaped the British but little else did. Within minutes they were in possession of White Hill, Bordentown, and Bristol. All American naval stores were burned. Any cannons found were spiked. In Bordentown, thousands of tent poles and pegs were discovered and used as kindling to burn down several patriot homes, Joseph Borden's among them (Hopkinson's home was spared; according to one story, it was used for a dinner party by the raiding officers).[122] By this time, the half-sunk *Effingham* and *Washington* were discovered, along with the *Lyon*, the *Mercury* packet, and forty others. They were "set on fire and consumed" in a fire that lasted two days.[123] Washington had ordered the frigates destroyed months earlier. Barry wouldn't, Hopkinson couldn't; the British could, and did.

Over the next two days, British fire parties burned no less than fifty-four American vessels, from the privateer *Sturdy Beggar* to the smallest row-galley. On hearing the news, Washington sent troops to drive the enemy away, "but they had compleated the Business by the time [we] reached the cross Roads," Washington wrote, getting one last lick in at the Navy Board: "Had the Commissioners of the Navy . . . scuttled and sunk the Frigates, it would have taken so much time and labour to have weighed them, that our force from all quarters could have been up to have prevented them."[124]

About his escape, and the final blow to his first frigate, Barry merely reported that the British "sent a party of men up and burnt the [*Effingham*] and the frigate *Washington*."[125] After a long day's ride he was back in Reading, reunited with Sarah. When he had left her, his career was in jeopardy and his reputation in question. He returned with his hero's mantle well-earned and intact.

In mid-June 1778, as the British army marched north, the British navy stood en masse down the Delaware, escorting three hundred merchant ships carrying 3,000 loyalist refugees. William Austin was among them.[126] The *Experiment* had already sailed, heading up the New England coast. Barry's successful escape was Wallace's first taste of defeat in the war. True, Barry had broken off the engagement, but not before burning two ships under Wallace's protection and nearly scuttling another. Even Wallace would have to agree that Barry had won this encounter.

There would be another.

CHAPTER EIGHT

THE RALEIGH

*W*ITH JOHN PAUL JONES ON A DIPLOMATIC ERRAND to France, Barry's hard-fought victories on the Delaware represented the only recent American naval successes. That spring of 1778, Barry learned about the tragic fate of a fellow captain and friend.

Nicholas Biddle sailed the frigate *Randolph* out of Philadelphia in early 1777. Over the next year he and his crew weathered storms while feasting on British shipping in the West Indies.[1] As Barry was taking his three prizes on March 7, young Biddle (he was twenty-seven) and his 32-gun frigate encountered HMS *Yarmouth*, a 64-gun ship-of-the-line, off Barbados. Rather than run, Biddle chose to fight. Severely wounded in the thigh, he ordered a chair brought to the quarterdeck so he could have his wound treated and still direct the action.[2] Without any warning there was a deafening explosion below deck–apparently a spark had ignited the ship's magazine; in that blinding flash, the *Randolph* disappeared, the remains of the ship and crew raining down on the stunned enemy sailors aboard the *Yarmouth*. Only four of the *Randolph's* crew of 315 survived.[3] Difficult as it was to build and send a frigate out against the British, the real loss was Horatio Nelson's former messmate: Biddle was irreplaceable. All of Philadelphia mourned. "Our little fleet is much diminished," the Marine Committee lamented.[4]

And much diminished it was. The *Randolph* tragedy–the largest loss of life in any naval action of the Revolution–was just one of many disasters that befell the Continental Navy over the previous year.[5] On September 19, 1777, the *Lexington* was taken by a British cutter as she was returning from France.[6] Lambert Wickes, whose bold raids on the English coast furnished some of the few pieces of bright news for the Americans, was lost at sea a few weeks later with his ship *Reprisal* off the coast of Newfoundland (in a Coleridge-like twist, only the cook survived).[7] On March 27, the *Columbus*, under Hoystead Hacker, attempted to run a British blockade of Narragansett Bay, Rhode Island, only to be discovered and pursued by British warships. Trying to avoid capture, Hacker ran the *Columbus* aground near Port Judith, where the British took possession of her. That same day another acquaintance of Barry's, Pennsylvanian John Young (number twenty-three on the captains' list), was forced to scuttle his sloop, *Independence*, on the Ocracoke sandbar in North Carolina.[8]

Three days later, James Nicholson, whose name topped that controversial captain's list, made his third attempt in nine months to get his frigate, the *Virginia*, past the British ships blockading the Chesapeake, much to the joy of the Marine Committee, already frustrated over Nicholson's year-plus delay in sailing *Virginia* into action. All was going well until the frigate got to the mouth of the bay, where her pilot ran the *Virginia* on the shoals, carrying away her rudder. While Nicholson's second-in-command, Lieutenant Joshua Barney, watched in open-mouthed surprise, Nicholson and a contingent of oarsmen abandoned ship via the *Virginia*'s barge. Barney wanted to cut the *Virginia*'s anchor cables, get her adrift and near Cape Henry, where she could be burned and kept out of British hands, but the other officers refused to obey him. Some sailors broke into the rum, getting drunk just as boarding parties from pursuing British ships captured *Virginia*. They took Barney and the crew prisoners without firing a shot.[9] It was April Fool's Day.

The next morning Barney witnessed more of Nicholson's colossal effrontery. Under a flag of truce, the navy's top captain had himself rowed to the British ship holding Barney and the other Americans. Once aboard, he reported that he had left his belongings on the *Virginia* due to his hurried departure. While Barney openly cursed his commanding office for his desertion, the British captain returned Nicholson's items to him. Most egregious of all was Nicholson's version of his surrender: he had abandoned ship "with such of my crew as was inclined to run the risque of getting on shore." The Marine Committee not only exonerated him but gave him another command.[10]

Then there was the *Raleigh*. A 32-gun frigate, she was another of the original thirteen ordered by Congress in 1775, and built in Portsmouth, New Hampshire, by John Langdon. Abandoning the original plans, Langdon redesigned the ship, building one of the most beautiful frigates ever seen. Launched on May 21, 1776–just sixty days from the start of construction–she was described in the *New Hampshire Gazette* as "one of the compleatest ships ever built in America." Langdon's vessel was 131 feet 5 inches in "length between the perpendiculars," displaced 697 tons, and mounted a figurehead of Sir Walter himself, bearded and vigilant. The cabin windows were handsomely decorated with carved vines. She had the rounded bow of her British counterparts, providing more living space in the fo'c'sle. A small lateen sail–similar to that found on a modern Sunfish–was set on the ensign staff at the stern, past the spanker, to steady her in strong winds.[11]

While construction raced along, rigging her proceeded at a snail's pace, and Langdon was forced to beg for rope and canvas that finally arrived a year later. Command of the *Raleigh* went to Thomas Thompson of New Hampshire, who ranked just ahead of Barry on the captains' list.[12] In August he put to sea for France accompanied by Elisha Hinman, commanding Barry's old ship *Alfred/Black Prince*.[13] The *Raleigh*'s 36 gunports (four more than originally planned) hid only a half a dozen guns; Thompson was to pick up the rest of his ordnance in France. Once under way, the frigate was breathtaking to behold. Her wales–the top edges of her sides, from fo'c'sle to quarterdeck–were low for a frigate, giving her an even sleeker look under sail. Despite the less-than-full complement of guns, their cruise to France brought the Americans a couple of prizes.

On the passage homeward the *Raleigh* constantly outsailed the slower *Alfred*. When the latter was overtaken by two smaller British ships, Thompson determined to run interference; but when he realized they had captured the old Continental flagship and were now heading for him, Thompson emptied his water barrels and threw everything overboard, including most of his French-made guns, leaving the British and Hinman in his wake. In a rare occurrence for that day, and unfortunately for Thompson, news that he abandoned the *Alfred* reached Boston before he did. An angry public demanded that he be removed from his post, if not sent to the gallows. When word reached the Marine Committee in May, they recommended to the Navy Board of the Eastern Department in Boston that they "forthwith suspend Captain Thompson from Command . . . until a full and fair enquiry can be made into his Conduct." However, "In the mean time it is not fit that the public should be deprived of the use of the *Raleigh* . . . and that the *Raleigh* be got ready Sea with all possible expedition. By the time this will happen the Committee will appoint a Captain to take Command of her."[14]

For the Marine Committee there was only one choice. Believing that command of the *Raleigh* was a fitting reward for Barry's recent deeds, they directed John Brown to give his friend the good news: "The Marine Committee having appointed You to the Command of the Frigate *Raleigh* now in the Port of Boston you will therefore instantly on receipt of this repair hither to receive the Instructions of the Committee."[15]

In Reading, Sarah Barry's joy at being reunited with her husband was muted by the ever-mounting emotional and financial toll the Revolution was taking on her politically divided family. As a sister of one of Philadelphia's most notorious turncoats (and sister-in-law of another), Sarah faced mounting problems. The war effectively put an end to her genteel lifestyle; she was now a surrogate mother for her half-sister's eight children. The property and goods of Reynold Keen's estate were being seized and auctioned off by zealous state officials in an effort to make examples of traitors and find revenue for a government that deemed itself as much in need of funds as a brood of motherless children. When Colonel Henry Haller, commander of the troops near Reading, ordered Keen's possessions sold, Sarah requested permission to retain or at least purchase some of Keen's furnishings and take them with the children back to Philadelphia. Forced to decide between his orders to commandeer an accused traitor's property and the pleas of the woman responsible for the care of the accused's children, Haller passed the buck to President Wharton and the Supreme Executive Council of Pennsylvania, begging "leave to Trouble the Honourable . . . Council" to make the decision for him. While Keen had indeed "gone over to the enimy," Haller did not want the responsibility of ruling on Sarah's request that "Kitchen furniture & Bedding for the children" be left for them, as well as "a Negro Girl" owned by the family.[16]

Wharton proved up to the task. As it was "Mr. Keen's business to take care of his family," Wharton suggested that Sarah or another relative "go into the city and inform Mr. Keen of the situation to which his conduct has reduced his helpless children." If Sarah elected to take the Keen children back to Philadelphia she could take some "decent cloathing" for her charges, but all furniture was to be left behind. Finally, Wharton ruled that "The Negro Girl cannot be permitted to be sent into the city, if she should be the property of Mr. Keen's debt."[17] As part of Keen's confiscated property, she could be sold by the state for a handsome profit.

Barry's furlough lasted less than two weeks. Once again, he packed his saddlebags, leaving Sarah alone to deal with her nephews, nieces, and traitorous relations. First he rode to York, still the refuge of Congress, to meet with Morris and the rest of the Marine Committee. He was also introduced to the French captain Pierre Landais, who had recently crossed the Atlantic with his ship's hold full of ammunition for the Continental Army and Navy.[18] Barry departed York on June 2, bearing a lengthy letter from the committee to the Eastern Navy Board that reviewed appointments, funding, and approval for construction in Portsmouth of a ship-of-the-line. The board was directed to get "Out the Vessels of war agreeably [and to] repair the loss and honor of our Navy." The letter ended with an introduction of the bearer: "This will be handed you by Captain John Barry whom we have appointed to command the Frigate *Raleigh*–He is a brave active Officer and we doubt not you will find him very attentive to his duty."[19]

Barry was just leaving Congress when Sam Adams pressed him to wait for a letter. As Adams painstakingly composed a message to James Warren, Barry's patience began wearing thin. While Adams informed his old friend that "The French Gentleman [Landais] ... *fed with promises* at Boston ... is highly esteemed by this Committee," and that the new 36-gun frigate being built in Salisbury, Massachusetts, originally to be christened *Hancock*, was instead to be named *Alliance* in honor of France's support of the American Cause and then placed under Landais's command, Barry's boots trod the hall floorboards a bit louder. Adams kept at his letter, mentioning that "Captain Barry ... is to take command of the *Raughly*," and expressing concern over the lack of news regarding his cousin John's earlier voyage to France, when Barry's footsteps became thunderous. At last, Adams got the hint: "The Bearer is in Haste. Adieu," he concluded.[20]

"The Bearer" reached Boston on June 24, handing over his orders and dispatches to Warren and John Deshon of the Eastern Navy Board.[21] Though Barry's credentials were in order and his exploits well-known to Bostonians, Warren and Deshon were reluctant to turn command over to an out-of-towner, especially while the *Raleigh*'s cabin was hosting one court-martial after another, forcing Barry to move into a lieutenant's quarters. Nor was Warren about to "agreeably" (i.e., immediately) get the *Raleigh* out to sea. Parochialism, a bothersome trait since colonial days, was especially rampant in New England, and Warren was consumed with it: "every Body acquainted with Seamen must know they will not Engage in a Ship till they know the Captain," he groused in his reply to Adams's letter. Regardless, the bottom line for Warren was obvious. The *Raleigh* "has no Men."[22]

Throughout June the trials continued in the *Raleigh*'s cabin. John Manley was acquitted for the loss of the first *Hancock*, followed by Hector McNeill's chance to defend accusations of dereliction of duty aboard the same ship. Next on the docket was Thompson, tried and found guilty in his own cabin. Then it was Hoystead Hacker's turn for running *Columbus* aground (he was exonerated). To Barry, his orders to get the *Raleigh* out to sea and restore some pride to the Navy with victories were being held up by the Navy's interminable review of her recent disasters.[23]

By now Boston harbor was host to five Continental vessels, whose captains included John Nicholson's brother Samuel, commanding the other frigate in port, the *Deane*. Barry was pleasantly surprised to find John Green in town, an old friend from the Willing & Morris days, captain of the *Queen of France*.[24] With so many Continental ships in port, Barry pressed Warren and Deshon to transfer the military proceedings to another vessel. He was supported by the Marine Committee, who never failed to mention in their correspondence their "Strong urgings" that the *Raleigh* "will shortly be manned."[25] Barry's lobbying efforts for a change of venue for the courts coincided with welcome news from New Jersey, where Washington's troops—forged with a steely resolve by a long winter of Baron Von Steuben's incessant drilling—attacked Clinton's rear guard and held the field at Monmouth Court House.

"We celebrated the 4th of July here yesterday with great parade & festivity," Warren wrote to Adams, now back in Philadelphia with the rest of Congress. After dwelling on the difficulties in getting the ships out to sea, Warren acknowledged he was getting to know Barry better: "Capt. Barry's Character scores high [and] his conduct is agreeable. I think therefore we should have but little difficulty in Manning his Ship tho' he is A Stranger."[26]

Warren finally approved relocation of the military courts, allowing the "Stranger" to move into the captain's cabin on July 5.[27] The *Raleigh* still had "no Men," no cannon, and no money. Indeed, the figurehead of Sir Walter Raleigh, sword in hand, was better armed than the ship. The frigate's bottom was still foul from Thompson's last voyage.[28] All Barry had was a promise from the Marine Committee via the Eastern Navy Board that "We shall without delay forward you as large A Sum of Money as can now be spared" so that the *Raleigh* could be refitted, remanned, and rearmed. They also informed their New England colleagues that America's new allies had finally arrived; a "Squadron consisting of 12 ships of the Line and four frigates under the command of Count D'Estaing" was at the mouth of the Delaware Bay. The committee hoped this piece of news would inspire Continental sailors to "step forth with alacrity and exert themselves in supporting our friends who have come so far to assist us to vanquish an enemy too long triumphant upon the Sea."[29]

With the trials moved elsewhere, Barry finally had the opportunity to thoroughly inspect his stores. He found them lacking, thanks to a woeful absence of discipline. "The ship had been Robb'd of a great many things," Barry reported to Morris, noting that the *Raleigh*'s officers could come and go from the ship "when they please" and were not held accountable for anything missing. To Barry, there was "no knowing where the evil will end or what things is on Board a Ship at any time." Once he took command, laxity aboard the *Raleigh* vanished. Even the dubious Warren recognized Barry's management skills: "You have Appointed a Good one," he reported to Adams.[30]

Lack of funds still prevented Barry from obtaining new ordnance and other supplies; the Navy Board could not even afford to have the *Raleigh*'s hull scraped and cleaned. "I am in Pain about the Ship in your Harbor," Sam Adams commiserated. Through his efforts, Congress sent $524,000 to Boston for refitting the Continental ships. Follow-up letters dispensed with any subtlety in prodding the Navy Board into action: "We have only to repeat our great desire to have the Continental Vessels at Sea, which no doubt you are using your endeavors to accomplish," one dispatch concluded. "We hope the *Warren* has gone to Sea and that the *Raleigh* will shortly follow her."[31]

But Warren's prediction that Barry would have difficulties enlisting a crew proved correct. The first rendezvous on the *Raleigh*'s behalf netted him less than one hundred men, most of whom were old hands from Thompson's days. A brainstorming session among Barry, Warren, and Deshon resulted in new ideas but nary a solution; one proposal to "borrow" French sailors from D'Estaing's fleet was floated, but the Marine Committee quashed that idea. A suggestion to enter into an exchange of prisoners was also rejected. The British, needing no sailors themselves, would simply drag out any negotiations—if they did not dismiss the idea altogether.[32]

Next, Barry and the Navy Board looked to the crew of the idle frigate *Trumbull*. Here Barry found not only some experienced tars but also the opportunity to replace the incompetent officers he had inherited from Thompson, keeping only George J. Osborne, Captain of the Marines. The fresh faces included a new second-in-command, first lieutenant David Phipps, and midshipmen Matthew Clarkson, who had ventured down the Delaware in Barry's barges; David Porter, the first in a family line of American Naval heroes; and young Jesse Jeacocks.

Barry still lacked marines. He knew it would be futile to sail without their presence on the fighting tops in battle; they were also indispensable in enforcing his authority among the crew. Barry's desperate situation called for a desperate solution. When the final muster rolls were complete, most of the *Raleigh*'s marines were British infantrymen taken prisoner at Saratoga.[33] Barry would not have proof of their newfound loyalty to the United States until he found a British ship to fight, and then see at whom they aimed their muskets.

By mid-August the frigate *Warren* and brigantine *Resistance* had departed Boston just as the *Alliance* entered Nantasket Road to procure the rest of her assigned cargo before sailing to France. The *Raleigh* still lay anchored in the harbor.[34] To Barry's frustration, many of her new guns were defective, and burst while being proven. But even the arrival of sound ordnance was not enough to get him out of Boston. Now it was the French fleet's turn to delay him.

D'Estaing's flotilla had come up the coast to New York, but was unable to cross the bar, the local pilots sure that the drafts of the large French ships would never clear. Sailing further north toward Newport, d'Estaing encountered "Black Dick" Howe's fleet. Try as both sides might, a full battle never took place: a huge storm sent the English and French ships in opposite directions, with d'Estaing's flagship losing her rudder. He slowly made his way into Boston harbor.[35] The sight of weatherbeaten French ships—Barry described them "in a most shattered condition"—was hardly the first impression long-suffering Bostonians expected from their new allies.[36]

Nevertheless, the harbor batteries fired a salute, followed by the pomp of a reception and dinner at Governor John Hancock's Beacon Hill mansion, with Barry in attendance.[37]

Over two months had passed since Barry's arrival in Boston. Now he fretted over a possible change in his orders, placing him under d'Estaing's command, which the Marine Committee was actually considering. "In my opinion [d'Estaing] will not sail from here for six weeks," Barry wrote to Morris. "I hope I shall not be obliged to wait till they are ready to Sail," he continued, "but . . . I am determined to Obey my Orders, let the consequence be what they will."[38] By late August his orders came: "Immediately Upon receipt of these our orders you will commence on a Cruize in Company with the Continental Brigt. *Resistance* Captain Bourke [Burke], before Cape Henlopen and Occracock on the Coast of North Carolina, with a view to take certain armed Vessels fitted out by the Goodriches, or any other of the enemies Vessels that may be infesting that Coast."[39]

Similar orders to sail under Barry's command were sent to Burke.[40] A follow-up letter from the committee was sent to Hampton Roads, Virginia, where Barry was to "call in at Hampton once a week . . . other Vessels [will be] ready for your convoy [and] you are to proceed with them as we shall direct."[41] The committee also wrote the Navy Board, adding the *Warren* and *Deane* to Barry's mission–unaware that these two ships and the *Resistance* had already sailed.[42] The *Raleigh* would be a squadron of one. These orders gave him a chance to return to the familiar waters of his glory days commanding the *Lexington*; he could do much more damage to Tory and British ships with the *Raleigh* than he did with that little brigantine. His mood now swung from worry about joining the French to ebullience over his anticipated venture. When the last shipment of ordnance rumbled down Boston's cobblestone streets to the docks along the Charles River, he gladly paid for "expenses to procure other guns" from his own pocket, buying enough "rum for the Waggoners" to make everyone happy.[43]

With a full crew, sound guns, and ample supplies, Barry put the finishing touches on his departure, writing letters to the Marine Committee and to Sarah. Her latest letter updated him on the dolorous state of Austin family affairs, including Reynold Keen's surrender to Pennsylvania authorities. Barry penned one final letter to Morris, ending it with a request for assistance regarding Sarah's plight:

> As I look on you to be my only and best Friend I have one favour to request of you . . . I have a Brother in Law, whom I believe you are acquainted with, his name is Re[y]nold Keen he has forfeited his Estate by the Laws of Pennsylvania; but I should suppose those Laws were made for People that have taken an active part against us, I should hope he never did, if he had I would not say one word in his favour . . . he lost the best of Wives, she left behind her eight small Children, all he had in the World [was] within the Enemy's lines, at that time very gloomy prospects on our side, and now he submits himself to the Mercy of his Country. If you think it consistant with your Heart to render him any service to recover his Estate, the Obligation will be forever acknowledged.[44]

On or about September 18, Barry departed Boston with the tide and stood down Nantasket Road, where the *Raleigh* languished in doldrums for another week. While he was in the roadstead, word reached Boston that "Lord Howe with a powerful Squadron is hovering between Rhode Island and Boston Bay."[45] In his letter to Morris, Barry mentioned "Twenty three Sail of Large Ships appear'd off this Harbour . . . but we have seen nothing of them since." Like the rest of Boston, Barry believed "they are gone off."[46]

Indeed, ships from Howe's fleet were patrolling the waters along that very area expecting, as always, to pick up American prizes, be they merchants or fighting sail. Among these marauders was the *Experiment.*

Few British officers on land or sea were as successful in the war as Captain Sir James Wallace, and few were more detested by the Americans: among the king's forces, only Walter Butler and Banastre Tarleton rivaled him in arousing such strong fear and loathing during the war. Born in England in 1731, Wallace entered the Royal Navy as a midshipman while in his teens, won his lieutenancy in 1755, and received his first command seven years later. By 1774, he was captain of the frigate *Rose*, twenty guns.[47] Lexington and Concord were months away when, under Admiralty orders, he sailed into Newport, Rhode Island, where his seizure of merchantmen and destruction of colonial property made him the archvillain of the British Empire in the eyes of New England colonists. His edicts were haughty and threatening, and he used the *Rose*'s guns to back them up.

He was especially determined to avenge the *Gaspee* affair, which occurred two years before his arrival. The *Gaspee*, a British schooner in pursuit of smugglers up Narragansett Bay, ran aground on the night of June 10, 1772. Seeing this, the smugglers boarded the crippled schooner, captured her crew after a short fight, and burned her. Despite a Crown offer of a £1,000 reward for information, not one name was disclosed.[48] Long before Wallace's arrival it was an open secret in Newport that the leader of the raiding party was Abraham Whipple. Wallace wrote him of his intentions: "You Abraham Whipple . . . burned His Majesty's vessel, the *Gaspee* and I will hang you at the yard arm." Whipple's reply was defiantly humorous: "Sir, Always catch a man before you hang him."[49]

Wallace began terrorizing Rhode Island, capturing every vessel he could get his hands on, burning coastal villages along the way. Evidence of the great animosity he inspired is found in a rambling, vituperative, open letter from one "J. P-ke" that was published in newspapers throughout the colonies. It began with the salutation "Though I have not the misfortune of personally knowing you" and described Wallace as a "pirate" and "assassin" with a "love of rapine."[50] Loyalist publications, in contrast, referred to Wallace as "ever vigilant and brave," and King George agreed, knighting Wallace while the Admiralty concurred, gaving him command of the ship-of-the-line *Experiment* in 1777.[51] Now, with other ships from Howe's fleet, he lurked outside the Massachusetts capes.[52]

At dawn on September 25, 1778, Barry gave orders to weigh anchor and the *Raleigh* departed Nantasket Road, accompanied by a brigantine and a sloop. Within two hours, Barry dropped off his pilot, "got the topgallant yards up," and "bore away E. b[y] S., the wind N.W." Barry then "set topgallants and steering sails." Canvas captured wind, and the frigate sped out to the open sea.[53]

The *Raleigh* made a good first impression on her new captain, cruising effortlessly to Cape Cod. "Only the best timber" had been used to build her, and her fine design allowed her to skim through the water.[54] She was "ten or twelve Leagues" north of Cape Cod when "The Man at the Mast head call'd out two Sail bearing about S.E." Barry raised his spyglass while he "ordered the steering and small sails to be ready to haul our wind should they be Ships of Force." Through his glass he saw that they were nothing more than "Fishing Schooners by their appearance," but with two ships under his protection, and in unfamiliar waters, Barry was being cautious–for now.[55]

Minutes later the cry "Sail Ho!" came down from the masthead again, and Barry asked, "Where Away?" The lookout shouted back: "two Sail bearing about S.E. by South, distance 8 or 10 Leagues." Peering again through his spyglass, it soon became evident to Barry that these were not fishing schooners; "one standing to the Northward, the other to the Southward, by their largeness and behavior I took them to be British Cruisers." He hailed the brigantine's captain, giving him orders to follow the *Raleigh* as close as he could, but the brigantine and sloop were soon lagging far behind. Barry resorted to signaling orders to his consorts, while heading *Raleigh* "by the wind to the Northward in hopes to get clear of [the cruisers]." No sooner had he changed course when "The Ship that was standing to the Southward . . . tacked and gave us Chase along with the other." Both British ships added sail to increase their speed, but the *Raleigh* showed them her heels; soon Barry put "a great distance to waindward" between his frigate and the enemy vessels.[56] All day long he raced northward in an effort to avoid a fight he neither sought nor wanted.

In outdistancing his pursuers Barry also lost sight of the other two American ships. "Night coming on the wind grew light and variable," Barry noted, "I embraced every opportunity to get in with the Land

and out of sight of the aforesaid ships." The British ships "kept their course after us," Barry recounted; however, "we closed upon a wind to the Northward, [and] at night we lost sight of them."[57] Just before the *Raleigh* went over the horizon at 9 P.M. John Ford, captain of the frigate HMS *Unicorn*, twenty-two guns, ordered his bow-chasers run out and "Fir'd several Shot" at the American ship." That night he entered the day's events in his log: "gave Chace to 2 Sail . . . at 9 they ran a Shore on Cape Cod." He also identified his partner in the pursuit: the *Experiment*.[58]

The next day, September 26, began with great sailing weather: a clear sky with fresh breezes. Through his spyglass Barry discovered what had become of his nautical charges: "saw the Aforesaid Ships, and a Brig: and Schooner bearing about SSW." Ascertaining that the brig was the one "which sail'd in [our] comp'y and was very near the first of the Night," Barry watched the schooner approach the two large cruisers: "The Schooner spoke one of the Ships, which partly convinced me the Brig had been taken in the Night and that the Schooner was Tender to one of the Ships"; the schooner, the *True Blue*, was actually tender of another warship, the *Rainbow*.[59] What Barry could not have known was that in capturing the brigantine Wallace learned what frigate he was pursuing and who her captain was. Barry's very name was music to Wallace's ears. Reports from the Philadelphia press and loyalist informants had informed Wallace as to who had bested him on the Delaware. Now Barry's appearance on the horizon gave Wallace the opportunity to even the score.

Only a few minutes passed when the *Raleigh* "heard several guns fired and Supposed them Signals to one of the Ships they being at that time a great distance a stern." Barry ordered the decks cleared for action and clapped on every yard of canvas. The "Chace" was on. Not knowing the lay of the shoreline, he conferred with his helmsman and Lieutenant Phipps, who suggested making for the safety of Portsmouth.[60] Barry agreed, and "continued our course for the land." The *Raleigh*'s swiftness testified to the efficiency of Barry's overhaul and refitting; she was soon running at 11 knots. Her speed proved too great for the British men-of-war. The *Unicorn*, smaller and lighter, was the better sailor of the two, outdistancing the *Experiment* but not gaining on the American frigate. By late afternoon Barry "lost sight of the said Vessels."[61]

In Barry's mind, the danger had passed: "thinking they had quitted chasing of us, as I could not perceive they gained anything the whole time, ordered the Ship to be kept away under a moderate Sail for fear of falling in with them in the Night and putting us in confusion." After heading east by northeast "by the Compass" at a speed of up to 6 knots, Barry ordered a change of direction at midnight to east by southeast. Believing that he had eluded the British, he decided that it was unnecessary to take refuge in Portsmouth.[62]

One wonders what would have happened, as the *Raleigh* slipped over the horizon, if another captain commanded the *Experiment*. Barry's past experiences against Hamond, Graeme, and Hudson may have led him to believe that "out of sight, out of mind" was the norm for a British captain. Not so with Wallace. It had not been enough that he had retaken the *Alert* and forced Barry to burn the *Mermaid* and the *Kitty*. The *Raleigh*'s captain did not know who was pursuing him, but Wallace knew who *he* was pursuing, and was not about to give up so easily. As he had done at Reedy Island, Wallace put himself in Barry's shoes and on Barry's quarterdeck—and plotted his course accordingly.

A few hours before daybreak on Sunday, September 27, Barry ordered "all Sails to be handed 'till Sun Rise." The *Raleigh* was dead still in the water at dawn. From the quarterdeck Barry scanned the horizon with his spyglass. With "nothing in sight," he gave fresh orders. "We made all the sail we could and steered S.E.b.E in order to keep clear of Cape Sable," a course Barry would only have kept under the belief that he was no longer being pursued.[63] North Carolina and Goodrich's fleet beckoned; the *Raleigh* resumed her southerly course.

At 9:30 A.M., the cry "Sail Ho!" rang down from the masthead. Once more Barry asked, "Where Away? How many?" Two sail, the masthead's man replied, off the port bow and "bearing about S.S.W." The American and British ships, like two lines seeking an intersecting point, were on a collision course. The enemy was coming so fast that no spyglass was required for identification: "We soon saw them from the quarterdeck," Barry noted, "and found they were [the] Ships standing for us."[64] The canny Wallace now also had the weather gauge; the wind was on his side in the race, not Barry's. Wallace controlled the chase.

With a strong west wind Barry "immediately Wore Ship and haul'd the wind to the N.N.W. with all the sails the ship could bear."[65] Every inch of canvas was already set, but the *Raleigh* carried no royal yards—there was no spar to support a sail higher than the topgallant.[66] She did carry studding sails ("stun s'ls") on her fore and main masts—extra sails set outside the spars. They were set as fast as the hands could perform the task.[67] The masts gave a perceptible groan with the added pressure of more canvas and the sudden change of course.

For the next four and a half hours, Barry kept the *Raleigh* as far from the enemy as possible. "At 2 P.M. or thereabouts we saw the Land a head"–the southern coast of Maine. "We still continued our Course and the two Ships in full Chace, one of them which appeared the smallest came up with us very fast [while] the other kept her distance," Barry later reported. Ford had the *Unicorn* fairly sprinting ahead of the *Experiment*, which maintained her original speed. The *Raleigh* was again making 11 knots, but the wind began to lessen just as the land Barry sighted could be seen more clearly as islands and not a singular shoreline.[68]

The closest Barry had ever been to the coast of Maine was aboard the *Industry* five years earlier. With no knowledge of the land he viewed through his spyglass, he "asked both Officers and Men if they knew anything" about the shoreline. For one brief moment, their answers stunned him: "To my great Grief I found there was not one on Board who was acquainted with it." Some of the crew told Barry "if we were 15 or 20 Leagues further to the westward they could carry [the *Raleigh*] into a good Harbour," but it soon became obvious that no one had a clue where they actually were. "As soon as I got close in with the Land, which proved to be desolate Islands 12 Leagues from the Main [land] and not a tree on them," he later recalled, and with "the smallest Ship some distance a Stern and on our Weather Quarter, I thought it most prudent to Tack to the

Southward in hopes to get to the Westward and make a Harbour before the ships could come up."[69] No sooner had the idea come to mind than it was being ordered and carried out–but Barry was running out of options.

Two hours later he ran out of time as well. "At 4 PM Tacked and before 5 the smallest Ship crossed us within Gun shott," he recounted. Since her spurt past the *Experiment*, Barry had been studying the *Unicorn*: how she sailed, how many guns she carried, and whether the *Raleigh* could take her–or at the very least send her running. He decided to fight: "I found we were a Match for her and ordered the Continental Colours to be hoisted and gave her a Gun"–fired to leeward, the time-honored invitation to engage. It was about 5:45 P.M.; the autumn sun was setting. Barry's plan for survival now crystallized: beat the smaller ship back, then run westward in the darkness and escape. His two-step plan was quite a balancing act. It required engaging the *Unicorn* while maintaining a safe distance from the *Experiment*.[70] He still did not want this fight; he simply had no choice.

Ford accepted the challenge, and the *Unicorn* "threw up St. George's Ensign and gave us a Broadside," Barry wrote, "which we returned." At first, the firing from both ships "did little or no damage on either side." Unexpectedly, "A fresh Breeze" suddenly snapped at the canvas and Barry gave orders that the mainsail be "haul'd up to right the ship" and sail her flat, making best use of his guns.[71] The *Raleigh* and *Unicorn* were about a quarter of a mile apart when, without warning, the *Unicorn* came under the lee quarter. Now she was between the *Raleigh* and her westward flight. Another broadside was let loose from the *Unicorn*.[72]

Whether from this barrage of fire or the strain of sail–Barry referred to it as "some unforeseen accident"–there came a loud crack from aloft. Barry looked up and saw the foretopmast snap, and cried out a warning to the starboard gun crews as a tangle of wood, canvas, and rope hurtled toward the deck, taking with it the "Main top gallant Mast[,] Jebb [jib], and fore stay sail." The debris crashed onto four of the *Raleigh*'s starboard guns and crew, the canvas draping over the *Raleigh*'s hull, acting as a drag on her speed and crippling her ability to defend herself. Ford wasted no time in firing another salvo into the injured *Raleigh*, adding more dead and wounded bodies among the fallen wreckage (Wallace, as a witness to the fighting, erroneously entered in *Experiment*'s log that the mast was down on the first broadside).[73]

With not so much as a second available to curse his bad luck, Barry immediately ordered "the Wreck to be cut away," but for now the *Unicorn* poured fire into the American frigate without fear; as long as the wreckage hung over these starboard guns the *Raleigh* could neither sail freely nor fire back. The deadly cannonade prevented the Americans of "getting clear of the Masts and Sails then alongside as soon as I could have wished."[74] All Barry could do was maintain his cool, commanding presence despite this sudden disaster. In doing so he gave courage and heart to his crew—some of whom had served under Thompson and could recall that captain's panicky retreat months earlier.[75] But inside, Barry knew that any chance for escape was slipping away.

Grim as the situation was, he still sought a solution that would keep any chance of flight alive, just as the *Unicorn* tacked to port, bringing her up for another broadside.[76] The *Raleigh*, in her present condition, could not outfight the *Unicorn*. Barry also saw the *Experiment* slowly coming closer as well. Her 18-pounders could easily sink the crippled *Raleigh* and massacre his crew. No longer able to outsail his opponents, Barry was determined to at least outfight them, "Being disabled so much I thought it impossible to get clear with my Ship."[77] Just then, Ford gave his gunners the order to fire into the *Raleigh*'s starboard, just as the fo'c'sle hands were jettisoning the wreckage from the previous British broadside. The deadliest broadside yet turned the *Raleigh*'s deck into a slaughterhouse.[78]

Barry's choices now dwindled to two: board the *Unicorn*, or strike his colors. He "determined to Board the Enemy if possible." Desperate as this gamble was, if Barry could "take her before the [*Experiment*] could come up," he could still turn the tables on the British. He "ordered the helm aweather," putting the *Raleigh* to windward and sending her right at the *Unicorn*.[79] This would let the *Raleigh*'s crew board to the windward side, with the smoke of battle at their backs, blowing into the eyes of the *Unicorn*'s men.

The darkness now fallen over the scene only heightened the sense of peril aboard the *Raleigh*. Boarding parties were assembled and given both orders and hand-to-hand weapons: pistols, cutlasses, and pikes. Grappling hooks were distributed to the strongest of the crewmen who could swing these heavy iron hooks over their heads and throw them in unison into the *Unicorn*'s bulwarks, then pulled by all hands to bring the *Unicorn* right alongside the *Raleigh*. Those guns still working on the *Raleigh*'s starboard were reloaded with grape and canister. Barry's marines–the former British prisoners–remained at their posts in the fighting tops, with orders to sweep the *Unicorn*'s deck with musket fire.[80] Cutlass in hand, Barry stood on the quarterdeck, ready to lead the boarders himself. Now it would be the *Raleigh*'s turn to have the advantage; her broadside of grapeshot, combined with the marksmanship of her marines, would decimate the enemy.[81] By now the *Raleigh* was right on top of the *Unicorn*.[82]

From her fighting tops, the *Unicorn*'s marines returned fire while Ford parried Barry's planned thrust. Seeing his opponent's intention to board his ship, Ford abruptly broke off the engagement. Before a single grappling hook was thrown, the *Unicorn* shot ahead and tacked to windward, taking with her Barry's last chance to win the engagement outright.[83]

But if the battle could not be won, it could be prolonged. For the next two hours the *Raleigh* and *Unicorn* peppered each other, while the *Experiment* sailed closer and closer toward the action. By this time Barry had lost scores of men and yet, while Ford had fewer casualties thus far, the *Raleigh*'s gunners were proving their mettle. Both the *Unicorn*'s "Main and Mizen Masts [were] dangerously wounded," her "Stays and Running Rigging much damag'd [and] the Ship making a good deal of Water."[84] As Ford sheared away from the *Raleigh*'s boarding parties, Barry saw that the *Unicorn* was "much shattered, and I thought water logg'd."[85] With his ship in danger of being dismasted, and walls of green water rushing into the jagged holes perforating the *Unicorn*'s hull–courtesy of the *Raleigh*'s broadsides–Ford needed Wallace to bring the *Experiment* up with all possible speed. He fired his signal lights.

From the *Raleigh*'s quarterdeck, Barry saw "the signals of distress" rise into the cool September night air. He had beaten back the

Unicorn, but the hours it took to do so and the price he paid in damage to his own ship made the second part of his plan–escape–all but impossible. As for Ford, he now waited for Wallace to come up and finish the job.[86]

It was midnight. Aboard the *Raleigh*, Barry had a brief, intense council with Phipps and his other officers. He "thought it most prudent to wear The Ship and Run her on Shore on any place so that She or the People might not fall into the Enemy's hands."[87] He sent his top-men aloft to cut down the rag of a main topsail and ordered "another bent," while sending his ship toward several small islands–indistinct forms lying ahead in the darkness, just outside Penobscot Bay.[88] At that exact instant, the *Experiment* arrived on the scene of the battle, her guns run out, ready to resume what was already seven hours of nocturnal carnage. Barry called for the top-men to abandon their task: "I thought it impossible to get clear at any rate and ordered the Men to lett it Stand."[89] With agility and speed they descended to the deck, clambering down the shot-up ratlines and frayed rigging. The *Raleigh* continued her headlong rush toward the islands.

Wallace, having been a spectator to this grueling, bloody affair, now looked to finish off the *Raleigh* and "Got alongside"–but Barry was ready for him. "Fire!" he roared from the *Raleigh*'s quarterdeck, and her 12-pounders slammed a broadside into the *Experiment*.[90] But this spirited, violent show of defiance did not deter Wallace. The *Experiment*'s 18-pounders were in the hands of the best-trained gunners in the world. On Wallace's orders, they returned fire, staggering the *Raleigh* with their heavier guns. Incredibly, Wallace's gunners sent three broadsides into the crippled, retreating frigate in just over five minutes, while the mauled *Unicorn* managed to fire a round or two "on our lee quarter."[91]

But just as Wallace would not be stopped by a broadside, Barry would not quit his plan. Under his orders, the *Raleigh*'s gunners "returned our [fire] with redoubled vigor" as Barry continued his head-on course toward the craggy islands. Despite her battered condition, the *Raleigh* pulled ahead of her pursuers, her stern-chasers defiantly shooting back at the British. With the island in the center of this cluster being closest, Barry ordered his helmsman to beach

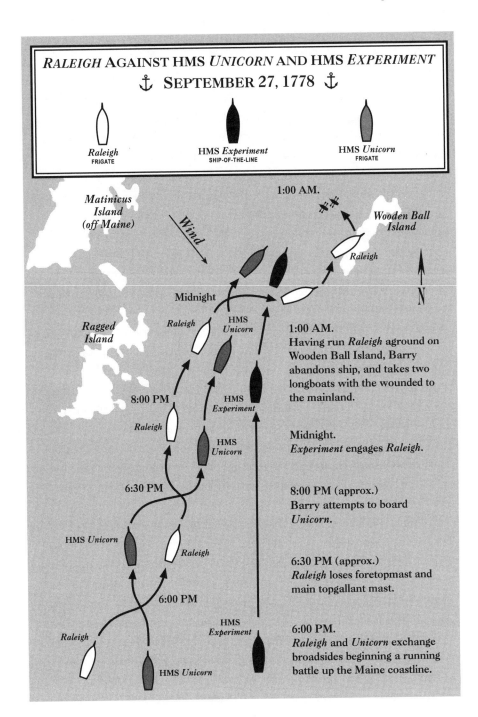

RALEIGH AGAINST HMS *UNICORN* AND HMS *EXPERIMENT*
⚓ SEPTEMBER 27, 1778 ⚓

Raleigh
FRIGATE

HMS *Experiment*
SHIP-OF-THE-LINE

HMS *Unicorn*
FRIGATE

Matinicus
Island
(off Maine)

1:00 A.M.

Wooden Ball
Island

Raleigh

Wind

Midnight

N

Ragged
Island

Raleigh   HMS
Unicorn

1:00 AM.
Having run *Raleigh* aground on
Wooden Ball Island, Barry
abandons ship, and takes two
longboats with the wounded to
the mainland.

8:00 PM   HMS
Experiment

Raleigh

Midnight.
Experiment engages *Raleigh*.

HMS
Unicorn

6:30 PM

8:00 PM (approx.)
Barry attempts to board
Unicorn.

HMS *Unicorn*

Raleigh

6:30 PM (approx.)
Raleigh loses foretopmast and
main topgallant mast.

6:00 PM

HMS
Experiment

Raleigh

6:00 PM.
Raleigh and *Unicorn* exchange
broadsides beginning a running
battle up the Maine coastline.

HMS *Unicorn*

the frigate there. As the crew braced themselves, the *Raleigh* struck sand–and struck it hard. She was aground.[92]

Beaching the frigate left her a sitting duck for British cannons, but Barry let his men know that they were not about to surrender; instead, he ordered the guns reloaded. One of his officers later recalled that "encouraged by our brave commander, we were determined not to strike." However, for the next five minutes striking his colors was the more prudent option. In that short span of time Wallace's gunners fired two more broadsides into the *Raleigh*. Then, after the second round, the *Experiment* "hove in stays"–made a quick tack. Anticipating this maneuver, Barry ordered his guns reloaded: now, for a few precious seconds, it was the *Experiment* that was vulnerable. Barry seized this "opportunity of raking [*Experiment*] which we did with our whole broadside."[93] The *Raleigh* was as dangerous as a cornered, wounded animal.

For the next fifteen minutes the Americans sent round after round of iron at the two British ships. It was the *Raleigh*'s last hurrah, but Barry's fierce pounding worked; the enemy ships "sheared off and came to an Anchor about half-a-mile Astern of us." Wallace, seeing his vessel "being close to the Rocks, tacked and Anchored about 1/2 a Gun Shott from her, as did the *Unicorn* in 20 fathoms Water." The last thing Wallace wanted was two British ships dashed on the rocks. It was now nearly 2:00 A.M. Barry knew what would come with daylight: broadsides and boarding parties. Wallace could turn in for a few hours, believing that Barry would be his prisoner by morning.[94]

If Wallace believed that a bombardment at dawn would pound the Americans into submission, he still did not know John Barry. No sooner had the battle broken off than Barry "got the Boat out in order to save what Men I could."[95] No one aboard knew the island at all; Barry's quick exploration "proved [it] to be rather a barren Rock than an Island." He determined that it was unsuitable ground to transfer any of the *Raleigh*'s guns to continue the fight (as at Turtle Gut Inlet two years earlier) being "about a solid Rock somewhat short of a Mile in length and a quarter of a Mile wide at the broadest place."[96]

In a repeat performance of his earlier fight with Wallace, Barry turned to fire to keep his ship out of enemy hands. With the island only good for a way-station, Barry issued new orders. Two boats, commanded by himself and Marine Captain Osborne, would take the wounded to the mainland. He placed young Midshipman Jesse Jeacocks and the *Raleigh*'s sailing master in command of a detachment of twenty men, and gave Jeacocks specific orders: pile up what combustibles he could find onboard, set fire to the *Raleigh*, then row with all possible speed for the mainland. Barry ordered the ship's lights kept lit as a ruse to cover the departure of the longboats. He sent the rest of the Raleigh's men to hide in the rocky crevices of the island, until the longboats could return and rescue them.[97]

The Raleigh's toughest hands manned the sweeps on the two longboats. Tired from the longest and most dangerous day of their lives, they rowed in silence toward the wooded shore. There were two dozen men to a boat. Barry determined it to be "12 Leagues from the Main land." Once again he miscalculated: it was nearly twenty miles–a vast stretch for men so worn out from chase and battle. Along the way they rowed past other islands, each equally as desolate as the one where they had left their comrades. After three hours of rowing they reached land, entering a small cove at daybreak. Roused from sleep, one of the inhabitants gave Barry the first reliable bearings of his whereabouts in three days, telling him the name of the barren island where he left ship and crew: Wooden Ball.[98]

Barry again set his spyglass eastward, looking for proof that Jeacocks had carried out his orders and that the *Raleigh* was destroyed, but no plume of smoke rose in the sky. For two hours he paced and fumed, not knowing what had become of his orders or his men. Finally, the third boat was sighted, manned by the sailing master and his band of saboteurs.[99] Once ashore, he told Barry what transpired after the captain departed.

The sailing master and his men immediately carried out their orders, piling combustibles below deck. All Jeacocks need do was ignite them and climb into the boat. The sailing master and men waited anxiously as the sun came up. At 5:00 A.M., from the quarterdeck of the ravaged *Unicorn*, Ford "discovered Rebel Colours flying still onboard the Enemy." He also "Observ'd many of her People ashore upon the Westpart of [the] Island." Two hours later, Wallace brought the *Experiment* near the *Unicorn* and anchored, where he "fired several Guns & hoisted out all our Boats Manned and Armed." In the forefront he "sent a Boat ahead with a Flag of Truce to offer them Quarters."[100]

As the only person left aboard the *Raleigh,* Jeacocks must have thought the British boarding parties were coming just for him. By this time he had doused the lanterns Barry ordered left burning, but he had yet to finish his assigned task. The sailing master called for the midshipman to hurry, but received no reply. Rather than send someone else (or himself) aboard to complete the mission, and seeing the British lowering their boats, the sailing master departed with the daylight. "The Master thought it most prudent to put off as they were within sight of the Enemy," Barry later explained.[101] The boat was well into Penobscot Bay when the *Experiment* resumed firing on the *Raleigh.*

Later, the American press labeled Jeacocks a spy; Barry called his actions "Treachery." Whether he was a traitor in their midst, or just plain scared, Jeacocks did find something to do aboard the *Raleigh* rather than obey his orders. When Wallace opened fire, Jeacocks hauled down the *Raleigh*'s ensign.[102]

Angry that Jeacocks had lost his nerve, sense of duty, or both; angry at himself that he could not be two places at once, to find a safe haven for his wounded and start a fire twenty miles away; and angry over his own error in judgment just twenty-four hours earlier, Barry again paced the spit of sand.[103] He ordered the boats back to Wooden Ball, hoping to rescue any Americans that might still be on the island, although he knew full well that the long row back, carried out by already physically drained sailors, would probably not get them there in time to save the others from capture. But maybe.

Maybe.

While the sailing master's boat entered the bay, Wallace and Ford put an end to the affair: "The Enemy on seeing a Flag of Truce . . . and Preparations for boarding her thought it prudent to haul down her Colours . . . the first Lieut. with 123 men soon after Surrendered on the island the Captn and remainder of the Crew made their Escape."[104]

Having "surrendered on a Summons of Truce," as Wallace put it, Phipps and most of the *Raleigh*'s crew laid down their arms. Only thirteen successfully concealed themselves behind the rocks on Wooden Ball. From their hiding places, these few watched as their shipmates were brought aboard the *Experiment*. Then, with high tide approaching, they saw "boats from the *Experiment* with our Longboat employed in heaving the *Raleigh* off, at 3 they hauled her off and brought her to an anchor off the Island." With the *Raleigh* no longer aground, the British crews went to work repairing the frightfully damaged *Unicorn*.[105]

The *Raleigh*'s boats did not approach Wooden Ball until evening, picking up the lucky thirteen under cover of darkness. They got back to the mainland at dawn on the twenty-ninth, informing Barry of his ship's fate. By October 1, both the *Raleigh* and the *Unicorn* were seaworthy enough to depart Penobscot Bay. Along with the *Experiment* they made for Cape Ann, with the battered *Unicorn* still "giving Chace" to every sail sighted. Ironically, the *Raleigh* fared better in the fight; the *Unicorn*'s hull was so shattered that she was finished as a frigate in His Majesty's Navy.[106]

"Saved 85 in number," Barry later reported. After requisitioning supplies from the village, he left those too seriously wounded to travel in one of the village homes with the *Raleigh*'s surgeon.[107] At dusk, Barry and the rest of his crew began the long row south, hugging the New England coastline. Nine days later, their clothes and appearance showing the wear of their journey and the tear of battle, the Raleighs reached Boston.[108] His uniform soiled and sweat stained—no longer the bright blue and red of its earlier days—Barry went at once to see Warren and Deshon, while his fellow survivors described their odyssey to the people of Boston.

Ironically, Bostonians did not take the news of the *Raleigh*'s loss as the latest in a long line of nautical disasters. While sharing Barry's disappointment in losing his ship, they reveled in the tale of its spirited defense, although not quite getting the names correct: "The *Rawley* frigate belonging to the States, Captn Bary, that lately sailed from this place, is taken by the enemy. She fought it is said, the *Diamond*, a British ship of war many hours, when a 60 gun ship came up to the aid of the *Diamond.* Captain Bary made a most gallant defense."[109]

Warren and Deshon lost no time in writing the Marine Committee: "perhaps no ship was ever better defended . . . We shall add no more, but that Captn Barry's conduct is highly approved here, and that his officers and men are greatly pleased with him." Upon hearing the news, Washington—no stranger to hard-fought defeats—praised Barry's "gallant resistance."[110] Soon newspapers on both sides of the Atlantic were telling the story.

A court of inquiry investigated the loss of the frigate and Barry's role in it. His "Defence of the *Raleigh*" laid out the facts in stark detail with no excuses, and included his error in changing course on the morning of September 27. Typically, he downplayed both his own courageous example and the horrific danger in the fight, dryly describing "the engagement" as "being very warm."[111] His only rancor was saved for young Jeacocks, and his only vagaries regarded how many of his sailors were killed or captured, as "The reason I could not tell how many of our Men were made Prisoners was because there was no return of the kill'd on Board."[112] The court not only "Honorably acquitted" Barry but also commended his bravery and leadership.[113] The Marine Committee wrote to Warren that while "the loss of the *Raleigh* is certainly a very great misfortune . . . we have the consolation in reflecting that the spirited and gallant behaviour of her commander has done honor to the flag."[114]

Warren urged him to remain in Boston; a new, 36-gun frigate was under construction in Norwich, Connecticut, believing she would be turned over to Barry's command upon completion.[115] Barry, who for three years had seen how a planned assignment like this usually went to someone with much better political connections, wisely decided to go home and await his next command. It had been months since he had seen Sarah, who could certainly use his assistance in handling her burdens.

Once again he packed his saddlebags and began the journey to Philadelphia. Along the way he passed an express rider carrying the latest messages from Congress, including a letter from the Marine Committee that informed the Navy Board that "Captain [Seth]

Harding has been appointed to the command of the Frigate at Norwich named the *Confederacy* which prevents our giving the Ship to Captain Barry."[116]

In New York, the libel and condemnation of the *Raleigh* was already under way, extolling "Sir James Wallace Knight, Captain and Commander" and "John Ford, Esquire, Captain and Commander" while awarding them their shares for the *Raleigh*'s capture. Testimony from both British and American officers was heard, including that of Phipps and the unlucky midshipman Matthew Clarkson, who survived Barry's Delaware River adventures only to be captured on that desolate rock in Penobscot Bay. The depositions from both sides are readily interchangeable–one side's testimony can easily be interchanged with the other; such was the honor of men over two hundred years ago. Both Clarkson and Phipps testified that the "crew of the said ship were partly American and partly European"–alluding to the captured British troops that comprised Barry's Marines.[117]

Wallace could justifiably feel that he had settled accounts with Barry, especially when the *Raleigh* was "taken into the British service . . . the command of her given to a lad" who was an admiral's nephew.[118] Yet Barry remained at large, with even more recognition for his fighting skills. Both men would continue to sail in harm's way throughout the war. But they would never face each other again.

CHAPTER NINE

PRIVATEER AND JUDGE

N JUNE 1778, WHILE HER HUSBAND WAS HEADING to Boston and the *Raleigh*, Sarah Barry and her brother Isaac took their nieces and nephews back to Philadelphia. Any happiness at coming home was mixed with dread over what awaited them.

Brother and sister discovered that the Austin mansion survived enemy occupation, but much of their city was a wretched mess. A stench permeated the streets and alleyways, coming mainly from a huge pit next to the State House, which had served as a British military hospital. For eight months the redcoats heaped garbage, dead livestock, and an occasional corpse into the pit. The odor was so foul it forced Congress to find other accommodations until time and nature remedied the situation. Many of the city's homes and buildings were ravaged; some had been converted into stables, their elegance spoiled by manure and vermin.[1] Returning Philadelphians were greeted by nine hundred American soldiers freed from the Walnut Street Prison, where they survived starvation and torture at the hands of the sadistic commandant. Although lice-infested and gaunt from a diet of leather, rats, and beef from diseased cows, they were the lucky ones. The bodies of more than a thousand of their fellow captives lay buried a block away, in unmarked graves.[2]

Shortly after Sarah's return to Philadelphia, the family scandal made the papers: "William Austin, yeoman, late keeper of the New Jersey ferry" was "attainted of High Treason to all interests and purposes, and shall suffer such pains and penalties, and undergo all such forfeitures as persons of high treason are to do."[3] He was one of 109 Loyalists accused of treason, some of whom were still in Philadelphia, hoping to receive clemency from Washington. The mansion could be seized at any time by the Supreme Executive Council. Soon they announced the scheduled sale of "the household goods and a Negro Wench of William Austin, late of this city."[4]

Washington appointed his protégé, Benedict Arnold, military governor of the city. Arnold faced the task of repairing both Philadelphians' structures and their spirits. Restoring homes and morale was easy when compared to Congress' battle with spiraling inflation, now a nationwide epidemic. The city needed to reestablish the West Indies trade, but merchants faced a severe shortage of ships.[5] Robert Morris had seen this coming; in 1776 he observed that a "ship that in common times sold for £1,000 by a sudden demand is raised in Value to £4,000 & seamans' wages jum[p] from £4 to £14 per mo[nth]."[6] Three years later, those expenses were bargains.

Prices for goods skyrocketed. Grain, the driving commodity of Philadelphia's mercantile establishments, was virtually nonexistent, supplies having been consumed by both armies over the past eight months.[7] Soon Continental currency was worth a paltry 5 percent of its original value.[8] This affected the navy as well: in 1775, Congress believed that $700,000 would build the original thirteen frigates. By 1780, Congress seriously mulled over a request for a million dollars to refit and supply just one.[9]

Barry arrived in Philadelphia amidst this sea of troubles, making his return "At a very Grate Expence" on October 27.[10] Once settled in, he joined Isaac in sorting through the affidavits and bills that would hound them for years. News of the *Raleigh*'s last battle preceded his arrival, and the Marine Committee presented him with a new assignment. An invasion of Florida was being planned under General Benjamin Lincoln, with an army comprised of Continental and militia forces. Barry was to lead a flotilla of armed galleys from Maryland

and Virginia.[11] His compensation for this campaign would be not in dollars but in Florida land grants.[12]

He viewed both the plan and proposed reward as foolhardy. Already owed over $3,000 in back pay, the offer of swampland in Florida, then a Spanish territory, was hardly appealing. Being placed under Lincoln's orders carried potential conflicts: would Lincoln overrule him on naval matters? Commandeering Maryland and Virginia galleys and then sailing them away from those states was totally unfeasible. Reading between the lines, Barry saw through the committee's instructions. They gave him authority to ask for the galleys but not to requisition them. Their encouragement to "cultivate harmony" among their officers and sailors was another veiled warning to Barry: be prepared for squalls when southerners found themselves under northern command.[13] Even Congress foresaw that if Barry had trouble as an out-of-towner recruiting in Boston, what would it be like to enlist Southerners?[14] Having begun the year accused of insubordination by Hopkinson, he was not about to end it with a mission that undermined his authority fore and aft. For Barry, the choice was clear: he did not want this assignment.

But how to say no? Having endured one fight on the floor of Congress, he was not anxious for another one. He made his feelings clear to John Brown, who suggested taking a different tack that would guarantee that the penurious Congress would let him off the hook. Barry's subsequent requests for everything from "a Secretary" to "a Table" were considered "extraordinary demands" by Henry Laurens, then President of Congress. Laurens, wise to Barry's ruse, informed Lincoln that "I believe Capt. Barry to be a brave & active Seaman, but I am told . . . that the intended service is not pleasing to him."[15] The campaign in Florida was tabled altogether.[16]

Barry found himself free to spend Christmas at home with Sarah. The break between assignments also gave him a chance to review his grim financial situation. With the estate of Sarah's mother still unsettled, and now entangled with William's infamous affairs, the Barrys were living on John's past earnings as a merchant captain and his prize shares from the *Lexington*'s glory days.[17] January came and went with no new offers from the Marine Committee. Ironically, although the captains' list was shrinking–Biddle and Wickes dead; McNeill and Thompson relieved; Nicholson and Alexander having lost their respective ships; Manley and Hacker court-martialed (and acquitted, but without commands)–there were still fewer ships than captains. Technically, Barry was now number four, but lack of Continental ships, his grim economic situation, and his fervent desire to stay in the fight left him only one option: turn privateer.

Privateer. The word had repugnant connotations in Congress. Many representatives, especially those involved in the establishment and survival of the navy, were fighting a war on two fronts: one against the British, and another with American merchants who employed privateers and benefited from their activities. "In all Transactions of America nothing has given me more Concern than that kind of irregular Conduct on b[oar]d the Am[erican] Privateers that savours more of Moorish Piracy than Christian Forebearance," Robert Morris wrote.[18] As a congressman, he officially looked down on the practice: "I have not hitherto had any Concern in Privateering," he wrote to a colleague. Then, without period or comma, he offered to personally bankroll such a venture.[19] Nor was he the only congressman to do so.

Since the war's outbreak, merchants saw potential wealth in a "letter of marque": a license from Congress allowing merchant-captains to make war on British shipping. Under international law, possession of this document meant that the seizure of an enemy ship and confiscation of its goods was a legal act; without it, the captain and his crew were nothing more than pirates. Merchants offered significantly better wages and shares than the navy's rates while still reaping sizable profits. Their biggest risk was the loss of the ship itself; a risk lessened when they considered that the only alternative was leaving the ship in port, bringing in no money at all.

"Such has been the Demand for Seamen [that] Wages have risen to ab[ou]t Twenty Dollars P[er] month–the Privateers give One Hundred Dollars P[er] man Advance," John Langdon grumbled to Morris.[20] Sailors thought nothing of signing on a Continental ship, then turning around and signing on for a privateer's cruise–usually short, with potential for a rich haul–to the consternation of congressman and navy captain alike.[21] With such a small navy, fighting the largest and best in history, it was no wonder that Congress viewed privateers as a necessary evil—and, by 1779, one could eliminate the word evil. "The excessive rage for privateering," as Benjamin Rush called it, was now a military and economic necessity.[22] American merchantmen were well suited for it. In 1779, a privateer's vessel of choice was a fast-sailing schooner or brig carrying about ten guns with a crew of up to fifty men (by the end of the war, many privateers carried "a score of heavy cannon" and upwards of two hundred and fifty sailors).[23]

Congressmen were in a high dudgeon over the methods and profits of privateers, but needed only to look in a mirror to find who was responsible. The government's pay scale and allotment of prize shares were scoffed at by captain and sailor alike. It was as if Congress thought they could hoodwink seamen by offering larger percentages of shares than their British counterparts—after Congress had deducted their half—thinking that a sailor's mathematical skills were relegated only to fathoms and knots. A sailor could add and subtract, especially when it came to his account book.

Two merchants who successfully made the switch from peacetime trade to wartime privateering were Matthew and Thomas Irwin. The brothers' reputation for blockade running and eluding enemy cruisers was such that they consistently recruited the best Philadelphia seamen and captains available.[24] Irwin-owned ships sailed to the West Indies with their holds full of boards, hoops, and staves, returning with sugar, molasses, rum, and coffee—all to be sold at phenomenal profits in Philadelphia.[25] A letter of marque issued to the Irwins was a safe bet.

Knowing that Barry was without assignment, the Irwins offered him command of their best ship, the brigantine *Delaware*. After receiving a leave of absence from the Marine Committee along with assurances that his commission and rank were secure, Barry was free to announce at the annual meeting of the Sea Captains Club that he was going "a-privateering," bound for Port-au-Prince.[26]

As with practically everything else during his war years, this venture had a rocky beginning. For weeks, boisterous mobs had been protesting conditions in the streets of Philadelphia. Their mood soon infected the waterfront just as Barry began hiring a crew. On January 12, sailors, dockhands, and shipyard workers staged a strike that went from ugly to dangerous. Boarding outbound vessels, the men unrigged them, creating mayhem on ship and shore.[27] Sailors refused to come aboard ship, dockhands refused to lift one bale, and ship-yard workers touched nary a spar, rope, or sail.

The issue was money. Rather than give in to workers' demands, merchants opted to recruit sailors from French ships anchored in the Delaware, and Barry followed suit. In doing so he unwittingly gave his very recognizable name to this blatantly undiplomatic solution. The vice consul of France began registering protests to both Congress and the Pennsylvania Supreme Executive Council, which issued a warning "to all owners and masters of vessels against employing or harboring" French deserters.[28] As Barry responded to these accusations in such a manner that the council was "satisfacto-rily redressed," tensions eased along the waterfront, and Barry soon had his complement of forty-five sailors—mostly English speaking.[29] While Barry was given a crash course on negotiating Continental loan certificates and the nebulous worth of Continental currency in the West Indies, the *Delaware*'s hold began to fill with construction goods, tobacco, and flour.[30]

Philadelphia's newest privateer had a busy day both professional-ly and personally on February 15. That morning he and Matthew Irwin registered "the Brigg *Delaware*," and Barry received his letter of marque, purchased by Irwin with a $10,000 bond and signed by the new President of Congress, John Jay.[31] Afterward, he and Sarah walked over to Walnut Ward and St. Joseph's Church, where he stood godfather to his newborn niece, Thomas's daughter Anna.[32]

The next day, accompanied by another Irwin brig, the *Lady Gates*, and several merchantmen, the *Delaware* departed Philadelphia. She was two hundred tons and mounted ten 4-pounders; Barry was back to *Lexington*-size cannon, and he immediately put his crew to their gunnery exercises. To deter any attacks by Goodrich's raiders, the ships sailed as a loosely kept squadron. For the first time in five years Barry was bound for the Caribbean. It was a swift passage; the *Delaware* entered the Channel de St. Marc and Port-au-Prince around March 15.[33]

Three months later Barry was home with the *Delaware*'s hold "loaded with West-Indies produce and dry goods."[34] With no naval appointments on his horizon, he refitted the brig for another voyage.[35] His small fleet of privateers included the brigantine *Impertinence*, commanded by Barry's friend John Young, late of the *Independence*. As before, the Irwins put the little squadron under Barry's command, and gave him a new title: "For the sake of regularity and good order we have appointed John Barry Esq Commodore of the Fleet."[36]

Among his crew was a seventeen-year-old boy. John Kessler had no idea of the adventures that lay in store for him when he signed on, nor did he know he was about to begin a friendship that would last nearly a quarter of a century. Born in 1761, Kessler was the son of German immigrants, and spent his teens in a series of apprenticeships to a drygoods merchant, a brewer, and a tobacconist. He partook in military exercises with a "voluntary" company of apprentices, drilling on the grounds before the statehouse. He began his service under Barry "in the three fold capacity of Clark, Steward, & Capt'n of Marines."[37] He had never been to sea before.

The "fleet" departed Philadelphia on July 14. As they passed Chester, Barry and his men got a glimpse of the frigate *Confederacy* riding at anchor, the very frigate James Warren wanted him to have. What envy Barry may have felt was short-lived: two days later, the commodore had his first prize. She was "the sloop of war *Harlem*," a happy Barry wrote to Mathew Irwin. It was just like old times; he had snatched another ship from "Goodrich's navy."[38]

Barry landed the prisoners at Sinepuxent, Maryland, only to discover that Maryland patriots were not comfortable guarding Tories who were also friends or extended family. After a detachment of local militia abandoned Barry's small contingent of sailors on the beach—forcing them to guard the sixty-four prisoners overnight by themselves—Barry and Young went into Sinepuxent themselves the next morning. After raising hackles with a local official, they left his loyalist neighbors in his hands. A prize-master and crew took the *Harlem* back to Philadelphia, along with a letter protesting the lack of cooperation by the patriots of Sinepuxent.[39] Blood was still thicker than water along the Chesapeake.

The fleet reached Port-au-Prince in August, and by early September was homeward bound.[40] North of the West Indies "a merchant vessell of Liverpool was taken," but she "came to be taken by the noted Guttridge [Goodrich] and carried into Bermuda."[41] Barry's squadron reached the Capes of the Delaware Bay without further incident.

At Cape Henlopen, one of Henry Fisher's intrepid pilots told Barry about the press gang from the *Confederacy*, news that brought out anger and anxiety among Barry's crew. Most of them were Philadelphians, married, and as resentful of possibly serving under a New England commander as New Englanders were the year before at serving under Barry on the *Raleigh*. Quite a few of them "desired to be put on shore." Calling for all hands, Barry addressed them: "My lads if you have the spirit of freemen you will not desire to go on shore, nor tamely submit against your wills to be taken away, altho the force of all the Frigates boat crews were to attempt to exercise such a specie of tyranny."[42]

Once he "implied his consent to their defending themselves," the crew "resolved to do it at all hazards."[43] The *Delaware* continued upriver, reaching Chester the next morning and thwarting the press gang.[44] When they docked in Philadelphia on October 5, Barry's decision to protect his crew that day became the talk of the wharf taverns in Philadelphia.[45]

Nor did he let the *Confederacy* incident remain in the waters off Chester. Once he checked in with the Irwins, he reported the affair to his friends on the Marine Committee and in the State Assembly. They in turn protested Harding's unsavory methods that "left families in a distressed situation," and demanded their immediate discharge. The committee determined "that no Commander of any ship or vessel of war in the service of the United States shall impress" any sailor without his state government's permission. They also commanded Harding to "Head inland immediately to discharge" any pressed sailors.[46]

Once home, Barry found himself in the midst of another crisis. Efforts by the State Assembly to combat inflation (including a resolution calling for wage and price controls) failed outright. Inflation now averaged 17 percent a month. Mobs still demonstrated in the streets, their numbers recently padded by unpaid militiamen. Benedict Arnold was forced to use Continental troops to maintain order. Climbing prices went hand in glove with the merchants' rise to true political power. They had moved quickly to fill the vacuum created by the Quaker abdication of civic leadership when the British evacuated Philadelphia. Meetinghouse names were being replaced by those from Christ Church–Morris, Willing, Nixon, and Clymer foremost.[47]

Another was James Wilson: lawyer, merchant, signer of the Declaration, and incurable land speculator (Wilson also provided much of the timber that went into the *Effingham* and other Continental ships). The day before Barry returned, a handbill circulated in Philadelphia demanding that the militia apprehend any "Loyalists" and/or "Profiteers" and run them out of town. A gang of disgruntled militiamen and unemployed Philadelphians gathered at a favorite tavern on the poorer side of town at Tenth between Race and Vine. Given the usual effects of spirits on the dispirited, the gang became angrier as they became drunker. Wilson's name kept cropping up, and soon he was the source of everyone's ills. The now frenzied mob headed for his palatial home. Pleas on his behalf from Charles Willson Peale and Dr. James Hutchinson went unheeded. Somehow Wilson was able to get Thomas Mifflin and twenty other friends to come to his aid. Mifflin led them in military drills outside Wilson's mansion in an effort to cower the mob, but once Mifflin ordered his "troops" into Wilson's house, the attack on "Fort Wilson" began. It ended when Arnold dispatched a troop of cavalry to the rescue. They arrived in a swirl of dust, circling the house with sabers drawn. By then five were killed and seventeen wounded.[48]

Barry was informed of the incident by Morris and Brown while making his report, and offered to assist Wilson, promising "everything in his power" to "prevent repeated and continual insults."[49] Guilty of the mob's suspicions as Wilson was (land speculation failures eventually landed him in prison), Barry was not about to bite a hand that fed him once and hopefully would again. He approached Wilson with a plan to "unite and strengthen us" that Wilson believed would "awe the insurgents."[50] But with Mifflin's troops remaining to guard "Fort Wilson," nothing came of Barry's offer.

For once, happy news awaited him at home. As a surprise for her husband, Sarah had converted to Catholicism. She was baptized at St. Mary's on July 21, with sister-in-law Ann serving as her sponsor. Another household member also converted: "Judith, slave of Captain John Barry," was baptized, sponsored by the priest's servant. It is not known if Judith was the young slave belonging to Reynold Keen.[51] Barry also learned that his intercessions to Morris on Keen's behalf were proving effective. The Supreme Executive Council approved Keen's petition "that the sale of his Estate . . . be postponed."[52] William Austin's case was another matter: he was now officially "guilty of high treason." The family estate, being in his name, went on the auctioneer's schedule.[53]

Like most captains, Barry found he liked privateering. For one thing, he was being paid handsomely, and on time.[54] Now he was sought after by other merchants, who viewed Barry's availability as baseball owners do a prize free agent. He was about to accept command of another "ship of twenty-four guns in the merchant service" when Congress came calling. A ship—actually more of a project than a ship—was in need of his talents.[55] He was offered "Command [of] a new Continental Ship . . . now on the Stocks at Portsmouth in New Hampshire." Duty won out over profit. Barry was ordered "to repair to that place and hasten as much as may be in your power the compleating of that Ship which we are desirous to have done with all dispatch."[56]

Barry was to report to John Langdon and oversee completion of the largest ship the Continental Congress would ever build, a seventy-four gun ship-of-the-line.[57] In Royal Navy parlance, she was a third-rate ship, one of three originally proposed back in the heady days of 1776.[58] Now she was the only one being built. While her keel had been laid two years before, she was still a long way from completion; due to lack of funds, only twenty-four carpenters were currently assigned her. There was also talk of cutting her down in size to carry fifty-six or sixty guns. In June, Congress told Robert Morris to get the ship finished.[59]

Quick goodbyes were now second nature for the Barrys. John departed on November 7, with orders to report to the Eastern Navy Board.[60] The approval of Barry's request that George Osborne be again appointed his captain of marines (as "he may be useful in doing many matters relative to that Ship") was one of the last acts of the Marine Committee. Congress was replacing it with a "Board of Admiralty" yet to be named.[61]

Once in Portsmouth, Barry saw there was no need for marines, sailors, or George Osborne for that matter. Barry and Langdon reviewed the stunning lack of progress on the ship-of-the-line. While both agreed she should remain a seventy-four, they found the work yet to be completed overwhelming. As his mission became more of an errand than an assignment, Barry determined to carry the report back himself.[62] Before departing, he encountered Thomas Thompson. The *Raleigh*'s old commander was still fighting to clear his name over the loss of the *Alfred*, and implored Barry to use his influence with Morris to give Thompson a second chance. He found Barry empathetic but noncommittal. Barry did not lift a finger on the disgraced captain's behalf–one of the rare instances in his career that he did not offer support to a fellow captain.[63] To this day, some naval historians believe Thompson deserved better.

After a visit to Boston to win over James Warren and John Deshon regarding his proposals for the ship-of-the-line, Barry rode back to Philadelphia, arriving on December 20, 1779.[64] He presented his findings to the new Board of Admiralty, consisting of Morris, Brown, and naval stalwart William Ellery of Rhode Island (by now the navy was in such low regard few congressmen offered to serve on the board).[65] Having only been home for one Christmas with his first wife, Barry was able to spend the third in as many years with Sarah. Before the New Year, Brown presented Barry with mixed season's greetings: the seventy-four would be completed pursuant to Barry's suggestions, but the "Treasury is so nearly exhausted that it will be impossible to furnish [the] monies" for the job.[66]

Barry began the new decade with a new expense: a horse, purchased for anticipated trips to New England. He petitioned the Admiralty for compensation, and he was not the only patriot shocked at the cost of keeping horseflesh: "our Board and Horse keeping have from the beginning cost us more than our pay," one Congressman complained.[67] Brown endorsed his friend's request "that his horse be permitted to be kept at the Continental stables."[68] Winter came and went. On St. Patrick's Day, Congress officially decreed that they "had no money to go on with the building" of the ship-of-the-line; therefore there was no need to send Barry north, nor reason to pay for his four-legged transportation.[69] Anxious to put to sea again, Barry obtained another leave of absence from the navy.[70]

With spring came a bitter task. He had last seen his brother Patrick in 1774. Since then Patrick had served as a privateer with his own share of adventures, including an international incident on the Mississippi involving the Spanish government and a British ship, the *Atalanta*.[71] In 1778, Patrick sailed the brig *Union* to Bordeaux, where he was entertained by Madame de Lafayette.[72] That August, the *Union* sailed into the treacherous Bay of Biscay, and was never heard from again. By 1780, with Patrick's fate ascertained, John was appointed executor of his estate.[73] As with the Austins, the settling of his brother's affairs would take years, and placed further pressure on him to assure that Patrick's widow and four-year-old daughter would be cared for.[74] Barry seemed trapped between family entanglements, a stalled career, and dwindling finances. The lure of the sea and a letter of marque–a fatal combination for Patrick–was John's only hope for solvency. Providentially, an offer to go to sea came to his door.

The firm of James Caldwell and Co. was one of the few still thriving in Philadelphia. Caldwell offered Barry command of the brig *American,* fourteen guns: in exchange for just a one-sixteenth investment on Barry's part for the ship, her cargo and command was his. This was a common practice by merchants to attract the best captains and, had Barry's finances been in a better light, he would have leapt at this prospect. Despite her being "a Very fine Leter of mark," he was forced to decline. John Brown, however, also viewed the proposal as a worthy investment–especially if Barry were to be the *American*'s captain. He offered to pay half of the price, and Barry readily agreed to scrape up the rest. With a hold full of lumber and tobacco and a crew of seventy aboard, the *American* departed Philadelphia on June 3 for St. Eustatia and was back in less than two months. Heartily pleased with both the *American*'s performance and his new employer, Barry believed he had "a fine prospect of retrieving hiss loss sustained in Public Service."[75] Another voyage was planned. At last Barry could see a pleasant change in his financial outlook.

The new Board of Admiralty, however, altered Barry's plans. He received orders to ride again to Boston. There he would find intrigue, scandal, and the finest command in the Continental Navy. Awaiting him was the frigate *Alliance*–but first he must put an end to the career of her previous captain, Pierre Landais.

————————

For generations, the Landais family supplied France with sailors.[76] Pierre entered the French Navy as a boy, rising in rank over the years until he became a *capitaine de brulôt*–commander of a fire ship, an appropriate assignment for one whose easily aroused temper found an outlet in dueling. A cameo of Landais reveals a uniformed officer with a long, aquiline nose, small chin, and genteel features that belie his combativeness and unbalanced personality.[77] He resigned his commission in 1775.[78] After covering Silas Deane with fawning flattery, he was given command of an American supply ship bound for Philadelphia. Among his fellow passengers was Baron von Steuben.[79] Making maximum use of Deane's recommendations, Landais became a cause célèbre of the Adams-Lee faction, who had members in both Congress and Paris–Sam Adams and Richard Henry Lee in Philadelphia, John Adams and Arthur Lee in Paris. Arthur Lee, who never hid his hatred of Franklin, saw Landais as the perfect foil for Franklin's satellite, John Paul Jones, cheered by the French for his recent triumphs commanding the *Ranger*. Lee and John Adams promoted Landais as a "Lafayette of the Seas," using him as a pawn in their chess game against "old Ben."[80] In Landais they had a very willing player.

Once in Philadelphia, Landais captivated the Adams-Lee faction in Congress. Their influence assured him command of the *Alliance* (he was also the first sent to review the ship-of-the-line in Portsmouth).[81] Paid sixty dollars a month, Landais dove into his role, if not his responsibilities. James Warren found him "An Ingenuous & well Behaved Man," but warned Sam Adams that, like Barry with the *Raleigh*, he would encounter recruiting difficulties with the new frigate: "I fear he will never Man her unless with Frenchmen & I suppose that would hardly be Agreeable to Congress."[82] Warren was right: where Barry was able to depart Boston in September, the *Alliance* did not sail for another ten months. Her prize passenger on this voyage was the Marquis de Lafayette, sent to France by Washington to update Louis XVI on the war and Washington's personal plea for more of everything.[83]

The voyage was an omen of what lay ahead for Landais. Once at sea he abandoned his unctuousness, but his dictatorial style did not play well with the crew. Several days before they arrived at Brest, a mutiny broke out, but the mutineers' plan to cast Landais adrift and put Lafayette in irons was just barely suppressed.[84] In Paris, Landais's true nature was clear to an alarmed John Adams, who now saw his former *bon ami* as "jealous of every Thing, jealous of every Body," and concluded that "he knows not how to treat his officers . . . nor any Body else."[85] Landais was dangerous, a ticking time bomb.

After keeping the *Alliance* in Brest for six months, Landais finally acquiesced to orders that he join the squadron under Jones for a raid against British shipping in the North Sea. It vexed Jones sorely to stand on the quarterdeck of his flagship, the ancient East Indiaman *Bonhomme Richard*, and watch the *Alliance* sail alongside him.[86] At first, Jones considered Landais a "sensible, well-informed man."[87] He would soon change his opinion. In the battle off Flamborough Head, where the *Bonhomme Richard* defeated the British frigate *Serapis*, Landais's conduct–steering clear of the fighting, when the *Alliance*'s participation could have ended the conflict much sooner (and saved countless lives), only to return and twice fire broadsides into both ships–is well documented.[88]

Jones's victory, along with the loss of the *Bonhomme Richard*, ensured his taking command of the *Alliance* away from Landais. The frigate spent the next several months in port while Jones, back in Paris, was awarded the title *chevalier* by Louis XVI and basked in well-deserved acclaim. But while Jones played, Landais burned, using his contacts with the equally resentful Arthur Lee to have his command restored.[89]

Landais's machinations perfectly suited Lee. Appointed with Deane and Franklin to serve as commissioners in France, Lee begrudged Franklin both his fame and his lifestyle. Better educated than Franklin–Lee was both a doctor and a lawyer–he was an eligible bachelor whose main task in France seemed to be scheming against Franklin. Fair-haired and blue-eyed, with a high forehead and thin lips, he wore a perpetual look of disdain. "I bear all his rebukes with patience," Franklin once wrote, "but it goes a little hard with me."[90]

Jones made a cruise with the *Alliance* that proved unrewarding and only enflamed the enmity between Landais's officers and those Jones brought aboard from the *Bonhomme Richard*. When orders arrived from the Board of Admiralty for the *Alliance* to sail home with munitions, uniforms, and supplies for Washington's army, Lee and Landais set their trap. Lee was to return home as well, and Jones, aware of Lee's enmity, hoped to win him over during the voyage. Lee arrived at L'Orient with an entourage of aides and servants and an excessive amount of baggage. The *pièce de résistance* was his personal coach, which he insisted be brought aboard. Choosing between Washington's supplies and Lee's frivolous demand was easy for Jones, who denied Lee permission to replace French weapons and uniforms with his French carriage. Lee now urged Landais to stir up the original *Alliance* officers, who were as resentful of Jones as Landais was. While Jones attended parties a hundred miles away in Nantes, Landais boarded the *Alliance* to the cheers of his officers. He ordered the men from the *Bonhomme Richard* clapped in irons.[91]

Upon hearing this, a furious Jones went to Paris to protest, while Lee's carriage was loaded aboard the *Alliance* and Washington's desperately needed goods were tossed back onto the dock. Jones returned to L'Orient with orders to retake command and authority to have French warships fire on the *Alliance* if Landais attempted departure. It was an order Jones could not bring himself to give. He watched the *Alliance* sail away.

The *Alliance*'s voyage to America was, in a word, bizarre. Within hours of departure Matthew Parke, captain of marines, was thrown in the brig after refusing to take an oath of loyalty to Landais, joining the *Bonhomme Richard*'s crew in irons.[92] When the *Alliance* reached the Grand Banks, the other sailors asked permission to fish, a custom in those times, especially when rations were low or spoiling.[93] Landais refused. On one queer day of sailing he suddenly ordered all canvas reefed and direction changed, to the consternation of his American seamen who were more than anxious to get home.[94]

Landais even turned on his benefactor. When Arthur Lee complained about the drinking water to his protégé, he received a virulent scolding from Landais that he could "drink from the common scuttlebutt" with the sailors.[95] At dinner one night, Lee reached for a slice of roast pig at the captain's table. An enraged Landais brandished his carving knife under Lee's nose—no one took meat before *le Capitaine*. Now even the self-centered Lee had had enough.[96] On August 11, he led several men into the captain's cabin, informing Landais that they were turning the ship over to the second-in-command, Lieutenant James Degge, currently under arrest.[97] Degge brought the *Alliance* into Boston eight days later—a closer destination than the scheduled one, Philadelphia. Bedridden in his cabin, Landais fired off a letter to the Eastern Navy Board announcing his arrival, in his unique English: "We were bound to Philadelphia . . . but two revolts of the crew have prevented . . . the officers and passengers have had in it. . . . Never before were such things seen or heard of and I conjecture this the first step when on shore will be altogether to give me a bad character. Before God! . . . You will find them out but there are vary cunning ones among them."[98]

The *Alliance*'s arrival was greatly anticipated by Washington and Congress alike.[99] From France, Franklin worried that "her crew . . . infected with disorder and mutiny, may carry her into England."[100] Upon discovering that Franklin's fears were correct in everything but destination, the Eastern Navy Board immediately convened an inquiry regarding the mutiny, and sent a rider to Philadelphia, informing Congress of its decision. Upon receiving the news, Morris, Ellery, and Brown dispatched orders authorizing the inquiry to look into every detail of the voyage, as soon as the *Alliance*'s newly appointed captain reached Boston. Then they sent for Barry.[101]

Once in the Admiralty offices—a stone's throw from the State House—Barry was informed of his new command. He received the news with mixed emotions: he was being awarded the finest ship in the navy, but as with the *Raleigh*, there was no crew and no money. Barry was also to preside over Landais' court-martial, which promised to be time-consuming and a potential diplomatic nightmare. For second-in-command, Morris had chosen the unlucky Hoystead Hacker. The Eastern Navy Board would pick the rest of Barry's officers, giving "preferences to seniority where qualifications were not wanted." To assist in obtaining funding for the *Alliance*, William Ellery would accompany Barry and Hacker to Boston.[102]

Hacker's luck had not changed since he lost the *Columbus*. Given command of Jones's old sloop *Providence*, he lost her in the disastrous Penobscot Campaign, a fiasco that resulted in heavy casualties and a slew of inquiries regarding the misconduct of surviving officers (including Paul Revere).[103] Later, after the further misfortune of being captured when the British took Charleston in May 1780, Hacker was paroled to Philadelphia and recently exchanged.[104]

Well mounted, the trio departed Philadelphia on September 10. Once they reached Rhode Island, Ellery said goodbye; Morris and Brown wanted him to seek both money and sailors in Newport for the *Alliance*. The Continental Navy was now down to five ships: frigates *Trumbull*, *Deane*, *Confederacy*, and *Alliance*, and the sloop of war *Saratoga*, now commanded by John Young.[105] No wonder Morris wanted Landais out of the picture and the *Alliance* back to sea so quickly.

The journey to Boston gave Barry time to reflect on how to handle Landais. While an embarrassment to both France and America alike, his nationality and political connections posed a problem of how to effectively dispose of him once and for all. The trial would require pristine tact on the part of each officer chosen to be judge and jury—particularly its president. In awarding Barry the *Alliance*, the Board of Admiralty also handed him a grand problem to unravel: a mutiny of American sailors against a French captain, instigated by an American diplomat. The solution would require navigational skills one did not learn with a sextant.

Barry and Hacker reached Boston on September 19. By now Washington had learned what had crossed the Atlantic in the *Alliance*'s hold for his near mutinous army, and he raged at Thomas Jefferson: "The Cloathing by the *Alliance* was as deficient of the expected quantity as that of the Arms."[106] The mutiny was the talk of Boston; "That poor vessel was the sport of more than winds and waves," Abigail Adams wrote her husband in Paris, adding that "Barre [Barry] has got command of her now."[107] Meanwhile, Arthur Lee was telling anyone and everyone in Boston that the Frenchman was completely insane. Soon Sam Adams, loyal to a fault, was Landais's only remaining champion.[108]

Since the *Alliance*'s docking in Boston, Landais remained in his cabin; now, with Barry's arrival, he was ordered ashore. For three days he refused to go.[109] Force would be required, and force was used: a detachment of marines broke the lock on the cabin door, overcame the scuffling Landais, and carried him, kicking and screaming, out of the cabin and down the gangplank. The manic Frenchman now took on the role of martyr. Spitefully, he haunted the hallway of the Navy Board offices, insisting that Warren and Deshon let him sleep on the floor.[110]

There was no one to greet Barry when he boarded the *Alliance* after Landais's departure. He found his cabin ransacked; furniture and linen had "disappeared" during his predecessor's stay (perhaps Landais was using the tablecloth as his blanket on the floor of the Navy Board's headquarters).[111] Despite the ignorant welcome, the *Alliance*'s new captain saw for himself the ship's fine lines and construction.[112]

Efforts at raising a crew proved even more difficult than with the *Raleigh*. Barry did succeed in signing on officers: the grizzled veteran Hezekiah Welch, second lieutenant; Patrick Fletcher, third lieutenant; John Buckley, sailing master; Joseph Kendall, surgeon; Samuel Gardner, purser; and Benjamin Balch, chaplain. Matthew Parke re-enlisted as captain of marines; his two lieutenants, Thomas Elwood and James Warren, also signed on for another cruise. Among the new midshipmen was John Kessler.[113]

Kessler had remained as clerk aboard the *Delaware*, although the ship's luck changed with Barry's departure. In 1780, she was "captured by three British frigates" and her crew "were landed and put in prison at Kingston in Jamaica." Later, Kessler and fifteen others made a daring escape and, after "meeting many disasters," reached Port-au-Prince. From there the teenager signed on a letter of marque bound for Salem, Massachusetts, where he found himself "an utter stranger, penniless and wretchedly clad, having left most of my Clothing in the prison."[114]

In Salem he heard that Barry was in Boston, commanding *Alliance*. Kessler immediately made his way there as well. Looking every inch the vagabond sailor he now was, he ascended the gangplank and "presented myself to Capt'n Barry." To Kessler's great relief, Barry instantly recognized the boy, his "shabby appearance" notwithstanding: Barry "was glad at seeing me and invited me to go with him in the Frigate as a Midshipman."[115] In a city of strangers, Barry was just as glad to see a friendly face as the youngster was to find his former captain and mentor.

An October rendezvous proved discouraging. The lure of privateering remained popular in Boston, and, thanks to Landais, *Alliance* was in low repute among Boston tars. When Kessler signed the meager muster roll, most of the names and marks belonged to British prisoners, who viewed sailing for the enemy preferable to the cold, damp hospitality of a Boston jail. This was not an uncommon practice. Some captured American sailors chose fighting beside the enemy to rotting in the prison hulks in New York harbor. Barry did not like the idea one bit—but few Yankee hands were forthcoming.[116]

As if he did not have enough troubles, Barry now got his first taste of James Nicholson's game-playing. After losing the *Virginia*, Nicholson was given the frigate *Trumbull*, and actually showed true mettle against a British privateer. But Nicholson was full of self-regard. After all, as he was first on the still controversial captains' list, should not the prize American command, the *Alliance*, be his? He wrote to Congress suggesting just that.[117] John Brown responded quickly with a combination of facts and common sense. While "it was an established rule of the Marine Committee in appointing

Commanders . . . to give preference to seniority when merit is equal," and Nicholson's claim was "reasonable," he "was out at sea" and therefore "Capt. John Barry was appointed . . . for his great activity and popularity with Seamen."[118] Nicholson might have chafed, but he accepted the reasoning, and saved further invective for another captain he deemed beneath him: John Paul Jones.

Barry's labors over the *Alliance* took a backseat on November 20, when the court-martial finally convened.[119] The panel included Hacker, Fletcher, and Nicholson's brother, Samuel. Thomas Dawes, Jr., served as judge advocate.[120] The *Alliance*'s cabin, returned to the spit and polish that Barry was accustomed to, hosted the affair. All wore their recently cleaned blue and red uniforms. The tall Barry sat at center, flanked by the other officers, their clerks and orderlies in tow. To ensure privacy and confidentiality throughout the proceedings, the closed cabin door was guarded by two marines. Only called witnesses gained entrance. The late autumn New England winds blew over the Charles, giving the cabin a wintry chill. Barry kept the stove's fire going, with lanterns lit to offset the shorter daylight hours.[121]

Accusations were culled down to four specific charges: that Landais "came away with the ship *Alliance* . . . without the knowledge of Dr. Franklin"; that Landais "permitted private goods" (i.e., Lee's excessive "luggage") aboard; that he "abdicated . . . command"; and that he "refused to deliver the ship *Alliance*, her cabin & furniture to John Barry Esq. when appointed to command of said ship."[122] For the next four weeks Barry's court reviewed the evidence. Witnesses' testimony, staggering in its vehemence, made clear how unfit Landais was for command.[123] Sailors and passengers openly cursed at him from the witness chair. No prodding or leading questions from Dawes were necessary. Witnesses could not wait to tell their side of the tale.

From the beginning, Barry gave latitude whenever necessary while ensuring the proceedings stayed on course.[124] When testimony provoked laughter, Barry could chuckle with his colleagues, yet still treat the accused with the courtesy and respect due his rank. His example guaranteed that the other officers did likewise. The right follow-up questions were asked and an appropriate tone of voice was applied, Barry skillfully using his wry humor to keep the proceedings from turning into a verbal lynching. After four long weeks, Dawes was finished; Barry granted Landais a two-week extension to finish his preparations. The transcripts for the prosecution totaled over one hundred pages of testimony and exhibits.[125]

On Tuesday, January 2, 1781, Landais personally presented his defense. For the next four days he rationalized his actions as best as a man traveling in and out of lucidity could. Barry gave him leeway to explain the unexplainable while keeping the defendant from getting lost in sophistry.[126] Landais rested his case that Friday.

Early the following morning the court met to deliberate. Barry walked the officers through the evidence point by point. His summation was a thorough reading of the facts in the case. Of all Barry's papers, it serves as the best example of his thinking and decision making. Acknowledging that the court "labr'd in this tedious & interminable Case, with all the patience and attention which honor & humanity could dictate," Barry reviewed the evidence and Landais' own testimony:

> Whether Captain Landais permitted goods to be brot' in the ship to America . . . that he at least connived at it, which in effect is permission, can't be doubted . . .
>
> . . . Reporting Captain Landais' abdicating his command... That there should be a coincidence of all the passengers, all his officers and all his crew against him for no reason is a phenomenon: That every action of theirs to him is diabolic and every action of his to them, divine, is another; and to believe such things requires a great share of credulity . . .
>
> Cap. Landais insisting upon living in the office of the Navy Board amongst the public papers . . . that he only wanted the floor to sleep upon . . . looks too much like courting persecution.[127]

Barry's harshest words were not directed at Landais. Instead, he saved them for Lee. For Landais to have taken "the advice of the hon[ora]ble Arthur Lee, a gentleman learn'd in the Laws and high in

Office," seize the *Alliance,* and abandon the army's desperately need-ed supplies was, to Barry, "repugnant." No time was lost in debating the verdict. The court ordered Landais "to be broke and rendered incapable of serving in the American Navy for the future."[128] Found guilty on all charges, Landais was the last captain tried by the Continental Navy.[129]

Next, the court reviewed Lieutenant Degge's role in the mutiny, and found him guilty as well. He, too, was "broken from the serv-ice"–not quite the reward he expected for bowing to Lee's sub-terfuge.[130] Ironically, Congress, in approving Barry's report, approved the mutiny while cashiering its lead officer. The Landais affair con-cluded, Barry turned his full attention to the *Alliance.*

Now three years old, the *Alliance* was even bigger and faster than Barry's previous frigate, the ill-fated *Raleigh.* Built by the Hackett Brothers, she was 178 feet long, with a 36-foot beam and 12 feet 6 inches depth of hold. Her draft was 16 feet 6 inches; she displaced 910 tons.[131] She mounted thirty-six guns. So beautiful was she to the nautical eye that one French official declared that "there is not in the King's Service, nor in the English Navy a frigate more perfect and more complete in materials or workmanship."[132] That said, she still lacked men and supplies. As the winter winds scoured Boston har-bor, Barry and the Eastern Navy Board did what they could to reach a full complement of sailors, while Congress came up with a mission for him.

Four months earlier, General Washington was stunned by the dis-covery of Benedict Arnold's treason. He had endured the slings and arrows of Generals Gates, Charles Lee, and Thomas Conway, but Arnold's betrayal hit him hardest. As 1781 began, matters only wors-ened: having gone a year without new clothing or pay, a thousand Pennsylvania troops mutinied at winter quarters in Morristown, with plans to march on Congress. To quell the insurrection, Washington was compelled to shoot two of the ringleaders. With the British in possession of the southern states, and little money (worthless at that) to provide for supplies, the war seemed lost.[133] Grim as the two pre-vious winters at Valley Forge had been, that of 1780-1781 was the bleakest of all for Washington, his army, and his country. "We are naked, shabbily naked," Lafayette wrote to Franklin.[134]

As before, in December 1776, Thomas Paine's pen crystallized the moment, and it was Paine who proposed a solution. In October, at his own expense, he published *The Crisis Extraordinary,* a short treatise in which he brilliantly argued for raising taxes by pointing out that if England won, Parliament would tax the defeated Americans to pay for the war. He also called for Congress to plead with France for more money—one million pounds sterling a year for the duration of the war, to be exact.[135]

After wrangling over the amount, Congress finally determined to ask the French for another loan of 25 million livres. During these sessions most congressmen reached the conclusion that Arthur Lee's open hostility toward Franklin required sending a different envoy back to Paris to better present their request. After Washington's aide Colonel Alexander Hamilton refused, stating that he was "not sufficiently known to Congress" to represent them with authority, they turned to another member of the General's staff: Henry Laurens's son John. He accepted, but only after being persuaded by Paine, who offered to accompany him.[136]

Only twenty-six, Colonel Laurens spoke perfect French and had studied law before the war. He was already a seasoned veteran, experienced with intrigue as well as battle. Laurens loved Washington and was loved by him in return.[137] This affection drove him to defend Washington's honor against Charles Lee on the field of honor. Facing Lee at the murderous distance of six paces, Laurens wounded him in his side.[138] The younger Laurens was also quite handsome, his pointed nose counterbalanced by large, light-colored eyes, and a fine jaw. In the spring of 1780 his father had embarked on a diplomatic mission to Holland, but his ship was captured, and he was imprisoned in the Tower of London.[139] Son John had no wish to join his father.

Carrying specific instructions from Congress, Laurens set out for Boston in January with Paine and Major William Jackson, stopping to pay their respects to Washington at his winter quarters.[140] After recapping the horrid state of the war as he saw it, Washington had Laurens ghostwrite a letter to Hancock in Boston, eliciting the governor's assistance in "Manning and fitting [the *Alliance*] for sea" and warning Hancock that any delays "would be fatal to the objects of [this] mission." Washington wanted "every effort of influence and authority" Hancock could provide. Lafayette's cousin, the Viscount de Noailles, would also accompany Laurens to Paris.[141]

Laurens and his companions reached Boston on January 25 and met with Barry the next day.[142] The two had met three years earlier at Valley Forge, and Laurens had admired Barry ever since.[143] In sharing his orders, Laurens unwittingly aroused Barry's frustrations. He appreciated Laurens's resolve for the undertaking, but laid out the grim facts: "two indispensables, men and money, were wanting to fit the *Alliance* for sea."[144] Barry's muster rolls consisted of castoffs from the Boston wharves and British prisoners of war: hardly a prime lot to tackle a mid-winter voyage across the Atlantic and fight whatever enemy they encountered.[145] For the moment, he told Laurens, his crew was happy enough to fight on land against America's only ally; earlier, some of the Alliances got into a tavern brawl with their counterparts from two French frigates in port. The fight soon became a riot. One of Barry's sailors was stabbed to death. Several others were wounded.[146]

When another letter from Washington informed Laurens that "We are at the end of our tether," the young colonel desperately sought any ideas that might get his mission off the ground and out to sea.[147] Barry mulled over one solution he found ironic, considering his encounter with the *Confederacy* on the Delaware eighteen months before. Conferring with Laurens and Warren, he raised the issue of impressment.[148] Barry believed the practice loathsome, knowing that press-gangs raiding the waterfront establishments and dragging protesting "recruits" to the *Alliance* would certainly have an adverse effect on his "popularity with Seamen" both in New England and back home, once word got out attaching his name to such an abhorrent practice.[149]

Warren raised no objections, and Laurens could only express his gratitude that Barry would even propose it. Barry's hunch that this would damage his reputation proved correct; news that he was considering press-gangs "so frightened the seamen [of Boston] that many hid themselves and others left town."[150] Nevertheless, the three men petitioned the Massachusetts General Court, requesting permission to press local sailors into service on the *Alliance*.[151] Citing his mission's importance, and the risk of sailing with so many British prisoners among the crew, Barry and the Navy Board made their case. The court quickly ruled against them. Laurens fumed, "private masters have superceded the general good."[152]

The ruling deepened Barry's black mood. If his only source of filling berths was with imprisoned British sailors, he confided to Laurens, the chance that his crew would fight when necessary was slim, and the possibility of mutiny would increase the closer the *Alliance* got to England. When several Bostonians inquired about passage to France aboard the frigate, Barry only agreed "on condition of [their] serving on the quarterdeck in case of an encounter." Laurens saw the wisdom in Barry's thinking, reporting to Congress that "they will reinforce the party of the officers in case of a mutiny."[153]

Actually, Barry did not want to sail at all, believing that the idea of mutiny would spring from the prisoners' "ancient connexions" to their homeland. Common sense was on his side, and only an appeal to his patriotism by Laurens changed his mind. *We are at the end of our tether.* Undaunted, Laurens wrote Congress that he would "insist upon Captain Barry's putting to sea with the crew he can obtain."[154] Not for reason or risk would Laurens let his beloved Washington down.

Won over by Laurens's fervor, Barry joined him on a new strategy. While he held another rendezvous, Laurens went to see General Lincoln, now commanding the troops in Massachusetts. Lincoln gave Barry "authority to engage such of the recruits of this State and soldiers of the invalid corps as might be qualified for the marine service," but this gambit "afforded us but few men." Next, Laurens "obtained permission from Governor Hancock to enlist volunteers from the guard of the castle."[155] Again, hardly any volunteers responded. There was some good news: Warren somehow raised enough money for supplies, munitions, and "commissioned a merchant of popularity and influence among the seafaring men to offer a tempting bounty" to entice the better hands among Boston's idle sailors. After that ploy, too, failed, Barry and Laurens embarked on door-to-door visits of each merchant captain in port, imploring them to relinquish some seamen—again with no success.[156]

Now at the end of *his* tether, Laurens threw all of his sincerity, eloquence, and passion into a new petition to the General Court on February 5. His appeal to duty, patriotism, and "a sum of specie to raise volunteers from the Continental troops" carried the day. The "sum of specie" added enough names to the muster roll that Laurens joyfully wrote Congress two days later that the *Alliance*, "barely in condition to go to sea," was nonetheless going to sea. "I shall embark today," he exulted, "and expect Captn. Barry will sail with the first wind."[157]

If Laurens was ecstatic, Barry was not. He needed experienced sailors. What he got was army castoffs, castle guards, and invalids. How many of them had even been in a rowboat we do not know, but judging from the high percentage of landsmen on board, Barry's bos'n, the man responsible for whipping the crew into shape, would not be sufficiently rewarded for his efforts were he to be paid in Crown jewels. There were 236 souls aboard—about three-quarters the expected complement—not enough to adequately sail or defend the frigate. After settling his bills with Warren and Deshon, Barry ordered his passengers aboard. The *Alliance* stood down Nantasket Road on February 11.[158]

From the minute Barry weighed anchor he could not help but be preoccupied with questions about the British prisoners among his crew: they knew how to sail, but would they? They could fight, but would they? Only the staggering importance of Laurens's mission made Barry risk this voyage with a crew of insufficient number and questionable loyalty. He knew "how essential it was to my Country that Col. Laurens should be landed in France with the greatest expedition," but each minute on deck he witnessed "how poorly the ship *Alliance* is mann'd and the great risque we run'd in coming to Sea with Such a Paltry Crew."[159]

As he took her eastward on the North Atlantic, Barry made two very different observations: "*Alliance* is a fine Ship," but "there was not ten men who could steer her."[160] Accordingly, he spread his few salts among each watch in hopes of teaching the landsmen some degree of seamanship–but after the first day at sea he discerned that "there are no seamen aboard . . . but disaffected ones."[161] The *Alliance* was the finest ship yet under Barry's command, and he had put to sea with his worst crew.

CHAPTER TEN

MUTINY

F BARRY HAD TREPIDATIONS ABOUT GOING TO SEA with an undersized crew consisting largely of landsmen and British prisoners, his passengers were thrilled to be leaving Boston. John Laurens and William Jackson were joyous that they were finally at sea; Viscount de Noailles anticipated a warm welcome from family and friends and a brief respite from war; and Tom Paine was just glad to get away from the political backbiting that had been dogging him for a year. That said, Paine bore his own anxieties about the voyage. On his previous trip across the Atlantic he became seriously ill and, as the man whose words stoked the flame of independence, he feared the consequences of being captured. Already no lover of sailing, he learned just before departing Boston that the ship he had hoped to book passage on prior to the *Alliance*'s departure was lost at sea with all hands.[1]

Paine's qualms about this voyage were soon justified. In sailing across the North Atlantic, the *Alliance* followed the time-honored winter passage to Europe. With British ships ensconced in safe harbors until spring, Barry viewed the weather as an ally. The biggest fear in winter for the *Alliance* was not enemy ships, or even storms: it was ice.

And ice the *Alliance* found. On the night of February 16, she was about two hundred miles southwest of Newfoundland under "exceedingly dark" conditions, when her sleeping captain was awakened by a sharp, slamming thud, "attended with a rushing noise." From above, Barry heard the sailors shout that the ship "was either a ground or on a rock." Instantly bounding up on deck, he saw what the problem was: icebergs, dead ahead, to port and to starboard. They seemed like glowing, frosty behemoths of unknown size both above and below the water line. Some were higher than the mainmast. There was no moonlight to allow Barry to accurately discern their size. The least bit of bad luck, and one of them would rip into the *Alliance*'s hull and send her sinking into the numbingly cold sea. All hands began arriving on deck. Paine was one of the first, his awe at the sight temporarily suppressing his fear, "finding ourselves Surrounded with large floating bodies of Ice against which the Ship was beating." Laurens, assigned a cabin in the *Alliance*'s larboard gallery near the captain's cabin (a small balcony built just outside the hull where the officers' head was also located), soon joined Paine.[2]

Minus a true wind due to the height of the bergs, Barry discovered *Alliance* to be at the whim of the current. Suddenly, the ship began to pitch and roll; the wind, coming from the stern, had picked up strength. Barry gave orders to "heave the lead," and a sailor came to the rail with the lead line: a rope long enough to reach 20 fathoms, tied to a drop-lead weight of about twenty-five pounds. Swung once, twice, three times overhead, it made a distinct "whoosh" sound through the air before being pitched into the sea to find the depth of water. The weight caught on the nearest iceberg below the waterline. The rope flew out of the lead man's hands, taking with it some skin off his palms and fingers. Barry called for a second line to be brought on deck, and this "Second tryal gave us the fathoms" but no bottom.[3]

Soon the wind "encreased to a Severe Gale," and Barry ordered all sails taken in. Before the top-men reached the ratlines, they heard a harsh, ripping sound, as one sail "was torn in two from top to bottom." Standing on the quarterdeck, Barry informed Paine that "Nothing could be done but to lay the Ship to and let her take her chance." The ship's safety was at the mercy of nature—a fact that did not sit well with anyone onboard. To Paine, "The Ice became every moment more formidable, and we began to apprehend as much danger from it as when we first supposed ourselves a Ground. The Sea, in whatever direction it could be Seen, appeared a tumultuous assemblage of floating rolling Rocks, which we could not avoid and against with there was no defence."[4]

With nothing to do but hope that his calm demeanor would inspire the same, Barry remained on the quarterdeck, sending the crew off-watch back below. Laurens and de Noailles returned to their berths, but Paine remained riveted to the deck, watching as Barry and the helmsman negotiated the *Alliance* between icebergs. Barry sent some hands along the rails, carrying the *Alliance*'s fenders: canvas bags of cork and other pieces of canvas, set outside the rail to protect the ship when bumping up against a dock. Now Barry hoped they would do the same against ice. Sailors at the bow sang out the distance and size of each approaching berg as best as they could guess, while others held the guns' rammers, sponges, and spars—anything of length to keep an approaching wall of ice from causing further damage. Each sailor, British or American, did whatever Barry asked without question: when the enemy is nature, one's country no longer matters. For two hours, the large frigate scraped and banged against the icebergs, "breaking on the Ships sides," but without breaking the ship apart. Paine described the loud crunches of ice as "Thundering."[5]

At 11 P.M., what Barry and his crew feared most happened. Laurens had just left his cabin—or, perhaps, the head—to rejoin Paine on deck, when another iceberg struck the *Alliance*, ripping into the larboard gallery. The barrage of frozen shards just missed piercing Laurens and killing him. Every man aboard watched the floating mountain of ice pass by the frigate, doing no further damage. For five more terrifying hours, the endless "Succession of Icy Rocks" floated by; to Paine, "no judgment could be formed . . . of the magnitude of these we had still to encounter." All Barry could do was steer the *Alliance* clear of the ice and hope that what he saw above the waterline wasn't masking a wider, deadlier obstacle below. Just before dawn, the gale died down; then, to their great relief, the Alliance's heard "the agreeable noise of the water round the Sides of the Ship and felt her roll easily." The last mountain of ice floated past them. It was estimated that the icebergs spanned twenty miles. Paine spoke for every man-jack aboard when he wrote that this frightening passage would "not be easily worn from our memories."[6] The *Alliance* may have seemed jinxed under Landais and Jones, but she was one lucky ship that morning.

As the Atlantic returned to a more peaceful nature, Barry examined the "considerable damage" to his ship's side, but within a few days, repairs were completed, and he took the *Alliance* on a week of fine sailing, with "a glorious breeze which carried us for nine to twelve miles an hour."[7] Each evening Barry's cabin offered decent dining and, with such diverse guests in nationality, social status, and philosophy, a wide array of topics for conversation.[8]

If Barry took Laurens into his confidence regarding his motley crew, it is doubtful he revealed anything to de Noailles or Paine. It did fall to these two gentlemen to provide some black comedy. While Midshipman Kessler later wrote that nothing occurred on the voyage "worth notifying" (including, apparently for Kessler, the battle of the icebergs), he did record "Paine's duel with the French officer."[9] Neither party in the duel, nor Barry or Laurens, documented what caused it, or the weapons chosen. If the viscount's aristocratic airs and breeding clashed with the pamphleteer's common touch, at least no actual wounds were sustained in their encounter. The *Alliance* continued eastward.[10]

Smooth sailing returned, and with it the surly mood of the British sailors: grudgingly obeying Barry's commands above deck, while hatching sinister plans below in the lantern-lit fo'c'sle. Barry's hunch was correct: their disposition for mutiny grew more noticeable as the *Alliance* got closer to their homeland. Their ringleader was Barry's quartermaster, John Crawford. Crawford quietly sounded out his fellow Englishmen on the sly to determine who could be counted on to help him seize the ship. Once he had a sufficient number of mutineers, his plot crystallized. On his signal, they would seize what weapons they could get their hands on and kill every officer on board save one who would agree—at knifepoint if necessary—to navigate a course sending the *Alliance* to Ireland or England. A Bible was found, oaths were sworn, and a round-robin was signed; the signatures forming a circle, thereby giving equal weight in the conspiracy to each mutineer. All that remained was to decide when to act.[11]

Barry knew nothing of the murderous scheme but, sensing something amiss, planned accordingly. Having already parceled out the British seamen among the watches, he gave his officers specific instructions to keep alert and report to him even the smallest of suspicions. He ordered Mathew Parke to have the marines patrol the decks around the clock. Arms were stowed aft, with every chest and door padlocked and guarded. Barry left nothing to chance.[12]

The closer the *Alliance* got to France, the better the odds of sighting sail. Only once did Barry let an urge for prizes overcome his desire to get his charges to France as quickly and safely as possible. When two ships were sighted off the coast of Greenland, he ordered weapons issued to all hands, including duelist Paine. The ships were British vessels, and soon showed Barry their heels.[13] On March 4, just outside the Bay of Biscay near Belle Isle, sail was sighted yet again. Two ships approached the *Alliance*. When they were close enough that Barry could identify them as a schooner and merchantman he hailed them. Receiving no reply, he ran up his colors and gave orders to fire a warning shot from a bow-chaser. The cannonball no sooner splashed into the water when both ships hove to.[14]

The schooner was the *Alert*, ten guns, a privateer from Glasgow. The merchantman was her prize, the *Buona Compagnia*, a neutral from the Republic of Venice and loaded with glass bottles, pepper, and indigo. The *Alliance*'s boarding party found her captain, Tomaso Lombardo, clapped in irons below deck and brought him to Barry. A spate of Italian and English commenced on the deck of the *Buona Compagnia*. After examining the ship's papers, Barry determined that the *Alert*'s seizure of Lombardo's ship was an act of piracy. "After a short consultation," Laurens wrote, "Capt'n. Barry and his officers very readily acceded to the liberation of the Venetian, and the complete restitution of the cargo and property, which was very valuable." Declaring the merchantman's seizure "contrary to the Laws of Nations and every principle of justice," Barry ordered Lombardo "left at liberty to pursue his voyage."[15]

The *Alert*'s status was another matter; Barry placed a prize crew aboard the schooner, and she accompanied the *Alliance* to France. Laurens viewed Barry's actions regarding the Venetian as a "happy opportunity of manifesting the determination of Congress to maintain the rights of neutral powers." Paine was equally elated: "The opportunity of doing an act of humanity like this . . . of relieving insulted distress, [is] esteemed preferable to the richest prize that could have been taken." Barry's recognition of the *Buona Compagnia*'s neutrality would go a long way in promoting international goodwill toward the young United States.

The following day, two more sails were sighted–a brigantine and a "dogger"–a ketchlike vessel popular among European privateers for coastal raiding. Barry gave chase, but only so far as to not take him off course so close to France. He spoke a Dutch ship and French brig the next day, and sighted "Land bearing E by N Distance about 5 or 6 Leagues" on March 7. Running the frigate along the coast of Brittany, he picked up both a pilot and some fog on March 8, the latter keeping the former from carrying out his job until the following day. The *Alliance* dropped anchor along Ile de Groix, the rocky island just outside of L'Orient, having made the journey, ice and all, in a remarkably quick twenty-six days. The *Alliance*'s pinnace–the frigate's eight-oared boat–propelled captain and passengers to shore.[16]

L'Orient stands where the Scorff and Blavet rivers empty into the Bay of Biscay and was one of the four main ports of France, along with Cherbourg and Brest on the Atlantic coast and Toulon on the Mediterranean. Originally built as a fortress called Port-Louis, it had come into its own in the mid-seventeenth century, when the Compagnie des Indes Orientale, France's own East India Company, flourished. Paine found L'Orient "a clean, agreeable town," with "streets Strait but not in general at right angles."[17]

The town commandant greeted them effusively, saving his warmest welcome for Paine, whom he congratulated for the "great success and spirit" of Paine's publications. Laurens immediately sent word to Congress of their arrival via a departing American ship. His mission had already become an obsession; he wanted to get to Passy–and Franklin–as quickly as possible.[18]

Barry also put pen to paper, writing the first in a series of letters to Franklin, going into great detail regarding his orders. As Franklin was in charge of the purse strings for American interests, Barry also requested funds to sheath the *Alliance*'s hull with copper. He knew all too well the damage wooden hulls sustained after months at sea from barnacles and the *teredo*–a long, worm-like mollusk that ate its way through wood. Copper sheathing would protect the *Alliance*, allowing her to maintain her speed and sailing capabilities. While a common practice for the British and French navies, it was expensive, and therefore rare for an American ship. Barry did his homework, discovered that "it will Cost in this place one third as much to Clean [*Alliance*] as it would to Copper her," and urged Franklin to "weigh this matter seriously," as "it will be rending the Continent a vast service."[19]

Before departing for Passy, Laurens joined Barry in a visit to the counting house of Moylan and Goularde in L'Orient. James Moylan, yet another Irishman, was held in high regard by American captains; when John Paul Jones sought a new command in 1779, it was Moylan who found *Le Duc de Duras*, which Jones renamed the *Bonhomme Richard*. Later, Jones stayed at Moylan's home while the *Alliance*, then under his command, was being refitted–a generous gesture on Moylan's part, having just married an ardent seventeen-year-old French girl.[20]

Barry briefed Moylan on his orders, and Moylan informed him that a "Ship with Continental Stores on board will be ready to sail in a few days." This was an old French Indiaman renamed the *Marquis de Lafayette*, under charter of Franklin's nephew, Jonathan Williams. In her hold were uniforms and munitions worth up to one million livres (and not one American diplomat's coach to displace them), with orders to sail within a week.[21]

Laurens delayed his journey to Paris, having been informed that the Minister of Marine, the Marquis de Castries, was en route to L'Orient while "on his way to Brest." Realizing that this was an opportunity to convey to de Castries the urgency of his mission, Laurens waited until March 11 to leave for Paris, but not before he and Barry learned that "twenty-five sail of the line ready for sea, with ninety transports" were heading to the West Indies and America with thousands of French troops. After meeting de Castries, and carrying Barry's letter to Franklin, Laurens departed for Paris.[22]

Barry spent most of his first days ashore, scouring the wards and ships in search of his biggest need–American sailors. There were none to be found. When he was "informed by good Authority that there is fifty Americans on board a French privateer at Nantes," he quickly wrote again to Franklin: if the *Alliance* were called on to convoy the *Marquis de Lafayette* home, Barry estimated that "we should have thirty or forty more men, for at present she is not more than a match for a small Frigate." Recalling earlier troubles manning the *Delaware*, he informed Franklin that "we Cannot take a French Sailor either here or in America into our Service." Therefore, the logical Barry believed "we have a right to take our Subjects out of French vessels." All Barry needed was Franklin's blessing to do so. Expecting that Franklin, a fellow Philadelphian, would assist him in padding his muster rolls with American seamen, he dispatched the letter.[23]

This request was one more sign that the pressure aboard the *Alliance* was intensifying. Matthew Parke also wrote Franklin on another urgent subject, money: "It is near eighteen months since the *Serapis* and *Countess of Scarborough* were taken by us . . . and not a farthing of Prize money is yet paid." Parke added that "the detention of said Prize money has been a very great detrim [ent] to the American Navy in America for which I appeal to John Barry, Esquire our commander." Parke, writing on behalf of the other members of *Bonhomme Richard*'s crew now serving on the *Alliance* as much as for himself, was beginning to vent his dissatisfaction with the state of affairs regarding money and morale, although he did inform Franklin that "We are exceedingly happy in our present Commander who is disposed to do everything in his power for the Honor of the United States & his Officers & Men."[24]

Discontent found its way into the *Alliance*'s log as well. On March 13, 1781, "Martin Crooks was Put in Irons for Gitting drunk Abusing the Officers & Dam[n]ing the Congress. Danniel Dunavin was Put in Irons for Gitting drunk & striking Hugh Mallery with a Sharp Clip on the head wich Lay his head open to the Scull." Four days later,

"Mr. Donnell, the Boatswain's mate, was put in Irons for Gitting drunk & Fighting.[25]

On March 19, the cat-o'-nine-tails made its first appearance under Barry's command of the *Alliance*. "All hands to witness punishment" shouted the bos'n. Parke ordered his marines to fall in, their muskets loaded and bayonets shining in the sunlight. Midshipmen took their place on the side of the deck, while Barry, Hacker, and the other officers stood on the weather side, the wind at their backs. Crooks, Dunavin, and Donnell were brought before Barry on the quarterdeck. "Rig the grating," Barry ordered, and ship's carpenter Charles Drew, along with his mates, took two of the hatch gratings, laid one flat on deck while setting the other up by the gangway. "Ship's company: off hats!" was the next order. Barry then read from the Continental Navy's Articles of War regarding the offenses. As Congress had ordered the Articles "hung up in some public place of the ship," each of the accused knew what he was in for.[26]

When told of his transgressions, Crooks was asked if he had anything to say; in most cases, the sailor's answer was "No." The bos'n's next order was but one word: "Strip." Once Crooks's shirt was off, the bos'n barked "Seize him up," and Crooks was bound at the wrist to the upright grating. Another of the bos'n's mates produced a red baize bag, and pulled out the cat-o'-nine-tails.[27]

Correct use of the "cat" took training and a strong arm. One learned the art of flogging by using a cask or barrel as the "victim." At the order, "Do Your Duty," the bos'n's mate advanced to within a few feet of Crooks's bare back. Bringing his arm back and low, he swept the cat forward. The force of the blow to Crooks's back would have leveled him were it not for being bound fast against the grate. It knocked the wind out of him; an involuntary groan came through his lips. Each of the nine leather "tails" held metal beads or bits of wire. The first "stripe," or lash, took the skin off his back anywhere the flaying leather strips landed. The mate brought the cat back to his free hand and wiped it to make sure the cat would strike "clean."[28] Then his arm went back again; the cat whistled through the air, followed by another fearful, slapping sound, and another groan from Crooks. A slow, cruel, paralyzing rhythm formed.

John Adams's "Regulations" aimed for a more humane navy than the British counterpart. Only twelve lashes were permitted without a court-martial. Three dozen were quite common in the Royal Navy. Crooks still had ten more lashes coming, and the bos'n's mate couldn't spare him by "easing up"; any leniency in his "duty" and he would wind up on the other side of the cat himself, if Barry were so disposed.[29]

Crooks's back was becoming a bloody mess. One recipient of the lash recalled the experience as "an astounding sensation between the shoulders under my neck, which went to my toenails in one direction, and my fingernails in another . . . I felt my flesh quiver in every nerve . . . the pain in my lungs was more severe, I thought, than on my back."[30] At the count of "twelve," Crooks's ordeal was over. Then came Dunavin's turn; when his flogging ended, he and Crooks were "Sent to their duty" while "Mr. Donnell," Barry recorded, was "Lett out of Irons and forgave."[31] The crew witnessed the whippings in silence. Barry believed that flogging never improved morale, and was known as a captain loath to let the cat out of the bag. But he believed the surly demeanor among the many British salts aboard the *Alliance* warranted a display of both corporal punishment and captain's authority.[32]

Punishment over, the crew was dismissed, with Crooks and Dunavin turned over to Dr. Bradford for care.[33] Bradford's ministration only added to their pains; washing their backs in stinging brine stopped the bleeding but increased their suffering. Salt packs were applied as a dressing and to ward off infection.[34] Barry hoped the day's punishment would serve as a warning to the malcontent British sailors. All it did was harden their resolve.

His other act as captain that day bore better results. His application for condemnation of the *Alert* was speedily handled. She was soon sold and the prize money was distributed to the crew upon receipt, providing a morale booster beyond measure—until it was spent in the taverns and brothels of L'Orient.[35]

Still hopelessly searching for American sailors, Barry was given a new problem: the *Marquis de Lafayette*. Seeing that the *Alliance* might be several weeks at L'Orient, Moylan urged the *Marquis's* captain, Monsieur de Galatheau, to sail his ship to Brest and join the large fleet Laurens had written home about. Instead, de Galatheau refused, requesting that Barry and the *Alliance* accompany him to Brest. If the fleet had already departed, he wanted Barry to escort the *Marquis* to Teneriffe in the Canary Islands, or "convey me as far as my destination"–Philadelphia.[36]

De Galatheau's brass came as little surprise to Barry, having seen the same in Pierre Landais. Knowing the *Marquis* was not ready, Barry decided that if de Galatheau wanted the *Alliance* for an escort, he would sail under Barry's orders. Wanting nothing to do with a trip to Brest, Barry pushed Moylan to step up his assistance in refitting the *Alliance* and was soon ready to depart.[37] All he needed was the much anticipated letter from Franklin, and he got it. It was the beginning of two years of frustrating correspondence with the Minister Plenipotentiary:

> I received the honor of yours dated the 10th Instant acquainting me with the Orders you have recev'd relating to your Ship, Sailing & c. I have none relating to your Ship and therefore cannot take upon me to sheath her with Copper tho' I think with you it would be a good thing; nor can give any Directions for you to apply to any Person for Supplies of what you may want; but I suppose you naturally fall under the Care of Mr. Schweighauser of Nantes in the Absence of Mr. Palfrey he being Agent.[38]

William Palfrey, the most recently assigned American agent, had not been heard from since his ship left home three months before (it was soon discovered his ship was lost at sea).[39] J. D. Schweighauser, a Swiss merchant and crony of Arthur Lee, was best known for his stinginess.[40] As far as Barry was concerned, only young Moylan was proving his worth. Barry's luck with American recruits did improve, by four: "Got one man out of A french Ship and 3 from a Schooner," he noted on March 21.[41]

On the twenty-third, with the *Alliance* ready to sail, Barry sent de Galatheau a copy of his orders from Congress and the signals they would use during the voyage.[42] He concluded with orders to "get

Your Ship ready for Sea Immediately & to proceed under my Convoy."[43] That letter was easy to write, compared to his response to Franklin. Throwing diplomatic tact to the wind, Barry acknowledged "The Honor to receive yours dated the 17th Inst. But it leaves me Intirely in the dark.–As I have no Orders from you . . . and to Comply with my orders from the Honble. the Admiralty I have took the Ship the *Marquis delafayette* with public Stores onboard under my direction and shall as soon as I can get ready (which will be on sunday or Monday next) proceed to Deleware with her under my convoy."[44]

This letter set the tone for Barry's communications with Franklin for the remainder of the war. Barry would write a simple, terse letter reporting his situation and/or requesting authority from Franklin to do what he felt necessary to refit, sail, and fight. Franklin usually responded with polite, Cheshire catlike dismissivness, rarely taking sides on an issue or fully answering any of Barry's questions. When Franklin did offer assistance, it was out of surety that any action on his part would not meet with any reproach from Congress. Barry's replies, such as this one, are politely worded, but one can feel his jaw clench and fist close as he dictated or wrote. Such was the correspondence between warrior and diplomat.

Both ships were ready to sail on March 26, but the winds were uncooperative. Barry remained ashore, penning one more response to Franklin, who had requested that Barry remain in port until a courier arrived from Passy, bearing Franklin's correspondence for Barry to take home. "I sail in a few hours for Philadelphia in Company with the Ship that has Continental Stores on board and Sundry other Vessells," an exasperated Barry wrote. "I am Sorry I cannot wait for your Dispatches the Reason is . . . with the Stores on board [the *Marquis*] being of such Consequence to the United States that I think I am Duty bound to convey her safe in my Power."[45] At least the philosopher in Franklin could be amused at the different personalities of the *Alliance*'s captains. Jones would not sail; Landais was not supposed to sail; Barry could not wait to sail.

Barry was no sooner aboard and the moorings cast off when a sudden, fierce squall severely fouled the foretopsail, hampering the frigate's sailing abilities; the Alliances "Made our Moorings Again

Fast."[46] While the storm raged, Barry was called on deck by one of his lieutenants: a signal from shore was requesting Barry's return. Moylan greeted him at the dock and introduced him to Jonathan Williams, fresh from Nantes and not the least bit happy about the *Marquis de Lafayette*.[47]

Williams proceeded to inform Barry about the ship's manifest: 450 tons of public stores including cannons, gun barrels, saltpeter, leather, 10,000 uniforms and enough bolts of cloth to make thousands more. Yet, as if 450 tons of cargo wasn't enough, Williams suspected the *Marquis* was even heavier in the water due to smuggled goods not listed on her cocket. With fraud an ongoing sideline in shipping munitions and Franklin's career in a state of precariousness at home, Williams worried that a possible scandal over his ownership of the *Marquis* would do irreparable damage to Franklin's reputation. To allay his fears, Barry offered to examine the *Marquis*'s hold before it was unloaded in Philadelphia.[48]

Humors aboard the frigate were as foul as the hail, wind, and rain battering the ship. Surgeon Bradford was put "under An Arrest" and replaced by Dr. Joseph Kendall, recently retired from the Continental Army. The weather finally cleared on the twenty-eighth, and Barry "Hoisted a Red and White Pennant at the Mizzen Peak as a Signal for the *Marquis* to get under way."[49] De Galatheau recognized the prearranged signal, but simply ignored it.[50] The following morning, "Clearing with fresh Breezes of wind at ENE," Barry again "made the Signal for the *Marquis* to get under Sail." Once again, the "Red and White Pennant" was hoisted; once again, the signal was ignored. When a third signal was raised and not obeyed, the *Alliance*'s pinnace was lowered, and Barry went to confront the Frenchman.[51]

Perhaps de Galatheau spoke English. We know Barry spoke no French, but his invective and tone regarding the blatant disregard of his signals probably did not require translation. Luckily, he found an ally aboard, Captain William Robeson from South Carolina, who promised to keep an eye on de Galatheau. In a moment of premonition, Robeson also gave Barry his trunk to stow aboard the *Alliance*. At 4 P.M. the *Marquis* was under way; the *Alliance* followed her down the roadstead, discharging the pilot an hour later.[52]

Now Barry ordered men aloft to "Set a Reef out of each T[op] S[ail]," sending his frigate homeward. Soon she was making seven to eight knots, a fast clip for unfamiliar waters. The sun had set and night was in full blackness when the watch heard a splash come from the stern. The cry of "Man Overboard!" brought all hands on deck.[53]

Barry ordered the ship "hove to," and all eyes searched the *Alliance*'s wake for signs of her lost sailor, who fell into the sea when a "tall tackle" gave way. Finally, "Seeing nothing of him," Barry gave orders to get under way, passing the Ile de Groix in the darkness. The weather, "squally with rain," continued into the night. "Lost a man over Board," Barry entered in the log, "named Patrick Duggan." He was one of the British sailors.[54]

Being unaware of the coming mutiny, Barry did not know that Duggan was one of its ringleaders. The conspirators, however, were more than a little unsettled by Duggan's demise. Retreating below to the berth deck, where sailors stowed their hammocks, they spoke in hushed but passionate voices. There is no proof that Duggan's death was accidental or a result of foul play, but it dampened the mutineers' zeal for murder and mayhem. A number of them were losing their nerve, and wanted the round-robin destroyed. They saw Duggan's death as a premonition of doom—not for the American officers and crew, but for themselves. The round-robin was torn up and given to one of the conspirators to throw overboard. The bits of paper floated in the breeze before joining Duggan in the waters off Ile de Groix.[55] The mutiny was still on, but with fewer mutineers.

March 30 found the *Alliance* entering the Bay of Biscay—France's stormy, dangerous doorway to the Atlantic.[56] Here John Paul Jones, in his latest command, the sloop of war *Ariel*, saved ship and crew from a furious storm only after chopping down her masts.[57] For the *Alliance*, the morning began with company: "At 6 A.[M.] saw a Sail Bearing W at 11 Saw a Sail Bearing about SW." A five-mile chase ended when she proved to be a neutral from Venice en route to Hamburg.[58]

As daylight waned, a sailor—Kessler calls him "an Indian (one of the Forecastlemen)"—asked to see Barry. Shown into the captain's cabin, he proceeded to tell Barry of the plot "among the Crew for the purpose of taking the ship." With Barry coolly urging him on, he went into great detail, and "pointed out 3 who had known to prevail upon him to be concerned therein." He named them for Barry: the quartermaster, John Crawford, and two "Able Seamen," Patrick Shelden and William McEllany.[59]

When the sailor finished his story, Barry thanked and dismissed him, then called the ship's officers aft to his cabin. The twin difficulties of being undermanned and the capricious whims of de Galatheau now seemed mere trifles. Keeping his voice down, Barry related what he just heard. With their lives in the balance, the meeting took on the aspects of a council of war—a war against some of the ship's own crew.[60]

Continuing in hushed tones, Barry outlined a brutal, simple plan. Parke and the marines were immediately put on alert. The captain and his officers reviewed which of the Americans in the ship's crew could be trusted with arms. These men and the marines would remain on deck throughout the night. Next, Barry ordered Parke to assemble an armed detail, go below without delay, arrest Crawford, Shelden, and McEllany as speedily as possible, and clap them in irons while officers issued weapons to the trusted hands. The slender, handsome Parke, whose wide-set eyes missed nothing, swiftly carried out his captain's orders. That night, Barry scribbled in the log how he put the conspirators "in Irons for ~~Mutity~~ Mutiny"; his crossed-out misspelling the only evidence of any anxiety. The next part of his plan would take place at daybreak.[61]

Only the bone-weary slept soundly that night. Marines stood watch, with most of the American-born sailors above deck. In the fo'c'sle, British sailors off watch looked upwards and wondered what was to come in the early morning hours, knowing by now that their comrades were in irons. It was plain to even the most fanatical of the mutineers that the jig was up. Their main concern was whether they too would wind up in irons—or worse.[62]

Throughout the night, Barry paced the quarterdeck. Outwardly, he revealed nothing to the Alliances but a grim visage, keeping his own anger, frustration, and degree of dread locked deep inside. Conversations above deck were whispered. The sound of the ship's bell, signaling the change of the watch, tolled ominously, as if for a funeral . . . or an execution.

To the loyal contingent of sailors it must have seemed that daybreak would never come. When it did, Barry brought the *Alliance* into the wind. Bos'n John Lewis and his mates–including the "forgiven" Donnell–piped all hands on deck. As they climbed up to daylight, Lieutenant Hacker ordered them to the forecastle deck. When that was filled, the rest of the sailors were ordered out along the booms and gangways. The marines, along with other American sailors, "strongly guarded the quarterdeck, the Storage & main deck to keep the remainder of the crew together."[63] Any mumbling was quickly silenced; the anxious and inquisitive glances exchanged among the British tars were the only forms of communication between them.

Barry sent Parke and a detachment of marines below to fetch Crawford, Shelden, and McEllany. The crew could hear the clanking of their shackles as they awkwardly came up the hatchway steps. Marines knelt down and unlocked Crawford's leg irons. Barry dispensed with the public reading of their violations as to the Naval Regulations and the Articles of War: this was no time for formalities. Calling the three by name, he told them they were charged with mutiny, and that their punishment would be less severe if they named their accomplices.[64]

Barry's "offer" hung out in the wind. The only noise came from the creak of the ship, the squeak of rope on wood, the breeze snapping loudly at flag and sail.[65] There was no need for Barry to order "all hands to witness punishment"; everyone on board knew what was coming next. With a nod of his head to Lewis, Barry gave the signal to begin. By then some of the crew noticed that no grating had been set up for a flogging.

Lewis and his men immediately seized Crawford, stripped him, and took him aft toward the mizzen stay. With dispatch, the bos'n's mates knotted small cords around Crawford's thumbs, tied them to a sheet, and hauled him up the mizzen stay–just high enough that his feet could not reach the deck. His entire weight, twisting in the breeze, was being held by his thumbs. In seconds, the ligaments and tendons were pulling apart from his bones. Crawford tried desperately to get his toes to reach the deck, but to no avail.

Then came the cat. Again and again, the bos'n's mate lay into his duty. There was no sequential count to the stripes; there was no counting at all. This was life or death. Crawford had vowed to kill his fellow sailors, his officers, and his captain. Now Barry's angry voice rang out–"Talk!" and "Who are they?!"

Crawford was enduring "a very severe whipping," but whether it was hatred, blind courage, or both, though he screamed and moaned, he did not reveal one name. Soon he was joined on the mizzen stay by his accomplices, their thumbs also carrying all of their weight while the flesh was being torn off their backs.[66]

Eventually, they broke. As each of the three mutineers moaned a name, Hacker called that accomplice to the quarterdeck, where he was "Strip(p)ed and tyed to the ridge rope of the netting." The same brutal justice was administered, stopping only when names were given. "At 11 found out a number more that were Concern'd in the Mutiny," and Barry later added the names of eight more mutineers to the log. By Kessler's recollection, "The names of 25 of their accomplices were obtained from them before the whipping was discontinued." Among those names were congressional critic Crooks and the "broken-headed" Hugh Mallady.[67]

By now the bos'n's mate wielding the cat was bloodstained, though himself unbloodied. He was also exhausted. Barry called for a break; then, "After an interval of some time Began to punish again and Ended About 3 p.m." The "whipping of all continued until it was thought all was discovered that could possibly be obtained." It lasted at least seven hours. The mutineers having "relinquished their designs," Barry ordered the three ringleaders put back in irons and sent below for the remainder of the voyage, "kept on bread and water."[68]

All through this horrific day, Barry watched the reactions of the mutineers to discern who was truly a threat to everyone else's safety. Satisfied that the three original ringleaders were the only ones that could not be trusted, Barry approached the other eight culprits, writhing in fear and pain. "After being admonished by Capt'n Barry

& on their solemn declaration to conduct themselves well," they were allowed to return to duty—at least, what duties men in their wretched condition could perform.[69] They swore to Barry they had abandoned their plan. His actions that day ensured it would stay abandoned. Savage as they were, Barry's methods were his only recourse; they saved the lives of his officers and loyal sailors, as well as his own.

"Pleasant weather and Clear. The *Marquis* in Company" was his summation of the rest of the day.[70] The mutiny over, Barry began scanning the horizon for the one thing that would unify his crew: action.

Weather-wise, April picked up where March left off: "The first part Breezy and Clear with the *Marquis* in Company." The ships were about six hundred miles west of L'Orient on April 2 when the *Alliance*'s lookout "Saw a Sail Bearing about NW." Barry had found his action, and "made all the Sails we could and Gave Chace." "Beat to quarters!" he roared, signaling the *Marquis* to accompany the *Alliance* in the chase. Gazing through his spyglass, Barry saw from their size and sail that his quarry were brigs. He fully expected them to show their heels. Surprisingly, they did not; instead, "They Stood for us." Both ships sailed boldly toward the *Alliance*. Barry let them come.[71] With his gun crews standing at the ready, and his marines aloft in the tops, the Alliances prepared to greet the oncoming brigs.

In those days, the code of naval warfare began with a polite hail from the captain, asking for the other ship's name and nationality while gauging his counterpart's intentions. The brigs were closing in on the *Alliance* under the delusion that she was a merchantman ripe for picking. By the time they reached the *Alliance* they realized their "prize" was a frigate cleared for action. It was too late to turn and flee.[72]

Both British captains decided it was also too late for any pleasantries. Without a hail, they "passed us to Leeward," giving the *Alliance* "a broadside Each," and high ones at that. After firing "the whole broadside at us," Barry saw "everyone of them run off their deck." His response to their neglect of battle etiquette was immediate and punishing; returning the broadside "Double Foul'd," the

Alliance's 12-pounders swept the decks of both vessels, abandoned though they were. The second broadside from the *Alliance* tore apart the larger ship's rigging, decimating her sailing capabilities so severely that her captain struck his colors. The smaller brig sheered off, making a desperate retreat eastward.[73]

After signaling de Galatheau to take charge of the surrendered brig, Barry sent the *Alliance* speeding after the smaller one. Once in range, Barry's bow-chasers fired incessantly until "She hove too about eleven o'clock" and also struck. She "proved to be the *Minerva*, Captain J[ohn] Lecoster commanding, mounting 8 four [pounders] & 55 men." A boarding party took command of her, and the *Alliance* escorted prize number two back to the *Marquis* and prize number one.[74]

In firing "high," the British brigs did not kill or wound any of the *Alliance's* crew with their shots. British warships often purposely fired broadsides high as a means of crippling an enemy ships' ability to maneuver by wrecking masts, sails, and rigging. This left the hull intact so that it could be taken without any danger of sinking. An angry Barry examined the damage done to his ship: her rigging was shredded, with one twelve-pound shot lodged into one of the steering sail booms. What should have been a short jaunt back took a long time. Barry's mood, usually jovial after taking a prize, was darkening by the time the *Alliance* rejoined the *Marquis*. He learned that the larger brig "proved to be the *Mars* of 20 twelves 2 sixes and 12 four pound cohorns 111 men." Furious at the injuries the *Alliance* sustained "in consequence of their firing on us with no intention of gravely fighting," Barry was not about to be magnanimous in dealing with her captain, John Proveaux: "All were put in Irons (without distinction)."[75]

Barry placed the *Mars* and fifteen hands under Patrick Fletcher's command, and turned the *Minerva* over to a prize crew picked from the *Marquis de Lafayette*. Still suspicious of de Galatheau, Barry was not happy about turning the *Minerva* over to the Frenchman. He spent the next day being rowed in the *Alliance's* pinnace between the prizes and the *Marquis*, giving strict orders that the three ships keep up with his frigate. If that proved impossible they were to make straight for Philadelphia. Unknowingly, Barry's orders to the French prizemaster countermanded those from de Galatheau, who secretly ordered him to sail the *Minerva* back to France, so de Galatheau could keep the prize money for himself.[76]

April 4 began with "pleas[a]nt Breezes," the last clear weather for some time. For two straight weeks the four ships sailed through "Very Heavy Squalls" and "a Large Sea from the North." But while the *Alliance*, "Laboring much in the Sea," plowed through the successive storms, Barry was forced to keep "false fires" burning as "signals for the other ships to keep with the *Alliance*." On April 18, tragedy struck again; with winds "Blowing Hard" and "a Ruff Sea and some Rain," the *Alliance* "lost a man off the M[ain] T[op] S[ail] Yard by name of John Burke." Barry immediately "Hove too but could not Save him."[77]

Later that day, Barry noticed the *Minerva* was missing. For the next week he kept false fires burning as "the Ship one Brig in Comp'y" struggled through the stormy seas. Even with her jury-rigged repairs, the *Alliance* was a far better sailor than either the old French merchantman or the little brig. But while Barry did everything possible to keep his consorts in view, de Galatheau kept waiting for an opportunity to break free.[78]

On April 25, the inevitable happened: "About 7 O'Clock in the morning (the *Marquis* close by us) we split our foresail and soon after our Four stay Sail which deprived us of any Head sail." Here was de Galatheau's chance, and he took it; "the *Marquis* being bent under her Fore Sail she soon shott ahead of us out of sight." On the quarterdeck of the *Marquis*, Captain Robeson gave de Galatheau a thorough tongue-lashing and "remonstrated with him that the *Alliance* Could not Steer that Course, & that he Must inevitably loose [lose] his Convoy." Barry raised signal flags and fired guns in an effort to bring the *Marquis* back on course and de Galatheau back to his duty, but to no avail–the *Alliance* "lost sight of the *Marquis*." Although Barry "Showed a false fire Every Hour" through the next day, even the return of "Calm and Clear Weather" showed no *Marquis de Lafayette* on the horizon. Barry spent two more days sailing back and forth, his spyglass scanning the horizon for de Galatheau. Finally, on the twenty-ninth, he resumed his homeward course.[79]

The return of fair weather did little to ease Barry's concern over the disappearance of the other ships. He could only hope de Galatheau had obeyed orders and continued west to Philadelphia. On May 1, Barry acknowledged observation of Saint Tammany's Day–the patron saint of the Revolution–in the log. He did not note how much grog or celebration he permitted the crew.[80]

At dawn on May 2, the mast-header "saw two Sails upon the Weather-Bow," and the chase began. Soon the bow-chasers were run out and brought to bear on the closest target–another brig. Two warning shots put her into the wind. She was the *Adventure*, recently split from the Jamaican fleet, then making its annual voyage to England. After an afternoon pursuit Barry caught up with the other vessel, a "Snow from Jamaica bound for Bristol." Combined, both ships carried over five hundred hogsheads of sugar and a bonus for Barry aboard the snow: four recruits–a seaman and three boys, who decided life on the *Alliance* would be better enjoyed in her employ rather than in the hold among the growing number of British prisoners.[81]

Barry placed prize crews aboard both ships, turning the *Adventure* over to young midshipman Edward Kirby and instructing both prizemasters that, "in Case of Separation [they] were ordered for Philadelphia, which was the Case a Short time afterwards in a hard Gale of Wind." Shortly thereafter, to westward, the mast-header sighted the entire Jamaica fleet–"Ab't 65 sail convoyed by 10 Sail of the line." Barry kept watch over the fleet by night, and then slipped away in the dark, by good fortune neither pursued nor captured.[82]

Barry escaped the Jamaica fleet's ships-of-the-line, but de Galatheau was not so lucky. He had, in fact, willfully disobeyed Barry's orders; Robeson's protests fell on deaf or noncomprehending ears. De Galatheau's comeuppance came five days later. The huge British convoy spied the *Marquis* and soon the *Egmont*, a seventy-four-gun ship-of-the-line, was joined by the forty-four-gun frigate *Endymion* in pursuit. For three hours de Galatheau put up a "smart, running fight," Robeson later admitted, trading blow for blow with the *Endymion* as the *Egmont* closed in. By the time the *Egmont*'s guns were in range, the *Marquis* was "Reduc'd to a perfect hulk." With heavy casualties among his small crew and his ship no longer navigable, de Galatheau surrendered. So damaged was the *Marquis* that the British had to tow her back to Edinburgh, where the contents of her hold were determined to be worth "£300,000 sterling."[83]

Unaware of de Galatheau's fate, the *Alliance* continued westward. Still slowed by her jury-rigged repairs, she was off the coast of Newfoundland. From this point on lay the greatest chance of encountering enemy warships. In addition to his ship's troubles, the *Adventure* was in a bad way, compelling Barry to "Repair her She being much in want of it." The *Adventure's* sailing difficulties were also too much for young Kirby to handle. Barry decided to replace Kirby with the more experienced midshipman Nicholas Gardner, sending him in the pinnace over to the *Adventure* and assume command.[84]

But Gardner's promotion got off to an inauspicious start. The sailor securing the pinnace to the *Adventure* used a very lubberlike hitch. Had it been properly done, the rolling sea and wind would have stretched the line taut; as it was not, the line slackened, and slid down the *Adventure's* hull. The pinnace departed on an unmanned voyage of its own. Someone aboard the *Alliance* alerted the captain. Barry thought he had seen everything on this mission: icebergs, dueling, mutiny, disobedient French captains, storms, and disappearing consorts and prizes. Now even his pinnace was deserting him. This was too much for his Irish sense of the absurd. Laughing through his own orders, Barry "gave chase," recapturing the longboat by late afternoon.[85]

By May 4 there were more than one hundred British prisoners in the *Alliance's* hold, and concerns that the mutineers "returned to duty" might resurrect their original plan–especially with so many fellow countrymen just a padlock away–were raised by Barry's officers. He ordered "a bright Look out" kept, but once the story of his actions on March 31 found its way into the hold, any thoughts of another insurrection dissolved.[86]

Bad weather also returned with a biblical vengeance. "In a hard Gale of Wind" on May 12, the *Adventure* and the nameless snow were lost to sight, vanishing in the rain and darkness. After several days of "Ruff Seas," adversity struck again. "On the 16th May . . . in a Severe Gale of Wind," the *Alliance* was beset by a tempest worthy of the Book of Jonah. Suddenly a bolt of lightning "cut a Main Top Mast in two." Like a finger from God, the lightning bolt flew down the mast and "knocked down twelve or fifteen men on Deck some of which it burnt some of their Skin off."[87]

Now dealing with fire as well as wind and water, Barry roared over the elements and the agonizing cries of his suffering sailors for Surgeon Kendall to come on deck. There were "A number knocked down and several much burnt," but Kendall's care for the stricken sailors proved effective.[88] "I thank God all of them have done well," Barry later wrote about their recovery.[89] The next week was spent on repairs: a new topmast was stepped in and the foremast was "fished," but Barry found no spar long enough among his supplies to replace the mainyard destroyed by the lightning bolt.[90] Further encumbered in her sailing abilities, the *Alliance* continued eastward.

The frigate's situation was deteriorating before Barry's eyes. When he departed L'Orient, he called her "a Ship never put to Sea in worse Condition as to Seamen"; the attempted mutiny proved him right. But even more alarming than her current condition was his negligible fighting strength: there were 241 men on Barry's muster rolls when he departed L'Orient; he added 8 more hands from the four prizes. Subtract from 249 the 2 lost overboard, the 36 assigned to sail the prizes to Philadelphia, the 3 mutineers in irons, at least 20 others under a cloud of suspicion, one arrested surgeon, and 50 on Kendall's sick list. That left him with 138 hands to sail a frigate that required more than twice that number for a full complement. Add more than 100 British prisoners to be guarded, in addition to the dictates of sailing and fighting, and one can easily understand Barry's course of action—or inaction—on May 19, when the *Alliance* "fell in with two Ships."[91]

Barry soon "took them to be [British] Merchantmen," but he would not pursue them, "being so poorly Manned." Summoning up every ounce of self-control, Barry sailed the *Alliance* far enough that he "did not speak them."[92] His decision galled him: two merchantmen, unescorted by British warships—a rarity, indeed—that he did not pursue. Give Barry a full crew, even just a few dozen more men, and there would have been two more prizes entered in his log. What lay in their holds would easily have been as rich as the £300,000 in the *Marquis de Lafayette*. Free from certain capture, the merchantmen sailed on to England, while the *Alliance* and her frustrated captain continued homeward.

On May 27, 1781, Barry was about two hundred miles from Cape Sable–the southernmost part of Nova Scotia. The following evening, the lookout sighted two sails on the weather bow. The two ships "hauled [their] wind & stood [their] course," sailing parallel to the *Alliance*. Soon Barry could make them out: "an armed Ship & a Brig about 1 League distance." Barry gave orders to keep the *Alliance* abreast of their course and speed. Even in the dark of night that was easy to do–their lanterns showed their position, and also their intent: obviously on the prowl, with Barry's frigate their intended prey.[93] The gales that bullied the *Alliance* across the Atlantic would have been welcome this night, but they were gone; replaced by an inter-mittent, fluttering breeze, allowing the two nautical wolves to main-tain their course while keeping out of range of the *Alliance*'s long guns. Despite the frigate's superior size and firepower, the two British captains were showing Barry that they were unafraid.

One of those captains, Sampson Edwards, standing on the deck of the "armed Ship," employed private signals that Barry could not answer–clear proof of the *Alliance*'s nationality. Edwards was that rarest of British captains: an officer with generations of family influence who nonetheless earned his rank with talent and courage. Both his father and uncle had died post-captains; another uncle was naval hero Admiral Richard Edwards. Now in his early thirties, Sampson had fought the French at Pondicherry, the Spanish at Manila, and the Americans wherever he found them. His "armed Ship," the *Atalanta*, was the Admiralty's reward for his "long and incessant services" to the Royal Navy. The brig was the *Trepassey*, acting Captain Smyth. They were both rated as sloops of war. Edwards was senior officer; the decision to face or flee the *Alliance* was his to make, and "Finding her a large ship, opposed to a two decker, and night coming on we hauled our wind and sailed in sight of her all night."[94]

While Edwards did not see the *Alliance* as a ship to avoid as much as a chance for prize and glory, he was not foolhardy. He based his judgment with the weather conditions in mind. The sea was still, and the "little puffs of wind" kept Barry from escaping, while allowing Edwards to stalk the *Alliance*.[95]

Dawn found the ships "in about north latitude 40° and west longitude 63°"–four hundred miles south of Nova Scotia.[96] The enemy ships closed in: "they hoisted English Colours & beat their drums," Kessler recalled. Seeing and hearing the call to battle, Barry aboard his battered, ill-manned ship did the same, later writing in his plain language: "We fell in with two [of] his Britannic Majesty's Sloops of War."[97]

CHAPTER ELEVEN

ATALANTA AND TREPASSEY

ITH BARRY'S ORDER, "BEAT TO QUARTERS!" ringing in their ears, the Alliances rushed to their battle stations: gun crews to their assigned cannon, marine sharpshooters to the "fighting tops," and the rest to their duties with rope and sail-assignments that looked to be of little benefit this day.

Below deck, acting surgeon Joseph Kendall entered the cockpit—the dark, cramped quarters for the midshipmen and master's mates. Aided by ship's carpenter Charles Drew and his mates, Kendall prepared for eighteenth-century triage.[1] They laid down a platform of planks about ten feet square which they covered with a stretched sail. Bedding was carried in, as were some beds for wounded officers.[2] Kendall then set out his equipment:

> [Surgical] instruments, needles and ligatures, lint, flour in a bowl, styptic, bandages, splints, compresses, pledges spread with yellow basilicon or some other proper digestive . . . the medicine chest . . . wine, punch for grog, and vinegar aplenty. . . . A bucket of water to put sponges in, another to receive blood from operations. . . Dry swabs to keep the platform dry . . . A water cask . . . to be dipped out as needed.[3]

Thus prepared, Kendall, his mates, and the "Loblolly Boys"—youngsters named after the gruel served in sick bay—were ready for the horrors to come.[4]

Up on the quarterdeck, Barry ordered his colors hoisted. Once raised, they hung limply on the flagstaff like a dolorous telltale. With little wind, the ships made progress by inches, drifting toward the coming confrontation on an ocean surface smooth as glass. It was noon before the British vessels came up on either side of the *Alliance*: the *Atalanta* on her starboard, with the *Trepassey* slowly approaching but not yet "on [*Alliance*'s] larboard quarter." Edwards determined that the *Alliance* was "about two cables lengths to leeward [when] she hoisted Rebel colours."[5] Barry estimated the distance as "within Pistol Shott."[6] Taking his speaking trumpet, he leaned over the quarter-rail and hailed the *Atalanta*: "Ship Ahoy! What ship is that?"

"*Atalanta*, Sloop of War, belonging to His Britannic Majesty," Edwards replied.

"This is the Continental Frigate *Alliance*, John Barry, I advise you to haul down your colours."

"I thank you, Sir," Edwards replied. He paused a moment. Then, with understated bravado, he added, "Perhaps I may, after a trial."[7]

Edwards hoped to keep the conversation going long enough for the *Trepassey* to come up into position, but Barry had eyes. He knew what lay behind these prolonged pleasantries, and saw no reason to delay the inevitable when, just at that moment, the wind completely died. For a second or two, the only sound aboard the ships was the useless flapping of canvas against the masts and spars above the silent and ready gun crews. Barry broke the silence. "Fire!" he commanded.[8]

The broadside raked the *Atalanta*, smashing into her bulwarks and taking out some of her rigging. Edward's second-in-command, Lieutenant Samuel Arden, was struck by a cannonball that took his right arm off. Taken below, he only stayed long enough to have his stump cauterized by the surgeon "and the instant it was dressed, resumed his [station]."[9]

After his initial broadside, Barry gave the order to "wear ship"—but while the *Alliance*'s helmsman could turn her, there was no wind to propel the frigate. Aboard the *Atalanta*, Edwards commanded his men not to fire. The *Trepassey* was moving up, using the one advantage she and the *Atalanta* both had over the *Alliance* this day: oars.[10]

Immediately Edwards ordered his men to "Man the sweeps" while the *Trepassey's* crew rowed hard and furiously, determined to assist their comrades aboard the *Atalanta*.[11] Their exertion backfired. The *Trepassey* was going too fast. Edwards watched in horror as, "With too much way and in heading [*Alliance's*] Quarter," the *Trepassey* "shot abreast of her." Smyth's overzealousness proved fatal. As his ship glided past them, the *Alliance* opened fire. The still waters gave Barry enough time to slam two devastating broadsides into the *Trepassey*, sending splinters flying around the deck, slicing the rigging to bits and killing several men, including Smyth, who dropped where he stood and was dead before he hit the deck.[12]

Winslow, the master's mate, was standing close to Smyth when he fell, and "sent to Lieutenant King to acquaint him [of Smyth's death], in order to his resuming the command." King ordered the men to keep rowing, now in a frantic attempt to get the *Trepassey* out of the range of the *Alliance's* heavier guns.[13]

By now Edwards had the *Atalanta's* sweeps out. In a move of sheer courage and audacity, he ordered his men to row the *Atalanta* between the *Alliance* and *Trepassey*, taking yet another fearful broadside that further damaged her masts and rigging, but of small consequence as long as there was no wind. Once the *Trepassey* was safe, Edwards's crew kept right on rowing until the *Atalanta* was in a position of minimum danger and maximum advantage. With the *Alliance* "laying like a log," the British ships were "athwart our Stern and on our quarters": the *Atalanta* on the *Alliance's* starboard quarter, with the *Trepassey* "on the leeward side."[14] The *Alliance* was now caught in a deadly crossfire. Between the two enemy ships, fifteen 6-pounders were brought to bear, their crews taking calculated aim against the nearly defenseless Americans.

Barry had dealt with the treacherous Atlantic winds during this entire voyage, but this absence of any breeze was the cruelest trick of all. Unlike her sister ship the *Confederacy*, the *Alliance* was not a galley—she had no sweeps, nor could Barry lower long boats to row her out of danger, for any Americans manning them would be slaughtered. Without a wind, the *Alliance* could not get close enough to board either ship. She may as well have been mired in mud.

Seeing Edwards's strategy unfold, Barry ordered his gunner, Benjamin Pierce, to remove some of the 9-pounders from their lines and bring them into an improvised position where they could be used against the enemy.[15] Smoke from the cannon fire hung over the deck like an acrid, stinging fog. Although they were just yards away, the ships could hardly see each other. Soon the only thing the combatants saw was the flash of cannon fire lighting up the hanging smoke, followed by the instant crash of the iron splitting their wooden walls.

The battle was now over an hour long, and clearly going against the *Alliance*. Barry's gun crews manned the 9-pounders and cohorns, while Parke's sharpshooters kept up their volleys from the tops.[16] Unerringly accurate as the marines were, they could not equal the pounding their shipmates were being subjected to below. The *Atalanta* and *Trepassey* were now alternating their fusillades, mixing cannonball with grapeshot, which consisted of clustered, walnut-sized balls mounted on a wooden disc or packed tightly in a canvas bag. Upon discharge they separated, and ripped indiscriminately into ship and sailor alike.[17] At such close range, Edwards also ordered the guns' powder charges reduced: this eighteenth-century technological trick ensured that the cannonballs striking the *Alliance* would tear longer and deadlier flying splinters through the air.[18]

Aboard the battered *Alliance*, "We could not bring one-half our guns nay oft times only guns out astern to bear on them," Kessler recalled. Soon he was hit, wounded in the leg.[19] Bulwarks and rolled hammocks were poor enough defense when ships fired on each other half a mile away. They provided little protection now.

In a situation growing more and more hopeless, Barry stood tall on the quarterdeck. Throughout the battle, he directed the best defense he could for his men and his ship. He gave commands in a clear, steady voice, and his presence, unaffected by the iron and lead flying around him, gave hope and renewed confidence to the Alliances, even as their comrades fell around them. In the fighting tops, Marine Lieutenant Samuel Pritchard suffered a direct hit by a 6-pound ball.

Marine Sergeant David Brewer, son of an army colonel, was shot through the head and died instantly at his post. George Green, one of the mutineers, was impaled by a flying splinter.[20]

Below deck, it was all that Kendall could do to not be overcome by the sheer numbers of dying and wounded placed one after another on his makeshift operating table. His experiences as an army surgeon, traumatic as they were, had taken place a safe distance from the battlefield, under a tent and on solid ground. Now he was forced to perform his duties while sand and more sand was continuously poured on the floor to sop up the blood and keep Kendall and his aides from slipping in gore. At least the still waters minimized any unexpected movement while he did what he could with scalpel, tourniquet, and saw, using what laudanum he had to tend to the wounded and dying.

Sometimes several men were brought to Kendall at once, forcing him to prioritize and order his assistants to use stopgap measures for those who had to wait for care. He turned a deaf ear to the cries and moans of his patients, not out of cruelty but in order to keep his focus: looking, probing, and assessing each wound.[21] He took on different roles at a moment's notice: that of bos'n to the slightly wounded, patching them up and gruffly sending them back into the carnage above; and that of a skilled "sawbones," using the swiftest means possible to save a life. There was no time to be father confessor for those poor souls like Pritchard, only a quick glance, then, "Next!" and they were carried away—and another victim was immediately placed before him.

By now the wounded sailors who could move were assisting their comrades above, bringing up gunpowder and cannonballs to maintain the fight. They handed these to the ship's boys (not yet known as "powder monkeys"), who scurried back and forth between the hatchway and their stations. The number of fighting sailors was thinning out. Barry and his men were soaked in grime and sweat. The air smelled of blood and sulfur. The *Alliance* was being taken apart, not by the wind but by the lack of it.

At nearly three o'clock, thick clouds of smoke seemed to rise from the water, enveloping the three ships as if they were Macbeth's witches, and the motionless Atlantic their cauldron. The ocean was still enough to perfectly reflect the carnage above it. Aboard the *Trepassey,* another broadside of grapeshot was being loaded. The gun crews went through their steps, and on "fire!" linstock touched base ring. With a loud roar, grapeshot flew in a withering volley at the *Alliance's* quarterdeck.[22] Until this instant, John Barry had gone untouched in his battles with the British.

Not now. A grape ball slammed into his left shoulder. The impact threw him on his back, and he hit the quarterdeck with a sudden thud. Dazed and shocked, he got halfway up, not yet feeling any pain. Still trying to clear his head, the pain hit him hard, and blood began soaking his uniform. Hacker and the other officers ran to him, offering to help him below. Once back on his feet, he waved them off. He would not be moved from his post. For a few minutes he remained on the quarterdeck, directing the action, while his voice grew noticeably weaker. Bleeding profusely, he became lightheaded, and standing became difficult. Barry's remaining on deck was not adding further inspiration to his officers and men. Instead, it was changing their focus from their duties to their commander's well-being—a sentiment that endangered them as well. Once more, Barry's officers begged him to go below.[23]

Finally, he relented, having remained "on the quarterdeck untill by the much loss of blood he was obliged to be helped to the cockpit." Turning the quarterdeck over to Hacker, he let the wounded Kessler and several others carry him below.[24]

In the cockpit, Kendall received word of Barry's being brought below, and the captain became his immediate priority upon arrival.[25] With a loblolly boy to assist him, Kendall removed Barry's coat and cut away his shirt, checking the hole to see how much of the shirt may have gone in with the ball. The surgeon ordered Kessler and the other men who had carried Barry below to remain. He would need every available hand to hold Barry down while he began his examination. If Kendall had any laudanum, he gave the captain a dose; if not, a pannikin of straight rum would be administered, to hopefully dull the pain.[26]

A single grapeshot was about an inch and a half in diameter—larger than a musket ball. To further complicate Barry's condition, grapeshot was made of iron, not lead as used with musket balls. Lead deformed on impact, but iron did not; therefore the soft tissue damage to Barry's shoulder was maximized. Whether it struck the collarbone or the top of the shoulder is not known; as Kessler said, he was removed from the quarterdeck "after much loss of blood," which leads one to question whether the brachial artery had been hit.[27]

American naval surgeons, trained according to British precepts, took quick and aggressive action in treating such a wound, believing that to be the more humane approach. While a probe was one of the tools of the trade, a finger was used as often as not. One surgeon from these times insisted that a finger be used; "I could never bring myself to thrust a pair of long forceps the Lord knows where, with scarce probability of any success."[28] The practice of bleeding the wound to extract "impurities" was not necessary–Barry had lost enough blood already.

Next, Kendall used his retractors, widening the wound further. The resulting pain would send any man into pure agony. If the brachial (or any other artery) was damaged, they were tied off or cauterized. If the grapeshot had splintered the clavicle, Kendall cleared out any bone fragments, and expelled any grumous blood from the wound.[29]

The wound thus opened, and with Barry flat on his back in quiet suffering, Kendall took his bullet forceps–a scissorlike instrument with cupped ends–to reach the projectile, and cut into the wound. Widening around the grapeshot (and adding more suffering to Barry's condition), Kendall grasped the forceps around the projectile. Slowly, he removed it from Barry's shoulder. The original 1 1/2-inch hole was considerably wider now. With the grisly piece of iron removed, Kendall let the wound bleed awhile. Then he cleaned the area out, using straight turpentine or a mixture of turpentine and egg yolk. Either would send the most stoic of souls into further agony. Finally, after leaving a channel open to permit the wound to drain, Kendall dressed Barry's shoulder with lint dipped in oil.[30] By this time, Barry could very well have lost consciousness or gone into shock.

No sooner had Barry been carried below deck when another broadside slammed into the *Alliance*, just missing Hacker but instantly killing quartermaster William Powell at his post, manning the ship's wheel. The Alliances returned fire. While they were reloading, a shot from the next British cannonade carried away the American flag. The *Alliance*'s silent guns "led the Enemy to think that we had struck the colours"; the British tars "manned the[ir] shrouds & gave three cheers."[31] These "huzzahs" came from the cracked lips, parched mouths, and lungs raw with smoke of a jubilant, exhausted enemy, gratefully believing that their encounter in this deadly hornet's nest had ended, and that they were victorious.

But it was not over. Two of the *Alliance*'s officers stepped over Powell's body; one took his place at the helm, while the other snatched the stricken Stars and Stripes, and "the colours were hoisted by a miz[z]en brail." Before Edwards could take his speaking trumpet and inquire through the manmade fog if the Americans were surrendering, the *Alliance*'s "firing began again," and the British realized their mistake. Both enemy ships resumed their onslaught. Aboard the *Alliance*, seaman David Cross was killed; Fitch Pool, Barry's clerk, went down with a severe wound.[32]

From the quarterdeck, Hacker watched the unrelenting dismemberment of ship and seamen with growing concern. He was a six-year veteran of the war, but he had never been in a battle like this. Nor was he very lucky when it came to fighting. Wherever he looked, he saw mounting defeat: sails full of holes, rigging in tatters, the deck awash with blood and strewn with debris–all on a frigate crippled by lack of wind. He conferred with the surviving officers about the deteriorating state of the fight, getting the gist of the ship's condition and the "butcher's bill" of casualties. Then he left the quarterdeck for the cockpit.[33] It took unquestioned bravery to face enemy fire, but for Hacker to go below and tell Barry what he had in mind took every speck of his courage.

Having stanched the bleeding, Kendall was applying a bandage to Barry's shoulder when Hacker approached. Barry shot a dark, quizzical look Hacker's way, then asked why the lieutenant was not on deck, directing the fight. Speaking fast, Hacker told him about "the shattered state of the sails and rigging, the number of killed and wounded, and the disadvantages under which they labored, for the want of wind." Breathlessly laying out the facts as he saw them, Hacker asked–he was not fool enough to suggest–"if the colours should be struck."[34]

Barry's reply was immediate and thundering. Struggling against Kendall's ministrations (and doubtless starting his shoulder bleeding again), Barry became a wounded lion. "No!" he roared. "If the ship can't be fought without me, I will be carried on deck." He dismissed Hacker back to the fighting and began arguing sharply with Kendall about getting dressed, determined to return to the battle. To Hacker's credit, he left any resentment of Barry's tongue-lashing below. Bounding up the hatchway, he returned to his post and "Made known to the crew the determination of their great commander." Informed of their captain's decision to keep fighting, the crew "one and all resolved to 'stick by him.'"[35]

Now, even Nature seemed to respond to Barry's exhortations. With unannounced quietness, and ever so gently, the wind returned. Kessler forever remembered this instant as "a small breeze of wind happening."[36] Every sailor on deck could feel it on their sweat-stained cheeks. They breathed it into their lungs, and held it in for a second, then exhaled as they watched it slowly, surely, puff out their tattered sails. The combination of Barry's scalding Irish temper and the return of the wind unleashed the pure warrior in Hacker. Immediately, he bellowed orders as the ship responded to the long awaited, simple change in the weather–a soft breeze. The *Alliance* answered her helm, sailors manned the braces, and the battered frigate moved into a position that would allow her to finally fight back with all of her might.

After dispatching Hacker to his duties, Barry continued to insist on getting dressed and returning to the quarterdeck. Kendall, seeing that there was no chance in keeping him below, assisted him in getting shirt and coat over the right arm and around the left. The task of rerigging the captain coincided with the crew's getting the *Alliance* under way.[37]

Now, for the Alliances, the old adage "He that sails without oars stays on good terms with the wind" came true at last. The breeze touched British cheeks as well, but for Edwards and King, it carried

ALLIANCE AGAINST ATALANTA AND TREPASSEY ⚓

MAY 28-29, 1781

Alliance FRIGATE HMS *Atalanta* SLOOP-OF-WAR HMS *Trepassey* BRIGATINE

Dusk.
Atalanta and *Trepassey* "haul their wind" to pursue *Alliance*.

HMS *Atalanta*

HMS *Trepassey*

Light Winds

N

Alliance

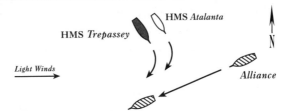

Noon.
Alliance and *Atalanta* begin engagement as winds abate.

HMS *Atalanta*

Puffs, No Wind

HMS *Trepassey*

Alliance

12:30-3:00 PM.
Manning sweeps, *Atalanta* and *Trepassey* take positions on *Alliance*'s stern quarters.

HMS *Atalanta*

Alliance

HMS *Trepassey*

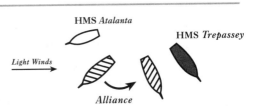

3:00 PM.
With the return of light breeze, *Alliance* turns to fire a broadside into *Atalanta*, then changes course to fire on *Trepassey*. *Trepassey* surrenders.

HMS *Atalanta*

HMS *Trepassey*

Light Winds

Alliance

3:00-3:30 PM.
Alliance changes course, goes around *Trepassey* to fire upon *Atalanta*.
Atalanta surrenders.

Alliance

HMS *Trepassey*

HMS *Atalanta*

Alliance

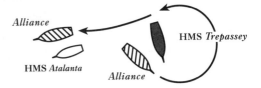

defeat, not victory. Before they could try to sail or row out of range, the first broadside from the *Alliance*'s starboard guns—fourteen 12-pounders—came smashing into the *Atalanta*.[38] The proximity to the *Alliance* had been an advantage for Edwards's small 6-pounders when coupled with the *Alliance*'s inability to move. Now such nearness was folly. Round shot shredded British rigging and further battered the *Atalanta*'s masts, already damaged from the battle's opening broadside. Seconds later, the fourteen guns on *Alliance*'s portside were loaded, primed, aimed, and fired at the *Trepassey*. One blistering salvo from the *Alliance* was enough for King. With his ship "Quite disabled," he ordered his colors struck.[39]

Aboard *Atalanta*, Edwards was not yet inclined to surrender, and quickly reviewed his other options: continue the fight, or try to flee. Either action required getting his ship away from the *Alliance*. He decided to break off the engagement. But in his attempt to sail the *Atalanta* out of danger, the strain on her injured masts reached the breaking point. Edwards and his crew heard a sharp crack, then another. They knew at once what was coming next. Pulverized by the *Alliance*'s guns, the fore and mizzen masts gave way. The *Atalanta*'s crew scrambled in an effort to avoid the wood, canvas, and rigging crashing onto the deck. Meanwhile the *Alliance* was wearing again, her guns ready. On the uproll, Hacker cried, "Fire!" This last, raking broadside did the trick: "The *Atalanta* . . . was a wreck." Reluctantly, Edwards, too, struck his colors.[40]

Barry was still struggling up the hatchway when all went silent above him.[41] Then he heard another chorus of hoarse cheers, only this time they came from the Americans. After the second British ensign fluttered down, they left their posts, leaping into the shrouds and along the bulwarks, roaring in exhausted jubilation. Recognizing why his sailors were cheering, Barry allowed Kendall's assistants to change his course, and get him to his cabin.

The battle had lasted nearly four hours.[42]

A much relieved Hacker found Barry in his cabin and relayed the news of his victory. Barry gave orders that Kessler take the pinnace and bring the vanquished British commanders back to the *Alliance* to discuss terms. Kessler reached the *Trepassey* first. Finding Smyth dead, he proceeded to the *Atalanta*, where Edwards greeted him with the usual courtesies, then accompanied Kessler back to the *Alliance*. Edwards's pleasant demeanor, first exhibited when he engaged Barry in conversation before the first broadside, had cloaked any personal anxiety over the coming fight. Now it masked the disappointment he bore in surrendering two of His Majesty's vessels over to a rebel captain.[43] The climb up the *Alliance*'s gangplank must have been very steep for such a man.

Once at the gangway, Edwards presented Hacker with his sword, only to be told that the *Alliance*'s captain was "confined in his cabin." After a knock on the door, Edwards was admitted, where he found "Capt'n Barry then there seated in an Easy chair his wound dressed." Again Edwards proffered his sword, this time to the correct officer. Using his right hand, Barry received it from Edwards, then "immediately returned [it] to him," saying, "I return it to you Sir[.] You have merited it, and your King ought to give you a better Ship." To Edwards's further surprise, Barry continued, "Here is my cabin at your service, use it as your own." He then ordered that Lieutenant King also be brought aboard.[44]

While Kessler returned to the *Trepassey* to escort King, Edwards told Barry his reasons for taking on his frigate in battle. He was "confident that they would subdue the *Alliance* . . . when the disadvantages under which the *Alliance* labored are considered." Barry, hurting as he was, must have suppressed a chuckle; had Edwards really "known all [the *Alliance*'s] disadvantages"—Barry's woefully undermanned ship, the frigate's sad condition, and all those British prisoners—Edwards certainly "had more reason to "flatter [himself] with success" then he knew.[45]

Once King arrived, he and Edwards reported their casualties and crew sizes. The *Atalanta* had five killed and fifteen wounded of her 125; the *Trepassey*, including Captain Smyth, had six killed with ten wounded of eighty aboard.[46] Barry did the arithmetic in his head. The captured crews put the number of his prisoners at over three hundred, far too great a number for the *Alliance* to hold, let alone feed.[47] They would rekindle fears among his officers of another uprising. Both Edwards and King reviewed the condition of their injured vessels. Sailing both the *Atalanta* and *Trepassey* to an American harbor, even with the smallest of prize crews, would leave *Alliance* far too diminished in manpower. Barry came up with a solution to this logistical nightmare: if one of the British ships sailed back to St. John as a cartel with all of the captured British aboard, would the British admiral exchange a similar number of captured Americans? With the admiral in question being his uncle, it was an easy question for Edwards to answer. He assured Barry that a fair exchange would be carried out.[48]

By now it was "too late in the day to effect removal."[49] Barry sent a prizemaster and crew aboard each British ship, with orders to keep close by the *Alliance* overnight. Edwards and King were to stay aboard the *Alliance*, along with the other officers and British wounded.[50] They were Barry's hostages, guaranteeing both his conditions for surrender and Edwards's word on prisoner exchange.[51] Barry requested that Edwards and King address their crews regarding the terms, and they agreed. Borrowing Barry's speaking trumpet, Edwards spoke across the lapping water to his men, informing them of Barry's generous terms and that he had assured Barry of their "orderly behavior during the night." King then did the same. Their orders had "the desired effect," resulting in a peaceful night after this violent day.[52]

At sunup, the *Atalanta*'s crew heard a familiar, cracking sound, as the mainmast snapped and fell on the deck, to be heaved over the side. Later that morning, Hacker updated Barry on the conditions of the three ships along with the latest casualty report. The *Alliance*, "shattered in the most shocking manner . . . wants new Masts, Yards, Sails and Rigging."[53] Her casualty list was five killed and twenty-four wounded. Three of them, including Pritchard, soon died of their wounds.[54]

Despite the *Atalanta*'s condition, Hacker told Barry that she was a prize worth taking home. Not only was "she the larger of the two vessels," but "her hull was sheathed in copper." While Barry ordered "Jury Masts upon her," different renovations were afoot aboard the *Trepassey*. Barry ordered her guns thrown overboard. Then, after her military stores were transferred to the *Alliance*, he placed her under command of her sailing master. The *Trepassey* was loaded with all of Barry's prisoners, save Edwards and the other officers, and sailed for Halifax that afternoon.[55] Repairs on the other two ships took another day. Barry gave command of the *Atalanta* to Hezekiah Welch, with orders to sail to Boston, being "the Nearest and safest Port." It was another day before the *Alliance* was seaworthy enough to sail. Barry was convinced that she would not make Philadelphia, being "In a Shattered Condition[,] very foul and hardly Men enough to work on Ship."[56] The wounded frigate "made all sail for Boston."[57]

Patrick Fletcher, lucky enough to avoid both bad weather and British warships, arrived in Boston with the "Guernsey privateer" *Mars* on May 12.[58] Assuming the same luck was with Barry, Fletcher reported that the *Alliance,* the *Marquis de Lafayette,* and Barry's prizes were not far behind. After three weeks passed, the *Alliance* was feared captured or lost—yet another tragedy for the American navy.[59]

On June 6, the *Alliance,* hardly recognizable from the trim, sharp frigate that departed in February, came up Nantasket Road, having eluded the British blockade off Cape Cod. With no spar of sufficient size to replace her main yard she sailed without one, her sails covered with countless patches.[60] It had been sixty-nine days since she departed L'Orient.[61] Crowds gathered along the waterfront, their jaws agape at the damage they saw to the frigate.

The *Alliance*'s docking could not come soon enough for Kendall. Barry was an uncooperative patient whose "wound was considered in a dangerous state." A crowd had already gathered along the wharf when the *Alliance*'s gangplank was run out. Accompanied by Kendall, Barry was carried on a stretcher and "immediately landed," then taken to a house along the waterfront. Once in his new surroundings, Pool and Kessler, both recovering from wounds, bivouacked in the house as well, and Barry put both to work. Sitting up in bed, with the *Alliance*'s log at his side, he dictated three long letters to Pool: one to Congress and the Admiralty Board, another to the Eastern Navy Board, and one to Sarah. He recounted the details of his voyages to L'Orient and back to Boston. "I am amongst the wounded," he reported, optimistically adding, "I shall be fit for duty before the Ship will be ready to Sail." As with Franklin, he asked permission for "Sheathing the Ship with Copper." Giving Kessler the letter to the Admiralty, along with a letter of safe conduct allowing him "to pass from hence to Philadelphia undeterred," he dispatched him "express to Philad'a to [fetch] Mrs. Barry."[62]

With Kendall's admonishment to remain in bed, all Barry could do was to wait for the arrival of his wife and his prizes. He heard that the "Snow with Sugars is in a Safe Port to the eastward," with "the *Atalanta* [expected] in every hour."[63] His anticipation of her arrival and that of the *Marquis* proved futile. While rumors swirled regarding the fate of the *Marquis*, Barry soon learned of the bad luck that befell the *Atalanta*. She was only a day or so behind *Alliance* when, on June 7, "Being near Cape Cod," she fell in with four ships from the British blockade "which retook the said sloop *Atalanta*, put a British officer & Seaman on board her & sent her safe into . . . Halifax."[64] The arrival in Boston of his prize the *Adventure* gave Barry some consolation.[65]

Barry displayed "high spirits" to his visitors, but his convalescence was long.[66] The wound healed slowly; sundered bone, tendons, and ligaments would mend as best as Kendall's knowledge of eighteenth-century medicine permitted.[67] Whereas tendons in the arms and legs could "be rejoined by relaxing the muscle and bringing the bones nearer" with a splint, the location of Barry's wound prevented such a remedy. Nor did his pain abate; to lessen it, Barry was given "one dram of bark every three hours," provided his stomach could handle it.[68] Weeks would pass before he was "in a fair way of recovery."[69]

While he recovered, news of his voyages and adventures appeared in Boston's *Continental Journal,* and then spread throughout the United States and across the Atlantic. The American press praised Barry's courage and leadership, while reassuring readers that he was recovering from his wound; British papers, of course, emphasized Edwards's gallantry. By mid-June Kessler reached Philadelphia. After giving a full narrative to the local press of the *Alliance's* triumphs over every adversity, and praising his captain's "unconquerable firmness and intrepidity," he escorted Sarah to Boston.[70]

Congressmen and other dignitaries extolled Barry's success (although one dour politician grumbled that the *Alliance* "was fortunate in capturing prizes but brought no Stores").[71] The rest of Congress was jubilant and laudatory, not only for his victory and captures but for his rescue of the neutral Venetian merchantman *Buona Compagnia.* They quickly passed a resolution applauding his "utmost respect to the rights of neutral commerce," and sent a copy to him that same day, along with a letter from the Admiralty commending his actions and expressing concern "that you was so ill of your wound."[72] Along with the narrative of his battle, the *Buona Compagnia* affair made the papers, eventually reaching Franklin in Paris.[73]

Barry also received a letter from John Brown, writing both as Admiralty Secretary and as his friend. While Barry was grateful for Brown's congratulations and "wish that your wound may be soon healed–that the use of your Arm may be restored and only an honorary Scar left behind," he was more pleased to read that "We have too directed that the *Alliance* should be sheathed with Copper," provided that there was "any person in Boston who knows how to put it on."[74] Much to Barry's delight, James Warren began "Entring on that business."[75]

CHAPTER TWELVE

REFITTING

ARAH AND KESSLER REACHED BOSTON at the end of June. Even though Kessler had prepared her about Barry's condition, she was still shocked at the sight of her husband laid so low. Her former suitor, usually the tallest and most striking of men in his uniform, was now sitting upright in bed, his usually tanned face as pale as his nightshirt, with newly etched lines from his suffering. Sarah immediately assumed round-the-clock care for him, her mere presence the best tonic. Throughout their marriage, she loved him totally and unabashedly, beginning each letter she wrote to him with the phrase "My dear Life."[1] Ironically, Barry's wound was, in a way, a gift for Sarah; while he remained dry-docked in this house he was completely hers. Slowly, surely, he began to rally.[2]

Sarah's arrival coincided with the court-martial of the ringleaders of the aborted mutiny. Testimony was taken, reviewed, and deliberated quickly and thoroughly, with the court's findings made public on June 28. All three were found "guilty of a breech of the twenty-Ninth Article in the Rules and Regulations of the Navy of the United States." The court hoped that its sentences would serve as a warning to Continental sailors:

Patrick Sheridan is guilty . . . and therefore adjudge that he be whipped three hundred and fifty four lashes upon the Naked back, One Hundred and Seventy Seven thereof alongside the ship *Alliance*, and the remainder thereof alongside the ship *Deane* Now in Boston Harbour . . . John Crawford is also Guilty...and therefore adjudged [to] wear a halter about his Neck and receive Fifty lashes upon his Naked back, twenty five at each of the ship's aforesaid . . . Sheridan and Crawford be Cashiered all their Shares, Prize Money and Wages . . . William McClahany is peculiarly Guilty and therefore adjudge . . . the punishment of death and that he be hanged by the neck on the starboard fore Yard Arm of the said Ship *Alliance* until he is dead.[3]

McEllany had the dubious honor of being one of the first sailors in the American navy ever sentenced to be hung.[4]

From his sickbed, Barry heard Boston's celebration of the Fourth of July, and marked his fourth anniversary with Sarah. Congratulatory letters continued to arrive, but they were mixed with bad news. Months earlier, Seth Harding finally had enough sailors for the *Confederacy*. Along with the *Deane*, under Samuel Nicholson, and the schooner *Saratoga*, under the intrepid John Young, Harding was convoying three dozen merchantmen from the Caribbean, bound for Philadelphia. A storm separated the three warships; afterward only the *Confederacy* remained to protect the merchant fleet. On April 14, a British sail was sighted off the Delaware Capes. After signaling the merchantmen to keep their course, Harding made for the enemy. It was the *Orpheus*. Soon another of Barry's old nemeses appeared: the *Roebuck*. Sizing up his chance of victory or escape as nil, Harding surrendered without firing a shot. The *Alliance*'s sister ship was welcomed into the British navy, renamed the *Confederate*. After the storm separated them, the *Deane* sailed onward to Boston, but the *Saratoga* was never heard from again: she had gone down with all hands. The news hit Barry hard; Young, an old friend from "the Sea-Captain's Club," left a wife and small children.[5]

A letter arrived from John Donaldson, one of the co-owners of the brig *American*, Barry's previous command. Donaldson updated him on the latest news of their investment. The British had taken St. Eustatia, capturing enough Yankee-owned goods that one loyalist cackled about the "ruin [of] all the rebel merchants in America." Donaldson gave Barry a detailed profit-and-loss statement, informing Barry that he had insured the brig for £3,000. Further, Donaldson had no sooner heard of Barry's recent prizes than he had placed an insurance policy worth 6,000 livres on them. Realizing that this sounded as if Donaldson might be profiting on Barry's risks, he explained: "I did not think it prudent to mention the matter to Mrs. Barry As she was at the time very unhappy at not hearing from you And my proposing a matter of this kind to her would induce her to believe I had apprehensions for your Safety."[6] Whatever chagrin Barry may have felt at earning income from insurance claims was countered by the fact that he would make any income at all. Then a letter arrived from James Nicholson.

For six years, Barry had steered clear of the intrigues that were constantly swirling around his fellow captain, John Paul Jones. Connections and coincidences intertwined the careers of the two most successful American captains: from the *Alfred/Black Prince* to the *Alliance*, from Landais to Franklin. So far Barry had yet to be entangled in any of Jones's ongoing controversies. Now Nicholson sought to bring Barry into the web that was forever being spun by, about, and around Jones.

In February 1781, Jones arrived in Philadelphia aboard the *Ariel*. Despite the fact that there were nearly as many congressmen against him as for him, he was justly recognized by that body for his heroism, with resolutions celebrating his "distinguished bravery and military conduct."[7] On the same day that Congress acknowledged Barry's diplomatic stroke on behalf of Venice, they unanimously appointed Jones "to command the ship *America*."[8] This news was all Nicholson needed for him to draw his poison pen. Having already complained about Barry's appointment to the *American* and then to the *Alliance*, it was in the natural order of Nicholson to launch a series of tirades in an effort to undermine, if not stop, Jones's appointment. Before he took quill in hand, Nicholson then learned that a congressman had leaked to Mary Peale Read that Congress might make Jones a rear admiral–a rumor that must have damaged Nicholson's gall bladder for the excessive bile it produced.[9] His letter to Barry was wondrous for its transparent "concern" for the welfare of the navy and the threat Jones posed to Barry's career. No jealous, petulant schoolgirl could have done better: "The Chevalier [Jones] ever since his arrival in [Philadelphia] has devoted his time, privately, by making personal application to the individual members of congress to give him rank at the head of our navy...I immediately took my Hat and with very little Ceremony waited on the President of Congress at his house & informed him of what I had heard...Many things pretty severe of the Chevalier's private as well as Public Carrector too odious to mention."[10]

Nicholson continued, hissing to Barry that he had spoken to "Bob Morris the Financier"–as Nicholson condescendingly called him–that the *America* should be offered to the captains still serving and ahead of Jones on that regrettable list (Morris quickly dismissed that idea).[11] From there, he went into false humility in praising Barry's exploits, and their effect on Jones:

> Your arrival and success came very opportunily and I did not fail to make use of it I mean outdoors in presence of Capt. Jones & some of his advocated Members, by observing that you had acquit yourself well, which they acknowledged. I then told them they could not do less than make you Admiral also. I had not a sentense of reply. It irritated the Chevalier so much that he was obliged to decamp . . . I am convinced he will never get [the *America*] to sea. It will suit his Vanity & only tend to expose himself and his friends to Congress.[12]

If Barry wrote a response to Nicholson, it did not survive. Considering his abhorrence of political infighting, it is reasonable to guess that this letter went unanswered. Nicholson's offensive, augmented by the Adams-Lee faction in Congress, guaranteed that Jones would not receive his admiralship.[13] Having succeeded in his smear campaign, Nicholson departed Philadelphia on the *Trumbull*, only to be captured by two British ships, originally the Continental vessels *Hancock* and *General Washington*.[14]

On July 25, Barry felt well enough to "hope in 3 or 4 days to be able to attend my duty."[15] One week later he was back at work. The *Alliance*'s copper sheathing was moving with surprising speed, yet Barry still discovered that "money would be wanting" to get her refitted with masts, rigging, and canvas.[16] On August 3, the *Trepassey* sailed into Boston harbor, crammed with 130 freed American prisoners from Halifax. Her service as a cartel over, Barry began her libeling procedures; she was sold on August 27.[17]

He was also happy to learn that Sampson Edwards's exchange was pending. Already an admirer of Edwards's courage, Barry was glad to discover that his foe's uncle, Admiral Richard Edwards, was well regarded (even by flinty-hearted New England merchants) for his humane treatment of captured American sailors throughout the war—quite a different approach than that found on the inhumane prison hulks lying in New York harbor.[18] With Barry's prizes in port, the Admiralty awarded the Alliances a two-thirds share, with the remaining one third going to the still missing *Marquis de Lafayette*, which resulted in a protest by the French Consul to Congress, who demanded a half-share.[19] Barry's problems with de Galatheau continued, with or without de Galatheau.

Still looking for ways to improve his finances, Barry turned to his prize, the *Mars*, as an opportunity to take part in privateering again, and joined a hastily formed group of investors spearheaded by Boston merchant Henry Mitchell. Taking his money from the *Trepassey*, Barry bought a one-sixteenth share of the *Mars*, which Mitchell refitted and renamed the *Wexford* in honor of Barry's home county.[20] Former navy captain John Beck Rathbun was given command.[21] Respected as "a man of known Courage and conduct," Rathbun was a brilliant decoy artist, once capturing a British merchantman by pretending to be a royal escort and inviting the captain to come aboard, which he did—for a little tea and captivity.[22] With orders from the owners to cruise in "the Chops of the Irish and English Channels," Rathbun departed Boston on August 20.[23] No sooner did the *Wexford* reach her destination when she was caught: a quick end to the joint venture of Messrs. Barry, Mitchell, et al. Loss of the *Wexford* nearly bankrupted Mitchell, who owned seven-sixteenths of the ship. "Money in this place has got to be so scarce," he lamented to John Brown.[24]

On August 25, the French frigate *la Resolute* sailed into Boston "after a passage uncommonly tedious," with Laurens and Paine aboard, loaded with supplies for Washington's army, and double-casks containing 2.5 million silver livres Congress so desperately needed.[25] Whether it was Laurens's charm—and, in one meeting, some saber rattling—that brought this latest manna from the French, or Franklin's deft greasing of diplomatic wheels, did not matter (although Gouverneur Morris tartly attributed any success to the "young beggar instead of the old one"): the money was as welcome as a military victory.[26] With the grateful permission of Congress, Laurens left the theater of diplomacy, rejoining Washington and the theater of combat.[27]

Late in August, a rented phaeton, drawn by three horses, stopped at the Boston waterfront, and John Paul Jones stepped out. He had been accompanied by Robert Morris and Richard Peters from Philadelphia as far as White Plains, where the Continental Army was encamped. Morris, Peters, Washington, and French General Rochambeau were too busy planning a new campaign and awaiting news of the French fleet's whereabouts to pay Jones much heed. He went on alone, but not before being warned by one of Washington's staff that his chevalier's cross would not play well in Puritan New England.[28] En route to Portsmouth and the uncompleted *America*, Jones stopped over in Boston. He and Barry shared breakfast on August 29.[29]

The two captains had not seen one another in nearly five years, when Jones was a lieutenant on the *Alfred*, and Barry in charge of her refitting. If the conversation over their meal reflected their personalities, Jones did most, if not all, of the talking. Their accents must have seemed particularly odd to the puritan Boston ear: Jones's with a touch of a burr, while Barry's still carried traces of a brogue. There was certainly a great deal to discuss—the *America*, the *Alliance*, Landais, and the war itself. One item Barry was careful not to bring up was his letter from Nicholson. Jones delighted in describing a new cockade he had designed for naval officers: red for "the glory and

Friendship of Spain," white to represent "the spotless purity of intention and the sincere Friendship of our illustrious Ally [France]," and blue "as the natural cockades of America, leaving the *Black* to England which is a true emblem of the character of that *Dark Minded* Nation."[30]

Their breakfast finished, they stepped out into the street. They made a rather incongruous pair walking along the Boston waterfront: the short, darkly handsome Scot, in a blue and buff uniform of his own design, and the tall, big shouldered Irishman, still wearing his official blue and red Continental uniform. Jones departed for Portsmouth the next day. The following week, he sent Barry "the cocade I promised" along with a letter mentioning that he knew he was "the Subject of a Letter you recd. some time ago from Philadelphia mentioning my Name." Without mentioning Nicholson by name, Jones was confident that Barry knew "how to credit such information."[31]

Jones' recent visit only heightened Barry's frustrations regarding the *Alliance* and his desire to get back to sea. From the docks, Barry had a perfect view of the entire Continental Navy, moored in the Charles River: the *Alliance* and the *Deane*, both lying idle, in need of men, supplies, and, of course, money.[32] The *Alliance*'s hull was copper-sheathed and back in the water, but not one spar or inch of new canvas was aboard.

When news reached Boston that the *Marquis* had indeed been captured, Barry decided to escort Sarah back to Philadelphia and meet with Morris, determined to personally plead his case to refit the *Alliance* and *Deane*.[33] He rented a coach for the trip.[34] Arriving home on October 12, they found the city awaiting news from Virginia. Weeks earlier, using feints and false encampments, Washington and Rochambeau stealthily departed New York and swiftly marched south to meet de Grasse's fleet, trapping Cornwallis and his army on the Yorktown peninsula.[35]

In Congress, other changes were afoot. The Admiralty Board, not yet a year old, was already ineffective. The victories of Barry and Jones were far outnumbered by the lack of success among other captains, and some of the navy's original champions had grown bitterly disheartened over the lack of money, sailors, and success. Exhausted from his efforts, William Ellery resigned, lamenting that "the next time American goes to war I hope she will have a respectable Navy. Our few little ships remaining don't deserve that name." Even the navy's most ardent supporter, John Adams, wrote from France that, after looking "Over the long list of vessels belonging to the United States, taken and destroyed," he found "it is very difficult to avoid tears."[36]

As summer waned, Congress plotted what would be its final course of action concerning naval affairs. Throughout 1781, they had placed more and more tasks on the broad shoulders of Robert Morris. As Superintendent of Finance, Morris now ruled supreme over all fiscal matters in Congress. By September the Seal of the Admiralty was also lying on his desk. While others had despaired of the navy's plight, Morris still had hopes for what was left of it.[37] With the title "Agent of Marine"–similar in scope to that of First Lord of the Admiralty in England–he took over total responsibility for "our unfortunate navy" with the same ardor and shrewdness he applied throughout his life to any task.[38] He was, literally, dictator of both the Treasury and the Continental Navy.

The Navy Boards were dissolved; their members and agents were immediately ordered to send their outstanding expenses to Morris for payment.[39] Morris sent the ever reliable John Brown to Boston, with orders for Barry to get the *Alliance* and *Deane* back to sea (the Barrys and Brown unknowingly passed each other on the coach roads between Boston and Philadelphia).[40] Morris's long list of directions to Brown were all encompassing and encouraging:

> I want to hear the most precise and accurate State of the marine Department . . . proceed to Boston, with all convenient Speed. . . the Governour to give you Aid on all occasions . . . he will furnish money for fitting out the frigates *Alliance* and *Deane*. . . you will take the Necessary Measures for sending the *Alliance* and *Deane* to sea immediately. . . you will find enclosed a letter to Capt. Barry and one to Capt. Samuel Nicholson. . . the Crews must be engaged for a Year, as the *Alliance* in particular being now Coppered, will only need occasionally to run

in for Provisions and Stores. . . The Men enlisted for a year may be better disciplined.[41]

Morris, unaware that Barry was in town, was surprised when the captain visited his office. After Morris inquired about his recovery, congratulated him on his successes, and summarized the details of the letters Brown took to Boston, Barry reported on the dire state of the two frigates. When Morris told Barry that Sam Nicholson might "decline going in the *Deane*," and that Brown was instructed to offer command of her to Nicholson's brother John, Barry must have breathed an inward sigh of relief that it was not going to the other brother (and Barry's senior), James.[42] Before departing, Morris presented Barry with two gifts: a week's furlough, and command of a joint cruise by the *Alliance* and the *Deane*–as soon as both ships were manned and "ready for sea."[43]

With Morris now in charge, and Brown as his direct contact, Barry had plenty of reason to be optimistic about the future. The navy might be down to two active ships, but the days of bureaucratic intrigue looked to be over. Robert Morris was no Francis Hopkinson. And a cruise with both frigates–Morris' appointment promised great things. Barry's step was lighter as he strode over the cobblestone streets back to the Austin mansion.

A week was not nearly enough time for Barry to review his in-laws' legal affairs. While he was home, the commonwealth announced that the "two story frame messuage, lot of ground and ferry wharff, on the north side of Mulbery Street . . . late the estate of the said William Austin" was for sale.[44] The battle to keep the Austin fortunes would have to be fought without him.

With orders to "sail immediately," he wrote Thomas McKean, now president of Congress, about his three mutineers, still in the Boston jail, requesting that Congress rule on their verdicts before he went to sea. Upon receipt of Barry's letter, McKean sent for a copy of the proceedings. None could be found, prompting a resolution that "the Superintendent of finance take [the] means for obtaining a copy of the proceedings, etc."[45] It was not enough, in McKean's eyes, for Morris to finance the war and save the navy–now he was finder of lost documents. After reviewing the case, Congress magnanimously commuted the sentence if the three "would serve during the war." As Barry would not have them back under any circumstances, they were "pressed" into the army.[46]

Before departing for Boston, Barry received new orders from Morris. Brown had written that "the *Deane* will probably not get manned as soon as the *Alliance*." That being the case, Barry was "to proceed to sea as soon as your ship be ready."[47] There would be no cruise in tandem with the *Deane*, after all. Once again, he parted with Sarah, mounted a horse, and left to report for duty.

He was barely two days north of Philadelphia when Tench Tilghman, Washington's aide-de-camp, rode into the city from the south with momentous news: Cornwallis had surrendered to Washington at Yorktown on October 19. Tilghman had ridden like Paul Revere, spreading the news along the way that the redcoats were leaving—at least Cornwallis's redcoats. He reached Philadelphia at two-thirty in the morning, bursting into McKean's home. Overcome with joy, McKean ordered the bells to be rung from Independence Hall. It was now past three o'clock and the German-born night watchman happily cried, "Gorrnvallis ist gedaken!" From Arch Street, Sarah and Isaac watched the town celebrate the news with cheers, booming cannons, and fireworks.[48]

Express riders carrying the news beat Barry to Boston, reaching the port on October 26. When Barry arrived the next day, he found the city awash with jubilation. He also learned that Brown had accomplished much since his own arrival, diligently carrying out Morris's instructions. Having made "pressing Solicitations" for refitting the frigates "as Decency [would] permit," he found a benefactor for the navy: Thomas Russell, one of Boston's wealthier merchants. Russell agreed to advance Brown enough money to make the necessary repairs on the *Alliance*. By the time Barry arrived, all that was needed was what was always needed—sailors. There were barely a hundred on Barry's muster rolls. In Philadelphia, Barry was one of the few captains whose men gladly reenlisted under him. However, this last crew, which Kessler considered "grossly amiss"—a rather mild description for mutineers and prisoners—was not the sort Barry wanted back.[49]

He also needed new officers. Hoystead Hacker had accepted a letter of marque. Marine lieutenant James Warren was still incapacitated by his wound, and both Chaplain Benjamin Balch and Dr. Kendall declined to return.[50] The surgeon was furious that Barry had not increased his wages once he assumed the surgeon's position while Joseph Bradford "was under an arrest"; Barry never made Kendall's promotion permanent.[51]

Barry, Brown, John Nicholson, and the lame-duck Eastern Navy Board met on October 30 to come up with a plan to make the next rendezvous a surefire success. They were joined by Samuel Nicholson, who had reconsidered his decision about leaving the *Deane*. When the meeting concluded, they arranged for their broadside to be emblazoned on the front page of the next edition of the *Continental Journal*: "ALL able-bodied Seamen, ordinary Seamen, and Landsmen, Are herby informed, that the two fine fast sailing Continental Frigates ALLIANCE and DEANE the first commanded by JOHN BARRY, Esq.; and the other by SAMUEL NICHOLSON, Esq.; are bound in Concert on a Cruise against the Enemy, and will sail soon, with every prospect of making a very advantageous Cruise."[52]

Set in huge type and placed dead center of the page, it was the largest advertisement yet seen in an American newspaper. All sorts of new incentives were promised. On this cruise, captured prizes would not be split with Congress: 100 percent of the proceeds would go to officers and crew. A bounty for each captured cannon would be issued. Bonuses would be paid upon enlistment: ten dollars to any seaman, six dollars to any landsman. Clothing and slops were to be provided at cost. Wages and bonuses were to be doled out "punctually in Silver or Gold."[53]

Finally, the advertisement offered an insurance policy. Anyone wounded in action would receive a $200 bonus prior to the divvying up of prizes, along with their shares. It was guaranteed that the subsequent care for the wounded—at a public hospital—would be free of charge, and those permanently disabled would receive half-pay for the rest of their lives.[54] So desperate were Barry and company to sign on a full crew that they turned to the incentive of "medical insurance"—first put into use by the Caribbean pirates a century earlier.

Despite the more generous terms, the rendezvous was unsuccessful. Barry soon discovered why: some of the *Alliance*'s former officers, led by Kendall, had entered into a whispered campaign of innuendo regarding Barry and his recent voyage. For the other conspiring officers, the main complaint was over back pay—but that was not enough for Kendall. Convinced he had been slighted financially and professionally, Kendall now "Propagated falsehoods to those properties of [Barry's] character," in hopes that any new recruits would sign on the *Deane* at the expense of Barry and *Alliance*, satisfying Kendall's spite if not his account book.[55]

As soon as Barry discovered the plot and its source, he wrote the not yet defunct Eastern Navy Board, making several counter charges regarding Kendall's "mis-conduct on the passage & Quitting the ship after her Arrival without leave" and requesting a court-martial. Honor compelled the captain to "request that [the Navy Board] Appoint a Court of Inquiry on my Conduct the last voyage." To Barry's consternation, the board took their time in responding. Eventually they assured him that they had heard nothing spoken against his character. Further, as Kendall had resigned his commission and was no longer in the service, he could not be brought before a court of inquiry.[56] By then Barry had found another physician to take Kendall's place—Dr. John Linn of Boston.

The *Alliance*'s other vacancies were also being filled: Matthew Parke, still justifiably aggrieved over back pay from his *Bonhomme Richard* days, agreed to return as captain of marines. Barry named the recently exchanged Hezekiah Welch his second-in-command, and moved Patrick Fletcher up a notch to Welch's old position. Nicholas Gardner was promoted to third lieutenant, his misadventures with *Alliance*'s pinnace forgiven if not forgotten.[57]

On December 1, two new officers signed on: James Geagan, a veteran naval surgeon, was appointed chaplain, and young William Morris (who counted among his relatives Francis Hopkinson) completed the officers' roster, signing on as a lieutenant of marines.[58] Aware of Barry's difficulties in amassing a crew, Robert Morris wrote him on November 9, hoping "that by the Time this Letter reaches you the *Alliance* will be ready for Sea." Morris understood that "men may be wanting," and promised that "a Letter from the Minister of France" would soon arrive, finally permitting Barry to recruit sailors from French ships in port. "This will I trust enable you to get a considerable number of good Seamen," Morris cheerily believed, concluding that Barry was "to wait my further Orders which shall soon be dispatched to you."[59] Since assuming control of the navy, Morris had made sweeping changes in policy, but this one puzzled Barry. Why, after two years of denials and reprimands for recruiting French sailors, was Barry at last allowed to do so?

Barry kept his officers out in the Boston cold, seeking every nationality of seamen with the exception of those loyal to King George; after Barry's first voyage commanding the *Alliance*, no English need apply. On December 10, he heard the bells ringing from Old North Church and other places of worship. They did not peal to herald a victory but an arrival. America's favorite Frenchman, the Marquis de Lafayette, had entered Boston with an entourage of relations and staff, including the Count de Noailles. He also carried orders to Barry from Robert Morris. The Marquis was returning to France–aboard the *Alliance*.[60]

CHAPTER THIRTEEN

SHOALS

OR YEARS, AMERICAN SCHOOL CHILDREN erroneously learned that the Revolutionary War ended with Cornwallis's surrender at Yorktown in October 1781. The first person to actually believe this, however, was Lord North. Upon hearing the news, he broke down: "My God! All is over," he cried, as much for his bankrupt ministry as for the looming outcome of his war.[1] Across the Atlantic, Washington knew better. Two British armies were still at large in South Carolina and New York, and Admiral de Grasse had sailed his fleet south for the winter. A disappointed Washington marched his Continentals back to New Jersey to keep a watchful eye on his old nemesis, Henry Clinton.[2]

Barry met Lafayette upon his arrival, and the Marquis handed over Morris's latest orders. Lafayette's mission–another fundraising venture–was "of the utmost importance to America." And, in restating his hopes that the *Alliance* was "manned and in every respect ready for Sea," Morris gave Barry a boost in reaching full strength quickly: he directed that Samuel Nicholson turn over some of the *Deane*'s crew to the *Alliance* "so as to complete her Compliment."[3]

That was the good news. In the same letter, Morris declared that Barry could not reward his men as promised in the recent advertisements. Safely delivering Lafayette and his entourage of fifteen to France was "of such importance" that Barry was "to avoid all Vessels, and keep in mind, as your sole object, to make a quiet and safe passage to some port in France." Morris piled one stipulation upon another. No other passengers were permitted. The *Alliance*'s new copper sheathing should ascertain "she will not want anything done to her." Barry was to "lay in the necessary Stores" for the accommodation of his aristocratic guests, but "not to expend one Livre more than is absolutely necessary, at any time during this voyage." Finally, giving Barry permission "to go on a Cruize" after safely landing his passengers in France, Morris wished him success—after hamstringing him from cabin to fo'c'sle.[4]

Having attached his name to broadsides promising sailors better prize shares and cash payments, Barry believed he had given his word on that subject to every man that signed on. Morris's orders were mortifying to an officer whose integrity was heretofore unquestioned. Barry knew full well that the promise of a cruise after crossing the Atlantic would not placate sailors that signed on under the conditions advertised throughout Boston. "Few of the ships belonging to the United States were . . . sent on private service and ordered not to go out of their way but to keep clear of all Vessels whatever," an exasperated Barry wrote.[5]

Despite distaste for his orders, Barry finished readying the *Alliance* for his passengers. When a final rendezvous brought in only seventeen Boston "landsmen," he reluctantly ordered Samuel Nicholson to send forty of the *Deane*'s hands to the *Alliance*. Nicholson bristled: "If Captain Barry has any power or Authority to Order my Men from the ship," he wrote, "I beg to be made acquainted with it . . . such a proceeding is quite new to me and I believe unprecedented." But Barry would not be denied, and eventually, Nicholson acquiesced.[6] But only a few men from the *Deane*—a far cry from forty—came over to the *Alliance*.

Barry found a more willing ally in Lafayette, himself "impatient to leave" and wishing he "had rather be under sail than at anchor."[7] His intercession with the French ships in port brought aboard 37 "Sick and About Naked" sailors, giving Barry 255 men for his voyage.[8]

"After a long struggle with much difficulty, I am at Last got on Board the *Alliance* in order to comply with your orders," Barry wrote Morris on December 22. He mentioned his spat with Nicholson, believing that "a proper mode of Court Martial" would have resulted in Nicholson's arrest, adding that Nicholson "is determined not to obey a Senior Officer." Keeping his critical remarks aimed at rules and not at Morris, Barry warned that regulations must be upheld, or "you can never expect anything from your Navy."[9]

Barry ordered the *Deane* on a cruise, echoing Morris's insistence on frugality while changing the nationality of the currency, commanding Nicholson "not to expend a Shilling of the Publick money more than absolute Necessity calls for." He wrote a last note to Sarah, and two letters to his friend Brown. One was a thorough "Acct. of Stores under the Care of the Several Officers belonging to the Continental Ship *Alliance*," and the other his detailed account of back pay and prize shares due him: the United States owed John Barry $5,229.36. With passengers and "a Poor Ship's Crew" aboard at last, the *Alliance* stood down Nantasket Road on Christmas Eve.[10]

"Nothing of note passed on the passage," the alliterative Kessler wrote, "except the oft time expressed wish of the crew 'that the Marquis was [already] in France.'"[11] Among the Americans, Barry found "very few Seamen" aboard; ironically, the best salts on the *Alliance* were the thirty-seven Frenchmen.[12] While the scarcity of prey on a wintry sea was a blessing, the very fact that the crew knew that he carried explicit orders to avoid any confrontation was enough to set them to belly-aching. "Discontent was so apparent that the Capt'n could not but be sensible of it," Kessler recalled.[13]

Finally, a sail was sighted "which appeared (as the crew expressed it) as if she could give them sport." The crew turned toward Barry, anticipating his cry, "Beat to Quarters!" Indeed, to the others on the quarterdeck, Barry's features were an open book, revealing "the conflict in his mind between the calls of his duty & his inclination" to give chase. Duty won out. A change in course was ordered, and the crew obeyed with noticeable resentment and muttering. Barry could not help but see the borderline insubordination. To Kessler's amazement, "instead of his reprobating & promptly punishing what on other occasions would have been the case, he was governed by a sullen silence," as if "propriety would have permitted him to break, [and pronounce] 'I also wish the Marquis was in France.'"14

While it is doubtless where Barry's sentiment lay, he never revealed it to his passengers. Instead, he played the perfect host; the Marquis called this passage on the *Alliance* "a happy voyage."15 Barry and Lafayette were embarking on a genuine friendship. When Barry confided to the Marquis his concerns over his crew's temperament and capabilities, Lafayette pledged to assist in finding better sailors once in France. The *Alliance* arrived at L'Orient on January 17, 1782.16

The *Alliance* no sooner docked when Barry called on Monsieur Clouet, the port commissary, to return his French sailors back to French command. Clouet gladly took them off Barry's hands, but when Barry handed him a detailed bill of £70 for the "almost Naked" Frenchmen's slops, Clouet replied he had no authority to pay it. That was a matter for Antoine de Thévenard, *l'Intendant* for the French navy at L'Orient. The duplicity in taking the sailors and not paying for their expenses was too much for Barry; Clouet "was not dealing candid with me," his voice raised with steely disdain, "& [I] assured him, I should not take his word again." Without waiting for Clouet's reply, Barry turned on his heel and went out the door, making headlong strides down the cobblestone streets of L'Orient and back to the *Alliance*, telling Lafayette what happened. Lafayette and his retinue departed for Paris the following morning. Some days later, a French officer visited Barry and handed him a purse bulging with French coins. Lafayette had come through again.17

In a letter to Franklin, Barry announced his arrival and that of his famous passenger, and also requested Franklin's help. As "My orders is to immediately go on a Cruize til the first of March, at which time I am to return here, to receive your dispatches," the French sailors "taken out of my ship" made it "out of my power to go to sea." And, while Lafayette promised "to speak to the Minister for 50 or 60 french Seamen," Barry implored Franklin "to back their solicitations." As for Barry, he hoped "to have it in my power, to release some of my poor Countrymen in english prisons."18

Franklin's reply was immediate—and vague: "French sailors ... are too much wanted to be spared to us," Franklin sadly clucked, but

Barry should find "a Number of Americans at L'Orient who have lately escaped or been exchanged from the Prisons of England." After flattering Barry that his "Desire of redeeming some of them is noble," Franklin came to the favor *he* wanted: "Let me know if, when you return to America, you can take any of the Congress Goods."[19] Hard as he looked, Barry could not find the slightest promise of assistance anywhere in Franklin's letter.

Thomas Barclay, American consul in L'Orient, was in Holland, so Barry reconnected with deputy consul James Moylan.[20] Aware that there were American sailors on French privateers near Brittany, Moylan suggested appealing to Thévenard for assistance.[21] To Barry's surprise, Thévenard granted his request, so he dispatched Chaplain Geagan to Morleaux, with expectations of Geagan's returning with dozens of Yankee tars. He came back with nine.[22] For the next two weeks Barry wrote Barclay requesting the consul's written assistance if not his physical presence, as "There are a Number of Americans on board French and Neutral Ships [but] it is out of my Power to procure one of them."[23] There was no news from Lafayette, and Franklin only seemed interested in filling the *Alliance*'s hold and not her muster rolls.[24] Barry saw Franklin's commiseration with his plight, while not giving him any assistance, for what it was: a refusal to help.[25] That being the case, Barry declined to help Franklin.

With barely cloaked contentiousness, Barry wrote Franklin that in "taking public Goods I have no Orders on that head." Recalling how turning the *Alliance* into a freight ship helped bring about Landais's downfall, Barry anticipated that "there will be fast sailing Vessels here bound to Philadelphia [and] I shall give them as safe a Convoy as possible." He closed with a polite warning: "my Orders being to sail the first of March I could wish not to be detain'd after that time–by your dispatches or any Goods which may be put on board."[26]

Luckily, Barry found an old acquaintance in port. Thomas Truxton, one of the more successful American privateers, was preparing to return to Philadelphia, and happily accepted Barry's latest letter to Morris detailing his frustrations with Franklin and Barclay. "I am deprived of any Assistance," he fumed.[27] From Passy, Franklin also wrote Morris, noting that the *Alliance* might not make her cruise "for Want of Hands."[28] Franklin looked to be correct.

Barry, awaiting permission from Thévenard "to Deliver all the Americans on board French Vessells, and in L'Orient," had acquired eighteen American tars; a net loss of nineteen sailors after subtracting the thirty-seven Frenchmen.[29]

While the *Alliance* took in supplies, Barry wrote to his late brother Patrick's agents in Bordeaux regarding Patrick's affairs, their "being the only People that can know any Knowledge of what he may have at Bordeaux."[30] At the same time, Barry's personal bad penny, de Galatheau, returned via post. The French captain, recently exchanged, renewed demands for his "shares" in the *Alliance*'s prizes. Barry fired back, "double-fould": "You say you suppose you have a right to a part of the Prizes the *Alliance* took after you were taken. . . . You may as well Suppose you have a right to a part of all the Prizes the *Alliance* may take, as long as She bears that name."[31]

Addressing the hijacking of the *Minerva*, Barry asked de Galatheau, "what has become of your Officer who run away with the Briggt *Minerva*, or had he your Orders Contrary to mine to Come to France."[32] If Barry's previous reprimands yielded no results, this last salvo did the trick. De Galatheau never bothered Barry again. Later, when Congress investigated de Galatheau's actions, Barry willingly cooperated, turning over his letterbook and logs. His earlier assertion that the *Marquis* "appeared very deeply laden" unwittingly played into Arthur Lee's hands. Lee made sure that any suspicions of fraud were laid "at Dr. Franklin's table"–which did little to warm the chilly relationship between Franklin and Barry.[33]

Despite the lack of manpower, the *Alliance* sailed out of L'Orient on February 9, heading for the turbulent Bay of Biscay and accompanied by privateer John Angus and his brig *Antonio*, bound for Philadelphia.[34] Before the two ships parted ways, Barry sent over two letters for Angus to deliver in Philadelphia. To Morris he pessimistically wrote, "I do not expect to make any thing of a Cruise as almost all the Trade in Urope is Carried on in Neutral Bottoms."[35] He penned a more personal letter to Brown, humorously referring to his crew as "a great number of half built Gentlemen," and asking Brown to look in on Sarah while keeping an eye out for a new home for the Barrys, "near the Bridge or that part of town."[36]

The letters were no sooner in Angus's possession when a suspicious sail was sighted. For the first time in two months, there was a chance at action and a prize. Through his spyglass Barry could see the ship clapping on all sail and jettisoning her guns, boats, and anchors. Nevertheless, the *Alliance* easily overtook her. To Barry's chagrin, she was another American privateer and, thanks to Barry's pursuit, now completely defenseless. All he could do was place her under Angus's protection as the two vessels sailed westward to America.[37]

Barry's cynical prediction to Morris about the "Urope" trade proved correct. For two weeks, the *Alliance* prowled the shipping lanes between England and Portugal, usually a great fishing hole for prizes. Barry sighted no less than sixteen ships, all neutral.[38] The cruise brought "nothing but Gales of wind" and, with most of the "half built Gentlemen" in his crew seasick and useless, Barry returned to L'Orient, arriving on February 26.[39] To his surprise, the *Alliance* was joyously welcomed: word had reached France she had been captured. The rumor was as empty as the *Alliance*'s hold, and as barren as Barry's mailbox: not one letter from Barclay or Franklin.

The temptation to quickly refit and return to Philadelphia was outweighed by Morris's orders to await Franklin's dispatches until March 1. But what dispatches? None had arrived yet. Still, duty was duty; just because Franklin had not written to Barry, Barry could still write to Franklin. He composed a dryly worded report about his empty-handed return and informed Franklin that Barclay's prolonged absence prevented "putting some public Goods on board." Promising to wait "for the [next] Return of Post" for Franklin's dispatches, Barry forewarned that "it will be out of my power to wait an hour longer if the Wind be fair."[40]

While Barry was on his unlucky cruise, Lafayette again aided his new friend, requesting Thévenard to release any American sailors to the *Alliance*. Thévenard assured the Marquis that Barry would be given "all American sailors in any French harbor." Upon his return, Barry discovered that there was "a Number of Americans on board Vessels in this place," and assumed Thévenard's word to Lafayette would be enough to have them transferred to the *Alliance*. But

Thévenard's heart had hardened, and he would not let the Americans go. "Trumpt up" charges kept several Yankee sailors in L'Orient's jail. With both Barclay and Moylan now out of town, Barry believed "it is out of my power to advance the money" to free them. Seeing through Thévenard's ruse, he did the only thing he could do—another letter to Franklin.[41]

But before Barry could finish his next letter, a letter from Franklin arrived—minus his dispatches. Countermanding Morris's orders to Barry, Franklin ordered him "to go to Brest, take in what he could of our Goods"—including a large supply of gunpowder—and sail for America with the French fleet that would be leaving in mid-March.[42] As further sign of Franklin's cavalier disregard for Barry's mission, he sent his dispatches to Brest, anticipating Barry's willingness to let his orders supercede those from Morris.[43]

Offended by Franklin's unconcern for both his orders and his situation, Barry let Franklin know it was "entirely out of my power to go to Brest being determined at all events to Comply with my Orders."[44] Barry closed his letter, noting that he would order Franklin's dispatches sent from Brest to L'Orient: "I shall wait for them until the Return of this Post, which is stretching my Orders further than I wish for." Then he signed off with a grander flourish than usual.[45]

In fairness, Barry's problems were small compared to Franklin's Herculean labors at Versailles: begging for money and military assistance while enduring troublesome (and often inept) colleagues, growing resistance from the king's advisers, and the presence in court of British spies (including his own secretary). But Barry was also a first for Franklin. When Lambert Wickes, Gustavus Conyngham, and John Paul Jones sailed to France, they visited Paris and fell under Franklin's spell as much as the city's charms. Nor were they reluctant to follow Franklin's "suggestions." Barry, however, was not so inclined. Perhaps he abstained from a visit to Versailles out of concern that he would feel out of place, or because he viewed any absence from the *Alliance* as being derelict in his duty. Maybe it was a combination of the two. In all, Barry made three voyages to L'Orient. He never went to Paris.

Word that Barry was in France reached American prisoners in England, and several soon wrote him of their plight. One of the six hundred in Plymouth Mill Prison—a "Pilot from Philadelphia"—asked if Barry "would get me exchanged out of this place," or at least "send me a little money as I want to buy some Cloth[e]s." John Green, another Willing and Morris captain, also wrote. Barry dispatched a heartfelt response, telling Green how, several months earlier, he had seen "Mrs. Green and all your little ones but John who has gone to Sea with his uncle." Barry promised he would do whatever was possible to get Green exchanged. He also heard from Stephen Gregory, the very same lieutenant who tried to press Barry's *Delaware* crew. Taken to England after the *Confederacy*'s capture, Gregory escaped, arriving in Nantes. Command of a merchantman bound for Virginia had been offered him, and he requested Barry's permission as senior officer in France for a leave of absence that produced both a way home and a job. It was gladly given.[46]

These letters put Barry in a more conciliatory mood regarding his fellow Philadelphian in Passy. Feeling a tinge of regret, he wrote a more explanatory and respectful letter to Franklin, apologizing for his "oversight" while pointing out "a Frigate is by no means calculated to carry Goods . . . especially if they Chace ev'ry Vessell they see."[47] If, in reading this, Franklin recalled Lee's carriage being placed aboard the *Alliance* two years earlier, he might have remembered that Landais was not in the habit of chasing every vessel *he* saw.

Franklin was not the only dignitary looking to ship public or personal goods. The Chevalier de la Luzerne, French Minister at Philadelphia, did succeed in getting a shipment of claret and a "small box" stored in the *Alliance*'s hold, and Barry also transported items Brown personally requested. Several Americans inquired of berths, including privateer John Foster Williams (recently escaped from Forten Prison, England), Boston physician Aaron Dexter, and Captain Samuel Smedley of Connecticut. An odd appeal for passage came from one Alexander Thomas, who informed Barry that, while "not a Son of Marrs," he required passage and space "in the Ship [for] two or three Trunks," smugly adding, "I will pay you handsomely for such indulgence."[48] Barry, a "Son of Mars," responded accordingly:

I would advise you, to Ship yourself and Trunks in some other Vessel than the *Alliance,* for I assure you, you shan't go in her, as I am determin'd to Keep Clear of the Censure of all your Character—You say you can't Fight neither, and yet you want to go on a Frigate—a verry unfit Vessel I assure you. I advise you to take passage in a Vessel without Guns, and then you need not be under any Apprehension for fear of being hurt.[49]

On March 15, the post arrived in L'Orient with Franklin's dispatches. One of these, unbeknownst to Barry, was a letter to Morris, with more than just a jab or two at Barry—who "think[s] himself too much confined by your Orders to allow himself to go to Brest as I desired."[50] The Minister Plenipotentiary was piqued; Barry was departing "without taking any of our supplies." Franklin viewed his requests as benign, but believed Barry viewed them as "throw[ing] every Burthen" upon his shoulders, which Franklin concluded "put him out of humour." Franklin called Barry "a great man," but "sometimes influenced by small Matters."[51] His opinion of Barry never changed, nor would he forget Barry's perceived disobedience to his requests.

Now it was nature's turn to wreak havoc on Barry's plans. Scarcely two days off the coast of France, powerful storms struck the *Alliance,* pulverizing two longboats and taking away her bowsprit. Ships sighted in the torrential rains were pursued and spoken, none of them British.[52]

There were black clouds below deck as well. Having gotten their wish—the Marquis *was* back in France—the Alliances who weren't seasick thirsted for action and prizes. After all, wasn't this the captain who had captured no fewer than six ships just a year ago? John Linn, the ship's surgeon, suffered "from a weak constitution," and his caustic bedside manner was only exacerbated by the appallingly large list of ill sailors. At least five of the crew died before the *Alliance* was thirty days at sea. Barry consoled himself that at least he was homeward bound, but with his passage delayed by storms and so many of his inveterate sailors ill to the point of death, it was small wonder that he wrote to Morris that he would never again "Risk my Reputation with such a crew."[53]

The gales persisted, driving the frigate southeast into warmer climates that added to the sick list. Three more sailors were buried at sea. By April 28, the *Alliance* was five hundred miles north of the Leeward Islands; she had been at sea forty-three days. That day, the mast-header sighted a veritable host of sail: a large fleet standing south. Not waiting long enough to see if they were English, French, or Spanish, Barry gave orders to steer clear. Once the fleet was out of sight, Barry sent the *Alliance* northward, reaching Cape Henlopen in twelve days.[54] If the winds continued to blow the *Alliance*'s way, Barry would be reunited with Sarah in only a tantalizing day or two.

But Whorekiln Road was not clear. The British fleet, now under command of Admiral Sir Robert Digby, had resumed guard-dog duties along the coast with a vengeance.[55] From the Jersey shore, Gouveneur Morris observed that "Prizes are every Day going in great Numbers to New York and that [the British] flatter themselves with the Hope of ruining our Commerce." He then voiced concerns for Barry: "I tremble for the *Alliance* as the Coast is lined with their Vessels and she must be near it."[56]

From the *Alliance*'s quarterdeck, Barry saw "A very large ship with her tender." Taking her to be the ship-of-the-line *Chatham,* and with the wind blowing northward, Barry gave immediate orders to reverse course. Both enemy vessels pursued the *Alliance* down the Delaware coast. The larger British ship tried to gain on the *Alliance,* but Barry kept her at a safe distance, despite his jury-rigged bowsprit. Clapping on every inch of canvas yet again, the *Alliance* showed why she was considered the finest American-built frigate of her day, and was soon flying at fifteen knots, showing "a good deal of Superiority in Sailing." Barry resorted to his old *Lexington* tactics, running his frigate into waters too shallow for the larger British cruiser to enter, yet ready to overpower the tender if she sailed too close. His knowledge of the coastline and sailing skills kept the *Alliance* from being yet another in a long line of captured Continental vessels. The British ships eventually "gave up the chace."[57]

No sooner had the British ships disappeared over the horizon when the wind shifted, allowing Barry to reverse course. Once more the *Alliance* approached Cape Henlopen only to find other enemy ships. Try as he might, Barry "could not get into the Delaware Bay." The odds of success were too long, and with "Provisions being short," he ruefully "put away from this place." With "the wind coming from the southward," the *Alliance* headed north, setting the crew to grumbling again. Off Sandy Hook, more enemy ships were sighted, and Barry's frigate "was likewise chac'd two Day(s) after by two Ships which I took to be Frigates." With all sails set, the *Alliance* sped past Long Island, rounded Montauk Point, and made for Long Island Sound. At twilight Barry reached Fisher's Island, where he picked up a pilot to take his ship up the Thames River (pronounced "Taymes") to the port of New London, Connecticut, arriving on May 12. Barry's "long and tajous [tedious] voyage" had taken fifty-nine days.58

Tory spies found it "somewhat extraordinary" that the *Alliance* "should have been able to reach a port in America, notwithstanding the boasted vigilance of Admiral Digby's Cruzers."59 But Barry had sailed into a friendly port in name only.

While Boston had welcomed the *Alliance* and her wounded captain the previous spring, New London's inhabitants were almost to a man indifferent at the arrival of one of the two remaining American frigates. Barry came ashore in search of the Continental agent for New London, Thomas Mumford, only to learn that he was twelve miles upriver at his home in Norwich. With two of his passengers heading that way, Barry gave them a letter announcing his arrival and requesting Mumford's immediate presence to help refit the *Alliance*.60 Returning to his ship, Barry was approached by Welch, warning him that the men wanted their pay, and shore leave to spend it. Lacking money for the former and fearful of mass desertion if he granted the latter, Barry denied both requests. The crew's mood, already surly, grew most foul.61

The next day the *Alliance* had a visitor. Thomas Mumford, too busy to meet Barry, sent his son Giles instead. When Barry apprised the youth of his needs—everything from a new bowsprit and two rowboats to provisions and slops—Giles, merely an errand boy, deferred to his absent father. Upon the subject of money, Giles Mumford was mum. Barry was torn over what to do next: if he rode to Philadelphia to personally relate his woes to Morris, he would be leaving command to Welch, who was woefully lacking in maintaining authority with the best-natured of crews. But if he remained, would a messenger succeed in getting from Morris exactly what Barry needed? He decided to go to Philadelphia. With strict orders to keep his crew on board and busy, sending only a few hands ashore with de Luzerne's claret and John Brown's bales, Barry began the long ride home.[62]

That morning a shallop approached the *Alliance* with a supply of meat that Barry ordered while ashore. Lieutenant Gardner, officer of the watch, called for hands to unload the beef. His orders were ignored. The crew refused to report to this or any other duty. Gardner went below and confronted the disgruntled sailors on the berth deck, repeating his orders. The sailors responded with curses, shouting "Liberty and back allowance!" Seaman Peter Jennings, menacingly swinging a barrel-hoop in his hand, escorted Gardner back to the hatchway and watched him ascend.[63]

Awakened by the growing din, sailing master John Buckley started from his cabin. He, too, confronted Jennings and the other malcontents–then scrambled up the hatchway, accompanied by more cries of "Liberty and back allowance!" On deck he found Gardner, Bos'n Joseph Lewis, and Matthew Parke–all armed, and discussing their next move. When a gang of sailors massed to rush the hatchway, the officers menacingly brandished their weapons. The mutineers hesitated just long enough to allow the other officers to arm themselves, taking weapons stashed in the captain's cabin. Once they joined their colleagues at the hatchway, the sailors retreated; Lewis fired a warning shot over their heads to show that the officers meant business. When the echo of the shot stopped ringing below deck, John McDaniel–one of the twenty-five "lesser" mutineers from the *Alliance*'s last voyage from France–fired off a string of curses at the officers.[64]

The uprising was too much for Welch. To the other officers he seemed either frozen in fear or overly cautious. Taking unofficial command of the situation, Gardner and Buckley sent a midshipman into town with orders to get a mount and keep riding until he found Barry. Below deck, the mutineers held sway over the rest of the crew, their shouts awakening Bryan Pierce, the gunner. Leaving his cramped cabin, he asked that the hatchway ladder be put up, and

McDaniel gave permission. Pierce no sooner reached the top step than he realized that the key to the powder magazine was still in his cabin, and sent a boy to retrieve it "with as little notice as possible." After a few minutes passed with no sign of the youngster, Pierce leaned over the hatchway. Someone flung an iron stand at him, missing his head by inches.[65]

Two cabin boys, trembling in their bunks below, heard one of the mutineers call for hands to break into the magazine, take a half-barrel of gunpowder, and blow up the quarterdeck. "No! Let's take the quarterdeck," McDaniel replied, to the raucous approval of the other mutineers. "Damn the officers," they replied, flinging an occasional plank through the hatchway, until the officers covered it with its grating. By mid-afternoon the mutineers' fury abated, and the cooler heads among the other sailors began addressing the folly of their actions. Their warnings that carrying out the mutiny would only result in floggings at best (and hanging at worst) made sense to most of their shipmates. At the very least, they argued, they had no arms, while the officers did.[66]

Twelve miles away, on the coach road from New London, the galloping midshipman caught up to his captain, and they hastened back to town. Then, abandoning their lathered and exhausted horses, they were rowed from dock to ship. It was dusk when Barry, himself in a great sweat, came aboard the *Alliance*. He immediately ordered the hatchway opened, his big voice easily recognizable to the crew below. Some, recalling his reaction to the attempted mutiny a year earlier, knew full well what might await them.[67]

Furious, Barry commanded the crew to come on deck, one at a time, accosting each man as he came up the hatchway. Some answered in quaking, respectful tones; others avoided his glare and approached in silence. He sized up each sailor's manner, determining who would be sent forward with a sharp rebuke, or seized and taken aft under guard. When he was finished, sixteen men were in irons below deck. The rest of the crew finally obeyed Gardner's order and unloaded the shallop in the black of night.[68]

The next day Barry sent every sailor ashore who was too ill for duty. Then, lacking enough officers to convene a court-martial for the mutineers, he decided to hold a one-man inquiry "to find out the

Ringleaders." Marines stood guard as he summoned the *Alliance*'s officers and crew individually into his cabin, where he peppered each "witness" as to what transpired while he was absent. After discerning that there were exactly three ringleaders in this latest insurrection, he transferred them to the harbor guard ship. The other thirteen were reprimanded and returned to duty.[69]

Having dealt with mutiny, Barry became entangled in diplomatic minutiae with the French again. Chevalier Louis-Alexandre de Quémy, commanding officer of the frigate *l'Emeraude* near the Connecticut coast, sent Barry a message inquiring about any British ships in Long Island Sound. Barry gave a short, informative reply–a professional courtesy to an ally.[70] Two weeks later, the mail brought orders from Morris regarding de Quémy: the *Alliance* was to assist *l'Emeraude* on a mission of "both secrecy and dispatch." His mind on all things fiscal and naval, Morris jumped to the conclusion that ten days in New London were enough to repair, refit, and reenlist a crew for the *Alliance*. Therefore, Barry was to "not loose a Moment" in putting to sea.[71]

Outside of the *Alliance* still needing repairs and men, there was one other factor in these orders that got Barry's blood boiling. "Not withstanding any seniority in Rank," Barry was to receive his "signals & ca. from Mons. Quernay [Quémy] and to the utmost of your power Comply with his Views." Lest any of this be misconstrued, Morris made things crystal clear: Barry would "be under the Orders" of de Quémy who, while he was actually a lieutenant, was rumored in New London to be a mere midshipman.[72] Morris was putting his captain under a junior officer's command –and a foreign one at that. Barry not only viewed this as an affront to his seniority; he was personally insulted. That such an order came from Morris, of all people, made it worse.

His reply to Morris was detailed and forthright. First, as to the state of the *Alliance*, and Mumford's lack of commitment: "All I have heard from [Mumford] is fair Promises–In Short There is no one here that I See Cares a Curse for any thing but their own Interest . . . I have not seen Mr. Mumford here this ten Days–& I think you need not expect any thing from him unless he has Some Self Views in it."[73]

Barry then broached the topic of reporting to a lesser officer, writing as one of the few Continental captains who deserved better, having served so well for over six years. If de Quémy was "a Captain in his Most Christian Majesty's Service, I shall with pleasure not only take his Signals but obey his orders in every Respect"; but "if he is a Lieutenant that you do not expect me to be under his orders." Choosing his words carefully, Barry hoped Morris "would be more tender of the Rank of a Continental Captain." Unpaid for years, Barry observed that his rank was "all I have got for Serving my Country."[74]

His next letter was a brief note to de Quémy. Rather than tell the Frenchman he did not want to serve under him, Barry used his "Want of a Boatsprit" as the reason for his delay in joining up with *L'Emeraude*. He also received a letter from Brown, just arrived in Boston from Philadelphia. Brown expressed joy at Barry's "Safe Arrival" after "so many narrow escapes" and sorrow "that you have not had any Success in capturing Prizes." Brown was sending a wagon to New London to pick up his goods, and closed, "I should have been happy to bring Mrs. Barry but she chose to wait until she hears from you." Barry read the end lines regarding Sarah with disappointment—he did not see himself getting to Philadelphia any time soon. It would be some days before he sent Brown a reply.[75]

For Barry to feel completely besieged in every aspect of his life only required a family matter to crop up, and that surfaced when the New London Commissary informed him that William Austin, while aboard a British ship, was taken prisoner when the vessel was captured.[76] The letter implied that Austin was a passenger on board. What Barry learned next flabbergasted him.

When the Barrys had returned to Philadelphia from Boston the previous fall, they heard of Washington's laying siege to Yorktown, assisted by the French navy. What they did not know was that Austin was in Yorktown as well—although he took a rather circuitous route. Upon arriving in New York with Clinton's army, Austin immediately offered his services to Lord Admiral Howe. As a master's mate, he made a round-trip voyage to Lisbon aboard the ship *Pelican*. When he returned in 1780, he was given "Command of an Armed Vessel called the *Rambler* 18 Guns" and went to the Chesapeake" in an expedition led by Benedict Arnold, now a general in the British army.[77] Arnold's army of loyalists laid waste to Virginia from the Chesapeake to Richmond, even threatening Washington's Mount Vernon.[78]

Arnold eventually departed, but Austin did not; he and the *Rambler* were soon part of Yorktown's defenses. Austin–"with Lord Cornwallis when he was taken"–was placed "on board the *Bonnetta*" with other captured loyalists and "confined in New York after Capitulation." Not only was his property confiscated, but his wife died in New York, leaving him a widower with several small children. Soon all but one of them would die as well.[79] William Austin paid a dear price for his loyalty to the Crown.

In an effort to free the black sheep, Barry went right to the top. He began a letter to Washington by paying his respects and updating the general on British naval activities. Then he made an unsubtle shift to the true reason for his correspondence, tactfully omitting anything he knew as to Austin's latest adventures:

> The Commissary in this place... informs me that no persons is Exchang'd without your Excellency's orders I have one favor to ask . . . that you will Suffer a Captain by the name William Austine to be exchang'd or go in on Parole . . . He is an Old acquaintance of Mine, and a particular Friend–if your Excellency will be pleas'd to grant the above favour I shall ever esteem it as a Mark of your Friendship.[80]

For the rest of his life, Austin caterwauled to his family that his actions saved their fortune from the British. So far they had brought about only heartache and bitterness, but Barry believed that blood was truly thicker than salt-water. In truth, he genuinely liked Austin, and respected him.

The next two weeks saw the same lack of progress as when the *Alliance* first docked in New London; a rendezvous signed just one sailor. De Quémy responded to Barry's message in a tone both sincere and patronizing: "I am afraid your BowSprit may be a hindrance," he penned, while "the *Chatham* & other British vessels . . . are cruising by the Bay of Boston." Mumford promised bread, beef, and "two or three caulkers," but no boats or bowsprit; "In finis I find

Cash is demanded for everything your Ship needs," he lamented. When Barry rebuked Linn regarding the lack of improvement among the sick *Alliance* crew, Linn was livid: "I shall be happy to retire (and *perhaps* you may find a person that will suit you better)."[81]

On June 4, Brown's promised wagon arrived in New London minus Brown, ordered back to Philadelphia. Having yet to answer Brown's earlier letter, Barry did so now; not writing to the Secretary of the Marine, but to a friend, dispensing with any euphemisms about his situation. "I was never in such a Damb country in my life," he began, and then poured out everything: Mumford, New London, Morris, and *l'Emeraude*:

> By the by I wood not trust [Mumford] farther than I could see him . . . Mr. Morris sent me orders by the express that your letter came by to Join the French Frigate at Road Island and be under his command. Mr. Morris must be unacquainted with his rank or he must think me a drol[l] kind of fellow to be commanded by a Midshipman I don't feel myself so low a Comm[ander] as to brook to such orders however I don't see it will be in my power to sail this year of our lord as I have not One hundred men on board . . . I suppose I will write Mr. M[orris] To morrow On the subj[ec]t I suppose he will be much offended.[82]

Barry's letters are not nearly as voluminous as those of other officers-paltry when compared to John Paul Jones. But in this letter, Barry hit rock bottom; ground down, exhausted from fighting with his own side. Continuing to write, energy returned to the warrior:

> I assure you all tho I serve the country for nothing, I am determined that no Midshipman in any service shall command me Let him be a Chev[alier] or what he will.[83]

I serve the country for nothing. Not permitted to seek prizes on his way to France–and not lucky enough to find any on his way from France–now, in spelling out his willingness to obey his orders, yet maintain his earned rank, he refocused on his calling, determined to do whatever was necessary to succeed.

He did not direct his rediscovered defiance at Morris. Rather, it went to the man who signed his commission for the *Lexington*. From Massachusetts, Governor John Hancock sent Barry a biting letter regarding a Massachusetts marine, Ephraim Wales. "While in the service of this commonwealth," Wales was captured by the British, taken to London, and from there escaped to France, where "My informant tells me you forc'd him on board your Frigate." Hancock threatened Barry: "Discharge Mr. Wales from his Confinement," or Hancock would "pursue such measures as will affect his release–which will be as Disagreeable to me as you."[84]

Barry was still reading the letter when he received word that two British frigates were rumored to be sailing up the Thames. If true, the odds were too great to stop both enemy frigates with the *Alliance* alone.[85] Waiting for more facts, Barry primed his pen and aimed it right at Hancock, in bold strokes the governor could read without his spectacles. First, he stated the whole truth about Wales, "Put on board the *Alliance* in France as he was a public nuisance to the People there, Having spent all the money that Doct. Franklin advanc'd him & my Ship wanting Men . . . I have been through necessity & contrary to my Inclinations oblig'd to keep Mr. Ephraim Wales on board–Not that he owes of any Service to the Ship only that as an American he may help to keep the Mutineers under."[86]

Then Barry fired a broadside at Hancock: "With respect to his Connections or any threats against me or my Conduct I bid them all Defiance–& a few Lines from you would have answered the ends of the threatening Letter I have Receiv'd–be assured that I will take Care to walk upright that a Request from a Friend will answer the Same as a threat."[87]

Fortunately, the enemy frigates proved a false rumor. Repairs on the *Alliance* were still stalled; with the ship still in disrepair "and not sixty . . . actual working people aboard," sailing from New London was impossible. Barry felt "as much in the Dark as ever." What of this he discussed with his officers is unknown, but they could size things up for themselves. Seeing firsthand the lack of supplies and manpower, they put in their own written protest: "As officers in our Country's Service, we think that the ship ought not to go to Sea."[88] Rather than merely concur with them, Barry decided to go to the one place where seamen would rally to his banner: Philadelphia.

He dashed off a quick note to Morris, not so much asking permission to come home as to let Morris know he was doing just that: "I hope you have no Objection [if] I visit Philadelphia as I have done every thing in my power to get men and never could procure them once since my arrival."[89] Five days later, on June 23, he was there, with a loving reception awaiting him at the Austin home. Sarah, now twenty-eight, had "grown very fat"–a phrase sometimes used in colonial days to suggest pregnancy. The stress she was under from the war's impact on her family was robbing her of her youthful smile and natural sense of happiness, and Barry was concerned about both her disposition and her health.[90]

William Austin's capture was just one piece of news the three shared. Reynold Keen had reclaimed both his citizenship and his children months ago, and Isaac was pursuing every possible means to reclaim title to their home. Earlier, the Supreme Executive Council put the estate up for auction. Isaac was the highest bidder, but when he disputed their terms, they re-auctioned the property. Again, Isaac outbid all others. However, his wrangling with the council continued, so they awarded the property to the trustees of the University of Pennsylvania. Isaac was appealing the decision. Among the trustees was Francis Hopkinson.[91]

Receiving word that Barry was back, John Brown paid a visit that evening, updating his friends on his growing responsibilities over naval affairs and assuring Barry that he had done right in coming to Philadelphia to recruit, having just written Barry that "Were you at this port [want of men] would easily be remedied." Brown also guaranteed that Morris would be happy to see him.[92]

Barry and Morris greeted each other warmly the next day. The war had aged both of them. Morris was heavier, which did not go unnoticed by much thinner Philadelphians, many of whom openly accused Morris of war profiteering. Barry, while still years away from gaining weight, had flecks of gray in his hair and, thanks to British iron, an aching left shoulder that would forever give him early warning of approaching squalls. Although Morris had been Barry's superior since 1774, their relationship was based on mutual admiration.

Now unfettered by distance and the written word, Barry spoke as plainly to Morris as he had written to Brown. Morris found his rationale for coming home sound, and reassured Barry of his unwavering support, even approving Barry's dealings with Franklin. Weeks earlier, he had defended Barry in a letter to Franklin, gently remonstrating the plenipotentiary that Barry's "Orders were such that he was right not to stay longer than he did in France, and therefore I must pray you to excuse his Inattention to your Requests."[93]

When Barry broached the subject of de Quémy, Morris offered no argument. In fact, Morris guaranteed that he would never come under de Quémy's command. Rather, he asked Barry as a favor to simply acknowledge the Frenchman's signals, should they put to sea together, citing a letter awaiting Barry in New London. "It is far from my Inclination on this or any other Occasion to require of you any thing that would be derogatory to your Rank," Morris wrote; "On the contrary it will always afford me particular pleasure to support it to the utmost of my power."[94]

Having been written, now it was said. Barry had hoped that Morris was still "too much of a friend" to ask him to do such a thing; now, Morris proved him right. With assurances of help in getting the *Alliance* to sea, Barry left Morris's offices a happier man than when he entered. While he prepared his rendezvous, Morris sent explicit instructions to Mumford and other New England agents to provide Barry "with Such Supplies as may be found necessary."[95] To his further delight, Barry's Philadelphia rendezvous was as successful as his New England ones were fallow. Within a week he had seventeen new hands, most of them far more experienced than the crew in Connecticut. Before long, the *Alliance* was "tolerably well manned." After observing the sixth Fourth of July and their fifth anniversary together, Barry left Sarah for Connecticut with no less than fifty seasoned sailors in tow.[96]

His overland route allowed for a courtesy call to Washington at his encampment along the Hudson. They discussed Barry's voyage with Lafayette, the whereabouts of the French fleet, and William Austin. Washington, acknowledging that "Some Disputes between the Contending Parties at Present" were preventing prisoner exchanges, had written to Governor Trumbull on "Capt[ain]

Austine's behalf."⁹⁷ Barry bade the general farewell and reached New London on July 20.⁹⁸ Little was accomplished during his absence, and Mumford was still less than amazing in his diligence: Barry found Brown's "waggon" right where he left it.⁹⁹

There was also a pile of letters, including one forwarded to Barry by a friend in Boston, sent from County Wexford. It was the first news from Ireland in over a year—and immediately put an end to his good humor: both of his parents were dead. His two sisters, Margaret Howlin and Elinor Hayes, and their families, were destitute.¹⁰⁰ Barry was heartsick. Their plight was so "very moving to me" that he arranged an annual stipend of twenty guineas, the money going through a London bank.¹⁰¹

Missing from surviving correspondence of this period is any letter from Sarah or Isaac. If Sarah was indeed pregnant, she must have suffered a miscarriage after Barry left Philadelphia. From New London, Barry penned a warm, solicitous letter to her, deeply concerned about her condition and her state of mind, imploring her not to withdraw from the outside world: "It is clever to visit ones friends now and then," he tenderly suggested; "besides it is helpful to good health."¹⁰²

Barry now devoted his waking hours toward escaping New London. First he addressed three departures among his officers. In an overly flattering letter, Marine Lieutenant Morris resigned, citing a "business necessity" as his reason for quitting.¹⁰³ Cutting through the homage, Barry recalled an unpaid $30 expense Morris billed to Barry's account, and listed him as "a Deserter from the Ship."¹⁰⁴ Parke lost no time in recommending a replacement, but Barry believed there was "a Sufficient Number of Marines Officers on board already." Carpenter Charles Drew was missing, having "Defrauded the Public from a Vast deal of Property." Suspecting that Drew, one of the married New Englanders whom Barry had advanced two months pay, was heading back to hearth and home, he asked Boston authorities to jail Drew "as a Deserter."¹⁰⁵ The third was a godsend; when Surgeon Linn resigned "with regret," Barry pounced, taking "the liberty to grant your request" and naming *Alliance*'s medically trained chaplain, James Geagan, to replace him. Linn, he told Morris, was "naturally of a weak constitution and . . . very Disagreeable to the Officers . . . I thought it best to get Clear of him."[106]

On July 27, Elisha Hinman, Seth Harding, and three other officers arrived from Boston for the court-martial of the mutiny's ringleaders. Each one was found "guilty of Mutiny and Sedition" and sentenced to receive between twenty and ninety lashes. The following morning, the punishment was carried out "on board the continental Ship *Alliance* at the Gangway."[107] Still needing a few sailors, a reluctant Barry returned McDaniel and Jennings to their duties, sending Anderson back to his Massachusetts regiment, his scarred back a lifetime memento of his sailing days.[108] To complete his crew, Barry took on several local slaves, whose owners could claim their wages and prize shares upon the *Alliance*'s return.[109]

By August the *Alliance* was seaworthy, and Barry's interminable stay in New London came to an end. "I sail tomorrow with a Good Ship's Company," he wrote Morris on August 2.[110] This was Barry's third voyage commanding the *Alliance*, but for the first time he had a loyal and capable crew. He also put to sea with no diplomatic encumbrances. Not since his second voyage on the *Lexington* had he sailed with such high hopes.

CHAPTER FOURTEEN

THE ALLIANCE

HE *Alliance* NO SOONER ESCAPED NEW LONDON on August 4, 1782, when a prize dropped into Barry's lap: a "Brig[ant]ine for Rhode Island bound to Hispaniola." Barry found her cargo of lumber and fish "not very Valuable, but it is making a Beginning." He headed south, hoping to replicate his earlier successes with the *Lexington*; but now, commanding the *Alliance*, there would be no turning tail at the sight of an enemy frigate. Six days later he came upon a second prize, a schooner "bound to Hallifax." If leaving New London was an immeasurable relief to Barry, these two quick prizes were a tonic both to him and to his crew. Euphoric, he informed Brown that "I have a good healthy ships Company, much beyond my expectation. My Jaunt to Philadelphia was of Great Service."[1]

Indeed, it was the happiest, most industrious crew ever to serve on the *Alliance*. John Kessler certainly benefited from Barry's tutelage, rising "from the state of a Rated Midshipman" to "acting as a Master's Mate."[2] Years later, Kessler recalled Barry's bond with his sailors:

> Innocent mirth of the Seamen was his delight–oft was heard the Boatswains call of "all hands to play" . . . inviting to

free & indiscriminate enjoyment of mirth & good cheer–on those occasions his . . . good humor would even extend to permit himself to be the subject of Joke and mirth–It sometimes happened that when any one had neglected or done anything wrong & when asked by Capt'n Barry how he came to neglect it…the person would begin to state, he thought so and so, Capt'n Barry would hastily say who gave you a right to think so, & which occasioned the crew among themselves to address their comrades with "who gave you a right to think, don't you know that Capt'n Barry thinks for us all"–and on one of those times of play he heard it, and required and received an explanation with the greatest good humor.[3]

Barry's skills as a sailor and commander were visible to officers and crew alike. "He knew how to perform all the duties of a Seaman from Stem to Stern," Kessler marveled, adding, "The promptitude and propriety of his decisions on sudden emergencies was wondered at & admired." Barry, even when "waked out of sleep," was "on deck in an instant, & all hands set to work wether it being the case of a vessell in sight, a violent gale or otherwise."[4]

Approaching Bermuda, Barry decided on a plan that was noble in thought. Since 1775 the island had been a haven for loyalist privateers, using the town of St. George's to refit, sell their plunder, and drop off their American prisoners.[5] On August 19, flying British colors, the *Alliance* glided into St. George's harbor; once safely in, Barry raised the Stars and Stripes. As Blackbeard did at Charleston and Wallace had done at Newport, the *Alliance* acted as a one-ship blockade. Barry notified the governor that if he did not release his American captives, the *Alliance* "would remain . . . to hinder any vessel going in or coming out." It was not an idle threat; "*Alliance* was more than ship enough" for the task.[6]

For one day neither side acted. The governor did not send out his prisoners, and the *Alliance* rocked at anchor in the mouth of the harbor, her gunports open. The following morning Barry saw "a small sloop . . . supposed to be coming with the prisoners." But the sloop's timing was poor: Barry's lookout had just sighted two sail to the westward and he ordered the *Alliance* "in chase."[7]

Five days after his abrupt departure from St. George's and without any additional prizes, Barry spoke "a brig for Guadeloupe bound for Rhode Island" and learned "of the sailing of a large fleet:" eighty-eight merchantmen, recently departed from Jamaica.[8] For Barry, this was course-changing news. It was the famed "Jamaica fleet."

He already knew two facts about the fleet. One, it always sailed north to Newfoundland, and thence home to England. Two, it would be well protected by numerous ships-of-the-line and frigates. Still, if the *Alliance* kept her distance, Barry could make a quick strike to cut out a merchantman or two . . . or three. For nine days, the *Alliance* plowed northward, racing to the Newfoundland Banks. On September 8, Barry claimed another prize: a Nantucket whaling brig he sent to Boston "on account of their having Adm'l Digbys protection & permission to bring their Oyl to New York."[9]

For several days the *Alliance* was trapped in the tail end of a storm which "tossed the ship about"; then, on September 18, the mast-header sighted another sail, and Barry soon came alongside his first prize from the Jamaica fleet: another brig, whose captain reported that "their convey [convoy] foundered in a gale, & that the fleet was scattered." The storm that the *Alliance* encountered was the tail end of a huge, destructive hurricane that had decimated the Jamaica fleet.[10]

Nine ships-of-the-line protected the fleet, including the *Ville de Paris*, de Grasse's former flagship and considered the largest ship of its time.[11] Captured by British Admiral Sir George Rodney in his masterful victory at the Saintes, she was the prize consort in the convoy. The fleet sailed under command of young and unlucky Admiral Thomas Graves, aboard his flagship, the *Ramilies*. The storm—two hellish days of winds, rain, and mountainous, crushing waves—overwhelmed the fleet off Cape Sable. The *Ville de Paris* and two other ships-of-the-line went down with all hands. Many others were dismasted and battered to the point of foundering. Thirteen merchantmen were at the bottom of the sea. The storm claimed 3,500 lives.[12]

After repairing the brig with jury-masts, Barry sent her back to Boston and sailed the *Alliance* east, in search of other disabled merchantmen.[13] She sailed through a tragic flotsam of cargo bobbing in

Portrait of John Barry as a successful merchant captain, c. 1775, possibly by James Peale. (*Bruce Gimelson Gallery/Private Collection*)

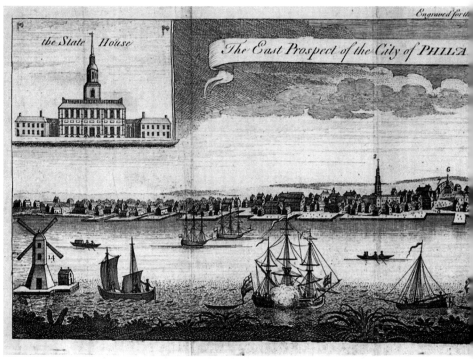

Within the image: *the State House* · *The East Prospect of the City of PHILA* · *Engraved for th*

View of Philadelphia in 1761, the year after John Barry arrived and made the city his home. (*Independence Seaport Museum, Philadelphia*)

View of St. Eustatia in the 1770s. (*Library of Congress*)

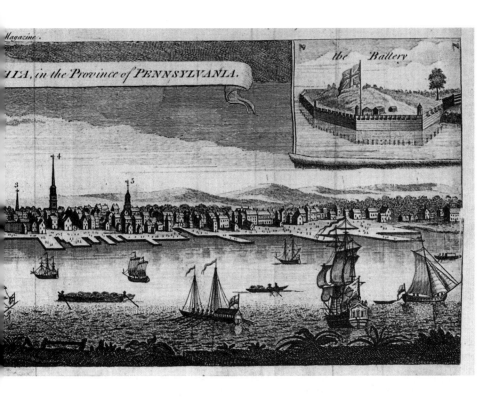

Robert Morris painted by Charles Wilson Peale. Morris gave John Barry captaincy of his finest merchantman, the *Black Prince*. Barry served under Morris before, during, and after the American Revolution. (*Library of Congress*)

Detail from the log of the *Black Prince*, Monday, September 11, 1775, in Barry's hand, marking 237 miles sailed in 24 hours, the longest known distance of a ship recorded in the eighteenth century. (*Independence Seaport Museum, Philadelphia*)

John Brown, Secretary of the Marine Committee and lifelong friend of John Barry. (*Cumberland County Historical Society*)

Andrew Snape Hamond, the British naval officer who failed to defeat John Barry despite numerous attempts to capture the elusive American captain. (*National Maritime Museum*)

The *Lexington* commanded by John Barry fires a broadside into the British sloop-of-war *Edward* on April 7, 1776. The *Edward* struck her colors shortly thereafter, the first enemy warship taken in battle by the Continental Navy. (*Nowland Van Powell, Naval Historical Center*)

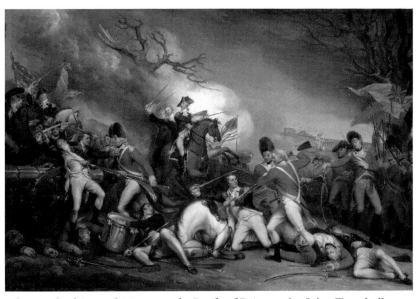

The Death of General Mercer at the Battle of Princeton by John Trumbull. Barry and other naval personnel distinguished themselves on this battle-field. (*Yale University/Art Resource*)

General Anthony Wayne. (*Library of Congress*)

John Laurens. (*Independence National Historical Park*)

Francis Hopkinson. (*Alonzo Chappel*)

Matthew Parke. (*Naval Historical Center*)

Pierre Landais. (*National Archives*)

Thomas Paine. (*Library of Congress*)

The *Alliance* with a missing mainyard, right, passing the Boston lighthouse in 1781, painted at the time by Matthew Parke. (*Naval Historical Center*)

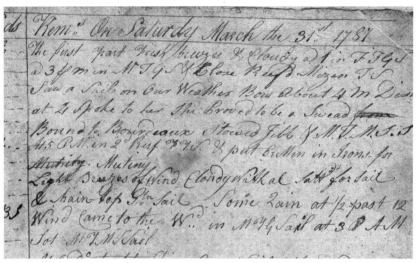

Detail from the log of the *Alliance*, March 31, 1781, where John Barry records the failed mutiny. The tenseness of the situation is revealed where Barry first misspells the word "mutiny," crosses it out, and then writes it correctly. (*Independence Seaport Museum, Philadelphia*)

The *Alliance* (center) battles the British warships *Atalanta* and *Trepassey* on May 28, 1781. Here, John Barry successfully defeated two ships simultaneously. (*Mariner's Museum*)

A late eighteenth-century illustration of *Alliance* battling the *Atalanta*; the *Trepassey* stands inaccurately in the background. This was a celebrated event of the American Revolution. (*Independence Seaport Museum, Philadelphia*)

A cameo of John Paul Jones once owned by John Barry. (*Hepburn Family Collection*)

Marquis de Lafayette. (*Library of Congress*)

Benjamin Franklin in French society. Unlike his contemporaries, John Barry never travelled to Paris to see the American plenipotentiary; he chose to write letters instead. (*Library of Congress*)

Off Cape Canaveral, Florida, on March 10, 1783, the *Alliance*, left, under John Barry, engages HMS *Sybil* in the final battle of the American Revolution. The *Sybil* sheered off due to damage from Barry's frigate as well as the appearance of the French ship-of-the-line *Le Triton*, on the horizon. (*Nowland Van Powell, Naval Historical Center*)

James Vashon, captain of the *Sybil.* (*National Maritime Museum*)

Richard Dale. (*Library of Congress*)

Thomas Truxtun. (*Library of Congress*)

James Josiah, first mate of the *Asia.* (*Peter McCausland Collection*)

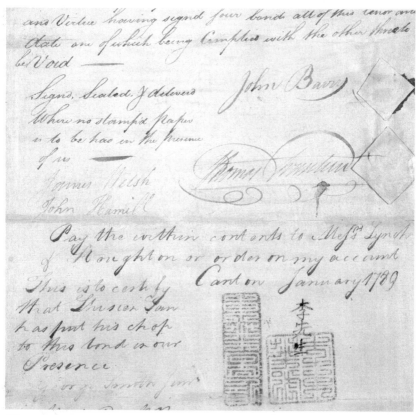

The "chop" signed by John Barry and Thomas Truxtun, a document that allowed them to trade in China. (*Independence Seaport Museum, Philadelphia*)

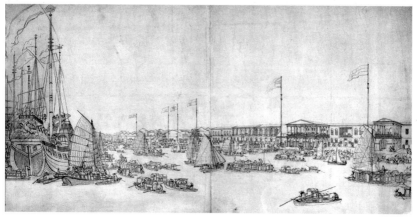

The factories at Canton in 1785. (*Peabody-Essex Museum*)

A teacup and saucer emblazoned with John Barry's initials from a set he ordered during his trip to Canton, China. (*Independence Seaport Museum, Philadelphia*)

George Washington painted in 1794, the year he gave John Barry his commission as the first flag officer in U.S. Navy history. (*Library of Congress*)

Henry Knox, Secretary of War in George Washington's cabinet. (*Library of Congress*)

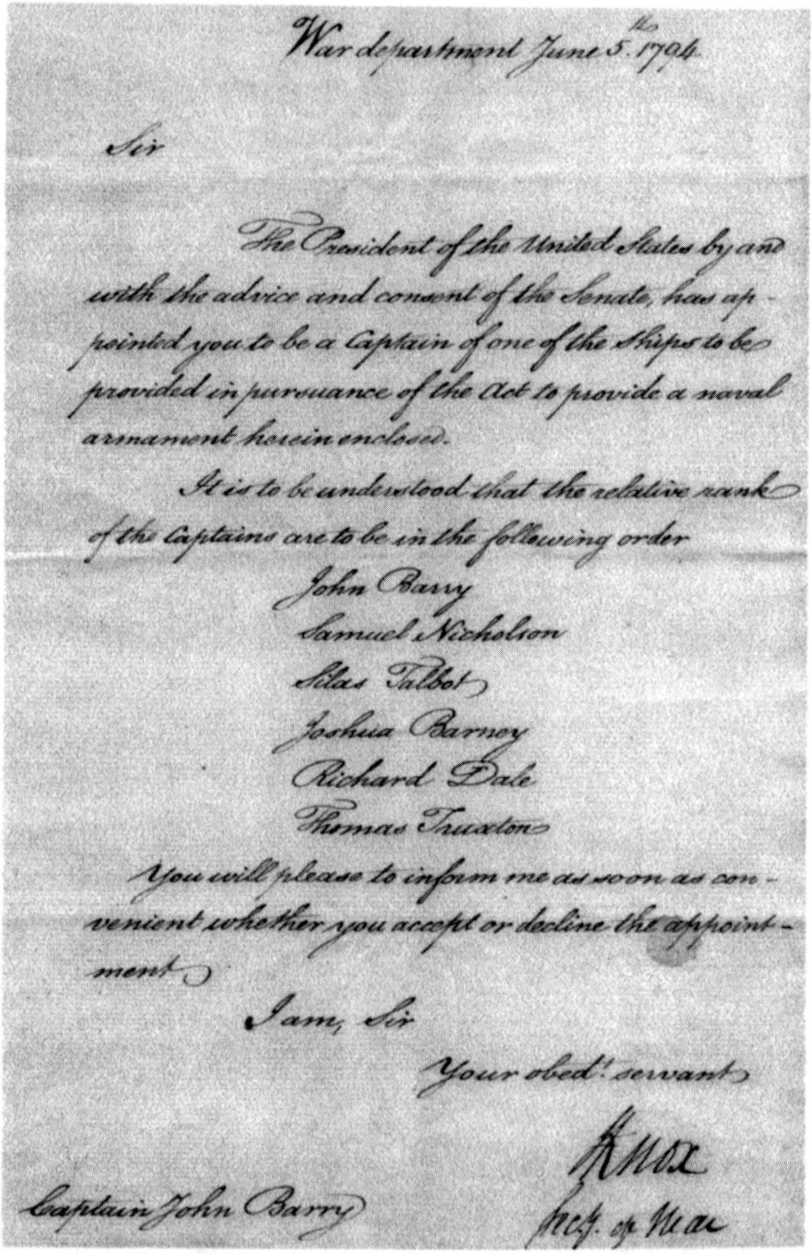

War department June 5. 1794.

Sir

The President of the United States by and with the advice and consent of the Senate, has appointed you to be a Captain of one of the Ships to be provided in pursuance of the Act to provide a naval armament herein enclosed.

It is to be understood that the relative rank of the Captains are to be in the following order

John Barry

Samuel Nicholson

Silas Talbot

Joshua Barney

Richard Dale

Thomas Truxton

You will please to inform me as soon as convenient whether you accept or decline the appointment

I am, Sir

Your obed! servant

Knox

Secy of War

Captain John Barry

The letter sent to John Barry by Henry Knox formally notifying Barry as having been selected to be the first captain in the new U.S. Navy. (*Independence Seaport Museum, Philadelphia*)

Benjamin Stoddert, Secretary of the Navy under John Adams. (*Department of the Navy*)

President John Adams navigated the undeclared war against French privateers in the Caribbean. (*Library of Congress*)

The frigate *United States,* designed by Joshua Humphreys and commanded by John Barry. (*Private Collection*)

The cutlass used by John Barry that hung in the Oval Office during President John F. Kennedy's administration. (*John F. Kennedy Presidential Library and Museum*)

Dr. Benjamin Rush, one of Barry's most trusted friends. (*Library of Congress*)

John Barry's niece, Elizabeth "Besty" Hayes, in later life. (*Hepburn Family Collection*)

The statue of John Barry greets visitors outside of the south entrance to Independence Hall. (*National Park Service*)

the Atlantic. Masts, spars, floating hogsheads, and puncheons were strewn along the fleet's wake. As they maintained their gruesome course, Barry's crew began to wonder if any other ships survived. Six days later, on September 24, the *Alliance* overtook two more merchantmen before darkness fell, their damaged condition belying their rich holds. Their masters told more horror stories of the hurricane—how they watched as the furious winds took one ship-of-the-line apart, plank by plank—until the walls of angry waves swallowed her up with all her men, their cries lost in the wailing wind.[14]

Barry's stalking of the fleet's derelicts netted him two more prizes while bringing him halfway to Europe. Now sharing provisions with an overload of British prisoners, and becoming shorthanded due to the number of prize ships, Barry decided "to proceed to France . . . with a determined view to get those [prizes] I already had taken in safe."[15] To the prizemasters, young Kessler among them, Barry gave explicit orders, including how to trick any British warship: "You will take Care to keep in Sight of the *Alliance* & at all times make all the sail you Can. Should you be separated from us . . . make the best of your Way for L'Orient. . . . In Case of falling with any of ye fleet, Personate the Captn. & go by your Papers, taking Care to keep these Orders & my Signals private."[16]

As before, Barry treated his prisoners well. They enjoyed "no confinement, no abridgement of food or any labors regard of them." Among them were officers from the *Ramilies*, who took note of Barry's hospitality, and "blush [ed] for their country" when they recalled England's treatment of captured Americans.[17] Barry's frigate and prizes reached L'Orient on October 17, but the *Alliance* had sustained damage during a heavy storm and was now drawing more water at her bow than stern.[18] Wasting little time, Barry set up an "Acct. of Disbursement" the next day.[19] To his surprise, American consul Thomas Barclay was actually in town, but his assurances to Barry of quick repairs and prize sales proved worthless.[20] In fact, L'Orient was teeming with American naval activity. Sixteen prizes were in port: Barry's four plus an even dozen taken by Yankee privateers, who also conducted a scavenger hunt with the remains of Jamaica fleet.[21]

Barry wrote Morris that the plunder from his prize-taking binge included "1280 hogsheads of sugar and 400 hogsheads of rum, a quantity of coffee, logwood & ca."[22] He was optimistic about his plans: "After repairing the damage [to the *Alliance*] I shall put to sea on a cruise."[23] Anticipating a ten-day layover, Barry entertained offers of "a Draught of Porter, Cheese . . . a Room & Bed" from friends in port.[24] The turning over of his prisoners was "more like the separation of old friends than that of individuals of nations at war," highlighted by one of *Ramilies*'s officers, who wrote Barry the most solicitous of thank you notes before departing on the cartel for Plymouth: "Accept my thanks for the genteel treatment we castaway dogs received on board the *Alliance*. I daresay I'll have an opportunity in more tranquil times than these, to assure Captain Barry how much I am Obliged to him."[25]

Barry found L'Orient awash with rumors of peace. Negotiations had been dragging on since April. Still smarting over the disastrous defeat at the Saintes, France's ministers now concerned themselves with Russia's growing lust for the Crimea, but wanted this war to end before starting another.[26] This did not bode well for Barry or his crew: as peace rumors inched closer to reality, delays in condemnations would drive down the sale of prizes.[27]

Nevertheless, Barry longed for one more cruise before a treaty bore signatures. Not a man to live by gossip, he wrote the one person in France he believed would tell him what truth lay between the rumors: Lafayette. After passing on Washington's concerns about the Marquis' health, Barry popped his question, asking if Lafayette knew of "anything new at Court, or any Expectations of Peace Soon." Three days later, the Continental ship *General Washington* arrived in port. Her captain, Joshua Barney (commander of one of the barges at Turtle Gut Inlet), carried secret dispatches marked for personal delivery to Franklin.[28] Barry handed Barney another.

He had delayed in writing to Franklin, there never having been any warmth or regard between them, save the transparent niceties of eighteenth-century correspondence. Recalling his disregard of Franklin's earlier orders stated as "suggestions," Barry "Therefore thought it would be only Troubling your Excellency to Write as I was . . . in expectation of being to Sea before an answer Could Come from Paris." Now Barry turned to his agenda: "if you [Franklin] mean [the *General Washington*] to go on a Cruize, I think you would render Great Service to the United States to order her out with the *Alliance*." He hoped Franklin's reply would, at the very least, give him some assurance as to the state of peace talks.[29]

But Barry would be in no condition to receive a reply. By day's end, he was seriously ill, and he summoned Dr. Geagan, who found him suffering from "a billious fever." The attack–a fever that would not spike–raged for several days. When his temperature finally subsided, the giant captain was as weak as a newborn. Correspondence went unanswered; the *Alliance*'s refitting, and the sale of her prizes was left to subordinates. It would be weeks before Barry got his sea legs back. The sentence "I was very much Indisposed with a fever which . . . Confined me to my Chamber These Ten Days," opened most of his subsequent letters.[30]

Once he could sit up he reviewed his mail. Lafayette's letter was pleasant ("With pleasure I break your Seal of 24th Inst . . . no Man feels for your Success more than I"), but with no substantial news on the negotiations. It ended with an invitation to Paris, inquiring if he was the same "Capt. Barry" who had met Lafayette's wife in Bordeaux years before. Barry's reply was friendly but frail: "As far as my going to Paris this time, it is out of my Power as the Ship is ready to Sail, only waiting my Recovery. . . . It was my Brother that had the Honor in Bordeaux (meeting Mme. Lafayette), who is since lost at Sea."[31]

Another old friend, Captain Henry Johnson, writing from Brest, regretted that he could not "get my affairs done [in] time enough to get to L'Orient," as he had "two or three Volunteers with me who would please you for Officers."[32] In his reply, Barry aired his frustrations over "Superannuated" Hezekiah Welch, who "has no more Command on board than one of the Smallest Boys on the Ship." Barry intended "to leave him here to take Charge of the Prizes. . . . He is not fit for a Ship of War."[33]

But his plans for Welch were suddenly tabled. Having stopped one mutiny at sea by British sailors before it could start, and quashed a second by American tars in New London, Barry now faced a third if unofficial rebellion coming from his own officers. Six of them, including Fletcher, Parke, and Geagan, had asked Barry to act as their agent for "our parts of Prize property taken by the *Alliance*." Still bedridden and "Determined to sail This Week if Wind and Weather permit," Barry balked.[34] Parke, unpaid for nearly four years, saw Barry's hesitation as proof that they would not be paid yet again.

This was too much. Had there not been promises of pay from Morris prior to their departure from New London? Had they not heard that the officers aboard the *General Washington* had "rec'd considerable compensation?" With Morris's assurances in their minds, and four captured Jamaicamen right before their eyes, they requested that Barry obtain notes for them, payable "on our Order in three four or five Months."[35]

While "Certainly [having] as Much reason to Complain as any of you," Barry replied, he believed the officers showed "a poor oppinion of your Country or Mr. Morris's Word" in "taking Notes payable in Six Months to receiving your wages in America where that money will be of more value to you." Further, he vowed "that if your Wages are not paid every farthing on our arrival in America, I will Join with you in any Petition or Remonstrance you may think proper."[36]

Still confined to bed, he awaited their reply. None came for four days, although he learned that the officers literally jumped ship, taking rooms in a nearby inn. Then, on November 24, he had a visitor: Parke, appointed by the others to make their latest demand in person. They wanted two-thirds of their back pay, or they would not report for duty. It took considerable courage to come into Barry's room and defy him, but Parke and his fellow officers misread Barry's promise of deferred assistance as a weakness. Barry sent Parke and the others a blistering reply: "Sir–Your Visit to me a few moments ago, convey'd threats... and you may be assured shall not pass over so light as you may expect–I have no power to pay your wages and it is impossible for me to do it here."[37]

As Parke "refused to go on board the *Alliance*," Barry placed him under arrest, then sent each officer a letter demanding they report aboard ship "this afternoon & there do your Duty til my further orders." Each one refused. They, too, were put under arrest with "no more to do with [the *Alliance*] till . . . try'd by a Court Martial in your country."[38]

Curiously, it was not what Barry did next, but what he did not do, that begs an explanation. While the officers were notified of their arrest, Barry sent no marines to arrest them, nor made arrangements for a court-martial. He was content to leave them ashore. Reports to Barclay, Morris, and Brown leave little doubt that he was angry over their behavior—which he wryly described as "the Drolest Manner you ever heard of."[39] But he did not jail them—he literally marooned them in L'Orient. Why? The answer was money, not pay: the money he hoped to raise through one more cruise before peace became a reality. It was more important to him to get back to sea than to remain in port one second longer than necessary—especially for a time-consuming court-martial.

He had no recourse but to order the "superannuated" Welch to resume his duties as second-in command. Welch immediately obeyed, giving Barry two senior officers still on his side—Welch and Marine Lieutenant Elwood. By the end of November, Barry's health was sufficiently recovered for him to be "ready to put to sea," even without a full complement of officers.[40]

Now Barclay shocked everyone. Despite having four unsold ships on his hands, Barclay ordered prize shares for the Alliances. A grateful Barry dealt them to everyone save the insubordinate six. He asked Barclay to oversee his shares once the prizes were sold, and that "Should peace come & you Can buy a Vesel or two Cheap, I should have not objection to be Concern'd a Quarter in each of them to go from here to Liverpool & from there to Phila." One might as well plan for the future. As for the six officers, he would leave them "to get to America as well as they Can, where I hope they will be Tried by a Court Martial and merit their desserts."[41]

Before the *Alliance* was ready to sail, Joshua Barney returned from Paris, with orders to remain in L'Orient until Franklin's latest dispatches regarding the peace negotiations arrived. Such news only hastened Barry's fervent desire to depart. On December 6, the dispatches came: "Peace between us and England is not concluded,"

Franklin wrote Barney, "yet the preliminary articles are signed and you will have an English passport."[42] The passport would provide safe passage to an American ship, demonstrating to any British captain that his government now recognized the new nation.

The last thing Barry wanted was an English passport. Once the *Alliance* was ready, he dashed off two letters. To Morris he wrote of his quarrelsome officers, his plans, and "the Joyous news of peace–As we have great Reason to Suppose it is about Concluded–I sail Tomorrow. I believe I Shall run down the Coast of Guinea," he closed, then "return to America Via Martinico [Martinique]."[43]

His letter to Brown was less restrained, telling him to expect his shares from Barclay, dryly asking that Brown "keep the money in your Hands 'till you are certain that I am not in the Land of the Living."[44] The *Alliance*'s muster book showed a hasty list of promotions, including Kessler as master's mate.[45] "I think it . . . my duty," Barry wrote, "to proceed to sea with such officers I have on board, as I have no expectation of getting any others." He was aware that "they are not adequate to the Duty of the Stations I Shall be Oblig'd to put them in," but, he concluded, "necessity has no law."[46]

Barry departed on December 7, the wind howling out of the northeast: cold, raw, and strong enough to send the *Alliance* speeding into the Bay of Biscay at ten knots. Two days later she was off the northwest coast of Spain. Bitter winds were blowing across England as well. On December 5, 1782, a forlorn George III ordered his ministers "to prohibit the further prosecution of offense of war upon the continent of North America."[47]

On December 11, Barry sent the *Alliance* south to Africa and spoke one ship, bound for home. He wrote a quick note, "On board the Frigate *Alliance* at Sea" to his acquaintance William West, a Philadelphia banker. While keeping his recent port of call secret, he did share his biggest news: "I was Inform'd that the preliminaries of peace was Sign'd . . . This you may rely on & I would have you Govern yourself accordingly."[48]

The *Alliance* soon reached the Madeira Islands, a volcanic archipelago some four hundred miles west of Morocco, where Barry changed course and headed westward to Martinique, plunging through the Atlantic. The year ended appropriately, as far as Barry was concerned: "Cloudy with Small Showers of Rain." New Year's Day began optimistically enough with "Light Winds and Pleasant Weather," as the *Alliance* continued toward the New World.[49]

Four days later the mastheader "Saw a Sail at 3:00 P.M. discovered her to be a very large two decker standing to the Northward." The chase was on. Barry "Halled our Winds to the Northward and Set all the Staysails." With the wind blowing east, the *Alliance* took her change of course effortlessly, going from "WNW to NNE," a transition easily accomplished by her seasoned crew. Her escape was so fast that Barry decided to spit in his pursuer's eye: "At 1/2 past 5:00 P.M. Tack'd Ship to have an Opportunity of seeing her Broadside better." Confident of his ship's sailing abilities and his crew's skill, he slowed to see if the dog in the hunt had two sets of teeth. She did. The *Alliance* resumed her flight until the ship-of-the-line abandoned the chase that evening.[50]

Barry soon found himself among the islands of his youth. On January 8, "at 2:00 p.m. made the Island of Domenica"; just a half hour later, the *Alliance* "made the Island of Martinico." After the ship "Came Too in the Road of St. Peir's [Pierre]," Barry saw "Several American Vessels and French Lying there." In port Barry was handed a dispatch from Morris, sent to Martinique back in October. The *Alliance* was "to proceed with all convenient speed to Havannah" where further orders awaited. Needing to "rigg a fresh top mast" and "a fresh supply of water," Barry put his men to their tasks with a sense of urgency, and they responded accordingly. Over the next two days, under "small Showers of Rain," the Alliances "Got the For Top Mast hooped & ready" and brought aboard "42 Puncheons" of drinking water.[51]

Once ashore, Barry informed the editor of the small *Martinique Gazette* about the preliminary accord for peace, and how articles had been signed: no more, no less. He was no sooner out the editor's door when the wharves and taverns were abuzz with the news. Barry departed the next day, unaware of what word of mouth was doing to his accurate report. Sailors aboard various ships departing St. Pierre embellished Barry's honest item of news with a furor of exaggeration. The paper's next issue excitedly confirmed that "dispatches to the Congress, announcing the signing of the preliminaries of peace" were seen by "Capt. Bary, the 2nd Commodore of the continental marine and an officer of credit."[52]

By February, the news reached American ports. Barry's hometown papers breathlessly reported that "hostilities had absolutely ceased in Europe." Soon the *Boston Evening Packet* reported that the *Alliance* had sailed into Martinique, Barry carrying an English passport, bearing news that "ARTICLES of PEACE were SIGNED on the 22nd Day of December last!"[53]

The *Alliance* sailed toward Cuba under "A Fine Wind about NE and Moderate Weather." On Tuesday, January 18, she "made St. Eustatia," the site of Barry's smuggling voyages for Reese Meredith. As the *Alliance* rested at anchor off "the Golden Rock"—now under French possession—a "cutter...with a Number of Gentlemen" approached. Barry hosted as lavish a dinner as a Continental frigate could provide. Among the dozen guests was yet another Barry, named David, who was a captain in Walsh's Irish Brigade and one of the legendary Wild Geese. He departed "in Raptures" over both his namesake and the *Alliance*. His guests gone, Barry left St. Eustatius with the tide just before midnight, heading for Cuba.[54]

Over the next eight days, as the *Alliance* cruised past the islands that dot the Caribbean, she was pursued several times, giving Barry the opportunity to show off his frigate's speed and excellent handling. "Off Hispaniola" (now Haiti and the Dominican Republic), peering through his spyglass on January 17, he found more than a few ships interested in the *Alliance*: "I fell in with the English fleet 17 sail which gave me chace." Already wearing all her canvas, the *Alliance* veered north, sprinting with the wind ahead of Lord Hood's fleet.[55]

Conditions became more harrowing on January 20. "Light Winds and Fair Weather" soon turned into a squall; then, "At 8:00 a.m. Saw 2 Sail Bearing WNW Standing for Us after the Squall Cleard away." They were an "English 74 and a Frigate." The *Alliance* "Made All Sail and Stood for the Land." The chase was no sooner under way when the *Alliance*'s wind died. The enemy ships fared better; they "took a

Breeze at NNW which bro[ugh]t them within 2 miles of us." The situation did not look good. While the lack of wind was reminiscent of Barry's battle with the *Atalanta* and *Trepassey*, these two ships were the sizes of the *Experiment* and *Unicorn* from his *Raleigh* days. But luck was with Barry: "We got the Breeze [still] not so much Force with us as with them." Using what "Force" there was to keep a safe distance, Barry skillfully kept the *Alliance* out of the enemy's clutches until stronger winds filled her sails and, "a few hours after, we left the 74 several Miles astern."[56]

The other pursuer, however, was not yet ready to give up her quarry: "the frigate held us a close chace for some time." Now, however, it would be either a fair race or a fair fight. Nearing the coast of Hispaniola, and with his orders present in his mind, Barry chose the former option. The *Alliance* pulled further away.[57]

Both captains were close enough to the fortress at Cap François (now Cap Haitien) to see her guns run out, ready to support the *Alliance*. After the frigate "chac'd us close under the Guns of the Cape," she, too, sheared off. Under cloudy skies, the Alliances "Hoisted the Cutter and Pinnace" and Barry went ashore.[58]

Cap François was so elegant in comparison to the other Caribbean ports that it was called "The Paris of the Isles." It had one of the largest roadsteads in the Western Hemisphere, capable of holding four hundred ships in a harbor naturally protected by a promontory that rivaled that of St. Eustatius in size. As the richest of the French colonies, her landowners lived like the transplanted scions of French royalty some of them actually were, dressing in tropical splendor. Sugar plantations abounded; slave labor was the driving force of the island's economy.[59]

Barry's pinnace no sooner reached the stone quay than he was quickly greeted by Seth Harding, late captain of the ill-fated *Confederacy*, last seen by Barry in New London.[60] With only the *Deane* and *Alliance* left of the American navy, Harding commanded a privateer that was captured by the British and taken to Jamaica, where he was once again exchanged.[61]

Both captains were pleasantly surprised by this turn of events. Harding wanted a passage home, and Barry desperately needed experienced officers. The two went to the Hôtel de la Coursonne, a favorite hostelry for mariners as well as a meeting place for the French gentry. After informing Harding of both the latest peace feelers and his orders, Barry asked Harding to join him. Harding, contemplating the offer of a French privateer, agreed to come aboard the *Alliance* as "Passinger," then treated Barry to a sumptuous dinner at the hotel.[62]

While provisions were stored and a pilot was engaged, Barry added another six seasoned Americans to his muster rolls. At 4:00 A.M. on January 22, he "called all Hands and got under Way in Company with the Ship *Apollo* Cap. Macky bound for Virginia and a Schooner bound for the Havannah." He left a letter updating Morris that he was "on my way to execute your orders, which I hope will meet with you Approbation."[63]

Sailing was peaceful but slow, the "Light Airs of Wind" allowing the other two ships to keep up with the frigate. But the next day, Barry found the schooner "still in Company," while the *Apollo* lagged behind. Exasperated with such lethargic sailing, Barry "took the Ship *Apollo* in Tow & made Sail." For the next four days the three lumbered toward the northern coast of Cuba, frequently traveling at only one or two knots. On the twenty-ninth, "Morro Castle"—the fortress at Havana's harbor—was sighted.[64]

In the early evening light, as the *Alliance* picked up a pilot and approached the harbor, Barry got his first glimpse of Spain's West Indies fleet, which had been lolling idly in Havana harbor for over two years. Ship after ship was anchored under the long shadow of the castle ramparts. The following morning, the *Alliance* entered the harbor with her pennants and colors snapping in the breeze, her 12-pounders peering out of their ports in a show of martial diplomacy. "At 1/2 past 10 came to & fir'd a Salute," the boom of her guns echoing around the harbor.[65] The salute was returned by the fortress guns. Barry clambered into his pinnace wearing his cleaned uniform, and an equally smart-looking band of tars manned the sweeps to row their captain ashore.

In Paris, negotiations proceeded despite the bickering between the three American ministers: Franklin, Adams, and John Jay, "the greatest quibblers I ever knew," a frustrated British diplomat commented.[66] Britain had come a long way since its initial offer of "an independent Parliament, and a Government similar to that of Ireland."[67] Shortly after Barry left L'Orient, the terms were finalized. The preliminaries were signed "in as short a time as a marriage agreement," Adams recalled.[68] From L'Orient, an exuberant Barclay wrote Delaware Congressman Nicholas Van Dyke that "the Preliminary Articles of Peace between France, Spain, and Great Britain were signed the 20th instant at Versailles."[69]

Like Barry, Washington stayed abreast on the twists and turns from Versailles while dealing with widespread discontent by Continental officers. As with the Navy, so with the Army: the issue was pay, and Washington's officers "were verging on a state which . . . will drive wise men mad."[70] Virtually bankrupt, Congress could do nothing but turn once again to Robert Morris, hoping he could pull one more golden rabbit out of his cocked hat.

Morris's solution lay in his orders awaiting Barry in Havana. Once Adams succeeded in obtaining a loan from Holland, Morris contacted his private banker in Europe and arranged for funds to be made available in Havana. Bills of exchange could be sold for specie, issued by a Spanish company with offices in Cadiz, Paris, and Havana. Morris had Franklin facilitate this transaction in Paris. The total specie came to 100,000 Spanish milled dollars, with five times that amount in American currency.[71]

Morris sent another ship to Cuba to escort the money in the event that the *Alliance* did not show: the *Duc de Lauzon*, twenty guns, under the command of Barry's old colleague John Green, late of Mill Prison.[72] As further sign of this mission's importance, Morris sent John Brown as the *Duc de Lauzon*'s supercargo.[73] Brown, given the task of collecting $500,000 in bills of exchange, could draw on only $67,422; he could have done better, he told Morris, had he used Morris's credit and not America's. The specie, rumored to be worth up to a half million, only totaled $72,447.[74]

The weather in Havana was beautiful on Saturday, February 1, 1783, when "Cap Bary the Governor & some Gentlemen came on board."[75] Besides Green and Brown, the "gentlemen" included James Seagrove, American Registrar in Havana: Don Luis Vizaga, Governor of Cuba; and Don Josef Solano, Admiral of the Spanish fleet.[76] The governor's finery and Don Josef's bright blue, red, and gold uniform contrasted with Barry's understated Continental issue as well as the subdued colors worn by Brown and Green. Barry arranged for dinner aboard the *Alliance*.

The cabin was a polite cacophony of Spanish, American, and Irish accents. After complimenting Barry on his frigate, Don Josef informed him that it would be some time before the *Alliance* left Havana. The port was closed until the idle Spanish fleet was ready to depart and join French forces in an invasion of Jamaica, England's richest island. He delivered this news in hushed tones, although it was a secret to the Spanish grandees only—everyone else was aware of it. Once the dishes were cleared and the port glasses drained, Barry bid *adios* to his Spanish guests with a thirteen-gun salute.[77]

Rather than get angry over the delay—Barry called it "an embargo"—he put the layover to good use. While the Catholic town observed Sunday solemnities (Barry could actually attend Mass), the Alliances were "getting Bread on Deck to Air" and acquiring "three Stays from the Shore." Before Monday's sunrise Barry "call'd all Hands" for one of the hardest tasks in the age of sail: careening.[78]

At the shallow end of the harbor, the *Alliance* was unloaded of cannons, stores, and ballast. Blocks, tackle, and harness—a symphony of creaking wheels and taut rope—droned endlessly in the background as Barry and his bos'n shouted orders. The strongest hands were sent to the harbor's "heaving down post," attached to a heavy floor embedded several feet below ground with buried rocks atop it. It was a literal land anchor for winch and cable. Next, the three new stays were lashed across the deck and run through the *Alliance*'s block and tackle, now made fast to a mast. Long iron bars were slotted into a capstan, located about ten feet from the post. Barry's men strained at the bars. Soon the taut stays stretched and slowly "hove down" the *Alliance* and "careen'd [the] Ship to port."[79]

Next came the tedious chore of examining the hull, scraping off barnacles, seaweed, and other souvenirs from every body of water that the *Alliance* had sailed through. Bare-chested, with kerchiefs tied around their heads in a futile effort to keep the sweat out of their eyes, the men worked feverishly. The stench of a raised hull was stifling in the Cuban humidity. At sunrise, professional help arrived: "21 Calkers came on board" who "fell to Work" so efficiently that by "4 P.M. [the crew] "headed the Ship to Starboard & got the Stays on the other Side . . . our people employ'd pricking oakum."[80]

The act of making oakum, usually a punishment, was attended to by all hands and given to the caulkers, who hammered it into the copper seams, resealing the hull. The noise of the hammers and mallets against the copper was so piercing it drove all of the gulls away. It was brought to Barry's attention that "the upper Streak of Copper on both Sides [was] a good deal ragged & Broke." Work dragged on until dark, beginning anew before dawn. There was no rest for the weary Alliances, "employ'd pumping, Scraping & overhauling the Sails." Once the careening was finished, they reloaded their provisions and stores. In three days the *Alliance* was presentable enough that Barry had "a Number of Gentlemen on Board to dine." On February 13, Barry requested the governor's permission for the *Alliance* and the American merchantmen in port to depart.[81]

Don Luis would not hear of it: "I have Maturely weighed the Motives you expressed... the port being Shutt which you are not Ignorant, for the sole object of Complying with secret Instructions from the King my Master, it is entirely out of my power to grant at present your Solicitation for Sailing, but you can assure yourself it Shall be the Soonest possible."[82]

Typically, Barry's next appeal to Don Luis was neither obsequious nor tactful–"I Cannot be Silent," he wrote. Conceding that the merchantmen could remain, Barry still could not fathom why "Ships of War" should be "restricted." Since Barry was not subservient to the governor's prompt response to his first letter, Don Luis let him simmer in "the Havannah's Pleasant Weather" for five days before he referred "the Affair to the Admiral," who feared "an unlucky accident" might befall Barry and Green, were they free to leave.[83] Brown advised his irate friend to ride out this period of inactivity as best as he could.

After ordering Green to careen his ship, Barry came up with a practical and noisy use of his own crew's time, directing them to "take care to exercise the Great Guns & Small Arms every Day." The daily drilling served several purposes: gun crews honed their timing and teamwork; their comrades improved their proficiency with musket and pistol; and the incessant barrage joined the piercing racket of the caulking hammers and mallets on the *Duc*, audible evidence of Barry's obedience to Don Luis's wishes. For the next two weeks the weather was idyllic. The only peals of thunder came from the thirty-six guns of the Continental frigate *Alliance*. But Barry's noisy presence did not change the governor's mind. Only *le Triton*, a "French 60 Gun Ship that . . . had on board [a] half Million of Dollars and bound to some of the French islands," was allowed to leave Havana.[84]

Supervision of gunnery practice went to Barry's newest officer, Robert Caulfield, a privateer from Maryland. Entered in the muster rolls as first lieutenant, Caulfield also led the crew in seamanship drills; Barry wanted them to "as often as possible loose the Topsails and lett the people Reef them in order to do it well."[85] Barry meted out shore leave to six sailors at a time, warning them that latecomers would be put in irons and leave cancelled for all—a parochial school approach meant to keep his crew from dallying too long in Havana's alluring taverns and brothels.

By March 5, the Spanish fleet was ready to sail, and the *Alliance* and the *Duc de Lauzon* "Wharp'd . . . towards the Moro." Two days later the fleet slowly paraded to the mouth of the harbor past Morro Castle. Its ancient cannons rumbled in salute, answered by the fleet's guns, with great cheering from sailors and spectators alike. No one was happier watching their departure than Barry. The following day, under "Pleasant Weather the Wind to the Southward," the *Alliance* "got under Way . . . in Comp[any] with the *Luzerne* . . . & a Number of Merchant Men."[86] With her hold full of "a large quantity of Dollars," a slower frigate carrying even more money, and a slew of merchantmen to escort, the *Alliance* sailed for home.[87]

Initially, Barry thought to accompany the Spanish through the first leg of the voyage, but with the "fleet a Great way to Leeward and heavy Sailers & not Knowing where they were bound, I thought it best to Quit them and make the best of my way."[88] He hailed Green, telling him of the change in plans; they would head for the Gulf of Florida, the water route above the Bahamas. The weather turned "Squally" as the *Alliance*, under full sail, tacked to the northeast, leaving the fleet far astern of her while also outdistancing the *Duc de Lauzon*. Barry "halled up the Main Sail" and reefed the topsails, letting Green's sluggish ship catch up. The Spanish fleet soon disappeared over the horizon. By three that afternoon, Barry spotted the Florida Keys, known as "the Martairs [Martyrs'] Rocks . . . about 5 or 6 Leagues" distant.[89]

The receding coastline was not the only thing in the *Alliance*'s range of vision. "Sail Ho!" the mastheader cried, and Barry saw "2 Sail bearing S.E." With "Top Gall[ant] Sails and Staysails" filling with the breeze, the *Alliance* headed back south toward the *Duc*. Both captains recognized the ships as "British Cruisers," but Green's suggestion that the American ships "stand more to the northward" stunned Barry, who immediately overruled him. They would maintain their southern course.[90]

Their pursuers were the frigates *Alarm*, thirty-two guns, under Captain Charles Cotton and the *Sybil*, twenty-eight guns, under Captain James Vashon. There were originally three ships, but the sloop *Tobago*, eighteen guns, under Captain George Markham, just "parted comp[any]" after weeks of prize taking along Florida's coastline. Cotton, the senior captain, signaled for Vashon to pursue as the Americans "bore away, and made sail from us."[91] Forty-year-old James Vashon had a lifetime of service in the Royal Navy under his belt, with stints under both Admirals Parker and Rodney during the war. As a reward for his valor in the Battle of the Saintes, he was given command of the *Sybil*, a captured French frigate.[92]

Seven hours passed. From his quarterdeck, Barry watched the British ships apply geometry to the variables of wind and water: "The Enemy [made] a Small angle on us if we Kept our Course, and Especially as we might be oblig'd to haul up a Little to Clear Cape

Florida and the *Duke de Luzerne* Sailing much heavier than us."[93] He ordered the decks cleared for action while reefing topsails and stay-sails to let the *Duc* catch up, while observing the British "in Sight standing for us." Before midnight, with "the enemy . . . within Gun Shott," the *Alliance* prepared to defend the *Duc de Lauzon*. Then, miraculously, Barry "saw the Spanish fleet." Both American and British mastheaders easily made out the lantern lights of the Spaniards under the starlit sky, and the British "left off Chace." The darkest hours before dawn were peaceful ones; the two American ships "Kept in Comp[an]y with the fleet all night."[94]

Daylight bore witness to an unwitting practical joke on the British. To Barry's amusement, he discovered that "the fleet" "were only 8 or 10 Sloops and Scooners"; not one warship among them but, as Barry wryly noted, "they answered our Ends." He and Green spoke several of the small Spanish sloops, inquiring as to the where-abouts of the real fleet, but no one could account for them, and Barry decided to "make the best of our way."[95] As they sailed northward, the *Alliance* sprinted ahead of the *Duc* with speeds up to ten knots over the next six hours. Cape Florida was soon sighted, and Barry shortened sail, allowing Green to catch up. They "made the Back of the Bahamia" early on March 8 and "tacked to the westward," sail-ing between Florida and Grand Bahama Island.[96]

Knowing that Morris would not have sent so slow a ship to carry such an important shipment, Barry became convinced something was amiss with the *Duc de Lauzon*. Her sluggish handling made her an ongoing risk. With the Spanish fleet a long sail away, Barry ordered "out the Pinnace" and "brought Capt. Green Mr. Brown & two other Gentlemen on board."[97] Entering Barry's cabin, they "held Consultation with respect to the Continental money placed on board the *Luzerne*."[98] Barry decided to lighten his consort's load, and transfer the bulk of the specie to the swifter *Alliance*–a move that would make the *Duc* faster and the specie safer.

Immediately the amicable discussion deteriorated. Green resent-ed his friend's order, and Barry let him spout a bit. But Barry suspect-ed that, like the *Marquis de Lafayette*, the *Duc de Lauzon* was carry-ing more than money in her hold. He believed that "Captn. Green had something on board that blinded him so much that he could not see as well as other people." Brown, however, readily saw the merits in Barry's decision, and the chests of specie were transferred. After adding his support to his friend's plan, "it was agreed between Capt. Greene, Mr. Brown & myself to have all the public money on board the *Alliance*." As little more than a sop to Green's bruised feelings, "thirteen thousand dollars or thereabouts" was left in Green's hold.[99] For the next several hours the pinnace ferried the chests of money to the *Alliance*. By evening the ships made sail. At sunrise they were just off Cape Canaveral.[100]

Barry's cautionary transfer of funds soon proved sound, for the Americans were on a collision course with their British counterparts from three days earlier. At 5:30 A.M. on March 10, 1783, under "Light airs, inclinable to be Calm," Vashon "saw two sail to the S'Wd."[101] Minutes later, aboard the *Alliance*, Barry "Saw 3 Sail bearing NBE" and another ship "Bearing SSW." The identity of the "3 Sail" was readily clear to Barry: they were the same ships that had chased them into the fishing fleet three days earlier, the sloop *Tobago* now back in company. Like three hungry wolves, the *Alarm*, *Sybil*, and *Tobago* made straight for their prey. Barry "made a Signal for Capt. Greene to make all the sail he could & follow me."[102]

He also kept an eye on the large sail further away to the southwest. At that distance, she was impossible to identify as friend or foe. The British were coming fast, with the larger frigate–Cotton's *Alarm*–far in the lead. After sizing up the situation, Barry determined "we had no business with them."[103]

Responding to Barry's signal, Green acknowledged the enemy's "superior force." Barry decided that sailing south toward the Spanish fleet–now a two-day race–was the best chance for survival. For him, the important thing was to save the money, even if it meant avoiding a fight and possibly letting the *Duc* be captured, even if his best friend–whose services were invaluable to the Navy–was aboard. "Not having an idea of being any service to [Green]," Barry "made all the sail I could" and sent the *Alliance* speeding southward, hoping that the *Duc* would keep up.[104] She did not. Soon the *Alliance* was as far ahead of her as the *Alarm* was from the *Sybil* and *Tobago*.[105]

Pursuit continued. By now both *Alliance* and the *Duc* had hoisted their colors, along with *Alliance*'s signals for the *Duc* to "Shift for herself." Despite her added cargo the *Alliance* was even quicker now, thanks to her cleaned copper hull; Barry "found I sailed faster than the Enemy." By mid-morning, the *Alarm* was within two miles of the *Duc*, with the others coming as fast as their sails could carry them. Suddenly Barry saw signal flags flying from the *Duc*: "Capt. Greene made a Signal to Speak with [Barry]," who "Shorten'd Sail" to find out what Green could possibly want to discuss at such a time.[106]

Barry was well aware that in returning to his consort, he was risking the money meant to save (or at least salve) America's dire financial straits. By 11 o'clock the *Alliance* was closer to the *Duc* than the pursuing *Alarm* and threw a scare into Charles Cotton. The closer the flying *Alliance* came, the more menacing her presence: with "the Squadron a long way a stern," Cotton "shorten'd Sail" to await his fellow captains.[107]

Barry, "determined to know what Capt. Greene wanted with me," was within hailing distance just as the *Alarm* and *Duc de Lauzon* exchanged cannon fire. The ships were not yet in range of each other; to Barry it seemed that Cotton wanted to feel out his opponent and see what the *Duc* was made of. He ordered his men to clew up the mainsail, take in the smaller sails, and clear the decks for action.[108]

While the *Alliance* showed no fear of the *Alarm*, Barry had eyes: the *Sybil* and *Tobago* now came on the *Alliance*'s heels, approaching her stern. Grabbing his speaking trumpet, he "spoke Capt. Greene, one of the Enemys 32 Gun Frigates then in Gun Shott of us, the other two . . . Coming up fast and Confident." Once more he ordered Green to make all sail and join the *Alliance* in a race for the horizon and the Spanish fleet.[109] Again, Green failed to comprehend the situation. "They [are] Privateers," he replied; "we could take them."[110]

Green's statement left Barry dumbfounded. This was no inexperienced captain, forgetting his prior signal of "superior force" two hours earlier. The British were coming off the horizon then. Now they were less than a mile away. "With myself," Barry thought, "I must have felt a sacrifice if I stayed with Capt. Greene."[111] What was Green thinking? What did he expect to happen, or hope to happen?

Barry's conclusion was simple: Green "would have made no Scruple to have Sacrificed my Ship and the public property"–meaning the transferred money. Further, Barry knew what a superior prize the *Alliance* would be for the enemy: "To have saved his own [ship] . . . I know if [the British] had agot me between them they would have paid little regard to his Ship."[112]

He choked back his anger, "begging to differ" with Green's ridiculous assessment: "It is very plain the ship to broadside of us to windward"–the *Alarm*–"is a thirty two gun frigate. The other two appear fully as large. I can stay with you no longer." He ordered Green to follow the obvious, time-honored (if not honorable) solution: "the only Chance he had to Get Clear was by heaving his Guns overboard to Lighten his Ship & try them [the British ships] before the wind."[113]

Almost immediately Green's crew began heaving their cannons overboard, keeping only her stern chasers for defense. That was the extent of Green's obedience. Instead of tacking to port and putting the wind behind him, he maintained his course, sailing parallel to the *Alliance* on her "weather bow."[114] This put the *Duc* directly along the *Alliance*'s starboard. In so doing, Green shortened the range between the *Duc* and the *Alarm*, whose bowchasers opened fire on the Americans. Green answered with the only guns he had left.[115]

Now the *Alliance*'s mastheader called attention to the other ship sighted that morning, and Barry "saw the Strange Sail tack and Stand for us." As quickly as possible, Barry processed the mystery ship's actions and what her intentions were. She had not sailed into the chase earlier–only after the exchange of gunfire between the *Alarm* and the *Duc*, and being able to see the British and American flags. If she were British, she would have entered the fray already; if she were neutral, she would have fled; and she was far too large to be American. She must be Spanish or French. Barry ordered signals run up for assistance.[116] Hoping that his hunch was correct, he now went to the rescue of the *Duc de Lauzon*.

At that moment the *Sybil* approached the *Duc*, just as "the head most and wind most of the Enemy"–the *Alarm*–"bore away a Cross Capt. Greene's Stern."[117] Why? Barry wondered, turning his gaze to the approaching stranger in this encounter. Why? Because Cotton saw the unknown ship's ensign seconds before Barry did. She flew the fleur-de-lis of France. It was *le Triton*–the very ship that had slipped out of Havana two days before the Americans departed. Now Barry knew why the *Alarm* was leaving the fight.

He also noticed there was enough space between the *Duc* and the *Sybil* for the *Alliance* to run a very risky screen play. Without losing a second, Barry "ordered the courses haul'd up and hard a Weather the helm."[118] His crew responded instantly: the helmsman turned the wheel over as the fore and main courses were hauled up. The *Alliance* changed directions so suddenly that wood, rope, and canvas made a collective shudder as the frigate ran between the *Sybil* and the nearly defenseless *Duc de Lauzon*.

This sudden yaw–dangerous enough in the most peaceful of traffic and tranquil of waters–was done quickly and successfully, allowing the *Alliance* to "Run Down between Capt. Greene and the Ship next to him in order to Give him a chance to Get by my bringing ye Enemy to Action which I did in a few moments."[119] Vashon watched as the *Alliance* "bore down to the Assistance of the small Ship."[120] Green proceeded to move as quickly as possible out of harm's way.

Barry had little time to get the crew ready for what was to come. A ration of grog was issued, doing as much as prayer to steel many a sailor's nerves.[121] It was in these incredibly tense moments, before carnage ensued, that Barry's leadership stood out. He "went from gun to gun on the main deck cautioning against too much haste and not to fire untill the Enemy was right abreast."[122] For seven years he had led his men through events such as these, but not since that long-ago-day when the *Lexington* faced the *Edward* had there been the semblance of a fair fight. Now, he had one. His own fears, if he still had any, were locked somewhere deep inside. Jocular and calm, he gave his men confidence. The gun crews, their cannons loaded and ready, hunched quietly over the starboard cannons as the *Sybil* sailed ever closer.[123]

Barry's opponent was doing much the same thing. Vashon was a bit of a braggart (the chapter about him in Ralfe's *Naval Biography of Great Britain*–while written in the third person–is written by himself), but he had courage, and his men respected him. It must have been demoralizing to see Cotton abandon him, but Vashon's crew was battle-tested.[124] While it seemed an eternity, only ten minutes passed since Barry sailed the *Alliance* in harm's way.

"At 50 Minutes past 11," the *Sybil* fired first—"a Bow gun, the Shott of which struck into the Cabin of the *Alliance*." The ball smashed windowpane and sash; flying glass and jagged splinters wounded everyone in the cabin, including the master's mate, Shubal Gardener.[125]

The *Sybil* tacked to fire a broadside from her port guns, but Vashon gave the order to fire before his gunners took aim, and they missed the *Alliance* entirely. The *Sibyl's* momentum carried her past the *Alliance's* starboard guns and brought her within Barry's favorite range: "half a pistol Shott." Now Barry "ordered the main top sail hove to the mast." After two solid weeks of performing this drill back in Havana, the top-men carried off the order perfectly. The *Alliance* slowed; soon the *Sibyl's* entire port side was exposed at close range. Finally, Barry gave his gunners the order they were waiting for: "Fire!"[126]

The *Alliance's* broadside was devastating, killing a lieutenant and wounding several sailors. The *Sybil's* rigging and stays were ripped apart, and her "Main Studding Sail" (Vashon had not hauled in his "stuns'ls" from his pursuit) was "shot away." The *Alliance* was so close to the *Sibyl* that Barry's crew could see the expressions on their adversaries' faces. Canvas, wood, and rigging littered the *Sybil's* fore-deck, severely hindering her ability to fight and sail. Both sides reloaded their guns, while marines poured lead across the enemy decks. The ships drew even closer. The *Alliance's* swivels were fired across the short distance of ocean. Loaded with musket balls, they sprayed like buckshot across the *Sybil's* deck.[127]

The next round from the *Sybil* did little damage to the *Alliance's* rigging but wounded several more Americans. Barry's replying broadside was again the more damaging, and the *Sybil's* "F[ore] top mast and F[ore] studding sails [were] shot away and lost over-board."[128] British casualties mounted swiftly; the cockpit, filling up with the dying and wounded, smelled of sawdust and blood.

The *Alliance* and the *Sybil* had locked horns for a half-hour. Even with his topmasts gone and his studding sails dragging in the water, Vashon doggedly sailed the *Sybil* alongside the *Alliance*, allowing

Barry's 12-pounders to punch a series of holes in the *Sybil's* hull. After the *Alliance's* next broadside, Vashon's ensign and truck (a wooden cap at the head of the flagstaff with small holes for the halyards that hoisted signals) were shot away. The *Sybil's* "guns were silenced, and nothing but musketry was fired from her," Kessler wrote; "she appeared very much injur'd in her Hull."[129]

Vashon assessed the sorry state of his vessel: "Our sails and rigging [were] cut all to pieces." He gave his carpenter orders to jury-rig one of the stays for the signal flags, then "hoisted a signal of distress." Vashon had had enough. The *Sybil* tacked to starboard as best she could and stood to the northwest.[130] The Alliances, sweaty and powder-stained, watched the "very much shattered" *Sybil* retreat before them. Barry observed that the *Alarm*, "which had it in his power to have come to action . . . put his helm a weather and sheer[ed] off."[131] While Vashon downplayed his casualties, one report later placed the dead at "37 killed and upwards of 40 wounded."[132] Vashon, curious and angry as to why the *Alarm* had deserted him, now added bitter chagrin to his state of emotions when he saw the signal flags flying from Cotton's ship: *Break off the engagement.*[133]

Quickly, Barry assessed the *Alliance's* condition and "the butcher's bill." Besides Shubal Gardener there were ten wounded, including Seth Harding; struck in the side, he would quickly recover. Damage to the *Alliance* was minimal: "My Sails Spars and Rigging hurt a Little, but not so much they would all do again," Barry believed.[134]

Much as he wanted to, Barry did not pursue the crippled *Sybil.* Doing so would put the *Alliance* and her specie at risk, in the event that the *Alarm* and *Tobago* took over the fight. The *Duc de Lauzon,* her guns jettisoned, could barely defend herself. No, the ship Barry wanted to catch was *le Triton*. The Frenchman had made sure to keep out of harm's way. Barry and Green "haul'd our Wind for the Strange Sail." The closer the American ships neared *le Triton* the angrier Barry became. Gradually the hulking giant's vague form took shape, from a distant sail to the magnificent ship-of-the-line she was. Her sixty-four guns were near twice that of the *Alliance.* Hailing her captain, Barry asked if he had seen the *Alliance's* signals, and why had he not joined the fight? The Frenchman's excuse was flimsy: *le Triton* "had on board half a Million of Dollars and [was] bound to the French

ALLIANCE AGAINST SYBIL ⚓ MARCH 10, 1783

| *Alliance* | *Duc de Lauzon* | *Le Triton* | HMS *Sybil* | HMS *Alarm* | HMS *Tobago* |
| FRIGATE | MERCHANTMAN | SHIP-OF-THE-LINE | FRIGATE | FRIGATE | SLOOP |

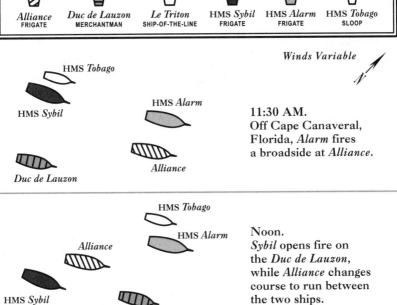

Winds Variable

HMS *Tobago*

HMS *Alarm*

HMS *Sybil*

11:30 AM.
Off Cape Canaveral,
Florida, *Alarm* fires
a broadside at *Alliance*.

Alliance

Duc de Lauzon

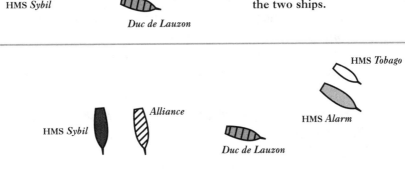

HMS *Tobago*

HMS *Alarm*

Alliance

Noon.
Sybil opens fire on
the *Duc de Lauzon*,
while *Alliance* changes
course to run between
the two ships.

HMS *Sybil*

Duc de Lauzon

HMS *Tobago*

Alliance

HMS *Alarm*

HMS *Sybil*

Duc de Lauzon

Le Triton

12:00-12:30 PM.
Alliance engages *Sybil* for 30 minutes.
Sybil sheers off due to damage from
Alliances's broadside and appearance
of French ship-of-the-line *Le Triton*.

Islands. The captain embellished further—he feared that the two Americans were captured prizes, and that Barry's signal for assistance was just a clever English trick to capture him.[135]

Barry did not buy a word of it. He considered the Frenchman's explanation a "foolish idea" that cost three prizes. Barry's "commencing the action was with the full expectations of the french ship joining & thereby . . . subdue part if not the whole of them."[136] When told the captain believed that the ensuing battle "was only a decoy," Barry's withering invective did not need translation.[137] However, now that the Frenchman knew his supposition to be erroneous, he offered to accompany the two American frigates and "give chace" to Scott's squadron.[138] No sooner said than done; the allies "tacked and Gave chace," but "at dark lost sight of them they being about 8 or 10 miles Ahead of the *Alliance* & the *Alliance* about two miles ahead of the french ship and three ahead of the *Luzerne*."[139]

It being his turn to be pursued, Vashon cut the *Sybil*'s wreckage and "Made sail from the Enemy" until "at 7 lost sight of them."[140] The *Sybil* eventually limped back to Jamaica.[141] *Le Triton* proved as slow as the *Duc*, which did nothing for Barry's mood: "Chace was made, but the French ship being unable to keep up . . . it was given over."[142] A fuming Barry watched *le Triton* bid *bon voyage*, and then signaled for Green and Brown to come aboard.[143]

While Brown was effusive in praise of his friend's skill and courage, Green was close to downright hostile. Barry weighed in on Green's entire conduct since leaving Havana, insisting that the remaining $13,000 be transferred to the *Alliance*. Green refused, but Barry did not take no for an answer, telling Green he would report everything to Morris, and that he "wanted an apology for [Green's] cool behavior." Even the diplomatic Brown was at a loss for words. The money was brought aboard the *Alliance*, while Barry transferred two 9-pounders to the *Duc*. By this time Green boarded the pinnace and returned to his ship, having severely damaged a long friendship.[144]

Three privateersmen who were passengers on the *Duc de Lauzon* now came over to the *Alliance* for the duration of the voyage, along with seventeen seasoned hands. Barry would have good use for them, once again being "short" due to his casualties. The two ships sat through the rest of the evening, and at dawn on March 11 weighed and continued their journey home.[145]

By late evening on March 18 they had sailed barely four hundred miles and were in the treacherous waters around Cape Hatteras. After Barry "Struck Soundings," he shared the information and ordered Green to "make all the Sail he could and follow me." The wind was picking up; even the dull-sailing *Duc* could accelerate to a satisfactory speed northward. But after midnight, an angry Barry "Saw Capt. Greene and in a Very little time lost Sight of him." With his closest friend aboard the *Duc*, Barry, "not being off the Deck the whole Night . . . did not Carry more Sail" so that Green "might have Kept up with us." The changing winds, the narrows around Hatteras, and the ever-present concern for British ships decided Barry's actions for him: he wanted the *Alliance*'s hold emptied in Philadelphia as soon as possible. Previously he had slowed down for the *Duc* to keep up. Now he did not tarry, or fret over his decision; Green's incessantly slow sailing, Barry concluded, "must be best Known to him, as I am Confident he might have Kept Comp[an]y with us if he had amind to."[146]

Giving orders to throw on every sail, Barry let the *Alliance* be the *Alliance*. Within twenty hours, she was outside Cape Henlopen–nearly as fast a day of sailing as he made with the *Black Prince* eight years earlier. The *Alliance* approached the gateway to home in a thick fog. Barry loved it. It was a rare instance during this war that the weather was on his side–the fog could certainly help him slip past British ships, pick up a pilot, and be safe at home with the money in Morris's hands. This fog was a godsend–unless, of course, it also cloaked the enemy. And it did: "On the 19 at 6:00 P. M. off the Capes of Delaware after a Thick Fogg I fell in with two British Cruisers . . . one of them appeared to be a two Decker, the other a twenty Gun Ship American Built."[147]

If Barry could not use the fog to get in, he could at least employ it to get out. It was better protection than any cannon could have been. After the *Alliance* "Got Clear," Barry played hide-and-seek with the enemy, still hoping to enter the Capes undetected. This attempt also failed; just "2 hours after" entering the bay, Barry "Saw [the enemy] in a Clear." They could not catch the *Alliance*, but their captains were smart enough to block her from her destination. Barry, "having Great Reason to Suppose the Coast was lined with the Enemy Ships, and no prospect of Getting in," took his last remaining option: "I thought it best to bear away."[148]

The "fogg" again lifted, showing the enemy to windward and "making chace."[149] With the wind to her advantage, the *Alliance* led them on a glorious race, flying at a rare speed for the 1780s. At one point Barry "hove the Logg myself" to gauge the speed of his beloved ship, which "was going 14 Knotts with a great deal of ease." In taking his pursuers on this joyride, Barry inadvertently opened the way for the *Duc de Lauzon* to enter the Capes safely, docking in Philadelphia on the evening of March 21.[150] When Brown later informed Barry of this, the captain realized he had once again saved Green's ship, if on this occasion, by happenstance: "Happy for you [Brown] you had parted company with me. By that means you got in safe."[151]

For a second day the *Alliance* sailed over two hundred miles. On March 20, in beautiful spring weather, she dropped anchor at Newport, Rhode Island.[152] Barry immediately wrote to Morris regarding his voyage, Green's bizarre behavior, and what to do "With 72 odd Thousand Dollars belonging to the public" in the *Alliance*'s hold. Barry did "not think it very Safe on board," and wanted a government official—any government official—to take the money off his hands. His crew, dutiful as they were, wanted to be paid, and Barry stood by them, telling Morris that "During the Action my Officers and Men behaved well," but "if the Ship is not paid off and Every man satisfied She will lye a long time without Men." He also believed that "if they are immediately paid I think we Can be Mann'd before the Ship is Repaired and I hope you'll be pleas'd to Give orders on that head." He finished his report requesting more officers, two 9-pounders to replace the ones given to Green, and recommending Robert Caulfield for a captaincy. Then, handing Caulfield the letter (along with one to Sarah), Barry sent him on horseback for home.[153]

With the *Duc*'s arrival in Philadelphia, it fell to loyal old Brown to counter Green's version of the story with what actually occurred. Brown also informed Sarah that her husband was safe—at least he had been two days earlier. She was worried; the most recent news of him came from the *Pennsylvania Gazette* in February, regarding his arrival in Havana "to take under his convoy the vessels that might be at that place bound for America." The same issue contained the latest news on the peace talks, letting patriot and loyalist know that they could expect "a just peace" unless "violent opposition" was made over "the restoration of Tory . . . estates"—something Sarah was all too familiar with.[154]

On March 23, 1783, the French sloop-of-war *Triomphe* picked up a pilot at Cape Henlopen and proceeded up the Delaware. Stopping at Chester, her most important cargo—news—leapt across the gangplank quicker than any sailor could have. A courier went galloping at breakneck speed to Philadelphia with the joyous news that the Treaty of Paris was signed.[155]

Shortly after the *Alliance*'s duel with the *Sybil*, Shubal Gardener, master's mate, died of the wounds he received in Barry's cabin and was buried at sea.[156] Gardener was the last Continental Navy sailor to perish from battle-related causes. Barry had fought the final engagement of the Revolution, unaware that the ink on John Adams's "marriage agreement" had been dry for seven weeks.

The war was over.

CHAPTER FIFTEEN

In Irons

O PHILADELPHIAN WAS HAPPIER ABOUT THE Treaty of Paris than Sarah Barry. Peace freed America from Great Britain, but more important to her, it freed her husband from the dangers of war, and gave her hope that a subsequent amnesty for her brother might reunite her family. Word of the treaty had not yet reached Newport so Barry, fearing "that my Ship is not Safe from the enemy," took the *Alliance* upriver to Providence. He also sent for Sarah.[1]

Barry was soon inundated with letters, some bearing good news. His friend William French warmly congratulated him on his arrival, wishing Barry "live long to enjoy the fruits of your Labour acquired with so much honor, Bravery and Danger." Morris sent word that the *Alliance* be "Imediately fitted for Sea," then off to Virginia "to take in a Cargo of Tobacco for Europe." Barry could not be happier: he had his old job back. For months he had given thought to a peacetime navy; now he poured out his suggestions to Morris, from using the *Alliance* "to Carry Cargoes," to reducing her crew to a number necessary "to Keep up the appearance of a public Ship."[2]

Other correspondence bore bitter tidings. While Barry was at sea, Joseph Kendall sued him over their payment dispute and won, recovering £180.[3] Having removed iron from Barry's shoulder, the troublesome surgeon now took money out of his account book. "I can hardly think that there is a Sett of Laws that will Condemn a Man who is fighting for them without being heard," Barry protested, berating one official that "I am in a fine Box after Serving the Country faithfully the Whole War to be oblig'd to learn [that] evr'y Man, even Deserters that have been under me can Sue me."[4]

As if unclaimed specie, no pay, and Kendall's revenge was not enough, Barry learned of another lawsuit. The American sloop *Fortune*, a prize Barry recaptured from the British in August, had been sold by a Continental agent without going through the legal condemnation process. Word of this reached her Connecticut owners who immediately sued Barry's agents in New England, sending him a summons which misspelled his name as "Barre." Barry called it the "Most rascaly writ couch'd with the most dirty Language I ever beheld . . . as for their Sueing me I care not a figg for them. I comply'd with my orders and I out them, or any Dirty Scoundrels like them to Defyance. . . . I observe in the warrant they have not spelt my name right, therefore it cannot be me they have Summon'd."[5]

After urging his agents to pay him "before they bring a properly spelt summons," he also addressed wages and shares for the slaves that served on the *Alliance*. While noting that his agent's two slaves earned their master "120 Livres each," he had troubling news for Congressman Ellery about his slave; Barry being unaware that "Caesar had a Master . . . A few days ago I Gave him Liberty to go to N[ew] Port, and I dare Say he is there now."[6]

Barry desperately wanted to visit Philadelphia, and requested leave "as my affairs in that place are lying in a Bad Way." While awaiting permission, two letters arrived. The first, from Morris, assured him "that the Ship should be paid off" by giving "each Man a Certificate that he belonged to the Ship." He reconfirmed Barry's upcoming European voyage and ordered him to "transmit your charges against these officers who staid in France and be prepared to Support them before a Court Martial."[7] In short, Morris gave Barry direction on everything but the most important item on the *Alliance*: the chests of money.

The second letter, from Brown, was personally "handed you by the most agreeable of Messengers."[8] Truer words were never written. The messenger was Sarah, accompanied by her teenage cousin, Mary Crawthorne.[9] Only eight months had passed since Sarah had seen John, but she was stunned at the changes in her husband. Though not yet forty, he had aged considerably. His perpetually tanned, leathered face was paler due to a cold and the last vestiges of the "bilious fever" that beset him in L'Orient. Damp days increased the chronic pain in his wounded shoulder. The crow's feet around his eyes were now as etched from worry as they were from sun and wind. His thick hair was graying well past his temples. Add the care-worn expression of an unpaid warrior collecting more lawsuits than laurels, and John Barry no longer looked the dashing captain Sarah had married six years earlier. Nevertheless, it was a joyous reunion, especially when Sarah told him she would accompany him to Virginia and Holland.[10]

Brown's letter offered no encouragement about Barry's financial morass. No matter where his goods were–L'Orient, Havana, or home, it was "Imposable to Sell a Single piece of any thing. . . . There is a Total Stop put to all kinds of Trade." Barry returned to his duties on the *Alliance*, winnowing the crew down to 142. Kessler and Welch were among the departed, leaving Lieutenant Elwood his only offi-cer. With no word from Morris about the once desperately needed money for the country (at least when it was not *in* the country), Barry ordered Elwood and his few marines to remain aboard the *Alliance*, standing guard round the clock over the Spanish milled dol-lars. To Sarah's consternation, he packed his saddlebags and rode to Philadelphia, arriving at the end of May.[11]

He found Philadelphians at peace with Britain but not among themselves. The once smartly painted houses looked old and dreary. The cobbled streets, in disrepair throughout the war, filled with mud after it rained. Inflation still ran amok; if something had cost one dol-lar in 1777, it now cost over one hundred. One citizen, watching the city awaken from its wartime nightmare, described Philadelphians dressed in clothing "of the coarsest form . . . made by the female's spinning in the house . . . *I know* that two lads, both afterwards commodores in the United States Navy, were both taught to be good spinners on the little wheel." A merchant despaired over the absence of trade goods such as tea, coffee, and sugar: "There was no *regular* business in anything," he lamented; even precious salt was "smuggled in women's pockets." Even the weather seemed to reflect Philadelphia's tempestuous mood; right before Barry's arrival a "hail storm believed the heaviest ever known here [struck] . . . stones fell of 1/2 an ounce–many windows were broken."12

Philadelphians, needing a scapegoat, found one in Morris. While he complained to Washington that "My Credit has already been on the Brink of Ruin," his enemies in Congress carped that it had "ever been a ruling principal with [Morris] to connect the public service with the private interest." Morris felt secure enough about his transactions to insist Congress review his books twice a year, and while James Madison attested that "I have seen no proof of malfeasance," nothing stilled the talk.13 Tired of the accusations, Morris submitted his resignation to Congress, who pleaded that he reconsider.

For ten days Morris held meetings with Barry, who presented an account of his service from the *Lexington* to the *Alliance*. After reviewing Barry's extensive documentation, Morris promised he would have the captain paid after an auditor's review, and finally made arrangements to free Barry from his Spanish milled dollars upon his return to Providence. They discussed upcoming plans for the *Alliance*'s voyage to Holland. Barry's request to pad his crew with Philadelphia sailors, so successful the previous summer, was denied, as was his request that Richard Dale be appointed second-in-command. Morris wanted Alexander Murray. He admitted that Barry's suspicions about Green's shifty behavior were well founded; Green had, indeed, loaded the *Duc de Lauzon* "beyond any Allowance [that] Captains are entitled to." Last, Morris informed Barry that he had been vindicated regarding his marooned officers: each had been found guilty of abandoning his duties.14

Visits with Brown were pleasant solely in companionship. Not only were Barry's stateside goods unsold; Barclay was still shipping more goods from France, bought with Barry's prize money and contrary to his directions. In his enthusiasm to be of service, the agent was making Barry's money disappear. Brown helped Barry draft a letter remonstrating Barclay. "I have lost a Great Dale of money," Barry stated, demanding "Interest for the money laying in your hands."[15]

John Paul Jones was back in town. He was supposed to be in Boston for the court-martial of both Captains Sam Nicholson and John Manley (a task that would have been very much to his liking), but Morris found him "so unwell that I gave up expectation of his going." When the two captains last met, Jones was off to Portsmouth, picking up where Barry left off, supervising completion of the ship-of-the-line *America*. Jones worked tirelessly to complete the task, and she was launched in November. But it was a hollow accomplishment. Lacking both money and sailors–Jones could ask Barry about that one–Morris saw the *America*'s launching as a twofold opportunity. He presented her to the French, both in thanks for their support and as a way to get the titanic vessel off Congress' books. In his last act as a captain in the Continental Navy, Jones turned command of the largest ship yet built in the western hemisphere over to the French. James Nicholson's petulant boast that Jones would "never get *America* to sea" was correct and incorrect at the same time.[16]

Among his peers Jones had few friends, but Barry was one. The Scotsman wrote a letter of introduction on Barry's behalf to the House of Deauville et Fils in Amsterdam, requesting that "As Captn Barry is an entire Stranger to Holland any civilities you may show will the more Oblige."[17] They parted company: Jones to recover his health at a Moravian sanitarium in Bethlehem, and Barry back to Providence. They never saw each other again.[18] Despite Barry's wound, mutinies, and money woes, the war had ended better for him than for *le Chevalier* Jones.

Barry returned to Providence, finding the *Alliance* nearly converted from man-of-war to merchantman and "perfectly sound."[19] The specie was transferred ashore, replaced in the hold by most of the *Alliance*'s guns: yesterday's arms were today's ballast. On June 20, Barry picked up a pilot and departed Providence. Sarah and her cousin watched from the quarterdeck as the *Alliance* stood down the Pawtuxet. The frigate never looked better, nor was her captain ever prouder.[20] The old superstition that women aboard ship were bad luck went unspoken. Virginia beckoned.

Then, in seconds, all happiness on board ended. The *Alliance* was "going four or five miles an hour" when disaster struck: "The Pilot ran her against a submerged Rock."[21] The impact was sudden and loud; the *Alliance*'s copper sheathing was no defense against stone. To Barry's horror, a series of heavy, splitting, cracking sounds came from *Alliance*'s hull. After the initial shudder, she stopped dead in the water.

Instantly, Barry sent the carpenter and his mates to assess the damage. Barry never documented what he called the pilot, but doubtless the invective was fitting—if less profane than usual due to the presence of the ladies. For two hours the *Alliance* lay trapped. When the carpenter reported that "the Ship made no more Water," Barry let the rising tide float her off the rock, with "hope [*Alliance*] received no Damage."[22] Embarrassed before his wife, of all people, at this turn of events, Barry again sent the *Alliance* downriver.

Now the ladies took their turn in this darkening comedy. Entering Narragansett Bay the wind picked up, the water turned rough, and the *Alliance* began reacting to the elements. Although a mariner's wife, Sarah and her cousin were landsmen. As their stomachs began to pitch and roll with the ship, their complexions went from rosy pink to a pale green, and the excitement of good winds and great sailing were lost on them. As quickly and as lady-like as they could, they returned to their cabins. For the next four days, the ladies held a death grip on two oaken buckets, sea-sick for the entire passage to Virginia.[23] With ship and spouse in poor health, Barry resumed his career as merchant captain.

For Sarah, as stoic and brave as any Philadelphian in the past six years, this was the most grueling ordeal of her life. Dreams of crossing the Atlantic were replaced with a vow that, if she lived through this, a coach back to Philadelphia would be her reward. "Mrs. Barry has been so sick on the passage here that she has given over going any further," her husband wrote.[24]

Barry and Morris incorrectly assumed the *Alliance*'s layover in Virginia would be five weeks, but Morris's Virginia agent, Daniel

Clark, was totally unprepared for Barry's arrival. Six weeks later the *Alliance* was still at anchor, but Sarah's companionship did wonders for Barry's mood: "it is all in vane to Grumble," he amiably rationalized. Finally, on August 20, the last of the tobacco was stowed. Slow as Clark was, he was thorough; Barry happily "put more tobacco in the two decks than I intended"–over five hundred hogsheads. He wrote Morris, "I flatter myself that my conduct will give Satisfaction and Shall always think myself happy and doing every thing in my power to merit your esteem."[25]

After watching the *Alliance* make sail and head for Holland, Clark saw the ladies to their coach, and they began their 400-mile journey over bumpy, eighteenth-century roads. Uncomfortable as the ride was, it was easier on their stomachs than the *Alliance.* Writing "from the Capes of Virginia on the 24th," Barry anticipated "a very good prospect before us." Back in his element, at the task he knew so well, and "with a Moderate breeze wind and smooth Sea," Barry foresaw a swift voyage, and a short stay in Holland.[26]

It was not to be: Barry's hopes were dashed by the same "sunken Rock" last seen in Rhode Island. The *Alliance* was entering the Atlantic when "we discovered all of a Sudden the Ship to make nineteen Inches [of water] per hr." This alarming discovery coincided with a change in the weather; "the wind in a short time after increased and of course made the Sea a little rougher and She then made one Inch and a half pr. Minute." The *Alliance* proceeded to prove a rule of nautical physics, "as the Wind and Sea increased . . . the Leake did also in proportion." Soon there was three feet of salt-water in the *Alliance's* hold, enough to ruin the "lower teare [tier] of Tobacco."[27]

Barry kept the pumps going through the night. By morning, with the *Alliance* "midway between the Capes of Virginia and the Delaware," he determined that only by heading home could he save the undamaged tobacco. In two days the *Alliance* was in the Delaware. Barry speedily composed a letter to Morris, sending it by courier from Bombay Hook. He was uncharacteristically philosophical: "As is often the Case…Peoples Expectations are buoyed up with great Prospects they frequently find themselves Disappointed."[28]

By the time the poor *Alliance* docked at his wharf, Morris enlisted a trio of congressmen to check the frigate's condition. They recommended that the tobacco be unloaded, "freighted to Europe on
the best terms," and that Morris "discharge the officers and crew"
and order a thorough inspection of the *Alliance*.[29]

Never before had Barry failed Morris, who bristled at the cavalier
tone of Barry's report. "The Misfortune which [the *Alliance*] has sustained" not only angered Morris, it mortified him. His first venture at
public trade never got out of American waters. "Repairing this Ship
cannot but be expensive," he fumed, calling the *Alliance* "an old
Vessel" for good measure. He discharged everyone but Barry,
Murray, and a few hands.[30] With Joshua Humphreys and Thomas
Read, they formed a committee to "survey and Estimate" the damage and cost of repairs.[31]

It had been years since Barry had had such a long stint at home.
He never really had the chance to accommodate himself to the
house he and Sarah purchased on Spruce Street, bought during the
interminable legal wrangling over the Austin estate.[32] For once, Barry
got to greet Sarah upon *her* return, but any pleasant surprise at this
twist ended when Barry shared the latest news of their perilous
finances. Barclay's latest update pleaded that Barry "not post any
Bills."[33] In Havana, Seagrove was "sorry to inform" that, while "a
great part of Capt. Barry's goods" were sold, Seagrove "was obliged
to give a credit" due to the fluctuating cost of cotton in Cuba.[34]

After learning that the State Assembly was offering half-pay and
land grants to resident army officers, Barry led his fellow navy officers in bombarding the Assembly with petitions in the hopes of
recovering similar financial rewards for their services. These
"Memorials" were flowery and, at times, desperately self-aggrandiz-
ing. Barry's–the first of several he would be compelled to write–
reviewed his naval career, mentioned the "Wound in his Shoulder,
which has proved very injurious," and concluded that

> the State of Pennsylvania, for whose commerce and whose
> trade he is assured reaped many Advantages from his
> Exertions on this Station and welfare he found himself deeply
> interested . . . will, he relies claim the indulgence of your

Honors so as to admit him to the emoluments of Land &Half-Pay . . . Your Honourable House has been pleased to extend to the Penna. Line . . . your Memorialist Sincerely hopes, that the prayer of his Memorial will experience a happy reception.[35]

Barry's memorial received a "happy reception" but not immediate results. It would be another year before naval officers received equity in the eyes of the Assembly. Like other veterans, he was heartened by Morris's decree that "American Officers and Soldiers" would receive "Certificates" that would entitle them to their pay along with interest—but when?[36]

Each workday Barry was rowed to the *Alliance* to oversee the survey. On one crisp autumn morning he had visitors: British Commodores Sweeney and Affleck, in Philadelphia on a diplomatic mission. Barry graciously welcomed them aboard. Another guest remarked how these "sons of Neptune [were] as intimate as brothers. To have seen them together it might readily have been supposed that they had been engaged throughout life in the same service." For several days they regaled each other with their war stories. Before departing, "Sweeney, taking Barry affectionately by the hand," was emotionally overcome. "Adieu, my countryman," he said. Barry was a bit puzzled. Politely, he replied, "Not exactly so . . . you, Commodore are Briton. I am an American." Sweeney good-naturedly disagreed, pressing his point:

> "I am," responded Sweeney "an Irishman, and so are you too, Barry, for if not you ought to be. You have too many of the strong features of a genuine Irishman for me to be mistaken . . . your attachment to the cause of the country for which you have fought and bled is both natural and highly to your honor—but, by God, you are too good a fellow for old Ireland to relinquish the claim that she has upon your best affections."

Barry laughed in acknowledgement, and, as his guests were rowed away, ordered a salute fired from one of the six guns remaining on deck.[37]

John Brown's wedding to a relative of Thomas Willing gave Barry a few hours' respite from his money woes and the frigate's structural ones, but by December his concern over the *Alliance* was dwarfed by worry over her crew.[38] There were constant visits from his men—more than a few destitute—asking, demanding, or begging for their "balance of Prize money." One sailor, though deathly ill, could not afford the cost of hospitalization. Hat in hand, Barry went to see what Morris could do: "Capt. Barry [came] to get a poor Seaman into the Hospital but as This Man had been discharged the Service, I could not meddle with it," Morris wrote in his diary.[39] It pained Barry to see so many of his men down on their luck and out in the streets, loitering outside the wharf taverns and the London Coffeehouse where, just months earlier, glasses were raised to their seamanship and courage. Now, discharged sailors aimlessly haunted the waterfront, hoping for a berth on a foreign merchantman.

Their plight led him to enter into an odd venture with Brown. With no money of his own, Barry borrowed two hundred dollars from the Philadelphia Bank. Then he and Brown bought up prize warrants from the neediest Alliances, after Brown convinced Barry that this was the only way he could provide assistance. They could not afford to pay face value, but most sailors were happy to settle for a lesser amount, remitted in cash. If this seems an unscrupulous scheme of making money on the hard-earned prize shares of Barry's sailors, it also kept quite a few out of debtor's prison, and others from starving.[40]

That winter he was "incessantly called upon and threatened with suits," forced "in several instances . . . to advance my own money to satisfy them which is very hard." He fired off angry letters to Barclay: for a year, Barry "had full confidence that you would have provided Funds for payment."[41] Where were they?

The winter was one of the coldest Philadelphians could remember. By Christmas, the Delaware was "frozen over opposite the city." Barry presented his report on the state of the *Alliance* to Congress the next day. He optimistically believed "the Ship will be fit for any Service for three or four Years" and stated, "The necessary repairs were estimated at 5,866 2/3 dollars."[42] Government coffers were so bare that Barry might as well have asked for a million. Morris, believing he had final say in the matter, wanted to wait until the only other Continental ship, the *General Washington*, returned to Philadelphia.

The New Year brought two days of warmth and a letter from Barclay. Both came with a downside. Philadelphians enjoyed "a most remarkable thaw," but with a "disagreeable, unwholesome vapour." Barclay's letter was like the weather—warm assurances, but sickly assets. "I am redly vex'd that you Should have been under any difficulties for want of money," Barclay commiserated. The total share of Barry's prizes in L'Orient came to over 30,000 livres, small comfort as long as they remained unpaid.[43]

By March, Barry was dead broke, and the bank's loan was due. The man who knew how to fight did not know who to fight anymore. He wrote two letters; one, to President of Congress Thomas Mifflin, included a bill of exchange for $260 that Barry "Should be glad to hear that you please took Steps to honor." The second letter was harder to write, let alone post. Setting pride aside, he reached out to his old rustling partner, Anthony Wayne, recently retired from the army and looking to restart his political career. As "the Bank has a demand on me for two hundred dollars," Barry asked if Wayne could "oblige me with that Sum."[44]

He received a warm response from Wayne, but no funds: just an empathetic letter from one penniless warrior to another. "I have met with serious disappointment from my Tenants & Others in the Payment of money due me," Wayne answered. However, being "in full confidence of receiving a very considerable sum . . . some days hence" from "Warrants that I obtained from Mr. Morris," Wayne asked Barry to "wait two or three weeks—as within that time I shall certainly receive Several hundred pounds."[45]

When the *General Washington* arrived, her captain, Joshua Barney, was dolefully candid with Morris regarding her condition. Having given the *America* to France and sold the *Bourbon, The Hague* (née *Deane*), and the *Duc de Lauzon*, Morris believed that, due to "the embarrassed state of our Finances," the best thing to do with the navy was to end its existence.[46] He was convinced that Congress should "make no Effort for the Purpose till the People are taught by their Feelings to call for and require it."[47] As his substantial livelihood was based on maritime trade, he understood better than anyone America's need for a navy, but as the man in charge of the nation's pursestrings he knew it was more luxury than necessity–at least for the time being.

Initially Morris got what he wanted. Congress approved the "sale at public auction of the frigate *Alliance* and Ship *Washington*."[48] Sale of the packet posed no problem to Congress, but a pang of nationalistic conscience overcame James Madison, who then urged his colleagues to keep the *Alliance*–without a clue how to pay for her repairs and upkeep.[49] Surprisingly, Congress agreed, "for the honour of the flag of the United States and the protection of its trade and coasts from the insults of pirates"–America's first act of homeland security.[50] With Barney discharged, Barry remained the only naval officer in Congress' employ, at sixty dollars a month.

As spring temperatures thawed the Delaware, trickles of money from all sources came Barry's way. From Cuba, Seagrove wrote Brown that "Our friend Barry's Goods are mostly sold . . . I shall Bring his Cash with me."[51] In May, Barry and Brown split 900 livres, their profit on the acquisition of the *Alliance*'s prize warrants.[52] He also billed Congress for $480–eight months' back wages.[53]

While work commenced on the *Alliance*'s repairs, Barry continued to receive inquiries from former naval officers, asking his advice on memorials, financial affairs, and merchant assignments, all trusting he was "at ease in Philadelphia after the tedious war." One officer Barry heard from looked to government "emoluments" to assuage his plight. Luke Matthewman had not changed his stripes much. Although in the same dire straits as his peers, he considered himself "one of the least of the sufferers" of the Revolution, although he believed "The exclusion of the Navy Officers" from land grants and monetary rewards "certainly unfair." The self-reliant Matthewman began a new career as a bounty hunter in "the disagreeable business of transporting free Negroes from [New York] to their respective homes" which "incurred the appellation of Kidnapper."[54]

Throughout 1784 Congress was deluged with memorials from former naval officers, and Barry sent a second one, with a unique twist. There had not been a commodore in the Continental Navy since unlucky Esek Hopkins. Now, with the navy consisting of one ship–his–Barry hoped that a request for the title might hasten remit-

tance of his back pay. It did not. Soon afterward, Congress had neither a "Department of Marine" nor an Agent of the Marine. Morris's
resignation was finally accepted on November 1, 1784, with no successor named. When Morris left, he gave Congress both a balanced
budget and a clean slate on any claims, an accomplishment equivalent to a battlefield victory.[55] He bought time for his government to
determine its own fate, just as more and more representatives began
seeing the ineptitude of the Articles of Confederation. But Morris's
mind was elsewhere: China.

By 1783 Morris saw China as both a source of public trade and personal wealth. Europeans had been trading with China for two hundred years, none more successfully than England's East India
Company. Morris wanted in on the action as both a public servant
and a private merchant and began recruiting investors from the
northern ports. In July, he found his first ship for the enterprise, a
square-sterned vessel of "about four hundred Tons Burthen." Graced
with a woman's figurehead, he rechristened her the *Empress of China.*
"I am sending some Ships to China in order to encourage others in
the adventurous pursuits of Commerce," he wrote to John Jay. The
Empress's hold was soon filled with cordage, wine, lead, iron, and
even some of Barry's Spanish milled dollars. The hottest commodity was ginseng, in high demand by the Chinese. Morris could not get
enough of it.[56]

The captaincy of the *Empress* was eagerly sought after, but Morris
had but one man in mind, one of his most trusted shipmasters before
the war. When offered the post, John Green accepted immediately.[57]

Whether Barry was even considered for the post, or if Morris disregarded him due to the *Alliance's* mishaps is not known. Any resentment Barry felt competed with ongoing frustrations over his
finances. His memorials and petitions went unanswered; back pay
was still owed, and expenses were still under congressional audit.[58]
The case of the incorrectly sold and ironically named *Fortune* was
still in the hands of lawyers. Other attorneys fighting over the tan-

gled morass of the *Alliance*'s prizes dogged Barry into 1785: "I beg I may not be troubled anymore about it," he wrote to one agent. Nor was the latest report from Cuba any better. Seagrove informed Barry that some unsold goods had been stolen—and that was the good news. "This is not the worst my very Good Friend," Seagrove confessed. "At present I cannot pay you."[59] Following Morris's resignation, Joseph Pennell became Commissioner of Accounts for the Marine. For over a year he ignored Barry's letters. It seemed that nobody could, or would, pay John Barry.

Barry joined Isaac Austin in both the settling of his mother-in-law's estate and in the battle to retake the Austin Ferry, both intertwined in William's traitorous status.[60] They publicly requested "all persons indebted to the estate of SARA Austin dead" make their payments.[61] For two years, Isaac beseeched the Supreme Executive Council to overturn the award of the ferry and houses to Hopkinson and the other University of Pennsylvania trustees. Each petition mentioned both Isaac's military service and his willingness to pay the Assembly's exorbitant assessment of the estate's worth: £1,800.[62] Each offer was turned down.[63] When the council finally held the auction, Isaac's bid was highest, but the council refused to transfer the property.[64] Now Barry went to work. Learning that William was in Nova Scotia, Barry requested his assistance, and William began a series of memorials and claims.[65] After some prodding, Barry's friends in the State Assembly presented a bill to the State's Committee of Grievances, who ruled in Isaac's favor.[66] When the council reviewed the matter, they unanimously supported the decision.

However, the man holding the estate, George Baker, refused to turn it over, having rented the houses and assumed possession of the ferry business. Rather than acquiesce to the will of the council, Baker went to his friend, Judge George Bryan. A future governor, Bryan issued a warrant against Isaac along with "a severe reprimand" for questioning Baker's authority.[67]

Isaac aired his side in a long, rambling letter to the *Pennsylvania Gazette*. Bryan's reply described how a violent Austin allegedly accosted a woman renting the Austin home "with a cow-skin whip, on the back part of her head whilst he struggled to divest her of her dwelling." Not to be outdone, Barry and Austin published affidavits of witnesses who refuted Baker's accusations while charging Bryan with being in "the company of certain miscreants" during the war. In December the council awarded to "Isaac Austin a certain messuage, wharf, ferry, and ferry landing," while the *Gazette* commented how a "certain Naval Officer" was instrumental in returning the Austin estate to the Austin family.[68] Philadelphians could readily guess who that was.

Isaac's victory presaged some judicial luck for his famous brother-in-law. To Barry's surprise, Congress ruled in his favor regarding the *Fortune* affair, granting "full discharge from the judgment against him" and sending Barry's shares his way.[69] Morris also assigned an attorney to represent Barry in a suit regarding another runaway slave from the *Alliance*.[70] Barry involved himself in another case concerning Joanna Young, widow of his friend John, lost at sea commanding the *Saratoga* four years earlier. Hearing that Congress approved half-pay measures to the widows of army officers, she petitioned for the same allowance. Congress decided that army officers were "subject to arduous duty without a prospect of booty," while naval officers "in a less severe service were in a situation of realizing substantial riches"–the very prize shares Barry and his colleagues were still trying to claim. "The prayer of the petitioner" was denied.[71]

Sad news arrived from Ireland: Barry's sister, Eleanor Hayes, had passed away, leaving her invalid husband, Thomas, a widower with three young children: Michael, Patrick, and Eleanor. After mentioning his own declining health, Hayes called Barry's contributions his "Only Relief," and "praised God for having such a friend in his later days." Barry assured Hayes that he would "prove a real Father to his Children" when the time came to do so. Barry's other sister, Margaret Howlin, was also widowed, living in poverty. He sent them what money he could spare whenever a Philadelphia merchantman was bound to Wexford.[72]

He began to receive a steady influx of letters from Ireland, looking for his assistance in helping the next generation find footing in the new world as he did, "putting [them] in the way of getting Bread,

Rather than they sh[oul]d Starve at home." From Cork came a letter from Jeremiah Teahan, a former Montserrat merchant and acquaintance from Barry's days on the sloop *Peggy*. Teahan, while asking Barry's "assistance" in finding employment for young Irishmen and knowing Barry's "influence to be great," did not wait for a yes or no answer. He sent the letter with a "poor young man"—a carpenter—begging Barry to "fix his Camp."[73] Nor was gender an issue regarding these requests. A Philadelphia ne'er-do-well sent for an indentured servant girl from Ireland, who arrived on board a ship at "the wharf below Race Street." When she refused to serve him, he decided that Philadelphia's most prominent Irishman should pay the forty dollars to free her from her indenture. After all, she was from "Rosswell by Donegall."[74]

One summer day in 1785 another letter was delivered by a young Irish émigré, "Matthew Doyle a lad of good repute . . . brought up to husbandry" and sent across the Atlantic by Barry's childhood hero, Uncle Nicholas. The letter young Doyle carried brought Barry about hard. Thomas Hayes was dead. Nicholas would send the three Hayes teenagers to Philadelphia upon Barry's request. Then, Nicholas raised another dolorous matter: there was no headstone for his parents' grave, and that "grieves and Troubles me Much your being So Worthy a Son to a Father and Mother, that there is no Memorial of them in the Church yard of Ruslare." In closing, he let John know that his "Cousin Richard Barry is now in Mexico or the Spanish Main" as "Commander of A Stout Ship belonging to Dublin." Yet another Barry had taken to the sea. It would be another year before John and Sarah sent for the Hayes children.[75]

At noon on May 11, a tired but elated John Green ordered a thirteen-gun salute fired as the *Empress of China* entered New York harbor. His odyssey had been immensely successful. New Yorkers were agog over the *Empress*'s "rich cargo of Teas, Silks, China, Nankins & Co.," calling Green's voyage an "eminently distinguished, and very prosperous achievement." Morris and company netted an astonishing 25 percent profit on their investment.[76]

Word of Green's triumph with his current command was sadly followed by news regarding Barry's last one. For over a year, the forlorn *Alliance* lay idly in Philadelphia harbor. The bold promise Congress made to repair and keep her for "the honour of the flag of the United States and the protection of its trade and coasts" was as empty as her decks, even as America was in need of her. The Philadelphia merchantman *Betsey*, Captain John Irwin (of the *Delaware* Irwins), had been captured by a Tangier corsair. It was America's first encounter with the Barbary Pirates, having been spared this embarrassment when under the protection of the British Empire and the tribute England paid the Barbary States. The Emperor of Morocco, Sidi Mahomet, who bragged of being the first leader to recognize American sovereignty (after all, he was an emperor; Louis XVI was only a king), used the *Betsey's* seizure as an opportunity to sign a treaty with America.[77]

Jefferson, America's minister in Paris, led negotiations on the *Betsey's* behalf, but advised Congress that the United States "will require a protecting force on the sea."[78] But Congress lacked the money for maintenance or manpower and placed this advertisement in the *Pennsylvania Gazette*:

> Board of Treasury, New York, June 13, 1785.
> SALE OF THE ALLIANCE.
> On the first Tuesday of August next
> WILL BE SOLD AT PUBLIC AUCTION AT THE MERCHANTS'
> COFFEE HOUSE IN THE CITY OF PHILADELPHIA.
> THE FRIGATE ALLIANCE
> Now lying in the River Delaware with all her Tackle and appurtenances (excepting her warlike appurtenances).
> A description of the ship and inventory of her tackle and appurtenances will be published on the day of sale.
> The payment for the convenience of the purchaser may be made in Good negotiable paper payable and four equal monthly installments.
> N. B. the sale will commence at twelve o'clock precisely.[79]

It now became the last official duty of the navy's last officer to prepare its last ship for decommission. By July 9, all vestiges of her status as a ship of war were removed. An unseasonable, vicious north wind accompanied a pelting rain on August 1, when a small crowd of onlookers joined merchants, carpenters, and chandlers as the coffeehouse auctioneer sold off everything that belonged to the *Alliance*. Even at 1785 prices she went for a fraction of her true worth. A consortium under Benjamin Eyre, the shipwright who had assessed her condition with Barry two years earlier, bought her for £2,887, the equivalent of $7,700. Eyre paid with "Morris notes"–certificates of public debt, purchased at 2 shillings 3 pence on the pound.[80]

Thousands of miles away in the Mediterranean, Algerian corsairs captured a second Philadelphia ship. Soon the press ran amok with rumors, including one that the *London Packet*, in Thomas Truxton's capable hands and bearing Benjamin Franklin home from France, was also seized. Her arrival at the Capes laid that story to rest. Secretary of Treasury John Jay's idea to build "five forty Gun ships" placed "under Direction of a brave experienced Commodore" was wishful thinking.[81]

This crisis and the sale of his beloved *Alliance* were not as present in Barry's mind as was his ongoing crusade to recover the rest of his back pay and prize money. Some prize shares had arrived, but his accounts were still under audit.[82] With Morris out of office, his bills were reviewed by men who did not know Barry nearly as well. Nor, did it seem to him, that they cared a whit if the debts to navy veterans were ever paid.[83]

Thomas Read was back in town. Richard Henry Lee, one of the earliest advocates for a navy, was now President of Congress. Read and Barry saw his appointment as a slim chance to be heard and, hopefully, paid. With many officers living hand-to-mouth and Congress's rejection of the Widow Young's petition, they delivered a joint memorial to Congress for themselves and "the other Officers of the Continental Navy." Possibly ghostwritten by John Brown, it was a logical plea for justice, calling attention to the fact "that they are the only Class of Officers in the United States who remain neglected and totally unprovided for," they petitioned "that they may be placed on a footing similar to that of their Brother Officers in the Land Services as to Half-pay or Commutation and Lands." Weeks passed. "We never heard anything of it," Barry complained. With Lee's compliance, the memorial died in committee.[84]

Two years had passed since Barry was last at sea, and he was restless, watching inferior captains get plum assignments. Now that Green (whom Barry still held in contempt) had proven Morris correct about China, friends like Truxton were being enticed to sail to the other side of the world for adventure and profit. With no results coming from his letters and memorials to Congress, Barry began to see China as his only way of restoring his financial fortune—and he had new reasons besides the simple justice of collecting his well-earned money.

His first was a new address. In the fall of 1785 he sold his Spruce Street home and, taking what money he and Sarah had, bought a "plantation"—actually a farm—called Strawberry Hill. Located three miles above Philadelphia in Northern Liberties, the estate consisted of sixty-two acres of fields and woods, and looked down over the Delaware River to Petty's Island. It shared a carriage path off Frankford Road with Elias Boudinot's estate, Rose Hill.[85]

The second reason was his health. He was forty, with thirty years at sea behind him. Besides his aching shoulder, he was having occasional difficulty breathing. Over time the attacks increased in length and frequency. Sometimes symptoms warned him of a spell; sometimes it came on without warning. Some ended in seconds, some fought him for days. It was asthma.[86]

Philadelphia had one of the hemisphere's foremost experts on the disease. Benjamin Rush first wrote a treatise on asthma back in 1770, advocating warm baths and questioning whether the disease was contagious.[87] Rush began treating Barry after his return from Virginia in 1783 and physician and patient became close confidantes for the rest of Barry's life. While "Bleeding . . . I believe, has done more harm than good," he did bleed Barry. The captain was confined to his home for a month; four visits from Rush, including a "physician's courtesy" discount, cost Barry £1.15.[88] In addition to bleeding, other remedies were prescribed and tried on Barry. One contemporary patient "obtained relief by the use of anti-spasmodic and expectorant medicines" although his "stomach was often disordered by their influence." His doctor used the patient's own words to describe the treatment's results: "I inhaled the medicated vapor . . . before going to rest. The first sensations it occasioned me, were slight fatigue and breathing, and an aching pain in the breast; which, however, subsided by degrees; and when expectoration took place . . . I felt completed relieved."[89]

If the hazards of years at sea combined with life in a dirty, eighteenth-century city were part of Barry's world, so too now was the life of an asthmatic. Over the years Rush tinkered with his patient's treatments, but the prognosis for Barry's health was grim. Physicians already knew that chronic asthma hardened the lining of the lungs, and the resultant effect on both breathing and the heart. By 1785 there was a host of treatments, from what was considered state-of-the-art science to folk cures. Different herbs were inhaled, as was turpentine and vinegar; one "fanciful idea" was "the desiccation of marshmallows."[90]

Strawberry Hill's bucolic setting made it as much a sanitarium as it was a country estate (it also extended Rush's travel time and, hence, his bill). The Barrys loved their new home, and the captain shared this joy in his correspondence. "I find you have entirely removed in the Country & bid adieu to the City," one friend wrote.[91]

That fall, Barry, along with his naval comrades, was recognized by his peers from the Continental Army—for service if not by payment—and elected to the Society of the Cincinnati. The group took its name from Cincinnatus, the legendary citizen-warrior who dropped his plowshare for his sword, defeated Rome's enemies, secured the restoration of its republic, and returned to his fields—an allegory obviously meant to flatter Washington. For Henry Knox, the society was an opportunity for officers to keep in touch through reunions, promote charitable interests, and serve as a tangible reminder that their cause—liberty—was an ongoing struggle. Washington was named the society's first president. Membership would be passed down to surviving sons. The organization's emblem—the bald eagle, and Cincinnatus himself—was embossed on certificates of membership and medals given to each member. The logo soon found its way to Canton, where it was etched on fine china ordered by society members. Thomas Paine, asked to write a song about the society, did so with enthusiasm.[92]

While Knox saw the society as a chance for peaceful camaraderie, and Washington welcomed it as a harmless organization honoring the service of his brave officers, others viewed it differently. Alexander Hamilton believed it was a wondrous opportunity for political advancement. Noncombatants viewed it with derision; to Samuel Adams, it was a "rapid stride towards a hereditary military nobility." Benjamin Franklin, calling it an "order of hereditary knights," acerbically suggested that membership be passed "up to parents rather than down to children." It inspired his essay nominating the wild turkey–"a bird of courage"–as the national bird, rather than the eagle–"a bird of bad moral character" and a "rank coward . . . by no means a proper emblem for the brave and honest Cincinnati, who have driven all the king birds from our country."[93]

Along with Jones and other naval captains, Barry accepted the offer to join, but like Washington, he stayed above–and away from– any vested partisanship found throughout the society. His pride as a member was documented for history; years later, when he sat for a portrait by Gilbert Stuart, his medal was prominently displayed upon his chest.[94]

By March 1786, the war had been over for three years, but Barry was still pursuing payment for some services he had rendered in 1776. When one of Pennell's bean counters finally answered Barry's inquiries with a condescending letter, Barry fired back a warning that he would gladly come to New York to demand his money. Another bureaucrat admonished him "that it is unnecessary for you at this time to come to New York," as "Congress had displaced Mr. Pennell with Colonel Benjamin Walker"–who also ignored Barry's letters regarding long overdue payment. When Walker finally answered one of Barry's posted broadsides, it was bureaucracy at its finest: "None of the books or papers of the *Alliance* in this office extend beyond 1781," he wrote, asking Barry to come up with the missing records. The shell game continued. Even after he presented the *Alliance*'s books, Walker begged "leave to refer you for more particulars."[95]

As best they could, John and Sarah were enjoying their new social life, hosting dinners at Strawberry Hill. In addition to meetings of "the Sea-Captains Club," Barry attended monthly dinners of the

Hibernian Fire Company. These overreaching "firefighters" were among the wealthiest and best-known Philadelphians, including Morris, Brown, Charles Biddle, and Matthew Meas, purser from the *Bonhomme Richard* (and badly wounded at Flamborough Head). Missing any meetings did not result in fines as long as Barry kept "his Buckets, Bags and Basket" in town.[96] Most members were budding Federalists, having witnessed first-hand the ineptitude of the Articles of Confederation.

William Austin continued writing Barry from Nova Scotia, grateful for the news of the restitution of the family property, which allowed Barry "to pay any person I am indebted to which will be a great consolation to me." Asking Barry "to keep this matter to yourself," Austin wrote freely, praising the "Bounty and goodness" of the British government "in making compensation to those poor people"–himself included–"who have suffered" the confiscation of their American property. Now persona non grata to his siblings, Austin asked his brother-in-law to "give my Love to my Sister and Brother." He also passed on to Barry how much Nova Scotia had changed "since you was here," sailing the *Industry* before the war, in what seemed a different lifetime.[97]

By the end of 1786 Barry and many former naval officers were past bitterness over lack of congressional recognition or assistance. They soon had company. In western Massachusetts, Daniel Shays, a veteran of Bunker Hill, organized the first revolt against farm foreclosures and skyrocketing tax assessments. A fearful Congress authorized Knox to lead a force against the rag-tag New Englanders. Shays's Rebellion illuminated the impotency of Congress. More and more Americans were coming to the conclusion already reached by groups like the Hibernian Fire Company–a stronger government might be the only way the infant United States of America would ever learn to walk.[98]

For Barry, public and financial issues took a back seat for at least one spring day in 1787, when he received word that the ship *Rising Sun* was approaching Philadelphia, back from a voyage to Wexford. Her captain was Barry's friend John Rossiter, another Wexford emigrant. Standing on the dock, the Barrys waited anxiously while the gangplank was lowered and the passengers disembarked. Then they saw Rossiter with two teenage boys, soon swept up in the welcoming arms of their uncle and tearful embrace of their aunt.[99]

Michael Hayes, the oldest at eighteen, explained his sister Eleanor's absence: recently married, she chose to remain in Ireland. Sixteen-year-old brother Patrick was slim and boyishly good-looking, possessing the family's cramped facial features above a well-defined jawline, his eyes more piercing than his uncle's. After a fine meal in town, the Barrys brought Michael and Patrick to their new home at Strawberry Hill.[100]

Michael soon returned to service on the *Rising Sun*, bound to Jamaica.[101] Patrick must have felt like a frog turned prince. Strawberry Hill was heaven to him. At that age Barry had already begun taking on the world, with no parental compass. Now he was determined to provide that guidance. Sarah was already a veteran at caring for a relative's children. The childless Barrys would raise Patrick as the son they never had.

By mid-1787 the China trade was no longer a novelty. No less than four American vessels were at the anchorage at Whampoa Reach, including the *Canton*–the former *London Packet*–with Truxton as captain and part owner. Even the *Alliance* sailed for China. Benjamin Eyre's partners could not afford her upkeep, and she was snatched up by none other than Robert Morris. With the same speed in which he and Barry refit peacetime vessels for war in the early days of the Revolution, Morris had her in prime condition, with James Read as captain and Richard Dale as first mate.[102]

Finally, Barry's turn came. No less than seventeen investors, Morris and Stephen Girard among them, were financing construction of the *Asia*, built specifically for the China trade. Her shipwright was Joseph Marsh, one of Philadelphia's best. At nearly four hundred tons, she was smaller than the *Alliance*, but better designed for trade than the old frigate. The *Asia* was the prototype of a new design, the Philadelphia China trader, and compared favorably to the classic merchantman of the East India Company. In June, her owners journeyed up Frankford Road to Strawberry Hill and requested the honor of having Barry serve as captain for her maiden voyage. While he did not need to be asked twice, he negotiated well for himself. His prospective shares in the undertaking could make him a wealthy man—if he was successful.[103]

His good news brought mixed emotions from Sarah. Happy as she was for her husband, she knew it meant a two-year separation, and became even more sorrowful when he announced that Patrick would accompany him.

Barry enthusiastically dove into his new responsibilities. His first mate was James Josiah, age thirty-six, a florid-faced, dark-eyed man who wore his hair in an eighteenth-century version of a mullet. He served in the war with Nicholas Biddle and later as a privateer. Josiah, like Dale, did not mind a subordinate position when it meant a chance for a voyage like this. His appointment was Barry's first entry in the *Asia*'s letterbook.[104]

By September most of his crew had signed on; within two weeks of the *Asia*'s launching, Josiah began overseeing storage of her cargo. Her hull and stern were beautifully decorated, and a handsome figurehead glistened on the bow, carved by the famous William Rush. It was said of Rush's craftsmanship on the *Asia*'s sister ship, the *Ganges*, that Calcutta residents "knelt and prayed to the River God figure head" he designed.[105]

Readying the *Asia* kept Barry occupied, commuting daily on horseback from Strawberry Hill. But throughout that summer he was working in the shadows of the Constitutional Convention, the most important meeting in Philadelphia since the drafting of the Declaration of Independence. Since May, most of America's best and brightest political minds (Adams and Jefferson were in Europe) were sequestered in the State House, scheming, quarrelling, stonewalling, and compromising, in order to form a more perfect union.

Every day Benjamin Franklin, now eighty-one and racked with pain from a kidney stone, arrived in a sedan chair carried by four inmates from Walnut Street Prison.[106] Washington served as president of the convention.[107] On September 17, under "unanimous consent of the States," the new government was announced.[108] It had taken four years to write and organize the Articles of Confederation. It took only four months to draw up the Constitution.[109]

Now attention turned to the states to ratify the new document. Well-drawn lines divided the political camps in the Pennsylvania Assembly. Most Philadelphians, along with their neighbors in the surrounding counties, favored the newly proposed federal government—it would assist and encourage business and growth. However, their counterparts from the rural counties saw it as the establishment of the divine rights of presidents, congressmen, and judges. In their eyes, any improvement in government efficiency, commercial growth, or a centralized monetary system was offset by perceived restrictions of the rights of the individual. For Barry and his navy friends, adoption of the new Constitution meant one thing: their last, best chance to finally get paid.

On September 28, Franklin's sedan chair carried him once again to the State House; the senior delegate to the recent Constitutional Convention was also President of the State Assembly. He informed his sixty-eight colleagues of his "very great satisfaction" on the convention's results (he also secretly revealed his closing remarks, the famous "rising sun" speech, to intensify public support).[110] Representatives from the backwoods counties were to a man against the Constitution, but their eastern counterparts, more numerous in number, were united in support of it.

Even though the Constitutional Convention was over, the assembly still gathered upstairs in chambers recently renovated as a carbon copy of their usual downstairs haunt.[111] The desks faced in the same direction, and the "gallery"—a cordoned-off area taking up about fifteen percent of the room—was filled with spectators. Anyone with a vested interest in the outcome could attend these sessions. Barry was a regular.

These sessions were Franklin's swan song. While slyly espousing that "I do not entirely approve of this Constitution," he desperately wanted it ratified, but followed Washington's example, keeping silent throughout the sessions. Speaker Thomas Mifflin read the long document to his colleagues. When he concluded, the gallery exploded in applause. The following day it was published in the local press, with five hundred copies printed in German for those Americans who did not speak English. The Constitution's supporters were led by men Barry knew well, including Mifflin, George Clymer, and recent convention delegate Thomas Fitzsimons. The opposition was led by James McCalmont, Jacob Miley, and James Barr.[112]

Fifty years old, McCalmont hailed from upper Strasbourg; at six feet four inches he was a figure to be reckoned with. He was a renowned Indian fighter, war hero, and major in the Pennsylvania militia, with a reputation as a great runner in his youth. His ability to load and accurately fire his musket at full sprint was legendary. He won Franklin County's first state election in 1784, and easily transferred his talents for confrontation, infighting, and gamesmanship from the backwoods to the Assembly chamber.[113]

The battle for ratification commenced. Words and blood pressure ran high; Clymer, leading the Federalists, tried to steamroller ratification, while McCalmont and the anti-Federalists, equally passionate, were determined to "oppose the measure by every possible argument."[114] To add to the tension, the debate was being fought within a shrinking calendar. The assembly was adjourning at the end of the month to allow members to go home and campaign for reelection.[115] Clymer's Federalists held a two-to-one advantage, but McCalmont's anti-Federalists skillfully stonewalled attempts at passage. If they succeeded, they could delay voting on ratification by a year—perhaps even defeat it. Barry's friends in the assembly wanted Pennsylvania to be the first state to ratify the Constitution. McCalmont's side wanted to kill it.[116]

Friday the twenty-eighth came; Mifflin called the assembly into order. When the issue of new business came up, Clymer rose to speak. Citing "business of the highest magnitude," he moved for a state convention to ratify the Constitution. As debate flew back and forth across the room, Fitzsimons proposed that the motion be amended, calling for "an election of delegates." A motion by the anti-Federalists to postpone the proposal was defeated. Clymer's brother Daniel argued that the Constitution was "too generally agreeable, and too highly recommended, to be assassinated by the hand of intrigue and cabal." A vote for the proposed selection of delegates would resolve the issue by December 1787; a vote against would delay debate to December 1788. While Barry and others watched intently, the Federalists began to shout "question!" in unison and the vote was called. The resolution passed, 43 to 19, and the gallery and Federalists lustily cheered. A motion to recess until four o'clock resoundingly passed, and the assembly went their various ways, in groups and individuals, leaving the building in search of a meal. Barry and the gallery followed.[117]

Around four, Barry rejoined the crowd in the gallery to witness the Federalists' victory. The representatives ambled in—only not nearly as many as had left earlier. The clock struck four. All nineteen anti-Federalists were missing. Their absence was their trump card: now, there was no quorum. There could be no vote.[118]

The sergeant-at-arms was ordered to search for them. Before long he returned; having found seventeen representatives at Major Boyd's boarding house, he reminded them of their duty, only to be told that "there is no House." Mifflin, reviewing the Assembly's by-laws, found no clause that forced members to attend, only a fine for their absence.[119] The Federalists had been outfoxed; one lamented, "If there was no way to compel them who deserted from duty to perform it, then God be merciful to us!" A collective groan came from the gallery as the forty-three Federalists cast dismayed eyes at Mifflin. Disgusted, he called a recess until 9:30 the next morning.[120]

Barry and the crowd stomped down the steps and out into the Indian summer weather. Everyone knew what would happen the next morning: another no-show by the anti-Federalists. Without a quorum, there would be no convention, perhaps no ratification for a year. How many absent assemblymen were needed to have a quorum? Barry knew the answer: two.

CHAPTER SIXTEEN

THE ASIA

*W*HILE OTHERS FUMED AND FRETTED, Barry rode home, turning over a plan in his mind. Before the assembly recessed, one member posed the problem: how do you compel the anti-Federalist "seceders" to attend? For Barry the answer was easy. Early on Saturday, the last scheduled session before adjournment, he was off to the State House–but not before he went to the waterfront.

It was a bright, crisp, autumn morning.[1] A large crowd gathered outside the State House well before 9:30, everyone hoping to find room in the gallery and see firsthand how events would unfold. Among the less genteel spectators was a gang of sailors, stevedores, and carpenters–wharf toughs whose appearance (as well as their language and smell) intimidated the more refined onlookers.[2] When the doors opened, they followed Barry up the stairs, joining the crowd packed tight behind the gallery rail.

Mifflin ascended to his chair, called the session to order, and read the latest resolution from Congress, calling for each state to hold a convention to vote on the new constitution. Next, he dispatched the sergeant-at-arms to Major Boyd's to fetch the truant assemblymen. Mifflin ordered a clerk armed with the congressional resolution to accompany him, in hopes of appealing to the anti-Federalists' collective conscience, if not to their sense of duty. Minutes later both men returned empty-handed, save for the resolution. Having celebrated their victory with a fine meal, spirits, and a good night's sleep, most of McCalmont's anti-Federalist allies had already left town. Only two were still tarrying at Boyd's: McCalmont and his roommate, Jacob Miley of Dauphin County, another tough frontiersman.[3] When accosted by the sergeant-at-arms, they simply ignored him and refused to return. Everyone in the room looked to Mifflin. Now what?[4]

With a nod to his companions, Barry and his men elbowed their way out of the gallery, jogged down the steps of the State House and out to Chestnut Street. Whether Mifflin was in on Barry's plan is not known—but as Barry's band exited, Mifflin "left the chair."[5] By doing so, he delayed adjourning the assembly.[6] Others in the gallery also followed Barry, but at a distance.

Barry's companions strode up Chestnut to Sixth, then turned and headed right to Major Boyd's. They forced their way in the front door, and then stomped upstairs to find McCalmont and Miley. The crowd trailing Barry turned into a mob, shouting curses and throwing stones through the boardinghouse windows.[7] Barry and company did not bother to knock before entering.[8]

As Barry's toughs circled the two assemblymen, he gave them a choice: they could walk to the State House under their own power, or be carried there.[9] Other politicians might have been struck with fear, but McCalmont and Miley were made of sterner stuff. They responded with their own profanity-laced declaration; they were not coming to the State House, despite the escort service confronting them. There was a second of silence. Then, "Take 'em!" Barry commanded, and the "compelling" began.

The two ex-militiamen put up a fight. Fists were thrown, clothes were torn, and fingers were bitten or pried off the banisters. The representatives of Dauphin and Franklin counties punched and kicked in every direction, but to no avail. Messrs. McCalmont and Miley bid adieu to Major Boyd's, without settling their bill.[10]

Once outside, the two men were hoisted up and carried, as one newspaperman reported, with "their clothes torn and after much abuse and insult." Slowly but surely, "they were finally dragged" down Chestnut Street.[11] By now the clamor could be heard on the second floor of the State House. Peering out of one of the windows, Mifflin saw his two colleagues being assisted back to work, and then quietly excused himself from the chamber.[12] Barry's gang reached the State House doors. Moving to and fro, sideways, backward, sideways, forward, his toughs got to the stairway. They scuffled up the first five steps to the landing while McCalmont and Miley squirmed to free themselves, lashing out at their bearers, whose fingernails dug into their necks and hands, drawing blood. Their clothes, torn in proportion to resistance, became shredded rags.

The next two flights of stairs were sixteen steps each. A five-foot wide stairway is more than broad enough for a crowd to use—the prisoners easily negotiated Franklin's sedan-chair daily—but this band, carrying two thrashing public servants, found it a narrow passage. The last flight of five stairs took the longest. To their credit, neither McCalmont nor Miley stopped fighting. When they could, they dug their feet into the stairs and flailed their arms. Finally, Barry and his men got through the doorway, literally throwing the two men over the rail that divided the gallery from the austere chamber of official government business.[13] Thanks to Barry there was bedlam, but also a quorum.

As the other assemblymen returned to their seats, Mifflin "assumed the chair, and the roll was called." The two manhandled legislators, bloody, bruised, and half-naked, glared at him. Panting heavily, they felt for cracked ribs and broken fingers. When their names were called by the clerk, they were still out of breath—but their colleagues happily responded for them. "HERE!" they cried. Mifflin acknowledged, to laughter and cheers, that a quorum was present. The session, delayed but not adjourned, began at last.[14]

Looking angrily at the gallery, McCalmont called to be recognized, protesting that his arrival and that of Mr. Miley was by force and force alone, "by a number of citizens he did not know."[15] Searching the faces of the ruthless gang that bore him there, he sought their ringleader. McCalmont continued to press his cause. He and Miley, present against their wishes, intended to leave.[16]

Thomas Fitzsimons spoke, ostensibly to commiserate. If a member of the assembly had done this to his esteemed colleagues, Mifflin should "mark such conduct with disapprobation." He was seconded by Henry Brackenridge, the Continental Army's old chaplain, who reasoned that McCalmont's beef was with the mob, not the assembly. Adding a rapier wit to Barry's bludgeoning, Brackenridge obligingly cited Franklin's difficulties: whether friend or foe brought McCalmont was immaterial; "if they brought [McCalmont] in a sedan chair . . . all we [need] to know is that he is here."[17]

The gallery erupted in laughter. Outnumbered, beaten in both body and vote, McCalmont fought on. He asked that the rules be read, and that he would abide by them. When the clerk noted that the penalty for preventing a quorum by premeditated absence carried a fine of five shillings, McCalmont shoved a bruised hand into his pocket and found his purse, miraculously still in his coat despite his rough journey. Disdainfully, he tossed the coins on the clerk's desk. Here was his fine, he said—now let him go—and the quorum with him. For once the crowd laughed with him. But Mifflin was up to the challenge, and won back the audience with a brilliant rejoinder: the representative assigned to collect fees, a fellow anti-Federalist, was absent. Therefore the fine could not be collected; therefore the quorum stood. To guffaws from the crowd, Mifflin politely assured McCalmont there was no fine for attending—he could keep his five shillings. Undeterred, McCalmont bolted for the door. With shouts of "Stop him! Stop him!" coming from the gallery, Mifflin yelled for the sergeant-at-arms to bar the way. In doing so he probably saved McCalmont's life.[18]

Rising to speak, Fitzsimons took command of the situation, bringing the matter to its climax. He had fought with Barry at Princeton, and would fight beside him now. In his offer of five shillings, it was McCalmont who "offended the greatest indignity to the Assembly," thinking that his pittance could stop the assembly from doing its duty. Brackenridge made a motion that a convention be held on the first Tuesday in November. McCalmont's protests fell on deaf ears (from the onset, Miley kept mute). The resolution passed 44 to 2. With no further business, Mifflin told McCalmont and Miley they were free to go; the assembly adjourned to tumultuous cheers, and the bells of Christ Church pealed throughout the afternoon.[19]

Before leaving town McCalmont learned the identity of the gallery's ringleader. Soon all Philadelphia knew, thanks to an inspired bit of doggerel regarding his civics lesson:

> *It seems to me I yet see B(arr)y*
> *Drag out McC(a)lm(o)nt.*
> *(By the Lord Harry,*
> *The might was right, and also Mil(e)y*
> *Was taken from an outhouse slyly,*
> *To constitute with him a quorum,*
> *For he it seems was unus horum.)*[20]

Admired as Barry was by Philadelphians and even members of Congress for his boldness, he quickly found himself without honor among the assembly whose face he just saved. On October 3, McCalmont presented a formal complaint, along with eyewitness accounts, to the Supreme Executive Council, declaring that "the inhabitants of Franklin and Dauphin [counties] had been grossly insulted by the treatment of their members." The council overwhelmingly agreed "that the Attorney General be directed forthwith to commence the prosecution against Captain John Barry, and such other persons as shall be found to have been principally active in seizing the said James M'calmont, or otherwise concerned in the riotous proceedings as sent forth."[21]

First to vote "yes" was Council President and Barry's old pen pal, Benjamin Franklin. It was an easy vote for him to cast—even though Barry's actions, harsh as they were, guaranteed the result Franklin wanted more than anything. Among the other members who voted for Barry's prosecution was his fellow "Sea Captain's Club" member, Charles Biddle, himself under pressure to vote against any investigation, especially since "some of the gentlemen ordered to be prosecuted were my intimate friends." As it turned out, only Barry was specifically named among "the gentlemen."[22]

Biddle, like Barry, possessed both integrity and courage, and broke the news to Barry over dinner that evening. During the meal they argued their positions. Barry was "displeased at first." Franklin's vote was no surprise, but he felt betrayed by Biddle, a good friend for twenty years. Biddle understood. He sincerely believed the resolution "a very disagreeable business," but he "concerned it to be my duty, and therefore voted for it." Biddle assured Barry that a warrant for his arrest was not coming any time soon, and that, while McCalmont looked forward to Barry's legal day of reckoning, the attorney general would assemble his evidence very slowly. After Biddle explained his reasoning, Barry "was soon satisfied it was right." By the time dessert was served, a friendship had been saved.[23]

On November 6, the Assembly vote for ratification of the Constitution barely passed, 46 to 23, and with it ended Barry's career as a political activist.

In December 1787 the *Asia* was registered by the state, and Congress approved the mission of "the Ship *Asia*, John Barry, Commander . . . american built and commanded and manned by Americans."[24] Barry was even notified by the Consul of Sweden that he could inform Swedish vessels that they "were required" to respect the *Asia* and give aid where necessary.[25] In addition to first mate James Josiah, John Sword was named second mate, old veteran Nathan Dorsey was appointed surgeon, and William Barry (no relation) signed on as steward. For supercargoes–the owner's agent in charge of his goods– Barry picked two young men from prominent Philadelphia families: Jonathan Mifflin and Joseph Frazier, who had already been to China in the first voyage of the *Canton*. Listed among the boys was William Vicary, who grew up to be a successful merchant captain, and Patrick Hayes, who could not wait to make this voyage with his uncle.[26]

Soon sailors and dock workers were loading a wide variety of goods into the *Asia*'s hold–not just ginseng, but iron, lumber, masts and spars from the Pennsylvania woods, and rum.[27] The stores for the *Asia*'s maiden journey were a bit unusual as well. The ship's cargo showed the wide interest of her owners, Barry, and their acquaintances. By the day of departure her hold contained "30 Casks of brandy" from Robert Morris, who directed Barry to use the casks to purchase the best India Nankeen" cloth.[28]

Others gave Barry money of various amounts for purchase of a wide array of Chinese goods. Letters accompanying these requests reflect 1780s elite consumerism at its best. Robert Colbys gave him "a bill of exchange amounting 276 Spanish milled dollars" for "any articles you may think as a good account." Henry Gurny, whom Barry had "been so Obliging as to offer to bring . . . any little matter," gave him $150 for a set of Nankeen china. John Nixon gave him "One Thousand Dollars . . . to be invested in the Annexed List" which included "Canton cloth . . . black scrimshaws" and "Black Satin," asking that Barry be "particularly attentive to the Quality of the goods as well as the Colours." Mary Crawthorne's new husband, John Montgomery, gave Barry "200 Spanish Mill'd Dollars" to invest in Chinese goods. Ira Boyle requested "a set of table China" and "Light Coloured Silks for Men's Coats." John Wilkes gave him $100 for "Serving Silk . . . and Nankeens of a Good Color." John Brown gave him $600 to "purchase . . . Nankeens of the Common kind" he hoped to resell in Philadelphia, promising Barry one third of the return. Finally, there was the extensive wish list of one Mrs. Hazelhurst, who must have imagined that the *Asia*'s hold was her personal treasure cave: no less than 205 pieces of china, each enumerated and signed, for which she gladly handed over $50.[29]

Barry also provided for his personal and business needs, obtaining £370 from a London bank and covering the loan with a £1,000 sterling insurance policy "for Cost & goods Shipped by me on Board the Ship *Asia* of which I am Captain."[30] Four 6-pounders and their carriages were stowed aboard, to be assembled when the *Asia* reached pirate-infested waters. By happenstance, the *Asia* was not the only Philadelphia ship making last-minute arrangements for a voyage to China: Truxton's *Canton* was preparing for her second voyage to the Orient.[31]

Ten years Barry's junior and a native Long Islander, Truxton first went to sea when he was twelve. At sixteen, the stocky boy was in the Royal Navy and tough enough to serve on press gangs. During the Revolution he made his reputation as a privateer; by war's end he succeeded John Paul Jones as Franklin's naval protégé.[32] Barry picked Truxton's brain thoroughly over what to expect on the voyage and at Canton. Truxton's knowledge would prove invaluable.

The two ships were both insured by the Irishman Benjamin Fuller, an old acquaintance of Barry's. After great success as a merchant before the war, the British occupation of Philadelphia and a debilitating illness had brought him to near financial and physical ruin.[33] The return of merchant trade to Philadelphia inspired his new career; his budding insurance company, along with investments in Morris's Bank of North America, was restoring his fortune. He covered the risk of Barry's venture with enthusiasm: "The Ship *Asia* Capt. John Barry Commander—a new Ship Completely fitted—four Six pound Cannon and Small arms with 30 Men—The Capt. esteem'd one of the most accomplished and complete Navigators belonging to this port."[34]

Truxton departed on December 8. Barry, facing a two-year absence from home, did not mind being beaten out of port. The Barrys had been together for four years, but that did not make parting any easier for Sarah. To keep her company at Strawberry Hill, Barry sent for her cousin Elizabeth Keen, twenty-three, called Betsy by the family. With his business affairs turned over to Brown, and assurances from friends that they would visit Sarah, Barry took Patrick to the ship. On the tenth, under wintry skies and a heavy frost, Barry and Sarah watched the *Asia* sail with the tide; Josiah would take her as far as Gloucester Point. After one last evening with Sarah, Barry picked up Doctor Dorsey and his two supercargoes. They took a carriage to League Island and came aboard the *Asia* there.[35]

Southwest winds blew so strongly against the natural flow of the Delaware that the *Asia* remained three days off Gloucester Point. Barry sailed the merchantman over to Reedy Island on the seventeenth to take on livestock and "Sundry other Preparations for sea," showing his nephew where he had battled James Wallace ten years earlier. "After a tedious time in the river" the breeze shifted to the west, and Barry sent the *Asia* to the Capes. "I cannot say much for the Ship's Sailing but She steers very well which is a good quality," he observed, further noting that "She is not so Stiff as I could wish but we must take the more care and she will be getting stiffer every day."[36] (A stiff ship does not roll or heel excessively.)

Optimistic as he was for his ship, he was positively jovial over his crew: "My officers and men please me very much for I can truly say I never had a Soberer Ships Company in my life." Nevertheless, Barry's third mate, a dark, quiet man named Marsh, gave him some degree of concern, but he remained convinced "We have a good prospect ahead of us."[37]

As soon as the *Asia* entered the Atlantic the sea gods welcomed back the long-absent captain with a terrific storm; thus began a series of violent weather. The elements seemed intent on testing the *Asia*, and the ship began showing her flaws. Furious waves broke against her hull and found her caulking less than sound. Inside his rocking cabin, keeping his writing hand as still as possible, Patrick wrote in his journal "Our Ship is very leaky . . . our decks constantly Full of Water." His uncle also kept a record of the beginnings of the *Asia*'s maiden voyage: "Soon after we left our Capes we met with hard gales of wind for several days." In one of the gales, "We Sprung our Bowsprit . . . we found The Spring not very bad we then secur'd it as well as possible."[38]

The bowsprit was no problem compared to the ship's leaky condition. Barry and ship's carpenter John Gatt searched for the principal source. Barry's initial observation over her lack of stiffness became a growing concern. "Our Ship [is] very Crank," he noted—a flaw in the *Asia*'s construction that made her lean too far to one side, which could result in capsizing. With a stretch of pleasant weather, the carpenter found the reason for the *Asia*'s leak, "a knot being rotten in her Starboard Wales." A good-sized knothole in a ship's plank was a serious issue, but Gatt plugged her well enough that Barry reported, "since we stopped her she has been tight."[39]

In the midst of yet another storm on the Atlantic crossing, as the crew fought rain and wind, "a heavy flash of Lightning struck our Main Mast." The blast "burst two of the Iron Hoops." Fortunately, sailing under bare poles, no one was aloft and in the bolt's path. The shock of the split hoops "Shiver'd the fishes," and Barry feared the mast would come crashing down. But despite the lightning strike, some luck was with the *Asia*—the impact was "not so much as to damage the Mast."[40] The *Asia* gamely plowed onward, running up and down the strong waves.

Finally the sun burst through the stormy skies, and, "under double reef'd topsails," with a steady northwest wind, the *Asia* started skimming across the waterline. "Tho a bad Sailer," Patrick Hayes wrote in his journal, the ship "was forced along at the rate of 8[,] 9 and 10 knots" until "we met the NE trade winds [and] we steered South." Soon Barry changed course to East by South, easing the *Asia* toward the Cape Verde Islands, three hundred miles off the coast of Senegal.[41]

He also ordered the 6-pounders brought up and mounted on their carriages. Gunnery practice began in earnest. For the older hands, ex-Continentals and privateersmen, it was an opportunity to show Hayes, Vicary, and the other landsmen the workings of a gun. The seizure of the *Betsy* was good enough reason for Barry to ascertain that his men would know how to defend themselves from any approaching Algerian or Moroccan ships.[42]

Eighteenth-century communications being what they were, Barry did not know that his drilling was unnecessary. Fed up with mounting losses at the hands of the Corsairs, Portugal declared war; their fleet kept the Barbary pirates blockaded in the Mediterranean. Americans were still debating the issue on both sides of the Atlantic. In England, John Adams foresaw war with the Barbary pirates in the future; languishing over America's inability to defend itself, he prophesied that "We ought not to fight them at all, unless we determine to fight them forever."[43]

Nor did Barry know that his pending arrest warrant was being pigeonholed. Shortly after the New Year, Pennsylvania's attorney general reported his investigation of the McCalmont affair to the Supreme Executive Council, requesting "advice of Council relative to the suit now carrying on by their order against Captain John Barry." Working behind the scenes on his behalf, Barry's friends in the assembly convinced their colleagues "that the Attorney General be informed that Council did not want to interfere," leaving "the matter intirely with him to act as he should judge best." The investigation quietly died. The actions of "the redoubted Captain Barry," as one supporter described him, were no longer subject to prosecution. Even Franklin kept silent.[44]

For some days, young Patrick could see the nine-thousand-foot volcanic mountain, Cano Peak, on the horizon; on January 23, 1788, the *Asia* "passed between the Cape Verde island." Barry sailed through the score of large and small islands–most of them just mountains jutting out of the East Atlantic, with no safe anchorage. The next day the *Asia* "struck Soundings off Cape Rochso [Roxo] on the Coast of Guinea.[45]

Throughout these days of gunnery practice and smooth sailing, the *Asia* was a happy ship, save for one: Marsh, the third mate. Inexplicably, his mood sank from gloomy to despondent. On February 3, while Barry "spoke a brig for the Persian Gulf . . . bound for Liverpool," young Hayes noticed that Marsh "apeared very much dejected." In the middle of the night, a single pistol shot rang out below deck and immediately roused Barry from slumber. He bolted from his cabin and down the dimly lit, narrow walkway where he found some fo'c'sle hands outside of Marsh's tiny berth. On his orders they broke down the door.[46]

The despondent Marsh had shot himself; "the ball entered his right breast and came out through his back." Dorsey was summoned and confirmed what the onlookers already knew: Marsh was dead. The next day, under a clear tropical sky, Patrick attended his first funeral at sea, and "We committed his body to the waves with the usual ceremony." Barry recorded the tragedy in the log with his usual brevity: "We lost Mr. Marsh on the Passage he shott himself." The incident troubled Patrick for days; Marsh "left no wrightings behind him to Justify the commission of so horrid a crime."[47]

Passing through the doldrums, the ship slackened its speed as it made for the southeast trades, and it grew oppressively hot above and below deck. Hayes noticed how the crew saw "round Spots on the sun with the naked eye one of them considerably larger than the rest . . . the sea seemed all on fire" as "we crossed the equator on 12 of february."[48] That day, Patrick and the other neophyte sailors who had yet to traverse the equator were forced to partake in the traditional hazing, "Crossing the Line":

Those of them who had never before passed being confined
below, about three o'clock our ship was hailed by the Old Man
of the Tropic who being desired by the Officer of the Deck to
come on board, entered over the bow, attended by his wife,
whence they were drawn in the chariot [one of the gratings]
by a number of sailors, as Tritons, to the quarter-deck, where
the captain and gentlemen received them. Their appearance
was truly ludicrous, having their faces black and painted, a
blanket over their shoulders, by way of a robe, and a large swab
on the head, instead of a crown, the long strands of which,
hanging down to the waists, served for hair etc.[49]

Next, Patrick was "Lathered with tar and grease, and shaved with
a notched stick." After making several vows to the "King (such as
never to drink small beer when there is strong, and never to kiss the
maid when he can kiss the mistress)," he was given Barry's speaking
trumpet to "hail the tropic." One last "handsome washing" by his
shipmates, and Patrick's ordeal—witnessed with delight by his uncle—
was over.[50]

Patrick's initiation was the only challenge he encountered in the
southeast trades. As his uncle did at the same age, Patrick took in
everything, describing it all with picturesque detail in his journal. He
was fascinated by how "the sky was always covered with flying
clouds of the day," with the night "cool and pleasant." He and the
others found themselves in a variable orgy of fishing: "We catched a
multitude of Fishes both large and small some of them weighing 100
lb. The sea all around us was covered with some of them about the
size of a shad."[51]

Nor were Barry's crew the only predators on this killing spree:
"sharks, bonetoes & other Large fishes destroy'd not a few of them."
Turning their attention to their competition, the armed sailors
"Lessened a number of those Tyrants Who spread terror and devas-
tation amongst the inhabitants of the ocean." For several days they
gorged themselves on fish until "several of our people was poisoned."
The sick recovered, but the Asia's crew returned to salt pork and
hardtack.[52]

Days later, slow sailing came to an end with "fresh Gales between
NW and West." Accompanying the strong gusts were several alba-

trosses, "very Large Birds their body head and under their Wings White the rest of their body of a rich dark brown Colour." Try as they might to catch or kill them, the sailors had no luck. Another sailor observed that "they must be exceedingly strong," recalling how "one of them, on being hooked, broke the deep sea line of the ship, to where the hook was fastened, and carried part of it away with him."[53]

By now the *Asia* was running southward again. On the morning of March 29, Barry "saw the Land bearing SE about 16 Leagues distant." By nightfall the *Asia* was "in the Table Bay in 5 fathoms water the Cape Town bearing NW one Mile dist." Barry brought the *Asia* about, and orders were given to dismantle the guns. The *Asia* was below Penguin Island, across the mainland known among mariners as "the Country of the Hottentots." "After a passage of ninety 9 days," the *Asia* was in Cape Town.[54]

Like Patrick, most of the men aboard had never seen Africa. Patrick vividly described the view: "Cape town lies a bout 40 Miles to the Northw'd of the Cape it is situated partly in a Val[le]y at the foot of a Chain of very lofty Mountains which forms a semicircle to the Southw'd of it there is only one passage by which you can approach the town." With daylight Patrick saw each peak of the mountain range. The highest peak, "called the TableLand . . . lies Due North of the town." The youngster's eyes swept southward: "The next is Called the Sugar Loaf on which the Dutch always keeps watch and who gives notice by Signals of what Country the Ships in Sight are of it lies S. W. of the Town. The next is Lions Rump it lies N. W. of the Town on which is kept a watch."[55]

Cape Town was founded in 1652 as a supply station for the Dutch East India Company. During the American Revolution a British fleet attempted to take over the Cape—an idea enthusiastically supported by the English East India Company, believing it could become "the Gibraltar of India." With assistance from a French fleet, the Dutch turned back the British invaders.[56]

Barry brought the *Asia* into Cape Town's accommodating anchorage, full of European ships and a few American ones, including the *Canton*. Barry went ashore to introduce himself, present his papers, and ask permission to trade. He learned that "Business is Caried on by Licence from the Dutch East India Company," which had everything a merchantman could want. To their pleasant surprise, Barry's crew need not load their water barrels on their boats and run them ashore in order to be refilled. A pipe ran the length of one of the piers, from which all the fresh water they needed could be taken directly aboard–state-of-the-art eighteenth-century technology.[57]

Once permitted, Barry began unloading those wares the owners deemed best suited for trade in Cape Town: tar, iron, and lumber. No sooner had the crew begun this task than the weather turned "very rough." Barry hoped to "be able to sail in ten days," and put the men to work repairing the damaged bowsprit and re-caulking the *Asia*'s problematic seams. Shore leave was scheduled in shifts. While the supercargoes handled provisions and trade Barry gave his nephew shore leave, admonishing him to keep his eyes and ears open and write down his observations. Patrick willingly obeyed.[58]

Patrick and the rest of Barry's crew found Cape Town "well built of Stone and bricks the houses two Story high with flat Roof, others are covered with Thatch." Like Philadelphia, Cape Town was laid out in a square; "the Streets are Straight and parallel the Town contains about 1200 houses," which were kept "Clean and elegantly furnished and well painted." Patrick found the Dutch to be vigilant; "allways keep[ing] a large body of troops in the town." The townsfolk "were generously well dressed . . . the Small Sword and Cockade complates the dress of every Man who wishes to appear like [a] gentleman." The trappings and estate of the Dutch East India Company were incredibly impressive: acres of sumptuous gardens bordered with oak trees with a "Collection of Strange beasts and birds," including ostriches, secretary birds, baboons, zebras, and "the Tygar Cat Leopard."[59]

Even the common livestock struck Hayes as uniquely odd. Being Irish he was no stranger to the sight of sheep, but here they were "Remarkable for their large Tail which weigh about 4 to 6 pounds." For all of its exotic sights, the young orphan found two things in common with his new home, Philadelphia: "a well built Church with a steeple and two clocks" and slaves. Slavery had been abolished in Pennsylvania in 1780–although the act did not free any slaves, it stopped the abhorrent practice–but the trade was still legal here and Patrick witnessed "dutch Neggroes and Indians from different part of the East" serving as "Slaves in this place." Dutch settlers told the inquisitive boy that all Africans "prove as troublesome to back Settlers here as the americane Indians do to the back Settlers in [our] Country."[60]

Cape Town justice was swift and merciless to its guests as well: "people Convicted of Capital crimes are broke on the wheel and gibbeted for the most bafling crime they will sentence a man to 15 or 16 years hard a labor." Cape Town was a puzzling place for Patrick, who found the idyllic at odds with the draconian. On one hand, there was "the wholesome air" for the "very corpulent" Dutch to enjoy. On the other, there were the "3 gibbetts one fore the sailors one fore the soldiers and one fore the Slaves."[61]

By April 11, Barry "finished our business here." The layover's success was mixed: "We did not sell the Spars," and the carpenter could only jury-rig the bowsprit "as well as it is in our Power," assuring Barry it would last until the *Asia* reached Canton. Further, some of the barrels in the hold had proved to be irreparably damaged in crossing the stormy Atlantic: "Fourteen Kegs of Cargo Rum" and "all the Spirits of Turpentine" were empty. Barry did find a replacement for Marsh, John Sutton, "taken off the Brig *Navigator*." Once more the *Canton* left ahead of the *Asia*, beating her out of Cape Town by two days. Barry "put to Sea on the thirteenth."[62]

For the next ten days it seemed as if every gale and storm came to call on Barry's vessel. Waves the size of canyon walls threatened her very existence, toying with the *Asia* as soon as she left Table Bay. "On the 14th it blowing very harde," the *Asia* lost another soul: "One of our Seamen Jack Kennedy was washt off the bows." The cry of "man overboard!" was instantly followed by a log and rope tossed in Kennedy's direction. "We did all that we could in our power to save him," Patrick sorrowfully wrote, "but it was to no purpose." Young Hayes stood on the poop deck with his uncle, watching helplessly as Kennedy rose and fell in the throes of the deadly wave, and then disappeared.[63]

The *Asia* "continued running to the southw'd and Eastw'd as well as the wind would permit," but "the Sea ran very high, the wind varying . . . from the Eastw'd and squally continuously . . . and very Cold Weather." On April 23, the bowsprit sprung again and the topmast was lost; Barry ordered every sail reefed as "it blew agale of wind with a heavy Sea." Beaten up and leaking, the *Asia* was truly imperiled when, fortunately and improbably, "the wind abated and the sea fell." Barry gave hurried orders and the crew jury-rigged a spare top mast and new lines to reset the *Asia's* rigging. To a relieved Patrick, "the weather seemed to wate for us to complete the necessary Job." It did not wait one second longer: "At night we had a violent Gale of wind at ENE," he wrote. The punishing weather continued with "Severe gales of wind varying every day from SW to S and SE." The wind seemed to be attacking the *Asia* from all sides at once. Nor was she making progress; for a solid week "we gained nothing."[64] To the crew, just keeping the *Asia's* hull in the water–and themselves out of it–was success enough.

This entire leg of the passage had been one long storm, save for the precious hours that allowed the bowspirit's repair. Seeing that keeping to his original course was futile, Barry threw the helm over and headed due south. He discussed his decision with his nephew, already copiously recounting the storms, wind directions, and ship's location in his journal. Judging from Barry's existing writings, Patrick's summary of his uncle's decision to change course reads like a direct quote: "Ships bound to the East Indies which happened to come in this Latitude would do well to turn the ship's head to the Southw'd if they expect to meet with a fresh Gale from the westward."[65]

On May 10, Patrick looked to starboard and saw the Island of St. Paul. "It is Remarcably high," he wrote, but "a desolate Island." The *Asia* reached it the following day.[66] St. Paul's sits like the dot on an "i" at 40 degrees latitude, giving one pause when gazing at a map of the world–how far it is from Cape Town, how much farther yet to China, and how incredibly far it is from Philadelphia.

The crew could hardly believe the sudden change in the weather. "The day was clear and serene," and "we dried ourselves and our cloaths which were Sufficient[ly] Soaked." From St. Paul's, Barry headed northeast; indeed, the passage up the Indian Ocean was the most pleasant leg of the voyage. On May 25, the ship "crossed the Tropick of Capricorn." Fresh breezes continued for four more days, as "the Clouds [seemed] to move in every direction," and "the Wind shifted that evening and got very calm."[67]

With daylight the next morning the crew made another odd discovery. They could see "the Surface of the Sea covered with something that looked like dirt." Was it a red tide? The thermometer registered eighty-four degrees; soon Patrick saw "a multitude of boobies arrived in the water." Few birds match their unique appearance. One sailor described them as "generously gray, about the size of a tamed duck, have a long, pointed beak, webbed feet and long wings." The men found them entertaining, yet slow-witted; laughing as the birds caught flying fish and swallowed them whole. The boobies were easy to kill, but less than appetizing: "lean, very fishy, but indifferent food."[68]

On June 2, the *Asia* entered the waters of the Malayan pirates, and Barry issued new orders. The crew "mounted our guns and got the Small arms on deck and cleaned them." Gunnery practice resumed. Piracy was every bit a threat in the South China Seas as it was in the Caribbean or the Mediterranean; while Barry's voyage came twenty years before the rise of the female pirate Ching Yih Saou and her thousands of cutthroats, the scores of Malayan and Chinese pirates warranted gunnery practice and a weather eye on the lookout. For the next three days the *Asia* worked its way up the coast of Java, six hundred miles long and the southwest guardian of Indonesia. Fifty-four days had passed since the *Asia* left Cape Town at dusk "on the 6th of June," when "we saw the land bearing NNE it looked like the top of a Conical mountain." What Patrick was viewing in the darkening sky, and believing to be Java Head, was actually the volcano on Krakatoa, only a few miles distant.[69]

The next day the *Asia* was attacked "by a deluge of rain a heavy Sea settling on shore the night very dark so that our Situation was very dangerous." Once more Barry and his men battled the elements, keeping the ship from smashing into the unknown, forbidding coast. When the storm finally died down, the sailors beheld Java Head, "a height close to the water rising gradually into [a] lofty Mountain." By "8 o'clock in the Evening," Patrick jotted, "we were abreast of Java Head."[70]

Next the *Asia* came to another treacherous passage—the Sunda Straits. With Prince Island (now called Panaitan) to port and Java

Head to starboard, the *Asia* began her entrance. Already grateful to Truxton for the information he shared about his previous voyage to Canton, Barry found himself especially appreciative during this passage. On his earlier trip, Truxton relied on the British Tables register, a veritable bible of navigational information. Afterward he determined that the British erred, placing Java Head one hundred miles off to the eastward.[71]

Amateur sailors have seen what happens to the wind when passing a group of houses—it dies, leaving them dealing with the current until they work their way past the buildings. Such was the western entry into the Strait of Sunda: "the Wind died away where we got to leeward of the Head which is very high," Patrick wrote, and his uncle "found a very Strong Current Setting out to Sea so that it was 11 o'clock at Night before we got [into] Mew Bay." Once in the Mew, the *Asia* "came too anchoring in 23 fathom Soft bottom" where Barry found several streams spilled into the bay, and ordered that the nearly empty water barrels be refilled. The next morning the crew saw "Several Rocks called the carpenters [in] the Strait between this and Java Head." The Sunda Straits were only "2 Leagues wide between [Prince] Island and Sumatra [where] it is too Deep to anchor." Almost instantly the *Asia* had company—"a Danish Ship which left the cape of Good hope Several Days before we came too at the same time."[72]

By 1788, Java was a well established Dutch settlement. Its capital, Batavia (now Jakarta), was the largest Dutch settlement in the East Indies. A contemporary of Barry's described the city as "handsome, built with white stones" with a network of canals running through it. The Dutch worked their Malayan slaves "without mercy and if they die, heave them overboard like a beast."[73]

As in Cape Town, western architecture clashed with western racism. What Java lacked, however, was health. The primary illness "was a swelling in the bowels, the other a pain in the breast." The water, "being salt peter ground," was boiled "in rice or barley, then being so hot, it was like physic to us when we had to drink it." One American sailor called it "the most unhealthy place I ever was in." Nor was it remotely stable politically. Barry reported home that "the Dutch and Malaese are engaged in war throughout the Chinese seas."[74]

Hayes soon lost his romantic notions of the island. On the morning after the *Asia* dropped anchor, "we Saw Several Canoes but none of them came to us." When several sailors asked if they could follow them to trade for fresh food, Barry nodded. Patrick and some others gave chase to one of them "in our Jolly boat and soone came up with her in her was Malayans they had 2 Turtle Cocoa Nuts . . . Benannoes [bananas] & several Monkeys aboard . . . we under stud from Their Signs that the Dutch would put them to death if they Catched them Selling Turtle or dealing for any Sort of produce to foreigners." Hayes was shocked to find the Malayans "Quite naked Save a piece of Stuff to cover their naked ness." Using "slap-sign" to indicate they would not tell the Dutch about any breach of international trade, the Americans won the natives over, and "With Some provisions and the Sight of Some money They Sold us the Turtle for two Dollars."75

The jollyboat was no sooner alongside the *Asia* when "a dutch officer came on board of us in a proe"–a Malay sailing boat and a favorite of Indonesian pirates, about thirty feet long with a sharp stern–"of a curious Shape with an oblong Sail." With the crew having just told their captain about their encounter with the Malayans, Barry gave quick orders to take the turtle below, just as the Dutchman climbed up *Asia*'s side. He was the customs officer at Angiertown, "stationed here for the purpose of taking an account of all vessels which passed this way." Barry presented his papers; after some perfunctory conversation, learned that the Dutchman also had a boatful of wares to sell. Barry "bought 9 Turtle and Some fish for a barrel of flower."76

The next morning, Barry gave orders to weigh anchor and proceed through the Sunda Straits. Passage took several days. All the while the *Asia* had company who were much less inhibited than their first native visitors: "We had a grate number of canoes along Side every Day the Malayans did not Seem the least Shy their canoes had outriggers to keep them from over Setting their paddles Were flat both ends . . . they trade a great Number of [sugar] Canes aboard for which they asked Extraordinary prices we likewise bought Several fowls of[f] them." The natives kept their canoes filled with island produce: "pepper Sugar Tobacco rice Coffee and coca Nuts plaintains and other tropical Fruit," which they held in outstretched arms up to the American sailors. Then the haggling began. Neither seller nor buyer spoke the other's language; the bartering was done by waving fingers, making gestures, and speaking pidgin English until a deal was made.[77]

On June 11, two other ships from Philadelphia came through the straits: Truxton's *Canton* and another merchantman captained by John Keene. Truxton, having sailed Barry's route on his previous voyage to China, had skimmed along the West African coast, then into the Indian Ocean—a longer route than Barry's but without the storms that had whipped the *Asia* to a virtual standstill before reaching St. Paul's. What Truxton did not know until years later was that a Royal Navy brig was just a few days behind him—HMS *Bounty*, bound for Tahiti and a mutiny. When the three American ships cleared the straits, Barry waved farewell as the other Philadelphia captains headed to starboard and Batavia, while Barry "Steered NNE for the Straits of Banca."[78]

Banka Strait, a narrow, twisting passage even more harrowing than the Sunda Straits, divided Sumatra from Banka Island. Winds were light, and soundings varied from "12 fathom Water" to a few feet. The water was so murky Barry could not make out the bottom; all he and his men could see were snakes "between three & four feet long," with "dark brown backs, yellow sides and bellies" and "black and white stripes or checks on the tail."[79] The presence of islands in the strait further slowed Barry's progress, but the most dangerous factor was the flood tide, which ran "very Strong to the Westward above us," threatening to send the *Asia* aground on the Sumatra side of the strait.[80]

Passage was painstakingly slow. Each night Barry dropped anchor, letting the *Asia* rock to and fro in the murky water, while young Hayes and the crew marveled at another eerie sight: "Every Eveneng a multitude of monstrous bats took their flight out of the Woods and directed their course towards Banca where they stay all night [and] return in the like number be fore Sunrise the next morning[.] They are as large as [a] fishing hawk and every way Shape like

THE EAST INDIES
AND THE
SOUTH CHINA SEA

0 100 ————————— 500
SCALE - MILES

CANTON

Great
Ladrone

Macao

HAINAN

S i a m

A n n a m

(COCHIN CHINA)

Gulf of Siam

Malay Peninsula

Strait of Malacca

Two Brothers

SOUTH CHINA SEA

Saddle
Island

B o r n e o

Sumatra

— EQUATOR —

Banka Strait

Banka
Island

Two
Sisters

Sundra Strait

BATAVIA
(Jakarta)

J a v a

S e a

Prince Island
JAVA HEAD

Mew Bay

J a v a

N

a bat their wings are 6 or 7 feet long and as wide as their body is long."[81]

After four days, the *Asia* passed through the strait. On summer's eve she recrossed the equator and was in the South China Sea, greeted, appropriately enough on this voyage, with another storm. The following morning Barry and Patrick saw a "small Island bearing

NNE of us about 9 leagues. . . . We found it to be Saddle Island so Called for its being like a Saddle." From there Barry set a course "NE by N," keeping the ship east of the Malay Peninsula.[82]

Unfettered by any straits, and blessedly unbothered by pirates, the *Asia* sailed up the South China Sea, with one last set of squalls for company. Barry sent the ship past the Gulf of Siam and around the islands called "two Brothers," bringing her closer to her destination.[83]

––––––––––

Back in Philadelphia, the city was putting the final touches on a special Fourth of July celebration. New Hampshire had just become the ninth state to ratify the Constitution, making it the law of the land. Once word reached Philadelphia "a general joy pervaded this city . . . the bells of Christ Church were rung, accompanied with a salute of cannon." The *Pennsylvania Gazette* printed the news in its July 2, 1788 issue along with word that, "By Capt. Swaine from Madeira, we have advice that a Guineaman, who put into that island, spoke the *Asia*, Captn. Barry, from Philadelphia for Canton, on 2nd of February . . . out 43 days, all well."[84]

Responsibility for Philadelphia's "completely Federal" parade was placed in the hands of the city's resident poet and tunesmith, Francis Hopkinson. The tiny lawyer was determined not to disappoint, envisioning a gala of *Meschianza*-size proportions. He had it all planned: how, after a "bell peel of the Christ Church, the ship *Rising Sun* would present a salute and lead a flotilla of ten vessels, all bedecked in signal flags," up the Delaware. Next would be a parade of eighty-seven floats up the city streets, including one portraying "the Federal ship *Union.*" The *Union* was actually the *Alliance*'s barge; Hopkinson put it under the command of John Green. On June 30, Hopkinson reviewed his plans for the extravaganza, happily anticipating the cheers from appreciative Philadelphians.[85]

That same day, on the other side of the world, John Barry stood on the *Asia*'s poop deck and beheld something he had never seen before: China.[86]

CHAPTER SEVENTEEN

THE CHINA TRADE

HEN CATHAY'S KUBLAI KHAN FIRST GREETED the Venetian adventurer Marco Polo back in the thirteenth century, it was impossible to imagine that European traders would begin reaching China by water in two hundred years. The first Portuguese ships reached Macao in the 1500s, the sailors having no idea they were meeting the peoples found in Polo's writings. Putting that together took time; after all, Columbus was still alive and trying to make sense of his discovery, thousands of miles away.[1]

Over the next three centuries, trade relations and the exchange of cultures evolved into a workable system between Chinese emperors and European traders. The first westerners to make a significant impact on the Chinese were not traders but Jesuit priests, whose extravagant gifts established their influence, later perpetuated by their skills in mathematics, astronomy, chemistry, and geography. They drew the first maps of China for their countrymen, and did their utmost diplomatically to make up for their sailors' behavior. Efforts to establish missions were not always successful: twice Chinese soldiers massacred Christian settlements in retribution for the mistreatment of Chinese women by traders and sailors.[2]

By the time Spain, Holland, France, and England sent their ships to Canton, the Chinese had established a system of rules and laws controlling both trade and behavior. The island of Macao–the entryway to Canton–was given to the Portuguese, in return for promises to assist in fighting pirates and explaining the rules of trade to any and all arrivals. Macao was where Barry obtained both a pilot and a pass that permitted him to proceed up the Chu-Kiang River, known by westerners as the Pearl.[3]

When the *Asia* reached Macao, China was under the rule of the great Emperor Ch'ien Lung. Now seventy-eight years of age, he had led China through over a half-century of prosperity, cultural awakening, and peace. His empire included Mongolia and Tibet; it had expanded to the borders of India and Assam (now Vietnam). His love of history and the teachings of Chinese philosophers led to a renaissance in building and renovations, including the restoration of the ancient Temple of Heaven to its former grandeur.[4]

Ch'ien Lung's view of the western world was similar to those of his predecessors. In his eyes, China was the center of the world. Having no conception of the powers that had been unleashed–for good and bad–by the west upon other continents and their inhabitants, he wrote to other leaders with the most polite condescension, commanding George III, in one piece of correspondence, that he be "trembling to obey," for "It behooves you, O King, to respect my sentiments and to display even greater loyalty in the future so that, by perpetual submission to our being, you may secure peace and prosperity for your continuing hereafter."[5]

For centuries, Canton, "the City of Rams," was the only sanctioned destination for western traders. To Ch'ien Lung, the behavior of the first western visitors indicated that nothing should change. Entreaties and memorials to establish other ports of trade at Ningpo, Chisau, and Tientsin were all rebuffed. Canton was suitable enough. After all, the westerners were barbarians, and nothing could change that. In Chinese eyes, they were "like beasts and not to be relied on the same principles as citizens . . . therefore to rule the barbarians by misrule is the true and best way of ruling them."[6]

Before leaving America, Truxton had briefed Barry that the "rules of the trade" began right at Macao. Barry ordered the *Asia*'s anchor dropped in the Macao Road and, with supercargoes Frazier and Mifflin, he was rowed ashore. Truxton had warned him of the onslaught of different "taxes" that were an established fact of Canton's life: "No charge attends going on shore Macao in the [*Asia's*] boat," but if Barry boarded a Chinese boat, "4 doll[ar]s will be exacted."[7]

By 1788 there were 7,000 Chinese and 4,000 Portuguese in Macao, most of whom made their living attending to arriving and departing western traders.[8] Barry was struck by the sheer number of western ships–dozens of them, moored all the way from the roadstead to the twin harbors. Once he got ashore he got his first glimpse of Praya Grande–the beautiful, crescent-shaped beach that stretched above Macao.[9] Above the twin harbors loomed an old, dilapidated fortress.[10] Although the town was an amalgam of western and eastern architecture, it was more a reflection of European occupation than Chinese dominion. Macao was dotted with western buildings and houses. Even grand estates had been erected. From Macao, foreign men could proceed to Canton, but women could not. The wives of European merchants and dignitaries got no closer to mainland China than the beach at Praya Grande. Forbidden by Chinese law to come one step closer to Canton, Macao was their home away from home. And it was dangerous to break the law: at one dinner, enraged Cantonese officials discovered a British captain's cabin boy lacked an Adam's apple; it took force of arms to rescue the the captain and the cabin boy–his wife.[11]

Once ashore, Barry presented his papers to the customs house clerk. After giving the documents the required scrutiny, he informed Barry that a "chop"–his pass to Canton–would be forthcoming in a day or two. Chops were never issued immediately, as permission for them came from Canton–a 160-mile trip. With the clerk's consent, Barry next met with the head of the customs house. With unfailing politeness and somewhat recognizable English, the official explained how patience with Chinese practices would be as appreciated as it would be tested over the coming months. Western traders might exhibit a sense of urgency, but never the Chinese–after all, they were not going anywhere. Barry would get his chop and pilot when they arrived. It was that simple. We do not know if Barry tried the oft-used method of discreetly passing cash to the official, as another captain did, who learned that, while "There is nothing to be gained by endeavoring to hurry these people into giving up a Pilot by loud talking . . . coaxing and greasing the palms of hands being the only means of doing it."12

At the customs house Barry picked up a comprador—the Chinese agent assigned to be his representative for the duration of his stay at Canton. There were many of them, each one confident in his abilities to assist with "soliciting in attending the ship." It was a decision Barry was forced to make by instinct, as "there is no great certainty of getting a good one for they can all provide good recommendations from those they have served before." While Barry never described his new business associate, a watercolor sketch of "a Chinese comprador" from those days shows a short man wearing a long, white, uncollared shirt over dark pants and ornamental slippers. An intelligent face looks serenely at the artist, his long hair pulled back in a braid that runs down his back.13

After calling on the governor of Macao to introduce himself, there was nothing left for Barry to do but return to the *Asia* and wait for his chop. It came the next day, along with a pilot, hired for thirty dollars—an exorbitant rate for those days. The journey up the Pearl began.14 As the *Asia* entered the river's mouth, Barry and his crew were struck by the remarkable resemblance of the Pearl to their home waterway, the Delaware. The mouths of both rivers are almost the same width, curving and narrowing exactly alike as if they were twins.15 Unfortunately for the sailors, the views were similar too. There was nothing exotic at all about their passage upriver: it was muddy, with drab shorelines and nondescript little islands that bore faint resemblance to romantic tales of the Orient.16

The pilot soon proved himself worth his high fee, as the *Asia* was approached by men poling sampans—small, flat-bottomed skiffs—which acted as tugboats, keeping the *Asia* away from the subtly treacherous shoals and sudden appearance of shallows. The pilot paid them out of his own pocket.17 Working back and forth across the river, tacking and reaching, the *Asia* passed Lintin Island, then Lankeet, called "the Dragon's Den," where "a tongue of land runs out onto the river on the opposite side, which bears the name Chuen-pee, or the 'Bored Nose' from a single rock which forms its most striking feature, perforated through." From there the pilot brought the ship to Boca Tigris—called "the Bogue" by westerners; named by the Chinese for its resemblance to a rising tiger.[18] The pilot put the *Asia* into the wind, and Barry gave the order to drop anchor.

This time the officials came to the *Asia*. Ornately decorated sampans, armed with carriage guns, came alongside Barry's ship. The *Asia* was boarded by a mandarin, whose job was to guarantee that trade went smoothly and strictly according to Chinese law. He was followed up the gangway by two guards. Barry handed over his chop to the mandarin while the comprador described the *Asia*'s cargo and mission. On Barry's order, the cook brought a bottle of wine on deck and had it opened—a ritual Truxton prepared him for. After a series of toasts and best wishes, the mandarin and pilot disembarked, leaving the two guards aboard. Once the chop was countersigned by the officials at the port, it was returned to Barry by another new pilot who would bring the *Asia* up to Whampoa.[19]

The sun was setting as the pilot climbed up the *Asia*'s side. There was a quick conversation among the guards, the comprador, and the pilot. Barry wanted to continue upriver, but the guards would have none of it. The comprador explained their orders to Barry, but the guards' determination that the *Asia* stay put for the night required no translation. Seeing how "these Small gentlemen [were] vary tenacious of their case," Barry could only agree to wait until morning to proceed further.[20]

At sunrise the *Asia* weighed anchor and pressed onward. Barry noticed that any approaching sampans, filled with poor Chinese and whatever goods they carried, immediately changed course when they saw the easily recognizable "mandarin Soldiers." For himself, Barry did not find the guards threatening—he saw them as duplicitous. While "the object of their Stay on board is to prevent Any Smugling trade," he learned otherwise: "they cannot be safely trusted when there are any light articles of value." Such behavior was nothing new to Barry, and his solution was time-honored (if not honorable) in every port: "if a bottle of rum and some provisions are given them they will return to their Boat which rides astern and give no farther trouble."21

The *Asia* passed "the Bogue" and with it, the far bank called Anung Hoy–the "Lady's Shoe."22 Now the scenery became "more inviting"; the Americans saw "several plantations of bamboos, bananas, and rice." The landscape here was as colorful as the previous day's had been drab. Beyond the high riverbanks were dense forests, where the tops of centuries-old pagodas could be seen. Small hamlets and fishing villages soon dotted the landscape, but the Americans' excitement at what they were seeing was tempered once they came closer. The towns were crowded and filthy. When the *Asia* sailed by flatlands abundant with peach and orange trees, it only added to the incongruity: such a beautiful setting dotted with such squalor.23

The *Asia* no sooner passed the fortress near Whampoa when she was approached by another flotilla of sampans acting as towboats to get "past the fort and sand bars."24 As before, the pilot paid for the assistance from his fee. Then, with the harbor in sight, came another hazard: traffic.

As the *Asia* neared Whampoa it became necessary for the pilot to slow her already sluggish pace. The river was a veritable logjam of sampans. Barry could not possibly count them all. They came out of the streams and clogged the river by the thousands, each one a floating household. They were filled near to swamping with men, women, and children, the youngest of whom had blocks of wood tied to their backs, to prevent them from drowning should they fall into the water. They carried eggs, chickens, and pigs to sell to the foreigners; most were filthy beyond measure.25 In muted horror, Barry watched as these "poorer Chinese [fed] upon the lice of their own bodies." Their utter poverty shocked him to his core. Barry had witnessed his share of wretched conditions in Ireland, Philadelphia, and the West Indies, but nothing like this. The sight stayed with him for the rest of his life.26

Before long, larger craft came into play: junks, those odd, exotic vessels, with large eyes painted on their square prows (to ward off evil). Other mandarin boats glided by, with red sashes adorning their carriage guns. Sampans carrying barbers and vendors hawking their services and produce sailed alongside barges transporting gaudily dressed theatrical troupes and fortune tellers, trolling for an invitation to perform and predict.[27]

Last came the "flower boats," whose passengers were the colorfully dressed "harlots of the harbor," their hands and necks arrayed in jewels, enticingly chatting up any onlooker for a little paid companionship, provided in the privacy of small but serviceable lattice cabins. All of these moved quickly out of the way of the junks of war, those imposing vessels maintaining their course regardless of whom or what was in their path. Almost every craft mentioned carried an ornamental joss house, a small bamboo structure containing the idol worshipped by the boat's passengers. At night the little shrines were candlelit, and Whampoa took on the appearance of a vast, illuminated, river of stars.[28]

At last the *Asia* nestled into Whampoa Anchorage, as international a port as any Barry ever visited. Here were Dutch East Indiamen, alongside their British counterparts: huge, bluff-bowed ships dwarfing the *Asia* and other merchantmen from Spain, Holland, Denmark, and France. With the recent departure of the *Alliance*, there were no other American ships in port. Barry, working as best he could with a foreign pilot, gave orders to "warp ship." Using the kedge anchor, his crew maneuvered the *Asia* around the other ships in the harbor until she reached her temporary mooring. It was July 7, 1788; after 198 days and 18,000 miles, Barry spent his eleventh wedding anniversary as far away from his loving spouse as one could get in this world. He ordered a thirteen-gun salute fired from his little 4-pounders. It was returned by the other ships in port; for several minutes cannon fire filled the air.[29]

His job completed, the pilot disembarked and went to report the arrival of the *Asia* to a Hoppo—one of the many customs officials (some of whom were mandarins) on duty at a station near the *Asia's* mooring. The pilot did not identify the ship by her name, but by that of her captain. Already aware of the exorbitant four-dollar fee for being rowed ashore in a Chinese boat, the frugal Barry ordered the longboat made ready. With papers and chop in hand, and his two supercargoes and one comprador in tow, Barry turned command of the *Asia* over to Josiah. He nodded acknowledgment to the "mandarin Guards" still furtively watching their American guests. They would remain aboard the *Asia* until she departed for America, ever vigilant in discouraging any illegal trade except their own.[30]

Whampoa Reach lay twelve miles below Canton. From what Barry had seen the day before, he expected traffic on the river to be excruciatingly slow. It was. Paintings of Whampoa from the 1780s depict a gridlocked waterway. In one, the view from Dane's Island looking toward Whampoa Island itself shows a vista dotted with western and eastern vessels, while the Great Pagoda and warehouses rise above the shoreline.

Barry beheld a grand view of the Great Pagoda in Canton, standing "near groves of banana, orange, peach, and lichie trees." At nine stories, it dominated the landscape, with its long shadow serving as a virtual sundial for native and foreigner alike. As the *Asia* slowly glided by, the Americans saw more denizens of the river: "thousands of ducks, under the care of their keepers." The din from their incessant quacking was soon joined by manmade noise: "the crash of gongs, and the hum of business heard from every quarter, presented a scene full of life and hilarity."[31]

Further along, Barry glimpsed Canton on the north side of the Pearl, also known as "The Tigris" by some of their fellow barbarians, and, in westernized speaking, "The Choo-Heang." Looking southeast he saw "the factories." These were not places of manufacturing, but where western officers, supercargoes, merchants, and dignitaries lived, alongside the Chinese business agents, known as "factors." Just past the factories were the suburbs of Canton, a large, bustling market interlaced by "exceedingly narrow" streets. The suburbs ended at Canton itself, surrounded by a thick wall built of stone and brick, and divided by another wall, which crossed it from east to west. The northern of the two sections thus formed, was called the Old City, and the southern the New.[32]

The factories were built on "a narrow strip of land on the river's bank . . . about a quarter of a mile square outside the city walls." This would be the closest any barbarian got to the city itself. Barry would never enter Canton, much less "the suburbs." He had sailed the *Asia* thousands of miles around the world to find that he and his super-cargoes would only be allowed to live in a narrow strip of land one third of a mile long, already crowded with Cantonese natives and the rest of the barbarians.[33]

While his oarsmen remained at the boat, Barry, and his supercar-goes followed the comprador past the factories. Some of these build-ings, over fifty years old, had the look of an eighteenth-century municipal building, with their broad, flat walls, high windows, and whitewash to keep out some of the oppressive heat. Two large avenues divided the market: China Street, flourishing with stores sell-ing silk, china, and antiques; and Hog Lane, where one tavern or brothel was crammed next to another. Hog Lane ran through the Canton outskirts like an unclasped necklace, with grog shops for its beads—each owned by Chinese merchants whose aim in life was get-ting the barbarian sailors drunk and then robbing them. Brawling was frequent, whether between sailors from the same ship or coun-try, sailors from other lands, or sailors and the Chinese. It was an ugly, contentious issue between the mandarins and their western guests. In all the world, there was no tougher street than Hog Lane.[34]

The comprador led his charges up China Street to a handsome array of buildings called the "Consoo House" (Consul House), the official headquarters for trade. Barry received a polite greeting from one of the officials, who expressed pleasure at seeing another visitor from the land of the "flowery flag," as the Chinese called the Stars and Stripes. At the Consoo House, Barry was told to select three more representatives from the Chinese government to work with him during his stay: another comprador, who would be assigned to Barry's factory (his first would remain aboard the *Asia*), a "linguist" to translate, and one of the Hong merchants. "A Linguist is absolute-ly necessary," Truxton had told Barry, telling him that "The Linguist most uniformly preferred is named Chicqua." To Barry's pleasant surprise, Chicqua was available, and Barry paid his up-front gratuity of $216, called a cumshaw, and "understood to be his only emolu-ment." Chicqua arranged for the Grand Hoppo—the superintendent of customs—to visit the *Asia* and have her tonnage measured. Barry was now free to find his factories.[35]

Chicqua spoke much better English than the compradors and answered Barry's questions with an unfailing politeness as they headed back to the waterfront to locate available housing. Not much has changed since those days; the closer Barry got to the waterfront, the higher the rent–starting at $1,200 per season, to those further away from the docks, renting "200 or 300 d[olla]rs less." After a close examination, in which Barry saw that the buildings "differ greatly in point of elegance," he selected one with a real asset: "a Treasury or Strongly built appartment to keep the Silver in–and keep thieves out." Another $1,200 went to the factory owner. According to Chicqua, Barry was lucky to arrive in Canton when he did, as "Ships which arrive late . . . meet difficulty in procuring a factory."[36]

The factories were two-story structures, with the first floor or "godown" used as the ship's warehouse until the good were sold, then it was used to store returning supplies and goods until they were transferred to the *Asia*'s hold. The second floor served as living quarters for Barry, his supercargoes, the factory comprador, and any servants enlisted for the *Asia*'s stay.[37]

Leaving Frazier and Mifflin with the house comprador, Barry, Chicqua, and the *Asia*'s comprador went to meet with the CoHong, the nine top Canton business officials to whom complete authority over trade had been divinely given by the emperor. While the merchants and tavern owners Barry's sailors would encounter along Hog Lane reflected a wide range of business principles–or lack thereof–the CoHong were special: their success was a result of doing business under strict, ethical standards. They reported to the viceroy of Canton, the emperor's hand-picked governor. Like other men of importance, the CoHong paid the viceroy for their position–an "entrance fee" of as much as 200,000 taels was not unheard of.[38]

To the CoHong fell the task of serving two masters–three, if they looked in a mirror. There was pressure from above to generate high revenues: pressure from the viceroy to pad his accounts while still sending plenty to the emperor, and self-imposed pressure to keep their own income (and subsequent high taxes) on the rise. Doing so required a delicate balance of business acumen and tact. They affixed and regulated prices, kept their superiors above and the merchants below them happy, while maintaining a customer satisfaction with representatives of those countries which sailed around the world to buy nankeen and silk. They politely endured complaints and tirades from Chinese and barbarian alike with a combination of serenity, manners, and backbone. The reward for their success in this balancing act was seen in their financial status–they were among the richest men in the world. The most famous CoHong, Houqua, was worth over 25 million dollars when he died. The CoHongs made Robert Morris look like Poor Richard. Their ability to do business honorably and shrewdly won them scores of admirers from the visiting countries. It was rare for a CoHong to deceive; when he did, it invariably stained his reputation with western traders. After a CoHong loaded a Philadelphia ship with bad tea and chests of paper instead of chests of silk, he was cast out of the factory and blackballed.[39]

Barry's dealings with the CoHong reminded him of his merchant acquaintances in Philadelphia. They "super intend foreign trade," he wrote, "after the manner of a corporate Body responsible as a company for the failure of one of them and the exicution of any contract." These merchants presented their abilities with "a good deal of earnestness." Barry listened to their proposals, which included guaranteed prices of goods, delivery times, and testimonies to "their character." With Chicqua's help, he made his selection: a man named Shi Sien Song.[40]

When Chicqua told Barry to put the agreement with Song in writing, Barry knew why other Americans had so much faith in him. "In a full hand, on a large sheet of paper," the Chinese CoHong and American captain agreed to terms; the CoHong using "his Chop of Business" as a great seal. The contract, drawn up both in Chinese and English, proved to Barry that "to a people that cannot read our writing it might be supposed that this formality would appear triv[i]al– but it is the general opinion that when you have the name of a china man to his agreement he is much more observant of it."[41]

Once these tasks were accomplished, Barry bade Chicqua good day and returned to his factory. To his surprise, the factory comprador had the residence "furnished . . . in two hours with beds, tables, chairs and dishes." Now it was time to return to the *Asia*. As the longboat made its way downriver, Barry discovered that Josiah had secured her off French Island, best known among the locals for its barbarian cemetery. Once aboard, Josiah let Barry know that the crew was permitted access to both French and Dane's Islands, as long as they maintained decorum. Officers from other merchantmen had hailed Josiah with hearty welcomes and offers of assistance, a common courtesy to newcomers in port.[42]

Josiah had the *Asia* cleaned to perfection while Barry was in Canton. With the crewmen well groomed in "their Sunday Suits," they were ready to greet the Grand Hoppo for his official visit on July 9. Standing on the poop deck, Barry–looking every inch a ship's master in his finest clothes–saw a long, brightly decorated barge being rowed toward the *Asia*. Its appearance bespoke wealth and power. The ceremony of "cumshaw and measurement" was about to begin.[43]

Americans had learned the hard way as to how this ritual should be handled. When the Grand Hoppo first visited the *Empress of China*, he asked for his "sing-songs"–the clever toys foreign governments presented him as gifts. When Green explained he had none, the dignitary was politely understanding of the barbaric lack of manners, and said that he understood–this time. Barry had his "sing-songs" in readiness, and ordered a nine-gun salute, in honor of the nine Canton Hoppos.[44] As the barge bumped against the *Asia*, her numerous flags and pennants snapping in the wind, Barry stood at the gangplank to greet his visitors. A large cast of officials and servants followed the Grand Hoppo up the *Asia*'s side.

Barry had never seen anyone so colorfully dressed. The Grand Hoppo wore a series of dazzling robes, all richly embroidered. His hair was cut short around his head–only the top was long, and pulled back into a queue. A long mustache draped down the sides of his mouth. Once he touched foot on deck, the mandarin guards and the compradors knelt in a gesture of respect. Next to arrive on board were Chicqua and the *Asia*'s appointed CoHong, followed by several musicians–two carrying small drums and the rest bringing their Chinese pipes. Once assembled, they played a brief salute of their own, a tune one Englishman compared to "a harmony resembling a sow-gelder's horn and the cackling of geese."[45]

Next, Barry presented his gifts along with glasses of the finest wine aboard and fresh biscuits. With the formalities correctly observed, the "measuremark" began. The *Asia* was not measured according to western practices–the volume of the hold. The Grand Hoppo's servants produced a measuring tape; then, "from the center of her mizen to the center of her foremast is Measured for her length and close abaft her mainmast her breath the length and width multiplied and the product divided by ten gives the amount." When the sum was calculated, Barry discovered it was only part of "a much heavier charge." Once converted into "Fanqui" exchange, it came to "2708 1/3 dollars." Throughout the pacing back and forth, Barry did the numbers in his head (redoing them later on paper), and did not dispute the figure–having been informed by Chicqua the day before that the Grand Hoppo's charge, regardless of the *Asia*'s size, would approach three thousand dollars. Barry paid it, along with "another demand of 18 dollars" for "the Mandarin soldiers."[46]

Once payment was handed over, the Grand Hoppo presented the *Asia*'s captain and crew with "two bulls[,] a sack of dirty Sugar[,] and a few Bottles of Samshaw."[47] The transaction complete, Barry was informed that the Celestial Emperor would permit him to commence trade. With another short piece of shrill music, the Grand Hoppo departed. Barry did not record how quickly one of the bulls was slaughtered, but after months of salt beef and pork, it is reasonable to guess there was fresh meat for dinner that evening.

Barry summoned Josiah, Frazier, and Mifflin to his cabin and gave them their orders. Josiah would be in charge of the *Asia*, overseeing the unloading of the ship's hold, refitting, organizing work crews, and scheduling shore leave on French Island, "the resort of the gentlemen ... of all nations" and a privilege given to only American and French "common sailors." Josiah contracted some Chinese laborers to build a bamboo structure, called a "Bansall," on French Island, under supervision of one the *Asia*'s mates. Covered with a grass mat roof, it would be used to restore supplies and goods coming and going from Canton–and closely guarded around the clock. The supercargoes were assigned responsibility for negotiating the prices for the *Asia*'s goods and selling them. They would join Barry at the factory for the length of their stay.[48]

The *Asia*'s cargo was unloaded expeditiously, but the daily twelve-mile journey up the perpetually clogged Pearl slowed things considerably. The ship's comprador oversaw the supply of the *Asia*'s provisions; Delf Craig, the *Asia*'s cook, learned to rely on him to ascertain that the "Hoppo man" did not "impose bad provisions . . . at a high price." In Canton, Barry learned to keep the factory comprador's palm perpetually greased, for "the Comprador attends to his business with less docility and cheerfulness" if not continually paid.[49]

Josiah got to know Whampoa much better than Barry did. Its hot, humid climate was a breeding ground for mosquitoes by the millions. Each morning Josiah saw firsthand the disparity between the sky-high Grand Pagoda, and the absolutely wretched living conditions of the poorest Chinese, living beneath its shadow in "low, squalid hovels."[50] Each day, the *Asia* had visitors as far removed from the Grand Hoppo as could be imagined: poor families aboard their sampans, using baskets to pick up the refuse "what fell from the ships."[51]

The climate and mosquitoes guaranteed that sickness reigned over the barbarians as much as the mandarins. One American called Whampoa "about as unhealthy a quagmire as China affords, for the immense banks of alluvial mud, left dry at low water, give rise to pestilence, fever breeding exhalations." Soon the *Asia*'s crew was laid low with illness, and Josiah had three lists to update daily: sailors on work detail, sailors on leave, and sailors too sick for either.[52]

Barry, along with his nephew, supercargoes, and some of the luckier sailors settled into life at the factory—actually a group of buildings connected by narrow annexes. Its entrance was an arched passageway, with counting-rooms and storage areas on the first floor, along with the living area for the hong comprador and his entourage of assistants. The "treasury"—Barry's vault—was made of granite, with heavy iron doors, all the more an asset to his mission when he discovered that there was no bank in Canton. The comprador had furnished the place well, including scales and weights on a large table—essential to any deals as trade was usually based on weight. The second floor featured dining and sitting rooms. Barry and his men slept in amply sized bedrooms on the third floor. Outside, an American flag flew on the flagpole; for the remainder of Barry's stay, his factory was called "The Flowery Flag Hong." The factory faced the Pearl, just beyond a spot called "Jack Ass Point," and across from large Honan Island–nature's barrier to the city of Canton.[53]

Each day Barry was grateful that Truxton recommending Chicqua. "He procures permits to Land Cargo or take it on board," the captain wrote, "transacts all Business relating to the Customs and is Generally the advisor to be referred to in any questions respecting the usages and rules of Trade."[54]

With the *Asia* in Josiah's capable hands, and his experienced supercargoes having little difficulties with their duties, Barry's agenda was soon fairly open. His waking hours were divided between visits to the *Asia* and briefings at his factory. Now, only one major labor remained, darkening his calendar, a responsibility he could not ignore indefinitely. Sooner or later he would have to fulfill the voluminous lists he brought to China from the *Asia*'s owners, his relatives, and friends. Finally, armed with other people's lists and other people's money, John Barry went shopping.

Several times a week he took Patrick on his forays into the shops and stores that ran along China Street. This was a new experience for Barry. In truth, while he did his utmost, his success was sporadic at best. Gallantly, he plunged into a world of silks, dishware, and fine, dainty things. He dutifully reported his adventures with the same frank language found in his logs, memoranda, and reports of battles. Whatever the quest, he wrote pretty much the same "Invoice and Bill of lading for Sundries on Board the ship *Asia* on your Acct. which I pray God may come safe at hand."[55] While he did win some victories along China Street, the letters that survive prove undeniably that, as a shopper, Barry was a great sailor.

"After doing everything in my Power to Comply with your orders," Barry wrote Morris regarding his thirty casks of brandy, the captain was "obliged to barter for Teas" instead of "the finest Nankeen" Morris expected. He discovered that Mrs. Nathaniel Lewis had given him too little money for too much silk; "you and I would have been better Satisfied," he reported, "had we known the Price of Silk in China before I sailed from Phila." Nonetheless, despite the "Price of Sattin" being so high, he made the purchase–then factored the interest on his advance at 75 percent. He explained, "Believe me it is not as much as I could have made of the Money to have bought things in Canton and Sold them in Philad[elphia]."[56] The warrior whose mettle had been tested on the open sea, in battle, and amidst political chicanery was hoping this discretionary solution was the better part of valor.

Finally we come to Mrs. Hazelhurst and her request for all of China's . . . china. The intrepid Barry haunted the shops on China Street. "About the first thing I did, was to Enquire for china, the same Pattern you sent by me," states part of his first sentence in a very long, expository letter. Using the same quick-mindedness that had kept him out of British hands and saw him safely through each and every storm, he "made Application to the first China Merchant there to see if he Could get enough Nankeen to complete your order." Alas, despite his Herculean efforts over the next six months, Barry was "at the last minute Grievously disappointed" and spent her money on silks. "I hope Madam you will not Conceive an Idea that I did not do everything in my power to Serve you," he pleaded.[57]

All was not lost, however. He kept a constant lookout for any souvenirs in the Celestial Empire that would please Sarah, buying at least two sets of china and an array of silks and satins. He also commissioned some custom pieces of porcelain, including a punch bowl with the view of the Pearl River encircling the outer rim, with a detail of the *Asia* at the bottom of the bowl, and filigree along the inside edge. He also commissioned a "deep, flaring" punch bowl, its interior edge decorated in coral and gold, with a beautiful reproduction of the *Alliance* "flying an American flag" and "riding on a turquoise blue sea," with "John Barry, Esqr. *Alliance* Commander" on a banderole above the ship. It would be a family heirloom for generations.[58] Thus ended John Barry's international shopping career.

Shortly after work began unloading the *Asia*'s hold, the *Canton* came up Whampoa anchorage. Once ensconced, Truxton joined Barry in visiting other Hongs and ships' cabins for dinner with other merchant captains, one of whom recalled how "the foreign fleets form a city in themselves. . . . [The officers] visit and dine with each other, sail boats, amuse themselves with the Chinese, and brag about their ships." Their companions included Robert Berry, another old Willing & Morris captain, and Samuel Shaw, John Green's supercargo aboard the *Empress of China* in 1784. Shaw was a former major and aide-de-camp to Henry Knox, who had recommended Shaw to Morris. Shaw's integrity in dealing with the Chinese gave America a solid foundation to build their trading relationship with the Chinese, and he was appointed consul by Secretary of State John Jay in 1786.[59]

Through Shaw, Barry got an update on John Green. Shaw, like Barry, had soured on Green—only much more so: "I do not know a term in any language sufficient to express my detestation of him," he said. When the *Empress of China* first arrived at Canton, Green complained about the low price offered for his personal supply of ginseng; when it was shown to be inferior, Green merely blended it with the owners' supply—much to Shaw's angry disapproval. On his recent return to Canton, Green was rebuffed by Consul Shaw. To get even, Green told everyone who would listen that Shaw was no longer his supercargo, having caught him embezzling on the first voyage. Shaw immediately published a lengthy rebuttal showing Green to be as deficient in memory as he was in honesty. Shaw wanted to challenge Green—whom he considered a coward—to a duel, but Canton was no place to fight one. While the loser might die, under Chinese law the winner was sure to—by strangulation.[60]

Shaw's observations on every aspect of the trade were revealing, and he willingly shared these with Barry and Truxton. He advocated construction of larger ships, similar to the British and Dutch Indiamen—up to eight hundred tons.[61] The *Empress* had been joyously welcomed on the first voyage, but Shaw assured the two that they were not nearly as rapturously received by the Europeans as had been the case on the first arrival of the American flag. The novelty had worn off. The constant presence of American ships in Whampoa Anchorage meant more competition, particularly for the British. Portuguese and Dutch trade was lessening, and the East India Company had designs to establish a monopoly in Canton. With the young United States eager to expand relations with China, that would not happen now.

Still, relations with their old mother country were quite good in China, a fact Barry discovered whenever dining with the British at Canton. He also saw Shaw's influence in this camaraderie firsthand. At dinner in any British captain's cabin, Barry learned what Shaw already knew: "It was impossible to avoid speaking of the late war." Having "allowed it to have been a great mistake on the part of their nation," they "were happy it was over" and "hoped all prejudices would be laid aside." Further, they "added that, let England and America be united, and they might bid defiance to all the world."[62]

Following Shaw's example in cultivating friendships was easy for the gregarious Barry. It was the good life for the captains, supercargoes, and other shipmates living at the factories, enjoying decent food and good wine as they shared tobacco and war stories. That was not the case for Josiah and the men aboard the *Asia*. Under the vigilant watch of the guards, the *Asia*'s hold was finally unloaded and now on the first floor of the "Flowery Flag Hong," while Josiah and Nathan Dorsey were kept busy attending the sick. Dorsey's skills can be attested by the fact that none of the *Asia*'s sailors died at Whampoa; only John Galt, the carpenter, became so desperately ill that he requested relief from his duties. On his next visit to the ship, Barry "provided [Galt] Thirty Dollars" for his services, wished him well, and arranged to send him home on another ship.[63]

In August, Josiah informed Barry that "we have brought all the Casks out of the hold and stowed them in the 'tween-decks, as far as the Bulkhead of the Steerage" although "there still remains all the Ginseng and Provisions."[64] By September, Mifflin and Frazier had finished selling the *Asia*'s goods. Return cargoes started to fill up the godown. Soon thousands of chests, half-chests, and quarter-chests of tea, weighing between fifty and one hundred pounds, made their way to the "Flowery Flag Hong," borne on the backs of coolies.[65] The tea ranged from the cheapest variety, Bohea black, to Souhong, richer in aroma and taste (the finest black tea, pekoe, packed in small canisters by the mandarins and given as presents, would not survive an ocean voyage).[66]

Frazier and Mifflin purchased nankeen by the ton, in bales of one hundred pieces, twenty bales to a ton. This cotton cloth was usually yellow, but by 1788 Americans were ordering it in the higher-priced white and blue. Bales of silk were stored, rolled in oiled paper to waterproof it for the voyage; "Black Taffetty" was already a Philadelphia favorite.[67] Finally, china—each piece handmade by farmers in what spare time they had—was delivered by the Hong merchants, who had already assembled the pieces into complete sets for easier sale.

Not all of the goods were carried on aching Chinese backs. Some came via the "wheelbarrow fleets"—an ingenious, time-saving trick in which the wheelbarrow porters rigged a sail on a bamboo mast and sailed across the Chinese countryside—a curious transportation vividly described to the barbarians kept outside the Walls of Canton, but never seen by them.[68]

Stowing the cargo in the *Asia*'s hold brought an unforeseen challenge. "We received Sixty Two Boxes of China and this morning gott them stoad away, in the fire hole," Josiah informed Barry, but the large crates created a problem that "cumshaw and measurement" could not solve: the boxes ran "from the Step of the fore Mast to Midway of the Main Hatchway."[69] There was only room for "forty or fifty Boxes more," but only if "four or five Boat loads" of flour were unloaded. What to do?

Barry's solution was simple and ingenious. The *Asia* became a bakery. He gave Delf Craig orders to start baking fresh bread, and told Josiah to inquire among the international community if fresh "FanQui" bread would be a desirable commodity. It was. Within days, the *Asia*'s fresh bread was a hot item along Whampoa Anchorage: "I have made an inquiry on board those Ships I thought most likely to want Bread," Josiah happily wrote to Barry, letting him know that not only the British, but "The Dutch, Danes, and swedes" were "glad to have the price & Quantity you would wish to Dispose off."[70] If Barry failed as a shopper for Philadelphians, at least he succeeded in the bakery business for the other barbarians.

On October 9, Josiah sent him word "we have gott the mast and riggen Compleated," and that "The sick are Something Better than when you left us" with "more of them able to do Duty."[71] The hold was filling up so fast that Barry ordered either Josiah or second mate "Capt. Sword" to remain on the *Asia* at all times "as we have a valuable part of our Cargo on Board" and Barry had "no dependance but on you and him." Since the *Asia*'s bread delivery service was still the hit of Whampoa, Barry determined to sell off other goods; soon "247 Spars and 18 Mast[s]" were disposed of, as was a barrel of turpentine to another American ship.[72]

Barry began closing up operations in early December. Frazier and Mifflin busied themselves crunching numbers and squaring accounts. Josiah shut down the *Asia*'s bread business and completed the storing of cargo and the ship's refitting. Barry signed off on the official invoices of the cargo, "Shipped by the Grace of God in Good Order aboard the *Asia*, Riding at Anchor in Canton," detailing each item, and closing "so God Send the Good Ship to her desired Port in Safety."[73]

Barry and Truxton agreed to depart from Canton together, mainly as a precaution against pirates in the South China Sea. They co-signed a bond with Shi Sien Song "in the parcel Sum of thirteen Thousand Two hundred . . . Spanish Mill'd Dollars," with "their Goods, Wares and Merchandise" as "their Mortgages." As per the custom of the day, they agreed that "in Case of the loss of the said Vessel (which God Forbid) . . . by Custom shall become due on the Salvage." The document was "Signed, Sealed, and delivered" with both of their bold signatures, those of two witnesses, and the imprint of Shi Sien Song's chop.[74]

Christmas was celebrated with parties at the factories and extra rations of grog aboard ship. Shortly after the New Year, the factory's furniture was moved out as fast as it came in; on French Island, the banshall was taken down, goodbyes were said to Chicqua and Shi Sien Song, and the "flowery flag" was struck. Barry and Truxton each wrote letters to their wives and ship's owners, then exchanged them in the event one of them did not make it home. "We leave thus in Comp[an]y through the China Seas, as being the most dangerous part of the voyage," Barry wrote to his conglomerate of owners.[75]

While Barry's letter to Sarah is lost, the touching letter Truxton wrote to his ten-year-old daughter that he gave to Barry still exists.

It is full of instruction, written with the love of a mariner-father unsure if he will see his little girl again:

> I love you all and all alike. . . . you must carefully observe all the dictates of your good Mama, impress on your mind all her minute actions, take notice of every step as she walks and let her will (in all cases) be your criteria, for it is impossible for you to have a better pattern. . . . instruct [your siblings] all you can and inspire them. . . . be easy and affable but not over volatile. . . . [this is] the advice and early desire of an affectionate father from unforeseen and unexpected misfortune, is obliged, to his heartfelt pain, to be so great a proportion of his time absent from you.[76]

On January 7, 1789, the *Asia's* comprador entertained the crew with a small display of fireworks calculated "to awaken the gods to the vessel's departure and given her good wind and good water."[77] The next day, Barry and Truxton made their farewells at the factories, having received their departure pass–"the Grand Chop"–from the Hoppo.[78] At Macao, each ship dropped off their comprador. Getting to Macao took longer on this return trip, thanks to a final visit by the mandarins, who painstakingly reviewed all papers and duty receipts.[79]

Once they got there, Macao had plenty of activities for the American sailors: gambling, dancing, prostitutes, and opium.[80] The martial law atmosphere of the outskirts of Canton was nowhere to be seen. Macao officials were much more susceptible to being paid off for any show of illegality.[81] Ironically, the only evidence that indicates that Barry awarded his sailors shore leave in Macao is found in the last entry of Patrick Hayes's journal. After arrival in Canton, he dropped the detailed account of his adventures. All that remains is a transcription of the *Second Song of Solomon*, followed by an entry on January 16, 1789–*"Maddam: full of shame–"* and we will never know why.[82]

Neither Barry nor Truxton partook in another practice in the China trade—smuggling opium—although Philadelphia merchants like Stephen Girard would soon deal heavily in it. "We sail for Macao Roads the 12th Instant," was all Barry said of their layover.[83]

The *Asia* and *Canton* came safely through the South China Sea and back to the devilish Sunda Straits, where they anchored near an island and "filled their casks with water." News that two large Indiamen were recently captured by pirates only reinforced the two captains' decision to sail together—which was proving to be more of a task for Barry than originally thought. "The *Canton* Sails much faster than the *Asia*," Barry wrote to his owners, advising them "not to be uneasy for there is that difference in the Sailing of both Ships, and remainder of the passage has no more Danger than the Common Occurrences of a Voyage at Sea." He believed the *Canton* would "arrive fifteen or twenty days before us," even though he would do his utmost to sail the crank *Asia* as fast as possible. Still, "How long we shall be in Sight of each other, I do not pretend to say."[84]

Despite her "cranky condition," Barry remarkably kept the *Asia* in sight of Truxton's *Canton*: through the Sunda Straits, around Java Head, down the long run to St. Paul's, into the storms between that rocky island and the Cape of Good Hope, and back to Cape Town, where they watered again. Both ships departed Cape Town on March 21. Two days later a terrific storm caught them both, buffeting the two merchantmen throughout the day. When the sun returned, neither captain saw any sign of the other across the horizon.[85]

Once again Barry put his sailing skills to the test, sending the *Asia* through the Tropic of Capricorn, passing the equator to the Cape Verde Islands. From there he sent the *Asia* across the Atlantic "W by N," and up the American coastline to the Delaware Capes, reaching them June 3. The next day, Philadelphia newspapers announced the arrival of "the ship *Asia*, Captain John Barry, in five months and twenty days from Canton in China." It had been eighteen months since he was home; by far his longest absence. The voyages had also been the most idyllic of his career; Barry told anyone and everyone that "there had never been one dispute or angry word on board his vessel."[86]

He and Patrick wasted no time in getting mounted and riding to Strawberry Hill for a happy reunion with Sarah and family–but his joy at seeing Sarah was muted by the fact that the *Asia* actually beat the faster *Canton* home. Barry thought of Truxton's letters, locked in his sea chest, but kept his concern to himself. He decided to wait at least another day before visiting Mary Truxton, and setting her and Truxton's young children to worrying.[87] To Barry's great joy, the *Canton* came up the Delaware the next morning. The two ships had reached Philadelphia within a day of each other. Neither captain would sail for China again.

James Josiah and John Sword both did. Josiah left six months later as captain of the ship *Brothers*. On Sword's return voyage to China, he brought along a portrait of George Washington purchased from the artist, Gilbert Stuart. While in Canton, Sword had more than one hundred glass copies made of the painting, which he began selling once he returned to Philadelphia. Upon hearing this, an enraged Stuart swore out an injunction against Sword, barring the sale of the bootlegged copies of Stuart's artwork.[88] This may be the first instance of cheaper Chinese labor being used to pirate an American artist's work.

CHAPTER EIGHTEEN

FIRST AMONG CAPTAINS

*A*FTER BARRY AND PATRICK REGALED SARAH and family with their adventures she brought them up to date on what they had missed the last eighteen months. William Austin was back in England.[1] Isaac awaited the final decision regarding ownership of the Arch Street Ferry while running his watch-making business.[2] That spring, Sarah's niece, Betsy Keen, became seriously ill, warranting visits from Benjamin Rush.[3] When Rush had an opportunty to visit, he peppered Barry with questions about his trip, and the captain went into great detail about it. Barry's emotional recounting of the inhuman conditions of the poorest Chinese shocked Rush; years after Barry's death, the doctor could still recall Barry's vivid descriptions.[4]

The *Asia*'s return was front page news, and Barry's exotic cargo of "best Imperial Soo Long TEAS . . . Black and fashionable colored lutestrings, satins, dark brown and silver gray damasks, colored sewing silks" and "sets of very elegant TEA China" sold briskly and at great profit.[5] Although pleased with Barry's stunning success, the *Asia*'s owners were divided about her future. Not everyone remained enthusiastic about the China trade. New ventures beckoned, partic-ularly land speculation on the Ohio frontier, which offered quicker returns with less risk.[6] After weeks of wrangling, they decided to sell the *Asia*–but not before handing Barry his share of the voyage's profits. After years of chasing Congress for back pay, this prompt reward for his odyssey was truly wondrous: with this one voyage, Barry restored a great deal of his personal fortune.[7] When two of the *Asia*'s owners bought another ship and asked Barry to take her to Canton, he declined; at a later meeting of merchants and captains, he reasserted in no uncertain terms that he was not interested in returning to the Orient.[8]

Much had changed in his absence: the investigation into his role in the McCalmont affair had been dropped, the Constitution had been ratified, the federal government had moved to New York, and Washington had been elected president. Barry wrote him a congratulatory note mentioning both his successful voyage and what American ships were in Canton. The president replied, thanking Barry for his "polite mark of attention."[9]

For the first time in his life, Barry did something he had never done before: relax. With this sudden end to his money woes, he was content to assume a life of rural gentility. He set out to make Strawberry Hill every bit the captain's rest it could be, ordering new furnishings from England and buying a Douay Bible for six dollars from a New York publisher.[10] For his new carriage he purchased a pair of horses whose spirit appealed to him. His ownership of them was short; their eagerness for speed terrified Sarah. As "Mrs. Barry is so timid," he was forced to exchange them for a more docile team.[11]

He resumed his activities with the "Sea Captains Club" and the Hibernian Fire Company, dining frequently with the other members at the City Tavern or Isaac Warren's Fish House.[12] He was elected to the Hibernian Society for the Relief of Emigrants from Ireland, yet another charitable organization.[13] He began investing his restored fortune–but not in Morris's land speculation. He stayed in the business he knew best, purchasing shares in various ships and their goods with captains and owners he trusted.[14] He was determined to never, ever, be poor again.

If Barry swallowed the anchor, he encouraged the budding careers of his nephews. Michael remained with Rossiter on the *Rising Sun*, while Patrick embarked on a series of voyages free from his uncle's watchful eye. Romance was also blooming at Strawberry Hill. Betsy Keen and Patrick Hayes became inseparable, despite Betsy's being older than Patrick by six years. Although Michael was at sea and William Austin an ocean away in London, everyone else was home, and the Barrys enjoyed the merriest of Christmases in 1789.

The harsh winter of 1790 brought more visits from Dr. Rush.[15] Patrick returned to sea, while Betsy remained at Strawberry Hill. Along the riverfront of Barry's estate, the bare winter trees gave him an unobstructed view of Petty's Island, where there was a new, forlorn arrival that would remain there for over a century.

The *Alliance* was older than her years. That she could sail to China and back after her disastrous accident in 1783 was testament to the repairs made by Humphreys and Eyre.[16] In 1789, Morris loaded her with flour and sent her to Cadiz. She returned in such terrible condition that Morris found it cheaper to condemn the *Alliance* than make repairs, and had her "broken up for her copper and iron."[17] Dockhands stripped her of her copper sheathing; if a bolt connecting her ironwork could not be removed, the piece was merely taken with the plank attached to it. Any piece of her worth a single penny was ripped and hauled away. Once everything of value had been taken, a few hands sailed the hulk upriver to the north end of Petty's Island. Coming about hard, they ran her aground, a great crack coming from her hull and keel. After making sure she had been foundered so fiercely that no tide could free her to turn derelict, they manned her remaining longboat and abandoned her, not far from where other Continental ships were burned in 1777.[18] Time and the elements soon erased any semblance of her having once been the navy's finest frigate.

From Strawberry Hill, Barry watched the transformation. One daughter of an *Alliance* officer wrote, "Many a brave fellow, looking at the wreck muttered to himself, 'perhaps that will be Jack's fate one of these days.'"[19] "Jack" might have found it sad or even insulting to see what had become of his beloved frigate, but he was not ready to be cast aside yet. As storms broke the *Alliance* apart, Barry contemplated a return to battle with Congress for compensation for service in the war. Rather than present individual or tandem memorials, he decided to make this an all-out offensive, rallying Read, Murray, the Nicholsons, and even John Green to his banner. "I think the best Method we could fall upon would be to collect as many Officers as posable in New York and appoint a Committee to draw up a Petition and Present it," he told James Nicholson on March 6.[20] Naval officers flocked to his call, holding their rendezvous in New York later that month. A petition "from Capt. Barry and others for commutation" was read on a slow day of Senate business on March 26. Their appeal for similar "emoluments that were granted to the Officers of the late Continental Army may be extended to them" was tabled, and they vowed to meet again in May and make a concerted effort to win over enough votes for passage beforehand.[21]

When Barry, Murray, and Green returned to Philadelphia they discovered the city on the brink of mourning. Franklin was bedridden with pleurisy, fever and a wracking cough, for which Rush prescribed doses of opium.[22] He died on April 17 at age 84. Twenty thousand Philadelphians crowded the streets near Christ Church for his funeral. In Congress, Madison proposed a month of mourning, as did Charles Carroll in the Senate. Madison's motion passed unanimously, while Carroll's found such strong opposition that he withdrew it.[23] Jefferson, knowing that France would (and did) go into a ceremonial acknowledgment of mourning Franklin's passing, asked if "the Executive Department should wear mourning." Washington said no. To the president, such recognition smacked of old world royalty.[24] Franklin would have agreed.

In May, Barry led the navy captains in a second appeal to Congress. Surprisingly, some influential congressmen were agreeable to their petition, offering to establish a committee, review their case, and make a quick recommendation to Congress. Finally, it looked like the old salts might win their battle, and they celebrated with a grand dinner.[25] But their success was fleeting. Weeks later, when the "Committee on Memorial of the Officers of the Navy" informed their peers in Congress "that they do not find any reason sufficient to justify the difference" regarding the disparity in compensation, the more financially conservative congressmen protested vigorously. "Luke warm friends" soon abandoned the fight, and the committee's recommendation died.[26] "There is an end to the business," Nicholson sulked. Barry agreed, and let it go.[27]

Congress soon followed Barry back to Philadelphia, once more the temporary capital until a permanent one was built along the Potomac River.[28] By midsummer Barry was immersed in his improvements on Strawberry Hill. When another overture was made about Canton, his answer was unequivocal: he would "never Adventure again to the Indias."[29] The fall goldenrod, plentiful on the grounds around his home, triggered another consuming battle with asthma, and Rush made more "visits to the country" to care for his friend.[30]

While recovering, Barry heard that his Rhode Island friend John Francis had built a new Indiaman for a voyage to the Orient. The long months away, the dangerous storms, and the unnatural living arrangements of a mariner's life were weighed in his mind against the opportunity to return to what he was born for—command at sea. Just weeks after his emphatic refusal, he rushed a letter to Francis, declaring his availability and interest.[31]

To Sarah's relief, the offer was declined: Barry's "favor from Strawberry Hill did not reach Providence" until after the captaincy had been accepted by a New Englander. "Had I not been positively informed . . . that you are resolutely determined not to return to that part of the world," Francis empathized, "I should have most certainly made you the offer . . . It would have given me great pleasure to have appointed you to the Command of so fine a Vessel."[32] Whether Barry was bemused or disappointed, he returned to the beautification of Strawberry Hill, asking Congressman James Jackson to send him seedlings from his Georgia plantation, and asking William Austin to purchase an Axminster "Carpet for our best room."[33]

For Barry, Congress' return to Philadelphia meant more friends for company. He still avoided any political affiliation. While he had worked his way up the social ladder by dint of his sailing skills and courage, he was not at home in either of the partisan camps. He certainly had friends among the Federalists, Morris and Fitzsimons chief among them. He was a proud member of the Society of the Cincinnati—practically Federalist to a man. But his Irish roots kept him from joining a party so pro-British in their sympathies. And, while he counted ardent Republicans like Rush and Jackson as friends, their support for all things French ran contrary to his experiences with the likes of de Galatheau, Landais, and the L'Orient bureaucrats. No political faction could claim him. After all, Washington did not belong to a political party. Barry remained an outsider, politically independent and proud of it.[34]

Yet another Christmas was spent at Strawberry Hill minus Patrick, away on a voyage to Cuba.[35] By now Barry was becoming a regular patient of Benjamin Rush. The good doctor believed that most asthma attacks came "in the spring and autumn oftener than in the summer and winter," but the winter of 1790-91 included several "visits in the Country" to his patient.[36] Rush was experimenting with his remedies, and Barry was treated with "laudanum . . . mustard (treatments) to the feet," and bleeding.[37]

It was in these years that Barry's physical appearance noticeably changed. The tall figure, while never thin, had always been trim: he was hard, lean, and muscular throughout his thirties, with a life spent constantly on his feet. Now consumption of the rich foods of the City Tavern and Fish House, combined with the country squire's life, began to result in the country squire's build. Although his length belied his breadth—he was too tall to ever look fat—he was noticeably larger, adding to his already formidable presence.[38]

For the next two years, although not striding a quarterdeck himself, the sea came to him, in visits, letters, and business investments. Shipmasters paid him courtesy calls or sent letters about their latest voyages and the ports of call they visited. Stephen Decatur, Sr., had joined the merchant ranks, his growing financial success a necessity thanks to his burgeoning family.[39] Truxton visited Barry after a voyage to India, telling of a meeting with India's governor general, the charming Lord Cornwallis.[40] Rossiter, with Michael Hayes in tow, paid his respects before embarking for China, giving Barry opportunity to send his own shopping list, including "Eight pair of good Nankeen Brushes . . . one black Sattin Vest . . . a caddy of Hyson Tea . . . Three Doz. Cups and . . . Saucers of Blue and White Nankeen China" for which he gave Rossiter "forty Dollars."[41] Shades of Mrs. Hazelhurst.

He was open-minded in assisting other mariners, if not always willing. David Porter, one of the *Raleigh*'s officers, requested assistance in obtaining the port surveyor's position in Baltimore. A "letter to the President" from Barry would seal the deal for Porter, as Barry's "intercession alone would best Thirty or Forty Signatures to a recommendation."[42] Barry, unimpressed with Porter for some reason, did not intervene. He happily wrote a recommendation on Seth Harding's behalf about the sailor's "coming aboard the Frigate *Alliance*" and of his "conduct at the time we engaged one of the three British frigates."[43]

No visitor was more welcome at Barry's door than Richard Dale. After the *Alliance*'s demise, he made several voyages to Canton as master of the merchantman *Pigou*.[44] Whenever Dale visited Philadelphia he stayed at Strawberry Hill, where he met and fell in love with Mary Crawthorne's younger sister, Dorothy. In September 1791 Bishop White married them at Isaac Austin's house, with Barry and Sarah present. Yet another sailor joined the family.[45] It was a pleasant summer in Philadelphia, and Barry enjoyed his social obligations with the Hibernian Fire Company, the "Sea Captain's Club," and, most especially, his time with Sarah and their young relations. "Everyday we get more and more attached to Strawberry Hill," he happily wrote.[46]

By 1792, Philadelphia was shaking off the postwar depression of the 1780s; construction of the Lancaster Turnpike was as much a reflection of speculation as it was a harbinger of westward expansion. New houses–palaces in reality–reflected the opulent wealth of their owners. Washington settled into "the President's Mansion," where weekly state dinners–held every Thursday, at four o'clock sharp–were as well known for what Senator William MacLay called "dead silence almost" as for the excellent food.[47]

Letters from family, friends, and strangers constantly arrived at Strawberry Hill. Pleas from Margaret Howlin and other relatives were always answered with financial assistance. In 1792, Barry received a lengthy letter from James Corish, who had sat with Barry in that small, damp schoolroom in Wexford forty years before. Corish and his wife were in New York, looking to resettle in the

Mohawk Valley, and soliciting Barry's advice about their planned purchase. Barry, taking "great Pleasure to hear from an old Schoolfellow," was happy to oblige, as bluntly as ever:

> I am much at a loss to know whether you have a Family or not and what your Views can be to buy land on the Mohawk River[;] for a man of your Years to bury your self in the woods unacquainted I presume with cutting down trees or building logg houses far removed from anyplace to educate your children if you have any . . . if you can make it convenient to spend a few weeks with me at Strawberry Hill within three miles of PHILa . . . Mrs. Barry requests me to give her compliments to Mrs. Corish . . . and begs her to accompany you . . . *you cannot refuse my request as you will have a good dale of time on your hands this winter.*

He closed telling Corish that, while the weather in the summer months was similar between New York and Pennsylvania, the winters along the Mohawk were more severe; in that regard, "I find the People of N.Y. have all ready deceived you."[48]

Paradoxically, his favorite correspondent was William Austin. Throughout the years, he addressed only one salutation to the old loyalist: "Brother." In his letters home, William frequently complained of being treated as a disowned pariah–but never to Barry, who he knew resolutely stood up to the Austins as his champion. Over time they sent each other goods to be sold; in one letter Barry requested some books, coupled with his suggestion as to how to ship them: "You might send us a few of the best and newest Maga[zines] to pass away the long Winters. Thereby you will oblige me to send me *Tom Jones*[,] *Sir Charles Grandisson* and *Clovis Harlow*. I think the Phila Capts would put them in their chests for me and deliver them without bills of Laden."[49]

Out of the blue, a letter from James Seagrove arrived. Now living in Savannah, Seagrove had traded destitution for being land poor. After escaping his Cuban creditors and spending some time in New York's debtor's prison, Seagrove somehow made enough business deals to own "a quality of the best Land in Georgia, suitable for Rice,

Indigo, Cotton" as well as "Live Oak and other valuable Timber Lands, all on Navigable Rivers in this State." He now offered both Barry and the equally patient John Brown "any part of which is at your service if it suits you, in discharge of your deed against me." Barry and Brown declined the offer. They wanted their money.[50]

Throughout these two years Barry gave the impression of being at home on dry land, satisfied with life as never before, almost welcoming the end to his sailing days. "I have retired to a handsome competency," he wrote a friend, and one can almost see the trace of a smile on his face.[51] Barry genuinely loved his adopted land: When another Irish-born mariner expressed a desire to return to Ireland, Barry was puzzled; after all, he wrote, "There is every thing that the heart could wish for here."[52]

Across the Atlantic, life was not as kind to the Revolution's other naval hero. After the war ended, John Paul Jones lusted for another chance at glory. When the Dey of Algiers seized the *Dolphin* and *Betsy,* Jones desperately wanted a crack at bringing retribution to the shores of Tripoli. Instead, he found himself in Catherine the Great's navy. Dreams of new honors were lost to shame and scandal. The hierarchy of the Russian Navy used his plans without giving him credit, and when his prima donna tendencies became too overbearing, he was declared "Kontraband," accused of raping a ten-year-old girl.[53]

After a year of roaming Europe, Jones returned to Paris, shunned by Lafayette and the very French dignitaries who once fought for his company. He walked the streets "in faded naval uniform like the wine skin from which the wine is drawn, the ghost of himself!" America's Minister to Paris, Gouverneur Morris, dreaded his visits: "Paul Jones calls and gives me his time but I cannot lend him mine," he acidly commented. Morris finally visited Jones when he received "A message from Paul Jones that he is dying. I go thither and make his will." After dinner with his family and a visit to his mistress, Morris returned to Jones's chambers to find him dead in a kneeling position by his bed, his jaundiced, swollen body quite cold.[54]

Morris sold all of Jones's personal effects except the Chevalier's sword, sending it to Robert Morris. Wrapped in a winding sheet,

Jones was interred in a Protestant cemetery, soon joined by the Swiss Guards murdered at the Royal Palace while protecting Louis XVI and Marie Antoinette. One month later, orders arrived from Washington, naming Jones "Commissioner with full powers to negotiate with the Dey of Algiers for the ransom of American citizens in captivity"–the very assignment Jones had longed for.[55]

In America, Barry busied himself finding housing for newly arrived Irish immigrants, in one case personally providing a "Small Tenement" for "a poor reduced Irish Family" fresh off the docks.[56] He also received a very unusual gift from Robert Berry, back in China. Through a mutual friend, Peter Hodgkinson, Berry sent Barry "a Malabar boy, he is a fine fellow." Hodgkinson was happy "to send him on if you Please or bring him with me, when I next leave New York."[57] The youngster, whom Barry named James, became one more resident of Strawberry Hill listed in the recently completed first Census of the United States. The head count for the Barry estate was four whites and two blacks, or, in constitutional accounting, five and one-fifth persons.[58]

For all of the peace and tranquility Barry and his family enjoyed since his return from Canton, 1793 would test his ability to keep the outside world's troubles from Strawberry Hill. It was a year of political and social tumult, as European affairs and Caribbean diseases both landed in Philadelphia. For a long time it seemed that they would never leave.

The French Revolution was prying the factions in Washington's cabinet led by Secretary of State Jefferson and Secretary of Treasury Hamilton further and further apart, leaving Washington in the middle, often by himself. England and Spain declared war on France, the start of hostilities that would run into three decades. While Federalists raged at the Reign of Terror, and Republicans drank to "Liberté, Égalité, Fraternité," others like Washington and Barry were distressed to learn that France had swung from the tyranny of a king to the tyranny of the mob. It saddened them to learn that the Duc de La Rochefoucauld, the first to translate the Declaration of Independence into French and a friend to America from the beginning, had been stoned to death in front of his wife and mother. News of the beheading of the king and queen drove a further wedge into the government Washington was trying to hold together. Shortly after his brief second inaugural on March 4, he issued a Proclamation of Neutrality, guaranteeing unending partisan attacks on his leadership, character, and even manhood.[59]

In April, France's new emissary arrived in Charleston, South Carolina. Edmond Charles Genet had been an aspiring commoner at the court of Louis XVI, worming his way into a series of diplomatic assignments. Possessed of charm but utterly devoid of discretion, he was frequently recalled from his posts. With the new French government lacking experienced statesmen due to Madame Guillotine, Edmund Genet was offered the plum post in America. As Citizen Genet, he could not—and would not—refuse. He was rapturously received everywhere; Jacobin clubs sprouted wherever he laid his cockade. At each seaport, this short, florid man, whose nose was long enough for two ambassadors, spread the gospel of the French Revolution by day and an endless supply of money at night, inciting sea captains to join the French cause as privateers against British shipping.[60]

As if in anticipation of his arrival, a French frigate, l'Embuscade, pursued a British ship, the Grange, into the Delaware Bay. Once captured, the French sailed her upriver to Philadelphia where, "upon her coming sight, thousands and thousands of the yeomanry of the city crowded and combed the wharves." The British vessel's reversed flag brought "peals of exultation" from the crowd.[61] When Genet reached Philadelphia, a similar crowd escorted him to Oeller's Hotel, where a banquet in his honor was hosted by Barry's friend, Charles Biddle. The highlight of the affair was a series of symbolic toasts and responses. Someone stood and made a toast; then, at a signal from the window, a battery of cannon, placed just outside the hotel, fired a salute. Toast and fire; toast and fire.[62]

Biddle joined Jefferson in falling under Genet's spell, but Barry did not. He saw no reason to change his spots because of popular sentiment, and kept to Strawberry Hill. At "the celebration of the fourth of July with the Society of Cincinnati," Genet's behavior became *trés gauche*. Among the society's members in town was Lafayette's cousin and Barry's old passenger, the Comte de Noailles. Seeing the count at his table, Genet declined an invitation to sit; when pressed, he disdainfully "mentioned he could not sit down at the table" with an "Aristo." This only added to Barry's distaste for Genet.[63]

The dinner marked the beginning of the end of Genet's popularity. The more news that came from France about the atrocities of the Reign of Terror, the less Genet looked like an avenging angel and more a mouthpiece for violence and anarchy. Even Jefferson, his most ardent supporter, began distancing himself. The crowds were no longer at fever pitch. Soon there were no longer crowds: a real fever had arrived in Philadelphia.

By August, yellow fever was rampant throughout the city, striking down residents regardless of status. Rush and his colleagues tried to determine its source, never suspecting the mosquitoes. One doctor correctly suspected a ship from San Domingo–but not those bearing refugees from Toussaint L'Ouverture's revolt. Instead, he laid the blame on spoiled coffee bales of the *Amelia,* lately arrived from San Domingo.[64] To purge the air, the same cannons used to salute Genet were fired from dawn to dusk. Rush also believed that blacks were immune to yellow fever. Under the heroic leadership of two African American ministers, Richard Allen and Absalom Jones, black Philadelphians began the enormous task of saving white Philadelphians.[65] Black men worked as "Carters," filling their drays with the bodies of the white dead and carrying them off to new burial grounds, for the church cemeteries were full. Black women were quickly employed as nurses by white families who could afford such care.[66]

Rush made two visits to Strawberry Hill, charging one of his highest fees–£15–on each occasion. The patient was Barry himself, no stranger to seeing outbreaks of "Yellow Jack" in the West Indies.[67] Barry survived, despite his friend's ministrations: long a disciple of purges and bleeding, Rush now pursued these measures to dangerous levels. Rush ordered Barry to avoid coming to town, and to keep handkerchiefs dipped in vinegar or camphor nearby to ward off the feverish air. Barry also lit gunpowder, believing it a life-saving air freshener. Rush advised "all the families I now attend, that can move, to quit the city." Truxton fled with his family to Perth Amboy, New Jersey. Biddle remained in Philadelphia, where "the streets were almost deserted. I have stood at my door at noon," he wrote, "and looking up and down the street for sometime, could not see one person on it."[68]

By mid-September, calling Philadelphia a "ghost town" had more than its share of macabre connotations. Half of the population had fled, including the nation's leaders. Washington, knowing his continued presence provided one of the few signs of stability, stayed until fears for Martha's health compelled him to take his entourage to Mount Vernon. The Hamiltons were stricken; luckily, an old friend from Nevis, Dr. Edward Stevens, was in town.[69] Stevens administered large doses of "Peruvian bark"–quinine–along with a regimen of cold baths, brandy laced with burnt cinnamon, and a nightcap of laudanum. The Hamiltons survived. Stevens viewed Rush's treatments as medieval, while Rush scorned Stevens' more natural remedies. In a city rent by political factions, now even medicine was politicized. French and Caribbean-born physicians sided with Stevens. Rush found the slights to his reputation contemptuous, and went right on bleeding.[70] Soon so much blood had been poured into his backyard that he indirectly began to breed countless flies, and his property gave off a "sickening sweet stench."[71]

"Being myself used to seeing people in fever in the West Indies," Biddle "did not feel that uneasiness many of my friends did." He was however, shocked at how the Yellow Jack affected even the bravest of his friends, who succumbed to either fear of the disease or fear for their families–one in particular: "Some who were thought to be afraid of nothing were much terrified at this disorder, among others an old friend of mine, Commodore Barry, an officer of distinguished bravery, returned to his country seat, and would suffer no person from the city to come near his home."[72]

Barry obeyed Rush's orders; when provisions were needed at Strawberry Hill, he sent James into town. Not until the first frost, on

October 28, did the city begin to emerge from the deadly siege. Rush himself was taken ill, but recovered; there is no record as to how much he was bled. By then, Washington and some congressmen had returned–to Germantown, not Philadelphia. Once again, it was Washington who restored a sense of security. After a severe frost, despite the concerns and protests of his staff, the president rode into Philadelphia alone on Sunday, November 10, under clear skies with a cool breeze. Nodding his head to the few Philadelphians that stepped outside, Washington's very presence signaled the end of the long ordeal.[73]

By the end of 1793, old and new foreign affairs replaced the epidemic in the newspapers. Citizen Genet finally wore out his welcome when a French-captured British brigantine, the *Little Sarah*, sailed into Philadelphia, was refitted with cannon and an American crew, and renamed *la Petite Democrate*: a flagrant violation of US law. She went to sea just as the epidemic swept the city. The privateer sailed far enough off the coast that only a frigate could have overtaken her– a perfect assignment for the old *Alliance*. Genet was recalled. A return to France meant the guillotine. The magnanimous Washington granted him asylum. Genet married New York Governor Clinton's daughter and remained in the United States until he died.[74]

After years of bickering, both Jefferson and Hamilton anticipated and hoped that the other would quit Washington's cabinet. Jefferson blinked first, resigning on New Year's Eve. In France, the Reign of Terror was eating its own: Marat, Danton, and Robespierre were dead, and Americans sorrowfully learned that members of Lafayette's family were also executed.[75] The war pitting France against England, Spain, and Holland continued. At its onset, the French opened her West Indies ports for trade, and American merchants sent an endless supply of ships southward. Under Washington's policy of neutrality, the immediate resumption of trade provided a shot in the arm for both countries economically–a fact not lost on Great Britain, which responded with two Orders of

Council referring to the Rule of 1756, whereby England would not trade with neutral nations who were also trading with the enemy: if trade is illegal in peace, it is still illegal in time of war. The "Orders" empowered British ships to seize any American vessels whose holds carried French goods—and tacitly allowed pressing American sailors into the Royal Navy as well. British captains gave American sailors a choice: service in the King's Navy or death in the prison ships they kept in the Caribbean—descendants of the dreaded *Jersey*.[76]

This strident change in policy struck Strawberry Hill. To Barry's delight, Patrick Hayes's career had as meteoric a rise as his own; by 1793, Patrick was master of the brig *Florida*. Off Nassau, he was captured by a British warship and his "valuable Cargo" seized as "Contraband of War." Eventually, Hayes and his men were released and returned to their ship. With ballast instead of goods in the *Florida's* hold, Hayes sailed homeward.[77]

More bad news reached American ports. After long serving as mediator between Portugal and Algiers, British diplomatic efforts bore fruit. Portugal and Algiers signed a truce, lifting the Portuguese blockade, thereby freeing the Dey's Corsairs to prey again on ships in the Mediterranean and Atlantic. By the time Congress returned to Philadelphia in December to begin their third session, eleven American ships had been captured by Barbary pirates and their crews imprisoned. Washington's former aide David Humphreys took the commissioner's position intended for John Paul Jones. Humphreys soon urged Washington that "a naval force has now (to a certain degree) become indispensable."[78]

Washington's neutrality policy was being hammered by both Britain and France. While Genet's machinations tried his patience, Great Britain's Orders of Council openly provoked it. Jefferson's Republicans, having captured both houses in the last election, guaranteed Washington an even rockier course to steer. By March 1794, over 250 American ships were in British hands. The dey would have a hard time catching up to that number, but not for lack of effort. Firsthand reports from the captured Americans in Algiers were published; their tales of being "stript of all our Cloaths" and "put into Chains and put to hard Labour" inflamed the public. "It's not possible," bemoaned one captured officer, "to Live long in this situation."[79]

The weather turned cold and rainy in December. On Petty's Island, waves buffeted the *Alliance*. The wind and rain howled around Strawberry Hill as the Barrys and their adopted brood shared the escapades of the *Plays of the Carmelites* and *Peeping Tom*. In Philadelphia, Washington's annual message to Congress (the precursor to a State of the Union address) warned that "if we desire to avoid insult, it must be known that we are at all times ready for war."[80] Abroad, no one considered the United States a serious threat. It was obvious, even to some Republicans, that there was only one way to get their attention: create a navy.

Shortly after Washington's report, naval advocate Thomas Fitzsimons rode to Strawberry Hill, seeking Barry's input and advice. Fitzsimons and his allies wanted as much information on projected costs, construction ideas, and the time estimated to build and man whatever ships Congress might approve. Regarding manpower and organization, Barry was a logical source for ideas; for design and construction, there was another Philadelphian anxiously awaiting this day, Barry's friend Joshua Humphreys.

Humphreys was a contradiction—a Quaker with a genius for building ships of war. Six years younger than Barry, he was apprenticed at fourteen to the shipbuilder Jonathan Penrose. In addition to his successes with Barry in orchestrating the first Continental fleet, he had built one of the barge-galley prototypes that defended Philadelphia during the British invasion.[81] His most noteworthy advancement in naval construction was the Continental frigate *Randolph*, longer and faster than her British counterparts. Humphreys's reward for his services was double-edged: by 1783, he was considered the finest shipbuilder in the country, but disowned by the Society of Friends for building ships of war.[82]

Like Barry, Humphreys's career was inextricably connected to Robert Morris, who had been waiting ten years for Congress to recognize the need for a navy. One year earlier, Humphreys boldly and enthusiastically described to Morris the ship he would build if given the chance, condensing years of contemplation into four paragraphs, each sentence reflective of his genius. "I believe it is time this Country was possessed of a Navy," he wrote, "but as it is yet to be raised, I have ventured a few ideas on the subject."[83]

He first dismantled the need for ships-of-the-line: "the situations and depths of Water of our coasts and Harbours" made the larger drafts of these sailing giants as impractical for their size as their cost. Combining geography with economics, he envisaged what a divided Congress could afford, "As our navy must for a considerable time be inferior in number." His solution proved to be the starting point and saving grace of America's navy for years to come: he would build a bigger and better frigate, able to carry heavier and deadlier fire power–"28, 32-pounders or 30, 24-pounders on the main gundeck & 12-pounders on the quarterdeck." Humphreys wanted the frigates built with "Red cedar & Live Oak"–the best wood available. As America could not afford a fleet, Humphreys would provide his country with the largest, fastest, and most durable and powerful frigates in the world. Looking down the roadstead, Humphreys saw his country's nautical future, as if Neptune read Nostradamus: "If we should be . . . dragged into a War with any powers of the old continent, especially Great Britain . . . whether one large or two small Frigates contribute most to the protection of our trade . . . the large ones will answer best."[84]

Morris shared Humphreys's letter with Fitzsimons, who busily gathered every scrap of information his committee could use to support Humphreys's recommendations. Fitzsimons, a savvy politician, knew that there were more than enough Republicans who would still find an American navy "the maddest idea in the world." He was right: the vote in Congress to approve even this baby step was 46 to 44.[85]

Washington put the project in the hands of Henry Knox. The rotund former bookseller, artilleryman, and now Secretary of War had only one brief major bit of naval experience–freighting cannons over rivers during the Revolution. Throughout the winter months, Knox met at length with Barry and Humphreys, soliciting their thoughts and recommendations. Knox also sought out Humphreys's cousin, John Wharton, and John Hackett, builder of Barry's beloved *Alliance*. Each man gave Knox a plethora of ideas and plans that he relayed to Washington. Naval historian Howard Chappelle wrote that the landsman Knox "was in the position of a non-musician who was required to buy a piano; it seemed to him that the advice of men who could play the instrument would be the most necessary aid to make the correct choice."[86]

Barry, Humphreys, and Wharton took turns bending Knox's ear; when they held the floor, the old general kept still and listened intently. When he spoke, he went through a unique habit. Since the Battle of Monmouth, he had wrapped his left hand–mutilated that day on the field–with a handkerchief. As he talked, the right hand began unwinding the handkerchief, almost to the point of revealing the gruesome damage done by British shot. Then, he wound the handkerchief back around his remaining fingers, his ritual as second nature to him as breathing.[87]

By January 20, 1794, Fitzsimons's bipartisan committee presented their report, recommending construction of four forty-four-gun and two twenty-four-gun frigates. With the low estimate of $600,000 to build the ships and a $250,000 annual supporting cost, they finished their presentation, and the battle for the navy began.[88] For two months the debate raged, both sides eminently sure of their righteousness. The fight was going the Republicans' way when, in March, Washington informed Congress about further depredations by the Algerians. Merchants up and down the coastline demanded protection of American ships by an American navy.[89] Government bonds were sinking as American businessmen saw their safe European trade being decimated by the Barbary terrorists.

Finally, after nearly two months of broadsides across the aisles of Congress, a vote on the naval bill was called. A Republican measure to recommit the bill, which would surely have killed it, failed. The bill passed by a vote of 50 to 39. Republicans insisted on and received an escape clause: ship construction would be suspended if and when peaceful relations were restored with the Algerians.[90] Watered down as it was, the act was both a baby step and a giant step for the young nation. America was preparing to defend itself.

Humphreys presented Congress with designs for his frigates. It would be nearly three months before his official appointment, but he already had put his imagination to paper and wood. By April he had a half-model for Knox to admire. When built, the frigates would have a 147-foot keel, 43-foot beam, 14-foot hold, 6 feet between decks, 7= feet between waists, with thirty guns on the main deck. Humphreys's prototype was exactly what he described to Morris a year earlier–a bigger, faster, and stronger frigate than was yet seen on the seas.[91]

Much to Sarah's dismay (and, perhaps, consternation), Barry followed the debate with more than passing interest. He enjoyed his self-imposed retirement, but the very thought of a new navy going to sea without him was just too much to bear. Truth be told, his life of leisure, peaceful as it was, had become too peaceful. Barry was bored. The call of the sea was compelling enough, but the call of a new navy was irresistible. On March 19, he wrote his once and future commander-in-chief:

> Sir–Finding the Government have partly determined to fit out some Ships of War for the protection of our Trade against the Algerines I beg leave to offer my self for the Command of the Squadron concerning my self confident there to assuring your Excellency that should I be honored with your probation, my utmost abilities and the most unremitting attention to be exerted for the good of my Country, and also to approve myself Worthy of the highest honor shown by your Excellency.[92]

Hearing of Barry's involvement, other Continental captains wasted no time writing him (and anyone else they thought may have sway) about wearing their country's uniform again. Some letters went right to the issue. Samuel Nicholson, whose blasé conduct in 1782 almost resulted in Barry recommending a court of inquiry, began sending Barry letters in January, "reminding" him of Nicholson's commission, signed by "John Hancock on tenth December 1776," and presented to him by Franklin and Deane in Paris. In truth, Nicholson feared being forgotten, and hoped his rank on the old captains' list would still be in effect.[93] David Porter wrote, again requesting Barry's assistance, but Barry's silence was deafening.[94] Other appeals poured in. "I am your old Friend," began a plea from John Hopkins, stripped of his commission early in the

Revolution.[95] Hoystead Hacker bypassed Barry, turning instead to his good friend, Congressman Silas Talbot. Hacker believed his old comrade would surely plead his case, unaware that Talbot was actively championing himself.[96]

With Jones dead, no other captain rivaled Barry in deed or reputation. Washington and Knox sought his assistance in reviewing the countless applications, hoping to come up with a list of six captains. Washington's determination to get the navy on good footing required some degree of compromise on the names–political clout in Congress still mattered–but Barry admired Washington's ability to accommodate those with influence, as long as he believed they would be solid choices. "From the first," Barry wrote, the president "was determined to come as near to Justice as was in his power" to make the right appointments.[97] For the next two months, the search committee of Washington, Knox, and Barry continued their deliberations.

With spring came a long letter from yet another Wexford relative of Barry's: Anstis Doyle, the very cousin Aunt Margaret gave birth to while Barry's mother was bringing him into the world. "I have Been Married to a James Doyle no Better Man Could be as long as Health Permitted," she wrote. Now, he was deathly ill, and the Doyles were "reduced to a low Melancholy Situation." As the letter continued, her pride left pen and paper, replaced by despair. The Doyles were starving. Anstis, "hearing of your goodness and humanity to Others," now made her "Application thus in distress." Pledging that her prayers "will be for Your Spiritual and Corporal welfare"–all she could repay him with–she closed, her one post script informing him that "I live in a Cabbin in Chapel Lane in Wexford."[98] Her cousin, reading the letter from his estate an ocean away and recalling his own memories of Wexford cabins, responded as he always did, with a solicitous letter and money.

On June 3, in the Senate the president's secretary delivered a written message from Washington, nominating his six choices for captains of the proposed frigates. They were immediately approved.[99] Two days later, a courier rode to Strawberry Hill with a message from the War Department:

Sir: The President of the United States by and with the advice and consent of the Senate has appointed you to be a Captain of one of the ships to be provided in pursuance of the act to provide a naval armament herein enclosed.

It is to be understood that the relative rank of the Captains is to be in the following order:

John Barry
Samuel Nicholson
Silas Talbot
Joshua Barney
Richard Dale
Thomas Truxton

You will please inform me as soon as convenient whether you accept or decline this appointment.

I am sir, etc.

Henry Knox
Secy. of War[100]

Barry wanted to accept immediately. He did not–perhaps in deference to Sarah. After seventeen years of marriage, Sarah knew his decision was a foregone conclusion; she might as well have tried to turn back the tide were she to oppose his acceptance. She was proud of this honor–that is self-evident in her surviving letters. If she had any qualms about his return to the sea (and in a fighting capacity–when he accepted his commission in the fledgling Continental Navy, he was thirty years old, now he was forty-nine), her husband could placate her with the facts; his ship's design was not even approved yet, much less built. Barry's reply was sent to Knox the next morning:

Strawberry Hill June 6, 1794
Sir
The honor due me in appointing me a Commander to the Navy of the United States is gratefully Acknowledged and Accepted by Sir
Your most obedient, humbl. serv't
John Barry[101]

CHAPTER NINETEEN

THE UNITED STATES

CONGRATULATORY LETTERS FLOODED STRAWBERRY HILL, with Sam Nicholson's being the most fawning and titillating at the same time. While "there is none in this quarter that is not well pleased" with Barry's appointment, there were, he added cattily, "exceptions who wish themselves or friends in it." After inquiring "when and where our Ships are to be built," and if he could "possibly get my two sons in as Midshipmen," he then asked the question most important to him: "What is to be our uniform?" It was the first letter addressed to "Commodore Barry." Barry's reply answered all Nicholson's questions, whetting Nicholson's appetite for the uniforms: "Blue and buff" and, in Barry's opinion, "better than the old blue and red." Nicholson was like a young boy at Christmas: "Pray inform me when you put on your Uniforms," he replied.[1]

As with the Continental navy, political standing mattered; Nicholson's number-two commission was proof of that. Talbot, appointed a captain in the Continental navy after valiant service in Washington's army, had never commanded a ship. Lack of a Continental commission put Truxton last on the list, but his success as a privateer put him above other jealous applicants. Barney, irked about ranking below Talbot, declined his commission. After obtaining a midshipman's berth for his son, he enlisted in the French navy.[2] Dale and Truxton rose up a notch, and little-known James Sever was given position number six.[3]

In 1775, Barry and Humphreys helped start a navy by refitting existing ships. Now they created from scratch the ships Humphreys wanted to build and Barry wanted to command. Knox kept them both "in constant attendance" as discussions intensified over plans, sites, and staffing.[4] A project of this magnitude meant jobs, revenue, and a windfall of patronage. Congress distributed the six plums accordingly. The six frigates were delegated to six ports: the forty-four-guns went to Boston, New York, Philadelphia, and Norfolk; the thirty-sixes went to Portsmouth and Baltimore. Knox originally listed a thirty-six for Norfolk, but President Washington, being a Virginian, "suggested" a switch with Baltimore.[5]

On July 1, Barry swore "true allegiance to the United States of America and to serve them honestly and faithfully against all their enemies or opposers whomsoever." Appointed "Superintendent of the frigate to be built at the port of Philadelphia," he threw himself into his new responsibilities, hurriedly finishing his "Dimensions of the Masts and Yards of a Ship of 145 feet Keil 43 Beam 14 Feed Hold," leaving "a Sail maker to find out how much Canvas it will take." The firm of Gurney & Smith was appointed to "provide all the materials not otherwise provided by the Treasury." Humphreys, as "Constructor," was ordered to have the "moulds for the frigates prepared with all possible dispatch" for delivery to the other shipyards.[6]

The demands on Humphreys became overwhelming. He found help in Barry's friend Josiah Fox, another Quaker who first displayed his shipbuilding talents in England.[7] Fox and Humphreys hit it off immediately, and Fox was named Humphreys's assistant (a third shipwright from Southwark, William Doughty, largely forgotten today, actually drew up the plans of the thirty-sixes).[8] Knox's approach guaranteed an overlap not only of countersigning but also in authority. Frequently, Barry shared management duties but was totally responsible if anything went wrong.[9] As Knox saw it, if checks and balances were good enough for the Constitution, they were good enough for the ships that would include the *Constitution.*

Such work meant business before pleasure; an invitation from Senator Butler for Barry and Sarah to join him for a brief vacation on the Jersey shore was declined, being too "inconvenient" for Barry "to leave home more than twenty-four hours, as I must be in Philadelphia every Other day."[10] He was also scolded from afar for not writing by his sister Margaret, in a letter given to Michael Hayes while the *Rising Sun* was in Ireland.[11] By September, Humphreys had hired scores of men for the undertaking. Men, Philadelphia had. What the ship needed was wood. Humphreys's Yankee ingenuity required southern timber.

As Humphreys saw it, if "seven dog years" equal one human one, then five eighteenth-century ship years equaled one ship's life. Wooden ships lucky enough to survive perils at sea usually rotted out within a dozen years; even the much-admired *Alliance* was laid to rest at twelve.[12] Humphreys believed that with live oaking his ships would outlast their contemporaries by decades. Barry, Dale, and Truxton concurred, informing Congress in a joint letter that they considered live oak "the most durable wood in the world," and also "a great saving to the United States, as we are well satisfied (accidents excepted) that their frames would be perfectly sound a half-century hence."[13] Having bested a divided Congress, the builders and the captains now took on geography, nature, and the calendar.

Live oak–*Quercis Virginiana*–a member of the beech family, is found along the coastline from southeastern Virginia to the Gulf of Mexico. It grows to heights of seventy feet, with trunks over twenty feet around. Somewhere from five to eighteen feet aboveground, the first broad, strong branches expand. At their tallest and widest, their crown covers 150 feet, providing enough shade for over half of an acre. Furniture makers found little use for the heavy, curved branches, but shipwrights found them perfect for their line of work. As the densest and hardest oak, it also handled saltwater better than any other wood. Humphreys had used live oak before and was well acquainted with the results. To see a live oak tree is to understand why John Muir called it "the most magnificent planted tree I have ever seen."[14]

There were problems: the shipyards ranged from Portsmouth south to Norfolk, and the live oak woods were hundreds of miles from all but the latter. Slave labor was plentiful enough, but skilled northern hands were needed to teach and supervise.[15] Knox recruited well-known Boston shipwright John T. Morgan, who arrived in Savannah in June to seek out coastal landowners whose property teemed with Humphreys's favorite trees; not only live oak but also red cedar, white oak, yellow pine, and locust.

He found a promising forest on the island of Saint Simon, but once ensconced, Morgan's labor was better suited for Hercules than a Yankee shipwright.[16] The island was "almost under water"; and the rainy season would make it "impossible almost to get the timber from where the live Oak grows." He grew despondent, telling Humphreys that St. Simon's was "low Land and Swampy," and "there never was so much rain known in this country."[17]

In October, with no shipments yet from Morgan, Treasury Secretary Tench Coxe sent Barry to find Morgan and discover what timber "may be in readiness for the Frigate." He departed on the brig *Schuylkill*, whose shipment of oxen and horses to the islands were "recommended" to Barry's "particular care." One week later, Barry stood atop "Gascoigne's Bluff on the Island of Saint Simon," giving him a view of Morgan's activity. There was none. Barry found Morgan "With his two Boys Sick and not a man with him nor a stick of wood cut." With Morgan prostrate, Barry examined the "camp": a ramshackle sawmill and a couple of tents. Coxe suspected that Morgan was behind schedule; Barry could not even find a schedule. After standing on the "dry, sandy knoll," surrounded by Humphreys's much-desired trees, Barry unpacked, made sure "the oxen and horses was all landed in good order," and began working on a plan.[18]

He assumed total command, directing the camp from his tent as if it was his quarterdeck. When a "Revenue Cutter arrived from Savannah with part of the utensils for Cutting timber, part of the moulds and part of the provisions," he ordered everything unloaded and stored, then told Morgan that "if he could stand on his feet, he would be required to get back to work," sending him "into the Country to try to get hands." Morgan came back with six slaves from a nearby plantation. Barry requisitioned ten more from another planter and set them to "making a road to the Wood." His sea-captain's management style did not enthrall Morgan. "If I am to stay her[e] till all the timber is cut I shall be dead," he bitterly complained to Humphreys. "If you was here you would curse live Oak."[19]

Providentially, "eighty one men arrived from New London, via Savannah." They may have come from the "damb country" Barry cursed years earlier, but they were a welcome sight, and he instantly gave them a task: "make a place to cover them for the Weather." By dark the camp was truly a camp, not just a forlorn, jury-rigged sawmill. On the "next day they was sent to cut wood." After an attempt in Savannah to enlist more ships to transport the timber north, and promising Morgan both more men and a visit home, Barry sailed back to Philadelphia, with "live oak plants & acorns" in his bags–a present for Humphreys.[20]

Shortly after his arrival, Barry reported to Congress that he was "well satisfied with the exertions of Mr. Morgan," believing "the whole quantity" of live oak "will be cut between this month and the month of February." Truxton and Dale joined him with a rosy prediction that "the ships may be built, and completely equipped in the course of the next year." Beaming, Barry and Humphreys were watching laborers unload the timber from the *Schuylkill*'s hold when the *Anna* arrived, also loaded with rough-cut live oak. The elated Humphreys called the wood "the best that ever came to this place." The increased activity can be seen in Humphreys's "Waste Book." It is simple arithmetic not measured in deliveries of iron, copper, or hand spikes. "Rec'd 6 Gallons of Rum," Humphreys entered on November 3. Before long he was up to a hogshead–about 50 gallons a day for his burgeoning work crews.[21]

But the *Anna*'s live oak shipment was the last one Humphreys would see for months. Barry's erroneous prediction that the shipyards would have all the wood needed before the daffodils bloomed was a harbinger of things to come, for him and the new navy.

On December 23, a diarist described the weather as "remarkably mild and pleasant, perfectly clear." He finished his entry with the phrase: "Saw the Stem of the Frigate raised." The diarist was Washington. He had brought his step-grandson, George Washington

Parke Custis, along to Southwark with him. Barry and Humphreys greeted them. Washington was "awed and thrilled "on this, *his First Visit to an American Navy Yard!*" Years later, Custis recalled how Washington "expressed his admiration at the great size of the Vessel that was to be. Commodore Barry was present, & Mr. Humphreys explained to the President...the great principle which he had organized...all of which meant with Washington's approbation."[22]

Barry's Christmas festivities began that day. But while the Barrys celebrated the yuletide, Morgan penned him a plaintive letter from soggy St. Simon: "You promised me that you would see that I should Com from heair." Morgan's ongoing fever "has fed into all my Lims and I can not walk," and "all the fine oxen that you Brought is dead."[23] Climate and fever were still Morgan's personal harpies. His New Englanders either died or deserted. Only three of them were fit for work, along with the slaves who, while they could die, certainly could not desert.[24] The rain never stopped; the surviving four oxen could not move the weighted-down carts through the mire.

The New Year in Philadelphia started off propitiously enough, as Humphreys's expert craftsmen turned the huge pieces into the frigates' "lower futtocks and knees"–the ship's ribs and right-angled supports.[25] No more wood arrived over the winter months–not for Barry or any other captains. What was forecast in December––shipyards full of America's finest carpenters, sawyers, chandlers–was replaced by the sight of increasingly idle craftsmen. Work on all of the frigates, Barry's included, slowed, then stopped. From Boston, Barry heard again from Nicholson: "When we are to get our Commissions, what is to be our uniforms, and when we are to receive our pay and rations . . . I have A large family and wish . . . to receive my pay and rations Quickly."[26]

The first captain to look for other work was Richard Dale. Offered command of a China voyage, he requested Barry's permission for a leave of absence. With approval from Washington's new Secretary of War, Timothy Pickering (Knox having resigned after a disastrous investment in a New England land scheme), Barry gave his permission, along with "800 Spanish milled Dollars" for "one Thousand pieces of the best shirt Nankeens" and "one box of tea or twelve pound of the best Hyson Sulong Tea."[27]

Dale departed in March, missing a wedding at Strawberry Hill. Patrick Hayes and Betsy Keen had become engaged. On April 9, a fine spring day, the Barrys, Austins, Keens, and a retinue of distant relatives and friends filled the pews inside Christ Church. Michael Hayes was best man. The Barrys watched Patrick and Betsy stand before the same altar they had approached eighteen years earlier. William White, now a bishop, cheerfully presided. The reception at Strawberry Hill was a gala affair, made livelier by Barry's "Sea Captains Club" friends in attendance, including John Rossiter, about to take Michael with him on the *Rising Sun*'s first voyage to China.[28] Of the family, only William Austin, now living in Charleston, was absent.[29]

Eleven days later, Benjamin Rush made his way to Strawberry Hill. Barry's asthma was back; Rush believed it to be "the dry asthma [that] occurs most frequently in . . . middle life." This time Barry's "paroxysms" truly laid him low. Sarah was fearful, and Rush returned for two more visits in early May. Barry recovered slowly. It would be weeks before he ventured to Southwark.[30]

Earlier, a merchantman arrived in Philadelphia with news: John Jay had negotiated a new treaty with Great Britain. Washington hoped for a mutually beneficial solution to several pressing issues, including British seizure of American ships and sailors, but Jay returned with nothing to safeguard American sailors from British press gangs. Even the bone thrown to America–the opening of British ports in the West Indies–came with a proviso: ships were limited in size to seventy tons. When the treaty's contents became public, riots broke out in New York and Boston. Americans, still predominantly holding French sympathies, saw no good in the treaty at all. Few realized that Jay had probably postponed another war with England. Communications being what they were, British ships were unaware of the treaty's approval–a fact made clear when "a ship from Philadelphia was boarded by Admiral Murray's squadron in the latitude of Sandy Hook" and "stripped of her people." George III "had issued orders . . . to take all American vessels bound to France."[31]

In July Barry returned to his duties at Southwark. His stamina diminished by this latest bout of asthma, he purchased a chaise to carry him to work, adding the buggy's cost to his expense account. His riding days were over. He found little progress made in his absence; the most significant change at the yard was the absence of Josiah Fox. With no one named to replace Dale, Fox became de facto superintendent at Norfolk.[32]

From Georgia, Morgan continued begging for release from his contract. New England craftsmen and southern slaves baked in morning sun, only to be soaked to the skin by afternoon thunderstorms that drowned out their camps. They were attacked incessantly by mosquitoes and the swamps were also home to cottonmouth and water moccasins. Morgan's pleas to Barry and Congress were finally answered, and denied.[33]

What live oak was cut and shipped was never enough, and shipments were poorly planned. One shipyard got more futtocks and knees than needed, while another got none at all. Transferring the huge pieces was time-consuming and costly. Seeing that "the difficulties of getting the live oak" prevented "the carrying forward of six frigates at the same time," Pickering closed four of the shipyards. Only Philadelphia and Baltimore remained open. He handed Washington a list of names for the frigates, such as the *Terrible* and *Revolution*. The president chose more judicious titles: *Constitution, President, Congress, Constellation*, and, later, *Chesapeake*. Barry's flagship would simply be called the *United States*.[34]

Pickering demanded a report from Barry regarding the masting of the frigates, seeking a uniform plan. Tactfully, Barry replied such exactitude was impossible: "I have never found two People who pretend to find rules for masting ships to agree . . . I am of the opinion that the longer the ships the longer the yard should be and I am sure I am not alone in that opinion."[35]

While Barry dealt with Pickering as tactfully "as was in his power," Washington continued to weave his way between the three sources of potential war: England, France, and Algiers. Edward Randolph, Washington's Secretary of State, was privately accused by Pickering and Woolcott of treason and resigned. Attorney General William Bradford died. Washington's decision to replace Chief Justice John Rutledge with the publicly despised Jay could not win

Senate confirmation. Already stripped of his ablest advisors, Washington did what he could with his second team, moving Pickering to State and replacing him at the War Department with his former aide and drinking friend, James McHenry.[36]

Barry's final report to Pickering about his frigate's status was as glowing as his first, prompting Pickering to "procure the whole of the live oak timber by the month of May, 1796."[37] Publicly, Barry believed the live oak–built frigates "would last fifty years." Privately he must have wondered if it would take fifty years to build them.

Soon it would not matter: peace was made with Algiers. Hasou Bashaw, "Dey of the City & Regency of Algiers," agreed "not to damage plunder or impede in her voyage any american vessel"–for a price.[38] Negotiations, helped behind the scenes by the French Republic, included a million-dollar tribute paid to Algiers and delivery of an armed brig and schooner to be built by Humphreys.[39] For the Republicans, these terms meant a virtual execution of the navy before it could get off the ground and into the water.

But Washington still had a trick or two up his sleeve. McHenry assured Congress that "one forty-four and one thirty-six may be completed with great ease by the month of November" and the rest "launched and completely equipped" one month later (even the most ardent "navalist" would have been hard pressed to believe that). On March 15, Washington asked Congress to reconsider the navy's death sentence. His request was turned over to a committee comprised of three pro-navy Federalists. Two days later, the triumvirate proposed that three frigates be completed: two forty-fours, one thirty-six.[40]

Debate resumed with a new player leading the Republican opposition, Swiss-born Pennsylvania Representative Albert Gallatin, a legislative junkyard dog over expenses. Gallatin's name was already anathema to Federalists. Rising up to do battle for the navy was its champion, William L. Smith of South Carolina. When the smoke cleared, the three frigates at Norfolk, Portsmouth, and New York were "laid aside." Those in Baltimore, Philadelphia, and Boston were spared. The push was on to get them completed, and Barry and Truxton were sent to "visit Cecil furnace" and prove the cannon cast for the *United States*.[41]

Truxton met Barry at the Head of Elk, and immediately confronted his old friend about rumors that Talbot was now angling for his
ship. "Mortified . . . if I am superceded," Truxton poured out his fears
that Talbot's congressional cronies might steal the *Constellation* away
from him. Barry assured him that his position was secure. At the furnace they met with the ironmaster, Samuel Hughes, who informed
them that thirty-five cannon had already been "proved." Upon their
inspection of the guns, Barry and Truxton found many of them wanting. Hughes got testy. He had proved them out of professional courtesy—there was no call for him to do so in the contract, which he
provided for the captains to review.[42]

Proving guns was a small part of a bigger problem. Hughes's contract, signed by Tench Coxe, contained neither a stipulated deadline
nor a penalty for delays. The guns were being sold not by the piece,
but by the ton. Barry was appalled—"In all my life," he "never saw any
thing" as one-sided as this contract; under its terms, Congress could
not fine Hughes "one shilling" for any "noncompliance." Barry, unlike
Truxton, was no close friend of Coxe, and blamed Coxe for the situation. He returned to Philadelphia. Josiah Fox was sent to resolve the
issue and refine the specifications for the cannons.[43]

Back at Southwark, Barry was elated over Humphreys' progress.
The giant frigate rose over the rooftops, her mastless, great hull
looming over the neighborhood like Noah's Ark. Working several
stories above the street, laborers carried red cedar and white oak
plank, hoisted heavier pieces with block and tackle, while sawyers
and carpenters toiled below. Workers on the ship's bow could actually look *down* on the steeple of the nearby Swedish Church.
Philadelphians had never beheld such a mammoth structure.

One newcomer to the yard, a teenager, was a recent dropout of
prestigious Episcopal Academy. Using his father's connections with
Barry and Humphreys, young Stephen Decatur began working on
the *United States* under Humphreys' watchful eye.[44] Like everyone
else at the yard, Decatur's ears were subjected to the endless din from
scores of hammers, mallets, and saws. The noise could be heard
throughout the entire ward, from sunup to sundown: endless
cacophony to the Southwark residents, but music to Barry's ears.

There was also more noise at Strawberry Hill that summer—not as loud, but more joyous. On July 8, Betsy Hayes gave birth to a son. She and Patrick named him John Barry Hayes, much to the pleasure of John and Sarah, who considered him a true grandson.[45]

Congress recessed; Morgan began his third year in exile at St. Simon. Dale returned from China, only to find his frigate and status in limbo.[46] Humphreys and Fox, fast friends and allies for two years, began to find fault with each other. Barry immersed himself with reports and correspondence—anything to bring his ship closer to launching. In September he presented "An Estimate of the Expenses and Fitting out the Frigate *United States*." From "A Captain's salary of 75 dollars pr mo." to "one Drum/Fife," his grand total—"as near as I can possibly make" was $7,285.[47]

As the ship inched closer to completion, Congress ordered her guarded by soldiers, there being no marines or sailors for the task. Barry was less than impressed with both their appearance and attentiveness: "Such a Set of ragamuffins I never had to do with," he grumbled. When McHenry showed him Hughes's latest report from Cecil Furnace, Barry was unimpressed but silent. He knew enough of sailing and fighting in the wooden world to match his knowledge with anyone, but was on unfamiliar ground with proving guns.[48]

So he went and learned, talking to every expert he could find. He then sent McHenry an exhaustive account of how the British, French, and Dutch used different shot, weight, and wad to ensure a cannon's worthiness and safety. Recalling the horrid tales of Revolutionary era cannons that touched off disaster and not projectiles (there were condemned guns on the *Bonhomme Richard* that killed and maimed a substantial number of Jones's crew—something Dale saw firsthand), Barry was concerned that ineffective proving "makes men [more] afraid of their own Guns than they are of their Enemies."[49]

That autumn everything was overshadowed by the first true presidential campaign. The Federalists nominated John Adams, while the Republicans picked Thomas Jefferson. While Adams and Jefferson officially remained above the fray, the campaign was fraught with ugly partisanship. Although he had friends in both camps, Barry felt more sentiment for the pro-navy Adams, who caustically noted that the United States was "a country Impotent at Sea."[50] Following Washington's lead, Barry kept his choice to himself. As the electors' results would not be announced until February, he was perfectly happy reporting to his current commander-in-chief.

International intrigue soon came to the fore, regarding both the election and the nascent navy. In October, French Minister Pierre August Adet announced that French warships would treat American merchantmen exactly as the British had been doing: seize them and confiscate their cargo. Adet gave notice to both Congress and the pro-Republican Philadelphia newspaper *Aurora* on the same day, a gesture Federalists denounced as a ploy to assist Jefferson's candidacy.[51]

In December Barry submitted his third report to Congress regarding the *United States*. Humphreys had already delivered his annual message, emphasizing that significant progress was being made. Barry complemented Humphreys' account: "The Rigging is all made . . . the Yarn spun and ready to be laid into Cables . . . the Anchors and Iron ballast all ready, the Blocks Water casks Boats Lanthorns and all the tinwork on hand, Guns, Gun Carry's Masts, Yards, pumps, Sails and may other articles much behind."[52]

Barry enjoyed some respite over the winter, beginning with Christmas at Strawberry Hill. Everyone was in good health, Rush having made only one visit "for [the] negro girl"–Jude's malady quickly treated for less than a pound.[53] Barry returned to his duties after the New Year during a harsh spate of numbing cold that froze over the Delaware. Wagons from New Jersey, loaded with supplies for the frigate, crossed over the river's thick ice to Southwark, where workers kept fires going to keep warm.[54] In February, the election results were announced: Adams barely defeated Jefferson, by three electoral votes.

On Washington's sixty-fifth birthday, he issued "commission no. One" to Barry, "appointed CAPTAIN in the Navy of the United States, and Commander of the FRIGATE called *UNITED STATES*, to take Rank from the Fourth day of June, One Thousand Seven Hundred and Ninety Four." Shortly thereafter, Barry attended two dinners honoring Washington: the first at the Executive Mansion on

Eighth Street, accompanied by Charles Biddle and William Johnson, in which they presented the president with honors from the Society of the Cincinnati. There followed another affair, attended by "All the Military and Naval Officers" in Philadelphia. On March 4, Adams was sworn in as president.[55]

While work continued on the frigates, Congress was at an impasse over their future once again. A motion to purchase a "live oak preserve" (Humphreys's brainchild) was resoundingly defeated.[56] Fortunately for Adams and the Federalists, the Directory of France filled the void left by the Dey of Algiers. They refused to receive Charles Pinckney as America's new ambassador. Federalists were furious.[57] Adams, ensconced in Morris's old palace as Washington had been, called for a special session of Congress, hoping for a peaceful solution to his first crisis—but it would be nice if Barry's frigate would at least be in the water by then.[58]

One pleasant April morning, twenty-eight-year-old Benjamin Franklin Bache, Franklin's grandson and editor of the *Aurora*, went for a stroll.[59] He did not meander aimlessly past the blossoming apricot and peach trees, but headed south along the waterfront for the Southwark shipyard, to see firsthand the progress made on the *United States*: a strange destination for someone whose rants against the navy's officers and laborers were frequent entries in his paper. Bache's grandfather often called himself a frustrated sailor; the same could not be said for him.

Some townsfolk bade him good morning; just as many did not. Bache's political beliefs were well known, and he carried them with him like a portable lightning rod.[60] He saved most of his vitriol for one man: "If ever a nation was debauched by a man, the American nation has been debauched by Washington."[61]

Bache entered the shipyard unannounced. No one informed Barry or Humphreys of his arrival, but he was immediately recognized by Humphreys's son Clement, his father's assistant.[62] Clement may have come from Quaker stock, but he saw Bache's arrival as an opportunity to host a less than friendly welcome. His voice ringing among the hammers and saws, he called to his carpenters, almost to a man Federalist sympathizers, to come down into the yard.

Humphreys's derisive greeting bypassed any jocular harangue and immediately became physical. Clement's Quaker tolerance vanished with his first shove. While the laborers watched, he methodically assaulted Bache. Between punches, he shouted into Bache's ringing ears the newspaperman's very own words: how he "accused the ship's carpenters of being bribed" and "abused the President." By the time he called the reports "Tory pieces," Bache was thoroughly, brutally beaten.[63]

The clamor brought Barry and Joshua Humphreys running from their office and pulling Clement off Bache, who stood on his wobbly legs and staggered off the yard. The attack over–it hardly could be called a fight–Barry and the elder Humphreys sent the men back to their tasks. Soon authorities came and arrested Clement. Found guilty at his trial, he was fined $50 and ordered to pay a $2,000 peace bond. While Republican papers excoriated Clement, the Federalist tabloid *Porcupine's Gazette* (written by the English printer and wit William Cobbit, alias "Peter Porcupine") summed up Bache's thrashing in four words: "It served him right."[64]

Bache did not get the chance to see that the frigate was nearly completed: her hull planked, decks laid, and copper sheathing nearly finished, she was ready for her debut. Her latest addition was the striking figurehead completed by the artist William Rush, who described his work with hyperbolic zeal. One admirer recalled that it

> represented the Genius of America, wearing a crest adorned with a Constellation. Her hair escaped in loose wavy tresses, and rested upon her breast. A portrait of Washington was suspended from a chain which encircled her neck, and her waist was bound with a civic band. In her right hand she held a spear and belts of wampum–the emblems of peace and war. In her left hand was suspended the Constitution of the Union. Above was a tablet, on which rested three books, to represent the three books of government, and the scales of Justice. On the base of the tablet were carved the eagle and national escutcheon, and the attributes of commerce, agriculture, the arts and sciences.[65]

As the days lengthened, Barry and Humphreys divided their time between finishing touches on the *United States* and construction of the launch area. Workers toiled beneath her great shadow to complete her launching ways, the long, two-rail frame constructed to send the ship into the water. Once completed, they were connected to the bilge ways, set in their positions underneath the hull. By April 24, the frigate rested on her keel blocks. Her "launching plank, bilge ways, blocking wedges, crosspieces, and shims fore and aft" were "all prepared and fitted." Barry and Humphreys announced May 10 as the launching date, to "take place at 2 o'clock if weather permits."[66] Finally, after three years, the time had come for the complex, dangerous task of sending the wooden behemoth into the Delaware.

On May 9, "strong northwest winds" blew so powerfully they "kept back the tides"; the Delaware was "too shallow to permit the launch."[67] As artillery batteries and "other uniformed companies together with the regular troops" took positions to guard the ship overnight, Barry sent the workers home, with orders to return at sunrise. Then he and Humphreys departed.[68] Even the elements seemed to conspire against the baptism of the United States Navy.

But that night, the wind died down. Returning to the shipyard well before sunup, Barry and Humphreys found most of their men already there, equally relieved about the diminished winds. In the dark they could hear voices, audible evidence that a crowd was already gathering around the shipyard. As the sun rose, Barry was amazed at how many Philadelphians were at Southwark, jostling for the best spots to witness the launching. Although the ship lacked masts and guns, Barry lovingly prepared her to look every inch the belle of the ball. With no stays or rigging, Barry ordered the banners placed over the gunwales. Years later one spectator's daughter wrote, "I heard my father state how gaily the Commodore dressed the frigate."[69]

Philadelphians were coming by the thousands. Congressmen and other dignitaries, brandishing special passes, elbowed for position.[70]

Soon the neighborhood was so crowded that late coming notables could not get inside the shipyard. Each passing minute brought more and more on-lookers. Humphreys had two large anchors "sunk in the yard in front of the ship, and two large cables lashed through the hauseholes"–cylindrical holes for the anchor cables to pass through– "as well as one to each anchor."[71] Next, "a large careening fall was reeved through each pair and hove tight by a capstan."[72] At daybreak Humphreys "proceeded to launch down the bilgeways, in order to retallow the launching plank."[73] With the first rumblings of the ship along the bilgeways accomplished, Humphreys ordered the ways "re-tallowed," applying another coat of wax to speed along 1,600 tons of wood, copper, and iron.[74]

Accompanied by Dale and a hand-picked crew, Barry came aboard the frigate. On the ground, Humphreys reviewed the steps for launching: a sequence that held preciously small margin for error. The capstans were manned and the bow cables hove as taut as possible with "the spur shores fixed."[75] By 9 A.M. everything was in readiness. High tide came after 12.

With his frigate's copper sheathing blindingly reflecting the sunlight, Barry remained on deck through the agonizingly long wait for her delivery. By now every rooftop within sight was overcrowded; Swanson Street, the main thoroughfare in Southwark, was impassable. Eyewitnesses estimated the crowd at between twenty and thirty thousand.[76]

By noon, "adjacent points of the river were crowded with vessels of different descriptions": from schooners and sloops to shallops and rowboats, "gay with bunting and richly dressed dames."[77] Among them was the "Brig *Sophia*, Capt. O'Brien," hosting the cabinet trio of Pickering, Woolcott, and McHenry (the President was conspicuously absent: Adams had left town to fetch his wife, Abigail).[78] During lulls in the action, troops stationed in the shipyard paraded and drilled to the applause of the spectators while, almost unnoticed, thirty laborers moved under the ways beneath the ship.[79] So dangerous was their role that these men were usually volunteers; if there were not enough, convicts filled the posts, after being promised commutation of their sentence.[80]

Noon came and went. Humphreys waited for the right second to begin cutting the frigate's restraints. Any restlessness felt by the crowd during the long wait had passed. Tension was as visible among the horde as it was on the frigate's taut cables. Finally Humphreys gave the order. "55 carpenters on each side" swung their mallets in unison, driving the blocks out from under the ship. A roar broke from the crowd. Suddenly, without warning, "the ship began to move"–but the blocks were not completely out.[81] Aghast, Humphreys watched as the frigate's sudden movement "strained the spur shores"–the last restraints against the ship. He ordered them taken away. Now only her cables kept the *United States* from accelerating down the tallowed ways.

But if her cables held–and Humphreys knew they would hold–the frigate could break the ways and come crashing to the ground, killing every man beneath her. He yelled over the din to Dale for the cables to be cut immediately.[82]

The order was not necessary. From the quarterdeck, Barry saw what was happening, and had already called out to Dale to cut the cables. Axes flashed in the afternoon sun, severing them with dispatch. Fraying hemp flew through the hauseholes with a whipping sound. With nothing now to hold her back, the frigate slid down the ways, barely over the heads of the thirty workmen who rose up and cheered after she rumbled loudly over them. Released from Humphreys's restraints, the *United States* rushed headlong into the Delaware, striking the river's bottom hard as she entered the water, sending out two huge waves that rocked the countless ships and boats, nearly capsizing the smaller vessels, and threatening the "richly dressed dames" with an unintended swim.[83]

After the launch, "carpenters and citizens sat down in the ship yard to a collation and the resuming part of the day was spent in the utmost festivity," while Barry, his ship in the river at last, disembarked to enjoy "a round of beef and a drink of punch." It was hours before the crowd dispersed; in the evening, "Front Street and Second Street were still chocked with people going home." Not every Philadelphian was enthralled. Quaker Elizabeth Drinker entered the event of the country's first "Friget" launching in her diary. "I wish I could say it was the last," the pacifist noted.[84]

Despite the unforeseen hazards of the launch, and the embarrassing striking of ground (due to her launching ways being too steep), Humphreys's report to McHenry was self-congratulating–with good reason. His innovations would soon be marveled at by foreign shipbuilders, and the launching was proof of the soundness of his work. During a launch, a ship was prone to "hogging": the bow and stern bend as the keel and bottom arch upward. Humphreys knew that "large Ships hogg in launching nearly two feet"–an incredible strain. But the *United States* "arrived at one Block without Straining or hogging more than One and a quarter Inch." For Humphreys, this was "convincing proof . . . of the utility of the diagonal riders in long Ships."[85] In the fictional exploits of Patrick O'Brian's Captain Jack Aubrey, Humphreys' design is rightly considered a wonder from that "fascinating modern age."

On May 16, 1797, Adams addressed Congress about the "depredations on commerce" by the French. Still hoping to resolve these affronts by "amicable negotiations," he proposed sending Timothy Pickering, John Marshall, and Elbridge Gerry as envoys to France to resolve America's grievances.[86] As Congress debated Adams's request, McHenry sent Barry back to Cecil Furnace to prove more guns.[87] Barry was aware of the importance of his errand. Albert Gallatin's fiscal opposition to a navy was unwavering, even if there now *was* a navy–if only one ship.

Unfortunately his visit to Hughes's furnace was more disheartening than previous ones. Upon his arrival, Barry learned the only guns that "stood proof very well" were already assigned to Truxton's *Constellation*–still three months from launching. No tirade at Hughes could manufacture more guns. Such was Barry's mood that he went straight to Strawberry Hill without bothering to confer with McHenry, sending a less than tactful report the next day: "I am at a loss to know when the Guns will be got for the frigate as there is not another gun at that furnace fit for a Ship of War." He ended with a postscript aimed at Gallatin's anti-navalists: "I think it is highly necessary that some inquiry Should be made when and where they can be procured as in all probability the Frigate will be ready to take them on board in Short time not with standing all that has been said about her."[88]

Typically, McHenry did not reply. Although he was popular with his peers, he was astonishingly deficient in administrative skills.[89] The demands of his office overwhelmed him, and Barry found his lack of response and resolve exasperating. The days of reporting to a superior with the breadth, depth, and empathy of a Robert Morris seemed long gone.

Happily, Barry returned to Southwark to discover the "limbs" of his frigate–her masts and spars–were almost finished, along with her longboats, rigging, and sails. All he needed was guns. In an effort to speed up their procurement he informed McHenry and Congress "that the Ship may be rigged and completed for Sea in one month after the guns and lower masts are on board."[90] To his amazement, Congress "passed the Bill for completing and Manning the Frigates." On June 29, McHenry summoned Barry and Truxton to meet with him to discuss "the appointment of officers." That same day, in Portsmouth, New Hampshire, "the frigate *Crescent* of thirty-six Guns" was launched without a hitch.[91] The American navy was still trying to walk, but the Dey's frigate was one step closer to completion, mostly at the expense of the *Constitution* and *Constellation*.

Selection of officers was never far from Barry's thoughts, being deluged with recommendations. Some wrote flowery nominations for themselves, like William Foulk, who "Commanded Vessels at this Port" and believed himself "Qualified to perform any duty." Others came from Barry's friends; James Jackson championed a son of "The loan officer of Georgia"; being one of the few pro-navy Republicans, Jackson saw his request as eminently justifiable. Barry even received a request on a boy's behalf from an acquaintance he had not heard from in years: Robert Morris.[92]

With Philadelphia in the midst of a depression–foreign banks were calling in loans–Morris was the most prominent citizen being brought down by an avalanche of debt. Morris's few remaining friends (some also ruined from following his lead in speculative land investments) watched as the financier converted his summer house into a veritable fortress, nicknamed "Castle Defiance," in an effort to repel angry crowds of creditors. Barry and other friends feared for Morris's sanity.[93]

After months of mulling over applicants, Barry began making selections. For first lieutenant and second lieutenant he picked Richard O'Brien of Massachusetts and John Mullowny of Philadelphia. John Lockwood, an old acquaintance, was made sailing master, and George Gillasspy of New York was appointed ship's surgeon. The list of deck and marine officers came from states as far north as Vermont and as far south as Georgia. James Jackson's nominee, Alexander Wylley, was given a midshipman's berth, as was young Stephen Decatur, Jr.[94]

Summer was in full season, hot and humid. The Fourth of July was celebrated with the usual festivities and fireworks; Barry and "fifty citizens dined at Geisse's Point–no-Point" in nearby Bridesburg.[95] Three days later the Barrys observed their twentieth wedding anniversary, a much more stable marriage than Alexander Hamilton's, whose scandalous affair was banner headlines in the Republican papers.[96] The strangest occurrence in the city was an epidemic of dead cats "which began to render walking out exceedingly disagreeable."[97] Some carcasses, thrown in the river, drifted up against and past the *United States*.[98]

Although yellow fever returned in 1794 and 1796, Philadelphians were spared another epidemic. Now it was back, as threatening as in 1793. Led by Adams, the government fled the city. When it became "too dangerous to go to work" at Southwark, Barry and Humphreys sent their men home.[99]

Soon Barry succumbed, not to yellow fever but to gout. It attacked the joints in his feet and legs, and the incessant pain made walking impossible.[100] The embattled Rush paid a visit to his friend at Strawberry Hill, warning him to remain there until the epidemic subsided. (He also recommended a student, Doctor John Bullus, for the position of surgeon's mate aboard Barry's ship.)[101] With Southwark shut down, Barry could only sit things out anyway, waiting for the day when walking would not be too painful while watching his year-old namesake take his first tentative steps.

Then Barry got an idea that made sense in the days before Pasteur. Writing to McHenry, he asked permission to "move the Ship in the Stream," believing that sending Gillasspy, Bullus, and "forty or fifty men on board to get things in ready ness" would get the ship back on some kind of schedule while keeping his men away from the rampant disease ashore, albeit by only a hundred yards. For once, McHenry jumped on a suggestion.[102] Upon receipt of McHenry's letter, Barry prepared to head to town. A few minutes of trying to walk changed his mind. A letter was sent in lieu of a captain. Hurriedly writing, angrily crossing out sentences in frustration at his physical immovability, he ordered Mullowny "to have the Frigate in the Stream as soon as possible." In between crossed out lines, raging at his own feebleness, Barry explained that "I am not able to walk on my leg or I would have seen you this Morning." Three days later, Mullowny "moor'd the Frigate on the Shore a little below Kensington."[103] So far, so good.

Then fever struck the ship. Once on board, Gillasspy found the *United States* a veritable hospital ship, minus a doctor.[104] Practically everyone was down with yellow jack. Working around the clock, Gillasspy cared for the stricken officers, sailors, and landsmen. Cooler winds returned to Philadelphia, but this only sent the sick sailors shivering in the crisp night air: the *United States* still lacked glass for her window frames.[105]

A letter from Sam Nicholson did nothing for Barry's mood. Happy as he was about the arrival of his uniform, Nicholson sought Barry's advice on appropriate entertainment and catering for the *Constitution*'s launching. With his deathly ill crew barely a broadside from Strawberry Hill, and the gout still hobbling him, Barry answered Nicholson with another letter replete with crossed out phrases and ink blots, dismissing the idea of a party. "You say She is a fine Ship," Barry wrote, but "I have heard it reported here and by one of the Finest Ship builders in New England that her Knees is pointed in the wrong way." If that was the case, "It is preposterous to talk of launching so Soon you will be Sorry for it." He warned Nicholson to have everything in order before attempting the launch or "you would be much to blame." Barry's warnings proved prophetic; it took three attempts to launch the *Constitution* before she slid into the Charles.[106]

Some days later, Barry received cheerier news about the *Constellation*. "A Better Launch I never saw," beamed Truxton.[107] News from Barry's own ship was not good: a marine had died, followed shortly by John Lockwood, the sailing master.[108] Gillasspy, suffering "with a violent cold," made a personal report to Strawberry Hill, where Barry ordered him to remain until he was better. But the doctor returned to the *United States*. From Downingtown, McHenry ordered that Barry "Not expose yourself" to the ship, and risk his own health.[109]

With his gout-ridden leg on a pillow at Strawberry Hill, Barry requested his friend Rush "go on board and give his advice." Beset by the latest outbreak, Rush sent an assistant who reported "that every thing had been done for the Sick that was proper as could be done here." Barry fretted over the true hero in this crisis, Gillasspy, whom he called "a man of Great humanity." Gillasspy's "Spirits [were] Very low having no one to assist him," and Barry ordered his new sailing master, Edwin Meade, to have "the Ship Washed and fumagated as well as possible."[110] To Barry's relief, Meade carried out his orders to the letter.

As before, cooler weather mercifully ended the epidemic. The frail Gillasspy was sent to New York to recover. In gratitude, Barry's crew published a testimonial to the good doctor offering their "sincere and most grateful thanks . . . it is to him (under *God*) we owe our lives." Before leaving, Gillasspy thanked Barry for his "kindness and attention," adding "You and Mrs. Barry who feel for others woes, ought to have been blest with Children whom I am sure never would have been the foot ball of fortune."[111]

Routine life returned to Philadelphia and McHenry with it, innocently asking that Barry get the frigate ready "to meet a winter at sea." Instead, Barry, wondered if McHenry had bothered to read his reports: why send a ship of war to sea without guns? In an effort to prove that he *had* been reading the reports, McHenry noted that the ship had guns–fifteen of them. Exasperated, Barry attempted to bring McHenry up to date without bringing him up short. All fifteen guns were unfit; nor were there any "suitable at Cecil Furnace." Barry suggested that Gillasspy investigate the availability of guns in New York, and McHenry consented.[112]

Gillasspy came through again. In a few days, combing New York from Kinderhook to Redhook, and from Manhattan to Governor's Island, the doctor found "Smooth and Handsome" 18- and 24-pounders at four different sites, along with "timber for the carriages." "They appear much better than those at Philadelphia," he exclaimed.[113] Gillasspy found nearly sixty guns, some already proved. Leave it to a doctor to find cannon when the secretary of war could not.

After learning of Gillasspy's success, McHenry ordered Barry to prepare "An Estimate of Provisions" for a twenty-six-week cruise. Barry's tally included 70,798 pounds of bread, 30,342 pounds of beef, and 70,798 half pints of rum. This estimate joined his report about Gillasspy's found cannon on McHenry's desk. After reading them, McHenry filed them away.[114]

Adams and Congress returned to a fever-free Philadelphia, along with news of increased attacks on American merchantmen by French privateers.[115] Hundreds of American ships were seized upon departing port. From Kennebunk, home of the sloop *George*, seized near Puerto Rico, to Savannah, home of the brig *Maria*, captured off Jamaica, newspapers vividly described the manhandling of American ships by French (and occasional English) predators. Letters from "the Masters of Captured American Vessels" poured into Secretary of State Pickering's office, including news of "the schooner *Little John*, Captain Pease," a friend of Barry's from the "Sea Captains Club."[116]

On November 23, 1797, short, stout John Adams, utterly devoid of Washington's commanding presence, made his first presidential address to Congress. With no word yet from his envoys in Paris, his report on the "unpleasant state of things" came off as tepid. His only flash of passion was an exhortation to "protect our commerce and to place our country in a suitable position of defense."[117] The Senate's approval of Adams's remarks rekindled in the old patriot his 1775 advocacy of a navy: "A maritime marine and a military marine most grow up together; one cannot long exist without the other."[118] But

Adams's fervor was offset by the affable McHenry's report on the *United States*. While he hoped that the frigate "would have been complete for sea sometime in autumn," the "contiguous fever" made it "too late in the season to get the ship in complete order."[119] As 1797 ended, Jefferson summed things up perfectly: Congress "had absolutely nothing to do, but to wait for news from our Parisian envoys."[120]

Word arrived from John Marshall in early 1798. Adams's envoys received a frosty reception from Charles Maurice de Talleyrand, French Minister of Foreign Affairs and recently returned to Paris after seeking asylum in Philadelphia during the Reign of Terror. The Americans met with three of Talleyrand's subordinates, whom Marshall encoded in his writings as X, Y, and Z. French demands, including a ten-million-dollar loan (and another $250,000 for Talleyrand) were bad enough, but when the three sycophants insisted the United States pay for damages inflicted on French privateers as they seized American merchantmen, the demands went from the ridiculous to the absurd. Pinckney's response has been used in defiance ever since: "Millions for defense, but not one cent for tribute."[121]

In January, McHenry ordered Barry to "have the marines and seamen mustered monthly while in port" with "regular muster rolls made out alphabetically," but still no word about Gillasspy's guns.[122] The old Irish temper smoldered, but Barry soon learned that he was not alone in questioning McHenry's abilities. A Committee on Naval Affairs had begun investigating everything from the tedious construction and cost overruns to McHenry's leadership, and sought Barry out.[123] He measured each word carefully, couching each sentence in deference without losing his point. "I believe you will agree with me that it has been but indifferently managed hitherto that there might be some allowance made for Young beginners," he began, complimenting McHenry's youthful appearance while dismissing his administrative skills. Then he made proposals that were as sound as those made years earlier by John Paul Jones–minus Jones's fanfare:

> The first thing that ought to be done should be to place the department by It Self and put it into the hands of three able

Men skilled in Naval matters. They ought to be well acquainted with the . . . Ships of War and have full powers to furnish every Article . . . for getting Ships to Sea. [There should be] three Commissioners under the direction of the President one of them a Commander one a Merchant the other a Ship Builder . . . There should ought to be three places belonging to the Public where the Ships of War Should rendezvous . . . those places ought to be in a fresh water river where they would be safe . . . from an enemy if a War should brake out they should be near a large seaport town that less difficulty may arise in manning them.

In one page, Barry laid out the Department of the Navy–shipyards, manpower, resources, and expertise from the top down. Excepting the suggestion of a triumvirate at the helm, Barry's ideas became the basis for the navy's first century. Wary of who else might see his letter, he signed just his initials–*JB*–as if no one would know who *that* was.[124]

He also faced his own crisis of leadership. Discipline was lax aboard the *United States*, and "French leave" was commonplace.[125] As before, when Barry was frustrated at matters beyond his control –such as McHenry's inaction over Gillasspy's guns–he came down hard on issues he could put under his thumb. "You as Commanding Officer in my absence will order the Men on board to do such duty as is most proper for them," he reprimanded Mullowny. Then he laid out rules for discipline with an eye for justice and fairness:

> For the good government of the ship it is my orders that no officer on any pretense whatever beat or abuse any of the men on board or on Shore when on the Ship's duty more than one or two slight strokes to make him jump quick to their work if he deserves more he is to be put in irons and complaint made to me of the offense he committed. He is not to have any of his rations stopped without an order from me. It is my wish that at all times a good understanding should subsist between my Officers and myself and nothing can contribute more to it than a promptitude of the duty required.[126]

Young Mullowny took Barry's criticism to heart. The next morning the crew found themselves making "grounding for the Cables" and seven unfortunate souls were confined "for absenting themselves for a whole night at least, some more"–including one sailor named John Barry.[127]

Congress' growing lack of confidence in McHenry's leadership and the resultant delay in the ship's completion were provided with a deus ex machina. On March 4, Marshall's report of the XYZ Affair reached Adams's hands. The complete lack of success of the mission made the Jay Treaty look like a resounding achievement. For two weeks, Adams deliberated on the best course of action, while Philadelphia taverns were abuzz with rumors that the French had already declared war on the United States. Finally, Adams informed Congress of the mission's failure, and to prepare for war. Concerned with the safety of the American envoys, he withheld the details of the XYZ documents.[128]

This decision caused a near riot among Republican congressmen and newspapermen alike. Called a warmonger and worse, Adams coolly kept his hand to himself. It turned out to be one of the best bluffs ever run by a president against his opposition. Smelling victory, Gallatin demanded that Adams make the report public.[129] Once sure that the trio of diplomats were safely heading home, Adams released Marshall's account.[130] Gallatin got more than he wished for. Overnight, public opinion swung to Adams who, caught up in martial fervor, was soon seen wearing a military uniform.[131] The XYZ papers were also a godsend for the navy. The French threat "that if nothing were done the coast of the United States would be ravaged" did more to complete the frigates than McHenry ever could.[132]

Throughout the previous four years it seemed to Barry that the entire project called the United States Navy was perpetually coming apart at the seams. Now, with completion finally in sight, his frigate did just that. The ship's "Decks topsides and other parts" were "much opened" and "the oakum loosened." Orders to make repairs "with as little expense as possible," came with a stipulation. McHenry cavalierly bowed to complaints by several merchants, who felt that the large frigate in the Delaware "incommodes the Vesls. coming in and going out," and demanded that Barry move the *United States* to "where the Channel is wider."[133]

For Barry, waiting for word on guns, supplies, and men, this was ludicrous. He wanted to get things moving, and all McHenry wanted to do was move the frigate. But the angry captain complied, and "placed the frigate in the best and widest part of the channel" where "any ship may pass by with ease."[134]

Over the next several weeks McHenry bombarded Barry with orders to obtain the necessary equipment (including rammers and sponges) for his guns. Soon all he needed was a gun. Gillasspy's cannons still lay unclaimed in New York; Barry knew it would not be long before Truxton or Nicholson sniffed them out. When Samuel Hughes sent word he had "23 twelve pounders to prove," Barry headed back to Maryland. Anxious to acquit himself, Hughes accompanied Barry to the open range where eight guns were ready for testing. One burst; then another, and another. With nowhere to hide, Hughes watched six of the first eight cannons blow apart. Barry and Hughes returned to the field the next morning, the desolate wreckage cleared away. Only five guns burst—but just six were tested. By the end of Barry's visit forty-four guns were proved: twelve passed audition, but nine of them "were doubtful" in Barry's eyes. Furious, envisioning his crew being killed by their own weapons, Barry told Hughes he did not want even one cannon.[135]

While Barry's carriage carried him home, steps were being taken to make the navy a separate entity from the War Department. Like Barry, Adams and Congress had seen enough of McHenry. Using their capital from the XYZ affair, Federalists passed a resolution giving the navy its own cabinet status. Adams needed a new secretary. His first choice, George Cabot, an old Massachusetts friend, turned him down. He approached another political ally, Benjamin Stoddert, a successful Maryland merchant. Stoddert accepted, becoming the first secretary of the Navy.[136]

After beseeching McHenry for months for clearance to go and inspect the guns in New York, Barry finally received permission. Carrying a letter from McHenry to Governor John Jay, Barry was "to examine the cannon" Jay could "lend to the United States." Leaving

Mullowny with orders to "have the Ship Scraped fore and aft" and her gun ports painted a "yellow and black check," he set off for New York. At Governor's Island, a jubilant Barry "Proved twenty-five Guns" and approved twenty-three of them. The guns at Red Hook, also proved, were available "for two Dollars for each." Barry could scarcely believe good fortune was finally smiling on him, and departed for Philadelphia, presenting his report to McHenry as soon as he arrived. All McHenry need do was send Jay an official request and the guns would be aboard the frigate within a week. But it took over a week before the procrastinating McHenry even responded, asking Jay to make all speed as "no time should be lost in forwarding" the guns—at least not McHenry's time.[137]

Upon his return Barry noticed a marked difference in the size of the navy. Congress approved an additional $950,000 for expenditures, including the purchase of merchantmen to convert to ships of war.[138] It was 1775 all over again; soon the navy had three new ships, including the *Ganges,* still under Dale's command. Even McHenry jumped through hoops, ordering Nicholson to prove cannon for the *Constitution* and enlist "proper Characters" for his crew.[139]

The spate of activity brought back a youthful spring to Barry's "gouty legs" and a visible change in his personality. Poor Sarah was torn; the welcome changes in her husband's disposition were clouds on her own horizon, signs of his impending absence. Her husband busied himself with completion of a roundhouse he designed for the frigate's quarterdeck. The roof of the roundhouse served as the ship's poop deck.[140] Save for this addition, the *United States* was a twin to her sister ship, the *Constitution.*

A great deal of mail awaited answers. Nicholson's younger brother John asked Barry to "Mention me to any of your Acquaintances in congress" for a command. David Porter made another plea for assistance in obtaining a commission, adding that Truxton had taken his son aboard the *Constellation*" as a midshipman. Friends from as far as the West Indies sought his influence in getting berths for youngsters "very anxious to go on board your frigate."[141]

The most interesting letter came from a Bostonian, designing the latest type of gun for the navy. Years earlier, he had been "on board the French Frigate *Concord* to make a drawing of the brass *carronades* with their beds." Now his designs were "in the War office in Philadelphia"—pigeonholed in McHenry's desk—but he fervently believed them more "preferable and much better" than the French guns. Nicholson had already ordered several for the *Constitution*. The carronades "are of my casting," he closed, "by which you will judge of the Workmanship." With clear strokes he signed his name: Paul Revere.[142]

When word reached Philadelphia that a French privateer had seized several merchantmen off New York, activity along the waterfront reached a frenzy not seen since the British invasion. Another ship, the *Hamburg Packet* of Philadelphia, was "bought by the Congress" for $45,000, renamed *Delaware*, pierced for twenty guns, and placed under command of Stephen Decatur, Sr. At the same time, Barry's midshipmen were sworn in—including Decatur's son, and Richard Somers, William Keen's young brother-in-law from the Jersey shore. The younger Decatur was thrilled—Somers was a friend from his Episcopal Academy days whose coastal upbringing and visits to Strawberry Hill only whetted his appetite for a life at sea.[143]

On May 5, a dispatch from McHenry arrived at Barry's doorstep "to direct you to repair with all due speed on board the Frigate *United States*." Urging that "no time be lost in completing that which is yet to be done" (how Barry's eyes must have rolled with that directive coming from McHenry), the orders included the enlistment of marines and a rendezvous to complete Barry's muster rolls. McHenry added that "it is in the President's express orders that you employ the most vigorous exertion to accomplish the several objectives"—just in case Barry did not believe McHenry. Nevertheless, after four years, any letter that ended with the phrase "sail at the Shortest notice" was welcome indeed.[144]

In the streets of Philadelphia, war talk reached fever pitch. "Hail Columbia," a stirring new march written by Francis Hopkinson's son, John, brought down the house nightly at the New Theatre on Chestnut Street.[145] "Crippled, toothless Adams," as Bache disparagingly called him, enjoyed a level of popularity he had never experienced, and never would again. While Adams basked in his brief moment of glory, urging American youths "to arms especially by sea," Bache's home and press were attacked by anti-French, anti-Republican citizens.[146]

Taking advantage of the patriotic fervor sweeping the country, Barry sent Mullowny to New York to enlist "the Compliment of Seamen" for the *United States*.[147] Barry gave responsibility for the Philadelphia rendezvous to young Charles Stewart, who was to keep to his task "Morning, Noon, & Night."[148] Broadsides flooded the waterfronts, appealing "to all *able-bodied and patriotic Seamen* who are willing to serve their country" for one year at $17 per month.[149] Thanks to the nearby presence of French privateers, both Stewart and Mullowny quickly had more than enough signatures on their muster rolls. "I am apprehensive in having more Men Shipt than our compliment," a bemused Barry commented. (How he would have loved that luxury twenty years earlier!) His solution to the overflow was simple: "Capt. Decatur will take them."[150] Over the next several days the enlistees came aboard, a mixture of seasoned tars and landsmen: some seeking adventure and escaping the drudgery of their life ashore, others returning to the only work they knew.

Last-minute glitches in getting to sea came from Tench Francis, Jr., purveyor of public supplies, the forerunner of the Navy Supply Corps. After Barry complained about his lack of assistance, Francis—besieged with requisitions from every captain—denied Barry's allegations of dawdling. "I have nothing to do in this business," he wrote disdainfully.[151] Barry's opinion was just the opposite: "you are the main spring of that business," he retorted; "have the different articles ready as soon as you can."[152] From Baltimore, Truxton rejoiced; "every thing is Sent for and on board . . . and ready for Sea," while Barry awaited supplies and a new wrinkle—the carriages for the 24-pounders.[153]

There was now an unofficial race as to which ship would be the first to sail. The competition centered on the *United States*, the *Constellation*, and the *Ganges* (the *Constitution* was weeks away from readiness). Dale was a whirlwind in refitting out his command, reminiscent of Barry with the *Lexington* twenty-two years earlier. Uniforms, supplies, even orders went to Dale first. Barry noticed that a fourth ship was practically ready for departure: Decatur's *Delaware*, her 9-pounders having arrived at Southwark.[154]

On May 23, McHenry requested that Barry "have one of your Boats and a Crew in readiness for me tomorrow morning at ten o'clock to go on Board the *Ganges*." The next morning, under clear skies, Barry and McHenry were rowed to Dale's ship, where they presented him with his orders to protect "the Jurisdiction of the United States, on our coast" and to cruise "between the Capes of Virginia and Long Island." After congratulations all around, Barry and McHenry departed. "A salute was fired; immediately after which [the *Ganges*] weighed anchor, to proceed to her cruising station."[155]

Watching Dale's ship stand downriver was bittersweet for Barry, proud of his friend's accomplishment yet wishing that he had been the first to sail. The first ship to represent the new navy at sea was commanded by an officer who served under both Barry and Jones. The ceremony was McHenry's last official maritime responsibility. Barry and the navy were Stoddert's problem now.

Anxious to get under way, Barry decided not to wait for guns and supplies in the shallow waters by Philadelphia. Better to move the frigate downstream, have her supplies sent there, and mount all the cannon he could on what carriages were available. On June 7, with the morning tide, Barry gave orders to First Lieutenant David Ross to weigh anchor. The commodore looked resplendent in his new uniform. The sword in his scabbard first belonged to John Paul Jones. Once again, salutes were fired, crowds cheered, and the largest ship yet completed in America "sailed down the river" past Fort Mifflin "and came to about noon."[156]

CHAPTER TWENTY

QUASI-WAR

OR OVER A YEAR, ADAMS HAD DONE his utmost to avoid war with France, hoping desperately to follow Washington's policy of neutrality. But it was not to be: the XYZ Affair, coupled with the unending seizures of American merchantmen by French privateers, made conflict inevitable. But there was sufficient Republican opposition in Congress to prevent Adams from getting a formal declaration of war, and Adams's own Federalist party was bickering over who would command the new army. Washington was the logical choice to come out of retirement and lead it, but competition for second-in-command was fierce. To Adams's disgust, Hamilton campaigned relentlessly for the appointment.[1] As France's belligerent activities were taking place at sea, Adams went forward with the new frigates into America's first undeclared war, thereby giving the navy its martial baptism.[2]

In John Barry the president had a national hero to lead America's ships into battle. Disappointed that George Cabot had declined the new cabinet position of Secretary of the Navy, Adams did not realize that his friend's refusal was a blessing in disguise. Some congressmen thought Benjamin Stoddert would not accept it either; after all, the compensation was inadequate, and "the weights of the services and toils" of the job were daunting."[3] But he did accept. Stoddert was born for this job.

He came from Georgetown, Maryland, and was a partner in a mercantile firm that also kept offices in London and Bordeaux. The son and grandson of Scottish tobacco farmers, he was apprenticed to a Philadelphia merchant before the Revolution. Wounded at the Battle of Brandywine, he spent a year fighting Indians along the Susquehanna River before resigning his captain's commission to serve the army as a civilian in procurement—a post equal to the rank of major. There he honed his administrative skills, making contacts that would be useful for the rest of his life. Even without the official rank, he became known as "the Major."[4]

After the war, he married a merchant's daughter and began shipping tobacco to England and France, earning enough money to participate in Robert Morris's land speculation schemes. With his knowledge of the land around Foggy Bottom, George Washington and Thomas Jefferson chose him to purchase what became the District of Columbia.[5]

By 1798, things had changed. War between England and France ended the European tobacco trade, and Morris's collapse left Stoddert with $86,000 in notes from the ruined financier. Land poor, he accepted the $3,000 salary Adams offered, left his pregnant wife and six children, and set off for Philadelphia.[6]

Once in office he worked tirelessly to make the navy a model department: seeking expert advice without regard to his own ego, meticulously keeping current on the comings and goings of his ships, and assessing the talents and flaws of each officer so as to promote merit and winnow out mediocrity. Even Albert Gallatin was impressed with his mastery of the budget. He was scrupulously honest—a trait that boded ill for the hordes of job seekers that descended upon him on his first chaotic day at his Walnut Street office on June 19.[7]

Barry was one of Stoddert's first visitors. Entering the secretary's office he met a square-shouldered, well-fed man, with bright, piercing eyes set beneath a wide forehead, crested with a mountain of

whitened hair. Stoddert checked idle conversation at the door, allowing Barry to get right to issues. When the subject of cannons came
up, Barry watched in amazement as Stoddert instantly ordered them
shipped "by a fast sailing vessel," and "without delay." Stoddert asked
Barry to remain in town until the *United States* was completely armed
and fitted; the new secretary wanted his input and advice. Barry was
glad to oblige.[8] What a change from McHenry.

He returned to Stoddert's office the next day, brandishing a letter
from Lieutenant Barron; some of the gun carriages were defective.
Again, Stoddert responded with vigor. Over the next week he kept
Barry and Humphreys busy reviewing the state of naval affairs. Both
men felt that, at long last, someone of ability was in charge.[9]

Within days the 12-pounders arrived and the 24-pounders were
all safely mounted. On June 26, Barry watched the brig *Delaware*
"proceed to Sea with the first fair wind." Stephen Decatur was off to
support Dale on his patrol; further south, the *Constellation* "had
arrived at the Door of the Ocean." Barry and Stoddert were convinced that the *United States* would be out of the Delaware in a few
days, letting Decatur sail south and team up with Truxton. On July
3, Barry received his official orders. With Adams still feeling his way,
Stoddert hinted at more clarification to come: "These Instructions
confine you with in narrow Limits, and you can do little more under
them, than exercise your men along the Coast—It is scarcely to be
expected that the French Cruisers will have the Temerity to throw
Themselves in your Way. But it is not improbable that [in) a very few
days . . . you may be ordered on more Important Service with greater
Latitude."[10]

With orders to "hoist a Danish flag on the main top Mast head"
for recognition by "any Express but that may be dispatched after
you," and with the president's "entire Conviction that nothing on
your Part will be wanting to justify the high Confidence reposed by
him," Stoddert sent Barry on his way.[11]

Knowing Barry's departure was imminent, Humphreys sent him a
checklist. Like a fretful mother sending her child off to his first day
of school, Humphreys wanted Barry to note how the *United States*
fared on her shakedown cruise: from "the height of your Guns above

water" and if the frigate "pitche[d] in a heavy sea" to whether "she [was] easy on her rigging" and if she could carry "a heavy press of sail without laying over too much." The anxious shipwright concluded, "Point out every good & bad quality your ship possesses"–as if Barry would not.[12]

The moment Sarah dreaded arrived on Independence Day. Barry stepped out the front door at Strawberry Hill dressed in his blue and buff uniform; he seemed to be turning back the clock. He and James climbed into his chaise, and made for the waterfront. From there a longboat took him downriver to his frigate, in the midst of the city's celebration of "the Glorious Fourth."

The *United States* was moored near Newcastle, Delaware. As part of the ship's observance of Independence Day, the officers' oaths were administered by a local judge. At 4:00 P.M., once Barry's boat was sighted, the bos'n piped all hands; as the longboat pulled alongside the giant frigate, Barry climbed up the side to the cheers of his crew in their full dress uniforms. Only Charles Wadsworth, the purser, was absent–having gone ashore to bring back enough livestock to feed five hundred men. The following day, while Wadsworth got his menagerie aboard, Barry kept the gun crews at practice. On July 7, the *United States* made for the Capes.[13]

The next morning two sail were sighted heading upriver. Barry easily identified one as the *Delaware*. As she neared, Decatur hailed Barry, identifying the other ship as the French privateer *la Croyable*– the first American prize of the war. Exultant cheers swept the deck of the *United States* and young midshipman Decatur beamed with pride as the *Delaware* continued upriver.[14]

No sooner were the ships out of sight when a pilot boat approached with Stoddert's latest orders to "keep on and off the capes of Delaware…'til further orders," as "late Acts of congress make a variation in your instructions necessary."[15] Barry could do nothing more than sail downriver very, very slowly. The *Delaware* came alongside the *United States* the next day; as Decatur climbed the gangway another round of cheers greeted him, and the two old friends retired to Barry's sumptuous cabin.[16] Decatur brought Stoddert's latest dispatches, a letter from Sarah, and news. To attract a new generation of privateers, Congress returned to letters of marque, with instantaneous results: a cutter hastily refitted for Barry's squadron, renamed the *Pickering*. They also passed "An Act for the Establishing of a Marine Corps." Barry's friend Thomas Fitzsimons led a consortium of Philadelphia merchants in raising funds for the construction of another, smaller frigate, to be named *Philadelphia*.[17]

Decatur had no sooner left when Barry gave orders to head for the Atlantic. Returning to his cabin he opened Sarah's letter, finding her "not a little disappointed at our not taking the first prize," but happy "that there is a beginning made." Then he turned to Stoddert's orders–pages of them, spread throughout several letters. He was ordered to Boston to pick up two smaller ships to join his squadron and then make for the West Indies. No matter how many times Barry read the rest of Stoddert's voluminous orders, he found them contradictory. The secretary gave explicit directions to sail to the West Indies and "fall in with the Islands three or four degrees to the Windward of Barbados & thence keeping to the Windward of Martinico, Guadeloupe, & Antigua . . . to afford the greatest chance of falling in with the French-armed Vessels." Straightforward enough, but while Stoddert "pointed out [Barry's] course," he added, "you are not rigidly to adhere to It."[18]

He was also to save the merchantman *New Jersey*, "captured by the French" and carried into San Juan, Puerto Rico. Once there, he should "write a civil Letter to the Governor"–already ghostwritten by Stoddert and found in another dispatch–and rescue "the greater Part of our captured Seamen" from that port and bring them home. Again, well and good; but if Barry should "ever see an American Vessel captured by the armed Ship of any Nation at War with whom WE are at Peace, you cannot lawfully interfere to prevent such Capture"–a veiled reference, of course, to England, whose courts, Stoddert believed "will render Justice."[19]

Nor was Barry permitted to "recapture any American Vessel taken by any such Nation," as "The Law of Nations forbids it, and We must respect that law." He finally closed, noting that "Mrs. Barry I understand is well," and adding that Congress was deliberating over "a declaration of War against France." Stoddert expected Barry back "on our Coasts in two Months."[20] Folding up the pages, Barry had to admit that Stoddert had thought of everything.

At Cape Henlopen he discharged his pilot, giving orders to sailing master Meade: "West nor'west." The *United States* began her maiden voyage, bound for Boston. From commodore to cabin boy, everyone was enthralled with her effortless speed, moving through the water with commanding grace. She was built for fighting, but first and foremost, she was built for sailing. "No ship ever went to Sea answers her helm better," Barry marveled. The *United States* sped ahead of the smaller, slower *Delaware*, and Barry "shorten'd sail" to allow the brig to catch up. A sprung foretop mast barely slowed her speed; only the *Delaware*'s sluggish pace prevented the *United States* from reaching Boston in record time. "She will sail with anything that floats," Barry joyfully worte Humphreys.[21]

Thousands of Bostonians crowded the waterfront, waiting for the *Constitution*'s sister ship. Guns saluted her arrival, and Barry ordered the compliment returned, to the cheers of patriotic Bostonians. Among the onlookers was a beaming Sam Nicholson, his ample form constrained in his long-awaited uniform. The next day it was the *Constitution*'s turn to take her maiden voyage; the same Bostonians that greeted the *United States* and *Delaware* were thrilled that their frigate was off to sea at last. The two ships designated by Stoddert to accompany Barry south were not ready, so once repairs were completed on the foretop mast, he departed for the West Indies. His trip to Boston proved to be pointless.

Due to a heavy fog, passage down Nantasket Road to Boston Harbor was slow, but it only took thirty hours for the *United States* to get within four hundred miles of the North Carolina coast. There Barry's mast-header saw "a sail in Sight bearing S.S.W. 5 or 6 leagues." She was a frigate flying French colors, but soon proved to be the H.M.S. *Thetis*, commanded by Thomas Cochrane. His flying a French ensign was a common *ruse de guerre*, and understandable: to the experienced captain's eye, the *United States* was certainly not British. Cochrane, who years later would burn Washington and attack Fort McHenry, provided Barry with British signals to prevent a similar deception turning into a needless chase, and dined aboard the *United States*, becoming the first British captain to see Humphreys's ingenuity firsthand.[22]

On August 21, the Americans made Barbados, and with the commodore's broad blue pennant flying atop the main mast, the *United States* entered Carlisle Bay: thirty-two years after Barry's first arrival in the tiny schooner *Barbadoes*. After inquiring at the fort about any signs of French activity, Barry set sail for Martinique.[23]

At dawn a sail was sighted, five leagues off shore. By evening she was in range, and Barry "fire[d] a bow gun at the Schooner." Soon he was alongside his first French prize: "the *Sans Pareil* of Guadeloupe, Capt. Tourin eighty-seven men." The captured crew, a polyglot of French officers and islanders, were transferred to the frigate under a pelting rain.[24]

Barry's chase through the Martinique Passage put him leeward of the islands–a direct contradiction of Stoddert's orders. He decided "to cruise 4 or 5 days to windward of Guadeloupe," sending the *Delaware* and the *Sans Pareil* to meet him at St. Bartholomew, putting the two vessels at the northern point of the Lesser Antilles and back in compliance with Stoddert's directions. The two captains parted at sunset. In splitting up the ships, Barry disobeyed orders to stay "within protecting distance" of each other, but allowed him to follow Stoddert's directive "to do as much Injury" and "make as many captures as possible." His hunt for Frenchmen came to nothing more than a tour of the islands under balmy tropical skies: past Dominique, Montserrat, Antigua, St. Eustatia, and Guadeloupe–all familiar layovers from earlier days.[25]

Guadeloupe was the enemy stronghold in Barry's station. The French retook it from the British in 1794 under the leadership of Victor Hugues, an agent nicknamed "the Colonial Robespierre." Hugues fomented slave rebellion throughout the neighboring islands while sending out privateers to prey on American and British merchantmen, making himself very rich in the process.[26]

After taking on supplies in St. Bart's, the three ships made sail for Puerto Rico, reaching San Juan on September 3. The following morning, Barry ordered Decatur to take the *Delaware* and *Sans Pareil* into the roadstead: a sail had been sighted, and Barry "gave chase, all

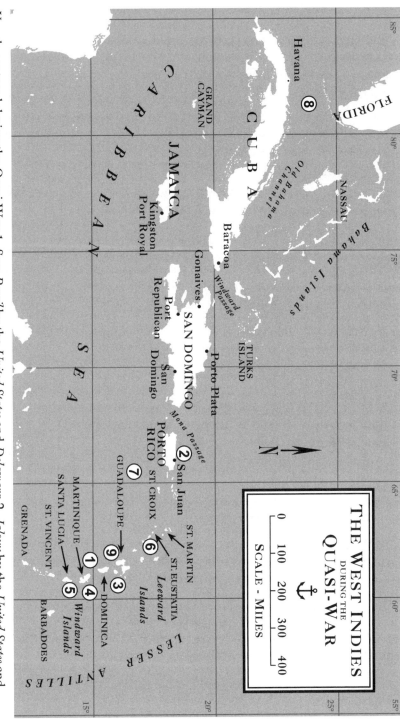

Vessels captured during the Quasi War: 1. *Sans Pareil* by the *United States* and *Delaware*; 2. *Jaloux* by the *United States* and *Delaware*; 3. *Retaliation* (U.S.) by *L'Insurgente* and *Volontaire*; 4. *L'Amour de la Patrie* by the *United States*; 5. *Tartuffe* by the *United States*, 6. *L'Insurgente* by the *Constellation*; 7. *Les Amis* by the *Montezuma* (U.S.); 8. *Marsouin* by the *Delaware*; 9. *Union* (Fr.) by the *Constellation*.

THE WEST INDIES
DURING THE
QUASI-WAR
⚓
SCALE - MILES

0   100   200   300   400

sails set." His prey, a sloop, led the *United States* on a twelve-hour chase under sunny skies, taking the frigate further and further west of Puerto Rico. Once she was in range of Barry's bowchasers, her captain ordered her "Bro't to all standing." She was the *le Jalouse*, from Guadeloupe, with a crew of sixty-seven. Barry's carpenters built another bulkhead below deck to provide larger accommodations for his prisoners.[27] It took two days of endless tacking through "contrary winds" before the *United States* returned to San Juan.

On the morning of September 7, the *Delaware* and *Sans Pareil* came in sight, and Barry sent for Decatur. Once in his cabin, Barry poured out his frustrations: a three-day sail for one lone prize; much of the ship's food was spoiled, and his frigate needed at least twenty more tons of ballast to sail efficiently. Furthermore, Stoddert expected both captains back home, and the hurricane season was upon them. Not wishing to risk his new frigate to tropical storms, Barry skipped his mission to rescue the *New Jersey* and her sailors, and the four ships departed the Caribbean, reaching Cape Henlopen on September 18. Barry disembarked at New Castle, where a coach took him to Philadelphia.[28]

Learning that Stoddert was in Trenton (owing to another outbreak of yellow fever in Philadelphia), Barry went to Strawberry Hill for an overnight reunion with Sarah. By daylight he was up, taking James with him to Trenton. Stoddert was dumbfounded to see his commodore back so quickly. Barry was put off by the secretary's reception, and reiterated that he merely complied with Stoddert's orders, sharing his "apprehensions for the Hurricanes in the West Indies at this Season." He then presented a detailed report on his shakedown cruise: "about 100 Frenchmen & negroes" were aboard the *United States*, with Decatur holding "30 or 40 more" along with the "Sloop & a Schooner took in the West Indies."[29]

Stoddert had little news for Barry regarding the actions of the other captains. Barry left the secretary and made the long ride back to Strawberry Hill, still uneasy about Stoddert's annoyance that he and Decatur were safely home. He was no sooner out the door when Stoddert dashed off a letter to Adams, addressed to the president's home in Quincy. Barry's captures were duly noted, but more than offset by Stoddert's simple, damning summation: "*Barry returned too soon.*" For Stoddert, Barry's first cruise fell "far short of my hopes."[30]

If Stoddert was dismayed to see Barry, the press was not. They reveled in his capture of "two French privateers...one which is reported to be the fastest sailing vessel the French pirates were possessed of." His arrival took Philadelphians' minds off the latest outbreak of yellow fever, which claimed the mayor and Benjamin Franklin Bache among the dead.[31] Barry's captures fueled the patriotic fervor still sweeping the city.

Once other captains returned to their home ports, their lack of results made Barry's short cruise look a resounding success. Despite extensive refitting, Dale's *Ganges* proved a woeful ship of war. Beset by structural issues and a mutinous crew, Truxton's cruise aboard the *Constellation* was disappointing.[32] And Sam Nicholson's one prize worth noting was a loyalist Frenchman, sailing with the British navy, which he maintained was legally his, despite all evidence to the contrary.[33] Yet none of this made Barry look better to Adams and Stoddert. Mere success was not enough; they needed spectacular results to offset any decline in public support for the war outside the walls of Congress, and Republican opposition within.

To get the *United States* back at sea by October, Stoddert threw his full support behind Barry's efforts to refit his frigate.[34] Various letters of introduction still poured in from acquaintances and strangers on behalf of various young men, seeking a midshipman's berth aboard the *United States*. One letter, from a Robert Boyce of Havre de Grace, Maryland, asked Barry to return a sailor from his crew: Thomas, "a Negro Slave belonging to me." Boyce expected Barry to "retain his pay in your hands until I may have an opportunity of getting him." Boyce was perplexed that Thomas would run off in the first place; as he was treated "with the least ill usage, threat or occasion."[35]

If Thomas were aboard the *United States*, he was among about fifty African-American sailors. By law, they were barred from joining the Marines, and Stoddert soon decreed "No Negroes or Mulattoes" were to be enlisted for the navy's revenue cutters.[36] Racism certainly existed aboard ship, but the mastery of skills required in the wooden world made a man colorblind in the split-second it took for another sailor's survival in the foretops or on a slippery deck in a storm. Many freemen saw sending their sons to sea as a path for advancement, just as Barry's own father did. By 1810 there was also an "African Marine Fund" for "the Relief of the Distressed Orphans, And Poor Members."[37]

On October 1, Stoddert ordered Barry to "proceed to sea as soon as your Ship is watered" and "protect the Trade from Delaware to New Hampshire." Stoddert saw "little danger of Enemy of Vessels on our Coast by the 15th of November" when Barry was to dock in Newport, Rhode Island. Adams approved Stoddert's plan, "sorry that Capt. Barry had not fully answered [Stoddert's] expectations" but happy that Barry was being sent out, as "The hurricanes are now passed."[38]

Immediately upon entering the Atlantic the frigate encountered powerful winds that prevented Barry from sailing northward. By the evening of October 17 "a heavy sea from the N.E." sent the *United States* to "pitching very much." The storm drove the frigate to the Virgina capes. For three days Barry's crew battled the "hard gales" and "violent squalls" while the frigate's sails and rigging were severely damaged. Soon the storm's warm winds loosened the stays; the masts began to shift in their steps, slamming into the keel and threatening to break the ship into bits. She was saved only after Lieutenant James Barron led a hardy band of topmen aloft with purchases, resecuring the masts by connecting them with new lines, moving perilously from one shroud to another in what historian James De Kay compared to "lacing a boot." By the time conditions allowed Barry to turn the ship northward he was off Cape Hatteras, and two men had died.[39] Adams was wrong: the hurricane season was not over, after all.

Due to the frigate's shattered condition, passage home was agonizingly slow. She reached Cape Henlopen on October 30, but nature was not through with the *United States*. "Snow, very thick" blinded the pilot, who ran the ship aground, forcing Barry to "get the Boats out." It took three days just to reach Newcastle. By then the sky was clear and the sun shining.[40]

The next morning Barry picked up Humphreys at Southwark and took him to Chester to see the damage firsthand, reaching the ship at nightfall. Once aboard they heard the sounds of horses, riders, and the metallic clang of scabbards along the way. Then, in a half hour, cheers wafted over the Delaware: "Genl. Washington [had] arrived at Chester, where the Troops of Horse for Philadelphia were to receive him." The most venerable of the old warriors had returned to serve his country once more, as Commander of the Army. As the sun rose, Washington and his escorts departed for Philadelphia. Barry ordered a fifteen-gun salute fired in his honor from the *United States*.[41]

After viewing the damage, Humphreys sent laborers to Newcastle to begin the necessary repairs, just as Adams, Stoddert, and Congress returned to Philadelphia. For his heroics, Barry recommended a captaincy for Barron, believing him "as fit to command as any in the service." He then raised the issue of his own rank: "Commodore" was not enough, especially as it was a courtesy title extended to all squadron commanders. Stoddert had been aggressively adding ships of all sizes to the navy: by the end of 1798 there were fourteen ships, with more on the way. Barry wanted to be the navy's first admiral. Stoddert saw no reason to honor the request; with no firsthand knowledge of the sea, he saw Barry's aborted cruise as one more failure to comply with orders. His answer was "wait and see," delivered with a poker face, not wanting to reveal his true feelings about his senior officer. With several other captains in port, Stoddert asked Barry to lead them in a review of the "extremely defective" Articles of War. Later, to his mentor and confidante, Hamilton, Stoddert's opinion jumped from the page: "Barry is old and infirm."[42]

As the captains huddled together over the articles while their ships were refit, reports arrived from Barry's friend, Alexander Murray, still stationed in the West Indies. Winter and the British navy all but eliminated the French menace on the Atlantic, but they were still prowling the Caribbean. There were "not less than 150 privateers out of Guadeloupe," and American merchants clamored for action. And, where previous reports listed "three Small frigates" as the largest French vessels, there now were two larger predators: *l'Insurgente*, forty guns, and the *Volontaire*, forty-four. The two had already captured the *Retaliation*–the new name of Decatur's prize *la Croyable*–commanded by William Bainbridge.[43]

Stoddert wanted to fill the Caribbean with American warships and decimate the French privateers. With Adams's blessing, he planned a four-squadron offensive of twenty-one ships led by Barry, Truxton, Decatur, and Thomas Tingey. Reluctant to give Nicholson a squadron, Stoddert was forced to place the *Constitution* under Barry's command along with the *George Washington*, thirty-two guns (commanded by Patrick Fletcher, one of Barry's "mutinous" *Alliance* officers), and the *Merrimack*, twenty-four, Captain Moses Brown. Stoddert sent Barry south with orders "to relieve our Commerce" from "the Piccaroons, and pirates, continually issuing from the Island of Guadeloupe." The island of Dominica would be his squadron's base. Barry was expected home in the spring, after teaching "the French and their colonies" to "respect, if not fear the power of the United States."[44]

At sundown on December 12, 1798, the *United States* began her third cruise. Immediately she showed the worth of Humphreys's repairs, reaching the waters off South Carolina in just two days, carrying nearly 40,000 square feet of canvas. She reached St. Rupert's Bay on December 30, where Murray's *Montezuma* was about to escort a fleet of merchantmen northward. A subsequent two-day cruise was only eventful diplomatically, as the *United States* was saluted by the British at Barbados and Barry was hosted at a dinner aboard Vice Admiral Thomas Harvey's flagship.[45]

While waiting for the rest of his squadron, Barry took his two ships to the French fox den itself–Guadeloupe–to see if Murray's reports were accurate. Once off the island he sent Fletcher eastward, and in a blatantly provocative gesture, made for the French stronghold at Deshaies. Recognizing the frigate as American, French forces ran out the guns from the fortress and two supporting batteries. Two cannonballs screamed over the frigate, while several others "Fell short"–Lieutenant Mullowny's brief comment about French marksmanship.[46] It was not Barry's intention to exchange cannonades with the batteries. Looking for French frigates and privateers, Barry found neither, and returned to Dominica.

The rest of his squadron had yet to arrive, but merchantmen were assembled for convoy. Out of deference to his friend and superior,

Murray requested that Barry take charge. He refused, and in so doing missed an opportunity to reconnoiter with Truxton, who encountered the convoy en route to Basseterre.[47] At another instance, when Barry learned that American merchantmen were "blocked up in Surinam" and needed military assistance, Barry sent the recently acquired cutter *Diligence*–not to Surinam, but to Truxton, ordering him to send a brig to the Spanish Main.[48] No captain enjoyed escorting merchantmen, finding the work tedious and unrewarding. In straightforward terms, Truxton mentioned Barry's behavior in a letter to Stoddert, who saw this as further proof of Barry's lack of initiative when, in fact, Barry went back in search of enemy warships–but returned empty-handed again.[49]

At Dominica he found the *Constitution*, whose captain's actions continued being the stuff of wonder. The swaggering Nicholson told Barry of capturing a British ship that was taken by *l'Insurgente* and given a French crew. After debating with himself whether or not an English ship captured by the French was a legal prize (it was), Nicholson released both British ship and French crew.[50] What the incredulous Barry thought has not been left for posterity. In fact, he was ill again. He did not mention whether it was his asthma or another attack of gout.[51]

When the *Merrimack* arrived, Barry's squadron was complete, and a pattern began to emerge. For the next two years Barry would command squadrons, but he rarely would sail them together *as* a squadron.[52] Pursuant to Stoddert's orders, he delegated his ships for convoy duty, but frequently broke off from them, sailing the *United States* in search of French frigates. Back home, the *Pennsylvania Gazette* erroneously reported that Barry "captured seven sail of French vessels," further raising Stoddert's expectations.[53]

The frigates continued to elude Barry's search, but privateers did not. On February 3, a sail was sighted and the *United States* gave chase. Pursuit took seven hours, but the Frenchman might as well have been a pigeon trying to escape a hawk; when her captain, "to the astonishment of all hands," put her to windward and "directly under our battery," she became a sitting duck. The third shot from an American 24-pounder put a gaping hole in her below the water line and she began to sink, as her crew "set up the most lamentable howl." Barry sent out longboats to save them. She was the schooner *l'Amour de la Patrie*, a notorious privateer "with great success in capturing our vessels."[54]

After making the rounds of the Windward Islands, collecting merchantmen for another convoy, Barry returned to St. Rupert's, proud that he had at least sunk one of the infamous French privateers. Learning that Hugues had been removed from office, he again handed off convoy duties to a subordinate, and took his French prisoners back to Guadeloupe for exchange. Barry put Mullowny on a longboat with a flag of truce with a letter to the new governor, General Edme-Etienne Borne Desforneaux. Again, the *United States*'s arrival was greeted with warning shots; again, Barry departed.[55]

Returning to Dominica, Barry picked up the *Constitution*, enduring another interminable visit from Nicholson. The bad news was that Nicholson had not captured anything–or, perhaps, that was the good news.[56] Frustrated as Barry was at his second failure to enter Guadeloupe, and in not finding the French frigates, he had at least captured a privateer of repute. The two forty-fours returned to Dominica where Barry found more ships sent by Stoddert for his squadron. There was also news: Truxton had captured *l'Insurgente*.

"The french Captain tells me I have caused a War with France," Truxton crowed; "if so I am glad of it, for I detest things being done by Halves." The French commander, Citizen Michel Barreaut (who recently assumed command from Joshua Barney, of all people), openly praised Truxton's "Honor, Courage and Humanity."[57] Add to these virtues Truxton's skills as a warrior, sailor, and correspondent, and one had Stoddert's template for a captain. Joyous as word of this victory was, it sealed Barry's fate with Stoddert and Adams. On paper, he was still first among captains, but both men would never think of him that way again.

———————

With seven ships under his command, Barry no longer needed Truxton's pressed brig. On February 22, 1799, after the squadron fired salutes "in honor to General Washington it being his birth day," Barry dispersed his ships, sending two to Surinam and the *Constitution* on a diplomatic mission to Antigua. Then, the *United States* sailed a third time for Guadeloupe, her hold full of captured Frenchmen.[58] This time Mullowny's longboat returned with company: Monsieur Deschamps, General Desforneaux's secretary. Deschamps replaced the gunfire of earlier visits with obfuscation. "We don't consider us in a State of War with your government," he said. Further, he had no prisoners to exchange, insisting "There is no americain life here Except those who mind to Stay." After going round and round in circles, Barry had had enough and simply sent his prisoners ashore.[59]

Another short cruise brought a prize and a glimpse of the atrocities of French privateers. Cruising off the island of Marie Galante, Barry's mast-header sighted two ships, and the *United States* gave chase, overtaking the slower of the two. She was the "ship *Cicero* of Liverpoole," recently "Taken by the [French ship] *Democrat.*" What the Americans found on board turned their stomach: dead and wounded British sailors left lying in their gore, including a cabin boy whose arm had been cut off when he refused to go aloft and haul down the British ensign. Barry resumed pursuit, confident of his ship's abilty to overtake any vessel yet pursued. But the captain of *le Democrat* used one of Barry's old tricks, running his ship into the shallows around Marie Galante where Barry's massive frigate dare not go: it was the *Lexington* and *Roebuck* in reverse.[60]

He returned to Dominica to deal with politics and logistics. His friend Daniel McNeill's ship, the *Portsmouth*, had departed for Surinam per Barry's orders, but not before McNeill pressed the crew off the injured ship *Scammel*.[61] To save money, Stoddert was sending supplies in ships from the United States, rather than pay the sky-high prices of island merchants, and the ships were overdue. Barry learned "War has been formally declared at Guadeloupe St. Eustatius & St. Martin by the French against the United States."[62] He searched among the pile of dispatches for a letter from Sarah and found none. Not that he had written her: just one short message announcing his arrival at Dominica weeks earlier.[63] The correspondence included a letter from Truxton, one of many he sent Barry over the past two months, most beginning with the remark, "I have heard Nothing from you."[64]

From Stoddert came two letters, months old, warning Barry of the "great clamor" against Nicholson and sending new instructions from the president. Adams, fascinated with exploring friendlier relations with Haiti's revolutionary leader, General François-Dominique Toussaint L'Ouverture, ordered Barry, "with the greatest part of the Fleet," to present himself "at Cape Francois, to Genl Toussaint, who has a great desire to see some Ships of War belonging to America." Stoddert believed Barry could "cultivate a good understanding" with the Caribbean hero. He closed, seeking Barry's input on "the merits of your Lieutenants–as promotions will take place before you return," and asking Barry to "Write me by all opportunities."[65]

Barry's reply was only the second he had written to Stoddert after three months at sea. (Unbeknownst to him, Stoddert was contemptuous of Barry's first dispatch, describing it to Hamilton as one long complaint about his poor health). Conversely, Truxton wrote Stoddert on at least eight occasions, long epistles with updates and ideas. Even Decatur and Murray caught on to the importance of communicating with Stoddert.[66] Throughout his career, Barry wrote his superiors upon arrivals and departures and rarely in between. This was good enough for him, and good enough for Robert Morris. He never learned that it was not good enough for Benjamin Stoddert.

In this letter Barry promised to "pay the most pointed attention" to Stoddert's wishes. Truly believing the French were avoiding him, he used the wry humor that had served him well with every superior (save Francis Hopkinson) in the past. He hoped to provide Stoddert "a good account of the French Cruisers and their Prizes, but it appears to me, they are all gone to some other part of the world."[67] Such a summary would have satisfied Morris, John Brown, or the old Marine Committee. Stoddert saw it as pure bluster, and continued to link Barry with Nicholson as one more impediment to American success in the war.

On March 20, the *United States, Constitution, Merrimack,* and *Eagle* "weigh'd anchor & put to sea"–but for Guadeloupe, not L'Ouverture in Haiti. Beating to windward under intermittent rain and squally winds, the strongest American squadron yet set sail in search of mischief.[68]

On the morning of March 22 Barry saw "two Large ships at Anchor supposed to be French Frigates" and "a Number of vessells at anchor" off Pointe-à-Pitre, Guadeloupe.[69] At last, Barry had a chance for a full engagement. The Americans "turned into the wind to reconnoitre the Harbour and reviewed the fortifications." Barry could attack the French stronghold, or bottle it up and force the French out to fight. Either outcome guaranteed the intense, bloody, smoking action Adams and Stoddert wanted to read about, and Barry desperately wanted to provide.

Then, nothing. As sailors beat to quarters and ran out their guns, Barry became aware of another critical factor in a sea fight—a "Very strong Current Setting to Leeward." The current put his ships at a distinct disadvantage, and made an attack foolhardy, if not futile. Barry had the squadron "lay too off Port Petre" overnight. That the ships remained within striking distance was proof that Barry hoped for better conditions to come with the sunrise, still spoiling for a fight.[70]

Not only did the current remain contrary; it prevented Barry's using his old ploy of "cutting out" any French ships without being pulled into shore and the ensuing enfilade from the fortress, shore batteries, and warships. Nor did the French see a reason to answer the challenge at their doorstep. They remained safely ensconced with both artillery and currents protecting them. Thwarted for a second day, Barry decided not to waste any more time. At noon the Americans "made sail and stood down the bay in Bassaterre Roads" in search of action—any action.[71]

"Running down below Guadeloupe & the Saints," Barry's mastheader "saw several small sail Close under the land." Soon there were more: "4 Ships at Anchor entirely strip't." Barry's ships gave chase only to find more intimidating company; "10 Schooners [that] appear to be arm'd & 7 Sloops three of which were arm'd," all dashing for the safety of the French stronghold. The wind was with them, and they were shortly under the protection of those numerous guns.[72] Within twenty-four hours, the opportunity for a fight presented itself three times. As frustrated as he was the day before, Barry must have been vexed beyond belief here, but refrained from any rash actions. His captains saw the wisdom of his forbearance, even if Adams and Stoddert would not (and did not) after reviewing the reports weeks later. Barry's squadron departed in unison and split up three days later.

Once divided the squadron had some victories, discounting the *Constitution's* chase and firing on another Englishman. March 27 found "the Commodore in chase" of two schooners that had separated from the fleet. Barry pursued them northward until they were below the Island of Antigua, where the schooners surrendered. They were the French privateers *le Tartuffe*, eight guns and a crew of sixty men; and a captured American sloop, *Vermont*, her cargo of tobacco, corn, and flour still in her hold. Barry immediately pressed *le Tartuffe* into service as his frigate's tender, and sent the *Vermont* to Martinique for libeling and condemnation.[73]

As if to atone for his enforced restraint at Guadeloupe, the fates placed another potential prize in sight of Barry's spyglass. On April 1, coming just north of the Leeward Islands, with the British ship *Syren*, Capt. Gosselin, in the distance, the cry "Sail ho!" came down from Barry's mast-header. She was a schooner, wasting no time showing her heels. The outcome was never in doubt as far as Barry was concerned, but the practice of throwing on extra canvas and mastering the wind to overtake a prize never lost its allure to commodore and crew alike. He soon had another prize, the captured American *Maria*. He placed a prize crew aboard and sent her into Martinique.[74]

Returning to St. Pierre on April 13, he learned that his squadron was performing capably; even Nicholson had caught and kept a legal prize.[75] Deschamps wrote to Barry that he was correct: there were American prisoners at Guadeloupe, after all. A Dutch ship was bringing them to Dominica.[76] There was more good news: two letters from Sarah. Truxton and Stoddert had chastised him for not keeping in touch; now came Sarah's turn: "I feel the same unreasonable disposition for scolding you as hitherto for not writing more fully you take not the least pains to descend to particulars if you know half how anxious my mind has been you'd omit not the smallest circumstance . . . your troubles my dear life must be great but may you never experience what I have . . . all is tolerably well with me at present God grant a continuance."[77]

There was also a kinder, gentler letter:

> By mere chance I have heard of a Vessel that's bound for Martinico that [allows] I shall be able to accomplish my desire of writing to my husband as fully as I wish...The world of trouble you have engaged inlays you my sweet life exposed to many dangers...I have not been an adventurer [i.e. investor] in any East Indian Vessels which I am really sorry for...the Navy likely to increase sizably I think we shall have in addition with others 6 Seventy fours.
>
> Your affectionate and loving Wife
>
> Sarah Barry[78]

On April 17, under winds so light Barry was forced to signal "for all boats to tow her out," the *United States* departed St. Rupert's Bay and began the voyage home, accompanied by the *Constitution* and thirty merchantmen.[79]

As Barry "steer'd NW by N" for St. Kitts, Stoddert was writing to Adams, again linking Barry with Nicholson and concerned that "these Gentlemen will return without an increase of reputation. Barry no doubt is brave," he continued, "well qualified to fight a single Ship." Adams, already "mortified" at some of Barry's decisions, readily agreed: "I Wish all the other officers had as much zeal as Truxton."[80]

During Barry's absence, the biggest news regarding the war came from Adams, not the navy. Having been aware of peace feelers from France since the hostilities began, Adams nominated William Vans Murray, minister at the Hague, to also serve as minister plenipotentiary to France. The groundswell of support Adams enjoyed at the war's onset no longer existed, largely because of the infamous Alien and Sedition Acts, passed by the Federalists in Congress. Aimed at restricting the immigration of "renegade aliens" and eliminating dissent from the Republicans at the same time, the acts further enflamed an already overly partisan political arena, where both sides used the press to hammer the public with rhetoric. Republican editors were fined for anti-Adams articles; one Congressman was even jailed for openly disparaging Adams. With domestic affairs spinning beyond his control, Adams turned his attention to ending the war, which further estranged him from his own party.[81]

On May 9, the *United States* entered the Delaware Bay. Barry had permission to come to the city but his men were quarantined aboard ship until it was determined they had not brought home any vestiges of the dreadful yellow jack.[82] Heeding duty first, Barry visited Stoddert, reporting on what he believed was a successful tour of duty.

In Barry's absence, Stoddert had worked like an evangelist on the navy's behalf, happily reporting "that Public opinion is getting more and more in favor of the Navy." After Barry made his recommendations for promotions, he raised the issue of reenlisting a crew. Stoddert's solution was novel; pay them off immediately. To the question, "what do you do with a drunken sailor?" Stoddert had a simple answer: sign him up as soon as he has spent his money. Even Barry had to admire that approach. After approving Barry's "returning to the River Delaware, with *United States*, with all possible expedition," Stoddert let him head for home.[83]

He was greeted at Strawberry Hill by Sarah, Betsy Hayes, and her children. Patrick was on a voyage to Canton with Rossiter. Michael, also at sea, was in love; Sarah described him as "full on matrimony" over one "Mollie L."[84] She also told Barry about the popular operetta in Philadelphia, *The Rival Soldiers*. The show's heroine sent her a warmly inscribed copy of its "hit," called "I am Here or There a Jolly Dog," with the chorus

> *When gallant Barry comes on aboard*
> *By all Columbia's sons ador'd,*
> *From him I sometimes pass the word,*
> *Tho' I'm an honorable midshipman.*[85]

Barry enjoyed many a hero's welcome before, but never in song.

Not so within the offices of Stoddert and Adams. During his meeting with Barry, Stoddert's congratulations masked the secretary's growing consternation and embarrassment. Ships were returning faster than he bargained for, and he had no one to blame for this but himself; his captains were returning home on his timetable. He needed a scapegoat, and with the unwitting Barry in town, he began a written onslaught to Adams, Hamilton, and even Truxton, questioning Barry's judgment, stamina, and courage. To Truxton he expressed displeasure at Barry's handling of prisoner exchanges. With a nod to *The Rival Soldiers*, he sarcastically wrote Hamilton that "Barry the brave" was "too infirm for active service." And, to Adams, "It was never intended that so many Vessels should be in port." Then he pinned the responsibility for it on Barry, who "came too soon, and ordered the return of those under his command, too soon."[86]

Anchored to his desk, fearing that another outbreak of yellow fever would strike his relocated family, Stoddert was dealing with intrigue more than battle plans: replacing Nicholson or Barry with Silas Talbot and the subsequent issue of rank between Talbot and Truxton (Dale, frustrated over lack of his own frigate, had received permission to make another voyage to China).[87]

Nicholson made the decision easy. After his embarrassing "captures," neither Stoddert nor Adams had a shred of confidence in him. Barry escaped being stripped of command by dint of his huge popularity among his fellow officers and with the public, especially as his hometown was the country's capital. And there was that damned song. Stoddert was pragmatic enough to see that Barry was not to be trifled with. Nicholson was given shore duty, superintending construction of one of the new seventy-fours. "Barry will go out in the *United States*," Stoddert glumly concluded.[88]

The secretary's incessant criticisms, however, stopped where Barry's junior officers were concerned. For vacancies and new positions to fill, he readily followed Barry's recommendations. With Alexander Murray down with yellow fever, Mullowny was named captain of the *Montezuma*–the first of "Barry's Boys" to move onward and upward. James Barron was promoted to captain and second-in-command of the *United States*. Decatur, Somers, and Edward Meade were notified of their upcoming promotions to lieutenants, cause for joy among the Keen family for Somers and a double dose of pride for Decatur, whose father was given command of the frigate

Philadelphia, a ship that would later play a major role in young Stephen's career.[89]

In filling his vacancies, Barry was approached by friends, politicians, merchants, and young men without influence who flooded Strawberry Hill with their appeals: a young immigrant from Dublin, "a waiter first and secondly a barkeeper in some of the best taverns"; "two young gentlemen" from "decided federalist" stock recommended by House Speaker Jonathan Dayton; and the son of Barry's friend from Savannah, Thomas Burke. Even Washington, who had "full determination not to apply to the Exertion in behalf of any person for appointment," put in a good word for one of General Spotswood's sons (other supplicants might be turned down, but who would deny Washington?).[90]

While Barry placed the chosen few in the capable hands of Lieutenant Charles Stewart, he turned his attention to another aspect of refitting the *United States*. He wanted to replace his 12-pounders with carronades: short, heavy, mortar-like guns that could throw heavier shells with deadly accuracy—a lethal complement to his 24-pounders. Once Stoddert approved the request, Barry sent Barron to New York to inspect the latest shipment, anticipated daily from London. Their delay stalled Barry's departure, prompting Stoddert to complain again behind Barry's back: "I wish I had not consented to his having them." They finally arrived on June 25.[91]

For all of Stoddert's grumblings, Barry soon had the *United States* refitted. He was also a bit richer, thanks to his prizes: libel and sale of *le Tartuffe* alone brought him several hundred dollars.[92]

The *United States* departed in July for a short, uneventful cruise of the American coastline, with orders to return to New York by September 10 "provided you can safely pass the Bar" or else put into Newport. Not one Frenchman was sighted during the cruise. The only development of note came during a dinner Barry hosted for other captains and officials while in Norfolk. Truxton had resigned, piqued that Talbot's return to command of the *Constitution* restored Talbot's rank above his own.

Pursuant to his orders, Barry finished his cruising on September 10; finding his frigate could not "pass the Bar," he arrived in Newport two days later.[93]

As the *United States* plowed up and down the coastline, a tug-of-war had been going on between Stoddert and Adams. Not wanting to waste his frigates on diplomatic missions, Stoddert had already dropped a planned joint voyage to Europe by Barry and Talbot, stopping short of calling the plan "Treason against the true Interest of the Country." But Adams faced different pressure: Congress wanted Minister Murray to have company during peace negotiations with France, and Adams wanted to end the war. He was determined to get his envoys to France, and wanted the French to see an American frigate firsthand: hence, Barry's coastline cruise. By September a worn-down Stoddert informed the president that the *United States* "has excellent accommodations for passengers." He wrote Barry to "hold yourself in readiness" in Newport. Stoddert was sending him two anchors and two envoys for a voyage to France.[94]

Barry awaited Stoddert's permission to visit Sarah. What he received was a condescending reminder of his duty, as "head of our Navy," to remain in Newport, thereby setting an example of restraint for his junior officers. Next came a flurry of dispatches, urging that the *United States* depart for France by November 1, stopping in Lisbon first. Stoddert suggested L'Orient as "the most eligible port" for landing his passengers, with Barry to "wait in port for their dispatches from Paris and then depart for the United States"–probably in February–then "come on yourself to Philadelphia." Then came the catch: "As you will sail to France and return as a Flag [of Truce], it would not be in your power to capture any thing on the Voyage." It would be the *Alliance*'s mission with Lafayette all over again, with this crew sure to resent such orders as the Alliances did. For once, Stoddert was empathetic, calling this "a mortification to which it is necessary you should submit."[95]

But his closing sentence erased Barry's resentment: "I hope to salute you an Admiral on your arrival." Admiral! Barry might have been unaware of the secretary's persistent backstabbing, but knew he was not held in any degree of esteem by Stoddert or Adams. Nevertheless, Stoddert could not have offered Barry a better incentive. Even word from his agent, John Leamy, that his six captures had netted him one thousand dollars was not better news.[96]

On October 31, the "Envoys Extraordinary," Chief Justice John Ellsworth and former North Carolina Governor W. R. Davie, reached Newport. Three days later, the *United States* took salutes from Forts Adams and Wolcott, accompanied by the cheers of the crowd on the waterfront. Soon she was slicing through the Atlantic with the same speed and handling Barry and the veterans in his crew were used to, although it was a special source of pride with these passengers aboard. Having an official captain—young Barron—to oversee day-to-day activities gave Barry time to spend with his guests and discuss politics, the navy, and the undeclared war itself. Passage went so quickly that Barry was but two days from the coast of Portugal on November 22, where he hailed a ship bound for Philadelphia, letting Sarah and the public know that all was well aboard the *United States*. On the twenty-fifth, the frigate was in the Tagus River a mile west of Lisbon, where the waters were deep enough to let the frigate safely ride at anchor.[97]

They spent four weeks in Lisbon, with several dinners hosted by William Smith, the American consul, who relayed to his guests the latest news from France. There had been a coup, and "the new Monarch of France is a Corsican." The consul's social calendar was too much for Barry, who bristled at the snobbery shown his young officers by Lisbon society. He preferred the hospitality of the Lisbon Assembly and their "Cards and Dancing on Thursday nights during the winter season."[98]

He also gave his officers a scare. Taking advantage of a beautiful day, he took some of them up a high hill for a panoramic view of Lisbon. Barry was soon lagging behind as they scrambled to the top. Finally, he joined them, but he was unable to appreciate the majestic view. The exertion was too much for his lungs; he could not get enough air into his bellows. The young officers anxiously watched this seemingly indestructible giant fight to do what came so easily to them—breathe. Slowly, his quick gasps became gulps, followed by a weary, wheezing rhythm of inhale and exhale. As the attack faded, he ordered, or maybe suggested, that they walk to the bottom. The attack was as severe as any Barry had yet suffered; years after his death, Rush cited the incident in a dissertation on asthma.[99]

The *United States* sailed for L'Orient on December 21. Aware of the treacherous Bay of Biscay, Barry still expected to reach the port in a week. After three days of decent weather, "a severe gale which blew with little intermission" assaulted the frigate. For two weeks the *United States* rode up the monstrous waves' crests, then plunged into the watery valleys between them. Unremitting wind and seas damaged masts, rigging, and canvas, even taking apart the figurehead, while keeping the sailors manning the pumps around the clock. The tempest drove her so far off course that at one point she had "drifted as far as Latitude 50, and to the West of Cape Clear": the southernmost tip of Ireland, and the closest Barry had been to home in forty years.[100]

By this time the ministers and their entourage were hopelessly seasick, begging Barry to put them ashore, anywhere. He made for Corunna, on the northernmost tip of Spain, known to sailors as "the Groyne." On January 11, the mast-header made out the port's ancient lighthouse, and Barry dropped his new anchor to wait out the storm. Even this went terribly wrong; under "a strain that would not have broken a two inch rope," the anchor snapped in two. As his helmsman strained every muscle at the wheel, Barry roared new orders over the gale, sending his crew to sheets and braces in an effort to keep the ship under control while the short anchor, saved for emergencies, was laboriously brought up from the waist and safely dropped. To add further to Barry's troubles, he had to land the envoys at a nearby village, where they were brought ashore by a fishing boat. From there they began their overland journey to Paris via Burgos, the old capital of the kingdom of Castile.[101]

Once the storm finally abated, the *United States* docked at Corunna, where Barry received grievous news from home: Washington was dead, within three weeks of seeing in the year 1800. In a letter William Smith wrote to Secretary of State Timothy Pickering which included a report of Barry's recent disastrous effort to reach L'Orient, Smith conveyed his sympathies. Pickering, who knew Washington well, "must feel his death with uncommon anguish."[102] The same could be said for Barry, who could recall meeting the general at Princeton, dinners at the President's Mansion in

Philadelphia, and the thank you letter a steel-nerved navy captain received for sending a jar of pickled oysters and cheeses to his equally steady commander-in-chief, while a nor'easter and a battle raged.

Barry did not deem the *United States* seaworthy enough to sail for home until mid-February, although there was no telling how the frigate would respond in a fight or another storm. Before his departure, a post rider from Burgos brought a dispatch from Davie and Ellsworth for Pickering. While not blaming Barry for their odyssey, they did not defend him or tell of the heroic efforts made on their behalf. Instead, the emissaries "regretted exceedingly the time that must be consumed in a long and painfull journey by land, in the most rigorous and unfavorable season of the year," calling their forthcoming overland trip to Paris "indispensable" due to the "ineffectual attempt to go to L'Orient." A lumbering voyage home was interrupted by just one severe storm, and the *United States* entered the Delaware Bay on April 2, 1800.[103]

While Barry was away, Stoddert dutifully made the case to Congress for his promotion to admiral. Stoddert actually requested six such advancements, declaring, "Justice and Honesty require that brave and experienced officers should be recommended"–words he no doubt felt better described Truxton.[104] Congress said no, and Adams expressed no interest in the matter. Weeks later, reading the uncomplimentary letter from Davie and Ellsworth that failed to give Barry any credit for his seamanship and hospitality, and seeing for himself the wretched condition of the *United States*, Stoddert decided that Barry had yet again come up short. He would never make admiral.

CROSSING THE BAR

HEN THE *United States* MOORED NEAR CHESTER, both ship and commodore showed excessive wear and tear. Leaving the frigate in Barron's capable hands, Barry stopped at Stoddert's office long enough to make his report and present the envoys' dispatches. Before he departed for Strawberry Hill, Stoddert reviewed the navy's activities in the Caribbean. Once again, Truxton's deeds shone brightest. Having rescinded his resignation and back commanding the *Constellation*, he found and fought another French frigate, *la Vengeance*. The Frenchman was about to surrender when the *Constellation* lost her mainmast, allowing *la Vengeance* to escape.[1]

The long separation was hard on Sarah Barry. Strawberry Hill's sixty acres required continuous oversight, and for the past two years both Barry and the Hayes brothers were away for months at a time. Sarah informed her husband that this recent separation would be the last in which she stayed at Strawberry Hill, miles away from family and friends, snowbound for weeks at a time during winter. She wanted to move back to the city, letting the estate serve as their summer residence as was the custom of Philadelphia gentry. That spring they purchased a house on Chestnut Street.[2]

While Rush attended to Barry, Humphreys attended to the *United States*.[3] The Bay of Biscay had decimated his pride and joy. With "most of the Wales Rotten," Humphreys decided to "take out most of her hanging knees"–the live oak supports for the ship's sides. Further examination compelled him "to take out everything from the extreme end of the ship." It was necessary to take the frigate apart in order to save her.[4]

That spring the federal government began moving to Foggy Bottom, Maryland–the swampland Stoddert and Washington had chosen for the nation's capital. Adams gave responsibility for the transfer of every lock, stock, and document to Stoddert, who was also called on to serve double duty in the cabinet.[5] Fed up over their never-ending subterfuge, Adams dismissed McHenry and Pickering, leaving him without a Secretary of War or State.[6] Until replacements were approved, Adams asked Stoddert to take over the War Department.[7] Once Stoddert accepted, Adams started out for the ramshackle capital of the nation.

With repairs on the *United States* looking to take months, Stoddert began dismantling Barry's crew. James Barron was given leave to visit family in Virginia. Before he left, Barry gave Barron a new signal book to be used by the entire navy that he had been working on for some time. Barry asked Barron to review it and have it printed.[8] Stoddert assigned Decatur to the brig *Norfolk*, bound for San Domingo. John Mullowny's *Ganges* was in port, and Stoddert ordered Barry to transfer thirty sailors to his protégé. In return, Mullowny left Barry a "box of segars" from Havana.[9]

Where Mullowny gave Barry reason to smile, Charles Stewart was giving him headaches. After Barron's departure, Barry turned over day-to-day command of the frigate's repairs to Stewart. Whether from another bout of ill health, or his own foul mood over lack of both promotion and action, Barry rode Stewart hard. When the lieutenant requested shore leave, Barry, preoccupied with other matters, dismissed him. Finding Stewart still ashore a day later, Barry laid into him for "willful neglect" of orders. His tirade wounded Stewart, who worshipped Barry. Soon his hurt turned into anger, and he pressed for "removal to another Ship; for I will no longer be the object of your unmerited Censure." The letter stung; Barry genuinely liked Stewart, and had high hopes for him. Whether it was the mellowing of age or the realization that the incident stemmed from his own crotchety behavior, Barry left Stewart's defiant note unanswered. In doing so he saved Stewart's career. Weeks later, when Stoddert promoted him to command of a schooner, Barry was "perfectly satisfied," hoping Stewart "will be more active when he comm[ands] then when he is comm[anded]."[10]

He also aided Midshipman James Caldwell, who asked Barry's "Advice on a Subject of the most Interesting Nature": money. Caldwell was intrepid, but also "a Young man of no Fortune." Recalling days when his own ambition clashed with lack of money, Barry engineered Caldwell's transfer to the *Constitution*. Talbot also saw merit in the boy, making him prizemaster of a captured schooner.[11]

In between courts of inquiry and overseeing work on both his new home and his ship, Barry waded through the thick packets of mail that included applications for officer's berths and other petitions. Two letters gave him a chuckle. One of Truxton's sailors, George Miller, due to "a bit of Frolick" and "too much Grog on board," was languishing in jail. The contrite tar begged Barry for a second chance, signing off piously, "may God Protect your undertakings." The other letter came from Samuel Chandler, "Brought up in the Church of England," and applying for the chaplain's berth. Knowing Barry's upbringing, he added, "I often visit the Catholic Church." Impressed by such ecumenism, Barry approved Chandler's request. Whether Chandler saved Miller's soul is not known.[12]

With Barry down to two lieutenants, Somers and Meade, Stoddert sent Talbot's son, Cyrus, to fill the vacancy left by Barron's departure. From Norfolk, Barron wrote Barry, "tired of an Idle Life" and asking Barry to help him get his own command. Barron had other news: the signal book Barry created and gave him for printing was finished. "I have ordered one hundred & fifty to be struck which will furnish each Vessel with three," he continued, predicting "thare Superiority to the System now practiced in the British Navy." The war had not brought Barry the success he hoped for, but he would always be proud that his signal book was used by the entire navy.[13]

As Humphreys had repairs well in hand, Barry decided to pursue the latest fad of Philadelphia society, a stay at the New Jersey shore. Long Branch was the most popular destination: not far from Monmouth battlefield and a two-day coach ride in good weather. Charles Biddle found it "the most agreeable place to spend some days in the summer," everything the well-off Philadelphian could ask for: "good living, a fine country to walk in, a number of vessels constantly in sight, and generally good society." Sarah was elated, and Barry urged Isaac Austin to close shop and come along, "as the benefit you would receive from the jaunt and batheing in the salt water" had "no comparison" for relaxation.[14] For three weeks they enjoyed a seashore vacation, eighteenth-century style. (Barry was one of Long Branch's first visitors of note; by the end of the century seven presidents had visited, including the mortally wounded James Garfield.)

The sun and salt air, a tonic for Sarah and Isaac, restored a youthful spring to Barry's step, and newfound determination to resume his duties. Newspaper headlines warned of the increase in "Captures made by Guadeloupe Privateers," and Stoddert wanted every idle warship heading to the Caribbean. Returning home, Barry expected that Humphreys had performed his usual miracles, with the *United States* back in fighting trim.[15]

He was dejected at the sight of her. "It is astounding to see the Condition she is in," he wrote Stoddert. "There was not a plank above the water what is rotten," he continued. After adding that "she will not be out of the Carpenters' hands before the first of October," Barry changed the subject: hearing that Truxton's expense accounts were reimbursed, Barry wanted the same done for him.

He then took a page out of Stoddert's book—actually, his letters— and mimicked the secretary's penchant for carping about dallying captains and idle ships: "it is very distressing to me to be confined so long in port when my country is suffering so much by captors." Citing the numerous French successes, he threw a jab at Stoddert and Adams, being "very much surprised when I hear so many of our merch[ant] vessels is captured": this did not happen on *his* watch. It was also a criticism of the squadron leaders in the West Indies.

Talbot, whom Barry hardly knew, was serving admirably if unspectacularly, an apt description of Barry's past two years. But Decatur, Murray, and Truxton were friends.[16]

By October 3, 1800, repairs on the *United States* were nearly finished; unbeknownst to Adams, Stoddert, and Barry, the Quasi-War was finished. Adams's envoys had successfully negotiated a treaty with Talleyrand, although it would be weeks before word reached American shores. From Washington, Stoddert sent orders to Barry to enlist a crew, and fill his officer vacancies.[17]

One application arrived as the muster rolls were nearly complete. To Barry's surprise, Stoddert nominated his own son: "I am afraid my Boy is too careless and too thoughtless ever to make a good sailor— I am afraid, too, you will be too kind to him, and he has already been spoilt by too much indulgence. I hope you will not treat him too well—nor excuse him from any of the duties performed by other boys his age and standings. I shall be much obliged if you would order him to be very attentive."[18]

While Barry was flattered by Stoddert's request, there were extenuating circumstances. Stoddert knew the war was about to end, and this might be young Ben's only chance at action on the high seas; the *Constitution*'s officers may have been prejudiced against a "southerner," regardless of who his father was; and Murray was known to have a heavy hand with his young officers. Nevertheless, Stoddert's reason may have been the obvious one: Barry was a master at molding officers. Truxton had been the war's hero, but even Stoddert could not deny that under Barry the *United States* had served as a de facto naval academy. The list of officers promoted from Barry's frigate was second to none: Ross, Mullowny, Barron, Decatur, Somers, Stewart, and Caldwell had all distinguished themselves on board what everyone knew to be "a happy ship."[19] Stoddert could not have done better for his son.

That said, the secretary continued complaining about Barry behind his back. Well aware that the combination of the commodore's seniority and his determination to return to the theater of action were politically insurmountable, Stoddert still did not want to give Barry the plum assignment of replacing Truxton at the head of the navy's largest squadron. He wanted that to go to Talbot, but in one letter indiscreetly bewailed, "I know not what to do with Barry if he is not sent thither." Finally, he decided that the *United States* "will leave the Delaware in time enough to escape the Frost—Barry will command her," confiding to Truxton that Barry's "rank and title" deserved "the Guadeloupe station."[20]

By November 10, Adams learned of the peace treaty, but the news came too late to affect the election. The peace Adams sought could not save his presidency. Stoddert knew his days, too, were numbered. From Philadelphia, Barry waited impatiently for final orders: "We have every thing ready for sailing," one young sailor wrote. The only noteworthy event was the delivery of a baby, "a young sailor born on board our ship," described as "a fine looking boy."[21] Who the woman was or why she was on board is not known.

The child was delivered by the frigate's surgeon, Edward Cutbush, who had joined Barry's staff a year earlier. A protégé of Rush, he was meticulous and far-sighted in ordering supplies, and had been advised by Rush in treating Barry's asthma attacks. A member of the American Philosophical Society with a passion for research, he was intent on studying the Gulf Stream on this voyage, and bought a sea thermometer for his studies. Cutbush, a real-life Stephen Maturin, was thrilled that Barry was both amenable and generally interested.[22] (On their return voyage, Cutbush diligently recorded air and water temperatures, skulking about the galley at all hours and frequently interrupting Barry's slumber in the process. He became convinced that "the Thermometer may become an Instrument of great utility in the hands of Navigators."[23])

A few days later, Barry received new orders. The wife of Philadelphian Edward Shippen had written Stoddert requesting passage to Antigua, on Murray's *Constellation*. Instead, Stoddert offered the *United States* as a substitute.[24] He assured Mrs. Shippen that Barry, "old as he is," would not mind. With this cavalier offer, Stoddert showed he considered Barry nothing more than commander of a packet, relegating the navy's flagship to that status just to make his point.[25] Barry had seen his share of slights and insults, but nothing cut like this.

Last-minute delays kept the frigate in the Delaware until December 6, when Stoddert finally ordered Barry to "assume the command of our Squadron, on the Guadeloupe station." Due to "The present state of uncertainty" about the treaty, Adams and Stoddert acknowledged that "it is difficult to prescribe the conduct to be pursued toward French National Ships." Accordingly, Barry was not to make "Encounters with Ships of this Description." As to privateers, however, Barry and his squadron were "to treat them as heretofore . . . unless Peace should be produced"–all this contingent upon the French navy and the privateers leaving American merchantmen alone.[26]

Just before departure Barry was laid low by another asthma attack. His lung capacity was deteriorating; one nineteenth-century physician, noting how the "hypertrophy of the bronchial muscles" resulted in "a permanent thickening of the walls and consequent narrowing of their caliber," could well have been describing the commodore's condition. Barry sent the frigate downriver in Cyrus Talbot's capable hands, coming on board at Bombay Hook on December 14; two days later, the frigate was "Off Cape Henlopen, Wind light, atmosphere clear."[27]

Two sails were sighted on New Year's Day; peering through his spyglass, Barry identified one as an armed schooner, then "tacked and chased her." This race was over before it started; that evening, the *United States* "brought to the Amer[ican] Brig *Sally* from New Haven." The prize crew of eight Frenchmen surrendered peacefully. The *Sally*'s captain told his rescuers he was "captured by the French schooner *Diamaid* the day before." An hour later, Barry "saw the French privateer to the leeward," and the game of cat and mouse continued as before. The schooner took the *United States* on an eight-hour chase, even losing the frigate at nine o'clock. But any relief the French captain felt was short lived when the *United States* soon reappeared on the horizon. In the wee morning hours, the frigate "came up with the prize."[28] The *Diamaid* was Barry's last capture.

One week later, Barry was at St. Kitts. The local newspapers carried the latest reports from America: "Governor Davie had reached

America," bringing the peace treaty with him. While waiting to relieve Truxton, more news arrived: Jefferson was elected president. Barry and his fellow captains could only surmise how this development would affect their future; most Republicans were no friends of the navy. On January 15, 1801, Truxton sailed into view on board the *President*, the latest forty-four-gun frigate. Like Barry, Truxton was flying the broad blue pennant of a commodore. He may have disputed Talbot's seniority, but not Barry's: one quick order from Truxton "hauled down ours & ran up a long one"–the banner of a captain. After assuring Barry of the scarcity of French privateers, he departed with his squadron for home.[29]

Barry proceeded to his most frustrating haunt, Guadeloupe, to see what kind of reception an American ship would receive. As before French guns were run out, and troops went to their stations. Only this time it was "to Receive the Commodore" and "fire a Salute," a far cry from Barry's previous visits. In return, he assured French officials that no fighting would start with the *United States*. The war had decimated the economy of Guadeloupe; beef soared to twenty dollars a barrel and flour twice as much.[30]

For two months, Barry kept his captains busy with cruises and convoy escorts. Finally, one captain, David Jewett, spoke for them all, seeking permission to "return to the United States as soon as [Barry] will permit." On April 12, supply ships arrived with Stoddert's latest orders: Barry was to send his squadron home and "make your best way to Philadelphia." The good news was relayed to his captains. Once the ships were resupplied, Barry saw no need to tarry. By evening he was "off the NW end of St. Eustatia."[31]

Barry was determined to see how the *United States* would fare on the sail home. He handled her cautiously heading to the West Indies; now, not even a "Heavy hard Sea from the Northward and West" kept him from pushing "his favorite" to her limits. She responded wonderfully, logging 220 miles one day. By April 21, she made Delaware Bay; Barry "Took a Pilot on board" and was greeted by springtime in the Delaware: "wind blows very heavy with Thunder and lightening." The severe storms forced Barry to proceed slowly upriver, not reaching Chester until April 28. It took just nine days to reach Cape Henlopen, but over a week to get to Philadelphia.[32]

Barry disembarked from the *United States* at Chester and took a carriage directly home, to find Strawberry Hill draped in black cloth. His nephew Michael Hayes had died. Whether he was lost at sea or died in Philadelphia is unknown. His small estate of five hundred dollars was divided between his sister Eleanor Kavanaugh and Betsy Hayes.[33]

From Strawberry Hill Barry sent word to Washington of his arrival. In February, Stoddert tendered his resignation to President-elect Jefferson, ironically citing his health as the primary reason (in fairness, his old wound from the Brandywine was giving him new pains that accompanied his aching financial condition), agreeing to stay until a successor was named.[34] Jefferson's search dragged into March, as one Republican after another declined to accept a cabinet post most believed would be of no consequence in Jefferson's pre-sumably antinavalist administration. Finally, Samuel Smith was per-suaded to serve on an interim basis.[35]

Before leaving office Stoddert wrote a flurry of proposals: selling "all the Public Vessels, except the [thirteen] Frigates;" reducing the navy's muster rolls; and recommending that only twenty-eight cap-tains be retained (Congress soon whittled that to nine). In his final act as secretary, he took the money from the unbuilt seventy-fours to buy the shore lands that became the navy yards in Washington, Norfolk, Boston, Philadelphia, Portsmouth, and New York—exactly what Barry suggested years earlier.[36]

Samuel Smith's first order to Barry came in early May: pay off his crew and keep only as many needed to sail the *United States* to Washington, "where it is intended she shall be laid up." This time Barry turned to family for his second officer, placing the frigate under Richard Somers' command as she slipped down to New Castle. The twenty-three-year-old was proud of his small success, bringing the ship downriver with "no Accident happening." The passage became one extended family affair; Patrick Hayes, just downriver in the *Hope*, "stayed and spent the evening" on board. After a fine dinner in his uncle's cabin, Patrick was rowed back to his ship in the early morn-ing hours, getting under way at daylight. Barry made for Washington under a "spare leading breeze from the Westw'd."[37]

He had already voiced concerns that the Potomac might be too shallow for the frigates draft, and he was right. The *United States* struck the river's soft bottom several times. Two schooners were dispatched; once alongside the frigate everything possible was unloaded to lighten her, from "2 Guns 24 Pounders" to "1 puncheon vinegar." Their holds bursting with ordnance and supplies, the schooners waddled like hippos upriver towards the new navy yard. Lighter by 700 tons, the *United States* was next waylaid by guests, including Jefferson and his new Treasury Secretary, arch antinavalist Albert Gallatin. Their visit was short and semisweet, with Barry saluting the president with his few remaining small guns. Barry continued up the eastern branch of the Potomac after officials assured him that "no injury [would] arise."38

They were right—only the ship rose. Despite her sluggish passage, the *United States* hit a bank of mud with such impact that "she scied seven feet"—her proud bow rising higher and higher into the air. It was the *Effingham* in reverse. Fortunately, Barry had kept the ship's block and tackle on board. All hands worked feverishly to get the frigate off the mud at high tide. It would take three more days before the *United States* was "moor'd at last."39

Barry found the new capital a shabby hamlet of shacks and cheap hotels, eventually locating the new Secretary of the Navy's office. Once he handed over his report and inventory, Smith handed him a letter from Sarah and told him he could leave the frigate under Somers' supervision and depart for Philadelphia "whenever it shall be agreeable." Returning to his cabin, he read Sarah's letter, written "by candlelight and With Out Spectacles." Commiserating over his troubles in getting up the Potomac, she was completely confident he "surmounted them all" and looked forward to "at least a few months of your society to make me happy."40 For twenty-four years, Sarah never failed to send letters like this one, encouraging her husband. All she asked in return was his companionship.41

Smith said he could leave Washington "whenever it was agreeable." That very hour was agreeable to Barry. He closed the door to his cabin and came on deck. The few remaining hands snapped to attention, the bos'n's whistle blew, and Somers ordered the broad blue pennant lowered. It fluttered to the deck in the humid air and was neatly folded. With one last salute, Barry climbed down the gangway, the first steps of his journey home.

———————————

At Strawberry Hill he found Sarah with Benjamin Rush, tending to Isaac. Only 49 years old, the watchmaker was dying. Sarah brought him to Strawberry Hill for its peace and quiet, Patrick's family having moved to their own home in town following the birth of a third child, Thomas. Isaac died on June 15. Sarah was devastated.[42]

After Isaac's burial, the Barrys spent a week at Long Branch, accompanied by James and Jude. While some Philadelphians felt the journey "too distant and rough for female participation," the trip was made as much for Sarah as for Barry's health. Whether the salt air and booming surf eased her broken heart, it did wonders for her husband. "Our good old uncle," Betsy Hayes wrote Patrick, "is much improved since his return."[43]

An artificially suspenseful letter arrived from Smith. Only nine captains were to be retained. Smith dragged out the obvious through several sentences before revealing that "the President has been pleased to select you as one of those who are retained." Barry was put on half-pay status "until called into actual Service." He did not see this as the first step to retirement. There might not be any official duties, but he was still intent on another command, holding out hope for becoming the navy's first admiral.[44]

News from the Barbary Coast was not good, especially the embarrassing treatment of William Bainbridge. After delivering the latest tribute to Algiers, Bainbridge's frigate, the *George Washington*, was commandeered to take the dey's ambassador, his harem, and a private zoo to Constantinople, flying the Algerian flag at the maintop in place of the stars and stripes. On the positive side, President Jefferson found the navy an invaluable resource for his foreign policies, and offered command of a Mediterranean squadron to Truxton. The hero of the Quasi-War again played the rank card, hoping Jefferson would do what Adams did not: place him above Talbot.

When Jefferson declined to do so, Truxton turned down his offer. In a twist, the president turned not to Talbot but to Richard Dale. It was an assignment Barry would have loved.[45]

All that summer, he invited visitors to Strawberry Hill in an effort to keep Sarah's spirits up. The Hayes family came for short stays, as did the remarried Reynold Keen, whose growing family overran Barry's estate, raising enough clamor that Barry was happy to see them one day and wishing he was away at sea the next. A happy Richard Somers visited in August with news; he was promoted to first officer of the frigate *Boston*, commanded by Barry's friend Daniel McNeill, who passed along his pleasure at "hearing of the reestablishment of [Barry's] health." Barry seemed pleased with his leisure time, but beneath the surface was an urge to get to sea. One more successful cruise and he could swallow the anchor on his terms.[46] He waited for word from Smith.

It came, instead, from another old colleague, Thomas Tingey, now superintendent of the Washington Navy Yard. By now Samuel Smith's brother, Robert, was Secretary of the Navy. Robert lacked Samuel's administrative skills, but at least someone had answered Jefferson's call. The president was contemplating sending another squadron to the Mediterranean and the *United States* was being refitted—the very news Barry hoped for. Acting at Jefferson's behest, Tingey inquired "whether you determined to command her yourself or to surrender your old favorite to be enjoyed and commanded by another."[47]

The letter reached Strawberry Hill on August 14, and Barry replied immediately: "If I am called upon and my health will admit I shall as a good citizen feel my self bound to come forward and do my might to Subdue any Enemy to my Country."[48] Barry waited, and waited, for further orders, not knowing Tingey's true feelings about him. Barry did not know that Stoddert had included Tingey in his diatribes about Barry, and Tingey had passed them along.[49]

With fall approaching, Barry made two investments: a new home, at 126 Spruce Street, and a joint venture with Patrick. Uncle and nephew purchased the schooner *Edward and Edmond*, along with a hold full of goods for $6,000. Barry handled the financial details while Patrick took the ship on a voyage to Cuba.[50]

Patrick no sooner reached the Capes when Barry received orders from Robert Smith—not to go to sea but to accompany Alexander Murray to prove some guns. Another letter from Smith followed shortly, requesting information on his "old favorite's" false keel. Barry asserted he "never discovered any deficiency in her" and that "her bottom is in perfect good order." Give his frigate "a Bower Anchor" along with "two Cables and some sails" and she would be ready; give him his orders and he would start rounding up officers and a crew.[51]

But that winter Barry's recent spate of good health abruptly ended. The asthma attacks were so severe that Murray wrote Smith: "Capt. Barry being too unwell to attend," he went alone to prove the guns.[52] Barry's inability to make a day trip was enough for Smith and Tingey. They began looking for a new squadron commander.

The year 1801 ended with a cold snap; Sarah Barry was particularly glad they were settled in their new home, closer to family and friends. For the first time in years the Barrys spent Christmas in Philadelphia, with Betsy Hayes and her three children, while Patrick was at sea.[53]

Throughout the winter Barry devoured the newspapers for developments from the Barbary Coast, learning of Charles Stewart's victory over one of the dey's warships and that Somers and the *Boston* were at Tripoli. Truxton refused yet another offer to command a Mediterranean squadron, believing his assigned frigate, the *Chesapeake*, too small for a commodore's command. Citing an attack of gout, he decided to "quit the navy." Richard Morris was given the assignment.[54] Barry was still "on the beach" as far as Smith and Tingey were concerned. His future seemed intertwined with that of his frigate, languishing at the Washington Navy Yard.

At Strawberry Hill that spring, Barry heard from his niece, Eleanor Hayes Kavanaugh. She received Patrick's letter about Michael's death "with a sorrowful heart," but not yet the money promised her from her brother's estate. Her husband's failing health and her suffering children compelled her to ask that at least a hundred dollars "be sent at once." Another letter came from Nancy Merriman Kelly, the cousin born to Barry's Aunt Margaret shortly after his own birth. Her mother's death was just one of "many other

Calamities," the worst concerning her husband, Michael Kelly. "I Lost my husband in the Disturbance"–her euphemism for the recent Irish rebellion against the British Empire–"in one of the Engagements." At fifty-nine, Kelly had joined "the Boys of Wexford" at New Ross on June 5, 1798, and was one of the first to die in three days of vicious fighting. For years, Barry's father had given her "half a Guinea" out of the money Barry sent home; could he send that to her, "Being in Such in Need?" He could.[55]

Barry also suffered a new wave of asthma attacks that spring, but after a visit to an Easton, Pennsylvania, spa he was well enough "to try some guns in Jersey." To the family, he seemed healthier than he had been in months; Sarah happily commented that "My dear Cap' Barry" was "quite well."[56]

He returned from New Jersey to find Strawberry Hill in a maelstrom. Sarah was gone, but the three Hayes children were there, under Jude's watchful eye. Yellow fever was again sweeping through Philadelphia, but Betsy, in the last days of another pregnancy, would not risk the carriage ride to Strawberry Hill, sending her children and a servant. Sarah left for Philadelphia the very next day, "determined not to quit until I see Betsy safe in bed."[57]

Just below Philadelphia, an embittered Patrick paced the deck of the *Edward and Edmond*. His voyage to Cuba had been a disaster; the schooner leaking, the value of the flour in her hold was plummeting due to a glut on the market, and his investors, including his brother-in-law, William Jonas Keen, were furious. Confined aboard ship for a quarantine of "ten tegious [tedious] days," he was worried over Betsy's condition. Fears of financial ruin overwhelmed him. Barry urged Patrick to "say nothing" further about the trip until he reached home, but it was Sarah who provided the wisest counsel: "We have another event to Keep us which I have already told you I am sure is in waiting for you," she wrote. "Do not my dear Nephew suffer your self to be so agitated. Keep your stren[g]th up," she finished, "there is not any thing to fear with the blessing of God."[58]

Her words were prophetic. The damage to the schooner was not severe. To offset his nephew's losses, Barry gave Patrick his shares in the venture. By August, Patrick was doubly blessed–command of the merchant ship *George Washington*, "as sound as though just off the stocks," and a fourth child, Isaac Austin Hayes. Barry was the infant's sponsor at his baptism.[59]

Summer's end found Barry battling asthma, a bureaucrat's cost report from his gun-proving trip, and joining Dale and Bainbridge in Philadelphia as they grilled midshipmen for their lieutenant's exam. In the Mediterranean, Richard Morris seemed more concerned with social affairs than duty (he brought his wife along, whom his officers called "the Commodoris"). Jefferson relieved him, fueling rumors that Barry would be offered command and spurring letters from other idle officers. One land-locked lieutenant, "very anxious to join your ship," implored Barry for a berth, "being heartily tired of doing nothing."[60] So was Barry.

In anticipation of his departure, Barry sold the home on Spruce, purchasing a larger, three-story house at Tenth and Chestnut Streets.[61] All through autumn he waited for Smith's letter. He was fifty-seven years old, and knew this command would be his last. In late November a package came from Smith, and Barry opened it with great expectation. There were no orders. Instead, he found a gold medal, struck by Congress to honor the "gallantry and good conduct" of Thomas Truxton for his service during the Quasi-War with France. As Barry was "Senior Officer in the Navy, and entitled to the most respectful consideration," Smith could not "resist the inclination I feel of presenting one [of Truxton's medals] to you."[62] Jones was the first naval hero to be so recognized, Truxton the second. For all his accomplishments in two wars, Barry was never similarly honored. Pride in his friend's accomplishment was mixed with the lack of news regarding his own appointment.

In December, the long-awaited orders from Smith came: "We shall have occasion to keep a small force in the Mediterranean, and upon the return of Commodore Morris we shall expect your services at that station. This information I consider it proper to give you at this time in order that when called upon you may be prepared to perform this duty without injury to your private affairs."[63] But the long-anticipated chance at "honor and success" was too late. Smith's letter came to a man no longer capable of going to sea. Barry's asthma was unrelenting, and Rush's treatments were becoming less and less successful.[64]

Barry began 1803 with a letter to Smith, sorrowfully declining the offer he had been yearning for. The captain who once easily clambered up the gangways of ships could barely climb a flight of stairs.[65] Smith was right about one thing: Barry began putting his "private affairs" in order. He sold some investments, including his shares in the "Schuylkill Bridge"–a venture that netted more than seven hundred dollars. In February, Rush told Barry what he already knew: time was getting short.[66]

Summoning William Jonas Keen, Barry dictated his will, a three-page document witnessed by John Brown, Reynold Keen, and young Somers, about to depart for his first command, the schooner *Nautilus*. Barry named Sarah, Patrick, and John Leamy as executors. While ashore, Somers brought Barry the latest news from the Barbary Coast. Following Barry, Dale also refused Smith's request to command a squadron in the Mediterranean; like Truxton, he was intent on being an admiral first, and a squadron commander second. Smith next turned to Edward Preble, who would prove to be the very man Jefferson and Smith were looking for.[67]

By May, Barry's condition was taxing Rush for new approaches for relief. He started bringing a colleague; "in consultation with Dr. Physick" now appeared regularly in his ledger. But even Philip Syng Physick, the leading surgeon of his day, could not delay the inevitable. Barry knew where he wanted to spend his remaining days: Strawberry Hill. Rush told Sarah the journey to the country was risky but worthwhile, and arranged transportation. On a May morning, several carriages and wagons lumbered out of Philadelphia, through the growing township of Northern Liberties. After a slow ride up Frankford Road, they turned onto the dirt path that led to Strawberry Hill.[68]

Summer did not pass peacefully. Barry's attacks became stronger, and Rush and Physick made several visits to Strawberry Hill. The spells were similar to his attack in Lisbon–a feeling of suffocation. Like Rush, Physick advocated bleeding, and while they continued in their use of emetics, the labida was now laced with laudanum, which relaxed Barry's spasms and suppressed his cough. The doctors showed Sarah how to administer a teaspoon under her husband's tongue, which quickly brought Barry a drugged calm. He was no longer a sick man. He was an invalid.[69]

The squadron that was to have been Barry's departed in July.[70] Preble's captains read like a reunion of Barry's officers: the *Siren*, Charles Stewart; the *Argus*, young Decatur; and the *Nautilus* under Somers.[71] Barry gloried in their promotions; if he could no longer fly his country's colors, at least they could. Betsy Hayes brought him Patrick's letters from the other side of the world, upbeat reports of his successful trading in Canton.[72] If Stewart, Decatur, and Somers were carrying Barry's legacy to the shores of Tripoli, Patrick was the able successor to his merchant days.

His condition steadily worsened, but he did not complain. To his visitors he seemed remarkably at peace. Sarah was alarmed, but he was not. On August 23, William Jonas Keen noted the changes and wrote Somers, "sorry in the first place to Inform you of Commodore Barry's Illness," adding, "he is now thought to be on his last tack." Keen found Barry resigned to his end: "He said to me this day that he was nearly done which I feel is true." Keen also wrote Betsy, staying at Somers Point, that Barry's brave front was "only flattering us to make the easier exit." Rush was summoned again; Keen, knowing the comfort Betsy was to Sarah, urged his sister to "pack up and come." He met her at the Arch Street Ferry, and brought her at once to Strawberry Hill.[73] By September 10, Barry was drifting in and out of consciousness. Sarah suggested returning to Philadelphia to be closer to his doctors, but Rush ruled it out.[74] The only thing to do was make his friend as comfortable as possible.

September 12, 1803, began as "a pleasant day" with winds "inkling to the east"–the telltale sign of approaching storms.[75] As Sarah, Betsy, and William looked on, Barry's breathing became shallow. With dawn came a steady rain. It continued through the morning when, in the great bedroom, Barry died. There were no conscious returns to storms pounding the *Barbadoes*, or battles fought from the *Alliance*'s quarterdeck, or to the grand vistas of China. Barry simply passed away.[76]

Word was sent posthaste into town. Funerals were frequently held the day after a death, and Sarah wanted word of her husband's passing printed in the afternoon papers. His body was carried down to the waiting wagon while Sarah, Betsy, and her children climbed into the carriage. The same small caravan that brought Barry to his beloved estate now took him back to Tenth and Chestnut Streets; Rush and Physick, making their final visit as physicians, were the first of his friends to pay respects to the widow. The afternoon edition of the *Pennsylvania Gazette* posted the announcement, ironically next to reports about "the dreadful rebellion in Dublin."[77] It stunned Philadelphia:

> BARRY.–The friends of the late Commodore Barry are requested to attend his funeral, to-morrow morning at 10 O'Clock . . . from his late dwelling, 186 Chestnut Street, The Members of the Cincinnati are particularly requested to attend the funeral of their deceased member.[78]

It was sunny but brisk on the fourteenth. At the appointed time, members of the Cincinnati led Sarah, her family, "Capt. Rush's well-disciplined volunteer corps," and the "numerous train of [Barry's] fellow citizens" to St. Mary's Roman Catholic Church at Fourth and Locust Streets. Sailor and landsman, merchant and dockhand, Republican and Federalist filled the pews as the colors of the sun-lit stained glass windows fell over them during the requiem mass. When the service ended, the mourners silently walked behind the church to the graveyard for the interment.[79] With bare heads they heard the priest utter the words *requiescat in pacem*, and then went home.

Newspapers spread word of Barry's death around the country, most reprinting the headline from the *Massachusetts Spy*: "At Philadelphia, Comm. John Barry, to his valour was owed much the honor acquired on the seas during the Revolution." Others mentioned "the scope of his character," his being "a warm and steady friend," and "a firm patriot."[80]

The will was executed. To Patrick and Betsy Hayes, Barry gave "one-thousand Spanish milled dollars," with his "wearing apparel" and "instruments of navigation" earmarked for Patrick. Each of their children received $100.00 except John Barry Hayes; the namesake received two hundred dollars. Barry wanted William Austin to have his silver-hilted sword "As a token of my esteem." The gold-hilted sword that belonged to John Paul Jones was given "to my good friend Capt. Richard Dale," who served both captains so well. To "my negro man James and my mulatto woman Jude" he provided freedom and "an annuity of twenty pounds lawful money" each year. Their manumission came with a caveat; it would only be granted upon Sarah's remarrying or her death. Until then, they were still her property. Everything else was bequeathed to Sarah.[81]

Moved by his own sorrow and the citywide depth of feeling at Barry's death, Rush wrote his old friend Jefferson, requesting official acknowledgment via a letter from Jefferson to Sarah, and the wearing of a black armband by federal government representatives as a sign of national mourning. While "No one would more willingly than myself pay just tribute due to the services of Capt. Barry," Jefferson refused. After citing his own appeal to Washington "that we might wear mourning" in observance of Franklin's death, and that Washington "thought it best to avoid it," Jefferson deemed "it is prudent not to engage myself in a practice that may become embarrassing."[82] There would be no official mourning.

Sarah accepted the well-meaning Rush's offer to write the eulogy for Barry's tomb. It was the first in an outpouring of flowery tributes and overblown poems that Barry would have found uncomfortable. It fell to two old friends, the sailor John Kessler and the Irishman John Brown, to sum him up as he lived: "the first of patriots, and best of men."[83]

AFTERWORD

ARMCHAIR HISTORIANS ARGUE ENDLESSLY OVER who was "Father of the American Navy," but Sarah Barry certainly has claim to being its mother. Young officers never failed to pay their respects whenever in Philadelphia, visiting her at 186 Chestnut Street. With Dale and Somers already in the family, Susan Bainbridge, daughter of William (who finally won his share of glory commanding the *Constitution*), married Sarah's grand-nephew Thomas Hayes in 1825. Sarah's home became "the pleasant resort of both the young and the old," and she became renowned in maritime circles as "a prudent and excellent adviser."[1]

She also increased the family fortunes with a series of astute transactions in everything from real estate to the Germantown Turnpike. Investment in ships became her passion. John Leamy handled countless transactions whereby Sarah loaned thousands of dollars to merchant captains or invested in their goods.[2] In 1805, she sold Strawberry Hill for the handsome price of $12,500, bringing her husband's estate to $27,000–far from the wealth of his friends Rush and Biddle, but better off than his old superiors Morris and Stoddert.[3] Sarah never remarried. She died on November 13, 1831, at the age of seventy-seven, having "commanded the respect, esteem and tender affection of all those who had the happiness of an intimate acquaintance with her."[4]

James and Jude never received their twenty-pound annuities. Thorough inspection of state and municipal records, newspapers, or church records uncovered no manumission papers, "runaway" notices or other documentation regarding them. They likely did not outlive Sarah and died her slaves. Upon James's death, his twenty pounds went to "the Trustees of the Roman Catholic Society worshiping at St. Mary"; Jude's to Margaret Howlin's family in Ireland.[5]

William Austin never returned to Philadelphia. Since 1801 he had lived in Charleston, South Carolina, where he became a merchant. Barry's death all but ended any correspondence with his family. His mercantile pursuits never matched his pre-Revolution success with the Arch Street Ferry, and by 1814 both his business and health were ruined.[6] On August 5 of that year he wrote Sarah, begging for the three hundred dollars bequeathed him in Isaac's will thirteen years earlier. "I have not for many years considered myself as belonging to the family," he wrote; only his "long and serious indispositions and the extream badness of the times" forced a quill to his hand.[7] He died four weeks later, before Sarah's check arrived.[8]

Patrick Hayes returned from China in 1804. He made one last voyage to Canton commanding the *Dorothea*, and then only invested in trade with China, restricting his voyages to the Caribbean. By the 1820s he owned a small fleet of merchant ships, including a brig christened *Commodore Barry*.[9] He also followed in his uncle's footsteps, joining the Sea Captains' Club and the Society of Cincinnati. When war with England was declared in 1812 he was forty-two, and considered too old to be offered a naval command. He served several terms as harbor master, maritime warden of Philadelphia, and director of the Marine Insurance Company. He became a naturalized citizen in 1822. Hayes lived to be eighty-six years old, dying in 1856, outliving his wife by three years.

Patrick and Betsy survived all their children save one. John Barry Hayes died at age eleven in 1807; Sarah Barry Hayes, sickly throughout her short life, died at twenty-three in 1821; it was the death Patrick took hardest of all. Thomas Hayes, who entered the navy as a midshipman at age fourteen in 1815, subsequently followed his father and became a respected merchant captain. He died at age forty-eight in 1849. Only Patrick Barry Hayes, born in 1809, outlived his parents, dying at fifty-three during the Civil War. Isaac and Patrick also worked in the "family business," each serving as a supercargo for their father's ships.[10]

At the time of Barry's death, Robert Morris was released from debtors' prison, living in a small house two blocks from Barry's Chestnut Street residence. Gouverneur Morris engineered an annuity for Robert's wife, as Robert's debts legally prevented him any possession of funds. The titan who carried the financial burden for the Revolution, once the epitome of success, died penniless in 1806. Few mourned his passing; only his Icarus-like fall from grace was remembered by the public.[11]

Francis Hopkinson had been in the ground twelve years when Barry died. He championed the Constitution, wrote a series of songs about and dedicated to George Washington, and was serving as a federal judge when he was "struck down by an attack of apoplexy" in 1791.[12]

After the Revolution John Kessler opened a grocery store across from Fanueil Hall in Boston and married a New England sailor's daughter. Over the next several years he lost his business, worked as a tax collector, and later was a fur trader with the Indians in Maine before finally returning to sea. After the death of two of his small children he and his wife returned to Philadelphia, where he became constable of Northern Liberties. By 1816 he was on a pension "for injuries received while in the service on board the Frigate *Alliance*." In 1813 he and John Brown wrote the "Life of Commodore Barry" for *Portfolio* magazine. He died in 1840.[13]

The years after the Revolution were not happy ones for John Brown. His wife died young, leaving him with an infant son to care for. The boy died two years later. Brown never remarried, and never retired from practicing law. He frequently visited Sarah Barry, who constantly relied on his advice and friendship. Like Barry, he provided for his relatives back in Ireland. When Ireland was threatened with an invasion by Napoleon in 1800, he sent for his late sister's children; one nephew later died on a voyage to China. In addition to his charity work with the Hibernian Society, he became a patron of the Pennsylvania Academy of the Fine Arts and the "City Dancing Assembly." He never remarried. When he died in 1833 at age eighty-five, the spyglass John Paul Jones used in his battle against the *Serapis* was found among his possessions.[14]

Joshua Humphreys continued shipbuilding for the United States Navy. His innovative designs revitalized navies everywhere; Czar Alexander I requested a Humphreys-built Russian Navy in 1824. The disowned Quaker lived to be eighty-six years old.[15]

Ben Stoddert's last years were unhappy ones both financially and politically. While Baltimore's maritime boom cut into Philadelphia's business, it demolished Georgetown's. Stoddert was ruined. Jefferson's election, followed by Madison's ascent in 1808, ended the Federalist Party that Stoddert so deeply loved. He died in 1813, as war with his old trading partner, Great Britain, raged—a war in which the navy he championed proved England's equal, frigate for frigate.[16]

Barry's Royal Navy opponents continued to distinguish themselves after the Revolution. He was right about Sampson Edwards; his bravery was rewarded with a better ship. Cleared of any negligence in the loss of the *Atalanta*, he was given command of the frigate *Diana* to cruise the Bay of Biscay and the West Indies. By 1801 he was a rear admiral, with two sons serving as lieutenants.[17]

James Vashon became captain of the *St. Albans*, a sixty-four, but in the eight years he commanded her "he never fired a gun in anger, nor saw an enemy." He resigned his commission in 1801. When war with France broke out again in 1803 he offered his services and was made admiral. His encounter with Barry stuck forever in his craw: whenever the subject of the *Alliance* versus the *Sybil* came up, he always insisted it was the *Alliance* that "sheared off when she had it in her power to continue the action."[18]

Andrew Snape Hamond was knighted in 1778, and commanded the fleet that helped take Charleston in 1780. Later that year he was appointed lieutenant-governor of Nova Scotia. Named a baronet in 1783, he served on the court of inquiry that tried the captured mutineers of HMS *Bounty*. He died in 1828, weeks shy of his ninetieth birthday.[19]

After the *Raleigh*'s capture, James Wallace continued his ruthless punishment of all things American. But in 1780, the *Experiment* was caught in a terrific gale off Savannah and dismasted. As the storm cleared, D'Estaing's fleet sailed over the horizon, capturing Barry's wiliest opponent. The Admiralty commended Wallace for his gallant defense of the wounded ship, rewarding him with command of the *Nonesuch*, sixty-four, and sending him to harass the French coast. He, too, was made an admiral. Sir James then served as commander-in-chief and governor of Newfoundland, returning to England in 1797. No portrait of Wallace is known to exist. Like Barry, he died in 1803.[20]

Pierre Landais never commanded another ship in the American or French navies. He moved to New York City, forever beseeching Congress for money and dreaming of the chance to meet John Paul Jones and challenge his old rival to a duel. In 1787, he saw Jones on a street corner talking with a friend. Coming from behind, Landais yelled, "I spit in your face!" in hopes of provoking Jones, who later stated he neither heard Landais nor was spat on.[21] No duel was fought; thirty-one years later, Landais died at the age of eighty-seven in New York, and was buried in St. Patrick's cemetery.[22]

Benjamin Rush died in 1813, still Sarah's physician and still championing her late husband's heroics. Over the years he maintained a vigorous correspondence with John Adams. In 1813, he responded to a letter from Adams regarding the origins of the American navy. "Your anecdotes of the laborious birth of our little navy," he wrote, "are truly interesting." Then Rush added how "I once saw from the pen of Paul Jones and heard from the lips of Commodore Barry. In the journal of the former are the following words: 'My hands first hoisted the American flag.' The latter with equal exultation once said to me, 'the British Naval flag first struck to me,' alluding to his having taken the first British sloop of war."[23]

The kindly doctor sought to augment and agree with the dour, ancient ex-president, but Adams treated Rush's letter like a shot across all New England's bow. Immediately Adams wrote to another old soul, John Langdon, who had his share of dealings with Jones and Barry while in Congress. Citing "an irresistible propensity to compare notes," Adams let fly: "Both these vain boasts I know to be false."[24] Langdon, slower of foot but still quick with pen, concurred. Ever parochial, Adams made the point that John Manley and other New Englanders were first. "Our poor old tame, good-natured pussy Massachusetts," lamented the not so poor or tame, but certainly prickly Adams.[25] After assaulting the unassuming Rush with two vociferous letters, Rush explained how "Capt. Jones meant only that the American flag was hoisted first on board a *national* ship by his hand, and Capt. Barry meant only that a British *national* ship struck first to his *national* flag."[26]

For Rush, it was politicizing yellow fever all over again, and he chastised Adams: "you do me great injustice in supposing I possess a single Pennsylvania or anti-New England prejudice."[27] There may not be any battles or plagues for the two old men to quarrel about, but there was still the American navy.

Thomas Truxton forever rued his decision not to take the command of the Mediterranean squadron. Subsequent offers to serve fell on deaf ears, even when his entreaties were accompanied with one of the hundred gold medals he personally ordered at his expense. Only one, Vice President Aaron Burr, lent a willing ear to Truxton's complaints over lack of use by Jefferson. On July 4, 1804, Truxton attended a dinner with Burr, sitting next to Alexander Hamilton. Truxton "had not the most distant idea of their being any differences between them." Days later, Burr killed Hamilton at twenty paces. Truxton's public association with Burr ended any chance of reinstatement. After Burr concocted his scheme to conquer Mexico, he approached Truxton to lead "Naval operations." Truxton would have nothing to do with it, and testified against Burr during his trial for treason. He never returned to the sea. Charles Biddle wrangled the post of "High Sheriff of Philadelphia" for his old friend. The gout-ridden Truxton died in Philadelphia in 1822, at sixty-seven.[28]

After distinguished service against the Barbary pirates, Richard Dale resigned his commission and went into the insurance business (at one point serving as director of the Insurance Company of North America), remaining active in the Episcopal Church and the charitable concerns of the Sea Captains' Club. When he died in 1826, his widow moved to a home close to Sarah's.[29]

Barry's "boys" earned more than their measures of glory and tragedy. When luckless William Bainbridge lost the frigate *Philadelphia* to Barbary pirates, Edward Preble approved a dangerous mission under young Stephen Decatur to sail the ketch *Intrepid* into

Tripoli's harbor and burn the frigate. Remarkably, he succeeded without so much as losing a sailor. The young man's rise was meteoric; by the War of 1812 he commanded the *United States* and captured the frigate HMS *Macedonian*. Decatur's deeds placed him in the phalanx of Barry and Jones; like Jones and Truxton, he was rewarded by Congress with a gold medal.[30]

Richard Somers chafed at being overshadowed by his old schoolmate. On September 1804, it was his turn to command the *Intrepid* on another daring mission. He loaded her with explosives, and sailed her back into Tripoli harbor, with orders to light the fuse where the explosion could do the most damage to the dey's fleet. The *Intrepid* never reached the pirate ships. Without warning, she exploded in mid-harbor, killing Somers and every man aboard. His remains lie buried in Libya.[31]

Charles Stewart accompanied Decatur on his hair-raising mission to burn the *Philadelphia*. True to Barry's hunch, he did command better than he had been commanded, distinguishing himself during the Barbary Wars. In 1813 he became captain of the *Constitution*. "Old Ironsides" had already won two victories in the war; now came Stewart's turn. On February 20, 1813, he fought and captured two British ships of war: the frigate HMS *Cyane* and the corvette HMS *Levant*. It was the *Constitution*'s last victory in the War of 1812.[32]

Fate was not so kind to James Barron. The young hero who saved the *United States* in that horrific storm was a commodore himself in 1807 and senior commander of the *Chesapeake* when she was fired upon and seized by the HMS *Leopard*, fifty guns, ostensibly searching for British deserters. The incident was a public relations disaster for Jefferson. A court-martial found Barron guilty and severed him from the service. When he applied for reinstatement in 1818, he found his most vociferous opponent was his old shipmate Stephen Decatur. Barron challenged Decatur to a duel. Decatur accepted. William Bainbridge acted as Decatur's second. In deference to Barron's near-sightedness, Bainbridge agreed to a distance of eight paces. Decatur was mortally wounded. Forever disgraced, Barron outlived all of Barry's officers, dying in 1852.[33]

Following the War of 1812, the *United States* was sent back to the Mediterranean and patrolled the Algerian coast until 1819, when she returned to Hampton Roads for decommission. Slowed by wear and age, she was known to her sailors as "the Old Wagon." She was still seaworthy; on one voyage in 1842 she rounded Cape Horn; among her crew was Ordinary Seaman Herman Melville. After being used to suppress the African slave trade, she was laid up in Norfolk and lay fallow until the Civil War, when the Confederate Navy re-christened her the *Confederate States*, nineteen guns, and used her to defend Norfolk's harbor. Later, when Confederates tried to sink her in the Elizabeth River, they discovered how well Joshua Humphreys built Barry's favorite. After countless axes failed to split her live oaking, they bored holes in her hull to sink her. The Union Navy raised her and brought her back to Norfolk. But once the United States was whole, the *United States* was broken up. This time saws and axes succeeded in breaking her apart, and her wood was sold.[34]

Four destroyers were named after John Barry in the twentieth century. The first, a *Bainbridge*-class destroyer, was appropriately built at the Philadelphia Navy Yard. Thousands attended her christening, the champagne bottle smashed by Barry's great-great-grandniece Charlotte Barnes. After patrolling the South China Sea and Pacific, she served in convoys against German U-boats. She was sold in 1920. The second, a 1,200-ton *Clemson*-class destroyer was built that same year in Camden, New Jersey. In World War II she played an active roll against the German U-boat "wolf packs." In 1945, off Okinawa, she was hit by kamikaze pilots on two separate attacks. The second sunk her. The third ship, a 2,800-ton *Sherman*-class, was built in Bath, Maine, in 1956. Her duties included action off Vietnam and later in the Persian Gulf. She is currently moored at Washington Navy Yard, where Patrick Hayes's descendants, the Hepburn family of Philadelphia, presented her commander with a copy of John Kessler's memoirs.[35] The fourth is an *Arleigh Burke*-class destroyer, built in Pascagoula, Mississippi, and commissioned in 1992. She has participated in operations in the Persian Gulf, and assisted in the evacuation of American citizens during the 2006 conflict between Israel and Lebanon.[36]

In 1939, Barry's logs, uniforms, swords, and other artifacts were auctioned in New York by the Hepburn family.[37] Most of the collection went to the Library of Congress and other museums. Barry's cutlass hung in the Oval Office from 1961 to 1963, where it bore silent witness as another Irish-American naval hero, John F. Kennedy, navigated his way through the most perilous thirteen days of the Cold War, using the U.S. Navy in the judicious manner that Washington and Barry envisioned in 1794.[38]

Naval historians will forever argue over who deserves the title, "Father of the American Navy." There are enough worthy nominees: Washington, Adams, Franklin, Congress, Joshua Humphreys, and Edward Preble among them. But Jones and Barry are the two that slug it out the most often—or at least their supporters do. In terms of personalities, Jones and Barry are the Babe Ruth and Lou Gehrig of the American navy. From their papers, it is easy to see which is which. Jones wrote prolifically, never afraid to toot his own horn. Barry, as we have seen, never wrote two words if one would do. Jones is a broadside, full of bravado; Barry is a shot across the bow. When a statue of Barry was dedicated at Independence Hall in 1913, thousands attended. (It was the second statue in his honor; there is also one from the Centennial of 1876 in Fairmount Park.) A year later a third statue was erected in Washington, D.C. Woodrow Wilson delivered the address. A fourth, in County Wexford, faces the harbor.

These ceremonies were cap guns, however, compared to the twenty-one-gun salutelike return of John Paul Jones to America. For over one hundred years his remains lay in a Paris cemetery. By 1905 it had been filled in, and was now beneath a laundry. President Theodore Roosevelt, one of the navy's greatest advocates, saw Jones as a valuable symbol in his ambition to make the navy second to none in the world. When Jones's body was discovered and returned to the United States Naval Academy in Annapolis, Roosevelt made a grand speech, extolling Jones's accomplishments. The president was the perfect champion for the brave but vain captain; in his daughter Alice's words, Roosevelt, like Jones, "wanted to be the baby at every christening, the bride at every wedding, and the corpse at every funeral."[39]

As it turned out, Barry and Jones were even buried in a befitting manner. Jones finally has the resting place of his dreams. You will find him beneath the Naval Academy Chapel (where Barry's Bible is displayed at the altar). Stairs take you below to a circular tomb; his crypt is dead center. Walking quietly around it one can see Jones's gold sword, the same one given to Barry and thence to Dale; a portrait of the bantam Scotsman, his certificate of membership in the Society of the Cincinnati, and the medals awarded him by France, Russia, and the United States. It is a grand tribute, but Jones is buried alone, the eternal warrior and bachelor.

At Independence Hall, one follows the direction Barry's statue points to, proceeding down Fourth Street to Locust and St. Mary's Church. Walking toward the graveyard one passes markers for the Bouvier family, ancestors of Jacqueline Kennedy Onassis; in the cemetery itself one finds Thomas Fitzsimons, Mathew Carey, and other friends of the old commodore. Front and center is Barry's tomb, where he is buried with his wives Mary and Sarah, along with Patrick and Betsy Hayes. It is not nearly as ostentatious as the crypt in Annapolis, but the hero is buried with his wives, his family and friends, in the city he adopted and that adopted him.

After lying forlorn for more than a century on Petty's Island, the *Alliance* disappeared, as much from neglect as natural causes. Through all that time only one Philadelphian took pity on her fate. In the early 1800s, a boat returned from the island with various pieces from her deck and bulwarks. Skilled hands went to work and produced a handsome, if rustic, tea caddy.[40]

For years its owner wheeled it out for appropriate social occasions. The tea was poured, and the guests, some in navy uniforms, found it quite a conversation piece, recalling the ship itself, bringing back to life the men who sailed her and the captain who trod her quarterdeck, shed his blood, and won honor for his country. Guests may have found such use of beams that once carried American sailors into battle an anomaly, but they politely congratulated its owner on the craftsmanship of the work and the cleverness of its use. The owner smiled and thanked them.

Sarah Barry was always very gracious.

NOTES

The following abbreviations appear in the notes.

APS   American Philosophical Society
BFP   Benjamin Franklin Papers
DHS   Delaware Historical Society
DNA   Department National Archives
FDR   Franklin Delano Roosevelt Library, Hyde Park, N.Y.
GWP   George Washington Papers
HCL   Haverford College Library
HSP   Historical Society of Pennsylvania
ISM   Independence Seaport Museum
JBP   John Barry Papers, Naval History Society Collection, New-York Historical Society
JCC   Journals of the Continental Congress
LCOP   Library Company of Philadelphia
LDC   Letters of Delegates to Congress
LOC   Library of Congress
MHS   Maryland Historical Society
NDAR   William Bell Clark, ed., *Naval Documents of the American Revolution.* Washington, D.C.: Naval History Division, Department of the Navy, 1964–2005.
NDBW   *Naval Documents Related to the Barbary Wars.* Washington, D.C.: U.S. Government Printing Office, 1939–44.
NDQW   Dudley W. Knox, ed., *Naval Documents Related to the Quasi-War Between the United States and France.* Vols. 1-7. Washington, D.C.: U.S. Government Printing Office, 1935-37.
NYPL   New York Public Library
PRO   Public Records Office (Admiralty Records, Kew, England)
RIHS   Rhode Island Historical Society
RMP   Robert Morris Papers
UVL   University of Virginia Library

CHAPTER ONE: OUT OF IRELAND

1 Van Powell, *The American Navies of the Revolutinary War,* 102.
2 Chappelle, *The History of the American Sailing Navy,* 89, 91.
3 Paullin, *Out-Letters,* vol. II, 109-110.
4 Wilbur, *Pirates and Patriots of the Revolution,* 75.
5 Pennsylvania Archives: Pennsylvania Collection (Miscellaneous), John Kessler Papers, "Rough Sketch of the Life of Commodore Barry," 2, 3.
6 Ibid., 3.
7 Ibid.
8 Ibid.

9 Ibid., 3, 4.

10 Ibid., 4.

11 Commodore Edward Preble, quoted in Gurn, *Commodore John Barry*, 296.

12 Ranelagh, *Ireland*, 109-112.

13 MacManus, *The Story of the Irish Race*, 441.

14 Ibid., 456-461, quotations on 461.

15 Montesquieu, quoted in ibid., 455.

16 Rafferty, "The Barry Hayes Papers."

17 Fraser, *Statistical Survey of the County of Wexford*, 12, 15, 7.

18 The Barry Family Bible, now at the U.S. Naval Academy, lists these as the names of Barry's parents, although there is still debate as to their accuracy.

19 Griffiths, ed., *Chronicles of the County Wexford to the Year 1777*, 141.

20 James, *Ireland in the Empire*, 212.

21 Several places in County Wexford claim to be the place of Barry's birth. There is a church in Rossiter with a record of births that list a "John Barry 1739" with a pencil mark placed there years ago. Celestine Rafferty, Senior Librarian of County Wexford, has done extensive work on the Barry family tree and believes he was born near Roostontown; given the date the family has entered in their bible, his birth date on his grave, and the date given in John Kessler's *Portfolio* magazine article (with Sarah Barry as his source) she believes (as does this author) that the date is 1745, and near Roostontown. The date, April 12, comes from the Julian calendar, in use in the British Empire until 1752. Converted to the Gregorian calendar, that date is April 23.

22 Independence Seaport Museum (ISM), Barry-Hayes Papers, Anstis Doyle to John Barry, March 20, 1794.

23 Ranelagh, *Ireland*, 119.

24 Ibid.

25 Ibid.; James, *Ireland in the Empire*, 235; Lecky, *A History of Ireland in the Eighteenth Century*, 90-91, 158-161.

26 MacManus, *The Story of the Irish Race*, 425.

27 Griffiths, *Chronicles of the County Wexford*, 259.

28 James, *Ireland in the Empire*, 201-202; ISM, Barry-Hayes Papers, John Barry Collection: Nicholas Barry to John Barry, 1785.

29 Lecky, *History of Ireland in the Eighteenth Century*, 151.

30 Conversation with Celestine Rafferty, Senior Librarian of Wexford County Council.

31 MacManus, *Story of the Irish Race*, 473.

32 Correspondence between Celestine Rafferty, George Willcox, and one Mrs. Willett from Wexford County, 2003; Clark, *Gallant John Barry*, Appendix, Barry Family Tree; 4.

33 Ibid. Griffiths, *Chronicles of the County Wexford*, 20-21.

34 Fraser, ISM, Barry-Hayes Papers Overview; Clark, *Gallant John Barry*, Appendix, Barry Family Tree.

35 James, *Ireland in the Empire*; ISM, Barry-Hayes Papers, Nicholas Barry to John Barry, May 1785; Clark, *Gallant John Barry*, 4.

36 Clark, *Gallant John Barry*, 5.

37 Lecky, *History of Ireland in the Eighteenth Century*, 43, 71.

38 JBP, Barry to James Corish, January 2, 1792.

39 Ibid., William Kearney to John Barry (no date).

40 ISM, Barry-Hayes Papers; Nicholas Barry to John Barry, May 1785; Clark, *Gallant John Barry,* 5.

41 Brown and Kessler, "Commodore John Barry."

42 Crawford, ed., *The Autobiography of a Yankee Mariner,* 14.

43 Wilbur, *Pirates and Patriots of the Revolution,* 17.

44 Ibid., 17.

45 Thomas, *John Paul Jones,* 19.

46 Wilbur, *Pirates and Patriots of the Revolution,* 39.

47 Ibid., 77.

48 Ibid., 50.

49 King with Hattendorf and Estes, *A Sea of Words,* 187.

50 Ibid., 394.

51 Wilbur, *Pirates and Patriots of the Revolution.* 54.

52 Clark, *Gallant John Barry,* 5.

53 ISM, Barry-Hayes Papers, letters from Nicholas Barry and Eleanor Howlin to John Barry.

54 The portrait of John Barry by Gilbert Stuart, completed around 1800, depicts these features (current owner anonymous).

55 Watson, *Annals,* vol. 1, 259.

56 Doerflinger, *Vigorous Spirit of Enterprise,* 12.

57 Kessler, "Rough Sketch," 1.

58 Tyler, *The Bay and River Delaware,* 15.

59 Engle and Lott, *America's Maritime Heritage,* 38.

60 Carse, *Ports of Call,* 197.

61 Historical Society of Pennsylvania, Penn Papers.

62 Interview with William Ward, Director of Education, Independence Seaport Museum, April 2004.

63 Nash, *First City,* 54.

64 Ibid., 62.

65 Craig, "Grounds for Debate," 168.

66 Watson, *Annals,* vol. 1, 265.

67 Engle and Lott, *America's Maritime Heritage,* 38.

68 Christ Church Records, 1760.

69 McCullough, *John Adams,* 83.

70 Nash, *First City,* 70.

71 William Ward, Director of Education at Philadelphia's Independence Seaport Museum, took this author on a walking tour of Old Philadelphia, pointing out the location of this tannery along the way. His tour was a wonderful complement to Watson's *Annals* and other sources.

72 Tyler, *The Bay and River Delaware,* 14-15.

73 Brown and Kessler, "Commodore John Barry," 4.

74 Craig, "Grounds for Debate," 150.

75 Brown and Kessler, "Life of Commodore Barry," 4.

76 Clark, *Gallant John Barry,* 6.

77 Cooper, "Sketches of Naval Men."

78 Doerflinger, *Vigorous Spirit of Enterprise,* 20.

79 *Pennsylvania Gazette,* September 12, 1754; December 4, 1760; November 4, 1762.

80 *Pennsylvania Gazette,* September 12, 1754.

81 HSP, Cadwalader Collection: Tonnage Records 1765-1775, Philadelphia Customs House.

82 Doerflinger, *Vigorous Spirit of Enterprise,* 100.

83 Ibid., 388 (to determine tonnage, multiply length times breadth times depth and divide by 95).

84 HSP, Cadwalader Collection, Series III, Duties of Incoming Vessels 1765-1775; PA Archives Vol. 1, Ships Registers 1762-1776, 395.

85 Clark, *Gallant John Barry,* 8.

86 Ibid., 12. City documents from that time found in the Philadelphia City Archives, have no mention of a "Cleary" or similar spelling.

87 Merritt, "Tea Trade, Consumption, and the Republican Paradox in Pre-Revolutionary Philadelphia," 131.

88 Lancaster, *The American Revolution,* 51-53.

89 HSP, Cadwalader Collection, Tonnage Records 1765-1775; Clark, *Gallant John Barry,* 9.

90 PA Archives, vol. 1, Ships Registers 1762-1776, 395; Clark, *Gallant John Barry,* 10.

91 Clark, *Gallant John Barry,* 10.

92 *Pennsylvania Gazette,* February 12. 1767.

93 Ibid.; *Pennsylvania Gazette,* February 1, 1770.

94 *Pennsylvania Gazette,* February 1, 1770, February 12, 1767.

95 HSP, Cadwalader Collection, Tonnage and Duties of Incoming Vessels, 1765-1775.

96 *Pennsylvania Gazette,* July 16, 1767.

97 Ibid.; *Pennsylvania Gazette,* October 29, 1767.

98 Philadelphia City Archives, Marriage Licenses, 1767. City tax records, 1767; Clark, *Gallant John Barry,* 12.

99 Clark, *Gallant John Barry,* 12.

100 *Pennsylvania Gazette,* February 18, 1768.

101 *Pennsylvania Gazette,* June 18, 1768; HSP, Cadwalader Collection, Tonnage Records 1765-1775, May 8, 1768; July 15, 1768.

102 *Pennsylvania Gazette,* June–September 1768.

103 HSP, Logbook, "Society for the Relief of Poor and Distressed Masters of Ships," 1769; Clark, "The Sea Captains Club," 44.

104 Lancaster, *The American Revolution,* 54, 58.

105 Fischer, *Paul Revere's Ride,* 25.

106 *Pennsylvania Chronicle,* August 21, 1769; *Pennsylvania Gazette,* September 14, 28, 1769.

107 HSP, Cadwalader Collection, Tonnage Records 1765-1775.

108 Library of Congress (LOC), John Barry Collection, Log of the ship *Barbadoes,* October 7, 1770.

109 Ibid., October 23, 25, 1770.

110 Ibid., October 28, 30, 1770; King with Hattendorf and Estes, *A Sea of Words,* 146.

Chapter Two: Storms

1 PA Archives, Kessler Papers, *Portfolio Magazine,* 4.

2 HSP, Cadwalader Collection, Tonnage and Duties of Incoming Vessels, 1765-1775; Eymal, "The Changing Situation of Philadelphia's Trade with the British West Indies," 166-67.

3 Doerflinger, *Vigorous Spirit of Enterprise,* 47-48, 50.

4 ISM, Barry-Hayes Papers, Nicholas Barry to John Barry, May 31, 1785; Wolf, *As Various as Their Land,* 99-100.

5 HSP, Cadwalader Collection, Tonnage Duties of Incoming Vessels, 1765-1775; HSP, Ships Registered before 1776, GN187; Clark, *Gallant John Barry*, 16.

6 Clark, *Gallant John Barry*, 16.

7 Illich, *Colonial Pennsylvania–A History*, 247.

8 Nash, *First City*, 68.

9 Some aspiring merchants did not survive–literally or figuratively. Protestants George Dunlope and William Glenholme came to Philadelphia from Ireland, set up by their fathers with credit, connections, and two brigantines–sleek, two-masted vessels perfectly suited for both Caribbean and Atlantic voyages. Flush with a shipment of marketable Irish flaxseed, they flaunted their good fortune, purchasing a racehorse as a side investment–an early example of a diversified portfolio. But the pace and risk of mercantilism overtook them. Cash for expenses flew out of their hands. Their high overhead and the planting season deadline were further encumbered by Delaware River ice and winter storms at sea. Glenholme, bedridden with a "nervous fever," was forced back to work after Dunlope suddenly went "numb in the limbs" and died walking home one night. Mounting debts were accompanied by news of a mutiny aboard one of the brigantines. When Glenholme learned of his slave's overtures to the firm's clients, representing himself as a bond servant whose imminent freedom would allow him to make better deals for them than his prodigal master, pressure won out over profits. The firm of Dunlope and Glenholme went bankrupt, advertising the sale of everything from office furnishings to a "very likely Negro boy" and "the famous horse Northumberland." Doerflinger, *Vigorous Spirit of Enterprise*, 12, 14.

10 *Pennsylvania Gazette*, December 6, 1770; Clark, *Gallant John Barry*, 16.

11 HSP, Cadwalader Collection, Tonnage Duty Book, 1765-1775; LOC, Barry Collection, ship's log, *Patty and Polly*, February 1771.

12 Pennsylvania *Gazette*, February 14, 1771; LOC, Barry Collection, ship's log, *Patty and Polly*, March 3, 1771.

13 LOC, Barry Collection, ship's log, *Patty and Polly*, March 13, March 23, May 20, 1771.

14 *Pennsylvania Gazette*, June 27, 1771; Clark, *Gallant John Barry*, 20.

15 HSP, Cadwalader Collection, Philadelphia Customs House records, August 21, 1771; HSP, Ships Registered before 1776, GN187; August 21, 1771.

16 Brown and Kessler, "Commodore John Barry," 13.

17 LOC, Barry Collection, Ship's Log, Schooner *Industry*, August 28, 1771.

18 Ibid.

19 Ibid., August 28-September 1, 1771, March 21, 1771, September 4, 1771; Clark, *Gallant John Barry*, 18.

20 LOC, Barry Collection, Ship's Log, Schooner *Industry*, October 21, 1771, November 4, 1771.

21 Ibid., November 4, 7, 9, 10, 14, 1771.

22 Ibid., December 5, 7, 12, 1771.

23 Ibid., January 5, 1772.

24 *Pennsylvania Gazette*, December 15, 1771, January 5, 1772.

25 LOC, Barry Collection, Ship's Log, schooner *Industry*, January 5, 16-19, 1772.

26 Ibid., March 13, 14-31, 1772.

27 Clark, *Gallant John Barry*, 25.

28 HSP, Cadwalader Collection, Philadelphia Custom House Records; *Pennsylvania Chronicle*, August 15, 1772.

29 Millar, *American Ships of the Colonial and Revolutionary Periods*, 12.

30 Clark, *Gallant John Barry*, 27.

31 Doerflinger, *Vigorous Spirit of Enterprise*, 44.

32 Clark, *Gallant John Barry*, 27.

33 HSP, Cadwalader Collection, Tonnage Duty Book, 1765-1775; Clark, *Gallant John Barry*, 28, 29.

34 Philadelphia City Archives; Tax Records, Walnut Ward, 1772.

35 Clark, *The Irish in Philadelphia*, 6; Wolf, *As Various as their Land*, 118–19; Bronner, "Village into Town, 1701–1746," 60–61; Thayer, "Town into City," 74.

36 HSP, Cadwalader Collection, Tonnage Reports, 1770-1775; Clark, *Gallant John Barry*, 30.

37 Mitchell, *Isles of the Caribees*, 150-52; Nash, *First City*, 18.

38 Tuchman, *The First Salute*, 19-20.

39 Ibid.; Clark, *Gallant John Barry*, 31.

40 Tuchman, *The First Salute*, 21-22.

41 HSP, Cadwalader Collection, Tonnage Reports, 1770-1775.

42 Ibid., 142.

43 Tinkcom, "The Revolutionary City, 1765–1800," 117.

44 Merritt, "Tea Trade, Consumption, and the Republican Paradox in Pre-Revolutionary Philadelphia," 143.

45 Library Company of Philadelphia, Tea Ship Broadside, November 27, 1773; Tinckom, "The Revolutionary City, 1765–1800," 108.

46 Nash, *First City*, 85.

47 Carse, *Ports of Call*, 206.

48 *Pennsylvania Gazette*, November 10, 1773.

49 Tinkcom, "The Revolutionary City, 1765–1800"; Clark, *Gallant John Barry*, 34.

50 Keen, "Descendants of Jöran Kyn," 486; Cooper, *Sketches of Naval Men*.

51 *Pennsylvania Gazette*, February 23, 1774.

52 Clark, *Gallant John Barry*, 35.

53 Ibid.

54 Wagner, *Robert Morris*, 1.

55 Ibid., 4–6.

56 Ibid., 8, 12; Doerflinger, *Vigorous Spirit of Enterprise*, 66.

57 Wagner, *Robert Morris*, 21.

58 PA Archives, vol. 1, Ships List, 1762-1777, 410.

59 HSP, Ships Registered before 1776, *Venus*, March 20, 1774; *Pennsylvania Gazette* 1773-1774.

60 Philadelphia Custom House Records, March 28, 1774.

61 *Pennsylvania Gazette*, June 10, 1774.

62 Fowler, *The Baron of Beacon Hill*, 170-172; Lancaster, *The American Revolution*, 70.

63 Fischer, *Paul Revere's Ride*, 26.

64 Doerflinger, *Vigorous Spirit of Enterprise*, 194.

65 Tinkcom, "The Revolutionary City, 1765–1800," 119-120; Illich, *Colonial Pennsylvania*, 272.

66 Wagner, *Robert Morris*, 24.

67 Doerflinger, *Vigorous Spirit of Enterprise*, 194, 256.

68 ISM, Barry-Hayes Papers, Memorial to Congress from John Barry and Thomas Read, September 1785.

69 HSP, Customs House Records, September 21, 1774.

70 Lancaster, *The American Revolution,* 70.

71 Ibid., 76.

72 Illich, *Colonial Pennsylvania,* 281.

73 Ibid.

74 HSP, Minutes Book, Society for the Relief of Poor, Aged and Infirmed Masters of Ships, and Their Widows and Children; Clark, *Gallant John Barry,* 38.

75 Fraser, "The Barry-Hayes Papers"; Clark, *Gallant John Barry,* 39.

76 ISM, Barry-Hayes Papers, Nicholas Barry to John Barry, May 31, 1785; Margaret Howlin to John Barry, 1794.

77 Millar, *American Ships of the Colonial and Revolutionary Periods,* 35.

78 Doerflinger, *Vigorous Spirit of Enterprise,* 194.

79 Millar, *American Ships of the Colonial and Revolutionary Periods,* 36.

80 HSP, Customs House Records, December 19, 1774.

81 HSP, Wharton Papers; Clark, *Gallant John Barry,* 41.

82 ISM, Barry-Hayes Papers: Log, *Black Prince,* January 2, 5-7, 10, 1775.

83 Ibid., January 16-20, 1775.

84 Ibid., January 22, 1775.

85 *Pennsylvania Gazette,* January 25, 1775.

86 ISM, Log, *Black Prince,* January 25, 1775.

87 King with Hattendorf and Estes, *A Sea of Words,* 395.

88 Brown and Kessler, "Commodore John Barry," 13.

89 Kessler, "Rough Sketch," 20.

90 ISM, Log, *Black Prince,* January 26, 27, 29, 1775.

91 Ibid., February 1-5, 1775; Clark, *Gallant John Barry,* 45.

92 Clark, ed., *Naval Documents of the American Revolution* (NDAR), vol. 1, 405, Richard Champion to Willing, Morris & Co., February 24, 1775.

93 ISM, Log, *Black Prince,* February 1–15, 1775.

94 Ibid., February 1775.

95 NDAR, vol. 1, 424, Champion to Willing, Morris & Co., March 6, 1775.

96 ISM, Log, *Black Prince,* February 1775; King with Hattendorf, *Harbors and High Seas,* 63.

97 ISM, Log, *Black Prince,* March 12, 14, 1775.

98 Ibid., April 3, 11, 21, 24, 1775.

99 Fischer, *Paul Revere's Ride,* 271; Young, *Robert Morris,* 29-30.

100 Young, *Robert Morris,* 29-30.

101 Wagner, *Robert Morris,* 26.

102 HSP, Christopher Marshall Diaries, April 26, 1775; HSP, Cadwalader Collection, Tonnage and Duty Records, April 26, 1775; *Autobiography of Charles Biddle,* 75-76, 85.

103 Tinkcom, "The Revolutionary City, 1765–1800," 123; HSP, Christopher Marshall Diaries, April 26-May 5, 1775.

104 ISM, Barry-Hayes Papers, Log, *Black Prince;* Clark, *Gallant John Barry,* 49.

105 HSP, Christopher Marshall Diaries, May 5, 1775; *Pennsylvania Gazette,* May 6, 1775.

106 HSP, Cadwalader Collection, Tonnage Duty Book, 1765-1775; ISM, Barry-Hayes Papers, Log, *Black Prince,* May-June 1775; Clark, *Gallant John Barry,* 49.

107 ISM, Log, *Black Prince,* May 7, 1775; Biddle, *Autobiography of Charles Biddle,* 76.

108 Clark, *Gallant John Barry*, 50.
109 ISM, Log, *Black Prince*, May 11, 1775.
110 Ibid., May 12, 22, 23, 1775.
111 Ibid., June 17, 24, 1775.
112 Clark, *Gallant John Barry*, 52; Lancaster, *The American Revolution*, 93.
113 Lancaster, *The American Revolution*, 93; *London Public Advertiser*, June 29, 1775.
114 ISM, Log, *Black Prince*, July 3, 1775.
115 Ibid., August 9, 1775; Clark, *Gallant John Barry*, 54.
116 ISM, Log, *Black Prince*, August 11, 1775; Clark, *Gallant John Barry*, 54.
117 ISM, Log, *Black Prince*, August 23, September 3-10, 1775.
118 Ibid., September 11, 1775.
119 Ibid.
120 Brown and Kessler, "Commodore John Barry," 14.
121 Ibid.
122 King with Hattendorf and Estes, *A Sea of Words*, 153.
123 ISM, Log, *Black Prince*, September 11, 1775.
124 Ibid.
125 Ibid.; Clark, *Gallant John Barry*, 56.
126 ISM, Log, *Black Prince*, September 23, September 13-October 4, 1775.
127 Millar, *American Ships of the Colonial and Revolutionary Periods*, 41.
128 Clark, *Gallant John Barry*, 59.
129 Jackson, *The Delaware Bay and River Defenses of Philadelphia, 1775-1777*, 5.

CHAPTER THREE: THE *Lexington*

1 *Pennsylvania Journal*, October 11, 1775.
2 PA Archives, *Journal of the Pennsylvania House of Assembly*, May 6, 1775; Brands, *The First American*, 499.
3 NDAR, vol. 1, 831, Minutes of the Pennsylvania Committee of Safety, July 6, 1775.
4 *London Advertiser*, "Extract of a Letter from Philadelphia, Dec. 6."
5 NDAR, vol. 2, 1163-1164, Caesar Rodney to Thomas Rodney, November 27, 1775; Lewis Nicola proposal.
6 Jackson, *The Pennsylvania Navy 1775-1778*, 15.
7 Ibid.; PA Archives, Series I, vol. 9, 638, Nat Irish to the Committee of Safety, July 26, 1775.
8 PA Archives, Series II, vol. 1, 376-377.
9 HSP, Minutes, Meetings of the Committee of Safety, September 20, 1775.
10 Jackson, *The Delaware Bay and River Defenses of Philadelphia, 1775-1777*, 7.
11 Fowler, "Esek Hopkins," 5.
12 Miller, *Sea of Glory*, 40.
13 Fowler, "Esek Hopkins," 6.
14 Tuchman, *First Salute*, 44.
15 Ibid.
16 Miller, *Sea of Glory*, 51.
17 JCC, III, 311-312, October 30, 1775.
18 McCullough, *John Adams*, 100.
19 JCC, III, 378-387.
20 NDAR, vol. 2, 896-97, John Adams to Elbridge Gerry, November 5, 1775.

21 Miller, *Sea of Glory*, 57.

22 Fowler, "Esek Hopkins," 7.

23 Butterfield, ed., *Diary and Autobiography of John Adams*, vol. 3, 350.

24 ISM, Barry-Hayes Papers, John Barry Memorials to Pennsylvania Assembly, 1783, and Congress, 1785; HSP, James Wharton Day Book, "Chandlery Supplied to the Continental Fleet," November 4, 1775–January 18, 1775.

25 Morison, *John Paul Jones*, 60; ISM, Barry-Hayes Papers, John Barry Memorial to Congress, 1785.

26 HSP, James Wharton Day Book.

27 Millar, *American Ships of the Colonial and Revolutionary Periods*, 35; Miller, *Sea of Glory*, 52.

28 *Dudley's Maryland Gazette*, November 20, 1775; *Morning Chronicle and London Advertiser*, January 20, 1776.

29 Butterfield, ed., *Diary and Autobiography of John Adams*, vol. 2, 221, November 27, 1775.

30 JCC, December 13, 1775, Resolution; JCC, December 14, 1775, Appointment of Marine Committee; NDAR, vol. 3, 101.

31 Committee Delegates to Continental Congress, John Trumbull, December 5, 1775.

32 Butterfield, ed., *Diary and Autobiography of John Adams*, vol. 2, 221, November 27, 1775; NDAR, vol. 3, 302; Thomas, *John Paul Jones*, 45.

33 JCC, December 5, 1775.

34 Fowler, "Esek Hopkins," 5, 6.

35 JCC, Hopkins' Orders from Congress, January 4, 1776.

36 Fleming, *Liberty*, 159-160.

37 Ibid., 160.

38 *Pennsylvania Evening Packet*, July 25, 1775.

39 NDAR, vol. 2, 920, Lord Dunmore's Proclamation, November 7, 1775.

40 Fleming, *Liberty*, 160.

41 Boyd, ed., *Jefferson Papers* 1, 260-61, November 16, 29, 1775.

42 Beck, *Letter Book of Esek Hopkins*, 18.

43 PRO, Admiralty 51/548, Journal of *HMS Liverpool*, Captain Henry Belew, February 5, 1776.

44 PA Archives, Colonial Records, vol. 10, 495.

45 Ibid.; ISM, Barry-Hayes Papers, Memorial to Congress, 1785.

46 HSP, Christopher Marshall Diary, March 23, 1776; Wilbur, *Pirates and Patriots of the Revolution*, 70.

47 ISM, Barry-Hayes Papers, Barry Memorial to Congress, 1785.

48 HSP, Joshua Humphreys Correspondence January–March 1776; Clark, *Gallant John Barry*, 71.

49 NDAR, vol. 3, 1054, John Barry, Receipts Related to the Maryland Ship *Defence*, January 30, 1776.

50 NDAR, vol. 3, 637-638, Naval Committee to Commodore Esek Hopkins, January 5, 1776.

51 Miller, *Sea of Glory*, 99.

52 Beck, *The Letter Book of Esek Hopkins*, 44.

53 NDAR, vol. 4, 56, Captain Andrew Snape Hamond, R.N., to Captain Alexander Graeme, R.N., February 23, 1776.

54 Beck, *Letter Book of Esek Hopkins,* 19; Morison, *John Paul Jones,* 68.

55 Rhode Island Historical Society, Hopkins Papers, March 3, 1776; Fowler, "Esek Hopkins," 11.

56 Morison, *John Paul Jones,* 69.

57 NDAR, vol. 4, 152, *Liverpool Journal,* March 3, 1776.

58 Maryland Historical Society, Maryland Council of Safety, March 9, 1776.

59 NDAR, vol. 4, 356, William Lux letter, March 15, 1776.

60 Maryland Historical Society, Carroll Papers, March 12, 1776; *Pennsylvania Packet,* March 11, 1776.

61 JCC, March 13, 1776.

62 Clark, *Gallant John Barry,* 72.

63 ISM, Barry-Hayes Papers, Memorial to Pennsylvania Assembly, 1783, and to Congress, 1785; NYHS, Barnes Collection, NY5-31, Certification affidavit, John Hancock, September 26, 1776.

64 Feldman, "Continental Navy Brigantine *Lexington* (1776-177)," 66-67.

65 HSP, Joshua Humphreys Papers, Wharton & Humphreys, Ship Yard Accounts, 1773–1795.

66 Millar, *American Ships of the Colonial and Revolutionary Periods,* 174, 176.

67 NDAR, vol. 4, 356, Receipts for Arms and Ammunition Received for the Maryland Ship *Defence,* March 15, 1776.

68 NDAR, Vol. 4, 399-400. Extract of a Letter from Philadelphia Dated 18th March 1776.

69 Matthewman, "Narrative."

70 HSP, Woodhouse Collection, Commissioners of the Continental Navy in Account with the Brigantine *Lexington,* March 28, 1776; Matthewman, "Narrative."

71 Fowler, *Rebels Under Sail,* 248.

72 Ibid.

73 Matthewman, "Narrative"; NDAR, vol. 8, 238-40, Monthly Return for the Continental Navy Brig *Lexington,* March [31] 1777.

74 PA State Archives, Group 27, Executive Correspondence: "Servant to Captain Barry, Petition to Committee of Safety."

75 Tuchman, *First Salute,* 45.

76 Miller, *Sea of Glory* 523.

77 Morison, *John Paul Jones,* 95.

78 Ibid.

79 JCC, IV, 213-215, March 13, 1776.

80 HSP, Wharton–Humphreys Papers, Charge Book; Clark, *Gallant John Barry,* 74.

81 PA Archives, Colonial Records, vol. 10, 524.

82 NDAR, vol. 4, 510, Henry Fisher to the Pennsylvania Committee of Safety, March 25, 1776.

83 PA Archives, Colonial Records, vol. 10, 525-528.

84 HSP, Christopher Marshall Diary, March 28, 1776; PA Archives, Colonial Records, vol. 10, 527-528.

85 HSP, Woodhouse Collection, "Commissioners of the Continental Navy in Account with the Brigantine *Lexington,* March 28, 1776.

86 HSP, Christopher Marshall Diary, March 28, 1776; Clark, *Gallant John Barry,* 75.

87 PA Archives; Pennsylvania State Papers, vol. I, 113-14.

88 PRO, Admiralty, 1/487, Journal of Captain Andrew Snape Hamond, March 20–25, 1776.

89 PRO, Admiralty, 51/796, Journal, HMS *Roebuck*, March 25–31, 1776.

90 Ibid.

91 University of Virginia Library, Hamond Papers, No. 4, March 28, 1776.

92 Wilbur, *Pirates and Patriots of the Revolution*, 44.

93 Morison, *John Paul Jones*, 63.

94 Wilbur, *Pirates and Patriots of the Revolution*, 44.

95 Ibid.

96 King with Hattendorf and Estes, *A Sea of Words*, 305.

97 Morison, *John Paul Jones*, 63.

98 Ibid.

99 Ibid., 63-64; Tuchman, *First Salute*, 118.

100 Wilbur, *Pirates and Patriots of the Revolution*, 46, 45; Tuchman, *First Salute*, 118.

101 Ibid.

102 Ibid., 75.

103 Conversation with Dr. Craig Symonds, USNA (retired), April 7, 2005.

104 NDAR, vol. 4, William Whipple to Josiah Bartlett, March 28, 1776.

105 PRO Admiralty, 51/796, Journal of HMS *Roebuck*, March 31, 1776.

CHAPTER FOUR: BATTLE

1 PA Archives, State Papers I, 113-115, April 1, 1776.

2 *Pennsylvania Evening Post*, March 28, 1776.

3 NDAR, vol. 4, Henry Fisher to the Pennsylvania Committee of Safety, April 1, 1776, 618-19; *Pennsylvania Gazette*, April 17, 1776.

4 *New York Journal*, April 11, 1776.

5 New-York Historical Society, Barnes Collection, John Barry Papers, April 8, 1776.

6 NDAR, vol. 4, 618-619, Fisher to the Pennsylvania Committee of Safety, April 1, 1776.

7 UVL, Hamond Papers, No. 4, April 7, 1776.

8 LOC, John Barry Collection, Libel Proceedings, HMS *Edward*, April 30, 1776.

9 JCC, IV, 270, April 7, 1776.

10 Kessler, "Rough Sketch," 16.

11 HSP, Aspinall Papers, vol. II, 780-784, April 26, 1776.

12 Docket of the Court of the Admiralty of Philadelphia, U.S. Customs House, Philadelphia, April 30, 1776.

13 King with Hattendorf and Estes, *A Sea of Words*, 196.

14 I thank Charles Brodine for his input.

15 *Pennsylvania Gazette*, April 17, 1776; London *Public Advertiser*, August 17, 1776.

16 Ibid.

17 *Pennsylvania Gazette*, April 11, 1776.

18 King with Hattendorf and Estes, *A Sea of Words*, p. 405.

19 *Pennsylvania Gazette*, April 17, 1776; NDAR, vol. 4, 702, Barry to Continental Marine Committee, April 7, 1776.

20 Ibid.

21 HSP, Anthony Wayne Papers, I, 44; Lt. Col. Johnson to Col. Wayne, April 10, 1776.

22 *Pennsylvania Gazette*, April 17, 1776.

23 Kessler, "Rough Sketch," 16.
24 Henkel, ed., *Confidential Correspondence of Robert Morris*, Silas Deane to Robert Morris, April 12, 1776.
25 Thomas, *John Paul Jones*, 50.
26 RIHS, Hopkins letter book, 61.
27 Morison, *John Paul Jones*, 69.
28 PRO, Admiralty 30/733, No. 10, April 4, 1776.
29 NYHS, Deane Papers, Robert Morris to Silas Deane, April 8, 1776.
30 Gurn, *Commodore John Barry*, 27.
31 NDAR, vol. 4, 665, Silas Deane to Robert Morris, April 4, 1776.
32 NYHS, Morris to Deane, April 8, 1776.
33 HSP, Wayne Papers, I, 44, April 10, 1776.
34 HSP, Christopher Marshall Diaries; LDC, vol. 3, Joseph Hewes to Samuel Johnston, April 11, 1776; *New York Journal*, April 18, 1776.
35 JBP, Congressional Marine Committee to Barry, April 11, 1776.
36 Naval Historical Center, Numb. 14626, *London Public Advertiser*.
37 JBP, April 8, 1776.
38 Ibid.
39 FDR Library, Barry to Captain Timothy Shalor, April 15, 1776.
40 PRO High Court of Admiralty, 3/733 no. 10, April 17, April 13, 1776.
41 NDAR, vol. 4, 1268-70, Hamond to Dunmore, April 26, 1776.
42 *Connecticut Courant*, May 20, 1776.
43 PRO, Admiralty 51/909, April 27, 1776.
44 Ibid.
45 *Connecticut Courant*, May 20, 1772.
46 HSP, Christopher Marshall Diaries, May 5, 1776; *Pennsylvania Journal*, May 8, 1776.
47 NDAR, vol. 4, 1268-1270.
48 Ibid.; PA Archives, vol. 4, 737.
49 HSP, Christopher Marshall Diaries, May 5, 1776.
50 *Pennsylvania Journal*, May 8, 1776.
51 NDAR, vol. 5, 493; NDAR, vol. 4, 669: Captures of the schooner *Hawk* and brig *Bolton*.
52 "Extract of a Letter from Esek Hopkins," *Pennsylvania Gazette*, April 17, 1776.
53 Beck, ed., *The Letter Book of Esek Hopkins*, 50.
54 Morison, *John Paul Jones*, 69-74.
55 Fowler, "Esek Hopkins,"12-13.
56 Morison, *John Paul Jones*, 91.
57 Docket of the Court of the Admiralty U.S. Customs House, Philadelphia, April 30, 1776; LOC, Barry Collection, *Edward* libel proceedings.
58 Ibid.
59 *Pennsylvania Gazette*, May 1, 1776.
60 JCC, April 3, 1776.
61 Morison, *John Paul Jones*, 92.
62 PA Archives, Colonial Records, X, 545-546.
63 PA Archives, 2nd series, I, Haywood et al., eds., 444.
64 JCC, IV, 415-416, June 4, 1776.
65 PA Archives; the date is approximate.

66 LOC, Letterbook, *Alliance,* Howland to Barry, March 31, 1783; Barry to Howland, April 8, 1783; Barry to Ellery, April 4, 1783.

67 UVL, Hamond Papers No. 4, May 5, 1776.

68 NDAR, vol. 4, Bache to Franklin, May 7, 1776, 1442-1443.

69 Haverford College Library, Charles Roberts Collection, Letters of Delegates to Congress (LDC), Vol. 3, Marine Committee to Barry, May 8, 1776.

70 Jackson, *The Bay and the River Delaware,* 24, 9.

71 UVL, Hamond Papers, No. 4, 5: Narrative, May 5-9, 1776.

72 PA Archives, 1st Series, IV, 750, Barry to Morris, May 9, 1776.

73 Biddle, *Autobiography;* NDAR, vol. 4, 1463.

74 Butterfield, ed., *The Adams Papers,* Series II, 406-407.

75 PRO, Admiralty, 51/548, *Liverpool Journal,* May 9, 1776.

76 NDAR, vol. 8, "Monthly Returns for the Continental Navy Brig *Lexington,*" March [31] 1777, 238-240.

77 HSP, Woodhouse Collection, Account with the Brigantine *Lexington,* May 21, 1776.

78 NDAR, vol. 5, p. 276, "Protest of Richard James, Master of the Snow *Champion,*" May 27, 1776; King with Hattendorf and Estes, *A Sea of Words,* 341.

79 Ibid.; PRO Admiralty, 51/548, *Liverpool Journal,* May 27, 1776.

80 PRO Admiralty, 51/548, *Liverpool Journal,* May 27, 1776.

81 Wilbur, *Pirates and Patriots of the Revolution,* 62.

82 U.S Coast Guard Geodetic Survey, Coast Chart No. 124, *Delaware Entrance,* W. W. Duffield, Sup., 1895.

83 PRO, Admiralty, 51/548 *Liverpool* Journal, May 27, 1776.

84 PA Archives, 1st Series, IV, 769-70, Henry Fisher to Pennsylvania Committee of Safety, June 7, 1776.

85 NDAR, vol. 5, Captain Lambert Wickes to the Committee of Secret Correspondence of the Continental Congress, July 11, 1776.

86 PRO, Admiralty, 1/484, Bellew to Shuldham, June 10, 1776.

87 JCC, June 14, 1776.

88 PRO, Admiralty, 1/484, Bellew to Shuldham, June 10, 1776.

89 Ibid., Bellew to Shuldham, April 24, 1776.

90 NDAR, vol. 5, 486, Fisher to Pennsylvania Committee of Safety, June 11, 1776.

91 Ibid.

92 JCC, V, pps. 420, 422-423, June 6, 1776.

93 PA Archives, 1st Series, V, 378, Davidson to Morris, June 19, 1776.

94 HSP, Emelin Knox Parker, "A Biographical Sketch of John Brown," 1-2; Catanzariti and Ferguson, editors, *The Papers of Robert Morris* (RMP), vol. 2, 208-9, 332.

95 LDC, Marine Committee to Lambert Wickes, June 10, 1776.

96 *Pennsylvania Evening Post,* July 11, 1776; *Pennsylvania Ledger,* July 6, 1776; *Connecticut Courant,* July 15, 1776.

97 PRO, Admiralty, 1/484, April 24, 1776.

98 LOC, William Bell Clark Collection, *Kingfisher* Journal, June 27, 28, 29, 1776.

99 PRO Admiralty, 51/479, *Orpheus* Journal, June 28, 1776.

100 LOC, Clark Collection, *Kingfisher* Journal, June 29, 1776.

101 Maryland Historical Society, Scharf Collection, Lambert Wickes to Samuel Wickes, July 2, 1776.

102 Ibid.

103 Montgomery, *Reminiscences of Wilmington Delaware*, 176-81.

104 LOC, Clark Collection, *Orpheus* journal, June 29, 1776.

105 MHS, Scharf Collection, Lambert Wickes to Samuel Wickes, July 2, 1776.

106 Ibid.

107 Ibid.

108 Ibid.

109 Ibid.; LOC, Clark Papers, *Kingfisher* Journal, June 29, 1776.

110 MHS, Scharf Collection, Lambert Wickes to Samuel Wickes, July 2, 1776.

111 LOC, Clark Collection, *Orpheus* Journal, June 29, 1776.

112 Montgomery, *Reminiscences of Wilmington Delaware*, 176-81.

113 MHS, Scharf Collection, Lambert Wickes to Samuel Wickes, July 2, 1776.

114 LOC, Clark Collection, *Orpheus* Journal, June 29, 1776.

115 Montgomery, *Reminiscences of Wilmington Delaware*.

116 *Pennsylvania Ledger*, July 6, 1776.

117 MHS, Scharf Collection, Lambert Wickes to Samuel Wickes, July 2, 1776.

118 Montgomery, *Reminiscences of Wilmington Delaware*.

119 MHS, Scharf Collection, Lambert Wickes to Samuel Wickes, July 2, 1776.

120 *Connecticut Courant*, July 15, 1776.

121 Ibid.

122 MHS, Scharf Collection, Lambert Wickes to Samuel Wickes, July 2, 1776.

123 Ibid.

124 LOC, Clark Collection, *Orpheus* Journal, June 29, 1776.

125 MHS, Scharf Collection, Lambert Wickes to Samuel Wickes, July 2, 1776.

126 Ibid.

127 Ibid.

CHAPTER FIVE: INDEPENDENCE

1 *Pennsylvania Gazette*, July 3, 1776.

2 HSP, Dreer Collection, Marine Committee to John Barry, July 2, 1776.

3 Ibid.

4 HSP, Dreer Collection, Marine Committee to John Barry, July 2, 1776.

5 PA Archives, Second Series, I, 621-624; PA Archives, Record Group 27, Supreme Executive Council Records, William Goodrich to John Goodrich, Jr.; *Pennsylvania Gazette*, August 7, 1776.

6 PA Archives, Record Group 27, Supreme Executive Council Records, William Goodrich to John Goodrich, Jr.; *Pennsylvania Gazette*, August 7, 1776.

7 PA Archives, Record Group 27, Supreme Executive Council Records, William Goodrich to John Goodrich, Jr.

8 *Maryland Gazette*, September 2, 1776.

9 NDAR, vol. 6, 63-64, Josiah Bartlett to John Langdon, August 5, 1776.

10 PA Archives, Record Group 27, Supreme Executive Council Records, William Goodrich to John Goodrich, Jr., September 5, 1776.

11 Ibid.

12 Dale, "Biographical Memoir of Richard Dale."

13 *Pennsylvania Packet*, September 10, 1776.

14 Butterfield, ed., *Adams Papers*, vol. 2, 74; NDAR, vol. 6, 63-64, Josiah Bartlett to John Langdon.

15 PA Archives, Record Group 27, William Goodrich to John Goodrich, Jr., September 5, 1776; NDAR, vol. 6, 1013-1014.

16 Dale, "Biographical Memoir of Richard Dale."

17 NDAR, vol. 6, 1011, Trial and Condemnation of the British Sloop *Betsey* in the Pennsylvania Admiralty Court, September 26, 1776; Clark, *Gallant John Barry*, 101.

18 Barry's Petition to Congress, quoted in Clark, *Gallant John Barry*, 102; ISM, Barry-Hayes Papers, Memorial, 1785.

19 *Pennsylvania Packet*, September 10, 1776.

20 NDAR, vol. 6, 877, Minutes of the Pennsylvania Council of Safety, September 17, 1776.

21 NDAR, vol. 6, 715-716, Extract from Marine Committee Minutes, Continental Navy Uniforms, September 5, 1776.

22 Thomas, *John Paul Jones*, 85-86.

23 JCC, VI, 860-862, 865.

24 Fowler, *Rebels Under Sail*, 228-229.

25 Morison, *John Paul Jones*, 118.

26 Thomas, *John Paul Jones*, 77.

27 Morgan, "John Barry: A Most Fervent Patriot," 51.

28 Miller, *Sea of Glory*, 284; Clark, *Gallant John Barry*, 106; *Pennsylvania Packet*, January 4, 1777; NDAR, vol. 7, 11-12, William Hooper to Joseph Hewes, November 1, 1776.

29 NDAR, vol. 7, 11-12, William Hooper to Joseph Hewes, November 1, 1776.

30 Millar, *American Ships of the Colonial and Revolutionary Periods*, 285.

31 NDAR, vol. 7, 78-79, Commodore Sir Peter Parker to Phillip Stephens, November 17, 1776.

32 PA Archives, First Series, V, 66; NDAR, vol. 7, 284.

33 Tinkcom, "The Revolutionary City, 1765–1783," 118-128.

34 HSP, Christopher Marshall Diaries, November 12, 17, 1776.

35 UVL, Hamond Papers, No. 6, November 25-December 31, 1776.

36 JCC, November 30, 1776.

37 HSP, Woodhouse Collection, "Commissioners of Naval Stores in Account with the Continental Frigate *Effingham*," March-December 1776.

38 HSP, Cadwalader Collection, "Return of Muster Rolls"; Clark, *Gallant John Barry*, 108; JCC, November 30, 1776.

39 Doerflinger, *A Vigorous Spirit of Enterprise*, 43.

40 HSP, Cadwalader Papers, Series II, Washington to Cadwalader, December 7, 1776.

41 HSP, Cadwalader Papers, Series II, "An Account of Artillery Officers," December 16, 1776.

42 HSP, Christopher Marshall Diaries, December 11, 1776.

43 Tinkcom, "The Revolutionary City, 1765–1783," 129.

44 NDAR, vol. 7, 528-535, Robert Morris to Deane, December 20, 1776.

45 NDAR, vol. 7, 528-535.

46 Fischer, *Washington's Crossing*, 396; Fleming, *Liberty*, 95. Contrary to legend, Rall was concerned about a possible American attack across the Delaware.

47 NDAR, vol. 7, 543, HSP, Cadwalader Collection, Colonel John Cadwalader to Pennsylvania Council of Safety, December 21, 1776.

48 Fischer, *Washington's Crossing*, 196.

49 NDAR, vol. 7, 595-596; LOC, GWP, Washington to Robert Morris, December 25, 1776.

50 LOC, GWP, Cadwalader to Washington, December 25, 1776.

51 Fleming, *Liberty,* 96.

52 UVL, Hamond Papers, no. 6, January 1777.

53 LOC, GWP, Cadwalader to Washington, December 27, 1776; Washington to Cadwalader, December 28, 1776.

54 Flexner, *Washington,* 97; Clark, *Gallant John Barry,* 110.

55 Quoted in Fleming, *Liberty,* 224, and Lancaster, *The American Revolution,* 166-67.

56 Fischer, *Washington's Crossing,* 327-334; Miller, *Sea of Glory,* 219; PA Archives, Second Series, I, 20.

57 Lancaster, *The American Revolution,* 167; Gurn, *Commodore John Barry,* 47; Fleming, *Liberty,* 224.

58 ISM, Barry-Hayes Papers, Memorial to Pennsylvania Assembly, 1783.

59 LOC, GWP, Washington to Cornwallis, January 8, 1777.

60 Ibid.

61 HSP, Cadwalader Collection, "Return of Muster Rolls"; PA Archives, Second Series, vol. I, 20.

62 Clark, *Gallant John Barry,* 115.

63 Cooper, "Sketches of Naval Men," 48; PRO/Admiralty, 51/674, December 20, 1776, Journal, HMS *Pearl,* December 20, 1776.

64 NDAR, vol. 7, 574-577, Robert Morris to Hancock, December 23, 1776.

65 NDAR, vol. 7, 929-932, Robert Morris to Deane, January 11, 1777.

66 NDAR, vol. 7, 954.

67 *Pennsylvania Gazette,* March 12, 1777.

68 ISM, Barry-Hayes Papers, Sarah Barry Correspondence; NYHS, Barnes Collection, Barry Papers Correspondence; Keen, "The Descendants of Jöran Kyn," 300, 484-91.

69 ISM, Barry-Hayes Papers, Last Will of Samuel Austin; Keen, "The Descendants of Jöran Kyn," 485.

70 Christ Church Records, 1760.

71 Pennsylvania *Gazette,* various issues from October 19, 1765 to April 2, 1767.

72 ISM, Austin Will.

73 *Pennsylvania Gazette,* September 24, 1767.

74 *Pennsylvania Gazette,* February 28, 1775.

75 Keen, "The Descendants of Jöran Kyn," 486.

76 Gurn, *Commodore John Barry,* 292-93

77 Keen, "The Descendants of Jöran Kyn," 486; PA Archives, vol. I, 234.

78 Keen, "The Descendants of Jöran Kyn," 486; Morison, *John Paul Jones,* 131.

79 David Library of the American Revolution (copy), PRO, A.O. 12/40/56: "The Memorial of William Austin, late of the City of Philadelphia," April, 1786.

80 HSP, Society Collection, Reynold Keen to Isaac Austin, August 5, 1776.

81 ISM, Barry-Hayes Papers, Last Will of Samuel Austin; Keen, "The Descendants of Jöran Kyn," 485.

82 Watson, *Annals,* vol. II, "Occurences of the War of Independence," 295.

83 HSP, Christ Church Marriage Records, July 7, 1777.

CHAPTER SIX: LOW TIDE

1 Brands, *The First American*, 170.

2 Hildeburn, "Francis Hopkinson," 315; Thayer, "Town into City, 1746-1765." 86-87.

3 Hastings, *Life and Works of Francis Hopkinson*, 68.

4 Peterson, *Patriots, Pirates, and Pineys*, 46.

5 Hastings, *Life and Works of Francis Hopkinson* 70-71.

6 Hildeburn, "Francis Hopkinson," 317.

7 Peterson, *Patriots, Pirates, and Pineys*, 46.

8 Ibid.

9 Fleming, *Liberty*, 248.

10 Peterson, *Patriots, Pirates, and Pineys*, 46.

11 NDAR, Vol. 7, 1261, Congressional Committee in Philadelphia to the Navy Board of the Middle District, February 22, 1777.

12 HSP, Gratz Collection, Central Navy Board to the Pa. Council of Safety, April 9, 1777; *Pennsylvania Gazette*, April 23, 1777.

13 NDAR, vol. 8, 282 John Adams to James Warren, April 6, 1777.

14 JCC, July 13, 1777.

15 Fleming, *Liberty*, 237-38.

16 McCullough, *John Adams*, 176.

17 Watson, *Annals*, vol. II, 283.

18 Tinkcom, "The Revolutionary City, 1765–1783," 132.

19 Doerflinger, *Vigorous Spirit of Enterprise*, 210.

20 NDAR, vol. 7, 940, Robert Morris to John Langdon, January 12, 1777.

21 JCC, July 3, 1777.

22 Quoted in Griffin, *The History of Commodore John Barry*, 48.

23 JCC, May 15, July 11, July 23, 1777.

24 JCC, July 24, 1777.

25 LDC, Henry Laurens to John Lewis Gervais, July 25, 1777.

26 State Historical Society of Wisconsin, William Bell Clark Estate, Central Navy Board to John Barry and Thomas Read, July 31, 1777.

27 Lancaster, *The American Revolution*, 173.

28 HSP, William Howe Proclamation, August 27, 1777.

29 McCullough, *John Adams*, 172, 173.

30 Chernow, *Alexander Hamilton*, 99.

31 Randall, *George Washington*, 335-36.

32 PA Archives, vol. 3, 153-54; Keen, "The Descendants of Jöran Kyn: The Founder of Upland," 485; Clark, 123.

33 Doerflinger, *Vigorous Spirit of Enterprise*, 210.

34 David Library (copy) and PRO, 12/40/56, "The Memorial of William Austin, late of the City of Philadelphia," April 1786.

35 Ibid.

36 Clark, *Gallant John Barry*, 123.

37 LOC, GWP, September 23, 1777.

38 Morgan, "John Barry," 52.

39 Watson, *Annals*, vol. II, 295.

40 ISM, Barry-Hayes Papers, Memorial to Congress, 1785; Barry's Petition to Congress, 1785, copied in Clark, *Gallant John Barry* (plate).

41 ISM, Barry-Hayes Papers, Barry Memorial to Pennnsylvania Assembly, 1783, and Memorial to Congress, 1785; Clark, *Gallant John Barry*, 124.

42 Clark, *Gallant John Barry*, 124-25.

43 Cooper, "Sketches of Navy Men."

44 Parker, "A Biographical Sketch of John Brown," 2; Wagner, *Robert Morris*, 49.

45 David Library (copy), PRO, AO 12/40/56, Austin Memorial; PA Archives, vol. 3, 153-154.

46 ISM, Barry-Hayes Papers, William Austin to Sarah Barry, August 5, 1814.

47 ISM, Barry Memorial to Congress, 1785. Barry's Petition to Congress, 1785, copied in Clark, *Gallant John Barry* (plate).

48 Marine Committee Letter-Book, 103, NA, September 26, 1777; NDAR, vol. 9, 969.

49 Jackson, *The Pennsylvania Navy 1775-1781*, 121.

50 Tinkcom, "The Revolutionary City, 1765–1783," 132.

51 Jackson, *The Pennsylvania Navy 1775-1781*, 122.

52 Watson, *Annals*, vol. II, 282-283.

53 ISM, Barry-Hayes Papers, John Barry to Congress, January 10, 1778.

54 *Pennsylvania Evening Post*, October 16, 1777.

55 Montresor, "Journal," 42.

56 Jackson, *Pennsylvania Navy 1775-1781*, 124.

57 Miller, *Sea of Glory*, 247.

58 NDAR, vol. 9, 976, Continental Navy Board of the Middle District to Governor William Livingston, September 28, 1777.

59 Lancaster, *The American Revolution*, 179-180.

60 LOC, GWP, Washington to Continental Congress Navy Board, October 27, 1777, 147.

61 ISM, Barry to Congress, January 10, 1778.

62 Miller, *Sea of Glory*, 248-249; Cooper, *History of the Navy of the United States of America*, 69.

63 Jackson, *Delaware Bay*, 20, 21.

64 Smith would recover and find himself, thirty-seven years later, commanding American defenses at Baltimore during the British attack on Fort McHenry, the inspiration behind "The Star-Spangled Banner."

65 Jackson, *Delaware Bay*, 21; Miller, *Sea of Glory*, 250.

66 Brands, *The First American*, 542.

67 Quoted in Clark, *Gallant John Barry*, 125.

68 LOC, GWP, Washington to Continental Congress Navy Board, October 27, 1777.

69 LOC, GWP, Barry to Washington, October 27, 1777; JCC, November 4, 1777.

70 LOC, GWP, Washington to Navy Board, October 27, 1777.

71 ISM, Barry to Congress, January 10, 1778.

72 Ibid.

73 HSP, Etting Papers, Navy Board to Barry, November 2, 1777.

74 ISM, Barry to Congress, January 10, 1778.

75 Ibid.

76 Ibid.

77 Ibid.

78 Ibid.

79 Ibid.

80 Ibid.; Clark, *Gallant John Barry*, 129.
81 Montresor, "Journal," 55.
82 ISM, Barry to Congress, January 10, 1778.
83 Prince, *The Autobiography of a Yankee Mariner*, ed. Crawford, 104.
84 Ibid.
85 HSP, Etting Papers, November 2, 1777.
86 ISM, Barry to Congress, January 10, 1778.
87 Ibid.
88 Ibid.
89 Ibid.
90 Ibid.
91 Hastings, *The Life and Works of Francis Hopkinson*, 223.
92 ISM, Barry to Congress, January 10, 1778.
93 HSP, Christopher Marshall Diaries, November 7-9, 1777.
94 ISM, Barry to Congress, January 10, 1778; Montrésor, "Journal," 56.
95 ISM, Barry to Congress, January 10, 1778.
96 Ibid.
97 King with Hattendorf and Estes, *A Sea of Words*, 301.
98 ISM, Barry to Congress, January 10, 1778.
99 Ibid.; LOC, GWP, Washington to Navy Board, November 12, 1777.
100 Montresor "Journal," 193; Miller, *Sea of Glory*, 251; Van Powell, *The American Navies of the Revolutionary War*, 64.
101 Clark, *Gallant John Barry*, 133.
102 Hastings, *The Life and Works of Francis Hopkinson*, 268-273.
103 Ibid.
104 LOC, Marine Committee to Navy Board, January 1, 1778; Clark, *Gallant John Barry*, 134. LOC, GWP, Washington to Navy Board, November 29, 1777.
105 NDAR, vol. 10, 598-601.
106 NDAR, vol. 10, 601-602.
107 HSP, Society of Small Collections, Cadwalader to Washington, November 1777.
108 LDC, Morris to Marine Committeee, December 19, 1777; Clark, *Gallant John Barry*, 135.
109 Continental Navy Board to Marine Committee, December 13, 1777.
110 LDC, Morris to Marine Committee, December 19, 1777.
111 Ibid.
112 Ibid.
113 PA Archives, Series, II, 154.
114 HSP, Christopher Marshall Diaries, December 28, 1777.
115 Watson, *Annals*, vol. II, 283-285.
116 JCC, December 30, 1777.

CHAPTER SEVEN: VINDICATION

1 Fleming, *Liberty*, 279.
2 Lancaster, *The American Revolution*, 186.
3 Fleming, *Liberty*, 280.
4 Ilich, *Colonial Pennsylvania*, 318.
5 Watson, *Annals*, vol. II, 283-284.
6 Ibid., 289.

7 Brands, *The First American,* 542.

8 Clark, *Gallant John Barry,* 137.

9 Parker, "A Biographical Sketch of John Brown," 3.

10 ISM, Barry-Hayes Papers, Barry to Congress, January 10, 1778.

11 Ibid.

12 JCC, January 10, 1778.

13 Ibid.; LDC, Misc. papers; Marine Committee letter book, January 13, 1778.

14 LDC, Misc. papers, Marine Committee to John Barry, January 29, 1778.

15 Jackson, *The Pennsylvania Navy 1775-1781,* 285.

16 Ibid.; NDAR, Vol. 11, 172-174, Lieutenant Colonel François-Louis de Fleury to John Laurens, January 20, 1778.

17 NDAR, vol. 11, 172-174, Lieutenant Fleury to Laurens, January 20, 1778.

18 Watson, *Annals,* vol. II, 336. This same writer acknowledged that "We are indebted to the facetious muse of Francis Hopkinson, Esq., for the . . . jeu D'esprit upon the occurrence." True enough: Hopkinson's subsequent poem, "The Battle of the Kegs," was a witty spin on another failed attempt at striking the enemy.

19 NDAR, vol. 11, 188, Continental Navy Board of the Middle Department to Washington, January 22, 1778.

20 JCC, January 29, 1778.

21 Ibid.

22 Ibid.

23 LDC, Marine Committee to John Barry, January 29, 1778.

24 LDC, Marine Committee to Middle Navy Board, January 29, 1778.

25 Clark, *Gallant John Barry,* 141.

26 HSP, Dreer Collection, Robert Morris to John Brown, January 31, 1778.

27 Clark, *Gallant John Barry,* 142.

28 LDC, vol. 8, January 29, 1778, Marine Committee to John Barry.

29 JCC Marine Papers, Marine Committee Letter Book, January 22, 1778.

30 LOC, GWP, Washington to Hopkinson, January 27, 1778.

31 Letters of Delegates to Congress, Vol. 8, January 29, 1778; NDAR, vol. 11, 605, Marine Committee to Barry, March 11, 1778; Clark, *Gallant John Barry,* 142.

32 Matthewman, "Narrative of Luke Matthewman," 178; NDAR, vol. 11, 605-606, Continental Marine Committee to Captain John Barry, March 11, 1778.

33 Matthewman, "Narrative of Luke Matthewman," 178.

34 PA Archives, Series I, 246-247; NDAR, vol. 11, 200-201, William Bradford to President Thomas Wharton, Jr., January 24, 1778; Jackson, *Pennsylvania Navy 1775-1781,* 285.

35 PA Archives, vol. 6, 243.

36 Abbott, "Blue Jackets of '76," quoted in Griffin, *The History of Commodore John Barry,* 71-72.

37 Clark, *Gallant John Barry,* 144.

38 ISM, Barry Memorial to Congress, 1785; quoted in Clark, *Gallant John Barry,* 144.

39 Matthewman, "Narrative of Luke Matthewman," 178.

40 NDAR, vol. 11, 321, Hamond to Commander James Watt, R.N., February 11, 1778.

41 Randall, *George Washington,* 351.

42 LOC, GWP, Wayne to Washington, February 25, 1778.

43 Ibid.

44 Matthewman, "Narrative of Luke Matthewman," 178.

45 LOC, GWP. Wayne to Washington, February 23, 1778.

46 Ibid.

47 LOC, GWP, Wayne to Barry, February 23, 1778.

48 Ibid.

49 Ibid.

50 NDAR, vol. 11, 420-21, Journal of HMS *Roebuck*, February 24, 1778.

51 LOC, GWP, Barry to Washington, February 26, 1778.

52 NDAR, vol. 11, 421.

53 LOC, GWP, Barry to Washington, February 26, 1778.

54 NDAR, vol. 11, 421.

55 NDAR, vol. 11, 421; LOC, GWP, Brigadier General Anthony Wayne to Washington, February 25, 1778.

56 LOC, GWP, Barry to Washington, February 26, 1778.

57 Ibid.; NDAR, vol. 11, 440, Master's Journal of HM Galley *Cornwallis*, Lieutenant Thomas Spry, February 26, 1778.

58 NDAR, vol. 11, 440, Master's Journal of HM Galley *Cornwallis*, Lieutenant Thomas Spry, February 26, 1778.

59 LOC, GWP, Barry to Washington, February 26, 1778; Clark, *Gallant John Barry*, 147.

60 LOC, GWP, Barry to Washington, February 26, 1778.

61 Ibid.

62 DHS, Deposition of Robert Porter and George Reynolds, February 25, 1778.

63 Montrésor, "Journal," 196-197.

64 NDAR, Vol. 11, 864, "Extract of a Letter from Captain James Ferguson to the Viscount Howe, Dated, *Brune* at Sea the 27th of March 1778."

65 Montrésor, "Journal," 196-197; LOC, GWP, Barry to Washington, March 8, 1778.

66 Clark, *Gallant John Barry*, 148.

67 LOC, GWP, Barry to Washington, March 9, 1778.

68 Ibid.

69 Ibid.

70 *Pennsylvania Gazette*, March 18, 1778.

71 LDC, Barry to Marine Committee, March 8, 1778.

72 *Pennsylvania Gazette*, March 18, 1778.

73 Clark, *Gallant John Barry*, 149.

74 LOC, GWP, Articles of Surrender of the British Army Schooner *Alert*, March 7, 1778.

75 Ibid., Barry to Washington, March 9, 1778.

76 Ibid.

77 LOC, GWP, Articles of Surrender of the British Army Schooner *Alert*, March 7, 1778.

78 LOC, GWP, Captain John Barry to General George Washington, March 9, 1778.

79 LOC, GWP, Barry to Washington, March 9, 1778; Smallwood to Washington, March 9, 1778.

80 Ibid.

81 LOC, GWP, Barry to Washington, March 9, 1778; "Letters of Major Baurmeister During the Philadelphia Campaign, 1777-1778," 161-62.

82 Clark, *Gallant John Barry*, 151.

83 LOC, LDC, Marine Committee to John Barry, March 11, 1778.

84 NDAR, vol. 11, 97, Journal of HMS *Experiment*, Captain Sir James Wallace, January 11, 1778, 120-21.

85 NDAR, vol. 11, 803-804, "Extract of a Letter from Captain James Ferguson to the Viscount Howe, dated *Brune* At Sea the 27th March 1778."

86 NDAR, vol. 11, 559-560, Journal of HMS *Experiment*, Captain Sir James Wallace, March 9, 1778; Montresor, "Journal," 196-197.

87 "Journal of Captain John Montresor," 197; HSP, Christopher Marshall Diaries, March 9, 1778.

88 LOC, GWP, Barry to Washington, March 9, 1778.

89 NDAR, vol. 11, 559-560, Journal of HMS *Experiment*, Captain Sir James Wallace, March 9, 1778; Journal of HMS Sloop *Dispatch*, Captain Christopher Mason, March 9, 1778.

90 LOC, GWP, Barry to Washington, March 9, 1778.

91 Ibid.

92 NDAR, vol. 11, 559.

93 O'Neill, *Patrick O'Brian's Navy*, 57.

94 LOC, GWP, Smallwood to Washington, March 16, 1778; Barry to Washington, March 9, 1778.

95 NDAR, vol. 11, 559-560.

96 Clark, *Gallant John Barry*, 152.

97 NDAR, vol. 11, 559.

98 Ibid., 560; Clark, *Gallant John Barry*, 153.

99 NDAR, vol. 11, 804.

100 Ibid., 559, 663, 560.

101 Ibid., 804.

102 Cooper, *History of the Navy of the United States of America*, 74.

103 NDAR, vol. 11, 560.

104 Ibid., 559.

105 *Pennsylvania Gazette*, March 21, 1778.

106 JCC, Marine Committee Letter Book, Marine Committee to Barry, March 11, 1778.

107 LOC, GWP, Washington to Barry, March 12, 1778.

108 LDC, William Ellery to William Varnum, March 16, 1778.

109 NDAR, vol. 11, 618, Hamond to Captain Charles Phipps, R.N., 312/78.

110 LOC, GWP, Smallwood to Washington, March 17, 1778; *Pennsylvania Ledger*, March 25, 1778; *Royal Gazette*, March 17 and 24, 1778, quoted in Griffin, *Commodore John Barry*, 76-77.

111 LOC, GWP, Barry to Washington, March 20, 1778; Smallwood to Washington, March 20, 1778.

112 LDC, Marine Committee Letter Book, Marine Committee to Barry, March 26, 1778.

113 LOC, GWP, Barry to Washington, April 6, 1778.

114 LOC, GWP, Barry to Washington, April 11, 1778; Washington to Barry, April 15, 1778.

115 JCC, Marine Committee to Navy Board, April 24, 1778.

116 Matthewman, "Narrative of Lieutenant Luke Matthewman," 178.

117 Jackson, *With the British Army in Philadelphia*, 226.

118 Clark, *Gallant John Barry,* 154.

119 PRO, M 60, Secretary of Admiralty, Philip Stevens; *Pennsylvania Packet,* June 16, 1778; *New Jersey Gazette,* May 13, 1778.

120 From a manuscript by Colonel James Read, quoted in Gurn, *Commodore John Barry,* 97.

121 Ibid.

122 *Pennsylvania Packet,* June 6, 1778; Hastings, *The Life and Works of Francis Hopkinson,* 229.

123 PRO 60, May 10, 1778; Taafe, *The Philadelphia Campaign, 1777-1778,* 189.

124 LOC, GWP, Washington to Philemon Dickenson, May 13, 1778.

125 ISM, Barry Memorial to Congress, 1785; Clark, *Gallant John Barry,* 155.

126 DNA, GWP, Barry to Washington, May 30, 1782; Jackson, *With the British Army in Philadelphia,* 260.

CHAPTER EIGHT: THE *Raleigh*

1 Van Powell, *American Navies of the Revolutionary War,* 58.

2 Miller, *Sea of Glory,* 311.

3 Fowler, *Rebels Under Sail,* 111.

4 LOC, Marine Committee Letter Book, Marine Committee to John Bradford, April 28, 1778.

5 Fowler, *Rebels Under Sail,* 111.

6 Miller, *Sea of Glory,* 302.

7 For a thorough story of Wickes's brilliant career, see Clark, *Lambert Wickes.*

8 NDAR, vol. 11, 1175, Eyewitness Account of Engagement Between Continental Navy Frigate *Randolph* and HMS *Yarmouth,* August 21, 1801; Miller, *Sea of Glory,* 322.

9 NDAR, vol. 11, 848-849, Journal of HMS *Richmond,* Captain John Lewis Gidoin, March 31, 1778.

10 Miller, *Sea of Glory,* 317-318.

11 Van Powell, *American Navies of the Revolutionary War,* 94; Millar, *American Ships of the Colonial and Revolutionary Periods,* 228, 253, 229; Chappelle, *The American Sailing Navy,* 69, 71.

12 Ibid.; Van Powell, *American Navies of the Revolutionary War,* 94.

13 Millar, *American Ships of the Colonial and Revolutionary Periods,* 234, 228-29; Cooper, *History of the Navy of the United States of America,* 70.

14 Miller, *Sea of Glory,* 314-315, 351; Cooper, *History of the Navy of the United States of America,* 74; LDC, Marine Committee to Eastern Navy Board, May 8, 1778.

15 ISM, Barry-Hayes Papers, John Brown to John Barry, May 21, 1778.

16 PA Archives, series II, vol. III, 154.

17 Ibid., 155.

18 LDC, Samuel Adams to James Warren, June 1, 1778.

19 MS Papers, Marine Committee Letter Book, May 30, 1778.

20 LDC, Adams to Warren, June 1, 1778.

21 *Boston Packet,* June 14, 1778.

22 LDC, Warren to Samuel Adams, June 26, 1778.

23 FDR Library, Barry to Robert Morris, September 3, 1778.

24 Clark, *Gallant John Barry,* 158.

25 Misc. Papers, Marine Committee Letter Book, Marine Committee to Eastern Navy Board, June 19, 1778.

26 Samuel Adams Papers, Vol. 11, 2194-2197, James Warren to Sam Adams, July 5, 1778.

27 Clark, *Gallant John* Barry, 159.

28 LDC, vol. 10, Marine Committee to Barry, September 28, 1778.

29 LDC, vol. 10, Marine Committee to Eastern Navy Board, July 11, 1778.

30 FDR Library, Barry to Robert Morris, September 3, 1778; LDC, Warren to Sam Adams, June 26, 1778.

31 LDC, vol. 10, Sam Adams to James Warren; Marine Committee to Eastern Navy Board, July 24, August 12, August 5, 1778.

32 LDC, vol. 10, Marine Committee to Eastern Navy Board, July 24, 1778; Marine Committee to J. Beatty, July 30, August 8, 1778.

33 *London Public Advertiser*, November 27, 1778, no. 12772; PRO, Admiralty Records, 32/441, Deposition of David Phipps; Smith, *Marines in the Revolution*, 174.

34 LDC, vol. 10, Marine Committee to John Barry, September 28, 1778.

35 Tuchman, *First Salute*, 160.

36 FDR Collection, Barry to Morris, September 3, 1778.

37 Fowler, *The Baron of Beacon Hill*, 235-37; Clark, *Gallant John Barry*, 162.

38 FDR Library, Barry to Morris, September 21, 1778.

39 LDC, vol. 10, Marine Committee to Barry, August 24, 1778.

40 Paullin, *Out-Letters,* vol. 1, 288.

41 LDC, vol. 10, Marine Committee to Barry, August 28, 1778.

42 Ibid., Marine Committee to Eastern Navy Board, September 14, 1778.

43 ISM, Barry-Hayes Papers, Barry to Continental Navy Board, Eastern Dept., September 17, 1778.

44 FDR Library, Barry to Morris, September 3, 1778.

45 LDC, vol. 10, Marine Committee to Johns Wadsworth, September 14, 1778.

46 FDR Library, Barry to Morris, September 3, 1778.

47 Government House, Newfoundland Website Project.

48 Fowler, *Rebels Under Sail,* 65.

49 Millar, *American Ships of the Colonial and Revolutionary Periods,* 35-36.

50 *Pennsylvania Evening Post,* "J. P-ke to Captain James Wallace, H.M.S. *Rose,* Newport," August 24, 1775.

51 *New York Gazette and the Weekly Mercury,* February 16, 1778.

52 PRO, Admiralty 32/436/10 Libel Papers, U.S. frigate *Raleigh,* October 14, 1778.

53 ISM, Barry's Defence of the *Raleigh,* 1778.

54 *New Hampshire Gazette,* May 2, 1776; ISM, Barry's Defence of the *Raleigh,* 1778.

55 ISM, Barry's Defence of the *Raleigh,* 1778.

56 Ibid.

57 Ibid.

58 PRO, Admiralty, 51/107, Captain's Journal, *Unicorn,* September 25, 1778.

59 Ibid.; ISM, Barry's Defence of the *Raleigh,* 1778.

60 Ibid.; Everett, "John Barry, Fighting Irishman," 23.

61 ISM, Barry's Defence of the *Raleigh,* 1778

62 Ibid.

63 Ibid.

64 Ibid.

65 Ibid.

66 Chappelle, *The American Sailing Navy,* 76.

67 King with Hattendorf and Estes, *A Sea of Words,* 355.

68 ISM, Barry's Defence of the *Raleigh,* 1778.

69 Ibid.

70 Ibid.

71 Ibid.

72 Cooper, *History of the Navy of the United States of America,* 79.

73 Ibid.; PRO, Admiralty, 331/1017, Captain's Journal, *Experiment.*

74 ISM, Barry's Defence of the *Raleigh,* 1778.

75 *Pennsylvania Packet,* October 22, 1778.

76 PRO, 56/1021, Captain's Journal, *Unicorn,* September 27, 1778.

77 ISM, Barry's Defence of the *Raleigh,* 1778.

78 Clark, *Gallant John Barry,* 165.

79 King with Hattendorf and Estes, *A Sea of Words,* 396.

80 Wilbur, *Pirates and Patriots of the Revolution,* 74, 71.

81 Cooper, *The History of the Navy of the United States of America,* 79.

82 ISM, Barry's Defence of the *Raleigh,* 1778.

83 Ibid.

84 PRO, Admiralty, 51/107, Captain's Journal, *Unicorn.*

85 ISM, Barry's Defence of the *Raleigh,* 1778.

86 Ibid.; PRO, Admiralty, 51/107, Captain's Journal, *Unicorn.*

87 ISM, Barry's Defence of the *Raleigh,* 1778.

88 "Bowles's New Pocket Map of the Most Inhabited Part of NEW ENGLAND"; Map of the New England Coast, American Revolutionary Org. NC 9, p. 22, Chapter IX.

89 ISM, Barry's Defence of the *Raleigh,* 1778.

90 PRO, Admiralty Records, Captain's Journal, *Experiment,* September 27, 1778.

91 *Pennsylvania Evening Post,* October 19, 1778.

92 ISM, Barry's Defence of the *Raleigh,* 1778; PRO Admiralty, 51/107, Captain's Journal, *Unicorn.*

93 Ibid. *Pennsylvania Evening Post,* October 19, 1778.

94 ISM, Barry's Defence of the *Raleigh,* 1778; PRO, Admiralty Records, Captain's Journal, *Experiment,* September 27, 1778.

95 ISM, Barry's Defence of the *Raleigh,* 1778.

96 Ibid.

97 *Pennsylvania Evening Post,* October 19, 1778.

98 ISM, Barry's Defence of the *Raleigh,* 1778; *Pennsylvania Packet,* October 19, 1778; Everett, "John Barry, Fighting Irishman," 25.

99 ISM, Barry's Defence of the *Raleigh,* 1778.

100 ISM, Barry's Defence of the *Raleigh,* 1778; PRO, Admiralty, 51/107, Captain's Journal, *Unicorn,* September 28, 1778; 51/331, Captain's Journal, *Experiment,* September 28, 1778.

101 ISM, Barry's Defence of the *Raleigh,* 1778.

102 Ibid.

103 Clark, *Gallant John Barry,* 169.

104 PRO, Admiralty, 51/107, Captain's Journal, *Unicorn,* September 28, 1778.

105 Ibid.

106 ISM, Barry's Defence of the *Raleigh,* 1778; PRO, Admiralty, 51/107.

107 ISM, Barry's Defence of the *Raleigh*, 1778; Clark, *Gallant John Barry*, 170.

108 LOC, GWP, George Washington to the Continental Congress, October 14, 1778; *Pennsylvania Packet*, October 22, 1778.

109 *Pennsylvania Packet*, October 20, 1778.

110 Ibid.; LOC, GWP, Washington to Continental Congress, October 14, 1778.

111 ISM, Barry's Defence of the *Raleigh*, 1778; *Pennsylvania Packet*, October 22, 1778.

112 ISM, Barry's Defence of the *Raleigh*, 1778. A review of the records on both sides would put the total of Americans killed at about fifteen.

113 *Pennsylvania Packet* October 22, 1778 ISM, Barry Memorial to Congress, 1785.

114 LDC, Marine Committee to Eastern Navy Board, October 15, 1778. One wonders if there may have been at least a faint coat of whitewash applied by the Navy Board and the subsequent inquiry, especially regarding Barry's decisions made before the battle and at its end. His error in thinking that Wallace had given up the chase was monumental. Naval historian Craig Symonds points out that Barry's assigning the *Raleigh*'s torching to a young, untested midshipman lacked foresight. When one recalls that Barry and another captain personally sabotaged the brigantine *Nancy* two years earlier, one wonders why he left Jeacocks in charge of destroying a much more valuable prize–a frigate–in the first place.

115 Chappelle, *The American Sailing Navy*, 84-85; Gurn, *Commodore John Barry*, 116.

116 LDC, Marine Committee to Eastern Naval Board, October 25, 1778; Clark, *Gallant John Barry*, 171.

117 PRO, Admiralty, HCA, 32/436/10, October 14, 1778.

118 *Pennsylvania Packet*, November 10, 1778.

CHAPTER NINE: PRIVATEER AND JUDGE

1 Tinkcom, "The Revolutionary City, 1765–1783," 143-144.

2 Watson, *Annals*, vol. II, 300.

3 *Pennsylvania Packet*, June 3, 1778.

4 *Pennsylvania Packet*, October 8, 1778.

5 Doerflinger, *Vigorous Spirit of Enterprise*, 210-212; Watson, *Annals*, vol. II, 302-303.

6 DNA, William Burley collection, Robert Morris to William Bingham; Doerflinger, *Vigorous Spirit of Enterprise*. 203.

7 Doerflinger, *Vigorous Spirit of Enterprise*, 210.

8 Tinckom, "The Revolutionary City, 1765–1783," 146.

9 Fowler, *Rebels Under Sail*, 69-70.

10 ISM, Barry-Hayes Papers, Memorial to the Pennsylvania Assembly, 1783, and to Congress, 1785; quoted in Clark, *Gallant John Barry*, 172.

11 LDC, Marine Committee to Barry, November 20, 1778.

12 JCC, November 10, 1778.

13 Ibid.

14 LDC, Henry Laurens to Benjamin Lincoln, November 24, 1778.

15 Ibid.

16 JCC, December 2, 1778.

17 ISM, Barry-Hayes Papers, Expense Report, March 1776-December 1781.

18 HSP, Bank of North America Papers, Morris to William Hooper, January 24, 1777.

19 NDAR, vol. 7, 368-369, Robert Morris to William Bingham, December 4, 1776.

20 NDAR, vol. 7, 205-206, John Langdon to Robert Morris, November 19, 1776.

21 Fowler, *Rebels Under Sail,* 245.

22 NDAR, vol. 7, 543-544, Benjamin Rush to Richard Henry Lee, December 21, 1776.

23 Fairburn, *Merchant Sail,* vol. I, 389.

24 Ibid.

25 JBP, 5-141, Wiiliam B. Clark Estate, "Shipping Order, Brigantine *Delaware,*" 1779; *Pennsylvania Packet,* June 5, 1779.

26 HSP, Minutes, "The Society for the Relief," January 1779.

27 *Pennsylvania Gazette,* February 17, 1779; Clark, *Gallant John Barry,* 176.

28 *Pennsylvania Gazette,* February 17, 1779.

29 From Clark, *Gallant John Barry,* 176; PA Archives, Record Group 27, Supreme Executive Council's Register of Letters of Marque, 1778-1782, February 15, 1779.

30 David Library of the American Revolution, Sol Feinstone Collection, Matthew Clarkson to Barry, February 13, 1779.

31 JBP, NY 5-141, Clark Estate, "Shipping Order, Brigantine *Delaware,*" 1779.

32 Archives, Archdiocese of Philadelphia, February 15, 1779.

33 PA Archives, Record Group 27, Supreme Executive Council's Register of Letters of Marque, 1778-1782, February 15, 1779; Clark, *Gallant John Barry,* 177.

34 *Pennsylvania Packet,* June 5, 1779.

35 DNA, Marine Committee to Eastern Naval Board, June 21, 1779; NYHS, Barnes Collection, Shipping order, Brigantine *Delaware,* July, 1779; PA Archives, Series 2, vol. I, p. 367.

36 Owners' Instructions, Brig *Delaware,* quoted in Clark, *Gallant John Barry,* 178.

37 Kessler, "Life of John Kessler," 1.

38 Haverford College Library (HCL), Charles Roberts Autograph Collection, Barry to Irwin, July 16, 1779.

39 Ibid.

40 *Pennsylvania Packet,* November 18, 1779.

41 Kessler, "Rough Sketch."

42 Kessler, "Rough Sketch," 2.

43 Ibid.

44 *Pennsylvania Packet,* November 18, 1779.

45 *Pennsylvania Gazette,* October 6, 1779.

46 DNA, Marine Committee to Harding, October 22, 1779; JCC, Reed to Marine Committee.

47 Doerflinger, *Vigorous Spirit of Enterprise,* 255; Tinkcom, "The Revolutionary City, 1765–1783," 147.

48 Doerflinger, *Vigorous Spirit of Enterprise,* 255; Tinkcom, "The Revolutionary City, 1765–1783," 147; Paullin, *Out-Letters,* vol. II, 264.

49 James Wilson to Robert Morris, October 4, 1779; quoted in Gurn, *Commodore John Barry,* 122.

50 Ibid.; Doerflinger, *Vigorous Spirit of Enterprise* 255; Tinkcom, "The Revolutionary City, 1765–1783," 147.

51 Archdiocese of Philadelphia Archives, Baptismal Records, St. Mary's Church, Philadelphia; Griffin, *The History of Commodore John Barry,* 108.

52 PA Archives, Colonial Records, vol. 12, 80.

53 *Pennsylvania Gazette,* April 10, 1779.

54 LOC, John Barry Collection, Mathew Irwin receipts, August 7, 1779.

55 ISM, Barry-Hayes Papers Memorial; Clark, *Gallant John Barry*, 183.

56 DNA, Marine Committee to John Barry, November 6, 1779.

57 Ibid.

58 Rates were based on number of guns; most frigates were fifth or sixth rated ships; King with Hattendorf and Estes, *A Sea of* Words, 308; Van Powell, *The American Navies of the Revolutionary War*, 86.

59 Chappelle, *The American Sailing Navy*, 80.

60 LDC, Marine Committee to John Barry, November 6, 1779.

61 Paullin, *Out-Letters*, vol. II, 131, Marine Committee to Captain John Barry, November 20, 1779; Miller, *Sea of Glory*, 421.

62 Paullin, *Out-Letters*, vol. II, 131.

63 Clark, *Gallant John Barry*, 185.

64 Ibid.

65 Miller, *Sea of Glory*, 421.

66 DNA, Board of Admiralty to John Langdon, December 28, 1779.

67 Samuel Adams Papers, vol. 11, 2194-2197, John Warner to Sam Adams, July 15, 1778.

68 DNA, Board of Admiralty correspondence, John Brown to Board of War, January 31, 1780; quoted in Gurn, *Commodore John Barry*, 126.

69 NYHS, "Received of Capt. John Barry one Continental horse Pack saddle," September 19, 1780; ISM, John Barry Memorial to Congress, 1785.

70 Clark, *Gallant John Barry*, 187.

71 NDAR, Vol. 8, 453-454, Captain Thomas Lloyd, R.N. to Governor Bernardo de Gálvez, April 27, 1777.

72 LOC, John Barry Collection, *Alliance* Letterbook. November 17, 1782.

73 *Pennsylvania Gazette*, May 24, 1780.

74 Archdiocese of Philadelphia Records, Baptismal Certificate, Eleanor Barry, July 2, 1775; from Griffin, *The History of Commodore John Barry*, 116.

75 ISM, Barry-Hayes Papers, John Barry Memorial to Pennsylvania Assembly, 1783, and to Congress, 1785; quoted in Clark, *Gallant John Barry*, 188.

76 Miller, *Sea of Glory*, 231.

77 Allen, *A Naval History of the American Revolution*, 528.

78 Miller, *Sea of Glory*, 231.

79 Landais, *Memorial to Justify Peter Landais' Conduct During the Late War.*

80 Morison, *John Paul Jones*, 232.

81 MHS, Adams Papers, Adams to Warren, June 1, 1778; LDC, Marine Committee to Eastern Navy Board, June 18, 1778.

82 Samuel Adams Papers, vol. 11, 2194-2197, Warren to S. Adams, July 5, 1778.

83 Morison, *John Paul Jones*, 231.

84 Miller, *Sea of Glory*, 374-375.

85 Bradford, ed., *The Adams Papers*, vol. II, 368.

86 Jones's second-in-command aboard the *Bonhomme Richard* was none other than Richard Dale, the young midshipman who Barry had persuaded to rejoin the American cause after the *Lexington* took the *Lady Susan*. Dale was on the *Lexington* when she was recaptured in 1777. A year after his imprisonment he escaped, walking right past the prison guards while dressed in a British uniform. He made his way to France and joined the crew of the *Bonhomme Richard*. To his dying day he never told anyone how he obtained that uniform. MacLay, *A History of American Privateers*, 64.

87 Thomas, *John Paul Jones,* 161.

88 The Battle of Flamborough Head is written about in great detail by Morison and Thomas in their biographies of Jones as well as in Fowler's *Rebels Under Sail* and Miller's *Sea of Glory.*

89 Fowler, *Rebels Under Sail,* 236.

90 Schiff, *A Great Improvisation,* 153.

91 Miller, *Sea of Glory,* 434–435.

92 DNA, MSS Division, Papers of the Continental Congress, "Barry's Summing Up of the Evidence at Landais' Court-Martial"; Morison, *John Paul Jones,* 359.

93 Ibid.; Ibid.

94 Morison, *John Paul Jones,* 359.

95 Ibid.

96 Fowler, *Rebels Under Sail,* 237.

97 Miller, *Sea of Glory,* 439.

98 De Koven, *The Life and Letters of John Paul Jones.*

99 LOC, GWP, Washington to Jeremiah Powell and John Trumbull, July 22, 1780.

100 Revolutionary Diplomatic Correspondence, BFP, Franklin to President of Congress, August 9, 1780.

101 Paullin, ed., *Out-Letters,* vol. II, Marine Committee to Barry, September 5, 1780, 261-262.

102 Ibid., 265-266, Marine Committee to William Ellery, September 9, 1780.

103 Miller, *Sea of Glory,* 413, 416. It also ended the career of its naval leader Dudley Saltonstall—once fourth on the navy seniority list.

104 Ibid., 423.

105 Paullin, ed., *Out-Letters,* vol. II, 265-266.

106 LOC, GWP, Washington to Jefferson, September 11, 1780.

107 Massachusetts Historical Society, Adams Family Papers, Abigail Adams to John Adams, October 15, 1780, October 8, 1780.

108 DeKoven, *The Life and Letters of John Paul Jones,* 142; Fowler, *Rebels Under Sail,* 237.

109 DNA, MSS, Barry's Report on the Landais Court-Martial, vol. II, 193; Clark, *Gallant John Barry,* 192.

110 DeKoven, *The Life and Letters of John Paul Jones,* 141-142.

111 DNA, MSS, Barry's Report on the Landais Court-Martial, vol. II, 193.

112 Clark, *Gallant John Barry,* 192.

113 LOC, Barry Collection, Muster roll, *Alliance,* 1781.

114 Kessler, "Life of John Kessler," 4.

115 Ibid.

116 DNA, RDC, vol. 4, Laurens to President of Congress, February 4, 1781.

117 JCC, November 13, 1780.

118 Ibid.

119 DeKoven, *The Life and Letters of John Paul Jones,* 142.

120 DNA, MSS DIR, Papers of Continental Congress, vol. II, 193, "Barry's Summing Up of the Evidence at Landais Court-Martial."

121 Clark, *Gallant John Barry,* 194.

122 DNA, MSS, Papers of the Continental Congress, vol. II, 193.

123 De Koven, *The Life and Letters of John Paul Jones,* 142-143.

124 Landais, *Memorial.*

125 De Koven, *The Life and Letters of John Paul Jones,* 142-143; Clark, *Gallant John Barry,* 195.

126 Ibid.

127 DNA, MSS Division, The Papers of the Continental Congress: "Barry's Summing Up."

128 Ibid.

129 Fowler, *Rebels Under Sail,* 237.

130 Miller, *Sea of Glory,* 439.

131 Chappelle, *The American Sailing Navy,* 85; Millar, *American Ships of the Colonial and Revolutionary Periods,* 45.

132 Morison, *John Paul Jones,* 235; French official Thevenard quoted in Clark, *Gallant John Barry,* 192.

133 Ellis, *His Excellency,* 129-130.

134 Brands, *The First American,* 589.

135 Keane, *Tom Paine,* 203.

136 Ibid.

137 Ibid., 204.

138 Chernow, *Alexander Hamilton,* 116-117.

139 LDC, vol. 16, Madison to John Jones, December 12, 1780.

140 Keane, *Tom Paine,* 206-207.

141 DNA, GWP, Washington to Hancock, January 19, 1781.

142 DNA, RDC, vol. 4, Laurens to President of Congress, February 4, 1781; Clark, *Gallant John Barry,* 197.

143 NDAR, vol. 11, 559.

144 DNA, RDC, Laurens to President of Congress, February 4, 1781.

145 Miller, *Sea of Glory,* 457.

146 Clark, *Gallant John Barry,* 198.

147 Washington to Laurens, quoted in Miller, *Sea of Glory,* p.457.

148 DNA, RDC, vol. 4, Laurens to President of Congress, February 4, 1781.

149 DNA, JCC, November 13, 1780.

150 DNA, GWP, Washington to Benjamin Lincoln, February 27, 1781.

151 Miller, *Sea of Glory,* 457-458.

152 DNA, RDC, Laurens to President of Congress, February 4, 1781.

153 Ibid.

154 Ibid.

155 Ibid.

156 Ibid., February 6, 1781.

157 Ibid., February 7, 1781.

158 Haverford College, Charles Roberts Autograph Collection, Account of Expenses for *Alliance,* February 9, 1781; Clark, *Gallant John Barry,* 200.

159 APS, Benjamin Franklin Papers, John Barry to Benjamin Franklin, March 13, 1781.

160 Ibid.

161 From Miller, *Sea of Glory,* 458.

CHAPTER TEN: MUTINY

1 NYHS, Thomas Paine to James Hutchinson, March 11, 1781; Keane, *Tom Paine,* 208.

2 NYHS, Paine to Hutchinson, March 11, 1781; Keane, *Tom Paine,* 175; e-mail, James Nelson, February 25, 2008.

3 NYHS, Paine to Hutchinson, March 11, 1781; King with Hattendorf, *Harbors and High Seas,* 229.

4 NYHS, Paine to Hutchinson, March 11, 1781.

5 Ibid.; King with Hattendorf, *Harbors and High Seas,* 164. I also wish to thank author/mariner James Nelson for his expertise in this area.

6 NYHS, Paine to Hutchinson, March 11, 1781;DNA, Laurens to President of Congress, March 10, 1781; e-mail, James Nelson, February 25, 2008; Keane, *Tom Paine,* 208.

7 NYHS, Paine to Hutchinson, March 11,1781; Keane, *Tom Paine,* 209.

8 Clark, *Gallant John Barry,* 201.

9 Kessler, "Rough Sketch," 5.

10 Keane, *Tom Paine,* 209; Clark, *Gallant John Barry,* 201.

11 Kessler "Rough Sketch," 5.

12 Miller, *Sea of Glory,* 458.

13 Keane, *Tom Paine,* 209.

14 DNA, vol. 4, John Laurens to President of Congress, March 11, 1781.

15 RDC, Laurens to President of Congress, March 11, 1781; NYHS, Barnes Collection, *Alliance* Letterbook, March 4, 1781.

16 ISM, Barry-Hayes Papers, *Alliance* log, March 6, 7, 9, 1781; APS, Benjamin Franklin Papers, Barry to Benjamin Franklin, March 10, 1781; King with Hattendorf and Estes, *A Sea of Words,* 285.

17 O'Neill, *Patrick O'Brian's Navy,* 16; King with Hattendorf, *Harbors and High Seas,* 237, 120; NYHS, Paine to Hutchinson, March 11, 1781.

18 Keane, *Tom Paine,* 210; DNA, RDC, vol. 4, Laurens to President of Congress, March 11, 1781.

19 APS, BFP, Barry to Franklin, March 10, 1781.

20 NYHS, Barnes Collection, *Alliance* Letterbook, August 1, 1782; From Griffin, *The History of Commodore John Barry,* 171: "An Attested Copy of what I related to the Committee of Congress in Philadelphia;" Morison, *John Paul Jones,* 222, 324.

21 APS, BFP, Barry to Franklin, March 13, 1781; JCC, July 15, 1782.

22 DNA, RDC, vol. 4, Laurens to President of Congress, March 11, 1781.

23 APS, BFP, Barry to Franklin, March 13, 1781.

24 APS, BFP, Matthew Parke to Franklin, March 13, 1781.

25 ISM, Barry–Hayes Papers, *Alliance* log, March 13, 1781.

26 Miller, *Sea of Glory,* 103; ISM, Barry–Hayes Papers, *Alliance* log, March 13, 1781; NDAR, vol. II, Appendix, "The Regulations of the Navy of the United Colonies."

27 Miller, *Sea of Glory,* 104.

28 Ibid.; Freidenberg, *Medicine Under Sail,* 101.

29 NDAR, vol. 2, Appendix, "Rules and Regulations;" Miller, *Sea of Glory,* 104.

30 Miller, *Sea of Glory,* 105.

31 ISM, Barry–Hayes Papers, *Alliance* log, March 13, 1781.

32 Kessler, "Rough Sketch," 14.

33 LOC, Barry Collection, Muster roll, *Alliance* Frigate, March 29, 1781.

34 Freidenberg, *Medicine Under Sail,* 101.

35 Clark, *Gallant John Barry,* 207.

36 JBP, *Alliance* Letterbook, August 1, 1782; Griffin, *The History of Commodore John Barry,* 170-171.

37 APS, BFP, Barry to Franklin, March 13, 1781; John Barry to Captain de Galatheau, March 23, 1781, from Griffin, *The History of Commodore John Barry,* 131-132.

38 APS, BFP, Franklin to Barry, March 19, 1781.

39 DNA, Wm. Sharpe to Thos. Burke, July 28, 1781; Ferguson, ed., *The Papers of Robert Morris,* vol. 3, 217.

40 Morison, *John Paul Jones,* 206.

41 ISM, Barry–Hayes Papers, *Alliance* log, March 17, 1781.

42 JCC, July 15, 1782; from Griffin, *The History of Commodore John Barry,* 170-171.

43 Barry to de Galatheau, March 23, 1781, quoted in Griffin, *The History of Commodore John Barry,* 131-32.

44 APS, BFP, Barry to Franklin, March 23, 1781.

45 APS, BFP, Barry to Franklin, March 27, 1781.

46 ISM, *Alliance* log, March 27, 1781.

47 JCC, July 15, 1782; from Griffin, *The History of Commodore John Barry,* 170-171.

48 JCC, July 15, 1782; from Griffin, *The History of Commodore John Barry,* 170-171.

49 ISM, *Alliance* log, March 28, 1781; Ferguson, ed., *The Papers of Robert Morris,* vol. 4, 556-557.

50 JCC, July 15, 1782; Griffin, *The History of Commodore John Barry,* 170-171.

51 ISM, *Alliance* log, March 29, 1781.

52 Captain William Robeson letter, January 22,1782, from Griffin, *The History of Commodore John Barry,* 174; ISM, *Alliance* log, March 29, 1781.

53 ISM, *Alliance* log, March 29, 1781.

54 Ibid.

55 Kessler, "Rough Sketch," 6.

56 King with Hattendorf, *Harbors and High Seas,* 91.

57 Morison, *John Paul Jones,* 364-367; Thomas, *John Paul Jones,* 236-243.

58 ISM, *Alliance* log, March 30, 1781.

59 Kessler, "Rough Sketch," 5; LOC, Barry Collection, Muster Rolls, *Alliance,* March 29, 1781.

60 ISM, *Alliance* log, March 31, 1781; Kessler, "Rough Sketch," 5.

61 NDAR, vol. 9; ISM, *Alliance* log, March 31, 1781; Kessler, "Rough Sketch," 5.

62 Kessler, "Rough Sketch," 5; ISM, *Alliance* log, March 31, 1781.

63 Ibid.; Ibid.

64 ISM, *Alliance* log, March 31, 1781; Miller, *Sea of Glory,* 474; Kessler, "Rough Sketch," 5.

65 Kessler, "Rough Sketch," 5.

66 Ibid.; ISM, *Alliance* log, March 31, 1781; Miller, *Sea of Glory,* 475.

67 ISM, *Alliance* log, March 31, 1781; Kessler, "Rough Sketch," 5.

68 ISM, *Alliance* log, March 31, 1781; Kessler, "Rough Sketch," 5-6; Boston Newspapers, vol. IV, June 14, 1781.

69 ISM, *Alliance* log, March 31, 1781.

70 Ibid.

71 ISM, *Alliance* log; Letter from Capt. John Barry to the Secretary of Congress, August 1, 1782, from Griffin, *The History of Commodore John Barry,* 170-72; Kessler, "Rough Sketch," 6.

72 ISM, *Alliance* log, April 2, 1781; from Griffin, *The History of Commodore John Barry,* 172-173.

73 ISM, *Alliance* log, April 2, 1781; from Griffin, *The History of Commodore John Barry*, 172-173.

74 ISM, *Alliance* log, April 2, 1781; Kessler, "Rough Sketch," 5-6; from Griffin, *The History of Commodore John Barry*, 173.

75 ISM, *Alliance* log, April 2, 1781; Kessler, "Rough Sketch," 6-7.

76 ISM, *Alliance* log, April 2-3, 1781; from Griffin, *The History of Commodore John Barry*, 144, 173-174.

77 ISM, *Alliance* log, April 3, April 18, 1781.

78 ISM, *Alliance* log, April 23, 1781; from Griffin, *The History of Commodore John Barry*, 174.

79 JCC, Barry to Congress, June 6, 1781, July 15, 1782; from Griffin, *The History of Commodore John Barry*, 171; ISM, *Alliance* log, April 25, 1781.

80 ISM, *Alliance* log, April 25, 1781.

81 Ibid., May 2, 1781; Boston Newspapers, vol. 4, June 14, 1781; Kessler, "Rough Sketch," 7.

82 ISM, *Alliance* log, May 3, 1781; JCC, Barry to Congress, June 6, 1781; Kessler, "Rough Sketch," 7.

83 From Griffin, *The History of Commodore John Barry*, 142, 174; Clark, *Gallant John Barry*, 217-218.

84 ISM, *Alliance* log 5, 1781; from Griffin, *The History of Commodore John Barry*, 144; JCC, Barry to Congress, June 6, 1781; Clark, *Gallant John Barry*, 219.

85 Clark, *Gallant John Barry*, 219.

86 JCC, Barry to Congress, June 6, 1781.

87 Ibid.

88 Kessler, "Rough Sketch," 7.

89 JCC, Barry to Congress, June 6, 1781.

90 See Mathew Parke's painting of *Alliance*; Clark, *Gallant John Barry*, 220.

91 JCC, Barry to Congress, June 6, 1781. Kessler, "Rough Sketch," 10.

92 Ibid.

93 Kessler, "Rough Sketch," 7; *London Daily Intelligencer*, August 6, 1781.

94 Ralfe, *Naval Biography of Great Britain*, vol. II, p. 362; *London Daily Intelligencer*, August 6, 1781.

95 Kessler, "Rough Sketch," 7.

96 *London Chronicle*, August 6, 1781.

97 Kessler, "Rough Sketch," 7; JCC, Barry to Congress, June 6, 1781.

CHAPTER ELEVEN: ATALANTA AND TREPASSEY

1 LOC, Barry Collection, *Alliance* muster roll, March 29, 1781; King, with Hattendorf and Estes, *A Sea of Words*, 129.

2 Friedenburg, *Medicine Under Sail*, 17, 18.

3 Wilbur, *Revolutionary Medicine 1700-1800*, 62-63.

4 King with Hattendorf and Estes, *A Sea of Words*, 235.

5 *London Chronicle*, August 6, 1781.

6 JCC, Barry to Eastern Naval Board June 6, 1781.

7 Kessler, "Rough Sketch," 8.

8 *London Chronicle*, August 6, 1781; Allen, *A Naval History of the American Revolution*, *Vol. 1*, 551.

9 *London Chronicle*, August 6, 1781.

10 Ibid.; Kessler, "Rough Sketch," 8.

11 *London Chronicle*, August 6, 1781.

12 Allen, *Naval History of the American Revolution*, 552; *London Chronicle*, August 6, 1781.

13 Ibid.; Ibid.

14 Allen, *Naval History of the American Revolution*, 552; *London Chronicle*, August 6, 1781; Kessler, "Rough Sketch," 8.

15 LOC, Barry Collection, *Alliance* muster roll, March 29, 1781.

16 Kessler, "Rough Sketch," 8; Brown and Kessler, "The Life of Commodore Barry," 7-8.

17 Wilbur, *Revolutionary Medicine 1700-1800*, 46.

18 Miller, *Sea of Glory*, 95.

19 Kessler, "Rough Sketch," 8.

20 LOC, Barry Collection, *Alliance* muster roll, March 29, 1781; Clark, *Gallant John Barry*, 223.

21 Friedenberg, *Medicine Under Sail*, 18.

22 Wilbur, *Revolutionary Medicine 1700-1800*, 49.

23 John Barry to the Board of Admiralty, June 6, 1781, from Griffin, *The History of Commodore John Barry*, 145; Kessler, "Rough Sketch," 8; Clark, *Gallant John Barry*, 224.

24 Kessler, "Rough Sketch," 8.

25 Ibid.

26 Wilbur, *Revolutionary Medicine 1700-1800*, 34; King with Hattendorf and Estes, *A Sea of Words*, 54; NDAR, vol. 6, 1488.

27 Laurence Todd, Detached Hospital, BB BAR, e-mail, October 18, 2005; Dr. Paul Kopperman, e-mail, October 18, 2005.

28 Dr. Paul Kopperman, e-mail, October 18, 2005; Ranby, *The Method of Treating Gunshot Wounds*, 2nd ed., 21, 34-35.

29 Kopperman and Todd e-mails, October 18, 2005.

30 Ibid.; Wilbur, *Revolutionary Medicine 1700-1800*, 34.

31 Kessler, "Rough Sketch," 8; LOC, Barry Collection, *Alliance* muster roll, March 29, 1781.

32 Kessler, "Rough Sketch," 8; LOC, Barry Collection, *Alliance* muster roll, March 29, 1781; Clark, *Gallant John Barry*, 224.

33 Kessler, "Rough Sketch," 8.

34 Brown and Kessler, "The Life of Commodore Barry," 8; Kessler, "Rough Sketch," 10; Clark, *Gallant John Barry*, 224.

35 Kessler, "Rough Sketch," 8-10.

36 Ibid., 8.

37 Brown and Kessler, "The Life of Commodore Barry," 9.

38 Ibid., 8; Allen, *Naval History of the American Revolution*, 552.

39 *London Chronicle*, August 6, 1781.

40 Ibid.

41 Ibid.; Brown and Kessler, "The Life of Commodore Barry," 9.

42 *London Chronicle*, August 6, 1781.

43 Brown and Kessler, "The Life of Commodore Barry," 9.

44 Ibid.

45 Ibid., 10.

46 *London Chronicle*, August 6, 1781.

47 *Pennsylvania Gazette*, June 27, 1781.

48 JCC, Barry to Congress, June 6, 1781.

49 Kessler, "Rough Sketch," 9.

50 JCC, Barry to Congress, June 6, 1781.

51 London *Chronicle*, August 6, 1781.

52 Kessler, "Rough Sketch," 9.

53 JCC, Barry to Congress, June 6, 1781.

54 Barry to the Board of Admiralty, June 6, 1781, from Griffin, *The History of Commodore John Barry*, 143-146; John Barry to Eastern Navy Board, 6, 1781.

55 JCC, Barry to Congress, June 6, 1781; King with Hattendorf and Estes, *A Sea of Words*, 117.

56 Ibid.; also Barry to Eastern Navy Board, June 6, 1781.

57 Kessler, "Rough Sketch," 9.

58 *Pennsylvania Packet*, May 26, 1781.

59 LOC, Joseph Bradford's Letter Book, May 14, 1781; Clark, *Gallant John Barry*, 227.

60 Matthew Parke's painting of the *Alliance* coming into Boston Harbor depicts this very accurately.

61 *Pennsylvania Gazette*, June 27, 1781.

62 Kessler, "Rough Sketch," 11; Clark, *Gallant John Barry*, 227; JCC, Barry to Congress, June 6, 1781; LOC, John Barry Collection, from the pages of the Pension Office.

63 LOC, John Barry Collection, Pension Office.

64 Allen, *Naval History of the American Revolution*, 555.

65 *Continental Journal*, June 14, 1781; LOC, Revolutionary Collection, Joseph Bradford letter book, Bradford to Board of Admiralty, June 14, 1781.

66 *Pennsylvania Packet*, June 23, 1781.

67 Laurence Todd, e-mail October 18, 2005.

68 Wilbur, *Revolutionary Medicine 1700-1800*, p. 34.

69 Boston Newspapers IV, *Continental Journal*, June 14, 1781.

70 *Continental Journal*, June 14, 1781; *Pennsylvania Gazette*, June 27, 1781; *London Chronicle*, August 6, 1781; *Pennsylvania Packet*, June 23, 1781; Brown and Kessler, "The Life of Commodore Barry," 9.

71 DNA, LDC, Richard Potts to Thomas Sim Lee, July 3, 1781

72 APS, BFP, Congressional Resolution, June 26, 1781; Haverford College Library, Charles Roberts Collection, Francis Lewis Lester to Barry, July 3, 1781

73 DNA, RDC, Franklin to McKean, November 5, 1781.

74 ISM, Barry-Hayes Papers, Brown to Barry, June 26, 1781.

75 Ferguson, ed., *The Papers of Robert Morris* (RMP), vol. 1, 308.

CHAPTER TWELVE: REFITTING

1 HSP; NYHS; Haverford College, Charles Roberts Collection: those letters from Sarah to John that survived all begin with the phrase "My Dear Life," although some, as we shall see, are more affectionate than others!

2 Barry to the Admiralty, July 25, 1781, quoted in Griffin, *The History of Commodore John Barry*, 148.

3 Extract of a letter from John Brown, Boston, January 4, 1782, RMP, vol. 3, 491-492.

4 Paullin, *Out-Letters,* 230.

5 Fowler, *Rebels Under Sail,* 84; Miller, *Sea of Glory,* 476; HSP, Logbook, "Society for the Relief of Poor and Distressed Masters of Ships"; LOC, William Bell Clark Collection, *Saratoga* papers.

6 Tuchman, *First Salute,* 217–218; John Donaldson to John Brown, quoted in Clark, *Gallant John Barry,* 231.

7 *Pennsylvania Gazette,* July 11, 1781.

8 JCC, June 26, 1781.

9 Morison, *John Paul Jones,* 377.

10 DeKoven, *Life and Letters of John Paul Jones,* vol. 2, 212-214.

11 Ibid.; Morison, *John Paul Jones,* 377.

12 DeKoven, *Life and Letters of John Paul Jones,* vol. 2, 211-214.

13 Miller, *Sea of Glory,* 478.

14 Morison, *John Paul Jones,* 378; Miller, *Sea of Glory,* 476-478.

15 Barry to Board of Admiralty, July 25, 1781, quoted in Griffin, *The History of Commodore John Barry,* 148.

16 DNA, RDC, Morris to Governor of Massachusetts, August 4, 1781; RMP, vol. 1, 308.

17 Early History Center, Washington Navy Yard, Boston Newspapers II, p. 85.

18 Ferguson, ed., RMP, vol. 2, 193-194.

19 JCC, July 15 and August 5, 1782; Clark, *Gallant John Barry,* 233.

20 From Clark, *Gallant John Barry,* 233.

21 Miller, *Sea of Glory,* 304-310.

22 ISM, Barry-Hayes Papers, Henry Mitchell to John Brown, September 4, 1781.

23 Quoted in Clark, *Gallant John Barry,* 233.

24 ISM, Mitchell to Brown. September 4, 1781; Clark, *Gallant John Barry,* 233.

25 RDC, vol. 4, Robert Morris to Ben Franklin, August 28, 1781; Keane, *Tom Paine,* 213.

26 Schiff, *A Great Improvisation,* 266-277.

27 DNA, LDC, vol. 18, Thomas McKean to John Laurens, September 6, 1781.

28 Morison, *John Paul Jones,* 380; Thomas, *John Paul Jones,* 249–250.

29 LOC, John Paul Jones Papers, Reel 6, Item 1339, September 7, 1781.

30 Ibid.

31 Ibid.; Clark, *Gallant John Barry,* 233. We do not know what Barry did with Jones's cockade, but we know that Barry held Jones's fighting skills and patriotism in high regard. A miniature portrait of Jones was among Barry's possessions at the time of his death, and treasured by his indirect descendants for generations. ISM, Barry-Hayes Papers, List of Articles for Auction, 1939.

32 RDC, vol. 4, Robert Morris to the Governor of Massachusetts, August 4, 1781.

33 JCC, Barry to Thompson, August 1, 1782.

34 Clark, *Gallant John Barry,* 234-235.

35 Flexner, *Washington,* 163.

36 Fowler, *Rebels Under Sail,* 84, 262-263.

37 Crawford, "Naval Administration Under Robert Morris," 2-3, 7.

38 HSP, Dreer Collection, Morris to Brown, September 19, 1781.

39 Fowler, *Rebels Under Sail,* 85.

40 Miller, *Sea of Glory,* 476; Clark, *Gallant John Barry,* 236.

41 HSP, Dreer Collection, Morris to Brown, September 19, 1781.

42 Ibid.

43 ISM, Barry-Hayes Papers, Henry Mitchell to John Brown, September 4, 1781; HSP, Dreer, Robert Morris to John Brown, September 19, 1781; Clark, *Gallant John Barry,* 237.

44 *Pennsylvania Gazette,* October 3, 1780.

45 JCC, November 28, 1781.

46 RMP, vol. 3 [enclosure], Sentence of the Court-Martial on Three Men of the *Alliance,* June 28, 1781; Clark, *Gallant John Barry,* 237.

47 Morris to Barry, October 17, 1781, quoted in Griffin, *The History of Commodore John Barry,* 152.

48 Tuchman, *First Salute,* 291.

49 HSP, Dreer Collection, Morris to Brown, September 19, 1781; Kessler, "Rough Sketch," 11; Clark, *Gallant John Barry,* 191, 238.

50 Barry to Congress, July 25, 1781, from Griffin, *The History of Commodore John Barry,* 148; RMP, vol. 4, 556-557; LOC, Robert Morris to Joseph Kendall, April 10, 1782.

51 RMP, vol. 4, 556-557; LOC, Robert Morris to Joseph Kendall, April 10, 1782.

52 *Continental Journal,* November 1, 1781, quoted in Clark, *Gallant John Barry,* 238-239.

53 Ibid.

54 Ibid.

55 Barry to Eastern Navy Board, from Clark, *Gallant John Barry,* 239.

56 Ibid.; RMP, vol. 4, 556-557.

57 JBP, Muster roll, *Alliance,* May 17, 1782.

58 Ibid.

59 JBP, 314, Morris to Barry, November 19, 1781.

60 HSP, Dreer Collection, Morris to Brown, November 27, 1781; Brown and Kessler, "The Life of Commodore Barry," 11.

CHAPTER THIRTEEN: SHOALS

1 Brands, *The First American,* 597.

2 Flexner, *Washington,* 168.

3 RMP, vol. 3, Morris to Barry, November 27, 1781, 260-263.

4 Ibid.

5 RMP, vol. 3, Barry to Morris, December 22, 1781; vol. 4, Barry to Morris, February 10, 1782.

6 Washington Navy Yard, Early History Center, Samuel Nicholson to John Barry, December 21, 1781.

7 LOC, GWP, Marquis de Lafayette to George Washington, December 21, 1781; RMP, vol. 3, Morris to Barry, November 27, 1781, 260-263.

8 APS, BFP, Barry to Franklin, February 29, 1782.

9 JBP, *Alliance* Letterbook, Barry to Morris, December 22, 1781.

10 JBP, *Alliance* Letterbook, Barry to Samuel Nicholson, December 22, 1781; Barry to Brown, December 22, 1781; Barry to Morris, January 30, 1782; Kessler, "Rough Sketch," 12.

11 Kessler, "Rough Sketch," 12.

12 JBP, *Alliance* Letterbook, Barry to Morris, February 10, 1782; Barry to Morris, January 30, 1782.

13 Kessler, "Rough Sketch," 12.

14 Ibid.

15 LOC, GWP, Lafayette to Washington, February 18, 1782.

16 APS, BFP, Barry to Franklin, January 31, 1782, Barry to Franklin January 17, 1782.

17 APS, BFP, Barry to Franklin, February 29, 1782; Morison, *John Paul Jones,* 235; Clark, *Gallant John Barry,* 245-246.

18 APS, BFP, Barry to Franklin, January 17, 1782.

19 APS, BFP, Franklin to Barry, January 24, 1782.

20 Ibid.

21 JBP, Barry to Morris, January 30, 1782.

22 APS, BFP, Barry to Franklin, February 29, 1782.

23 JBP, Barry to Barclay, January 27, 1782.

24 Lafayette was making entreaties at the court, but not for sailors. By now, Versailles was tiring of America's constant pleas for more money. Franklin put the Marquis' reputation, charm, and influence to immediate use. Eventually, Lafayette delivered; yet another six million livres were loaned to America. APS, BFP, 340, Franklin to Morris, March 4, 1782; Schiff, *A Great Improvisation,* 294.

25 APS, BFP, Barry to Franklin, January 31, 1782.

26 Ibid.

27 JBP, Barry to Morris, January 30, 1782.

28 RMP, vol. 4, 133, Franklin to Morris, January 28, 1782.

29 JBP, Barry to Thévenard, February 5, 1782.

30 Ibid.; Clark, *Gallant John Barry,* 248.

31 JBP, Barry to de Galatheau, February 9, 1782.

32 Ibid.

33 JCC, July 15, 1782; LBC, vol. 18, Charles Thompson to Barry, July 16, 1782.

34 APS, BFP, Barry to Franklin, February 27, 1782; Clark, *Gallant John Barry,* 249.

35 JBP, Barry to Morris, February 10, 1782.

36 Ibid.; JBP, Barry to Brown, February 10, 1782.

37 Clark, *Gallant John Barry,* 249–250.

38 Kessler, "Rough Sketch," 12.

39 APS, Barry to Franklin, February 27, 1782.

40 APS, Barry to Franklin, February 27, 1782.

41 APS, BFP, Lafayette to Franklin, February 29, 1782.

42 RMP, vol. 4, Franklin to Morris, March 4, 1782, 341.

43 JBP, Barry to Franklin, February 29, 1782.

44 Ibid.

45 Ibid.

46 JBP, NY 5-34, William Downs to John Barry, February 9, 1782; John Green to Barry, February 10, 1782; Barry to Green, March 13, 1782; Barry to Gregory, March 10, 1782.

47 APS, BFP, Barry to Franklin, March 4, 1782.

48 Ibid.; ISM, Brown to Barry, May 23, 1782; NYHS, NY 5/32, Samuel Smedley to Barry, March 8, 1782; Alexander Thomas to Barry, March 5, 1782.

49 JBP, Barry to Thomas, March 8, 1782.

50 RMP, vol. 4, 380-381, Franklin to Morris, March 9, 1782.

51 Ibid.; DNA, RDC, Franklin to Morris, March 30, 1782.

52 JBP, Barry to Morris, May 12, 1782.

53 Ibid.

54 Ibid.; Kessler, "Rough Sketch," 13.

55 ISM, Rear Admiral R. Digby Naval Order to British Commanders, December 1, 1781.

56 RMP, vol. 4, Gouverneur Morris to Robert Morris, April 8, 1782.

57 Kessler, "Rough Sketch," 13; Morgan, "John Barry," 59; NYHS, Barry to Morris, May 12, 1782.

58 JBP, Barry to Morris, May 12, 1782; Kessler, "Rough Sketch," 13; MHS, 2/40 John Barry to Brown, May 11, 1782; NYHS, Barry to Morris, May 12, 1782.

59 *London Daily Intelligencer*, August, 8, 1782, NNB, English Historical News, 15020.

60 JBP, *Alliance* Letterbook, Barry to Mumford no date; RMP, vol. 5, 254-255, Robert Morris to Thomas Mumford, May 24, 1782.

61 HSP, Proceedings of Court-Martial on board *Alliance*. July, 27, 1782.

62 Ibid.; JBP, Mumford to Barry, May 18, 1782, Barry to Brown, May 16, 1782.

63 HSP, Proceedings of Court-Martial on board *Alliance*, July, 27, 1782.

64 Ibid.

65 Ibid.

66 Ibid.

67 Ibid.; Clark, *Gallant John Barry,* 260.

68 HSP, Proceedings of Court-Martial on board *Alliance*, July, 27, 1782; NYHS, *Alliance* Letterbook, Barry to Morris, 5, 1782.

69 JBP, Barry to John Nicholson, May 18, 1782; Clark, *Gallant John Barry,* 262.

70 Ibid.; Barry to De Quémy, May 18, 1782; G. Lacour-Gayet, *La Marine militaire de la France sous le règne de Louis XVI*, 418, 674; Etienne Taillemite, *Archives de la Marine, Série B*, 248. With thanks to Michael Crawford.

71 RMP, Vol. 5, 248-250, Morris to Barry, May 24, 1782.

72 Ibid.

73 JBP, Barry to Morris, May 29, 1782.

74 Ibid.

75 JBP, Barry to de Quémy, May 29, 1782; ISM, Brown to Barry, May 23, 1782; JBP, Barry to Brown, June 4, 1782.

76 Ibid. Barry to Washington, May 30, 1782.

77 PA Archives, RG 27, AO 12/40/56: "The Memorial of William Austin," April 3, 1786.

78 Miller, *Sea of Glory*, 470–471.

79 Ibid.; Keen, "Descendants of Jöran Kyn," 485-86.

80 JBP, Barnes Collection, Letterbook *Alliance,* Barry to Washington, May 30, 1782.

81 JBP, Barnes Collection, Barry to Morris, June 5, 1782; De Quémy to Barry, May 31, 1782; NY 5-131, Linn to Barry, May 30, 1782.

82 Manuscript Collection of the U.S. Naval Academy Museum, No. 167, Barry to Brown, June 4, 1782.

83 Ibid.

84 Haverford College Library, Charles Roberts Autograph Collection, Hancock to Barry, June 3, 1782.

85 Clark, *Gallant John Barry,* 265-266.

86 HSP, Conarroe Papers, LS, Barry to Hancock, June 6, 1782.

87 Ibid.

88 JBP, Nicholson to Barry, June 1, 1782; Barry to Nicholson, June 10, 1782; Barnes, Letterbook *Alliance*, Officers to Barry, June 17, 1782.

89 RMP, vol. 5, 394.

90 JBP, Brown to Barry, June 20, 1782; conversation with Susan Klepp, Ph.D., Temple University, Department of History; Clark, *Gallant John Barry*, 269.

91 Keen, "Descendants of Jöran Kyn," 486; Rowe, "State Supreme Court," 55-56; PA Archives, vol. 13, 406-407.

92 JBP, NY 5-122, Brown to Barry, June 10, 1782; Clark, *Gallant John Barry*, 267.

93 RMP, vol. 5, 244, Morris to Franklin.

94 RMP, vol. 5, 448, Morris to Barry, June 19, 1782.

95 JBP, Trumbull to Barry, June 18, 1782.

96 JBP, Barry to Brown, July, 22, 1782; Barry to Morris, August 2, 1782.

97 LOC, GWP, Washington to Barry, June 12, 1782; Flexner, *Washington*, 169.

98 JBP, Barnes, Letterbook *Alliance;* Clark, *Gallant John Barry*, 268.

99 JBP, Barnes, Barry to Brown, July, 22, 1782.

100 Ibid.

101 JBP, Tracy to Barry, June 10, 1782; Barry to Tracy, July 21, 1782.

102 Barry to Sarah Barry, from Griffin, *The History of Commodore John Barry*, 175.

103 JBP, Morris to Barry, June 29, 1782.

104 JBP, Barry to Morris, July 22, 1782; Pennell to Barry, June 12, 1782.

105 JBP, Barry to Parke, July 30, 1782.

106 JBP, Linn to Barry, July 22, 1782; Barry to Linn, July 22, 1782; Barry to Morris, August 2, 1782.

107 JBP, Barry to Brown, July, 22, 1782; HSP, Proceedings of Court-Martial on board *Alliance*, July 27, 1782.

108 Clark, *Gallant John Barry*, 270.

109 LOC, Letterbook *Alliance*, Barry to William Ellery, April 4, 1782; Barry to Howland and Coit, April 8, 1782.

110 JBP, Barry to Morris, April 2, 1782; Barry to Brown, April 4, 1782.

Chapter Fourteen: The *Alliance*

1 JBP, Barry to Brown, August 4, 10, 1782.

2 Kessler, "Life of John Kessler," 5; LOC, List of Officers and Men on board the Continental Frigate *Alliance*, December 8, 1782.

3 Brown and Kessler, "The Life of Commodore Barry," 20.

4 Ibid., 19.

5 Ibid.; *Pennsylvania Packet*, December 17, 1782; NYHS, Samuel Tufts's Statement, August 23, 1782.

6 Kessler, "Rough Sketch," 13.

7 Ibid.; JBP, "Statement of Manassah Short," August 12, 1782; Clark, *Gallant John Barry*, 273.

8 Kessler, "Rough Sketch," 14.

9 Ibid.; *Pennsylvania Packet*, December 1782.

10 *Pennsylvania Packet*, December 17, 1782.

11 Tuchman, *First Salute*, 293; Clark, *Gallant John Barry*, 274.

12 JBP, Barry to Morris, October 17, 1782; Tuchman, *First Salute*, 293; Miller, *Sea of Glory*, 517.

13 JBP, Barry to Morris, October 18, 1782; LOC, Barry Collection, Orders/Private Signals, September 28, 1782.

14 LDC, Virginia Delegates to Benjamin Harrison, December 17, 1782; LOC, Barry Collection, Letterbook, *Alliance*, RMP, vol. 6, 625, Barry to Morris, October 18, 1782.

15 JBP, Barry to Morris, October 18, 1782.

16 LOC, Barry Collection, September 28, 1782.

17 Kessler, "Rough Sketch," 15.

18 King with Hattendorf and Estes, *A Sea of Words,* 197; NYHS, Barry to Morris, October 18, 1782.

19 Ibid.; Barry to Barclay, "Account of Disbursements on the American Frigate *Alliance* John Barry Esq. Commander 18th September [*sic*; October 18], 1782.

20 Giunta, ed., *The Emerging Nation,* vol. II, 54-56, Barclay to Livingston, October 23, 1782.

21 JBP, Barry to Morris, October 18, 1782.

22 Ibid.; LDC, Virginia Delegates to Benjamin Warren, December 17, 1782.

23 JBP, Barry to Morris, October 18, 1782; RMP, vol. 6, Barry to Morris, October 18, 1782, 625.

24 JBP, NJ44, White to Barry, October 26, 1782.

25 JBP, John Black to Barry, October 25, 1782.

26 Brands, *The First American,* 614-615.

27 Clark, *Gallant John Barry,* 277.

28 LOC, Letterbook, *Alliance*, Barry to Lafayette, October 28, 1782; RMP, vol. 7, Franklin to Morris, December 14, 1782; Clark, *Gallant John Barry,* 278-279.

29 LOC, Letterbook, *Alliance*, Barry to Franklin, October 31, 1782.

30 LOC, Letterbook, *Alliance*, various letters, November 1782.

31 LOC, Letterbook, *Alliance*, Lafayette to Barry, November 1, 1782; Barry to Lafayette, November 17, 1782.

32 Haverford College, Charles Roberts Collection, Henry Johnson to Barry, October 16, 1782.

33 LOC, Letterbook, *Alliance*, Barry to Johnson, November 18, 1782.

34 LOC, Letterbook, *Alliance*, Ship's Officers to Barry, November 17, 1782; Barry to *Alliance* Officers, November 19, 1782.

35 LOC, Letterbook, *Alliance*, Officers of *Alliance* to Barry, November 19, 1782; Clark, *Gallant John Barry,* 281.

36 LOC, Letterbook, *Alliance*, Officers of *Alliance* to Barry, November 19, 1782.

37 LOC, Letterbook, *Alliance*, Barry to Parke, November 24, 1782.

38 LOC, Letterbook, *Alliance*, Barry to Parke, November 25, 1782; Barry to Fletcher, November 25, 26, 1782.

39 LOC, Letterbook, *Alliance*, Barry to Henry Johnston, November 29, 1782; HSP, Dreer Collection, John Barry to John Brown, December 7, 1782.

40 LOC, Letterbook, *Alliance*, Barry to Henry Johnston, November 29, 1782; Griffin, *The History of Commodore John Barry,* 201.

41 LOC, Letterbook, *Alliance*, Barry to Barclay, December 14, 1782; Barry to Morris, December 7, 1782; Clark, *Gallant John Barry,* 285.

42 Quoted in Clark, *Gallant John Barry,* 285-286.

43 LOC, Letterbook, *Alliance*, Barry to Morris, December 7, 1782.

44 HSP, Dreer Collection, Barry to Brown, December 7, 1782.

45 LOC, John Barry Collection, *Alliance* Muster Book, December 8, 1782.

46 LOC, Letterbook, *Alliance*, Barry to Barclay, December 8, 1782.

47 Kessler, "Rough Sketch," 15; Giunta, ed., *The Emerging Nation*, Articles of Peace, November 30, 1782, 91.

48 LOC, LBA, Barry to William West, December 12, 1782.

49 King and Hattendorf, *Harbors and High Seas*, 78; ISM, *Alliance* Log, January 1, 1783.

50 ISM, *Alliance* Log, January 1, 1783.

51 ISM, Log, *Alliance*, January 8, January 10, 1783; RMP, vol. 6, 582, Morris to Barry, October 14, 1782.

52 *Pennsylvania Journal*, February 26, 1783; *Extract from the Martinique Gazette*, January 15, 1783.

53 *Pennsylvania Gazette*, February 12, 1783.

54 ISM, *Alliance* Log, January 13–18, 1783; Clark, *Gallant John Barry*, 290.

55 ISM, log, *Alliance*, January 15-20, 1783; LOC, Letterbook, *Alliance*, Barry to Morris, January 22, 1783.

56 LOC, Letterbook, *Alliance*, Barry to Morris, January 22, 1783.

57 Ibid.

58 Ibid.

59 Tuchman, *First Salute*, 231; Howard, *Seth Harding, Mariner*, 156.

60 King and Hattendorf, *Harbors and High Seas*, 304; ISM, Log, *Alliance*, January 10, 1783.

61 Fowler, *Rebels Under Sail*, 233; Howard, *Seth Harding, Mariner*, 153-156.

62 Howard, *Seth Harding, Mariner*, 153-157; ISM, Log, *Alliance*, January 21, 1783.

63 ISM, Log, *Alliance*, January 21, 1783; LOC, Letterbook, *Alliance*, Barry to Morris, January 22, 1783.

64 ISM, Log, *Alliance*, January 23–30, 1783.

65 ISM, Log, *Alliance*, January 31, 1783; Clark, *Gallant John Barry*, 293.

66 Quoted in Schiff, *A Great Improvisation*, 317.

67 Giunta, ed., *The Emerging Nation*, vol. I, 547, Lord Shelburne to Richard Oswald, September 3, 1782.

68 Quoted in Schiff, *A Great Improvisation*, 326.

69 LOC, Nicholas Van Dyke Papers, 181.

70 Flexner, *Washington*, 170, 171.

71 LOC, NY14-4, Morris Papers; ISM, Barry to Robert Morris, March 20, 1783; Miller, *Sea of Glory*, 518.

72 ISM, *Alliance* Log, March 10, 1783; Cooper, "Sketches of Naval Men," 272. The ship's namesake was an officer who distinguished himself at Yorktown and was later guillotined during the French Revolution.

73 LOC, JCC, May 14, 1783.

74 RMP, vol. 7, 467-468; ISM, Barry to Morris, March 20, 1783.

75 ISM, *Alliance* Log, February 1, 1783.

76 HSP, Society Collection, James Seagrove to John Brown, March 6, 1783.

77 LOC, Barry to Morris, March 20, 1783; Clark, *Gallant John Barry*, 293; Miller, 505; ISM, Log, *Alliance*, February 1, 1783.

78 Ibid. ISM, Log, *Alliance*, February 2, 1783.

79 ISM, Log, *Alliance*, February 2, 1783; Wilbur, *Pirates and Patriots of the Revolution*, 90.

80 ISM, Log, *Alliance*, February 3, 1783; Cordingly, *Under the Black Flag*, 95-96.

81 King with Hattendorf and Estes, *A Sea of Words*, 268; Wilbur, *Pirates and Patriots of the Revolution*, 12; ISM, Log *Alliance*, February 3-6, 1783; LOC, Letterbook, *Alliance*, February 13, 1783.

82 LOC, Letterbook, *Alliance*, February 14, 1783.

83 Ibid., February 15, 20, 1783.

84 Ibid., March 20, 1783; Howard, *Seth Harding, Mariner*, 159.

85 LOC, Letterbook, *Alliance*, February 22, 1783.

86 ISM, Log, *Alliance*, March 5, March 6, 1783.

87 Kessler, "Rough Sketch"; ISM, Log, *Alliance*, March 6, 1783.

88 LOC, Letterbook, *Alliance*, March 20, 1783.

89 ISM, Log, *Alliance*, March 7, 1783; ISM, "Barry's Account of Proceedings on the *Alliance* and *Duc de Lauzon*," March 20, 1783.

90 ISM, "Barry's Account of Proceedings on the *Alliance* and *Duc de Lauzon*," March 20, 1783; LOC, Letterbook, *Alliance*, March 20, 1783.

91 PRO Admiralty, 51/578, Journal *Sybil*, March 7, 1783.

92 Gouldsborough's *Miltary and Naval Magazine* (vol. II, 185), quoted in Griffin, *The History of Commodore John Barry*, 226.

93 LOC, Letterbook, *Alliance*, March 20, 1783.

94 Ibid.; ISM, Log *Alliance*, March 7, 1783.

95 LOC, Letterbook, *Alliance*, March 20, 1783.

96 ISM, Log *Alliance*, March 8, 9, 1783.

97 Ibid., March 9, 1783.

98 LOC, Letterbook, *Alliance*, March 20, 1783.

99 Ibid.

100 ISM, Log, *Alliance*, March 9, 1783.

101 PRO, 51/875, *Sybil* Journal, March 10, 1783.

102 ISM, Log, *Alliance*, March 20, 1783; LOC, Letterbook, *Alliance*, March 20, 1783.

103 LOC, Letterbook, *Alliance*, March 20, 1783; PRO, 51/875, *Sybil* Journal, March 10, 1783.

104 PRO, 51/875, *Sybil* Journal, March 10, 1783; ISM, Log, *Alliance*, March 10, 1783.

105 Kessler, "Rough Sketch," 16.

106 LOC, Letterbook, *Alliance*, Barry to Morris, March 20, 1783.

107 PRO, 51/875, *Sybil* Journal, March 9, 1783.

108 LOC, Letterbook, *Alliance*, March 20, 1783.

109 Ibid.

110 ISM, Barry–Hayes Papers, "An Account of the *Alliance* and *Duc de Lauzon*."

111 LOC, Letterbook, *Alliance*, March 20, 1783.

112 ISM, "An Account of the *Alliance* and *Duc de Lauzon*."

113 Ibid.; LOC, Letterbook, *Alliance*, March 20, 1783.

114 Kessler, "Rough Sketch," 16.

115 LOC, Letterbook, *Alliance*, March 20, 1783.

116 Ibid.; Kessler, "Rough Sketch," 17-18; ISM, "An Account of the *Alliance* and *Duc de Lauzon*."

117 ISM, "An Account of the *Alliance* and *Duc de Lauzon*."

118 Ibid.

119 LOC, Letterbook, *Alliance*, March 20, 1783; King with Hattendorf and Estes, *A Sea of Words*, 405.

120 PRO, 51/875, March 10, 1783.

121 Fowler, *Rebels under Sail,* 253.

122 Kessler, "Rough Sketch," 17.

123 Clark, *Gallant John Barry,* 301.

124 Ralfe, *Naval Biography of Great Britain,* Vol. 2; PRO, 51/875, Log *Sybil,* March 10, 1783.

125 Ralfe, *Naval Biography of Great Britain,* vol. 2; PRO, 51/875, Log *Sybil,* March 10, 1783; Kessler, "Rough Sketch," 17; Clark, *Gallant John Barry,* 300.

126 PRO, 51/875, Log *Sybil,* March 10, 1783; Van Powell, *The American Navies of the Revolutionary War,* 124-127; ISM, "An Account of the *Alliance* and *Duc de Lauzon*"; Kessler, "Rough Sketch," 17.

127 PRO, 51/875, *Sybil* Journal, March 10, 1783; Kessler, "Rough Sketch," 17; ISM, "An Account of the *Alliance* and *Duc de Lauzon*"; Wilbur, *Pirates and Patriots of the Revolution,* 50.

128 PRO, *Sybil* Journal, March 10, 1783.

129 Van Powell, *The American Navies of the Revolutionary War,* 124-127; PRO, *Sybil* Journal, March 10, 1783; Kessler, "Rough Sketch," 17.

130 Brown and Kessler, "The Life of Commodore Barry," 10; PRO, *Sybil* Journal, March 10, 1783.

131 Ibid.; ISM, Log, *Alliance,* March 11, 1783.

132 HSP, Society Collection, James Seagrove to John Brown, April 24, 1783.

133 Clark, *Gallant John Barry,* 301.

134 LOC, Letterbook, *Alliance,* March 20, 1783; Howard, *Seth Harding, Mariner,* 160.

135 LOC, Letterbook, *Alliance,* March 20, 1783; Kessler, "Rough Sketch," 17-18.

136 Kessler, "Rough Sketch," 18.

137 Brown and Kessler, "The Life of Commodore Barry," 10; ISM, "An Account of the *Alliance* and *Duc de Lauzon*"; LOC, Letterbook, *Alliance,* Barry to Morris, March 20, 1783.

138 ISM, "An Account of the *Alliance* and *Duc de Lauzon*"; Kessler, "Rough Sketch," 17.

139 ISM, "An Account of the *Alliance* and *Duc de Lauzon.*"

140 PRO, 51/875, *Sibyl* Journal, March 10, 1783.

141 HSP, Seagrove to Brown, April 24, 1783.

142 Brown and Kessler, "The Life of Commodore Barry," 10.

143 Ibid.; ISM, "An Account of the *Alliance* and *Duc de Lauzon.*"

144 ISM, "An Account of the *Alliance* and *Duc de Lauzon.*"

145 ISM, "An Account of the *Alliance* and *Duc de Lauzon*"; Clark, *Gallant John Barry,* 302.

146 LOC, Letterbook, *Alliance,* March 20, 1783.

147 Ibid.

148 Ibid.

149 Ibid.

150 RMP, vol. 7, Diary: March 21, 1783, 618.

151 Barry to Brown, April 19, 1783, Quoted in Griffin, *The History of Commodore John Barry,* 247-248; ISM, Barry–Hayes Papers, Brown to Barry, April 5, 1783.

152 LOC, Letterbook, *Alliance,* Barry to George Olney, Esq., March 20, 1783.

153 LOC, Letterbook, *Alliance,* Barry to Morris, March 20, 22, 26, 1783; RMP, vol. 7, 646-647, March 30, 1783.

154 *Pennsylvania Gazette*, February 26, 1783.

155 Ibid., March 26, 1783; JCC, LBC, Boudinot to Pritchard, March 23, 1783.

156 EHC, Boston Newspapers/*Continental Journal*, March 27, 1783.

CHAPTER FIFTEEN: IN IRONS

1 LOC, Letterbook, *Alliance,* Barry to Morris, March 22, 1783; Barry to John Coffin Jones, March 26, 1783.

2 LOC, Letterbook, *Alliance,* William French to Barry, 4, 1783; RMP, vol. 7, 437-438, Robert Morris to Thomas Russell, February 17, 1783; Letterbook, *Alliance,* Barry to Morris, March 31, 1781.

3 LOC, Letterbook, *Alliance,* Joseph Henderson to Barry, March 27, 1783; ISM, John Brown to Barry, May 28, 1783.

4 LOC, Letterbook, *Alliance,* Barry to Henderson, March 28, 1783; and Barry to John Lowell, Esq., April 5, 1783.

5 LOC, Letterbook, *Alliance,* Barry to Howland, April 8, 1783.

6 LOC, Letterbook, *Alliance,* Howland to Barry, March 31, 1783; Barry to Howland, April 8, 1783; Barry to Ellery, April 4, 1783.

7 LOC, Letterbook, *Alliance,* Barry to Morris, March 30, 1783; RMP, vol. 8, Morris to Barry, March 27, 1783.

8 LOC, Letterbook, *Alliance,* Brown to Barry, April 5, 1783.

9 Keen, "Descendants of Jöran Kyn, 493.

10 LOC, Letterbook, *Alliance,* Barry to Brown, July 8, 1783; Clark, *Gallant John Barry,* 306.

11 LOC, Letterbook, *Alliance,* Brown to Barry, April 5, 1783; Kessler, "Rough Sketch"; RMP, vol. 8, 182, Morris to Welch, June 10, 1783; RMP, vol. 8, 136, Morris Diary, May 31, 1783.

12 Miller, "The Federal City, 1783-1800," 156; Watson, *Annals,* vol. II, 299, 361.

13 Wagner, *Robert Morris,* 93, 95.

14 RMP, vol. 8, 22-106, 136-250 (diary entries), quotation 758, diary entry, April 29, 1783; HSP, Dreer Collection, Accounts of Prize Money due Officers and Crew of *Alliance,* April 15, 178; JCC, December 26, 1783.

15 JBP, Barry to Brown and Morris, May 21, 1783; 5/155, Barry to Brown, May 21, 1783, Barry to Barclay and Moylan, May 21, 1783.

16 Morison, *John Paul Jones,* 396, 377; RMP, vol. 8, 266.

17 JBP, Barnes, Jones to Deauville, June 4, 1783.

18 Morison, *John Paul Jones,* 396; Clark, *Gallant John Barry,* 310.

19 RMP, vol. 8, 49.

20 ISM, Barry-Hayes Papers, Barry to Brown, July 8, 1783.

21 Ibid.

22 Ibid.

23 Ibid.

24 Ibid.

25 Ibid.; JBP, Barnes Collection, Barry to Morris, August 20, 1783.

26 JBP, Barnes Collection, Barry to Morris, August 26, 1783; JCC, September 3, 1783.

27 Ibid.

28 JBP, Barry to Morris, August 26, 1783; Clark, *Gallant John Barry,* 312.

29 JCC, No. 28, 229; September 5, 1783.

30 RMP, vol. 8, 480-481, Morris to Elias Boudinot, September 1, 1783.

31 Washington Navy Yard, Early History Center, DC7, L584, Morris to Barry et al., October 6, 1783.

32 PA Archives, Tax Rolls 1782; Philadelphia City Archives, City Directory 1783.

33 LOC, Barry Collection, Barclay to Barry, August 12, 1783.

34 HSP Society Collection, Seagrove to Brown, August 25, 1783.

35 ISM, Barry Memorial to Pennsylvania Assembly, September 18, 1783.

36 Quoted in Griffin, *The History of Commodore John Barry,* 252-253.

37 From Alexander Garden, *Anecdotes of the American Revolution* (Charleston, 1828), quoted in Gurn, *Commodore John Barry,* 190-191.

38 Parker, "A Biographical Sketch of John Brown," 3.

39 JBP, Barry to Barclay, November 28, 1783; RMP, vol. 8, 835, December 23, 1783, Diary Entry.

40 JBP, Barnes Collection, Barry to Anthony Wayne, March 10, 1784; Griffin, *The History of Commodore John Barry,* 256, "An Account of Monies paid to the Officers and Crew of the Frigate *Alliance,* and also of the net profits on sundry shares purchased for the account of Captain John Barry and John Brown," January 12, 1785; Clark, *Gallant John Barry,* 317.

41 JBP, Barry to Barclay, November 28, 1783.

42 Miller, "The Federal City, 1783-1800," 155-156; RMP, vol. 8, 699, Barry et al. to Morris, November 1, 1783; JCC, December 18, 1783.

43 Watson, *Annals,* vol. II, 358; LOC, Barry Collection, Barclay to Barry, December 25, 1783.

44 JBP, Barnes, NY5/178, Barry to Mifflin, March 10, 1784; Barry to Wayne, March 10, 1784.

45 JBP, Barnes Collection, Wayne to Barry, no date.

46 JCC, April 8, 1784.

47 Nuxall, *The Early Republic and the Sea,* 3.

48 Ibid.

49 Fowler, *Jack Tars and Commodores,* 2.

50 Miller, *Sea of Glory,* epilogue.

51 HSP, Society Collection, Seagrove to Brown, March 27, 1784.

52 Griffin, *The History of Commodore John Barry,* 256, "An Account of Monies, etc.," January 12, 1785; Clark, *Gallant John Barry,* 317.

53 LOC, Barry Collection, Itemized Bill to Congress, July 1, 1784.

54 Ibid.; HSP, Roberts Collection, Murray to Barry, November 16, 1784; Clark, *Gallant John Barry,* 318; Matthewman, "Narrative of Lieutenant Luke Matthewman"; Statement of Luke Matthewman from the *New York Packet,* 1787.

55 JCC, December 16, 1784; Clark, *Gallant John Barry,* 318; Wagner, *Robert Morris,* 106.

56 Hayes, *To the Farthest Gulf,* 25, 16; Morris to Jay quoted in Gallagher, "Charting a New Course for the China Trade," 61.

57 Hayes, *To the Farthest Gulf,* 61.

58 JCC, May 10, 1784; Clark, *Gallant John Barry,* 319.

59 JBP, Barnes Collection, Department of Maritime, September 1, 1784, Barry to William Smith, September 18, 1784, Seagrove to Barry, October 28, 1784.

60 JBP, Barnes, 5/137, Barry to Keen.

61 *Pennsylvania Gazette,* November 1784.

62 PA State Archives, AO/13/5/74-25, "Wm. Austin's Loyalist Claim."

63 *Pennsylvania Gazette*, February 4, 1784.

64 Ibid.

65 David Library, Sol Finestone Collection, William Austin to Barry, April 7, 1786.

66 ISM, Barry-Hayes Papers, Report of Grievance Committee to Supreme Executive Council, 1784.

67 *Pennsylvania Gazette*, February 4, 1784.

68 *Pennsylvania Gazette*, February 4, 25, 1784, December 8, 1784; NYHS, Barnes, Personal and Private Correspondence, December 22, 1784.

69 JCC, 1774-1789, January 18, 1785.

70 RMP, vol. 9, 251, "Memorandum of James Read," April 13, 1784.

71 LOC, William Bell Clark Papers, Petition of Joanna Young, February 23, 1785.

72 ISM, Nicholas Barry to John Barry, May 31, 1785; From Griffin, *The History of Commodore John Barry*, 265, A bill for three months tuition of "Mr. [master] Howling £1.2.6 etc."

73 JBP, NY5/138, Jeremiah Teahan to Barry, August 12, 1784.

74 JBP, NY5/139, Mitchell to Barry.

75 ISM, Barry-Hayes Papers, Nicholas Barry to John Barry, May 31, 1785.

76 Christman, *Adventurous Pursuits*, 60; Smith, *The Empress of China*, 206; *New York Dispatch*, May 19, 1785; Doerflinger, *Vigorous Spirit of Enterprise*, 292. When he approached Canton, Green and the *Empress* were escorted into Chinese waters by the French man-of-war *Le Triton*–the same ship that played silent witness to the *Duc de Lauzon*'s flight from the *Sybil* the year before. Green found *Le Triton* as sluggish an accompanist as Barry had on board the *Alliance*. ISM, Log, *The Empress of China*, July 21, 1784.

77 Fowler, *Jack Tars and Commodores*, 4, 5.

78 Ibid.

79 *Pennsylvania Gazette*, June 22, 1785.

80 HSP, Christopher Marshall diary; Griffin, *The History of Commodore John Barry*, 258; Watson, *Annals*, vol. II, 339.

81 Fowler, *Jack Tars and Commodores*, 7-9; *Pennsylvania Gazette*, September 21, 1785; JCC, October 21, 1785.

82 HSP Collection, Seagrove to Brown, letters, 1784.

83 LDC, August 20, 1785, Abiel Foster to Unknown.

84 Ibid.; ISM, Barry Memorial to Pennsylvania Assembly, 1783, and to Congress, 1785.

85 Philadelphia City Archives, Settlement Papers, Strawberry Hill, September, 1785.

86 Salter, *On Asthma*.

87 Rush, *A Dissertation on the Spasmodic Asthma of Children*, 22.

88 LCOP, Benjamin Rush Journals, 1785.

89 Scudeman, *Cases*, 100-101.

90 Salter, *On Asthma*; Scudeman, *Cases*.

91 LCOP, Benjamin Rush Ledgers; Clark, *Gallant John Barry*, 328; NYHS, Barnes, NY5-81, French to Barry, March 7, 1786.

92 Chernow, *Alexander Hamilton*, 216; Keane, *Tom Paine*, 254.

93 Adams quoted in Chernow, *Alexander Hamilton*, 216-218; Franklin quoted in Brands, *The First American*, 668, 669.

94 LOC, Barry Collection, Society of Cincinnati Certificate; NYHS, James Nicholson to Barry, November 6, 1786; Morison, *John Paul Jones*, 399.

95 HSP, Charles Roberts Collection, Reed to Barry, January 17, 1786; NYHS, Barnes, NY5-80, Farrell to Barry, March 26, 1786, November 12, 1786; LOC, Barry Collection, Walker to Barry, November 2, 1786.

96 HSP, Fire Company Records, Hibernian Fire Company Minutes, 1763-1923, March 2, 1785.

97 JBP, NY5-48; Barry to Barry, December 19, 1786; David Library, Sol Finestone Collection, Austin to Barry, April 7, 1786.

98 Ellis, *His Excellency,* 172, 173; Brands, *The First American,* 677.

99 JBP, Rossiter to Barry, June 11, 1787; Clark, *Gallant John Barry,* 329.

100 JBP, Rossiter to Barry, June 11, 1787; Clark, *Gallant John Barry,* 329.

101 JBP, Rossiter to Barry, June 11, 1787.

102 Chandler, "Early Shipping in Pennsylvania," 26; Watson, *Annals,* vol. II, 339; Wagner, *Robert Morris,* 108; Clark, *Gallant John Barry,* 330.

103 Christman, *Adventurous Pursuits,* 71; *Pennsylvania Gazette,* August 22, 1787; JBP, *Asia* Registration Papers, December 6, 1787; Clark, *Gallant John Barry,* 330; JBP, John Barry to James Cornish, January 2, 1792.

104 ISM Collection, Portrait of James Josiah by Charles Willson Peale; Christman, *Adventurous Pursuits,* 71, 70; Clark, "James Josiah, Master Mariner," 453; LOC, Barry Collection, Letterbook *Asia.*

105 JBP, NY5/48, Barry to Barry, November 19, 1787; Josiah to Barry, August 28, 1787; Brewington, "Maritime Philadelphia 1609-1837," 108.

106 Brands, *The First American,* 674.

107 LOC, GWP, Washington Diary, May 13, 1787.

108 Miller, "The Federal City, 1783-1800," 163.

109 With respects to Fowler, *Jack Tars and Commodores,* 2.

110 Brands, *The First American,* 694; APS, BFP, September 18, 1787.

111 Discussion with Carrie Diethorn, Curator of Independence National Park.

112 Isaacson, *Benjamin Franklin,* 456; Alberts, "Business of the Highest Magnitude," 49; Seilhamer, "Old Mother Cumberland," 44.

113 Burgner, *Life and Times of Colonel James McCalmont,* 6-14; Seilhamer, "Old Mother Cumberland," 44.

114 *Pennsylvania Gazette,* October 10, 1787.

115 Miller, "The Federal City, 1783-1800," 163.

116 McDonald and McDonald, eds., *Confederation and Constitution,* 212.

117 Ibid., 60.

118 Ibid., 61; Scharf and Westcott, *History of Philadelphia,* vol. I, 446.

119 McMaster and Stone, eds., *Pennsylvania and the Federal Constitution,* 61-62.

120 From Griffin, *The History of Commodore John Barry,* 274.

CHAPTER SIXTEEN: THE *Asia*

1 HSP, Christopher Marshall Diary, September 29, 1787.

2 Burgner, "Life and Times of Colonel James McCalmont," 16; Biddle, *Autobiography of Charles Biddle,* 218.

3 Burgner, "Life and Times of Colonel James McCalmont," 16.

4 McMaster and Stone, eds., *Pennsylvania and the Federal Constitution,* 63.

5 Ibid., 64.

6 PA Archives, Colonial Series, vol. XV, 285-287.

7 Ibid.; HSP, Jacob Hiltzheimer Diary, 133, September 29, 1787.

8 Scharf and Westcott, *The History of Philadelphia,* vol. I, 446; *Pennsylvania Gazette,* October 10, 1787. One story circulated around Philadelphia that Barry and company actually found Miley in Major Boyd's outhouse.

9 *Pennsylvania Gazette,* November 19, 1787 and October 10, 1787.

10 Biddle, *Autobiography of Charles Biddle,* 218-219.

11 *Pennsylvania Gazette,* October 10, 1787.

12 McMaster and Stone, eds., *Pennsylvania and the Federal Constitution,* 64.

13 Seilheuer, "Old Mother Cumberland," 44.

14 McMaster and Stone, *Pennsylvania and the Federal Constitution,* 64; Scharf and Westcott, *The History of Philadelphia,* vol. I, 447.

15 McMaster and Stone, *Pennsylvania and the Federal Constitution,* 65.

16 Scharf and Wescott, *The History of Philadelphia,* vol. I, 447.

17 McMaster and Stone, eds., *Pennsylvania and the Federal Constitution,* 65, 66.

18 Ibid., 66-67, 70; Scharf and Westcott, *The History of Philadelphia,* vol. I, 446; Biddle, *Autobiography of Charles Biddle,* 218.

19 Flanders, "Thomas Fitzsimmons," 308; *Pennsylvania Journal,* October 2, 1787.

20 *Pennsylvania Gazette,* November 19, 1787.

21 LOC, LDC, Samuel A. Otis to Elbridge Gerry, January 2, 1788; *Pennsylvania Gazette,* October 10, 1787; PA Archives, Colonial Series, vol. XV, 285-287.

22 PA Archives, Colonial Series, vol. XV, 285-287; Biddle, *Autobiography of Charles Biddle,* 219.

23 Ibid.

24 JCC, December 1, 1787.

25 Griffin, *The History of Commodore John Barry,* 276-277.

26 ISM, Barry-Hayes Papers, Patrick Hayes Journal; King with Hattendorf and Estes, *A Sea of Words,* 337; "Advanced the people belonging to the *Asia* he Sums & Articles," quoted from Griffin, *The History of Commodore John Barry,* 277; *Pittsburgh Sunday Dispatch,* February 1999.

27 HSP, Customs House Records, Port of Philadelphia, Outward Entries, September 1, 1786-December 29, 1787.

28 LOC, Letterbook, *Asia,* Morris to Barry, December 10, 1787.

29 LOC, Letterbook, *Asia,* various letters, December 10-20, 1787.

30 Ibid.; John Barry to Peter Whiteside, December 8, 1787.

31 Ferguson, *Truxton of the Constellation,* 81.

32 Ibid.

33 Doerflinger, *A Vigorous Spirit of Enterprise,* 216.

34 HSP, Benjamin Fuller Letterbook, December 8, 1787.

35 HSP, Christopher Marshall Diary, December 10, 1787; HSP, Customs House Records, Port of Philadelphia, Outward Entries, September 1, 1786-December 29, 1787; LOC, Barry Collection, Letterbook, *Asia,* Various letters, December 10-20, 1787; Clark, *Gallant John Barry,* 335, 336.

36 LOC, Letterbook, *Asia,* Barry to Archibald McCall, December 20, 1787.

37 Ibid.

38 Ibid., Barry to McCall and Lewis, April 3, 1788; ISM, Barry-Hayes Papers, "Patrick Hayes His Book January the 19, 1787" (Hayes Journal).

39 LOC, Letterbook, *Asia,* Barry to McCall and Lewis, April 3, 1788; King, Hattendorf, Estes, *A Sea of Words,* 141.

40 LOC, Letterbook, *Asia,* Barry to McCall and Lewis, April 3, 1788.

41 ISM, Hayes Journal; LOC, Letterbook, *Asia*, Barry to McCall and Lewis, April 3, 1788.

42 Ibid.

43 Clark, *Gallant John Barry*, 338; Dudley, Crawford, Nixon, etc., 16.

44 PA Archives, Colonial Series, vol. XV, 389; LOC, LDC, Otis to Gerry, January 29, 1788.

45 ISM, Hayes Journal; King and Hattendorf, *Harbors and High Seas*, 91.

46 LOC, Letterbook, *Asia*, February 3, 1788; ISM, Hayes Journal.

47 LOC, Letterbook, *Asia*, June 11, 1788; ISM, Hayes Journal.

48 ISM, Hayes Journal.

49 Smith, *The Empress of China*, 89-90.

50 Ibid.

51 ISM, Hayes Journal.

52 Ibid.

53 Ibid.; Smith, *The Empress of China*, 126.

54 ISM, Hayes Journal; King and Hattendorf, *Harbors and High Seas*, 85; LOC, Letterbook, *Asia*, April 3, 1788.

55 ISM, Hayes Journal.

56 King, *Harbors*, 100.

57 LOC, Letterbook, *Asia*, Barry to McCall, Lewis, and Co. April 3, 1788; Clark, *Gallant John Barry*, 340; Ferguson, *Truxton of the Constellation*, 69.

58 Ferguson, *Truxton of the Constellation*, 69; ISM, Hayes Journal.

59 ISM, Hayes Journal.

60 Ibid.

61 Ibid.

62 LOC, Letterbook, *Asia*, April 11, 1788; ISM, Hayes Journal.

63 ISM, Hayes Journal.

64 Ibid.

65 Ibid.

66 Ibid.

67 Ibid.

68 Ibid.; "Narrative of Samuel Shaw," quoted in Smith, *The Empress of China*, 126.

69 Cordingly, *Under the Black Flag*, 75-78; ISM, Hayes Journal.

70 ISM, Hayes Journal.

71 Ferguson, *Truxton of the Constellation*, 70.

72 Ibid.; ISM, *The Empress of China* Journal, August 6 and 7, 1784; ISM, Hayes Journal.

73 ISM, Hayes Journal; King and Hattendorf, *Harbors and High Seas*, 162.

74 ISM, Hayes Journal; *Pennsylvania Gazette*, February 4, 1789.

75 ISM, Hayes Journal.

76 Ibid.; King and Hattendorf, *Harbors and High Seas*, 297.

77 ISM, Hayes Journal.

78 Ibid.; Ferguson, *Truxton of the Constellation*, 81.

79 "Narrative of Samuel Shaw," quoted in Smith, *The Empress of China*, 140.

80 ISM, Hayes Journal.

81 Ibid.

82 Ibid.

83 Ibid.

84 *Pennsylvania Gazette*, July 2, 1788.
85 Watson, *Annals*, vol. II, 343.
86 LOC, Letterbook, *Asia*, Barry to Josiah, December 27, 1788; Clark, *Gallant John Barry*, 344.

Chapter Seventeen: The China Trade

1 Hawes, *To the Farthest Gulf*, 3.
2 Ibid., 3-4.
3 Smith, *The Empress of China*, 147.
4 Hawes, *To the Farthest Gulf*, 5.
5 Ibid., 6.
6 Ibid., 7, 4.
7 ISM, Barry–Hayes Papers, "Memorandum relating to the Trade at Canton."
8 Ferguson, *Truxton of the Constellation*, 71.
9 Smith, *The Empress of China*, 140.
10 Ferguson, *Truxton of the Constellation*, 72.
11 Smith, *The Empress of China*, 160-161; Hawes, *To the Farthest Gulf*, 9.
12 Smith, *The Empress of China*, 147.
13 ISM, China Memorandum; Lee, *Philadelphia and the China Trade*, 40.
14 ISM, China Memorandum.
15 Smith, *The Empress of China*, 150-151.
16 Ferguson, *Truxton of the Constellation*, 72.
17 Ibid.
18 Smith, *The Empress of China*, 148.
19 Hawes, *To the Farthest Gulf*, 19; Ferguson, *Truxton of the Constellation*, 72.
20 ISM, China Memorandum.
21 Ibid.
22 Smith, *The Empress of China*, 148.
23 Ibid.; Ferguson, *Truxton of the Constellation*, 72; Corner, ed., *The Autobiography of Benjamin Rush*, 222.
24 Smith, *The Empress of China*, 148.
25 Ibid.
26 Ferguson, *Truxton of the Constellation*, 73; Hawes, *To the Farthest Gulf*, 18; Library Company of Philadelphia, Benjamin Rush Commonplace Book, 1792-1813, June 30, 1789.
27 Ferguson, *Truxton of the Constellation*, 73; Hawes, *To the Farthest Gulf*, 18.
28 Hawes, *To the Farthest Gulf*, 18, 19.
29 Ferguson, *Truxton of the Constellation*, 73, 83, 72; King and Hattendorf, *Harbors and High Seas*, 393; Hawes, *To the Farthest Gulf*, 19.
30 Smith, *The Empress of China*, 153; ISM, China Memorandum.
31 Smith, *The Empress of China*, 149.
32 Ibid.; Ferguson, *Truxton of the Constellation*, 74.
33 Smith, *The Empress of China*, 149, 9.
34 Hawes, *To the Farthest Gulf*, 21.
35 Ibid.; ISM, China Memorandum.
36 Hawes, *To the Farthest Gulf*, 21; ISM, China Memorandum.
37 Ferguson, *Truxton of the Constellation*, 74.
38 Ibid.; Hawes, *To the Farthest Gulf*, 8.

39 Hawes, *To the Farthest Gulf,* 8; Lee, *Philadelphia and the China Trade;* Smith, *The Empress of China,* 36.

40 ISM, China Memorandum.

41 Ibid.

42 Ibid.; Christman, *Adventurous Pursuits,* 73; PMHB, Haverford College, Charles Roberts Autograph Collection, Josiah-Barry Correspondence, August 28, September 25, October 9, 1788.

43 Smith, *The Empress of China,* 152; Ferguson, *Truxton of the Constellation,* 75.

44 Christman, *Adventurous Pursuits,* 60; Smith, *The Empress of China,* 152.

45 Ferguson, *Truxton of the Constellation,* 75.

46 Smith, *The Empress of China,* 153; ISM, China Memorandum.

47 Smith, *The Empress of China,* 153; ISM, China Memorandum.

48 Ferguson, *Truxton of the Constellation,* 83, 76; ISM, China Memorandum.

49 ISM, China Memorandum.

50 Christman, *Adventurous Pursuits,* 73.

51 Library Company of Philadelphia, Benjamin Rush Commonplace Book, 1792-1813, June 30, 1789.

52 Christman, *Adventurous Pursuits,* 73.

53 Lee, *Philadelphia and the China Trade;* Smith, *The Empress of China,* 40, 41; Hawes, *To the Farthest Gulf,* 23.

54 ISM, China Memorandum.

55 LOC, *Asia* Letterbook, various correspondence, January 1-8, 1789.

56 Ibid.

57 Ibid.

58 ISM, Barry–Hayes Papers, Auction Booklet for John Barry Auction, New York, 1939.

59 Ferguson, *Truxton of the Constellation,* 83; Christman, *Adventurous Pursuits,* 74, 59; NYHS, Barnes Collection, Peter Hodgkinson to Barry, no date; Hawes, *To the Farthest Gulf,* 17.

60 Christman, *Adventurous Pursuits,* 60, 65. Earlier, when a salute was fired from a British ship, a Chinese worker was killed. The viceroy ordered that the gunner be turned over to Canton authorities. The British refused. Mandarin soldiers then went to the British Hong and seized a supercargo as a hostage. Further, they recalled every comprador, hong, and linguist from all western ships and factories. Business came to a dead stop. Shaw spoke out on behalf of the British to representatives from the other western nations, believing that a show of unity would convince the viceroy to return the supercargo and rescind his request for the gunner's arrest. His argument fell on deaf ears: the Danes, Dutch, and French, fearing an end to trade, would not hear of it. The British exchanged the unfortunate gunner for their supercargo. Skipping a trial, the Chinese went right to a public execution, and the gunner was strangled. Ibid., 60-61.

61 Ibid., 66.

62 Hawes, *To the Farthest Gulf,* 19; Christman, *Adventurous Pursuits,* 60.

63 Quoted from Clark, *Gallant John Barry,* 347; NYHS, Barnes Collection, Josiah to Barry, September 25, 1788.

64 Haverford College, Roberts Collection, Josiah to Barry, August 24, 1788.

65 Ferguson, *Truxton of the Constellation,* 84.

66 Christman, *Adventurous Pursuits,* 31; Hawes, *To the Farthest Gulf,* 26.

67 Hawes, *To the Farthest Gulf,* 41.
68 Ferguson, *Truxton of the Constellation,* 84.
69 JBP, Josiah to Barry, September 25, 1788.
70 JBP, Josiah to Barry, November 29, 1788.
71 HSP, Gratz Collection, Josiah to Barry, October 9, 1788.
72 LOC, Letterbook, *Asia,* November 22, 1788.
73 JBP, Shipping Notice, December 26, 1788.
74 ISM, Barry and Truxton Bond and Grand Chop, January, 1789.
75 LOC, Letterbook *Asia.*
76 Ferguson, *Truxton of the Constellation,* 84-85.
77 Christman, *Adventurous Pursuits,* 77; Smith, *The Empress of China,* 202.
78 ISM, Lee, *Philadelphia and the China Trade;* Smith, *The Empress of China,* 202.
79 ISM, Barry and Truxton Bond and Grand Chop, January, 1789; Smith, *The Empress of China,* 202.
80 Hawes, *To the Farthest Gulf,* 35.
81 Portuguese officials were as ignorant of worldly affairs as they were of what went on in their own backyard. At a dinner in 1787, the Portuguese governor inquired how the war between England and her American colonies was going. ISM, Hayes Journal.
82 Ibid.
83 Lee, *Philadelphia and the China Trade;* Smith, *The Empress of China,* 41; LOC, Letterbook *Asia.*
84 LOC, Letterbook *Asia,* Barry to McCall, Lewis & Company, January 27, 1789.
85 Ibid.; Clark, *Gallant John Barry,* 350; Ferguson, *Truxton of the Constellation,* 82.
86 *Pennsylvania Gazette,* June 6, 1789; Library Company of Philadelphia, Benjamin Rush Papers, Correspondence Book 1789-91.
87 Ferguson, *Truxton of the Constellation,* 86; Clark, *Gallant John Barry,* 350.
88 Christman, *Adventurous Pursuits,* 77.

Chapter Eighteen: First Among Captains

1 JBP, Barry to William Austin, October 30, 1790.
2 Rowe, "Judicial Tyrant and *Vox Populi,*" 55-57.
3 LCOP, Benjamin Rush Papers, Ledger entries, 1779-1790; Journals, 1784-1791.
4 LCOP, Benjamin Rush Papers, Commonplace Book, 1789-1791.
5 *Philadelphia Independent Gazette,* June 5, 1789.
6 Doerflinger, *A Vigorous Spirit of Enterprise,* 285.
7 *Pennsylvania Packet,* August 12, 1789; Clark, "James Josiah, Merchant Mariner," 470; NYHS, Barnes Collection, John Barry to James Corish, January 2, 1792.
8 JBP, Barnes, Francis to Barry, November 22, 1790.
9 LOC, GWP, Washington to Barry, July 6, 1789.
10 JBP, PNP, February 18, 1790; Barry to William Austin, 10, 1791.
11 JBP, Barry Correspondence, August 6, 1789.
12 "Extracts from the diary of Jacob Hiltzheimer," 171; Smith, Lee, *Philadelphia and the China Trade,* 64.
13 HSP, Hibernian Society Notebook; ISM, *Constitution of the Hibernian Society for the Relief of Emigrants from Ireland,* 1790; Griffin, *The History of Commodore John Barry,* 284.
14 ISM, NYHS, various correspondences, 1790-1801.

15 LCOP, Benjamin Rush Ledger, 1779-1790; Journal, 1784-1791.

16 *Freeman's Journal,* July 24, 1788.

17 HSP, Commodore Barron to J. F. Watson, December 17, 1825; Griffin, *The History of Commodore John Barry,* 264.

18 Watson, *Annals,* vol. II, 339.

19 Griffin, *The History of Commodore John Barry,* 264.

20 ISM, Barry-Hayes Papers, Barry to Nicholson, March 9, 1790.

21 From Griffin, *The History of Commodore John Barry,* 283; MacLay, ed., *Journal of William MacLay,* 224; ISM, Barry to James Nicholson, March 6, 1790.

22 Brands, *The First American,* 710.

23 Gurn, *Commodore John Barry,* 288.

24 LCOP, Jefferson to Rush, October 3, 1803.

25 MacLay, *Journal of William MacLay,* 259.

26 NYHS, Captain Thomas Hartley to Captain Barry in care of Major Samuel Nicholson, June 25, 1790.

27 James Nicholson to Barry, June 25, 1790, quoted in Clark, *Gallant John Barry,* 356.

28 Flexner, *Washington,* 237.

29 JBP, John Francis to Barry, November 22, 1790.

30 LCOP, Rush Ledger.

31 JBP, Francis to Barry, November 22, 1790.

32 Ibid.

33 JBP, Barry to Austin, 10, 1791; Clark, *Gallant John Barry,* 360.

34 McCullough, *John Adams,* 436-37; Clark, *Gallant John Barry,* 358-359.

35 LOC, Barry Collection, Letterbook, *Asia.*

36 LCOP, Benjamin Rush, Papers, Ledger and Journal Books, 1784-1791.

37 HSP, Benjamin Rush Collection, Asthma Manuscript.

38 See Mathew Pratt's portrait of John Barry; Clark, *Gallant John Barry,* 360.

39 DeKay, *A Rage for Glory,* 11.

40 Ferguson, *Truxton of the Constellation,* 89-90.

41 JBP, Barry to Rossiter, March 10, 1793.

42 David Porter to Barry, quoted from Clark, *Gallant John Barry,* 362.

43 ISM, Barry-Hayes papers, Barry to Harding, March 9, 1790.

44 Lee, Smith, *Philadelphia and the China Trade,* 30.

45 Keen, "Descendants of Jöran Kyn," 494.

46 JBP, Barry to William Austin, October 30, 1790.

47 Doerflinger, *A Vigorous Spirit of Enterprise,* 285; Miller, "The Federal City, 1783-1800," 177.

48 JBP, Barry to Corish, January 21, 1792.

49 JBP, Barry to Austin, October 30, 1790.

50 JBP, Seagrove to Barry, July 7, 1792.

51 JBP, Barry to Corish, January 21, 1792.

52 Ibid, John Barry to David Barry, December 6, 1792.

53 Morison, *John Paul Jones,* 430, 459.

54 Thomas, *John Paul Jones,* 302; Morison, *John Paul Jones,* 467, 305, 474.

55 Callo: *John Paul Jones,* 176; Morison, *John Paul Jones,* 475-479, 473.

56 HSP, Dreer, Wm. Bingham to Barry, June 17, 1791.

57 JBP, Hodgkinson to Barry, no date.

58 ISM, Barry-Hayes Papers, various correspondences; John Barry's will, 1803; National Archives, Census Records, 1790.

59 McCullough, *John Adams,* 444, 443; Ellis, 222; Flexner, *Washington,* 286.

60 McCullough, *John Adams,* 444; Flexner, *Washington,* 289; Ellis, *His Excellency: George* Washington, 222.

61 *Jefferson's Works,* vol. X11, p. 348, quoted from Griffin, *The History of Commodore John Barry,* 290.

62 Biddle, *Autobiography of Charles Biddle,* 252.

63 Ibid.

64 Miller, "The Federal City, 1783-1800," 180, 181; Niderast, "Capital in Crisis," 68.

65 Ferguson, *Truxton of the Constellation,* 95.

66 Millick, "The Wages of Blackness," 163-164.

67 LCOP, Benjamin Rush Ledgers.

68 Ferguson, *Truxton of the Constellation,* 95; Niderast, "Capital in Crisis," 68; Biddle, *Autobiography of Charles Biddle,* 256.

69 Chernow, *Alexander Hamilton,* 449.

70 Miller, "The Federal City, 1783-1800," 185; Chernow, *Alexander Hamilton,* 450.

71 Niderast, "Capital in Crisis," 70.

72 Biddle, *Autobiography of Charles Biddle,* 256, 257.

73 Ibid., 188; McCullough, *John Adams,* 447; Flexner, *Washington,* 304.

74 Flexner, *Washington,* 294-295, 312, 305.

75 Chernow, *Alexander Hamilton,* 453; Brodie, *Thomas Jefferson,* 360; McCullough, *John Adams,* 447.

76 Fowler, *Jack Tars and Commodores,* 16; McCullough, *John Adams,* 449; Flexner, *Washington,* 309.

77 LOC, Barry Collection, Patrick Hayes to Mr. Assurellen, April 25, 1793.

78 David Humphreys to Washington, quoted in Fowler, *Jack Tars and Commodores,* 16.

79 Chernow, *Alexander Hamilton,* 455, 459; Wood, *Live Oaking,* 24.

80 Washington's address to Congress December 3, 1793, quoted in Fowler, *Jack Tars and Commodores,* 17.

81 Humphreys, "Who Built the First United States Navy," 386-387.

82 Chappelle, *The American Sailing Navy,* 63-65.

83 Ibid.

84 Ibid.

85 Chappelle, *The American Sailing Navy,* 119; Fowler, *Jack Tars and Commodores,* 18.

86 Fowler, *Jack Tars and Commodores,* 18, 20; Chappelle, *The American Sailing Navy,* 118, 117.

87 Ibid., 118; *National Portrait Gallery of Distinguished Americans,* Vol. 2 (Philadelphia, 1836), unnumbered page.

88 Fowler, *Jack Tars and Commodores,* 18.

89 Smelser and Powers, "The Fleetless Nation," 39.

90 Ibid., 40.

91 Humphreys, "Who Built the First United States Navy," 390; Chappelle, *The American Sailing Navy,* 120.

92 JBP, Barry to Washington, March 19, 1794.

93 JBP, Nicholson to Barry, January 27, 1794

94 JBP, Porter to Barry, March 15, 1794.

95 John Hopkins to Barry, quoted in Clark, *Gallant John Barry,* 366-367.

96 Fowler, *Jack Tars and Commodores,* 22; Fowler, *Silas Talbot,* 100-101.

97 JBP, Barry to Nicholson, June 24, 1794.

98 Ibid. ISM, Barry–Hayes Papers, Anstis Doyle to John Barry, March 20, 1794.

99 LOC, JCC, June 3, 1794, Senate Executive Journal.

100 ISM, Barry-Hayes Papers, Knox to Barry, June 5, 1794.

101 New York Public Library, Ford Collection, Barry to Knox, June 6, 1794.

CHAPTER NINETEEN: THE *United States*

1 Samuel Nicholson to John Barry, June 14, 1793, quoted from Griffin, *The History of Commodore John Barry*, 293; JBP, Barry to Nicholson, June 25, 1794.

2 Barney, ed., *Biographical Memoir of the Late Commander Joshua Barney*, 182-186.

3 Fowler, *Jack Tars and Commodores*, 23.

4 ISM, Barry-Hayes Papers, Knox to Barry, August 7, 1794.

5 Fowler, *Jack Tars and Commodores*, 22; Smelser, *The Congress Founds the Navy*, 73.

6 JBP, July 1, 1794. ISM, Barry-Hayes Papers, Knox to Barry, August 7, 1794; NYHS, Barnes, Barry to Knox, June 7, 1794; HSP, Knox to Humphreys, July 24, 1794.

7 Humphreys, "Who Built the First United States Navy," 389; Chappelle, *The American Sailing Navy*, 120-121; Westlake, "Josiah Fox: Gentlemen, Quaker, Shipbuilder," 317.

8 ISM, Barry-Hayes Papers, Knox to Barry, August 7, 1794.

9 Fowler, *Jack Tars*, 42.

10 JBP, Barry to Butler, September 10, 1794.

11 JBP, Margaret Howlin to Barry, August 6, 1794.

12 Fowler, *Jack Tars and Commodores*, 24.

13 LOC, ASP, 1:8; Barry, Dale, and Truxton to Knox.

14 Wood, *Live Oaking*, 4, 16; Muir quoted on 6.

15 Fowler, *Jack Tars and Commodores*, 25; Wood, *Live Oaking*, 28; NYHS, Barnes, Barry to Coxe, November 10, 1794.

16 Fowler, *Jack Tars and Commodores*, 25; Wood, *Live Oaking*, 26.

17 HSP, Humphreys Letterbook, Morgan to Humphreys, August 30, 1794.

18 Tench Coxe to John Barry, October 3, 1794, quoted in Griffin, *The History of Commodore John Barry*, 300-301; *Pennsylvania Gazette*, October 8, 1794; JBP, Barry to Coxe, November 10, 1794; Wood, *Live Oaking*, 10.

19 JBP, Barry to Coxe, November 10, 1794; HSP, Humphreys Letterbook, Morgan to Humphreys, October 21, 1794.

20 JBP, Barry to Coxe, November 10, 1794; HSP, Roberts Collection, Humphreys to Barry, October 30, 1794.

21 "Copy of a letter from Captains Barry, Dale, and Truxton, to the Secretary of War, dated Philadelphia, December 18, 1794," from Griffin, *The History of Commodore John Barry*, 306-308; HSP, Humphreys Letterbook, December 20, 1794; National Archives, Joshua Humphreys Wastebook, 11, 1794–4, 1795.

22 LOC, GWP, *Diary of George Washington, Vol. VI*, 215.

23 JBP, Barnes, Morgan to Barry, December 29, 1794.

24 Wood, *Live Oaking*, 29.

25 HSP, Humphreys to Morris, 1793; King with Hattendorf and Estes, *A Sea of Words*, 174, 223.

26 HSP, Etting Collection, Nicholson to Barry, January 19, 1795.

27 JBP, Barry to Pickering, February 9, 1795; Flexner, *Washington*, 328; Chernow, *Alexander Hamilton*, 471.

28 JBP, Rossiter to Barry, May 1795.

29 HSP, Gratz Collection, William Austin to Barry, April 22, 1795.

30 LCOP, Benjamin Rush Ledger Book, April 20, 1795, May 4, 1795, May 12, 1795, Benjamin Rush Papers, "On Asthma"; JBP, Rossiter to Barry, May 1795; HSP, Letterbook Joshua Humphreys; Clark, *Gallant John Barry,* 376.

31 Flexner, *Washington,* 329; McCullough, *John Adams,* 456, 457; *New London Courant-Gazette,* June 18, 1795; Wood, *Live Oaking,* 27.

32 JBP, Barry Expenses, 10, 1795. Westlake, p. 319.

33 Wood, *Live Oaking,* 30; *Naval Documents Related to the Barbary Wars* ("NDBW"), vol. I, p. 80.

34 Wood, pps. 30-31; American State Papers, Naval Affairs, vol. 1, 17-21; Chappelle, *The American Sailing Navy,* 123; *Fowler, Jack Tars and Commodores,* 24.

35 JBP, Barry to Pickering, August 19, 1795.

36 Flexner, *Washington,* 335-337, 343-344.

37 NDBW, Vol. I, 122-124.

38 Ibid., 121-122.

39 HSP, Humphreys Correspondence, July 14, 1797; Fowler, *Jack Tars and Commodores,* 26.

40 NDBW, Vol. I, p. 127; Symonds, *Navalists and Antinavalists,* 40; Smelser, *Congress Founds the Navy,* 78.

41 Balinsky, "Albert Gallatin," 298-299; Symonds, *Navalists and Antinavalists,* 40-41, 46-47; *NDBW,* Vol. I, 150, 156; Smelser, *Congress Founds the Navy,* 82-83; JBP, James McHenry to Barry, May 16, 1796.

42 *NDBW,* vol. I, 124; Clark, *Gallant John Barry,* 379.

43 *NDBW,* Vol. I, 176; NYHS, Barnes, May 63, Barry to Truxton, May 22, 1796; Stein, *The Life and Correspondence of James McHenry* 181-182.

44 De Kay, *A Rage for Glory,*16-17.

45 ISM, Barry–Hayes Papers Patrick Hayes and Sarah Barry correspondence 1797-1802; Barry Family Tree from Clark, *Gallant John Barry,* Appendix.

46 *Pennsylvania Gazette,* March 9, 1796.

47 JBP, Barry to McHenry, September 19, 1796.

48 JBP, Barry to McHenry, August 28, 1796, September 20, 1796.

49 Ibid., Barry to McHenry, September 10, 1796.

50 Smelser, *The Congress Founds the Navy,* 89.

51 Ibid., 88-89.

52 JBP, Barry to McHenry, December 21, 1796.

53 LCOP, Benjamin Rush Letterbook, 12, 1796.

54 Watson, *Annals,* vol. I, 359.; National Archives, Joshua Humphreys Wastebook, 1797.

55 Griffin, *The History of Commodore John Barry,* 297, Washington's Diary, February 25, 1797, quoted in Clark, *Gallant John Barry,* 381; McCullough, *John Adams,* 418.

56 Smelser, *The Congress Founds the Navy,* 96.

57 McCullough, *John Adams,* 477.

58 Symonds, *Navalists,* 56.

59 Watson, *Annals,* vol. II, 361.

60 Scharf and Westcott, *The History of Philadelphia,* vol. I, 490; Smelser, *Congress Founds the Navy,* 53.

61 Philadelphia *Aurora,* December 23, 1796.

62 Clark, *Gallant John Barry,* 383.

63 Scharf and Westcott, *The History of Philadelphia,* vol. 1, 490.

64 Clark, *Gallant John Barry,* 383. Scharf and Westcott, *The History of Philadelphia,* vol. 1, p. 490; McMaster, *A History of the People of the Midland States,* Vol. II 322-323.

65 HSP, Humphreys Correspondence, vol. I, William Rush to Humphreys, April 30, 1795; quotation in Scharf & Westcott, Vol. I, p. 490.

66 HSP, Humphreys letterbook, April 24, 1797, Humphreys to McHenry, May 11, 1797; Philadelphia *Daily Advertiser,* May 3, 1797.

67 McMaster, *A History of the People of the Midland States,* vol. II, 322-323.

68 *Philadelphia Gazette,* May 11, 1797.

69 Sarah Smith Stafford to Capt. John S. Barnes, April 16, 1877, quoted in Griffin, *The History of Commodore John Barry,* 318.

70 McCullough, *John Adams,* 482.

71 King with Hattendorf and Estes, *A Sea of Words,* 195.

72 HSP, Humphreys letterbook, Humphreys to McHenry, May 12, 1797.

73 Ibid.

74 Ibid.

75 Ibid.

76 Philadelphia *Gazette,* May 11, 1797; McMaster, *A History of the People of the Midland States,* vol. 2, 324.

77 Philadelphia *Gazette,* May 11, 1797; McMaster, *A History of the People of the Midland States,* vol. 2, 323.

78 Scharf and Westcott, *The History of Philadelphia,* vol. I, 490. McCullough, *John Adams,* 482.

79 McMaster, *A History of the People of the Midland States,* vol. 2, 322-323.

80 Gillmer, *Old Ironsides,* 33.

81 HSP, Humphreys letter book, Humphreys to McHenry, May 12, 1797

82 Ibid.

83 HSP, Humphreys letter book, Humphreys to McHenry, May 12, 1797; Clark, *Gallant John Barry,* 383; JBP, Barry to McHenry, August 28, 1797.

84 Philadelphia *Gazette,* May 11, 1797; JBP, Barry to Nicholson, September 14, 1797. McMaster, *A History of the People of the Midland States* vol. 2, 324; HSP, Diary of Elizabeth Drinker, vol. 2, 916.

85 King with Hattendorf and Estes, *A Sea of Words,* 201; HSP, Humphreys letter book, May 11, 1797.

86 *Naval Documents Related to the Quasi-War Between the United States and France, Volume* 1, 6, Secretary of War to Thomas Truxton, June 29, 1797; McCullough, *John Adams,* 484-485.

87 HSP, Humphreys letter book, Humphreys to Truxton, June 11, 1797.

88 JBP, Barry to McHenry, June 20, 1797.

89 Fowler, *Jack Tars and Commodores,* 28.

90 Barry to McHenry, June 16, 1797, quoted in Griffin, *The History of Commodore John Barry,* 329-330.

91 QW 1, Secretary of War to Thomas Truxton, June 29, 1797, 6.

92 JBP, Foulk to Barry, February 5, 1797, Jackson to Barry, February 26, 1797; David Library of the American Revolution, Sol Feinstone Collection, Morris to Barry, August 8, 1797.

93 Winch, *A Gentleman of Color,* 80; Wagner, *Robert Morris,* 129.

94 JBP, Barry to McHenry, July 24, 1797.

95 Scharf and Westcott, vol. I, 491.

96 Chernow, *Alexander Hamilton,* 530-534.

97 *Pennsylvania Gazette,* August 16, 1797.

98 HSP, Diary of Elizabeth Drinker, p. 944; McCollugh, *John Adams,* 490.

99 McCullough, *John Adams,* 491-492; HSP, Humphreys Correspondence, Humphreys to McHenry, September 25, 1797; JBP, Barry to McHenry, August 28, 1797.

100 King with Hattendorf and Estes, *A Sea of Wordss,* 183.

101 LCOP, Benjamin Rush Ledger, September 9, 1797; NYHS, Barry to McHenry, August 28, 1797.

102 NDQW, vol. 1, p. 16, Secretary of War to Barry, August 30, 1797.

103 JBP, Mullowny to Barry, September 6, 1797.

104 JBP, Gillasspy to Barry, September 13, 1797.

105 HSP, Gratz, Barry to Francis, September 17, 1797.

106 HSP, Barry to Nicholson, September 4, 1797; Fowler, *Jack Tars and Commodores,* 27-28.

107 HSP, Joshua Humphreys Correspondence, Truxton to Humphreys, September 7, 1797.

108 JBP, Barry to Mullowny, September 13, 1797.

109 Tench Francis to Barry, September 13, 1797; quoted in Griffin, *The History of Commodore John Barry,* 332.

110 JBP, Barry to Mullowny, September 13, 1797.

111 *Porcupine's Gazette,* October 3, 1797; NYHS, Gillasspy to Barry, October 11, 1797.

112 JBP, Barry to McHenry, September 13, 1797; Gillasspy to Barry, November 21 and 26, 1797; State of the Frigate *United States* at the Close of 1797, as Reported to Congress, quoted from Griffin, *The History of Commodore John Barry,* 333-334; Clark, *Gallant John Barry,* 393.

113 JBP, Gillasspy to Barry, November 26, 1797.

114 JBP, Barry to Mullowny (no date); Clark, *Gallant John Barry,* 393.

115 Symonds, *Navalists and Antinavalists,* 66-67.

116 NDQW, vol. 1, 28-36, "Abstract of the Cases of Capture of American Vessels," 33; HSP, Sea Captains' Club Minutes.

117 McCullough, *John Adams,* 493; Symonds, *Navalists and Antinavalists,* 61.

118 Smelser, *The Congress Founds the Navy,* 125.

119 Quoted in Griffin, *The History of Commodore John Barry,* 333.

120 LOC, Thomas Jefferson Papers, Jefferson to John Wayles Eppes, December 26, 1797.

121 Chernow, *Alexander Hamilton,* 548-550; Smelser, *The Congress Founds the Navy,* 128; McCullough, *John Adams,* 495.

122 NDQW, vol. 1, McHenry to Barry, January 4, 1798.

123 Clark, *Gallant John Barry,* 394.

124 Ibid.; JBP, Barry to James Imlay, January 8, 1798.

125 JBP, *United States,* Muster roll, March 12, 1798.

126 NYPL, Barry to Mullowny, February 12, 1798.

127 HSP, Roberts Collection, Mullowny to Barry, February 14, 1798.

128 Chernow, *Alexander Hamilton,* 550; McCullough, *John Adams,* 491-497.

129 McCullough, *John Adams,* 497.

130 Ibid.

131 Chernow, *Alexander Hamilton,* 550.

132 Allen, *Our Naval War with France,* 25.

133 NDQW, vol. 1, 4, Secretary of War to Joshua Humphreys, March 23, 1797; JBP, McHenry to Barry, March 31, 1798.

134 JBP, Barry to McHenry, April 3, 1798.

135 JBP, Barry to Mullowny, March 26, April 2, 1798; Griffin, *The History of Commodore John Barry,* 339.

136 Symonds, *Navalists and Antinavalists,* 71; Palmer, *Stoddert's War,* 9, 12.

137 LOC, Barry Papers, McHenry to John Jay, April 18, 1798; NYHS, Barry to Mullowny, April 10, 1798, Barry to McHenry, 5, 1798; NDQW vol. 1, p. 70, Secretary of War to John Jay, May 7, 1798.

138 Symonds, *Navalists and Antinavalists,* 70; Fowler, *Jack Tars and Commodores,* 32.

139 NDQW vol. 1, 57, Secretary of War to Joshua Humphreys and Captain Thomas Thompson, April 25, 1798; "Purchase of Ship *Ganges,*" 62-63, 56-57.

140 Haverford College, Charles Roberts Collection, Sarah Barry to John Barry, June 1798. Chapelle, *The American Sailing Navy,* 122-123. King with Hattendorf and Estes, *A Sea of Words,* 315.

141 HSP, Porter to Barry, April 18, 1798. JBP, Barry to Barry, April 19, 1798; Clark, *Gallant John Barry,* 401.

142 HSP, Roberts Collection, Paul Revere to Barry, April 29, 1798.

143 NDQW, Vol. 1, p. 74, To Alexander Hamilton from James McHenry, May 12, 1798; 67-68, "Purchase of Ship *Hamburgh Packet,* May 5, 1798; Chernow, *Alexander Hamilton,* 553; Keen, "The Descendants of Jöran Kyn; De Kay, *A Rage for Glory,* 22; Clark, *Gallant John Barry,* 402.

144 LOC, Barry Papers, McHenry to Barry, May 5, 1798.

145 Ibid.

146 McCullough, *John Adams,* 500, 505, 506.

147 LOC, McHenry to Barry, May 5, 1798.

148 JBP, Barry to Stewart, May 10, 1798.

149 NDQW, Vol. 1, pps. 73-74, Captain Samuel Nicholson's recruiting advertisement for the U.S. Frigate *Constitution,* May 12, 1798.

150 JBP, Barry to Mullowny, May 20, May 23, 1798.

151 LOC, Barry Papers, G. Daws to Tench Francis, May 16, 1798.

152 Barry to Francis, May 10, 1798, quoted in Griffin, *The History of Commodore John Barry,* 342; Clark, *Gallant John Barry,* 404.

153 JBP, Truxton to Barry, May 23, 1798.

154 NDQW, vol. 1: 77, To Captain Richard Dale from Secretary of War, May 22, 1798; 84-87. "Military and Other Stores to be Delivered to Captain Barry," May 26, 1798; 82, To John Harris, storekeeper, from Secretary of War, May 25, 1798.

155 NDQW, vol. 1: McHenry to Barry, May 23, 1798, 77; Allen, *Our Naval War with France,* 63; Fowler, *Jack Tars and Commodores,* 35.

156 *Philadelphia Advertiser,* June 8, 1798; Palmer, *Stoddert's War,* 128.

CHAPTER TWENTY: THE QUASI-WAR

1 Chernow, *Alexander Hamilton,* 553-557.

2 Palmer, *Stoddert's War,* 6; Fowler, *Jack Tars and Commodores,* 31-32.

3 Smelser, *Congress Founds the Navy,* 157.

4 Carrigg, "Benjamin Stoddert," 61, Palmer, *Stoddert's War,* 12.

5 Palmer, *Stoddert's War,* 16.

6 Ibid., 17.

7 Carrigg, "Benjamin Stoddert," 62; Smelser, *Congress Founds the Navy*, 158.

8 NDQW, vol. 1, 122-123, To Jeremiah Yellott, Navy Agent, Baltimore from Secretary of Navy, June 18, 1798; Clark, *Gallant John Barry*, 409.

9 JBP, Barron to Barry, June 18, 1798; Clark, *Gallant John Barry*, 410.

10 JBP, Stoddert to Barry, July 3, 1798; NDQW, vol. 1, 133, Thomas Truxton to James McHenry, June 23, 1798.

11 JBP, Stoddert to Barry, July 3, 1798.

12 ISM, Humphreys to Barry, June 26, 1798.

13 NDL, U.S. Frigate *United States*, July 6, 1798; Midshipmen's Oaths of Allegiance, quoted in Griffin, *History of Commodore Barry*, 346; NDQW, vol. 1, 163, 169, Journal of Lieutenant John Mullowny, July 4, 7, 1798; Clark, *Gallant John Barry*, 411.

14 HSP, *Philadelphia Journal*, July 8 and 9, 1798; LCOP, "A Journal Kept by Thomas Wilkey on board the United States Ship *Delaware*," July 7-9, 1798.

15 LOC, Barry Papers, Stoddert to Barry, July 7, 1798.

16 NDQW, vol. 1, 201, Mullowny Journal, July 12, 1798; 203-204, July 13, 1798.

17 NDQW, vol. 1, 181, "An Act to Protect the Commerce of the United States," July 9, 1798; 96, T. Williams to Secretary Pickering, May 31, 1798; 215-16, "Agreement between John T. Morgan and Thomas Fitzsimons, July 7, 1798; Fowler, *Jack Tars and Commodores*, 36-37; Chappelle, *The American Sailing Navy*, 163-164.

18 Haverford College, Charles Roberts Collection, Sarah Barry to John Barry, July 9, 1798; NYHS, Stoddert to Barry, July 11, 1798; HSP, Gratz, John Barry to Sarah Barry, July 26, 1798.

19 JBP, Stoddert to Barry, July 12 and 14, 1798.

20 Ibid.

21 Ibid.; HSP, Joshua Humphreys Correspondence, Barry to Humphreys, July 22, 1798; NDQW, vol. 1, 211, Mullowny Journal, July 15, 1798; HSP, Joshua Humphreys Correspondence, James Morris to Humphreys, July 23, 1798.

22 NDQW, vol. 1, Mullowny Journal, 250, July 28, 1798; 265, August 1, 1798. Cochrane's young nephew, Thomas, would become the inspiration for Patrick O'Brian's character Jack Aubrey.

23 NDQW, vol. 1, Mullowny Journal, 325, August 21, 1798; 327, August 22, 1798.

24 Ibid., 331, August 23, 1798.

25 Ibid., 334, August 24, 1798; JBP, Stoddert to Barry, July 11, 1798.

26 Palmer, *Stoddert's War*, 75-76.

27 NDQW, vol. 1, 373, 375, 377, Mullowny Journal, September 3, 4, 1798; *Porcupine's Gazette*, September 21, 1798.

28 NDQW, vol. 1, 381, 384, 411, 424, 430, Mullowny Journal, September 7, 8, 16, 18, 20, 1798; Clark, *Gallant John Barry*, 423; Stoddert to Adams, September 21, 1798.

29 NDQW, vol. 1, 430, Stoddert to Adams, September 21, 1798; Clark, *Gallant John Barry*, 425.

30 NDQW, vol. 1, 430, Stoddert to Adams, September 21, 1798.

31 *Porcupine's Gazette*, September 21, 1798; McCullough, *John Adams*, 513.

32 NDQW, vol. 1, 158, Stoddert to Truxton, July 2, 1798; HSP, Truxton papers, Truxton to Stoddert, August 16, 1798,

33 NDQW, vol. 1, 449, Stoddert to Adams, September 24, 1798.

34 NDQW, vol. 1, 132, Stoddert to Francis, September 22, 1798

35 JBP, John Coste to Barry, no date; Rob Boyce to Barry, July, 28, 1798.

36 Fowler, *Jack Tars and Commodores*, 129; NDQW, vol. 1, 517, "Circular to the Commanders of Revenue Cutters," October 10, 1798.

37 Bolster, *Black Jacks*, 80, 160.

38 NDQW, vol. 1, 481-482, Stoddert to Barry, October 1, 1798; Adams to Stoddert, October 1, 1798, quoted in Griffin, *Commodore John Barry*, 361.

39 NDQW, vol. 1, 551, 552, 560, Mullowny Journal, October 19, 21, 24, 1798; De Kay, *Rage for Glory*, 28-29.

40 NDQW, vol. 1, 580, Mullowny Journal, October 31, 1798; NDQW, vol. 2, 6, Mullowny Journal, November 4, 1798.

41 NDQW, vol. 2, 14, 19, Mullowny Journal, November 9, 10 1798; Flexner, *Washington*, 381-82.

42 NDQW, vol. 2, 473-475, Barry to Stoddert, March 16, 1799; 313, Stoddert to Hamilton, February 6, 1799. Fowler, *Jack Tars and Commodores*, 38. NDQW, vol. 2, 55-56, Stoddert to Barry, November 29, 1798; 313, Stoddert to Hamilton, February 6, 1799.

43 NDQW, vol. 2, 57, Alexander Murray to Stoddert, November 29, 1798; Palmer, *Stoddert's War*, 71; Fowler, *Jack Tars and Commodores*, 37.

44 NDQW, vol. 2, 70-72, Stoddert to Barry, December 7, 1798; 77-78, Stoddert to Decatur, December 10, 1798; 84-85, Stoddert to Tingey, December 12, 1798. JBP, Stoddard to Barry, December 7, 1806.

45 NDQW, vol. 2, 87, 98, 109, 112, 129, Mullowny Journal, December 12, 19, 21, 23, 28, 1798; 205, 212, Mullowny Journal, January 3 and 4, 1799.

46 NDQW, vol. 2, 238, Mullowny Journal, January 13, 1799.

47 Fowler, *Jack Tars and Commodores*, 41; HSP, Truxton letterbook, January 17, 1799.

48 NDQW, vol. 2, 361, Mullowny Journal, February 15, 1799; 473-474, Barry to Stoddert, March 16, 1799; HSP, Gratz, Truxton to Barry, February 16, 1799.

49 NDQW, vol. 2, 265, 275, Pity Journal, January 19 and 23, 1799; 266, Mullowny Journal, January 19, 1799; HSP, Truxton to Stoddert, January 17, 1799.

50 Palmer, *Stoddert's War*, 92-93; JBP, Nicholson to Barry, January 24, 1799.

51 NDQW, vol. 2, 70-73, Stoddert to Barry, December 7, 1798; 467-648, Stoddert to Barry, March 15, 1799.

52 NDQW, vol. 2, Mullowny Journal, January 30, 1799.

53 *Connecticut Courant*, March 25, 1799; Palmer, *Stoddert's War*, 94; *Pennsylvania Gazette*, January 30, 1799.

54 *Pennsylvania Gazette*, January 30, March 20, 1799.

55 NDQW, vol. 2, 366, Mullowny Journal, February 16, 17, 1799; *Connecticut Courant*, March 25, 1799; Palmer, *Stoddert's War*, 69.

56 NDQW, vol. 2, 375, 382, Pity Journal, February 20 and 21, 1799.

57 HSP, Gratz, Truxton to Stoddert, February 9, 1799; Barreaut to Truxton, Truxton Letterbook, 1798-99.

58 NDQW, Vol. 2, 387, Daniel McNeill to Barry, February 22, 1799; 473-475, Barry to Stoddert, March 16, 1799; 388, Mullowny Journal, February 22, 1799.

59 JBP, Monsieur Deschamps to Barry, "28th Germinal 7th year of the French Republic."

60 *Pennsylvania Gazette*, April 17, 1799; NDQW, vol. 2, 473-475, Barry to Stoddert, March 16, 1799.

61 NDQW, vol. 2, 473-475, Barry to Stoddert, March 16, 1799.

62 NDQW, vol. 2, 409, Pity Journal, February 26, 1799.

63 HSP, Gratz, Sarah Barry to John Barry, February 18, 1799.

64 HSP, Gratz, Truxton Letterbook, Truxton to Barry, March 14, 1799.

65 Ibid.; NDQW, Vol. 2, 241-42, Stoddert to Barry, January 16, 1799.

66 NDQW, vol. 2, 313, Stoddert to Hamilton, February 6, 1799; HSP, Truxton Letterbook, 1798-1799.

67 NDQW, vol. 2, 473-475, Barry to Stoddert, March 16, 1799.

68 NDQW, vol. 2, 496-97, Pity Journal, March 20, 1799; Brown Journal, March 20, 1799; Mullowny Journal, March 20, 1799.

69 NDQW, vol. 2, 503, Pity Journal, March 22, 1799; Brown Journal, March 22, 1799.

70 NDQW, vol. 2, 496-497, Pity Journal, March 20, 1799; Brown Journal, March 20, 1799; Mullowny Journal, March 20, 1799.

71 NDQW, vol. 2, 503, Pity Journal, March 22, 1799; Brown Journal, March 22, 1799.

72 NDQW, vol. 2, 508, Pity Journal, March 23, 1799; 509, Brown Journal, March 23, 1799; Clark, *Gallant John Barry*, 445.

73 *Pennsylvania Gazette*, March 15, 1799; NDQW, vol. 2, 524; Ingraham log book, March 27, 1799; Clark, *Gallant John Barry*, 445.

74 NDQW, vol. 2, 524; Ingraham log book, March 27, 1799; JBP, Gay to Barry, May 11, 1799.

75 JBP, Memorandum regarding British Packet *Carteret*, prize of U.S. Frigate *Constitution*, April 4, 1799.

76 NDQW, vol. 3, Deschamps to Barry (with Enclosures), April 15, 1799.

77 Haverford Colege, Charles Roberts Collection, Sarah Barry to John Barry, January 25, 1799.

78 HSP, Gratz, Sarah Barry to John Barry, February 17, 1799.

79 NDQW, vol. 3, 63 and 66, Pity Journal, April 17 and 18, 1799.

80 NDQW, vol. 3, 66, Stoddert to Adams, April 19, 1799; 84, Adams to Stoddert, April 22, 1799.

81 Chernow, *Alexander Hamilton*, 575, 599; NDQW, vol. 3, 593; McCullough, *John Adams*, 523.

82 NDQW, vol. 3, 177, Stoddert to Barry, May 13, 1799.

83 NDQW, vol. 3, 301, Stoddert to Barry, February 2, 1799; 47, Stoddert to Barry, April 15, 1799.

84 Haverford College, Charles Roberts Collection, Sarah Barry to John Barry, January 25, 1799.

85 JBP, Barry Collection, "Love to Mrs. Barry from 'Miss Cray,'" 1799.

86 NDQW, vol. 3, 176-177, Stoddert to Adams, May 13, 1799; Palmer, *Stoddert's War*, 108; 185, Stoddert to Adams, May 15, 1799; 199, Stoddert to Truxton, May 17, 1799; 131-132, Stoddert to Hailton, May 3, 1799; 252, Stoddert to Adams, May 25, 1799.

87 NDQW, vol. 2, 300, Stoddert to Dale, February 1, 1799.

88 NDQW, vol. 2, 300, Stoddert to Dale, February 1, 1799; 313, Stoddert to Hamilton, February 6, 1799; Palmer, *Stoddert's War*, 111; NDQW, vol. 3, 186, Stoddert to Talbot, May 15, 1799.

89 NDQW, vol. 3, 252-53, Stoddert to Adams, May 25 1799; 371, Stoddert to Barry, June 20, 1799; 268-69, Stoddert to Mullowny, May 28, 1799; 252-253, Stoddert to Adams, May 25, 1799; 372, Stoddert to Stephen Decatur, Sr., June 20, 1799; Palmer, *Stoddert's War*, 139.

90 John Espy to Barry, May 21, 1799, quoted in Griffin, *Commodore John Barry*, 392; HSP, Gratz, Jonathan Dayton to Barry, June 17, 1799, and Thomas Burke to Barry, May 10, 1799; LOC, GWP, Washington to Stoddert, July 10 and 15, 1799.

91 NDQW, vol. 3, 324, Stoddert to James and Ebenezer Watson, June 10, 1799; 405, Stoddert to James and Ebenezer Watson June 25, 1799; 411, Stoddert to McHenry, June 27, 1799.

92 NDQW, vol. 3, 552, Stoddert to Barry, July 27, 1799; NDQW, vol. 4, 61-62, To Captain Thomas Truxton, U.S. Navy, from John Cowper, brother of Master Commandant William Cowper, U.S. Navy, August 11, 1799; 208, Stoddert to Adams, September 19, 1799.

93 NDQW, vol. 3, 552, Stoddert to Barry, July 27, 1799.

94 NDQW, vol. 3, 559-60, Stoddert to Adams, July 29, 1799; NDQW, vol. 4, 87-88, Stoddert to Adams, August 17, 1799; 71, Stoddert to Adams, August 14, 1799; LOC, Barry Collection, Stoddert to Barry, October 16, 1799.

95 LOC, Barry Collection, Stoddert to Barry, September 20 and October 1, 1799; NDQW, vol. 4, 304, Stoddert to Barry, October 21, 1799.

96 NDQW, vol. 4, 304, Stoddert to Barry, October 21, 1799; ISM, "Statement of Distribution of Prize Money," October 14, 1799.

97 NDQW, vol. 4, 350 and 411, Gibbs and Channing, Navy Agents, to Stoddert, November 3 and 11, 1799; *Pennsylvania Gazette*, March 12, 1800; King and Hattendorf, *Harbors and High Seas*, 156.

98 NDQW, vol. 5, 178, William Smith, U.S. Minister, to Secretary of State Pickering, February 1, 1800; Koedel, *Glory at Last!* 27; Clark, *Gallant John Barry*, 462; JBP, Lisbon Assembly Invitation, December 2, 1799.

99 LCOP, Benjamin Rush Collection, "On Asthma."

100 NDQW, vol. 5, 205, Ellsworth and Davie to Pickering, February 10, 1800.

101 Ibid.; NDQW, vol. 5, 384, Stoddert to James and Ebenezer Watson, April 4, 1800; King with Hattendorf and Estes, *A Sea of Words*, 332.

102 NDQW, vol. 5, 178, Smith to Pickering, January 21, 1800; NDQW, vol. 4, 558, "General Orders to the Officers of the U.S. Navy and Marines from the Secretary of the Navy," December 20, 1799.

103 NDQW, vol. 5, 205, Ellsworth and Davie to Pickering, February 10, 1800; *Pennsylvania Gazette*, April 9, 1800.

104 Carrigg, "Benjamin Stoddert," 70.

CHAPTER TWENTY-ONE: CROSSING THE BAR

1 *Pennsylvania Gazette*, February 26 and March 19, 1800; NDQW, vol. 4, 384, Stoddert to James and Ebenezer Watson, April 4, 1800.

2 NYPL, Barry to McCormick, May, 17, 1800; Clark, *Gallant John Barry*, 466.

3 LCOP, Rush Ledger, 1800.

4 JBP, Humphreys to Barry, May 2, 1800; King with Hattendorf and Estes, *A Sea of Words*, 194.

5 Palmer, *Stoddert's War*, 210-211.

6 McCullough, *John Adams*, 538-539.

7 NDQW, vol. 5, 565, Adams to Stoddert, May 26, 1800.

8 Haverford College, Charles Robert Collection, James Barron to Barry, June 4, 1800.

9 NDQW, vol. 5, 517, Charles Washington Goldsborough for the Secretary of the Navy to Stephen Decatur (Junior), May 15, 1800; 567, Mullowny Journal, May 26, 1800; JBP, Mullowny to Barry, May 25, 1800.

10 JBP, Stewart to Barry, June 4, 1800; Barry to Stoddert, July 31, 1800.

11 NDQW vol. 6, 183, Stoddert to Stewart, July 26, 1800; 422, Talbot to Stoddert, October 1, 1800.

12 NDQW vol. 6, George Miller to Barry, April 21, 1800; Samuel Chandler to Barry, April 21, 1800, quoted in Griffin, *Commodore John Barry*, 405.

13 Haverford College, Charles Roberts Collection, James Barron to Barry, June 4, 1800; Daniel McNeill to Barry, September 14, 1800; NDQW, vol. 7, 78, Extract from Log Book of the U.S. Frigate *President*, Captain Thomas Truxton, commanding, January 9, 1801.

14 Biddle, *Autobiography*, 269; JBP, Barry to Austin, July 1800 (no day listed).

15 Ibid., Barry to Stoddert, July 30, 1800.

16 Ibid.

17 McCullough, *John Adams*, 552; Chernow, *Alexander Hamilton*, 630-631; NDQW, vol. 6, 393-409, "Convention of Amity and Commerce between the United States and France," September 30, 1800; JBP, Stoddert to Barry, October 25, 1800.

18 LOC, Barry Collection, Stoddert to Barry, November 24, 1800.

19 Palmer, *Stoddert's War*, 223.

20 NDQW, vol. 6, 514, Stoddert to Stephen Higginson and Company, October 29. 1800; 522, Stoddert to Truxton, November 6, 1800.

21 NDQW, vol. 6, 525, Stoddert to Fitzsimons, November 10, 1800; *Connecticut Courant*, December 15, 1800.

22 APS, Edward Cutbush to John Vaughan, July 10, 1801; Cutbush, "Thermometrical Journal," 1800-1801.

23 APS, Cutbush Journal, April 12-21, 1801. Cutbush presented his findings to the American Philosophical Society on May 12 where it lay, as William Bell Clark noted, "dust covered and neglected" for over one hundred years. Cutbush's journal is the only surviving document from Barry's last cruise.

24 LOC, Barry Papers, Stoddert to Barry, November 28, 1800.

25 NDQW, vol. 6, 558, Stoddert to Mrs. E. C. Shippen, November 28, 1800.

26 NDQW, vol. 7, 14, Stoddert to Barry, December 6, 1800.

27 Salter, *On Asthma, Its Pathology and Treatment*, 138; Cutbush, "Thermometrical Journal," December 16, 1800.

28 Koedel, *Glory at Last!* 31.

29 NDQW, vol. 7, 76, Lieutenant Bartholomew Church, U.S. Marine Corps, to Lieutenant Colonel Commandant W.W. Burrows, U.S. Marine Corps, January 8, 1801; NDQW, vol. 7, 92, 94, *President* Log Book, January 15–25, 1801; HSP, Gratz, Truxton Letterbook, Truxton to Thomas Tingey, December 1, 1800; Truxton to Barry, January 15, 1801.

30 Koedel, *Glory at Last!* 32; Clark, *Gallant John Barry*, 471.

31 JBP, Captain David Jewett, USS *Trumbull*, to Barry, February 4, 1801; NDQW, vol. 7, 154, Stoddert to Barry, March 23, 1801; APS, Cutbush, "Thermometrical Journal," April 12, 1801.

32 APS, Cutbush Journal, April 12-21, 1801.

33 ISM, Barry-Hayes Papers, William Jonas Keen to Patrick Hayes, October 16, 1801.

34 LOC, Thomas Jefferson Papers, General Correspondence, Stoddert to Jefferson, February, 18, 1801; Paullin, *Out-Letters*, 229.

35 Palmer, *Stoddert's War* 232.

36 Carrigg, "Benjamin Stoddert," 71.

37 NDQW, vol. 7, 212, Samuel Smith for Acting Secretary of the Navy to Barry, May 1, 1801; JBP, Midshipman Noble W. Glenn to Barry, May 1801; Somers to William Jonas Keen, May 17, 1801.

38 JBP, Joseph Green to Barry, June 3, 1801; Clark, *Gallant John Barry,* 451; NDQW, vol. 7, 240, Smith to Barry, June 2, 1801.

39 NDQW, vol. 7, 240, Smith to Barry, June 2, 1801.

40 McCullough, *John Adams,* 541; NDQW, vol. 7, 240; JBP, Sarah Barry to John Barry, May 23, 1801.

41 Ibid.

42 ISM, Elizabeth Hayes to Patrick Hayes, July 2, 1801; Philadelphia Archives; ISM, Betsy Hayes to Patrick Hayes, October 16, 1801; Keen, "Descendants of Jöran Kyn," 486; Clark, *Gallant John Barry,* 483.

43 Watson, *Annals,* vol. 2, 464-465; ISM, Elizabeth Hayes to Patrick Hayes, July 2, 1801.

44 NDQW, vol. 7, 251, Smith to Barry, June 11, 1801; JBP, Barry to Tingey, August 14, 1801.

45 Fowler, *Jack Tars and Commodores,* 63–64, 66; NDQW, vol. 7, 45, Richard O'Brien, U.S. Consul General, Algiers, to William Kirkpatrick, U.S. Consul, December 24, 1800; Ferguson, *Truxton of the Constellation,* 215-218.

46 Keen, "Descendants of Jöran Kyn," 482-500; NDQW, vol. 7, 271, Robert Smith to Richard Somers, July 30, 1801; JBP, McNeill to Barry, August 12, 1801; Somers to William Jonas Keen, August 13, 1801; ISM, Betsy Hayes to Patrick Hayes, July 2, 1801; Barry to Truxton, August 14, 1801.

47 Fowler, *Jack Tars and Commodores,* 60-61; Thomas Tingey to Barry, August 11, 1801, quoted in Griffin, *The History of Commodore John Barry,* 409.

48 JBP, Barry to Tingey, August 14, 1801.

49 Quoted in Palmer, *Stoddert's War,* 224.

50 Philadelphia Archives; From Griffin, 415; ISM, Patrick Hayes to William Jonas Keen, November 13, 1801; Patrick Hayes to Elizabeth Hayes, November 13, 1801.

51 NDQW, vol. 7, 302, Robert Smith to Barry and Murray, November 14, 1801; 304, Murray to Robert Smith, December 1, 1801; LOC, Manuscript Division, Robert Smith to Barry, November 21, 1801.

52 NDQW, vol. 7, 304, Murray to Smith, Dercember 1, 1801.

53 HSP, Elizabeth Drinker Diary, December 1801; ISM, Patrick Hayes to Betsy Hayes, September 21, 1801; November 13, 1801.

54 Fowler, *Jack Tars and Commodores,* 69-70; Koedel, *Glory at Last!* 48-49; Naval Documents of the Barbary Wars, vol. 2, 94; Ferguson, *Truxton of the Constellation,* 224.

55 ISM, Eleanor Kavanaugh to Patrick Hayes, 3/24, 1802; NYHS, Nancy Kelly to Barry, May 20, 1802; Pakenham, *1798: The Year of Liberty,* 63-66; an email from Celestine Rafferty on June 12, 2006, mentioned finding Kelly's gravestone "on the Rebel side."

56 ISM, Barry-Hayes Papers, Sarah Barry to Betsy Keen, June 11, 1802; Elizabeth Hayes to Patrick Hayes, July 19, 1802.

57 ISM, Sarah Barry to Patrick Hayes, July 27, 1802.

58 ISM, Patrick Hayes to Elizabeth Hayes, April 22, May 19, June 26, 1802; Sarah Barry to Patrick Hayes, July 27, 1802.

59 ISM, Barry to Keen and Somers, August 5, 1802; Archdiocese of Philadelphia, Baptism Records, St. Mary's, October 17, 1802.

60 LCOP, Rush Ledger, August, 1802; JBP, Barry to Smith, August 8, 1802; HSP, Gratz, Barry to Robert Smith, August 25, 1802; from Griffin, *Commodore John Barry*, 409; Fowler, *Jack Tars and Commodores*, 72-81; HSP, Gratz, Lieutenant Charles Ludlow to Barry, September 25, 1802.

61 Philadelphia City Records, Real Estate Transactions, 1802.

62 From Griffin, *The History of Commodore John Barry*, 410.

63 Robert Smith to Barry, December 22, 1802, quoted in Griffin, *Commodore John Barry*, 410.

64 Interview with Carla Keirns, M.D., Ph.D., September 27, 2006.

65 Ibid.

66 ISM, M. McConnell to Barry January 16, 1803; LCOP, Benjamin Rush Ledger Books, 1802-1803.

67 NDBW Vol. 2, 398, Appointment of Richard Somers to command U.S. Schooner *Nautilus*, May 5, 1803; ISM, John Barry's Will, February 27, 1803; Fowler, *Jack Tars and Commodores*, 82-83.

68 LCOP, Rush Ledger, 1803; Richardson, "The Athens of America 1800-1825," 243; Clark, *Gallant John Barry*, 490.

69 LCOP, Rush Ledger, 1803, Interview with Carla Keirns, M.D., Ph.D., September 27, 2006.

70 Fowler, *Jack Tars and Commodores*, 83-85.

71 NDBW, vol. 2, 474-477.

72 ISM, Charles Higbee to Patrick Hayes, August 24, 1803.

73 Gloucester County Historical Society, William Jonas Keen to Richard Somers, August 23, 1803; ISM, Keen to Elizabeth Hayes, August 24, 1803.

74 Clark, *Gallant John Barry*, 491. From Griffin, *The History of Commodore John Barry*, 411.

75 HSP, Elizabeth Drinker Diary, September 12, 1803.

76 Ibid., September 13, 1803; *Pennsylvania Gazette*, September 13, 1803; conversation with Carla Keirns, M.D., September 27, 2006.

77 *Pennsylvania Gazette*, September 13, 1803; LCOC, Benjamin Rush Ledger, 1802-1813.

78 *American Daily Advertiser*, from Griffin, *The History of Commodore John Barry*, 412.

79 *Pennsylvania Gazette*, September 13, 1803.

80 *Massachusetts Spy* and *Worcester Gazette*, September 21, 1803, from Clark, *Gallant John Barry*, 492; *American Daily Advertiser*, from Griffin, *The History of Commodore John Barry*, 412.

81 ISM, John Barry Will, February 1803.

82 LOC, Jefferson Papers, Jefferson to Rush, October 11, 1803.

83 From Griffin, *The History of Commodore John Barry*, 416; Brown and Kessler, "Life of Commodore Barry," 13.

Afterword

1 *National Gazette*, from Gurn, *Commodore John Barry*, 292-93.

2 ISM, Barry-Hayes Papers, Sarah Barry Collection, receipts, 1815-17, 1822, 1823-24; Estate Accounts, November 31 [*sic*], March 2, 1832.

3 Philadelphia City Records, Real Estate Transactions, March 19, 1805; USNA, "Inventory of the Estate of John Barry of the Northern Liberty, County of Philadelphia, State of Pennsylvania," November 27, 1803.

4 *National Gazette*, from Gurn, *Commodore John Barry*, 292-293.

5 ISM, Barry's Will, 1803.

6 Keen, "The Descendants of Jöran Kyn," 485-486.

7 ISM, William Austin to Sarah Barry, August 5, 1814.

8 Keen, "The Descendants of Jöran Kyn," 486.

9 ISM, Barry-Hayes Papers, Patrick Hayes Papers and Correspondence.

10 Clark, *Gallant John Barry*, Appendix: "The Barry-Hayes Family"; ISM, Patrick Hayes Correspondence.

11 Wagner, *Robert Morris*, 132-134.

12 Hildeburn, "Francis Hopkinson," 324.

13 PA Archives, Papers of John Kessler; Mount Laurel Cemetery Records.

14 Parker, "A Biographical Sketch of John Brown."

15 Humphreys, "Who Built the First United States Navy?" 385-411.

16 Carrigg, *American Secretaries of the Navy*, 72.

17 Ralfe, *Naval Biography of Great Britain*, vol. II, 367-372; also quoted in Gurn, *Commodore John Barry*, 172-177.

18 Ralfe, vol. III, 369; quoted in Gurn, *Commodore John Barry*, 177.

19 University of Virginia, Hamond Papers, "Memorandum on the Papers of Sir Andrew Snape Hamond."

20 Ralfe, *Naval Biography of Great Britain*, vol. II, 413-419.

21 Morison, *John Paul Jones*, 417; Thomas, *John Paul Jones*, 265.

22 Griffin, *Life of Commodore Barry*, 120-121.

23 Butterfield, ed., *Letters of Benjamin Rush*, 1175-1176.

24 Adams, *The Works of John Adams*, vol. 10, 27-29.

25 Ibid., 29.

26 Butterfield, ed., *Letters of Benjamin Rush*, 1177.

27 Ibid, 1181.

28 Ferguson, *Truxton of the Constellation*, 256-260.

29 Keen, "Descendants of Jöran Kyn," 494-500.

30 De Kay, *A Rage for Glory*, 57-59.

31 Koedel, *Glory at Last!* 132-138.

32 Fowler, *Jack Tars and Commodores*, 252-253.

33 De Kay, *A Rage for Glory*, 199-204, 211.

34 Chappelle, *The American Sailing Navy*, 428, 556.

35 Historic Naval Ships Association, "Historic Naval Ships Visitors Guide."

36 USS *Barry* Web site.

37 American Art Association/Anderson Galleries, Inc.: "The Barry Collection and Other Historical Americana."

38 The sword is on display at the John F. Kennedy Presidential Library in Boston, Massachusetts.

39 Morison, *John Paul Jones*, 480-482.

40 Watson, *Annals*, vol. II, 339. Some of the *Alliance* remains at Independence Hall National Park, labeled as "timbers belonging to the ship *Alliance* commanded by John Paul Jones."

BIBLIOGRAPHY

MANUSCRIPTS AND COLLECTIONS

Abolition Records for City of Philadelphia. Historical Society of Philadelphia, Philadelphia.

Adams Family Collection: 1776-1914. Library of Congress, Washington D.C.

Adams Papers, 1639-1889. Library of Congress, Washington, D.C.

Samuel Adams Papers. Library of Congress, Washington, D.C.

Admiralty Records. Public Record Office, Kew Gardens.

Alliance. Ship's Letterbook. Library of Congress, Washington, D.C.

Baptismal, Marriage, and Church Records. Archdiocese of Philadelphia, Philadelphia.

Barnes Collection. New York Historical Society. New York.

John Barry Papers. Library of Congress, Washington, D.C.

John Barry Papers. New York Public Library, New York.

Barry-Hayes Papers. Independence Seaport Museum, Philadelphia.

The Barry Collection and Other Historical Americana. American Art Association/Anderson Galleries, Inc. New York, 1939.

William Bingham Papers, 1776-1779. Library of Congress, Washington, D.C.

Elias Boudinot Papers, 1776-83 Force Transcripts. Library of Congress, Washington, D.C.

Cadwalader Collection. Historical Society of Pennsylvania, Philadelphia.

Census Records, City of Philadelphia 1790-1830. National Archives, Washington, D.C.

City of Philadelphia, Marriage Records, Manumissions, Real Estate Transactions, Tax Records, City of Philadelphia Records, Philadelphia.

William Bell Clark Collection, 1770-1950. Library of Congress, Washington, D.C.

Correspondence of Continental Congress. Library of Congress, Washington, D.C.

Correspondence of Marine Committee. Library of Congress, Washington, D.C.

Correspondence of United States Congress. Library of Congress, Washington, D.C.

Tench Coxe Papers. Historical Society of Pennsylvania, Philadelphia.

Richard Dale Papers. Library of Congress, Washington, D.C.

Richard Dale Papers. Operational Archives Branch, Naval Historical Center, Washington, D.C.

Silas Deane Letterbooks, 1777-84, Force Transcripts. Library of Congress, Washington, D.C.

Stephen Decatur, Naval Papers, 1801-1820. Historical Society of Pennsylvania.

Dreer Collection. Historical Society of Pennsylvania, Philadelphia.

Henry Fisher Papers. Richard Rodney Collection, Delaware Historical Society, Wilmington.

Benjamin Franklin Papers. American Philosophical Society, Philadelphia.

Joseph Galloway Papers, 1779-1785, Force Transcripts. Library of Congress, Washington, D.C.

German Troops in America, 1776-83. Library of Congress, Washington, D.C.

Hamond Naval Papers, 1766-1825. Library of Congress, Washington, D.C.

John Hancock Papers, 1774-1776. Library of Congress, Washington, D.C.

Harwood Family Papers, 1767-1940. Library of Congress, Washington, D.C.

Hessian Officers, Letters, 1776-81. Library of Congress, Washington, D.C.

Hessian Troops, Papers, 1775-82. Library of Congress, Washington, D.C.

Jean Holker Papers, 1777-1822. Library of Congress, Washington, D.C.

Francis Hopkinson Collection, 1759-65. Library of Congress, Washington, D.C.

Joshua Humphreys Collection and Correspondence. Historical Society of
    Pennsylvania, Philadelphia.

John Paul Jones Papers, 1775-88, Force Manuscripts. Library of Congress,
    Washington, D.C.

John Kessler Papers. Pennsylvania Archives, Harrisburg.

Robert Morris Papers. Library of Congress, Washington, D.C.

William Penn Papers. Historical Society of Pennsylvania, Philadelphia.

Penn-Physick Papers, Edward Physick Letter Books, 1769-1801. Historical Society
    of Philadedelphia.

Pennsylvania Abolition Society Papers, 1775-1975. Historical Society of
    Pennsylvania, Philadelphia.

Philadelphia Customs House and Tonnage Duty Books. Historical Society of
    Pennsylvania, Philadelphia.

Franklin Delano Roosevelt Library, Hyde Park.

Benjamin Rush Papers, Correspondence, Ledgers, and Account Books. Library
    Company of Philadelphia.

Benjamin Rush, "On Asthma." Benjamin Rush Papers. Historical Society of
    Pennsylvania, Philadelphia.

Richard Somers Papers. Gloucester County Historical Society, Gloucester.

Stouffer Collection. Historical Society of Pennsylvania, Philadelphia.

George Washington Papers. Library of Congress, Washington, D.C.

Thomas Wilkey, "A Journal Kept by Thomas Wilkey on board the United States
    Ship *Delaware*." 1798. Library Company of Philadelphia.

BOOKS AND ARTICLES

Adams, Charles Francis. *The Works of John Adams*. Vols. VIII–X. Boston: Little,
    Brown, 1853.

Adams, John. *Diary and Autobiography of John Adams*. Ed. H. Butterfield. Vols. 1-4.
    Cambridge, Mass.: Belknap, 1961.

Adams, Russell B., ed. *The Revolutionaries*. New York: Time-Life Books, 1996.

Alberts, Robert C. "Business of the Highest Magnitude." *American Heritage* 22, no.
    2 (February 1971).

Allen, Gardner W. *A Naval History of the American Revolution*. Boston: Houghton
    Mifflin, 1913.

———. *Our Naval War with France*. New York: Houghton Mifflin, 1909.

The American Revolution, 1175-1783: An Atlas of Eighteenth-Century Maps and Charts.
    Washington, D.C.: Naval History Division Department of the Navy, 1972.

Anderson, William Gary. "John Adams and the Creation of the American Navy."
    Ph.D. diss. State University of New York, 1975.

Augur, Helen. *The Secret War of Independence.* New York: Duell Little, 1955.

"The Aurora and the Alien and Sedition Laws." *Pennsylvania Magazine of History and Biography* 77 (1952).

Balinsky, Alexander S. "Albert Gallatin: Naval Foe." *Pennsylvania Magazine of History and Biography* 82 (1957).

Barney, M., ed. *Biographical Memoir of the Late Commander Joshua Barney.* Boston: Gray and Bowen, 1832.

Baurmeister, Carl. "Letters of Major Baurmeister During the Philadelphia Campaign, 1777-1778." *Pennsylvania Magazine of History and Biography* 60 (1935).

Beck, Alverda S., editor. *The Correspondence of Esek Hopkins, Commander-in-Chief of the United States Navy . . . in the Library of the Rhode Island Historical Society.* Providence: Rhode Island Historical Society, 1933.

———. *The Letter Book of Esek Hopkins, Commander-in-Chief of the United States Navy, 1775-1777 . . . in the Library of the Rhode Island Historical Society.* Providence: Rhode Island Historical Society, 1932.

Biddle, James S., ed. *Autobiography of Charles Biddle, Vice-President of the Supreme Executive Council of Pennsylvania, 1745-1821.* Philadelphia: E. Claxton & Co., 1883.

Bolster, W. Jeffrey. *Black Jacks: African American Seamen in the Age of Sail.* Cambridge: Harvard University Press, 1997.

Bradford, James C. *Command Under Sail: Makes of the American Naval Tradition 1775-1850.* Annapolis: Naval Institute Press, 1985.

———. *John Paul Jones and the American Navy.* New York: Rosen Publishing, 2002.

———. "The Navies of the American Revolution." In *Peace and War: Interpretations of American Naval History,* 2nd ed. Ed. Kenneth J. Hagan. Westport, Conn.: Greenwood, 1984.

Brands, H. W. *The First American: The Life and Times of Benjamin Franklin.* New York: Anchor, 2000.

Breen, Kenneth C. "A Reinforcement Reduced? Rodney's Flawed Appraisal of French Plans, West Indies, 1781." In *New Interpretations in Naval History: Selected Papers from the Ninth Naval History Symposium.* Ed. William R. Roberts and Jack Sweetman. Annapolis: Naval Institute Press, 1991.

Breen, T. H. *The Marketplace of Revolution.* New York: Oxford University Press, 2004.

Brewington, Marion V. "American Naval Guns, 1775-1785." *American Neptune* 3 (1943): 11-18, 148-158.

———. "The Designs of Our First Frigates." *American Neptune* 8 (1948): 11-25.

———. "Maritime Philadelphia 1609-1837." *Pennsylvania Magazine of History and Biography* 63 (1938).

Brodie, Faun M. *Thomas Jefferson: An Intimate History.* New York: Norton, 1974.

Brodsky, Alyn. *Benjamin Rush: Patriot and Physician.* New York: St. Martin's, 2004.

Bronner, Edwin H., "Village into Town, 1701-1746." In Russell Weigley, ed., *Philadelphia: A 300-Year History.* New York: Norton, 1982.

Brown, John Howard. *American Naval Heroes, 1775-1812-1861-1898.* Ed. Gertrude Battles Lane. Boston: Brown and Co., 1899.

Brown, John, and John Kessler. "American Biography: The Life of Commodore Barry." *Portfolio Magazine* (July 1813).

Burgner, M. K. "Life and Times of Colonel James McCalmont: A Paper read before the Kittochtiny Historical Society 27th Ma, 1920." Chambersburg, Pa. (1923).

Burke, Edmund. *Irish Affairs.* Ed. Matthew Arnold. London: Cresset Library, 1988.

Butterfield, Lyman Henry, ed. *Diary and Autobiography of John Adams.* Vol. 3. Cambridge: Harvard University Press, 1961.

——. *Letters of Benjamin Rush.* Vol. 2. Princeton: Princeton University Press, 1951.

Callo, Joseph. *John Paul Jones: America's First Sea Warrior.* Annapolis: Naval Institute Press, 2006.

Carrigg, John J. *American Secretaries of the Navy.* Ed. Paolo E. Colletta. Vol. 1. Annapolis: Naval Institute Press, 1980.

Carse, Robert. *Ports of Call.* New York: Charles Scribner's Sons, 1967.

Catanzariti, John, and E. James Ferguson, eds. *The Papers of Robert Morris.* Vols. 1-8. Pittsburgh: University of Pittsburgh Press, 1984.

Chandler, Charles Lyon. "Early Shipping in Pennsylvania, 1683-1812." In *Philadelphia: Port of History.* Philadelphia: Philadelphia Maritime Museum, 1976.

Chappelle, Howard I. *The American Sailing Navy.* New York: Bonanza, 1949.

Chernow, Ron. *Alexander Hamilton.* New York: Penguin Press, 2004.

Christman, Margaret C. *Adventurous Pursuits: Americans and the China Trade 1784-1844.* Washington, D.C.: Smithsonian Institute Press, 1984.

Clark, William Bell. *Ben Franklin's Privateers: A Naval Epic of the American Revolution.* Baton Rouge: Louisiana State University Press, 1956.

——. *George Washington's Navy: Being an Account of His Excellency's Fleet in New England Waters.* Baton Rouge: Lousiana State University Press, 1960.

——. *Gallant John Barry.* New York: Macmillan, 1938.

——. "James Josiah, Master Mariner." *Pennsylvania Magazine of History and Biography* 79 (1954).

——. *Lambert Wickes, Sea Raider and Diplomat.* New Haven: Macmillan, 1932.

——. "The Sea Captains Club." *Pennsylvania Magazine of History and Biography* 81 (1956).

Clark, William Bell, William James Morgan, and Michael J. Crawford eds. *Naval Documents of the American Revolution.* Vols. 1-11. Annapolis: U.S. Navy, 1964-2007.

Coggins, Jack. *Ships and Seamen of the American Revolution: Vessels, Crews, Weapons, Gear, Naval Tactics, and Actions of the War for Independence.* Harrisburg: Stackpole Books, 1969.

Coletta, Paolo, ed. *American Secretaries of the Navy.* Vol. 1. Annapolis: Naval Institute Press, 1980.

Connolly, S. J. *Religon, Law, and Power: The Making of Protestant Ireland, 1660-1760.* Oxford: Oxford University Press, 1992.

Cooper, James Fenimore. *History of the Navy of the United States of America.* Vols. 1-2. Philadelphia: Lea & Blanchard, 1840.

——. "Sketches of Naval Men." *Graham's Magazine* (1839).

Cordingly, David. *Under the Black Flag.* New York: Harcourt Brace, 1995.

——. *Women Sailors and Sailors' Women: An Untold Maritime History.* New York: Random House, 2001.

Corner, George W., editor. *The Autobiography of Benjamin Rush: His "Travels Through Life" Together with his Commonplace Book for 1789-1813.* Westport: Greenwood Press, 1970.

Craig, Michelle L. "Grounds for Debate? The Place of the Caribbean Provisions Trade in Philadelphia's Pre-Revolutionary Economy." *Pennsylvania Magazine of History and Biography* 129 (April 2004).

Crane, Elaine Forman, ed. *The Diary of Elizabeth Drinker*. Vols. 2-3. Boston: Northeastern University Press, 1991.

Crawford, Michael J. ed. *The Autobiography of a Yankee Mariner: Christopher Prince and the American Revolution*. Dulles, Va.: Brassey's, 2002.

Crawford, Michael J. "Naval Administration Under Robert Morris." Presented at the conference "Founding Financier Robert Morris," New York. April 7 2000.

Dale, Richard. "Biographical Memoir of Richard Dale." *Portfolio Magazine* 3, no. 6 (June 1814).

Davis, Allen F., and Mark H. Haller, ed. *The Peoples of Philadelphia: A History of Ethnic Groups and Lower-Class Life*. Philadelphia: Temple University Press, 1973.

Davis, Joshua. *A Narrative of Joshua Davis, an American Citizen who was Pressed and Served on Board Six Ships of the British Navy*. Boston: B. True, 1811. Navy Department Library.

De Conde, Alexander. *The Quasi-War: The Politics and Diplomacy of the Undeclared War with France, 1797-1891*. New York: Scribner, 1966.

De Kay, James Tertius. *A Rage for Glory: The Life of Stephen Decatur*. New York: Free Press, 2004.

De Koven, Mrs. Reginald. *The Life and Letters of John Paul Jones*. Vols. 1-2. New York: Charles Scribner's Sons, 1913.

Doerflinger, Thomas M. *A Vigorous Spirit of Enterprise*. Chapel Hill: University of North Carolina Press, 1986.

Dorland, W. A. Newman. "The Second Troop, Philadelphia City Cavalry." *Pennsylvania Magazine of History and Biography* 47 (1923).

Dorson, Richard M., editor. *Patriots of the American Revolution*. New York: Gramercy Books, 1953.

Dudley, William S., and Michael J. Crawford, eds. *The Early Republic and the Sea*. Dulles, Va.: Brassey's, 2001.

Dull, Jonathan R. *The French Navy and American Independence: A Study of Arms and Diplomacy, 1774-1787*. Princeton: Princeton University Press, 1975.

Egnal, Marc. "The Changing Structure of Philadelphia's Trade With the British West Indies, 1759-1775." *Pennsylvania Magazine of History and Biography* 99 (1974).

Ellis, Joseph J. *American Sphinx: The Character of Thomas Jefferson*. New York: Knopf, 1998.

———. *Founding Brothers*. New York: Knopf, 2000.

———. *His Excellency, George Washington*. New York: Knopf, 2004.

Engle, Eloise, and Arnold S. Scott. *America's Maritime Heritage*. Annapolis: Naval Institute Press, 1975.

Everett, Barbara. "John Barry, Fighting Irishman." *American History Illustrated* 12, no. 8 (December 1977).

"Extracts from the Diary of Jacob Hiltzheimer, of Philadelphia 1768-1798." *Pennsylvania Magazine of History and Biography* 16 (1892).

Fairburn, William Armstrong. *Merchant Sail*. Vol. 1. Center Lowell: Fairburn Marine Educational Foundation, 1945.

Fanning, Nathaniel. *Fanning's Narrative: Being the Memoirs of Nathaniel Fanning, an Officer of the Revolutionary Navy . . . in the Library of the Rhode Island Historical Society.* Alverda S. Beck, ed. Providence: Rhode Island Historical Society, 1933.

Feldman, Clayton A. "Continental Navy Brigantine Lexington (1776-1777): Deriving New Plans from Original Data." *Nautical Research Journal* 49, no. 2 (2004).

Ferguson, Eugene S. *Truxton of the Constellation.* Annapolis: Naval Institute Press, 1956.

Fischer, David Hackett. *Paul Revere's Ride.* New York: Oxford University Press, 1994.

——. *Washington's Crossing.* New York: Oxford University Press, 2004.

Flanders, Henry. "Thomas Fitzsimmons." *Pennsylvania Magazine of History and Biography* 2 (1877).

Fleming, Thomas. *Liberty.* New York: Viking, 1997.

Flexner, James Thomas. *Washington: The Indispensable Man.* New York: Little, Brown, 1969.

Fowler, William M., Jr. *The Baron of Beacon Hill: A Biography of John Hancock.* Boston: Houghton Mifflin, 1980.

——. "Esek Hopkins: Commander-in-Chief of the Continental Navy." In *Command Under Sail: Makers of the Naval Tradition 1775-1850.* Ed. James C. Bradford. Annapolis: Naval Institute Press, 1985.

——. *A Gentlemanly and Honorable Profession: The Creation of the U.S. Naval Officer Corps, 1794-1815.* Annapolis: Naval Institute Press: 1991.

——. *Jack Tars and Commodores: The American Navy, 1783-1815.* Boston: Houghton Mifflin, 1984.

——. *Rebels Under Sail: The American Navy During the Revolution.* New York: Scribner's, 1976.

——. *Silas Talbot: Captain of Old Ironsides.* Mystic: Mystic Seaport Museum, 1995.

Fraser, Megan Hahn. "Barry-Hayes Papers Overview." *Independence Seaport Museum.* 2006.

——. "Guide to the Barry-Hayes Papers." *Independence Seaport Museum,* 2003-4.

Fraser, Robert, Esq. *Statistical Survey of the County of Wexford.* Dublin: Graiseberry & Campbell, 1807.

Freidenberg, Zachary B. *Medicine Under Sail.* Annapolis: Naval Institute Press, 2002.

Frey, Sylvia R. *Water from the Rock: Black Resistance in a Revolutionary Age.* Princeton: Princeton University Press, 1991.

Gallagher, Mary A. Y. "Charting a New Course for the China Trade: The Late 18th-Century American Model." In William S. Dudley and Michael J. Crawford, eds., *The Early Republic and the Sea.* Dulles, Va.: Brassey's, 2001.

Gilje, Paul E. *Liberty on the Waterfront: American Maritime Culture in the Age of Revolution.* Philadelphia: University of Pennsylvania Press, 2004.

Gilkerson, William. *The Ships of John Paul Jones.* Annapolis: Naval Institute Press, 1987.

Gillmer, Thomas C. *Old Ironsides: The Rise, Decline, and Resurrection of the USS Constitution.* Camden, Me.: Ragged Mountain Press, 1993.

Giunta, Mary, ed. *The Emerging Nation: A Documentary History of the Foreign Relations of the United States Under the Articles of Confederation, 1780-1789.* Vols.

1-3. Washington, D.C.: National Historical Publications and Records Commission, 1996.

Golway, Terry. *For the Cause of Liberty.* New York: Simon & Schuster, 2000.

Goodrich, Charles A., Rev. *Lives of the Signers to the Declaration of Independence.* New York: William Reed & Co., 1856.

Gough, Deborah Matthias. *Christ Church, Philadelphia.* Philadelphia: University of Pennsylvania Press, 1995.

Griffin, Martin I. J. *The History of Commodore John Barry.* Philadelphia: American Catholic Historical Society, 1897.

Griffiths, George, ed. *Chronicles of the County Wexford to the Year 1777.* Enniscorthy, 1902.

Gurn, Joseph. *Commodore John Barry.* New York: P. J. Kennedy & Sons, 1933.

Hastings, George Everett. *The Life and Works of Francis Hopkinson.* Chicago: University of Chicago Press, 1926.

Hawes, Dorothy Schumman. *To the Farthest Gulf: The Story of the American China Trade.* Ipswich: Ipswich Press, 1990.

Hawke, David Freeman. *Everyday Life in Early America.* New York: Harper & Rowe, 1988.

Henkel, S. V., ed. *The Confidential Correspondence of Robert Morris: The Great Financier of the Revolution and Signer of the Declaration of the Independence.* Philadelphia: S. V. Henkel, 1917.

Hildeburn, Charles R. "Francis Hopkinson." *Pennsylvania Magazine of History and Biography* 2 (1877).

Hill, Frederic Stanhope. *Twenty-Six Historic Ships.* New York: G. P. Putnam's Sons, 1903.

Howard, James L. *Seth Harding, Mariner.* New Haven: Yale University Press, 1930.

Humphreys, Henry H., Col. "Who Built the First United States Navy." *Pennsylvania Magazine of History and Biography* 40 (1915).

Illich, Joseph E. *Colonial Pennsylvania–A History.* New York: Charles Scribner's Sons, 1976.

Ireland, Bernard. *Naval Warfare in the Age of Sail: War at Sea, 1756-1815.* New York: Norton, 2000.

Isaacson, Walter. *Benjamin Franklin: An American Life.* New York: Simon & Schuster, 2003.

Jackson, Donald, and Dorothy Twohig, eds. *The Diaries of George Washington.* Vol VI. Charlottesville: University Press of Virginia, 1979.

Jackson, John W. *The Delaware Bay and River Defenses of Philadelphia 1775-1777.* Philadelphia: Philadelphia Maritime Museum, 1977.

——. *The Pennsylvania Navy 1775-1781: The Defense of the Delaware.* New Brunswick, N.J.: Rutgers University Press, 1974.

——. *With the British Army in Philadelphia.* San Rafael: Presidio Press, 1974.

James, Francis Godwin. *Ireland in the Empire.* Cambridge, Mass.: Harvard University Press, 1973.

James, William M. *The British Navy in Adversity: A Study of the War of American Independence.* London: Longmans, Green, 1926.

Keane, John. *Tom Paine: A Political Life.* New York: Grove Press, 1995.

Keen, Gregory. "The Descendants of Jöran Kyn: The Founder of Upland." *Pennsylvania Magazine of History and Biography* 4 (1879).

King, Dean, John B. Hattendorf, and J. Worth Estes. *A Sea of Words*. New York: Henry Holt, 1995.

King, Dean, and John B. Hattendorf. *Harbors and High Seas*. New York: Henry Holt, 1996.

Klepp, Susan E., and Billy G. Smith. eds. *The Infortunate Voyage and Adventures of William Moraley and Indentured Servant*. University Park: Pennsylvania State University Press, 1992.

Knox, Dudley W., Capt., ed. *Naval Documents Related to the Quasi-War Between the United States and France*. Vols. 1-7. Washington, D.C.: U.S. Government Print Office, 1935-37.

———. *Naval Documents Related to the United States Wars with the Barbary Powers*. Vols. 1-3. Washington, D.C.: U.S. Government Print Office, 1939.

———. *The Naval Genius of George Washington*. Boston: Houghton Mifflin, 1932.

Koedel, Barbara. *Glory at Last! A Narrative of the Naval Career of Master Commandant Richard Somers*. Somers Point, N.J.: Atlantic County Historical Society, 1993.

Lacour-Gayet, Georges. *La Marine Militaire de la France sous le regne de Louis XVI*. Paris: H. Champion, 1905.

Lancaster, Bruce. *The American Revolution*. Boston: Houghton Mifflin, 1971.

Landais, Pierr. *Memorial to Justify Peter Landais' Conduct During the Late War*. Boston: Edes, 1784.

Lanning, Michael Lee, Lt. Col. (Ret), *Defenders of Liberty: African Americans in the Revolutionary War*. New York: Citadel Press, 2000.

Lecky, E. H. *A History of Ireland in the Eighteenth Century*. Chicago: University of Chicago Press, 1972.

Lee, Jen Gordon. *Philadelphia and the China Trade*. Philadelphia: Philadelphia Museum of Art, 1984.

Lee, Robert E. *Blackbeard the Pirate*. Winston Salem: John F. Blair, 1974.

Lemisch, Jesse, ed. *Benjamin Franklin: Autobiography and Other Writings*. New York: Signet, 1961.

Lincoln, Charles Henry, ed. *Naval Records of the American Revolution, 1775-1788*. Washington, D.C.: Government Printing Office, 1906.

Ludenberg, Philip K. *The Continental Gunboat Philadelphia and the Northern Campaign of 1776*. Washington, D.C.: Smithsonian Institution, 1966.

MacLay, Edgar Stanton. *A History of American Privateers*. New York: D. Appleton and Co., 1899.

———. *A History of the United States Navy from 1775-1893*. Vols. 1-2. New York: D. Appleton and Co., 1894.

MacLay, Edgar Stanton, editor. *Journal of William MacLay*. New York: D. Appleton & Co., 1890.

MacManus, Seamus. *The Story of the Irish Race*. New York: Barnes & Noble, 1999.

Mahan, Alfred T. *The Major Operations of the Navies in the War of American Independence*. Boston: Little, Brown, 1913.

Maritime Dimensions of the American Revolution. Washington, D.C.: GPO, 1964.

Martin, Tyrone G., Captain, USS *Constitution*. *A Most Fortunate Ship: a Narrative History of "Old Ironsides."* Chester, Conn.: Globe Pequot Press, 1979.

Matthewman, Luke. "Narrative of Lieutenant Luke Matthewman." *Magazine of American History* 2, part I (1878).

McCullough, David. *John Adams.* New York: Simon & Schuster, 2001.

McCuster, John J., comp. "Ships Registered at the Port of Philadelphia before 1776: A Computerized Listing." *Historical Society of Pennsylvania.* September 1970.

McDonald, Forest, and Ellen Shapiro McDonald, eds. *Confederation and Constitution 1781-1789.* Columbia: University of South Carolina Press, 1968.

McKee, Christopher. *A Gentlemanly and Honorable Profession: The Creation of the U.S. Naval Officer Corps, 1794-1815.* Annapolis: Naval Institute Press, 1991.

McMaster, John B. *A History of the People of the Midland States.* Vol 2. New York.

McMaster, John B. and Frederick D. Stone, eds. "Pennsylvania and the Federal Constitution." *Pennsylvania Magazine of History and Biography* XIII (1888).

Meany, William Barry, M.D. *Commodore John Barry.* New York: Harper & Brothers, 1911.

Merritt, Jane T. "Tea Trade, Consumption, and the Republican Paradox in Pre-Revolutionary Philadelphia." *Pennsylvania Magazine of History and Biography* 129 (April 2004).

Metzger, Charles H. *The Prisoner in the American Revolution.* Chicago: Loyola University Press, 1971.

Millar, John F. *American Ships of the Colonial and Revolutionary Periods.* New York: Norton, 1978.

Miller, Nathan. *Sea of Glory: The Naval History of the American Revolution.* Charleston: Nautical & Publishing Co. of America, 1974.

Miller, Richard G. "The Federal City, 1783-1800." In *Philadelphia: A 300-Year History.* Ed. Russell F. Weigley. New York: Norton, 1982. 155-207.

Millick, Jacquelyn C. "The Wages of Blackness: African American Workers and the Measuring of Race During Philadelphia's 1793 Yellow Fever Epidemic." *Pennsylvania Magazine of History and Biography* 130 (August 2005).

Mitchell, Carleton. *Isles of the Caribbees.* Washington, D.C.: National Geographic Society, 1986.

Montgomery, Elizabeth. *Reminiscences of Wilmington, Delaware.* Wilmington: Johnston & Bogia, 1872.

Montresor, John. "Journal of Captain John Montrésor." *Pennsylvania Magazine of History and Biography* 6 (1881)

Morgan, William James. "John Barry: A Most Fervent Patriot." In *Command Under Sail: Makers of the Naval Tradition 1775-1850.* Ed. James C. Bradford. Annapolis: Naval Institute Press, 1985.

Morison, Samuel Eliot. *John Paul Jones: A Sailor's Biography.* Annapolis: Naval Institute Press, 1989.

Morris, Robert. *The Confidential Correspondence of Robert Morris.* Philadelphia: Kessinger Publishing, 1917.

Nagy, John A. *Rebellion in the Ranks: Mutinies of the American Revolution.* Yardley, Pa.: Westholme Publishing, 2008.

Nash, Gary B. *First City.* Philadelphia: University of Pennsylvania Press, 2002.

Niderast, Eric. "Capital in Crisis." *American History Magazine* 39, no. 3 (August 2004).

O'Connor, Raymond G. *Origins of the American Navy: Sea Power in the Colonies and the New Nation.* Lanham, Md.: University Press of America, 1994.

O'Neill, Richard, ed. *Patrick O'Brian's Navy.* London: Salamander Books, 2003.

Pakenham, Thomas. *1798: The Year of Liberty.* New York: Random House, 1998.

Palmer, Michael A. *Stoddert's War: Naval Operations during the Quasi-War with France, 1798-1801.* Columbia: University of South Carolina Press, 1987.

Parker, Emelin Knox. "A Biographical Sketch of John Brown." *Historical Society of Pennsylvania.* Carlisle, 1918 (revised 1928, 1935).

Parramore, Thomas C. "The Great Escape from Forten Gaol: An Incident of the Revolution." *North Carolina Historical Review* 45 (October 1968).

Paullin, Charles Oscar. *Out-Letters of the Continental Marine Committee and Board of Admiralty.* Vols. 1-2. New York: Devinne Press, 1914.

———. *The Navy of the American Revolution: Its Administration, Its Policy and Its Achievements.* Cleveland: Burrows, 1906.

Peckham, Howard H. *The War for Independence: A Military History.* Chicago: University of Chicago Press, 1958.

Pennypacker, Samuel, Hon. "Anthony Wayne." *Pennsylvania Magazine of History and Biography* 32 (1908).

Peterson, Robert A. *Patriots, Pirates, and Pineys.* Medford: Plexus, 1998.

Quarles, Benjamin. *The Negro in the American Revolution.* New York: Norton, 1973.

Quilley, Geoff. "The Image of the Ordinary Seaman in the 18th Century," website of the National Maritime Museum, Greenwich, England.

Rafferty, Celestine. "The Barry Hayes Papers, a Presentation for the Wexford County Library." Wexford, 2002.

Ralfe, James. *Naval Biography of Great Britain.* Vols. 2-3. Boston: Gregg Press, 1972.

Ranby, John. *The Method of Treating Gunshot Wounds, 2nd ed.* London: Robert Horsfield: 1760.

Randall, William Sterne. *George Washington: A Life.* New York: Henry Holt & Co. Inc., 1997.

Rankin, Hugh F. "The Naval Flag of the American Revolution." *William and Mary Quarterly* 2 (1954): 229-353.

Rannelagh, John. *Ireland.* London: William Collins, 1981.

Roach, Hannah Benner. "Taxables in the City of Philadelphia, 1756." *Pennsylvania Genealogical Magazine* 22 (1961-62).

———. "Taxables in Chestnut, Walnut, and Lower Delaware Wards." *Pennsylvania Genealogical Magazine* 22 (1961-62).

Ross, J. E., ed. *Radical Adventurer: The Diaries of Robert Morris, 1772-1774.* Bath: Adams & Dart, 1971.

Rowe, G. S. "Judicial Tyrant and Vox Populi." *Pennsylvania Magazine of History and Biography* 118 (1993).

Rush, Benjamin. *A Dissertation on the Spasmodic Asthma of Children in a Letter to Dr. Miller.* London: T. Gilhool, 1770.

Salter, Henry Hyde, M.D., FRS. *ON Asthmas, Its Pathology and Treatment.* London: John Churchill, 1860.

Salvucci, Linda. "Merchants and Diplomats: Philadelphia's Early Trade with Cuba." Historical Society of Pennsylvania website.

Sandwich, John Montague, 4th Earl. *The Private Papers of John, Earl of Sandwich, First Lord of the Admiralty, 1777-1782.* Editors. G. R. Barnes and J. H. Owen. London: Navy Records Society, 1932-38.

Scharf, J. Thomas, and Thompson Westcott, eds. *The History of Philadelphia.* Vols. 1-2. Philadelphia: Everts & Co., 1884.

Scheina, Robert L. "A Matter of Definition: A New Jersey Navy, 177-1783." *American Neptune* 39 (July 1979): 209-217.

Schermerhorn, Frank E. *American and French Flags of the Revolution, 1775-1783.* Philadelphia: Pennsylvania Society of Sons of the Revolution, 1948.

Schiff, Stacy. *A Great Improvisation: Franklin, France, and the Birth of America.* New York: Henry Holt, 2005.

Scudeman, Sir Charles, M.D., FRS. *Cases Illustrative of the Efficiency of Various Medicines Administered by Inhalation . . . In Asthma.* London: Longman, Reeves, Overe Brown and Green, 1830.

Seilhamer, George O., Esq. "Old Mother Cumberland." *Pennsylvania Magazine of History and Biography* 24 (1900).

Serle, Ambrose. *The American Journal of Ambrose Serle, Secretary to Lord Howe, 1776-1778.* Ed. Edward H. Tatum, Jr. San Marino: Huntington Library, 1940.

"Ship Registers for the Port of Philadelphia 1726-1775." *Pennsylvania Magazine of History and Biography* 28 (1904).

Smelser, Marshall. *The Congress Founds the Navy.* Notre Dame: University of Notre Dame Press, 1959.

Smelser, Marshall, and Steven T. Preiss. "The Fleetless Nation." In *American Secretaries of the Navy.* Vol. 1. Annapolis: Naval Institute Press, 1980.

Smith, Charles R. *Marines in the Revolution: A History of the Continental Marines in the American Revolution, 1775-1783.* Illus. Charles H. Waterhouse, USMCR. Washington, D.C.: U.S. Marine Corps, History and Museums Division, 1975.

Smith, Philip Chadwick Foster. *The Empress of China.* Philadelphia: Philadelphia Maritime Museum, 1984.

Somers, J. B., M.D. *Life of Richard Somers, A Master Commandant in the U.S. Navy.* Philadelphia: Collins, 1868.

State Papers and Publick Documents of the United States: from the Accession of George Washington to the Presidency, Exhibiting a Complete View of Our Foreign Relations Since that Time 1789-1796. Boston: T. H. Wait & Sons, 1815.

Steiner, Bernard. *The Life and Correspondence of James McHenry.* Cleveland: Burrows, 1907.

Stewart, Frank H., ed. *Letters and Papers of Richard Somers.* Reprinted from "The Constitution" April 8, 1942 to September 16, 1942. Gloucester County Historical Society.

Stout, Neil R. *The Royal Navy in America, 1760-1775: A Study of Enforcement of British Colonial Policy in the Era of the American Revolution.* Annapolis: Naval Institute Press, 1973.

Symonds, Craig L. *Historical Atlas of the U.S. Navy.* Cart. William J. Klipson. Annapolis: Naval Institute Press, 1995.

———. *Navalists and Anti-Navalists: The Naval Policy Debate in the United State, 1785-1827.* Newark: University of Delaware Press, 1980.

Syrett, David. *Shipping and the American War 1775-83: A Study of British Transport Organization.* London: Athlone Press, 1970.

Taaffe, Stephen R. *The Philadelphia Campaign, 1777-1778.* Lawrence: University Press of Kansas, 2003.

Taillemite, Etienne. *Archives de la Marine, Série B.* Paris: Imprimerie Nationale, 1969.

Thomas, Evan. *John Paul Jones.* New York: Simon & Schuster, 2003.

Tinckom, Harry M. "The Revolutionary City, 1765–1800." In Russell Weigley, ed., *Philadelphia: A 300 Year History.* New York: Norton, 1982.

Tuchman, Barbara. *The First Salute*. New York: Knopf, 1988.

Tyler, David Bradley. *The Bay and River Delaware: An Illustrated History*. Cambridge, Md.: Cornell Maritime Press, 1955.

Urwin, Gregory J. *The U.S. Cavalry: An Illustrated History*. Oklahoma City: University of Oklahoma Press, 1983.

———. *The U.S. Infantry: An Illustrated History*. Oklahoma City: University of Oklahoma Press, 1988.

U.S. Naval History Division. *The American Revolution, 1775-1783: An Atlas of 18th Century Maps and Charts: Theaters of Operations*. Comp. W. Bart Greenwood. Washington, D.C.: GPO, 1972.

Van Powell, Noland. *The American Navies of the Revolutionary War*. New York: G. P. Putnam's Sons, 1974.

Wagner, Frederick. *Robert Morris: Audacious Patriot*. New York: Dodd, Mead, 1973.

Warriner, Francis. *Cruise of the United States Frigate Potomac: Around the World during the Years 1831-1834*. New York: Leavitt, Lord, & Co., 1835.

Watson, John F. *Annals of Philadelphia Peoples*. Vols. 1-2. Philadelphia: Edwin Stuart, 1887.

Weigley, Russell, ed. *Philadelphia: A 300 Year History*. New York: Norton, 1982.

Westlake, Mark T. "Josiah Fox: Gentleman, Quaker, Shipbuilder." *Pennsylvania Magazine of History and Biography* 88 (1963).

Whipple, Addison B. C. *To the Shores of Tripoli: The Birth of the U.S. Navy and Marines*. New York: William Morrow, 1991.

Wilbur, C. Keith, M.D. *Pirates and Patriots of the Revolution*. Guilford, Conn.: Globe Pequot Press, 1973.

———. *Revolutionary Medicine 1700-1800*. Guilford, Conn.: Globe Pequot Press, 1973.

Winch, Julie. *A Gentleman of Color: The Life of James Forten*. New York: Oxford University Press, 2002.

Wolf, Stephanie Grauman. *As Various as Their Land*. New York: Knopf, 1988.

Wood, Virginia Steel. *Live Oaking: Southern Timber for Tall Ships*. Boston: Northeastern University Press, 1981.

Young, Eleanor. *Robert Morris: Forgotten Patriot*. New York: Macmillan, 1950.

Zacks, Richard. *The Pirate Hunter*. New York: Hyperion, 2002.

Newspapers

American Daily Advertiser. (Philadelphia)
Boston Independent Chronicle 1778-1783
Boston Packet
Connecticut Courant (Hartford)
Continental Journal (Boston)
Dudley's Maryland Gazette (Annapolis)
Liverpool Journal
London Chronicle
London Daily Intelligencer
London Public Advertiser. 1775-1782
London Morning Chronicle
Massachusetts Spy (Worcester)
National Gazette (Philadelphia)
New Hampshire Gazette (Portsmouth)

New Jersey Gazette (Bridgeton)
New London Courant-Gazette.
New York Journal (New York)
Pennsylvania Chronicle. (Philadelphia) 1775
Pennsylvania Evening Packet (Philadelphia)
Pennsylvania Evening Post (Philadelphia)
Pennsylvania Gazette (Philadelphia) 1765-1803
Pennsylvania Journal (Philadelphia)
Pennsylvania Ledger (Philadelphia)
Pennsylvania Packet (Philadelphia) 1765-1785
Philadelphia Advertiser
Philadelphia Aurora
Philadelphia Daily Advertiser
Philadelphia Gazette
Philadelphia Independent Gazette
Pittsburgh Sunday Dispatch
Porcupine's Gazette (Philadelphia)
Weekly Mercury (Philadelphia)
Worcester Gazette

Maps, Charts, and Atlases

The American Revolution, 1175-1783: An Atlas of Eighteenth-Century Maps and Charts.
  Washington, D.C.: Naval History Division Department of the Navy, 1972.
Canton River from the Second Bar Creek to the Upper Part of Whampoa Reach (Rare G
  7822 .65 P5 1816 .N4).
This Survey of the Canton River (Rare G 7822 PJ 1816 N4): D.R. Newell.
Cape Sable to Cape Hatteras (G 3321 .P5 1882 US) US Coast Guard Geodetic
  Survey.
Coast Chart No. 124, Delaware Entrance (United States Coast and Geodetic
  Survey): William Duffield, Superintendent, ca. 1895.
Delaware River to the Atlantic Ocean (G 3792.D44): J. Luffman, 1814.
Delaware River Estuary (Rare G 3824.P5; 2F6 S3 1777a.F58, .F583, .F585): Francois
  de Fleury.
Delaware River Estuary Etc. (Rare G 3832 .D4 P5 1794): Joshua Fisher.
The Island of Cuba: (Rare G 4920 1775 .J4): Thomas Jefferys
Mud Island with the Operations for reducing it: Dickey, Weissman, Chandler, Hoyt
  (copy).
National Charts – Caribbean Area (Rare G 4901 .P5 1824 >B5): Edmund Blunt.
National Geographic Family Reference Atlas of the World. Washington, D.C.: National
  Geographic, 2002.
The N. American Pilot for Newfoundland, etc. (Rare Bk. G 1106 N6 1788 Vol. 1):
  Thomas Jefferys.
Penobscot Bay, Maine (G 3732 P.5 1887 US).
West Indies Maps to 1800 (Rare G 4390 1762 .A2).
An Accurate Map of the West Indies with the Adjacent Coast (ca. 1762): ISM, copy.

INDEX

ACKNOWLEDGMENTS

ANYONE ATTEMPTING A BOOK ON the early American navy owes a debt to William Bell Clark, who spent most of his life championing early naval history and its heroes. He is the navy's Homer, and the best you can hope to do is stand on his shoulders. Fortunately, his prolific successors made themselves accessible. William Fowler at Northeastern University (and late of the Massachusetts Historical Society) gave a great interview and sent both documents and encouragement over the years. Craig Symonds, recently retired from the United States Naval Academy, had great suggestions regarding the *Raleigh*. At the Naval Historical Center, naval scholars E. Gordon Bowen-Hassell (retired) and Charles Brodine read portions of the manuscript and offered sound revisions. James Nelson, a skilled mariner and elegant storyteller, read the text and provided both literary and hands-on knowledge of square-rigged sailing and the wooden world. James Bradford of Texas A & M, the consummate authority on John Paul Jones, reviewed Jones's relationship with Barry. From the University of South Carolina, Michael Palmer shared his deep understanding of Benjamin Stoddert. These scholars' works on the navy and its figures are great reads and wonderful sources. This project was immeasurably helped by their assistance.

Original source material came from both sides of the Atlantic. Celestine Rafferty, County Wexford librarian and historian, provided insight and accuracy about Barry's family and eighteenth-century Ireland. From London, Roger E. Nixon combed the Admiralty archives on my behalf and sent me logs, journals, and newspaper reports that put flesh and bones on Barry's opponents in the Revolution. Douglas McCarthy of the National Maritime Museum turned up the portraits of Hamond and Vashon; he and Mathew Sheldon of the Royal Navy Museum were available for every question and request. In Paris, Jason Stump dug through French maritime archives.

Stateside, I received assistance from Bruce Gimelson of Garrison, New York, Thomas G. Lannon at the New York Public Library, Alycia Vivona at the FDR Library in Hyde Park, Gail E. Farr at the

Philadelphia branch of the National Archives, Evelyn James at the Dauphin County Historical Society, Ann Hull at the Franklin County Historical Society, June Sheridan at the Atlantic County Historical Society, Barbara Price at the Gloucester County Historical Society, Roger Applegate at the Beaver County Historical Research and Landmarks Foundation, John Mills of Princeton Battlefield Park, Brian McCartin at the Thomas Paine National Historical Association, Ellen Poteet at the Clements Library of the University of Michigan, George Carpenter at Cold Spring Presbyterian Cemetery at Cold Spring, New Jersey, Kate Farley at the Georgia Historical Society, Nicholas Noyes at the Maine Historical Society, Connie Cooper of the Delaware Historical Society, Claudia Jew at the Mariner's Museum in Newport News, Virginia, John Anderies and Ann W. Upton at the Haverford College Library, Susan Drinan of the Philadelphia History Museum at Atwater Kent, Debbie Miller and Richard Tritt of the Cumberland County Historical Society, Bente Polites at the Falvey Memorial Library at Villanova University, Richard Fraser at the Philadelphia College of Physicians Library, Nicole Joniec at the Library Company of Philadelphia, Regina Rush at the University of Virginia Library, and Heather Joynes of the John F. Kennedy Presidential Library and Museum.

It took some time to track down John Kessler's papers, thought to be anywhere from Massachusetts to Montana. They were found in a box by Jonathan Stayer of the Pennsylvania Historical and Museum Commission in Harrisburg, who subsequently uncovered documents on James McCalmont. Frank Grizzard was instrumental in guiding me through George Washington's papers (and helped lay to rest an old Barry legend). Adam Kane at the Lake Champlain Maritime Museum discussed at length the construction and use of Revolutionary War barges. Donald Hagist, Jim Kochan, John Houlding, Don Graves, and Linnea Bass reviewed naval ordnance. At the eleventh hour, Kathie Ludwig of the David Library of the American Revolution discovered documents regarding William Austin that showed why Barry remained such a staunch friend. The search for what happened to James and Jude, Barry's two slaves, was ably assisted by George Nagle of the Afrolumens Project. I'm grateful to Walter Palmer for his time and knowledge on the subject of slavery in Philadelphia. Susan Klepp at Temple took every question I had about family life and a woman's lot in colonial times.

Regarding Barry's health issues, Laurence Todd and Paul Kopperman put me right next to Dr. Kendall in the *Alliance* cockpit, treating Barry's wounded shoulder. Carla Keirns very generously shared her knowledge of the suffering and treatment of asthmatics in Barry's day.

Quite a few institutions put up with numerous visits and questions over the past seven years. Lorraine Baratti and Ted O'Reilly were gracious hosts at the New-York Historical Society. Jim Cheevers, Don Leonard, and Dolly Pantelides were always helpful at the Preble Museum at the United States Naval Academy. I was made welcome at the Library of Congress by Virginia Wood, Bruce Kirby, and the late Mary Wolfskill. At the American Philosophical Society, J. J. Ahern and Valerie Lutz were generous with their time, reviewing Franklin's relationship with Barry and digging up Dr. Cutbush's amazing journal. Visits to Christ Church allowed me to become friends with Neil Ronk, Bruce Gill, Tish Byrne, Carol Smith, and Trish Troilo, and a climb up the bell tower for the best view of Philadelphia the eighteenth century could provide. At Independence Hall, Karie Diethorn, Karen Stevens, and the intrepid Andrea Ashby provided everything from early American documents to measuring the stairways, which helped envision Barry's escort service for McCalmont and Miley. The Historical Society of Pennsylvania is a treasure trove of knowledge and terrific professionals, Lee Arnold, Dan Rolph, and Rob Medford among them (and my thanks to Max Moeller). At the Independence Seaport Museum, where this project began, I received invaluable assistance from Matt Herbison, Bob Doordan, Craig Bruns, and Bill Ward.

At Valley Forge, Bill Troppman set the scene for Barry's visit to Washington's headquarters. The late gentleman Don Stokes took me on his boat through the watery graveyard of the ships the British burned (and that he helped rediscover) near Bordentown. Larry Helmick had as much fun as I did while Airman Nicholas C. Lyman took us through the USS *Constitution* from the keelson to the . . . well, they wouldn't let us go aloft (Larry's consummate knowledge of sailing, much better than my own, has also been a huge help). And the best way to see the Delaware through Barry's eyes is to travel upriver on New Jersey's tall ship, the schooner *A. J. Meerwald*, skippered by Jesse Briggs, and accompanied by his crew and his energetic wife, Megan, whose Bayshore Discovery Project is nobly preserving the history and ecosystem of the Delaware Bay.

Indirect descendants of John Barry were enthusiastic and supportive, including John Barry Kelly and the Hepburn family: Austin Sr., Darcy, Doug, Marty, and especially Austin Jr., his wife Hannah, and their children, who were extremely kind, opening their home and hearts. From California, William Berret Kessler, Jr. was helpful in picking up John Kessler's story where the archives left off.

Fran O'Brien of the Philadelphia Port Authority provided an opportunity to produce a child's book on Barry for their reading program, which allowed me to work with my son Ted, an award-winning illustrator with global recognition for his art. My daughter Courtney–the real writer in the family–gave sound advice and assisted in typing the manuscript along with Carolyn Catona, Donna Thompson, and Delores McLaughlin. Russ Wylie, who must be related to Joshua from the amount of projects he takes on and completes, was instrumental in getting Barry's family papers microfilmed and later digitized. In Wildwood, J. F. Stocker, whose family has been in commercial boating and sightseeing at the Jersey shore for generations, provided charts and background on the coastal waters Barry knew so well. Author Jim Donovan offered suggestions and support during this undertaking. Author and adventurer Dean King's two books, *A Sea of Words* and *Harbors and High Seas,* were extremely beneficial.

From the second he expressed interest in this book, Bruce H. Franklin, Westholme's publisher, has matched my commitment about telling Barry's story with his own energy and drive. Trudi Gershenov's beautiful cover captures Barry's spirit perfectly. John Hubbard's excellent photography allowed several of illustrations to appear in the book. Tracy Dungan laid out the battle diagrams and maps, and Noreen O'Connor-Abel edited the manuscript and answered many queries about grammar and style.

Michael Crawford, who now holds the baton first carried by William Bell Clark, took every question and put up with every visit to the Washington Navy Yard. He never failed to provide smooth sailing with the manuscript, sources, or ideas. Greg Urwin, of Temple University, is a highly regarded authority on military history whose passion is matched by his generosity. He read every word of the manuscript and referred me to several of the names listed above. His assistance was truly invaluable. He was referred to me by Jim Hilty, another renowned, lifelong scholar of American history who first endured my company when

I studied under him at Temple. Thanks to the aging process, he has gone from being a mentor to a peer. In his low key, gentle way, he dared me to do this. Some professors never stop teaching.

Two women are responsible for your holding this book. Megan Fraser introduced me to the Barry-Hayes Papers at the Independence Seaport Museum, sending me down a path I had no idea was waiting for me. Now at UCLA, she has skills as a librarian and archivist that are second to none. I can never repay her for her kindness and friendship.

Finally, there's Cyd, the north star of our family. She read every word of this book, which has taxed her patience, her English major past, and her willingness to let every table in our home be covered with countless copies of letters, documents, logs, journals, and charts, and allowed a long departed sea captain to join the family. Thanks, Cyd. No man married better.